T0331604

Cases on Immersive Virtual Reality Techniques

Kenneth C.C. Yang
The University of Texas at El Paso, USA

A volume in the Advances in Multimedia and
Interactive Technologies (AMIT) Book Series

Published in the United States of America by
IGI Global
Engineering Science Reference (an imprint of IGI Global)
701 E. Chocolate Avenue
Hershey PA, USA 17033
Tel: 717-533-8845
Fax: 717-533-8661
E-mail: cust@igi-global.com
Web site: http://www.igi-global.com

Library of Congress Cataloging-in-Publication Data

Names: Yang, Kenneth C. C., editor.
Title: Cases on immersive virtual reality techniques / Kenneth C.C. Yang,
  editor.
Description: Hershey, PA : Engineering Science Reference, 2018. | Includes
  bibliographical references.
Identifiers: LCCN 2017059211| ISBN 9781522559122 (hardcover) | ISBN
  9781522559139 (ebook)
Subjects: LCSH: Virtual reality.
Classification: LCC QA76.9.C65 C376 2018 | DDC 006.8--dc23 LC record available at https://lccn.loc.gov/2017059211

This book is published in the IGI Global book series Advances in Multimedia and Interactive Technologies (AMIT) (ISSN: 2327-929X; eISSN: 2327-9303)

Advances in Multimedia and Interactive Technologies (AMIT) Book Series

Joel J.P.C. Rodrigues

National Institute of Telecommunications (Inatel), Brazil & Instituto de Telecomunicações, University of Beira Interior, Portugal

ISSN:2327-929X
EISSN:2327-9303

MISSION

Traditional forms of media communications are continuously being challenged. The emergence of user-friendly web-based applications such as social media and Web 2.0 has expanded into everyday society, providing an interactive structure to media content such as images, audio, video, and text.

The **Advances in Multimedia and Interactive Technologies (AMIT) Book Series** investigates the relationship between multimedia technology and the usability of web applications. This series aims to highlight evolving research on interactive communication systems, tools, applications, and techniques to provide researchers, practitioners, and students of information technology, communication science, media studies, and many more with a comprehensive examination of these multimedia technology trends.

COVERAGE

- Social Networking
- Multimedia Streaming
- Gaming Media
- Mobile Learning
- Audio Signals
- Multimedia Technology
- Digital Communications
- Web Technologies
- Digital Images
- Digital Technology

IGI Global is currently accepting manuscripts for publication within this series. To submit a proposal for a volume in this series, please contact our Acquisition Editors at Acquisitions@igi-global.com or visit: http://www.igi-global.com/publish/.

Titles in this Series

For a list of additional titles in this series, please visit: www.igi-global.com/book-series

Handbook of Research on Examining Cultural Policies Through Digital Communication
Betül Önay Dogan (Istanbul University, Turkey) and Derya Gül Ünlü (Istanbul University, Turkey)
Information Science Reference • copyright 2019 • 447pp • H/C (ISBN: 9781522569985) • US $265.00 (our price)

Advanced Methodologies and Technologies in Media and Communications
Mehdi Khosrow-Pour, D.B.A. (Information Resources Management Association, USA)
Information Science Reference • copyright 2019 • 752pp • H/C (ISBN: 9781522576013) • US $295.00 (our price)

Interface Support for Creativity, Productivity, and Expression in Computer Graphics
Anna Ursyn (University of Northern Colorado, USA)
Information Science Reference • copyright 2019 • 355pp • H/C (ISBN: 9781522573715) • US $195.00 (our price)

Trends, Experiences, and Perspectives in Immersive Multimedia and Augmented Reality
Emília Simão (Escola Superior Gallaecia University (ESG), Portugal) and Celia Soares (University Institute of Maia (ISMAI), Portugal & Polytechnic Institute of Maia (IPMAIA), Portugal)
Information Science Reference • copyright 2019 • 277pp • H/C (ISBN: 9781522556961) • US $185.00 (our price)

Cross-Media Authentication and Verification Emerging Research and Opportunities
Anastasia Katsaounidou (Aristotle University of Thessaloniki, Greece) Charalampos Dimoulas (Aristotle University of Thessaloniki, Greece) and Andreas Veglis (Aristotle University of Thessaloniki, Greece)
Information Science Reference • copyright 2019 • 213pp • H/C (ISBN: 9781522555926) • US $145.00 (our price)

Feature Dimension Reduction for Content-Based Image Identification
Rik Das (Xavier Institute of Social Service, India) Sourav De (Cooch Behar Government Engineering College, India) and Siddhartha Bhattacharyya (RCC Institute of Information Technology, India)
Information Science Reference • copyright 2018 • 284pp • H/C (ISBN: 9781522557753) • US $215.00 (our price)

Intelligent Multidimensional Data and Image Processing
Sourav De (Cooch Behar Government Engineering College, India) Siddhartha Bhattacharyya (RCC Institute of Information Technology, India) and Paramartha Dutta (Visva Bharati University, India)
Information Science Reference • copyright 2018 • 429pp • H/C (ISBN: 9781522552468) • US $235.00 (our price)

Real-Time Face Detection, Recognition, and Tracking System in LabVIEW™ Emerging Research and Opportunities
Manimehala Nadarajan (Universiti Malaysia Sabah, Malaysia) Muralindran Mariappan (Universiti Malaysia Sabah, Malaysia) and Rosalyn R. Porle (Universiti Malaysia Sabah, Malaysia)
Information Science Reference • copyright 2018 • 140pp • H/C (ISBN: 9781522535034) • US $155.00 (our price)

701 East Chocolate Avenue, Hershey, PA 17033, USA
Tel: 717-533-8845 x100 • Fax: 717-533-8661
E-Mail: cust@igi-global.com • www.igi-global.com

Editorial Advisory Board

Table of Contents

Section 1
The Emergence of Digital Reality Technology

Section 2
Emerging Themes and Practices in Digital Reality Research

Section 3
Applications and Best Practices in Digital Reality

Detailed Table of Contents

Section 1
The Emergence of Digital Reality Technology

Section 1 provides an overview of emerging digital reality technologies (such as augmented, mixed, virtual realities, and 360-degree video) in the contemporary media ecosystem around the world. This section will provide background on the technologies by examining their technological attributes, their global diffusion, theoretical paradigms, and consumer behavior implications that have been gradually felt among many countries around the world.

Chapter 1

Digital reality technologies have become a global phenomenon that attracts huge attention from researchers and practitioners around the world. ResearchandMarkets.com predicts that the global revenue for both augmented reality (AR) and virtual reality (VR) applications will reach $94.4 billion by 2023. As an introductory chapter to the edited book volume on the global impacts of digital reality technologies, this chapter examines the current state of digital reality technologies around the world. Global, regional, and country statistics are presented to shed light on the diffusion of a variety of digital reality technologies such as augmented reality, mixed reality, and virtual reality. Potential and existing digital realty technologies around the world will be examined in greater detail to provide readers with contextual information for the remaining chapters of the book.

Section 2
Emerging Themes and Practices in Digital Reality Research

The five chapters in this section deal with emerging research paradigms and practices in digital reality studies in different areas ranging from physical education and sport training, cultural industry, and higher educational context. This section is written by a panel of global experts in digital reality technologies to share their own research and implementation experiences in their individual countries, organizations, or research fields. As an emerging and converging technology, digital reality has been studied using a mixture of usability, experiment, focus group, survey, and text mining research methods demonstrating the contributions of engineering, education, humanity, and social science scholars to this burgeoning new field.

Chapter 2

Pooya Soltani, Aix-Marseille University, France & University of Porto, Portugal
João Paulo Vilas-Boas, University of Porto, Portugal

For effective learning and training, virtual environments may provide lifelike opportunities, and researchers are actively investigating their potential for educational purposes. Minimal research attention has been paid to the integration of multi-user virtual environments (MUVE) technology for teaching and practicing real sports. In this chapter, the authors reviewed the justifications, possibilities, challenges, and future directions of using MUVE systems. The authors addressed issues such as informal learning, design, engagement, collaboration, learning style, learning evaluation, motivation, and gender, followed by the identification of required elements for successful implementations. In the second part, the authors talked about exergames, the necessity of evaluation, and examples on exploring the behavior of players during playing. Finally, insights on the application of sports exergames in teaching, practicing, and encouraging real sports were discussed.

Chapter 3

Miguel Angel Garcia-Ruiz, Algoma University, Canada
Pedro Cesar Santana-Mancilla, Universidad de Colima, Mexico
Laura Sanely Gaytan-Lugo, Universidad de Colima, Mexico

Algoma University holds an important collection of Canadian objects from the Anishinaabe culture dating from 1880. Some of those objects have been on display in the university's library, but most of them still remain stored in the university's archive, limiting opportunities to use them in teaching and learning activities. This chapter describes a research project focusing on digitizing and visualizing cultural artifacts using virtual reality (VR) technology, with the aim of supporting learning of Canadian heritage in cross-cultural courses. The chapter shows technical aspects of the objects' 3D digitization process and goes on to explain a user study with students watching a 3D model displayed on a low-cost VR headset. Results from the study show that visualization of the 3D model on the VR headset was effective, efficient, and satisfactory enough to use, motivating students to keep using it in further sessions. Technology integration of VR in educational settings is also analyzed and discussed.

Chapter 4

Users sometimes lost their balance or even fell down when they played virtual reality (VR) games or projects. This may be attributed to degree of content, high-rate of latency, coordination of various sensory inputs, and others. The authors investigated the effect of sudden visual perturbations on human balance in VR environment. This research used the latest VR head mounted display to present visual perturbations to disturb balance. To quantify balance, measured by double-support and single-support stance, the authors measured the subject's center of pressure (COP) using a force plate. The results indicated that visual perturbations presented in virtual reality disrupted balance control in the single support condition but not in the double support condition. Results from this study can be applied to clinical research on balance and VR environment design.

Chapter 5

This chapter describes a study that was conducted in a semi-immersive desktop virtual reality environment. The study investigated teacher trainees' perceptions of their mental effort in Second Life, their satisfaction with the communication modalities, and their perceived social behavioral changes. In the first event, only the instructor (host) used voice to communicate while all participants as well as the in-text facilitator (co-host) used text chat only. In the second event, not only did both hosts use voice, but the participants also had the option to use voice rather than text. The majority of teacher trainees appreciated the freedom to choose either modality. The integration of voice was perceived as humanizing the discussion, increasing the flow, and making the conversation more engaging. However, the addition of multiple voices was believed to increase their mental effort. While some teacher trainees felt more relaxed and more open in a virtual discussion, others reported a lack of attention and honesty as well as a tendency to ignore social conventions.

Chapter 6

This chapter deals with the problem of including motion cues in VR applications. From the challenges of this technology to the latest trends in the field, the authors discuss the benefits and problems of including these particular perceptual cues. First, readers will know how motion cues are usually generated in simulators and VR applications in general. Then, the authors list the major problems of this process and the reasons why its development has not followed the pace of the rest of VR elements (mainly the display technology), reviewing the motion vs. no-motion question from several perspectives. The general answer to this discussion is that motion cues are necessary in VR applications—mostly vehicle simulators— that rely on motion, although, unlike audio-visual cues, there can be specific considerations for each particular solution that may suggest otherwise. Therefore, it is of the utmost importance to analyze the requirements of each VR application before deciding upon this question.

Section 3
Applications and Best Practices in Digital Reality

The six chapters in Section 3 demonstrate the applications and best practices of digital reality technologies. The pervasive applications of digital reality platforms have been seen in the marketing, creative cultural industries, higher education institutes, and formal and informal learning contexts, including special education for people with autism using an integrated approach to combine AR, MR, and VR technologies with other emerging platforms such as game and online learning platforms.

Virtual learning environments are receiving a growing interest due to exponential advancements in technology alongside the millennial users' preference for more modern rather than traditional means of studying. This chapter narrows down on optimizing edutainment in the classroom by strategically using the methods of flipped classroom, team-based learning, and the IDEAS method. The study provides an explained framework that highlights what needs to be implemented on behalf of the instructor and what outcomes can be expected as a result. An experimental study was conducted on students within a course at the graduate level in the United Arab Emirates (UAE). The main objective is to study the effect of virtual learning environment that incorporates the use of flipped classroom, Team-based learning and IDEAS methods on students' academic performance.

Recognition of the dramatically changing nature of what it means to be literate in the so-called "information age" has resulted in an increasing interest among the educational research community around the importance of students developing "multiliteracy" skills and engaging in multimodal learning. Nevertheless, for such learning to be meaningful, requires to reconceptualize delivery strategies and assessment of multimodally mediated experiences. The aim of this chapter is dual: First to introduce an alternative framework for formative assessment of multimodal interactions for learning. Secondly, the intention is to uncover the story of culturally and linguistically diverse students' multimodal experiences, resulting from engagement in the creation of a student-generated virtual museum during a design-based research implementation.

Drawing from the literature, analysis, and evaluation using the framework explained, it is evident that virtual museum-based multiliteracies engagement, benefits pupils' multimodal awareness, meaning making, and development as active designers of their learning.

When a student works on a VR game design project, the input scheme is often bypassed because it is considered to be one of the easiest things to implement. But should design affect the inputs, or the other way around? The author attempts to solve this with the creation of a unified communication tool among students, academics, and developers. This proposed tool will define which movement and/or interaction technique is best suited, depending on the following factors: platform, constraints, context, physique, space, immersion, and user experience. The game design framework will be described, discussed, and presented in a table format to address all of the above when working on VR games. This chapter will also include a section that will define what the player can do and how.

Chapter 10

This chapter deals with emerging augmented, mixed, and virtual reality platforms and their applications in cause-related marketing (CRM) campaigns. This chapter provides definitions and examples of augmented, mixed, and virtual realities and explains their importance CRM professionals. Compared with traditional marketing platforms, reality-creating technologies are characterized with their capabilities to interact with marketing contents through their geolocation specificity, mobility, and synchronization of virtuality and reality. These technological characteristics have made reality-creating technologies very promising for many cause-related marketing (CRM) campaigns. This chapter surveys current discussions in the existing literature and ends with three cause-related marketing (CRM) campaigns. The study concludes with an overview of emerging issues, future directions, and professional best practice recommendations.

Chapter 11

This chapter illustrates the use of VR applications in professional development and introduces an application used to assist teachers, learning support assistants (LSAs), and teaching assistants (TAs) to better understand autistic children's behaviors while in the classroom. One of the challenges faced in classrooms is how to understand the autistic children's behaviors and empathize with them. The proposed VR application repurposes a different form of narrative of the world of a child on the autism spectrum in an immersive environment designed for educators. The VR application in this chapter uses recorded footage through 360-degree cameras and special effects powered by Unity. In a context where integration is a key to today's learning and education, the researchers believe that the use of VR to assist the teachers in empathizing with their learners' traits and conditions may be of great benefit to the learners' school experiences.

Chapter 12

Yowei Kang, National Taiwan Ocean University, Taiwan

Digital reality technologies have become a key component of promoting creative and cultural industries in Taiwan. In 2016, Taiwan's Ministry of Culture funded 45 projects to promote creative and cultural industries in this island country. A total of USD$25.6 million dollars have been granted to this project. Among these projects, the applications of virtual reality (VR) and augmented reality (AR) technologies have been found to be the latest trend in Taiwan's creative and cultural industries. This chapter employs a case study approach to survey the current state of digital reality technology applications particularly in the area of creative and oceanic cultural industries in Taiwan. Using a detailed description of these best practices among creative and cultural industries to promote Taiwanese oceanic culture, this chapter aims to provide a detailed examination of digital reality applications in the creative and cultural industry sectors in a non-Western context.

Preface

EMERGENCE OF DIGITAL REALITY TECHNOLOGIES

Digital reality technologies are often used as an umbrella term to cover an array of emerging technologies and their applications in augmented reality (AR), mixed reality (MR), virtual reality (VR), 360-degree video, and other immersive platforms (Cook, Jones, Raghavan, & Saif, 2018). Recent advances in articificial intelligence and machine learning technologies have prompted many practitioners to claim immersive digital reality technologies will be the next step in many marketing activities (Pettey, 2018). A recent report in *Forbes* (Herschman, 2017; Tourville & Forbes Agency Council, 2018) point out there has been a growing interest in experimentation and actual implementation among brand such as Ikea, Porche, Lowes, MTV, TOMS, Warner Brothers, etc. to integrate immersive AR and VR into their marketing activities and communication campaigns to create consumers' different brand experiences. Rosy and optimistic predictions have prompted the rapid spending and investment on these immersive digital reality technologies. Total spending on AR and VR products and services is expected to reach $160 billion in 2021, according to International Data Corp. (IDC) (Cook et al., 2018). On the other hand, the AR industry is also expected to reach $100 billion in 2024, according to Grand View Research (Holger, 2016). Similarly heightened interest in these digital reality technologies is found in the retailing industry (Herschman, 2017). The usage of AR and VR software among retailing enterprises is expected to reach $1.6 billion in 2025 (Herschman, 2017). The impacts of the digital reality technologies (in particular, virtual reality) have been expanded to entertainment, gaming, and sports industries (Petrock, 2018).

However, the widespread and rapid diffusion of these technologies still depends on the willingness of corporate adopters to allocate their resources. According of 2018 Gartner CIO Agenda Survey of 3,160 Chief Informatin Officers (CIOs) in 98 countries, 37% of them indicate that they have paid attention to AR and VR, but still refrain from taking any plan to implement these technologies in their business activities (Petty, 2018). For these digital reality technologies to reach the mass market, *Digi-Capital*, a technology consultation firm, has identified seven key factors that could determine the business success of AR and VR (Grubb, 2015). These are affordability, flexibility, immersion, mobility, usability, vision, wearability (Grubb, 2015). Similar determinants of AR and VR diffusion are discussed after using historical data to understand how fast these technologies could permeate the society (Fink, 2017) and at what speed. These technical attributes are claimed to be critical to the success of digital reality technologies as a mass market product by offering consumers subsidized equipment purchase (i.e., affordability), excellent immersive experiences by means of easy to use, superb image quality, ubiquitous access (Grubb, 2015). The ultimate success of AR and VR technology will rely on if the technologies can become part of consumers' culture and fashion (i.e., wearability) (Grubb, 2015). In addition to these technological attributes to determine the adoption of digital reality technologies, the availability of reality-creating technologies also plays similarly important role (Holger, 2016). Citing a report by Perkins Coie, 37% of consumers say they are relunctant to adopt AR and VR technologies, due to concerns about content availablity to justify their expensive investment in these technologies (Holger, 2016). These two major inhibitors of widespread consumer adoption remain the same even after two years since Holger's (2016) predictions (Petrock, 2018). Other factors in affecting the success of AR/VR technologies also rely on consumers' knowledge about and interest in them. A large-scale online survey of over 8,000 consumers by Nielsen's Media Lab (2016) has observed that 18-54 years old consumers' knowledge about VR (27%) is comparable to that of 3D printers (24%), drones (24%), and wearable techologies (29%), while their interest in VR as a fan (36%) is also comparable that in Internet of Things (35%) and wearable technologies (35%) (Refer to Figure 1 below).

THE ECOSYSTEM OF DIGITAL REALITY TECHNOLOGIES

Digital reality technologies transform how human beings interact with the environment through new interfaces such as emotion, gesture, and gaze (Deloitte Consulting LLP & Consumer Technology Association, 2018) to give users a sense of presence (*eMarketer.com*, 2016). Consumers' immersive experiences are made possible through reality-creating technologies as shown in the digital reality ecosystem below to create business advantage (Figure 2) (Deloitte Consulting LLP & Consumer Technology Association, 2018).

Virtual reality is a digital technology that will create a fully-immersive digital environment to replace or enhance user's experiences in a real-world environment with the ability to navigate the virtual space through the use of head-mounted display (HMD) devices connected to controllers, smartphones, and other equipment (Deloitte Consulting LLP & Consumer Technology Association, 2018; *eMarketer.com*, 2016). Some popular HMDs include Facebook's Oculus headsets, Magic Leap One, Samsung Gear VR (Patrizio, 2017).

Augmented reality enables the overlay of computer-generated contents with physical objects in users' actual environment (Deloitte Consulting LLP & Consumer Technology Association, 2018; *eMarketer. com*, 2016). For example, Google Glass employs AR through its HMD to provide users with a different experience (*eMarkter.com*, 2016). Because mobile devices have become widely adopted, major players in the mobile AR market have included well-known companies such as Alphabet, Apple, Face, and Snap that offer either embedded AR capabilities in their smartphone (such as Google and Apple), or providing AR software applications (such as Facebook and Snap) (Seitz, 2018).

The introduction of 360 degree video, on the other hand, allows users to view their environment with a surrounded perspective (Deloitte Consulting LLP & Consumer Technology Association, 2018). Other immersive technologies, such as the latest *free viewpoint video* (Collet et al., n.d.; Pagés, Amplianitis, Monaghan, Ondřej, & Smolić, 2018), also provide similarly multi-sensory experiences to users (Deloitte Consulting LLP & Consumer Technology Association, 2018). The emerging *free viewpoint video* is defined as "a scene photographically captured in real-time that can be played back in real-time and appears like video from a continuous range of viewpoints chosen at any time in playback" (Collet et al., n.d.)

Recent advances in the digital reality technologies have led to the development of mixed reality which users to interact with an environment that blends digital contents with the physical world (Deloitte

Figure 1. Results from a large-scale survey on consumers' knowledge and interest in virtual reality

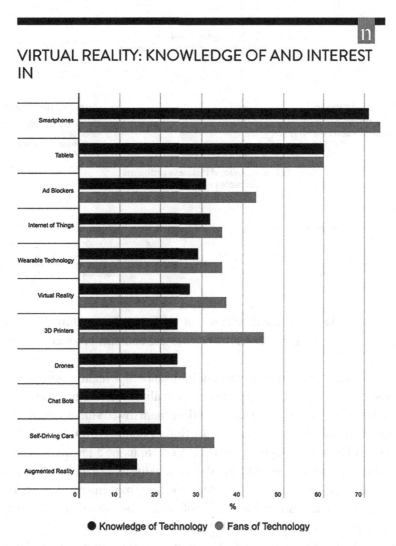

VIRTUAL REALITY: KNOWLEDGE OF AND INTEREST IN

● Knowledge of Technology ● Fans of Technology

Consulting LLP & Consumer Technology Association, 2018). The best definition of mixed reality is described as "experiences with real-time comingling of virtual and physical objects achieved by products like Microsoft's HoloLens" (*eMarketer.com*, 2016, n.p.). As one of the most recent innovations in the digital reality landscape, the adoption of MR is equally influenced by the corporate decision makers for adoption consideration (Arena, 2018). In a recent survey of 394 US executives in March 2018, about two-thirds of the executives indicate that they are currently testing the application of MR. However, only 20% of them express that they are current developing, producing, or deploying MR, despite the majority of them believe MR is a technology that will impact on their strategic plan in the future (Arena, 2018).

In their technical primer for digital reality technology, Deloitte Consulting LLP and Consumer Technology Association (2018) identify three areas of key players to take advantage of the ample opportunity in the emerging digital reality marketplace. These players can be broadly divided into 1) ap-

Figure 2. Digital reality ecosystem

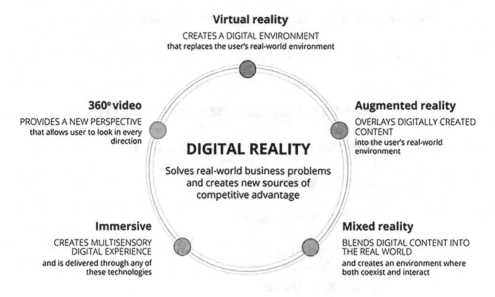

plication content (such as industry information and analytics); 2) infrastructure providers in data system, hardware, or head-mounted devices (HMD), etc.; 3) tools and contents producers (such as apps, capture tools, platforms, etc.).

The infrastructure component of the reality technology landscape mainly covers hardware/equipment to allow users to interact with digital reality contents (RealityTechnologies.com, n.d.). For example, head-mounted displays (HMD) are worn by users to allow them to see videos or images in the embedded standard LCD screen (RealityTechnologies.com, n.d.). Some popular HMDs include Facebook's Oculus, Google Glass, Microsoft HoloLen, Magic Leap, HTC Vive, to name a few brands (Patrizio, 2017). On the other hand, input/output devices constitute another area of the landscape by allowing users to provide sensory feedbacks to the HMD through their hand, feet, and body movements (RealityTechnologies.com, n.d.). These input/output devices also create a sense of actual interactions with the digitally generated objects through forces, motions, and vibration (RealityTechnologies.com, n.d.).

The platform component of the digital reality landscape is often composed of three sub-areas of the technologies: distribution platforms to access reality contents, process and engines of contents editing and creation, and reality capture tools (RealityTechnologies.com, n.d.). First, the distribution platforms are the gateway where users can access and distribute digital reality contents through closed/specific or open/agnostic HMD (RealityTechnologies.com, n.d.). On the other hand, software-based tools allow users or content developers to edit and create digital realities through computer image generating engines, file size compression technologies, and editing and stitching software (RealityTechnologies. com, n.d.). For example, Unity Technologies offers software and tools to facilitate the development of 3D game (Patrizio, 2017).

The final domain of this digital reality landscape is formed by a variety of applications and contents in business, education, entertainment, healthcare, gaming, marketing, sports, travel, etc. (RealityTechnologies.com, n.d.). This particular area of the digital reality ecosystem has seen most burgeoning developments by many start-up companies to create apps, tools, and contents (RealityTechnologies.com, n.d., https://www.realitytechnologies.com/companies/) that also converge with other new media platforms. For example, ScopeAR (www.scopear.com) offers the application of AR, Remote AR, in the workplace to connect experts to collaborate, while MindMaze (www.mindmaze.com) combines neuroscience, mixed reality, and artificial intelligence to develop "intuitive human machine interfaces." Social media giant, Snapchat, similar smartphone app to allow users to access a variety of AR applications (Patrizio, 2017). The convergence of digital reality with other information-communication technologies also prompts the startup, NextVR, which cooperates with major broadcasters (such as Turner Broadcasting) and major leagues to broadcast live virtual reality professional sports and music events (Patrizio, 2017). Porn industry is expected to be the third largest VR user, followed by NFL-game applications (McEvoy, 2018).

EMERGING RESEARCH QUESTIONS RELATED TO DIGITAL REALITY TECHNOLOGIES

The exponential growth of the digital reality technologies and related applications would unavoidably lead to avid interests among the academic community to explore their impacts on various aspects of contemporary human experiences. Academic journals have been established to deal with emerging AR, MR, AND VR applications, real-time visualization, and related research topics. For example, Springer's *Journal of Virtual Reality* was established in 1995 to publish original research in "the development and evaluation of systems, tools, techniques and software" in the areas of display, haptic, and tracking and interaction management through biosensors, eye gaze, gesture control, and wearables (*Journal of Virtual Reality*, https://www.springer.com/computer/image+processing/journal/10055). The open access electronic journal, *Journal of Virtual Reality and Broadcasting* (https://www.jvrb.org/), explores the interface and interaction among digital reality and existing broadcasting technologies and applications. Related topics in this journal include human machine interfaces, computer graphics, image processing, virtual set environments, and media technology. Other academic journals (such as *Media Tropes*) also published works that deal with how the design of HMD may affect virtual reality paradigms (Stein, 2016).

The study of AR, MR, and VR technology is multi-disciplinary in nature and this edited volume intends to reflect a wide spectrum of digital reality technologies, applications, and research around the world. The original call for chapters developed by the previous editor demonstrates his forte in the engineering and computer science expertise. This edited volume has thus attracted contributions in the area of virtual reality in games and game-based learning (Chapter 9 and Chapter 10), virtual reality and education (Chapter 2, Chapter 5, and Chapter 7), virtual reality and multimodal interaction (Chapter 8), evaluation and assessment for reality-based learning in different platforms (Chapter 5 and Chapter 6), interactions with a virtual environment (Chapter 2 and Chapter 3), and AR and VR applications for non-profit causes and organizations (Chapter 3). Upon the invitation of the IGI Global Publishers, the new editor has added chapters on more social scientific aspects of AR, MR, and VR technologies in the areas of their applications in cause-related marketing (Chapter 10), and creative and oceanic cultural industries (Chapter 12), and a general chapter on the global diffusion of reality-creating technologies (Chapter 1).

THEORETICAL FOUNDATIONS FOR DIGITAL
REALITY TECHNOLOGY RESEARCH

This edited volume does not contain a dedicated chapter to discuss major theoretical foundations to investigate digital reality technologies. This is attributed to the multi-disciplinary nature of digital reality research and practices. Furthermore, originally conceptualized as a book project that will be helpful for practitioners in game design, educational technology, human-computer interface, advertising and marketing applications, the discussions of relevant theories are often embedded in each individual chapter to address their discipline-specific relevance. Therefore, this preface attempts to provide an overview of theories that could be useful when studying the adoption, impacts, and designs of these digital reality technologies. This theoretical section aims to provide contextual information to better comprehend chapters written by authors from various background.

In general, the literature that provides timely research on the digital reality technologies and their applications can be broadly divided into six major areas of exploration that is often interrelated with each other to develop a successful AR, MR, or VR project: consumer-, system-, communication channel-/modality-, message-, environment-, and product-related factors.

Studies that are written by engineers or designers to describe the planning, development, and implementation of AR, MR, and VR technologies in different contexts tend to be a-theoretical and focus more on the technical aspects of these applications (Claudio & Maddalena, 2014; Hsu, 2017; Kang, 2018).

The Technology Acceptance Model (TAM) (Davis, 1989) and its derived Extended Technology Acceptance Model (TAM2) (Davis & Bagozi, 1989) offer a useful and integrative model to explain the relationships between consumer-. system design-, and product-related factors in explaining the adoption of AR, MR, and VR technologies. TAM and TAM2, originally developed from The Theory of Reasoned Action (TRA), emphasize the role of adopters' psychological determinants in explaining the decision-making process to use a variety of information technologies in different contexts (Huang & Liao, 2015; Phan & Daim, 2011; Rese, Schreiber, & Baier, 2014; Rese, Baier, Geyer-Schulz, & Schreiber, 2017; Roberts & Henderson, 2000). For example, Phan and Daim (2011) investigate factors affecting the acceptance/ adoption of mobile data services (Phan & Daim, 2011). Rese, Schreiber, and Baier (2014) use IKEA's mobile catalog app as an example to study the usefulness of TAM in predicting consumers' acceptance of this AR mobile app, when comparing with online review textual data. Huang and Liao (2015) focus on adopters' cognitive innovativeness to examine if this user characteristics will predict behavior toward an AR interactive technology. Their empirical findings observe that online users with a high innovativeness level tend to emphasize more on the aesthetics, service excellence perceptions, and usefulness of AR.

TAM and TAM2 attempt to explain what motivate users to adopt an information technology. Relevant to this edited book will be what leads to the adoption of AR, MR, and VR technology. Davis (1989) offers three technology-related attributes; that is, they are perceived usefulness (PU), perceived ease of use (PEOU), and attitude toward use (AU) to account for intention to adopt and actual usage behavior of a technology. To address the lack of external factors (such as image, subjective norms, and voluntariness), TAM2 has included both social influence variables and cognitive factors (such as job relevance and output, and result demonstrability) to better explain people's adoption behaviors (Maillet, Mathieu, & Sicotte, 2015). An extensive review of TAM, TAM2, and other adoption decision-making models is not a feasible task in this short preface (Refer to Taherdoost, 2017, for a complete review of adoption decision-making models). However, TAM and TAM2 have properly addressed factors related to system attributes, users' perceptions and behaviors, and technology products and services.

To explore the influence of communication modality and environment on the messages (contents) and interactions in a virtual environment created by AR, MR, or VR technologies, practitioners and researchers of digital reality technologies often employ the concept, immersion, to explain the feeling of flow and presence (Kim & Biocca, 2018), virtual presence and co-presence (Emma-Ogbangwo, Cope, Behringer, & Fabri, 2014) that are experienced by many users in a virtual space. The concept of immersion refers to "the level of physical or psychological submergence of a user within a virtual space relative to that user's consciousness of the real-world environment" (Emma-Ogbangwo et al., 2014, n.p.). Both psychological and technological immersion has been used to study its impacts on marketing applications (Queiroz et al., 2018; Yim, Chu & Sauer, 2017).

Similarly, Kim and Biocca (2018) use an experimental study to compare the effectiveness of immersive VR games with non-immersive 2D game, in the context of health-related psychical activity. They hypothesize that an immersive game will lead to better physical performance. Digital reality technologies are able to create an immersive virtual environment and offer users different levels of detachment from their physical environment, which is expected to influence human behaviors (Kim, Rosenthal, Zielinski, & Brady, 2014). For example, Kim et al. (2014) have researched different levels of immersion as embedded in technologies (i.e., low immersive desktop, HMD, to fully immersive media platforms) on users' emotional arousal and task performance among 53 college participants. Using a 3 (3 technologies with low to high immersive levels) by 2 (high- and low-stressful virtual environment), their study confirms that the fully immersive technology could induce the highest sense of presence and different emotional responses and task performance have been caused by immersive levels in the technologies. The applications of immersion in digital reality studies have been extended to the context of education and even neuroscientific research to examine the effect of fear in a virtual environment (Huff, Hernandez, Fecteau, Zielinski, Brady, & LaBar, 2011). Immersion, a characteristics of digital reality technology, continues to allow researchers and practitioners to explore its impacts on other aspects of digital reality research, such as system design, message/content creation and outcomes, and consumers' cognitive, emotional, and behavioral responses (Huff et al., 2011; Kim et al., 2014; Kim & Biocca, 2018).

ORGANIZATION OF THE EDITED BOOK

This edited volume has touched upon an important area of research and application in immersive digital reality technologies. This book has been written in a language that will be easy to read to both researchers and practitioners of immersive virtual reality technologies to better understand this emerging phenomenon around the world. Thanks to the country and organizational background of each contributing author, this edited volume has a rare strength of providing an international coverage to demonstrate the impacts of these technologies on various fields in their respective country. For example, Chapter 1 provides a thorough examination of the global diffusion of these digital reality technologies through a detailed secondary research of these technologies around the world. Chapter 2 discusses an European example, while Chapter 3 examines the digitalization of cultural objects in Canada. The potential applications of AR, MR, and VR in Taiwan's creative and oceanic cultural industries are explored in Chapter 12. This edited volume has also included three chapters to go over the applications of digital reality technologies in the U.S. Chapter 4 examines the visual pertubations effect on balance, while Chapter 5 similarly discusses a U.S. case in the relationship between communication modality, learners' satisfaction level, and mental effort. The potentialities of AR, MR, and VR technologies are not limited to the educational setting, Chapter 10 discusses the roles of these technologies in promoting social goods and cause-related marketing applications, while a similarly non-profit application of "living autism" is explored by a panel of experts in Chapter 11.

This edited volume has been conceptualized to target both technical and non-techical readers. As a result, a book with its coverage willl be also appropriate for both undergraduate and graduate classes that teach immersive digital reality technologies by focusing on their applications, social impacts, and system development. A well-rounded book like this has potential to meet the demands of audience without and with technical backgrounds in AR, MR, and VR. In addition to its potential uses in the textbook market, this volume is also useful for AR, MR, and VR practitioners and researchers who are interested in studying the global diffusion of a variety of reality creating technologies.

The editor has organized these twelve chapters into three thematic sections that explore the theoretical, academic, and practical implications of digital reality technologies around the world. The following narratives provide a summary description of each of the chapters as the authors have provided in their chapter abstracts. These summaries are modified minimally to reflect what these authors have presented in their chapters:

Digital reality technologies have become a global phenomenon that attracts immense attention from researchers and practitioners. Chapter 1 provides an overview of the global impacts of digital reality technologies. This introductory chapter aims to examine the current state of digital creating technologies around the world. Global, regional and country statistics are presented to shade lights on the diffusion of a variety of digital creating technologies such as augmented reality, mixed reality, and virtual reality.

Chapter 2 aims to fill the gap in the literature to study the integration of Multi-User Virtual Environments (MUVE) technology for teaching and practicing real sports. The justifications, possibilities, challenges, and future directions of using MUVE systems in the educational context are thoroughly scrutinized by two experts from France and Portugal. In the second part of this chapter, the necessity of evaluation, and examples on discovering the behavior of players during playing *exergames*. The authors conclude this chapter by offering their insights into the application of sports *exergames* in both teaching and practicing.

Chapter 3 shifts the focus to study the role of digital reality technologies in the context of cultural heritage visualization and education in Canada. Using the huge collection of Canadian objects from the Anishinaabe culture at Algoma University as a case study, Chapter 3 describes a research project on the VR-enabled digitization and visualization of cultural artifacts. The chapter shows technical aspects of the objects' 3D digitization process and explains a user study with students watching a 3D model displayed on a low-cost VR headset. Results from the empirical study have shown that visualization of the 3D model on the VR headset was effective, efficient and satisfactory enough to use, motivating students for continual use in the future.

The success of an AR, MR, and VR project is undoubtedly contingent on a superior system design. Chapter 4 focuses on the effect of visual perturbations on users' balance in a virtual environment. The authors investigated the effect of sudden visual perturbations on human balance in a virtual environment created by VR. This study employed the latest VR head mounted display to present visual perturbations to disturb balance as measured by double-support and single-support stance. The authors measured the subject's center of pressure (COP) using a force plate. Their results indicated that visual perturbations presented in VR disrupted balance control in the single support condition but not in the double support condition.

Chapter 5 describes a study conducted in a semi-immersive desktop virtual reality environment. Using the popular 3-D virtual world, Second Life, among educators, this chapter investigated the relationships among three study variables: teacher trainees' perceptions of their mental effort while using Second Life, their satisfaction with the communication modalities, and their perceived social behavioral changes. Results were discussed extensively in this chapter.

Chapter 6 studied the need and potential problem of integrating motion cues as perceptual cues in VR applications. Motion cues, generated in simulators and VR applications in general, are an important and necessary design element for VR applications. The authors argue that it is of the utmost importance to analyze the requirements of each VR application before deciding upon whether and how to integrate motion cues in each specific VR application.

Chapter 7 touches upon a growing application of digital reality technologies in the higher education context. The rise of virtual learning environment is partially attributed to meet the needs of the millennial students' preference for more technology-advanced approach of learning. Chapter 7 focuses on how to optimize edutainment in the classroom by strategically using the methods of flipped classroom, team-based learning and the IDEAS method in the United Arab Emirates (UAE). An experiment study was conducted on students taking a graduate level course to empirically study the effect of virtual learning environment, the use of flipped classroom, Team-based Learning and IDEAS methods on students' academic performance.

Chapter 8 addresses the importance of developing "multiliteracy" skills and engaging in multimodal learning in the Information Age. This chapter first introduces an alternative framework for formative assessment of multimodal interactions for learning. The study continues to explore the intention is to uncover the story of culturally and linguistically diverse students' multimodal experiences and engagement in a student-generated virtual museum. The author argues that virtual museum-based multiliteracies engagement is likely to benefit students' multimodal awareness, meaning making and development as active designers of their own learning experiences.

Chapter 9 develops a list of interaction and movement techniques to guide game design students and educators to determine what will be the best techniques to use in a VR design project after taking into consideration of factors such as constraints, context, platform, users' physique, space, immersion, and user experience.

Chapter 10 deals with emerging augmented, mixed, and virtual reality platforms and their applications in cause-related marketing (CRM) campaigns. This chapter provides definitions and examples of augmented, mixed, and virtual realities and explains their importance CRM professionals. Chapter 10 surveys current discussions in the existing literature and ends with several cause-related marketing (CRM) campaigns to offer directions for emerging issues, future trends, and professional best practice recommendations.

Chapter 11 provides an extensive discussion on the use of VR in professional development to assist Teachers, Learning Support Assistants (LSAs) and Teaching Assistants (TAs) to better understand autistic children's behaviours in the classroom. This chapter reports an actual VR application to record footage through 360-degree cameras and special effects powered by Unity to better help children with autism.

The authors argue that the use of VR will be able to assist the teachers in empathising with their learners' traits and conditions and ultimately help children with special needs to enhance their school experiences.

Chapter 12 examine the role of AR and VR in promoting creative and cultural contents in Taiwan. This book chapter employs a case study approach to survey the current state of digital reality technology applications particularly in the area of creative and oceanic cultural industries in Taiwan. The author employs a detailed description of several best practices that promote Taiwanese oceanic culture to describe and discuss potential digital reality applications in the creative and cultural industry sectors in a non-Western context.

IMMINENT ETHICAL AND REGULATORY ISSUES RELATED TO DIGITAL REALITY TECHNOLOGIES

The omnipresence of digital reality technologies as part of contemporary human experiences has spurred concerns about their potential ethical and regulatory implications (Goodmann, 2016; Gunkel & Hawhee, 2003; Johansson, 2018; McEvoy, 2018; Mullin, 2016; Polgreen, 2014; Poushneh, 2018; Spiegel, 2018; Virtual Reality Society, n.d.). These ethical issues are particularly pertinent, given the widespread of AR, MR, and VR technologies in the context of broadcasting, business, gaming, education, entertainment, sports, and healthcare sectors (RealityTechnologies.com, n.d.). The same ethical concerns are likely to appear even in the creative and cultural industry sector (such as museums and art exhibitions) that rely on location-sensitive AR-guide device (Chang, Chang, Hou, Sung, Chao, & Lee, 2014). For example, McEvoy (2018) identifies 10 potential ethical concerns that are caused by the advent of virtual reality, and similarly applicable to other digital reality technologies: 1) HMDs and sensory vulnerability due to limited access to other senses; 2) potential harm due to the lack of face-to-face interactions in an isolated VR environment (i.e., social isolation); 3) a sense of desensitization among heavy VR users in an immersive VR environment; 4) Inability to differentiate what can be accomplished between a real- and –virtual world (i.e., overestimation of users' own abilities); 5) uncertain psychiatric effects on users; 6) potential misuse or abuse of VR technologies in unpalatable contents (such as pornography); 7) unexpected misuse by authoritarian regime, military, or criminals to torture or interrogate; 8) manipulation of consumers by advertisers from profit-making purposes; 9) ethical roaming and re-creation of the physical environment to gain sensory pleasure; 10) tracking of users' interactions with virtual objects and potential privacy-invasion risks. Particularly, the desensitization and virtual criminality issues are also mentioned by Virtual Reality Society as two major ethical concerns.

Fundamentally, these ethical issues are related to the overall impacts that information-communication technologies have created and are grounded in more philosophical questions such as meaning, truth, representation, identity, and communication behaviors (Gunkel & Hawhee, 2003). Some of these ethical concerns are also evident in professional contexts such as medical and journalism (Spiegel, 2018; Polgreen, 2014). Specific to the medical field, Spiegel (2018) discusses four types of ethical concerns related to VR technologies.

Depersonalization/Derealization Disorder is one of the potential mental health risks caused by VR use. Furthermore, heavy use of VR technologies is also likely to cause users to ignore their own body and physical environment. VR technologies often blur the distinction between the real and the virtual. Finally, data about how an individual interact with the virtual environment is likely to invade personal privacy and manipulation (Spiegel, 2018). To address these potential issues, Spiegel (2018) and Goodman (2016) have proposed legal and policy amenties to better train health professionals to deal with the ethical impacts of VR and other digital reality technologies.

The potential impacts of digital reality technologies on journalism focus on the delimma that the technologies could create for more engaging and immersive storytelling (Polgreen, 2014). In Mullin's (2016) insightful discussion of VR applications in journalism, he raises the questions on how the use of digital reality technology could fundamentally challege conventional journalistic standards. Using the VR project, *The Displaced* (https://www.nytimes.com/2015/11/08/magazine/the-displaced-introduction. html), produced by *The New York Time Magazine*, to describe suffering children in the war-torn Ukraine, South Sudan, and Lebanon as an example, Mullins (2016) asks the following questions:

Do the technical requirements of virtual reality conflict with the long-held journalistic standards preventing photojournalists from influencing the scenes they record? Does its visceral nature require new guidelines governing explicit and traumatic imagery? Do its immersive experiences interfere with efforts to craft balanced narratives? And in the case of virtual reality that uses computer graphics to piece together scenes, how much reconstruction is permissible?

Some of his questions above also address several of McEvoy's (2018) ten ethical concerns related to digital reality technologies in terms of potential harms on unaware consumers of AR, MR, and VR technologies. To address these ethical concerns derived from these digital reality and other technologies, new regulations, international collaborations, and industry self-regulation best practices have been proposed (Barker, 2016; Horsfield, 2003; Lui & Lamb, 2018; Metivier-Carreiro & Lafollette, 1997). For example, taking a philosophical perspective, Horsfield (2003) discusses four ethical areas related to digital virtual reality: digital virtual reality contents, distraction and displacement questions, epistemological questions, and the question of power. Taken into consideration the lack of platform-specific regulations, Barker (2016) raises some pertinent issues that can also be applicable to digital reality technologies. For example, who will be responsible for the potential harms of digital reality contents (such as users' sense of desensitization and social isolation that McEvoy has discussed) since both the users and AR, MR, and VR designers "co-generate" such results?

Another equally important question may involve who should have control of users' behaviors in the virtual environment? This is also related to the question of power as brought up by Horsfield (2003). Finally, the massive amount of users' interaction and behavioral data with virtual objects in AR, MR, and VR applications unavoidably will lead to rising privacy concerns (Poushneh, 2018; Pridmore & Overocker, 2016; Spiegel, 2018). Scholars have begun to explore whether concerns about personal privacy may have effects on their satisfaction level (Poushneh, 2018). For example, using an experimental study, Poushneh (2018) examines how augmentation quality of an AR application in retailing may generate users' concerns over their access to their personal information and affect their satisfaction level. The empirical findings support that individuals do pay attention to the privacy concerns in an AR application and have significantly affect users' satisfaction level, despite the positive augmentation effects created by AR (Poushneh, 2018).

To sum up, the issue of privacy in an immersive virtual environment created by AR, MR, and VR technologies is of great relevance nowadays, when considering the advent of artificial intelligence (AI), Internet of Things (IoT), and Big Data that make personalized virtual experiences a possibility (Wortley,

2011). A recent survey by *eMarketer.com* (2018) of 260 participants from advertising agencies, brand advertisers, and tech vendors has found that data-dependent practices (such as audience targeting, audience segmentation, dynamic creative, and personalized offer) are ranked as top considerations. The growing dependence on individual personal data is likely to worsen similar privacy concerns in AR, MR, and VR applications.

CONCLUSION

To conclude, an edited book on the ever-changing digital reality technologies is less likely to keep abreast with the incessant changes in the field. However, this book hopes to open up more discussions to deal with less studied topics such as mobile multimodal system, machine learning and artificial intelligence, virtual reality datasets, fusion, representation, and validation, VR dialogue modeling, visual behaviors in social and multimodal interactions, to name a few. Issues related to the applications of digital reality technologies should be investigated to explore their impacts on various industry sectors and their convergence with gamification in game-based learning and marketing activities. As an increasingly ubiquitous technology, thanks for the popularity of smartphone, scholars should explore social, cultural, ethical, and regulatory concerns related to the applications of AR, MR, and VR that could touch upon every aspect of contemporary human experience.

Kenneth C. C. Yang
The University of Texas at El Paso, USA

REFERENCES

Arena, R. (2018, August 17). *Mixed reality not a reality for most companies, at least for now*. Retrieved on December 18, 2018 from https://www.emarketer.com/content/mixed-reality-tbd

Barker, K. (2016). Virtual spaces and virtual layers - governing the ungovernable? *Information & Communications Technology Law*, 25(1), 62–70. doi:10.1080/13600834.2015.1134146

Benes, R. (2018, October 11). *Five charts: How marketers use AI: Automated ad targeting is on the rise*. Retrieved on December 1, 2018 from https://content-na2011.emarketer.com/five-charts-how-marketers-use-ai

Chang, K.-E., Chang, C.-T., Hou, H.-T., Sung, Y.-T., Chao, H.-L., & Lee, C.-M. (2014). Development and behavioral pattern analysis of a mobile guide system with augmented reality for painting appreciation instruction in an art museum. *Computers & Education*, 71, 185–197. doi:10.1016/j.compedu.2013.09.022

Claudio, P., & Maddalena, P. (2014, January). Overview: Virtual reality in medicine. *Journal of Virtual Worlds Research*, 7(1), 1–33.

Collet, A., Chuang, M., Sweeney, P., Gillett, D., Evseev, D., & Calabrese, D. (n.d.). *High-quality streamable free-viewpoint video*. Redmond, WA: Microsoft. Retrieved on December 1, 2018 from http://hhoppe.com/fvv.pdf

Cook, A. V., Jones, R., Raghavan, A., & Saif, I. (2017, December 5). Digital reality: The focus shifts from technology to opportunity. *TechTrends*, 2018.

Davis, F. D. (1989). Perceived usefulness, perceived ease of use and user acceptance of information technology. *Management Information Systems Quarterly*, *13*(3), 319–340. doi:10.2307/249008

Davis, F. D., Bagozzi, P. R., & Warshaw, P. R. (1989). User acceptance of computer technology: A comparison of two theoretical models. *Management Science*, *35*(8), 982–1003. doi:10.1287/mnsc.35.8.982

Deloitte Consulting LLP & Consumer Technology Association. (2018, February 8). *Digital reality. A technical primer.* Deloitte Consulting LLP & Consumer Technology Association. Retrieved on December 8, 2018 from https://www2.deloitte.com/insights/us/en/topics/emerging-technologies/digital-reality-technical-primer.html

eMarketer.com. (2016, February 1). *Virtual reality is an immersive medium for marketers.* Retrieved on December 9, 2018 from https://www.emarketer.com/Article/Virtual-Reality-Immersive-Medium-Marketers/1013526

Emma-Ogbangwo, C., Cope, N., Behringer, R., & Fabri, M. (2014). *Enhancing user immersion and virtual presence in interactive multiuser virtual environments through the development and integration of a gesture-centric natural user interface developed from existing virtual reality technologies.* Paper presented at the International Conference, HCI International 2014. 10.1007/978-3-319-07857-1_72

Fink, C. (2017, December 13). Why consumer adoption of VR and AR will be slow. *Forbes.* Retrieved on December 8, 2018 from https://www.forbes.com/sites/charliefink/2017/2012/2013/why-consumer-adoption-of-vr-ar-will-be-slow/#2011f2783f28359f

Goodman, K. (2016). *Ethical considerations in the use of virtual reality.* Paper presented at the Home Ethics in Investigational & Interventional Uses of Immersive Virtual Reality (e3iVR).

Grubb, J. (2015, July 10). 7 factors that will make virtual reality and augmented reality worth $150b. *VB.* Retrieved on December 8, 2018 from https://venturebeat.com/2015/2007/2010/2017-factors-that-will-make-virtual-reality-and-augmented-reality-worth-2150b/

Gunkel, D., & Hawhee, D. (2003). Virtual alterity and the reformating of ethics. *Journal of Mass Media Ethics*, *18*(3&4), 173–193. doi:10.1207/S15327728JMME1803&4_3

Herschman, N. (2017, October 23). How AR/VR can create a "wow" experience at retail. *TWICE*, p. 14.

Holger, D. (2016, September 27). Report: VR adoption rates significantly jump in 2017. *VR Scout.* Retrieved on December 8, 2018 from https://vrscout.com/news/report-vr-adoption-rates-2017/

Horsfield, P. (2003). Continuities and discontinuities in ethical reflections on digital virtual reality. *Journal of Mass Media Ethics*, *19*(3&4), 155–172. doi:10.1207/S15327728JMME1803&4_2

Hsu, W.-Y. (2017). Brain computer interface connected to telemedicine and telecommunication in virtual reality applications. *Telematics and Informatics*, *34*(4), 224–238. doi:10.1016/j.tele.2016.01.003

Huang, T.-L., & Liao, S. (2015, June). A model of acceptance of augmented-reality interactive technology: The moderating role of cognitive innovativeness. *Electronic Commerce Research, 15*(2), 269–295. doi:10.100710660-014-9163-2

Huff, N., Hernandez, J. A., Fecteau, M., Zielinski, D., Brady, R., & LaBar, K. S. (2011). Revealing context-specific conditioned fear memories with full immersion virtual reality. *Frontiers in Behavioral Neuroscience, 5*(75). doi:10.3389/fnbeh.2011.00075 PMID:22069384

Johansson, A. (2018, June). 9 ethical problems with VR we still have to solve. *TNW*. Retrieved on December 10, 2018 from https://thenextweb.com/contributors/2018/2004/2018/2019-ethical-problems-vr-still-solve/

Kang, J. (2018, January). Virtual reality interfaces for interacting with three-dimensional graphs. *Wireless Personal Communications, 98*(2), 1931–1940. doi:10.100711277-017-4954-0

Kim, G., & Biocca, F. (2018, July 15-20). *Immersion in virtual reality can increase exercise motivation and physical performance.* Paper presented at the Virtual, Augmented and Mixed Reality: Applications in Health, Cultural Heritage, and Industry - 10th International Conference, VAMR 2018, Held as Part of HCI International 2018. 10.1007/978-3-319-91584-5_8

Kim, K., Rosenthal, Z., Zielinski, D., & Brady, R. (2014). Effects of virtual environment platforms on emotional responses. *Computer Methods and Programs in Biomedicine, 113*(3), 882–893. doi:10.1016/j.cmpb.2013.12.024 PMID:24440136

Levy, H. P. (2017, October 2). *Here's why CIOs will be the new executive leaders.* Gartner, Inc. Retrieved on December 7, 2018 from https://www.gartner.com/smarterwithgartner/heres-why-cios-will-be-the-new-executive-leaders/

Lui, A., & Lamb, G. W. (2018). Artificial intelligence and augmented intelligence collaboration: Regaining trust and confidence in the financial sector. *Information & Communications Technology Law, 27*(3), 267-283. doi:10.1080/13600834.13602018.11488659

Maillet, É., Mathieu, L., & Sicotte, C. (2015). Modeling factors explaining the acceptance, actual use and satisfaction of nurses using an electronic patient record in acute care settings: An extension of the utaut. *International Journal of Medical Informatics, 84*(1), 36–47. doi:10.1016/j.ijmedinf.2014.09.004 PMID:25288192

McEvoy, F. J. (2018, January 4). 10 ethical concerns that will shape the vr industry. *VB*. Retrieved on December 10, 2018 from https://venturebeat.com/2018/2001/2004/2010-ethical-concerns-that-will-shape-the-vr-industry/

Metivier-Carreiro, K. A., & Lafollette, M. C. (1997, September). Commentary: Balancing cyberspace promise, privacy, and protection--tracking the debate. *Science Communication, 19*(1), 3–20. doi:10.1177/1075547097019001001

Mullin, B. (2016, January 6). *Virtual reality: A new frontier in journalism ethics.* Retrieved on December 10, 2018 from https://www.poynter.org/news/virtual-reality-new-frontier-journalism-ethics

Nielsen. (2016, September 22). *Reality check: A peek at the virtual audiences of tomorrow.* Retrieved on December 8, 2018 from https://www.nielsen.com/us/en/insights/news/2016/reality-check-a-peek-at-the-virtual-audiences-of-tomorrow.html

Pagés, R., Amplianitis, K., Monaghan, D., Ondřej, J., & Smolić, A. (2018). Affordable content creation for free-viewpoint video and VR/AR applications. *Journal of Visual Communication and Image Representation, 53,* 192–201. doi:10.1016/j.jvcir.2018.03.012

Patrizio, A. (2017, July 12). Virtual reality companies: Top 20 VR companies to watch. *Datamation.* Retrieved on December 9, 2018 from https://www.datamation.com/mobile-wireless/virtual-reality-companies-top-2020-vr-companies-to-watch-2011.html

Paura, A. (2009, March). Virtual reality creates ethical challenges for journalists. *Digital Journalism.* Retrieved on December 10, 2018 from https://ijnet.org/en/story/virtual-reality-creates-ethical-challenges-journalists

Petrock, V. (2018, April 25). *Virtual reality beyond gaming: Solving business problems in industries.* Retrieved on December 9, 2018 from https://www.emarketer.com/content/virtual-reality-beyond-gaming

Pettey, C. (2018, January 4). *Immersive technologies are moving closer to the edge of artificial intelligence.* Gartner, Inc. Retrieved on December 7, 2018 from https://www.gartner.com/smarterwithgartner/immersive-technologies-are-moving-closer-to-the-edge-of-artificial-intelligence/

Phan, K., & Daim, T. (2011). Exploring technology acceptance for mobile services. *Journal of Industrial Engineering and Management, 4*(2), 339–360. doi:10.3926/jiem.2011.v4n2.p339-360

Polgreen, E. (2014, November 19). Virtual reality is journalism's next frontier. *Columbia Journalism Review.* Retrieved on December 10, 2018 from https://www.cjr.org/innovations/virtual_reality_journalism.php

Poushneh, A. (2018). Augmented reality in retail: A trade-off between user's control of access to personal information and augmentation quality. *Journal of Retailing and Consumer Services, 41,* 169–176. doi:10.1016/j.jretconser.2017.12.010

Pridmore, J., & Overocker, J. (2014, January). Privacy in virtual worlds: A US perspective. *Virtual World Research, 7*(1), Retrieved on December 12, 2018 from https://journals.tdl.org/jvwr/index.php/jvwr/article/view/7067

Queiroz, A. C. M. N., Moreira, A., Alejandro, T. B., Tori, R., De Melo, V. V., De Souza Meirelles, F., & Da Silva Leme, M. I. (2018). *Virtual reality in marketing: Technological and psychological immersion.* Paper presented at the 24th Americas Conference on Information Systems 2018: Digital Disruption, AMCIS 2018, Louisiana State University (LSU), College of Business.

RealityTechnology.com. (n.d.). *Reality technology market overview.* Retrieved on December 9, 2018 from https://www.realitytechnologies.com/market/

Rese, A., Baier, D., Geyer-Schulz, A., & Schreiber, S. (2017). How augmented reality apps are accepted by consumers: A comparative analysis using scales and opinions. *Technological Forecasting and Social Change, 124,* 306–319. doi:10.1016/j.techfore.2016.10.010

Rese, A., Schreiber, S., & Baier, D. (2014). Technology acceptance modeling of augmented reality at the point of sale: Can surveys be replaced by an analysis of online reviews? *Journal of Retailing and Consumer Services, 12*(5), 869–876. doi:10.1016/j.jretconser.2014.02.011

Roberts, P., & Henderson, R. (2000, April). Information technology acceptance in a sample of government employees: A test of the technology acceptance model. *Interacting with Computers, 12*(5), 427–443. doi:10.1016/S0953-5438(98)00068-X

Seitz, P. (2018, January 29). Augmented reality glasses still 23 years from consumer market. *Investors Business Daily.*

Spiegel, J. S. (2018, October). The ethics of virtual reality technology: Social hazards and public policy recommendations. *Science Engineering Ethics, 24*(5), 1537-1550. doi: 15 doi:10.100711948-11017-19979-y

Stein, C. (2016). Virtual reality design: How upcoming head-mounted displays change design paradigms of virtual reality worlds. *MediaTropes, 6*(1), 52–85.

Taherdoost, H. (2017, October 5-6). A review of technology acceptance and adoption models and theories. *Procedia Manufacturing, 22,* 960-967.

ThinkMobiles. (2018, April). *Augmented reality development companies in 2018.* Retrieved on December 9, 2018 from https://thinkmobiles.com/blog/augmented-reality-companies/

Tourville, S., & Forbes Agency Council. (2018, December 7). The power and promise of immersive technology in brand storytelling. *Forbes.* Retrieved on December 7, 2018 from https://www.forbes.com/sites/forbesagencycouncil/2018/2012/2007/the-power-and-promise-of-immersive-technology-in-brand-storytelling/?ss=leadership#49137b49132e49167b49135

Wortley, D. (2011). Immersive technologies and personalised learning: The influence of games-related technologies on 21st century learning. *Proceedings of the 4th Annual International Conference on Computer Games, Multimedia and Allied Technology, CGAT 2011 and 2nd Annual International Conference on Cloud Computing and Virtualization, CCV,* 74-78.

Yim, M. Y.-C., Chu, S.-C., & Sauer, P. L. (2017). Is augmented reality technology an effective tool for e-commerce? An interactivity and vividness perspective. *Journal of Interactive Marketing, 39,* 89–103. doi:10.1016/j.intmar.2017.04.001

Acknowledgment

I would like to thank the generous assistance from many people that took part in this book project. First, the excellent and visionary idea of the previous editor who developed the call for chapters and took on the first round of chapter solicitation and reviews. His foundational work has made my editorship much easier. Secondly, I am deeply indebted to the reviewers and the editorial advisory board members that took part in the review process to help shape and finalize this book project. This edited volume would not be possible without their time and effort.

Thirdly, special thanks will go to each one of the authors for their chapters that provide an significant addition to the current literature in virtual reality technologies, theories, and applications. These scholars have contributed their unique perspectives on the research of virtual technologies in their individual fields to broaden the coverage and depth of this book.

Finally, I dedicate this book to *Sanbao* who passed away unexpectedly on July 18, 2018 after his long and generous companion that brought immense happiness to my life.

Kenneth C. C. Yang
The University of Texas at El Paso, USA

Section 1
The Emergence of Digital Reality Technology

Section 1 provides an overview of emerging digital reality technologies (such as augmented, mixed, virtual realities, and 360-degree video) in the contemporary media ecosystem around the world. This section will provide background on the technologies by examining their technological attributes, their global diffusion, theoretical paradigms, and consumer behavior implications that have been gradually felt among many countries around the world.

Chapter 1
Reality–Creating Technologies as a Global Phenomenon

Kenneth C. C. Yang
The University of Texas at El Paso, USA

EXECUTIVE SUMMARY

Digital reality technologies have become a global phenomenon that attracts huge attention from researchers and practitioners around the world. ResearchandMarkets.com predicts that the global revenue for both augmented reality (AR) and virtual reality (VR) applications will reach $94.4 billion by 2023. As an introductory chapter to the edited book volume on the global impacts of digital reality technologies, this chapter examines the current state of digital reality technologies around the world. Global, regional, and country statistics are presented to shed light on the diffusion of a variety of digital reality technologies such as augmented reality, mixed reality, and virtual reality. Potential and existing digital realty technologies around the world will be examined in greater detail to provide readers with contextual information for the remaining chapters of the book.

INTRODUCTION

The Global Digital Reality Technology Market

The term, digital reality technology, is proposed by Deloitte Consulting LLP & Consumer Technology Association (2018), to refer to a set of technologies that are able to immerse users in a computer-generated virtual environment. Because of their technical capabilities and potentialities to separate users from their actual physical world through augmented (AR), mixed (MR), and virtual reality (VR), these technologies are also called *immersive technologies* in the literature (Forbes, Kinnell, & Goh, 2018) and trade publications (*eMarketer.com*, 2018a, b, c, d, e, f). Some scholars have expanded the scope of digital reality technology to cover video games, virtual worlds, and social networking technologies (Wortley, 2011).

Virtual reality (VR) is an immersive technology that aims to reduce users' other sensory inputs, except those presented to them through a head-mounted or helmet-mounted display (HDM) device (Herschman, 2017). Augmented reality (AR), on the other hand, is different from virtual reality (VR)

DOI: 10.4018/978-1-5225-5912-2.ch001

because, unlike the need for a specialized head-mounted display (HMD), AR can be easily accessed through user's smartphone and mobile devices (Petrock, 2018). AR users are able to interact with "[o] verlaying of images in physical contexts via the augmented reality feature" (de Gortari, 2018, n.p.). This technological advance has made digital reality technologies "closer to mainstream" (Petrock, 2018, n.p.). Furthermore, unlike VR, users need to rely on external audio and visual inputs as part of their interactions with the virtual environment (Herschman, 2017). Unlike AR and VR that offer mostly "synthetic" (graphic) contents, 360-degree video is able to offer real-world contents, captured by "omnidirectional camera rigs" (Pagés, Amplianitis, Monaghan, Ondřej, & Smolić, 2018, p. 192).

In Figure 1, the global AR, MR, and VR markets have grown from USD$9 billion in 2016, expects to grow to USD$25.6 billion in 2018, and will reach USD$40.6 in 2019 (Deloitte Consulting LLP & Consumer Technology Association, 2018). Divided by core AR, MR, and VR technologies, AR has surpassed VR in 2016 in terms of its market size of USD$5.2 billion vs. USD$3.7 billion in 2016. Due to rapid diffusion of smartphone and related apps, AR's growth is expected to continue and exceed other immersive technologies such as VR at USD$13.1 billion and MR at USD$0.3 billion in 2019 (Deloitte Consulting LLP & Consumer Technology Association, 2018). Despite the promising prediction of MR, its market size is relatively unimportant, growing from USD$0.1 billion in 2016, to USD$0.2 billion in 2018, and USD$0.3 billion in 2019 (Deloitte Consulting LLP & Consumer Technology Association, 2018). Refer to Figure 1 below for more details.

The global virtual reality market has been predicted to grow intensely between 2017 and 2027 (*Business Wire*, 2018). In particular, in the healthcare area, VR applications have seen a rapid growth (*eMarketer Editor*, 2018). In addition, entertainment, gaming, and sports account for the majority of VR applications (Petrock, 2018). According to a 2017 survey conducted by *eMarketer.com*, 74% of the respondents indicate that gaming will be most impacted by VR technology, followed by education (36%), architecture, engineering, and construction (32%), medical and healthcare (30%), creative and culture industries (such as broadcasting, film, and TV) (27%), and marketing communication sectors (27%) (Petrock, 2018).

Among four billion Internet users around the world, the ownership of a VR headset is comparatively low to support its full potential, even across different geographic regions (Petrock, 2018). In North

Figure 1. Digital reality technology market around the world

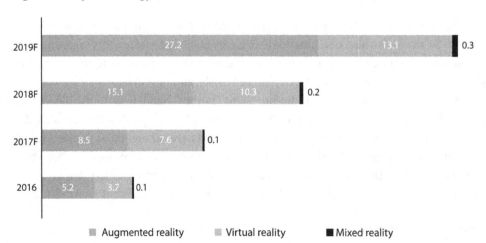

America, only 5% of respondents between 16 and 64 years old have owned a VR headset, the number is even lower among Internet users in Middle East & Africa at 2% (Petrock, 2018). Other regions only reach 3% of its population in terms of VR headset ownership (Refer to Figure 2) (Petrock, 2018).

The cost of a VR and AR handset could be an inhibitor to widespread adoption of these technologies. Citing IDC data, Gagliordi (2017) points out that AR and VR headset shipment is expected to increase from 10.1 million in 2016 to 99.4 million in 2021. Data from *CCS Insight* predict that by the year of 2022, shipment of smartphone AR and VR will account for 63% of the total shipment, compared with 32% for that of dedicated VR, 5% for that of AR smart glasses, and only 1% for that of enhanced AR (*eMarketer.com*, 2018a). Combined with the increasing number of immersive contents, industry pundits have a favorable assessment of these two technologies. In particular, the popularity of smartphone has prompted the usage of AR due to its ease of access. Disparities of AR and VR equipment can be found that commercial AR (18.78%) is more prevalent than consumer AR (2.80%) equipment in 2022, while the diffusion of VR among commercial and consumer adopters is more balanced (International Data Corporation, 2018)

According to *eMarketer.com* (2018b), a survey of 1,000 smartphone users above 18 years old has found that accessing AR applications or contents via user's smartphone is overwhelmingly preferred over a dedicated AR smart glass. For example, 87% of the U.K. smartphone users chose smartphone in social communication, while the number is 82% for connected packaging, 78% for task fulfilment, 71% for product trial before purchase, etc. (Mindshare & Zappar, cited in *eMarketer.com*, 2018b). In the U.S., ownership of VR headset among US Internet users has grown from 0% in 2014 and 2015, to 8% in 2016, to 10% in 2017, and to 8% in 2018 (*eMarketer.com*, 2018d). The number of augmented reality users in the U.S. has also seen a steady growth from 9.5% of the population (about 30.9 million) in 2016, to 15.5% (about 51.2 million) in 2018, and is expected to increase to 20.2% (about 67.5 million) in 2019 (*eMarketer.com*, 2018d). In terms of the age distribution of VR headset owners in Japan, the 30-39 years old segment is the major adopters (17% of respondents in this bracket), followed by the 15-19 year old bracket (14.8%) (Macromill, 2017). Other age brackets of Japanese VR headset owners have around 10% of each age group: 9.8% for 20-29 years old bracket, 9.6% for 40-49 years old bracket, and 10.1% for 50-59 years old bracket (Macromill, 2017). The higher than average adoption among 15-19 years old

Figure 2. Ownership of VR headset by region (2017 Q1)

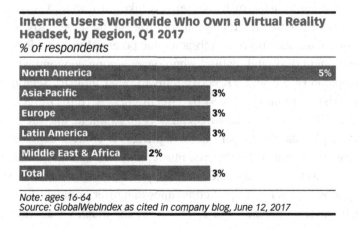

is likely attributed to the popularity of digital game in Japan and similarly around many economically developed countries around the world.

To conclude this section, different types of headsets have been developed, on the basis of hardware types to generate different levels and types of enjoyment (Clemmons, 2017). Clemmons has developed a virtual representation of how mobile AR, mobile VR, desktop/console VR, and dedicated AR technologies are related to each other in term of type of hardware and type of enjoyment. In Clemmons' map, four quadrants are created to describe the relationships between mobile vs. dedicated device (i.e., type of hardware) and simulated/separate vs. enhance/existing (i.e., type of enjoyment). According to the map, a dedicated device such as *Oculus*, *PlayStation VR*, and *VIVE* is able to generate simulated, but separate, enjoyment (in the left bottom quadrant), while *Samsung Gear VR* and *Google Cardboard* have the convenience of mobility and a relatively low cost (in the upper left quadrant) (Clemmons, 2017). On the other hand, mobile AR applications such as those provided by *Facebook*, *Vufonria*, and *Tango* are able to provide existing and enhanced enjoyment through mobile AR devices (in the upper right quadrant). *HoleLens* and *Meta* are both dedicated AR devices to offer enhanced and existing enjoyment (Clemmons, 2017).

BACKGROUND

The Digital Reality Technology Ecosystem

In a global study of marketers to learn the types of content that they will invest in 2018, 28.2% of all marketers in this survey show that they will invest in virtual reality, while 21.6% will spend on AR. (*eMarkter.com*, 2018g). However, there are noticeable country variations among marketers from Singapore who are most enthusiastic about the promise of VR (55.3%), while French and Singaporean marketers in the same survey are almost equally eager about the opportunities created by AR (35.6% and 35.0%, respectively) (*eMarkter.com*, 2018g). Australia is most lukewarm about either VR (19%) or AR (12.5%) among economically developed countries (such as France, Germany, UK and US) in this survey (*eMarkter.com*, 2018g). In the U.S. about 27.7% of the surveyed marketers will invest in VR, while 21.8% of them will allocate company resources to AR in 2018 (*eMarkter.com*, 2018g). The number for VR investment in UK is 23.3%, and that for AR is 20.9% (*eMarkter.com*, 2018g). Contrary to what many would anticipate, marketers in Germany is relatively lukewarm about VR (18.5%), what 10.2% will spend on AR, when compared with other European countries in the same study (*eMarkter.com*, 2018g).

Despite their cross-national variations in embracing the potentialities of AR, MR, and VR technologies, the vibrant development of digital reality technologies among economically-developed countries has prompted the expansion of AR and VR ecosystems to other industry sectors previously to be old and traditional media. Using a map produced by Greenlight VR (https://greenlightinsights.com/wp-content/uploads/2015/07/2015-vr-ecosystem-map.png) as an example, the VR ecosystem is composed of industry sectors in display hardware, peripheral haptics, VR content capture, content studios (i.e., cinematic, gaming, news & documentary, sports, music, and live actions), industry applications (i.e., education, healthcare, tourism, real estate, and finance), production, tools, and services, app stores, social etc. Each industry subsector is made up of companies that offer products, services, and professional skills to meet individual users' demands. For example, for the display hardware sector, *Sony*, *Oculus* and *Fove* manufacture HMD, while *Samsung Gear*, *LG*, and *Google* produce mobile VR devices. The convergence of digital reality technologies with existing and emerging media platforms such as film, news and documentary, social, media, and information/data service sectors demonstrates their pervasive impacts across national borders. For example, in the cinematic sector, companies such as *VR Playhouse*, *WEVR*, *PENROSE*, ad *StoryStudio* as emerged to produce VR-related contents, while *ALCHEMY VR*, *EXPEDITIONS*, and *SOLIARAX* create VR-related educational contents. Other emerging players include *UPLOAD*, *SVVR*, *VR Scout*, *ENTERVR*, among others in the media sector (Greenlight VR., n.d.).

Country-specific ecosystem maps are also widely available after conducting Google searches. For example, an ecosystem map that includes both AR and VR players in Australia has shown similar categorization of industry sectors (http://patriciahaueiss.com/augmented-virtual-mixed-reality-ecosystem-report-2018-highlighting-australias-innovation-capabilities/) while showing the variation of AR, MR, and VR technologies in different countries. Data published by *eMarketer.com* (2018g) has shown that Australia is the least enthusiastic about investment on either VR (19%) or AR (12.5%) when compared with France, Germany, UK and US. Nevertheless, the Australian government has been eager to take advantage of the rising USD$106.5 AR and VR market in the country (McLean, 2018). This Australian ecosystem map has included 10 major industry subsectors that range from software development, 360 degree video, arcade, agency, education, network, university, accelerator, platform, and corporate lab. Given the size of each sub-section as visually represented in the map above, software development and 360 degree video sectors have attracted the largest number of players. One of the noteworthy players in the Australian ecosystem is the important role of major universities to help with the research and development (R&D) of digital reality technologies. Some examples of these participating universities include University of Sydney, RMIT, Monash University, UNSW, etc. Unlike AR and VR equipment manufacturers that are dominated by well-know brands, the burgeoning software development and 360 degree video studio sectors are mostly occupied by local players such as *INSPACE XR*, *FRAME VR*, *PAND-AD*, *Oceanic VR*, *JUMPGate*, *CATALYST VR*, *PixelCase*, among others.

Research Objectives and Research Questions

The objectives of this book chapter are to better understand the current state of digital reality technologies around the world to identify and describe emerging issues in the applications of these technologies. In particular, this book chapter aims to answer the following research questions:

RQ1: What are current state of different types of digital reality technologies (such as AR, MR, VR, and other immersive technologies) around the world?
RQ2: What are the determinants of explaining the global diffusion of these digital reality technologies?
RQ3: What are the roles of businesses and consumers in the diffusion of digital reality technologies around the world?

Research Methods

To provide useful contextual information for the forthcoming chapters of this edited volume, this book chapter employs a secondary research method, defined as one type of literature review (Becker, 2007, cited in Curtis & Curtis, 2011) by examining data or research databases available offline or online in libraries, government and research institutes, research companies (such as Nielsen, *eMarketer.com*, *com.Score*, and other research firms) or from the Internet (Curtis & Curtis, 2011). The author has used keywords or phrases such as "augmented reality," "mixed reality," "virtual reality," "360 degree video," "immersive technologies", etc. to search for information for later analysis.

MAIN FOCUS OF THE CHAPTER

This book chapter will focus on two main areas to search, retrieve, and analyze articles, reports, and statistics that have been identified in the author's search efforts. This chapter will primarily emphasize two areas of inquiries: responses to digital reality technologies from the viewpoints of both business communities and consumers.

Business Potentials and Best Practices of Digital Reality Technology

The advent of digital reality technologies has particularly drawn ample interests among business communities. For example, advertising agencies in Europe is currently using AR (23%) and VR (22%), while 32% of them are considering AR and 22% are thinking of VR for future adoption (*eMarketer.com*, 2018h). The ubiquitous influence of AR, MR, and VR technologies can be seen in almost all aspects of business operations. Deloitte identifies five promising business opportunities in applying digital reality technology in a commercial and industrial context; those are *connect, explore, know, learn,* and *play* (cited in WIRED Brand Lab, 2018). From the perspective of businesses, digital reality technologies have been envisioned to connect capacities available to a business, regardless of their locations (WIRED Brand Lab, 2018). The practice of so-called "cooperation without co-location" (WIRED Brand Lab, 2018, n.p.) is most beneficial to businesses that can offer trainings and services to their customers and businesses from a remote location (WIRED Brand Lab, 2018). As stated by Facebook's Ash Jhaveri about this potential (WIRED Brand Lab, 2018, n.p.):

Our virtual reality products originally were targeted at consumers, but by addressing the social aspect and presence, VR can remove barriers that transcend distance and time in ways that can benefit the enterprise.

The exploration function of these digital reality technologies often refers to their applications in attracting customers to a company's experiences, products, and services (WIRED Brand Lab, 2018, n.p.). For example, home improvement brands such as *Ikea, Lowes*, and *Mayfair* have employed AR to allow users to simulate how a furniture would look like in their home to better explore their design choices (Alcántara, 2018). *Ikea* has developed its *Ikea Place* app to showcase over 2,000 *Ikea* products that allow consumers to virtually place their choice before placing their final order (Ikea, 2017). *Ikea's* VR station, *Virtual Home Experience*, also offers consumers with a simulated demonstration of its product at its brick-and-mortar stores (Shridhar & Herschman, 2017). Many retailers have also believed that consumers' virtual experiences with their products or services could eventually lead to higher purchase intention (WIRED Brand Lab, 2018).

The educational function (or "Know" according to Deloitte) refers to the potential applications of digital reality technologies to allow "knowledge workers" to access essential information to enable their professional practices (WIRED Brand Lab, 2018). For example, Butnaru and Girbacia (2009) explore the capabilities of the VR technology to create a collaborative pre-surgery planning to reduce the time in actual bone surgery. Using the networked *CAVE* systems and *Reachin Display* will allow surgeons to analyze patient's bones to reduce the operation time. Similarly, in the advertising and marketing industries, the combination of artificial intelligence and digital reality applications is likely to generate more personalized virtual experiences to make advertising and marketing campaigns more effective (Benes, 2018).

The educational function of digital reality technologies will let users to employ these technologies to learn and is most commonly used in a technology-enabled virtual learning environment (WIRED Brand Lab, 2018; Shin, 2017). Virtual learning made possible by digital reality technologies not only allows users to access educational contents online, but to learn new skills such as data visualization, spatial socialization, and sharing (Shin, 2017). AR technology has been used in creative and cultural industries (such as cultural heritage and virtual museums) to engage museum-goers to relive the life of ancient tribal men, to immerse themselves in the underwater exploration, or to explore an ancient Egyptian tomb. Chung, Lee, Kim, and Koo (2017) confirm the relationships between consumers' beliefs about AR, their satisfaction with AR, and subsequent attitudes and behavioral intention toward a tourist destination, suggesting the huge potential of these technologies in the consumption of cultural contents and products.

Many businesses have experimented or implemented different functionalities for AR applications, depending on what AR users would prefer in their individual trade (*eMarketer.com*, 2018d). In Figure 3, gaming is the most preferred AR application among different Western European countries (such as Belgium, France, Germany, Italy, Netherlands, Spain, Sweden, UK), followed by transportation and travel (22%), home improvement (17%), fitness (16%), and retail (15%). As shown in Figure 3, there are minor percentage variations to account AR users' preference in individual countries, but the overall trend is consistent what is ranked to be users' favorite applications.

Figure 3. AR applications in different Western European Countries

Industries in Which Augmented Reality Users in Select Countries in Western Europe Have Used AR, Nov 2017

% of respondents

	Gaming	Transport & travel	Home	Fitness	Retail
Belgium	81%	23%	17%	16%	18%
UK	79%	14%	10%	8%	8%
Sweden	78%	22%	17%	10%	15%
Germany	75%	25%	16%	16%	11%
Spain	69%	22%	16%	20%	12%
Italy	68%	29%	21%	26%	25%
France	68%	18%	16%	12%	12%
Netherlands	67%	23%	18%	18%	18%
Total	**73%**	**22%**	**17%**	**16%**	**15%**

Note: ages 18+
Source: Osborne Clarke, "The European connected consumer: A life lived online" conducted by YouGov, April 5, 2018

Business decisions to develop AR. MR, and VR applications are often contingent on managers' perceptions of their profitability potentialities. Figure 4 also reports findings from a global survey of 603 executives from China, Finland, France, Germany, Norway, Sweden, US, and UK. The survey attempts to understand if these businesses are experimenting or implementing AR and VR for industrial use (*eMarketer.com*, 2018e). Based on the statistics reported in Figure 4, VR experimentation has been adopted by a large percentage of these business users (64%), while only 36% of them are currently implementing AR and VR for industrial use (*eMarketer.com*, 2018e). Germany is the most eager country (77%), to experiment with VR in the business setting, followed by Finland, Norway, and Sweden at 72% (See Figure 4). Actual implementation with AR for industrial use seems to be on the rise (45%). Figure 4 also reports country variation data that might need to be explored further to explain what cause these differences from a country to another.

Consumers' Responses to Digital Reality Technology

Consumers' responses and acceptance of a technology have been two popular research topics. Consumer behavior models such as The Technology Acceptance Model (TAM) (Davis, 1989) and Extended Technology Acceptance Model (TAM2) (Davis & Bagozzi, 1989) have been widely used among academic researchers in the technical aspects of digital reality technologies to explore the relationships between perceived technical attributes (such as TAM's perceived ease of use [PEOU], perceive usefulness [PU]), attitude toward, intention to use, and actual use of a technology (Davis, 1989). Other consumer adoption behavior models have been developed to study determinants, processes, and outcomes of technology adoption (Refer to Taherdoost, 2017 for a thorough description of various adoption behavior models). Some other theoretical examples include The Theory of Reasoned Action (TRA), Uses and Gratifi-

Figure 4. West European executives' interests in AR and VR experimentation and implementation

Executives in Select Countries Whose Companies Are Experimenting with vs. Implementing AR & VR for Industrial Use, by Country
% of respondents, June 2018

	AR		VR	
	Experimenting	**Implementing**	**Experimenting**	**Implementing**
China	49%	51%	49%	51%
France	52%	48%	57%	43%
Germany	62%	38%	77%	23%
UK	64%	36%	67%	33%
US	41%	59%	58%	42%
Select countries*	85%	15%	72%	28%
Total	**55%**	**45%**	**64%**	**36%**

*Note: n=603 at automotive, manufacturing and utility companies that are at least experimenting with AR/VR; *Finland, Norway and Sweden*
Source: Capgemini, "Augmented and Virtual Reality in Operations," Sep 7, 2018

cations Model (U&G), Diffusion of Innovation Theory, The Theory of PC Utilization (MPCU), etc. (Taherdoost, 2017).

Regardless of what adoption models that have been used, consumers' awareness of a technology has been proven most crucial to its subsequent usage. This variable is often treated as the first phase of any consumer behavior phases. A survey of Western European countries have found that about 47% of the Internet users are aware of AR, but only 12% of them have actually used the technology (*eMarketer. com*, 2018f). It is apparent that there is a noticeable gap between awareness and actual usage of AR in West Europe. Countries such as Spain, Italy, and UK have over 50% the respondents who suggest they are aware of AR, but their actual usage often falls below 15% (*eMarketer.com*, 2018f). Netherlands and Belgium have about 34% and 37% awareness level, but their actual usage is comparable to Spain, Italy, and UK (*eMarketer.com*, 2018f). Refer to Figure 5 for more information.

Most consumer adoption theories postulate the linear process that knowledge follows awareness. Nielsen's (2016) online survey of 8,000 consumers offers the most descriptive relationship between knowledge and fan (i.e., holding favorable attitude toward) of a list of ICTs. As demonstrated in Figure 6 below, more well-known and mature technologies (such as smartphone and tablet), consumers tend to have the same level of knowledge about the technologies, compared to their more emotional responses to the same technologies (Nielsen, 2016). Technologies that are heavily hyped in the mass media tend to generate more favorable attitudes (i.e., fan) even though consumers might not know as much as an expert. Some examples of these ICTs are self-driving car (22% knowledge vs. 33% fan) and 3D printing (24% knowledge vs. 45% fan). For AR and VR, both have received a lot of hyperbole in the media, leading to a relative positive attitudes among consumers (in terms of fan-o-meter: AR at 20% and VR at 36%), even though knowledge level about these two technologies are observably lower with AR at 14% and VR at 27%. It is also observable from Figure 6 that there seems to be a positive correlation with the year of

Figure 5. Awareness of and interest in AR among internet users in West Europe

Usage and Awareness of Augmented Reality Among Internet Users in Select Countries in Western Europe, Nov 2017
% of respondents

	Awareness	Usage
Spain	58%	14%
Italy	55%	13%
UK	51%	13%
France	48%	12%
Germany	48%	9%
Sweden	46%	16%
Belgium	37%	10%
Netherlands	34%	11%
Total	**47%**	**12%**

Note: ages 18+
Source: Osborne Clarke, "The European connected consumer: A life lived online" conducted by YouGov, April 5, 2018

diffusion, and consumers' knowledge level. In other words, more established and mature technologies tend to generate a high level of knowledge among consumers: smartphone at 71% and tablet at 60%) (Nielsen, 2016). Latest technological innovations such as chat bots (16%) and AR (14%) tend to have lower knowledge level as expected (Refer to Figure 6).

In both academic and practical research, demographics of AR, MR, and VR users continue to offer useful insights into consumers' adoption behaviors. *eMarketer.com* (2018i) reports a survey of 703 participants to examine demographic profiles of mobile AR users in the U.S. The survey finds that AR has attracted a large percentage of female users (54%) (*eMarketer.com*, 2018i). The majority of them falls in the 25 to 34 age bracket (36%), followed by 35-44 years old (29%) and 18-24 years old (16%)

Figure 6. Awareness of and interest in AR among internet users in West Europe

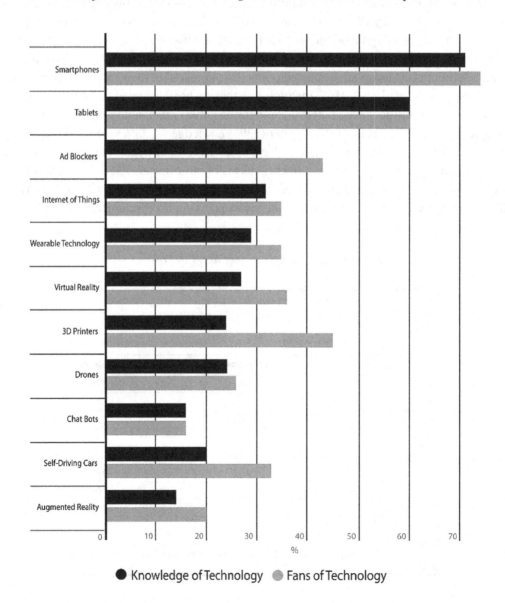

(*eMarketer.com*, 2018i). As expected, older users (above 55 years old) tend to be laggards in adopting this new technology (*eMarketer.com*, 2018i). Household income continues to account for the adoption behaviors of AR technology, along with other ICTs as anticipated in the literature and trade publications. Families who are making more $75,000 are the major adopter category of mobile AR (41%), when compared with those making less than $25,000 (*eMarketer.com*, 2018) (Refer to Figure 7).

CONCLUSION

As an introductory chapter, this book chapter has been written intentionally to be descriptive and data intensive to offer readers some background information about the global diffusion of AR, MR, and VR technologies. The detailed analysis of reports, statistics, and charts from the secondary research also attempts to provide economic justifications of why researchers and practitioners need to pay attention to these digital reality technologies as a global phenomenon that is likely to affect how businesses will be conducted. This book chapter ends with a quick survey of consumer-related consideration in research digital reality technologies. The present chapter is undoubtedly limited by the scope of secondary materials retrieved and analyzed, but readers are invited to explore discipline-specific chapters that offer more relevant insights into the planning, development, experimentation, and implementation of AR, MR, and VR technologies in their individual field.

A descriptive chapter on the current state of AR, MR, and VR technologies around the world is evidently limited by the timeliness and coverage of data. Given the large number of countries that this

Figure 7. Demographics of US mobile AR users

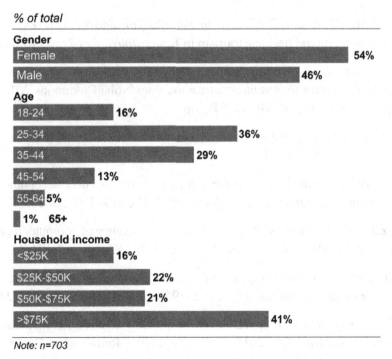

% of total

Gender
Female — 54%
Male — 46%

Age
18-24 — 16%
25-34 — 36%
35-44 — 29%
45-54 — 13%
55-64 — 5%
1% 65+

Household income
<$25K — 16%
$25K-$50K — 22%
$50K-$75K — 21%
>$75K — 41%

Note: n=703

chapter intends to cover, the analyses are unavoidably limited to economically-developed countries where research data are more accessible than their less developed counterparts. Future research will benefit the digital reality communities greatly by offering country-specific studies from these countries.

REFERENCES

Alcántara, A.-M. (2018, March). Brands are finally embracing augmented reality, but not without speed bumps. *AdWeek*. Retrieved on August 4, 2018 from https://www.adweek.com/digital/brands-are-finally-embracing-augmented-reality-but-with-speed-bumps-along-the-way/

Benes, R. (2018, October 11). *Five charts: How marketers use AI: Automated ad targeting is on the rise.* Retrieved on December 1, 2018 from https://content-na2011.emarketer.com/five-charts-how-marketers-use-ai

Burritt, M. (2017, December 11-24). Experts: Amazon's mixed reality software is a tool, not a solution. *Furniture/Today, 6.*

Business Wire. (2018, November 28). Global virtual reality (VR) market analysis & forecast to 2027 - increasing adoption of head-mounted displays (HMD) in the gaming & entertainment sector - research-andmarkets.Com. *Business Wire*. Retrieved on December 1, 2018 from https://www.businesswire.com/news/home/20181128005629/en/

Butnaru, T., & Girbacia, F. (2009). *Collaborative pre-surgery planning in a tele-immersive environment using VR technology.* Paper presented at the FMBE Proceedings of International Conference on Advancements of Medicine and Health Care through *Technology.*

Chung, N., Lee, H., Kim, J.-Y., & Koo, C. (2017). The role of augmented reality for experience-influenced environments: The case of cultural heritage tourism in Korea. *Journal of Travel Research*, 1–17.

Clemmons, N. (2017, June 8). Analyzing the false dichotomy of AR vs. VR. *Gamasutra*. Retrieved on December 1, 2018 from https://www.gamasutra.com/blogs/NolanClemmons/20170608/20299550/Analyzing_the_False_Dichotomy_of_AR_vs_VR.php

Curtis, B., & Curtis, C. (2011). *Social research: A practical introduction.* Thousand Oaks, CA: Sage Publications. doi:10.4135/9781526435415

Davis, F. D. (1989). Perceived usefulness, perceived ease of use and user acceptance of information technology. *Management Information Systems Quarterly*, *13*(3), 319–340. doi:10.2307/249008

Davis, F. D., Bagozzi, P. R., & Warshaw, P. R. (1989). User acceptance of computer technology: A comparison of two theoretical models. *Management Science*, *35*(8), 982–1003. doi:10.1287/mnsc.35.8.982

de Gortari, A. B. O. (2018). Empirical study on game transfer phenomena in a location-based augmented reality game. *Telematics and Informatics*, *35*(2), 382–396. doi:10.1016/j.tele.2017.12.015

eMarketer.com. (2017, December 4). *Planned change in spending on mobile content among smartphone users worldwide*, by content type, Nov. 2017 (% of respondents).* Retrieved on December 1, 2018 from http://totalaccess.emarketer.com/chart.aspx?r=215051

eMarketer.com. (2018a, April 9). *Chart: Virtual and augmented reality device shipment and sales share worldwide, by device type, 2022 (% of total).* Retrieved on Dec. 1, 2018 from http://totalaccess.emarketer.com/chart.aspx?r=219212

eMarketer.com. (2018b, April 24). *Chart: UK smartphone users who prefer using smart glasses vs. Smartphone for select augmented reality activities, April 2018 (% of respondents).* Retrieved on December 1, 2018 from http://totalaccess.emarketer.com/chart.aspx?r=220210

eMarketer.com. (2018c, April 5). *Industries in which augmented reality users in select countries in Western Europe have used AR, Nov. 2017 (% of respondents).* Retrieved on December 1, 2018 from http://totalaccess.emarketer.com/chart.aspx?r=219349

eMarketer.com. (2018d, November 12). *Ownership of VR headsets among US internet users, July 2014-Aug 2018 (% of respondents).* Retrieved on December 1, 2018 from, http://totalaccess.emarketer.com/chart.aspx?r=224365

eMarketer.com. (2018e, September 7). *Executives in select countries whose companies are experimenting with vs. Implementing AR & VR for industrial use, by country (% of respondents, June 2018).* Retrieved on December 19, 2018 from http://totalaccess.emarketer.com/chart.aspx?r=222816

eMarketer.com. (2018f, April 5). *Usage and awareness of augmented reality among internet users in select countries in Western Europe, Nov 2017 (% of respondents).* Retrieved on December 1, 2018 from http://totalaccess.emarketer.com/chart.aspx?r=219347

eMarketer.com. (2018g, March 13). *Types of content in which marketers in select countries will invest in 2018 (% of respondents).* Retrieved on December 1, 2018 from http://totalaccess.emarketer.com/chart.aspx?r=217368

eMarketer.com. (2018h, September 24). *Which emerging technologies are agencies and brands in Europe using in their marketing strategy? (% of respondents, July 2018).* Retrieved on December 1, 2018 from http://totalaccess.emarketer.com/chart.aspx?r=222826

eMarketer.com. (2018i, March 15). *Demographic profile of us mobile augmented reality users, jan 2018 (% of total).* Retrieved on December 1, 2018 from http://totalaccess.emarketer.com/chart.aspx?r=219053

eMarkter Editors. (2018, April 24). *Marketers' roundtable: Why the healthcare industry is embracing virtual reality and how organizations can get started.* Retrieved on December 1, 2018 from https://content-na2011.emarketer.com/why-the-healthcare-industry-is-embracing-virtual-reality

Forbes, T., Kinnell, P., & Goh, M. (2018, August 17). *A study into the influence of visual prototyping methods and immersive technologies on the perception of abstract product properties.* Paper presented at the NordDesign: Design in the Era of Digitalization, NordDesign 2018.

Gagliordi, N. (2017, March 16). VR, AR headset shipments will increase tenfold by 2021: IDC. *ZDNet.* Retrieved on December 1, 2018 from https://www.zdnet.com/article/vr-ar-headset-shipments-will-increase-tenfold-by-2021-idc/

IKEA. (2017, September 12). *IKEA launches Ikea place, a new app that allows people to virtually place furniture in their home.* Retrieved on December 12, 2018 from https://www.ikea.com/us/en/about_ikea/newsitem/091217_IKEA_Launches_IKEA_Place

International Data Corporation (IDC). (2018, September 20). *AR/VR headset shipments worldwide, commercial vs. Consumer, 2018 & 2022 (millions and CAGR).* Retrieved on December 1, 2018 from http://totalaccess.emarketer.com/chart.aspx?r=222930

Lesch, W. C., & Hazeltine, J. E. (2013). Secondary research, new product screening, and the marketing research course: An experiment in structured decision making. In J. Goodwin (Ed.), *Secondary data analysis* (pp. 1–16). Thousand Oaks, CA: Sage Publications, Inc.

Macromill. (2017, October 17). *Internet users in Japan who own a virtual reality headset*, by age, Sep 2017 (% of respondents in each group).* Retrieved in December 1, 2018 from http://totalaccess.emarketer.com/chart.aspx?r=213870

McLean, A. (2018, June 26). Australia looks to capitalise on $150b AR and VR market opportunity. *ZDNet.* Retrieved on December 1, 2018 from https://www.zdnet.com/article/australia-looks-to-capitalise-on-2150b-ar-and-vr-market-opportunity/

Nielsen. (2016, September 22). *Reality check: A peek at the virtual audiences of tomorrow.* Retrieved on December 8, 2018 from https://www.nielsen.com/us/en/insights/news/2016/reality-check-a-peek-at-the-virtual-audiences-of-tomorrow.html

Pagés, R., Amplianitis, K., Monaghan, D., Ondřej, J., & Smolić, A. (2018). Affordable content creation for free-viewpoint video and VR/AR applications. *Journal of Visual Communication and Image Representation, 53*, 192–201. doi:10.1016/j.jvcir.2018.03.012

Petrock, V. (2018, April 25). *Virtual reality beyond gaming: Solving business problems in industries.* Retrieved on December 9, 2018 from https://www.emarketer.com/content/virtual-reality-beyond-gaming

Seitz, P. (2018, January 29). Augmented reality glasses still 23 years from consumer market. *Investors Business Daily.*

Shin, D. (2018). Empathy and embodied experience in virtual environment: To what extent can virtual reality stimulate empathy and embodied experience? *Computers in Human Behavior, 78*, 64–73. doi:10.1016/j.chb.2017.09.012

Shrindhar, S., & Herschman, N. (2017, October 23). How AR/VR can create a 'wow' experience at retail. *TWICE,* p. 14.

Taherdoost, H. (2017, October 5-6). A review of technology acceptance and adoption models and theories. *Procedia Manufacturing, 22*, 960-967.

We Are Social. (2018, January). *Digital in 2018.* Retrieved on December 1, 2018 from https://wearesocial.com/blog/2018/01/global-digital-report-2018

WIRED Brand Lab. (2018). Digital reality: The focus shifts from technology to opportunity. *Wired.* Retrieved on December 12, 2018 from https://www.wired.com/brandlab/2018/2002/digital-reality-focus-shifts-technology-opportunity/

Wortley, D. (2011, April 25-26). *Immersive technologies and personalised learning: The influence of games-related technologies on 21ˢᵗ century learning.* Paper presented at the 4th Annual International Conference on Computer Games, Multimedia and Allied Technology, CGAT 2011 and 2nd Annual International Conference on Cloud Computing and Virtualization, CCV.

ADDITIONAL READING

Alelis, G., Bobrowicz, A., & Ang, C. S. (2015). Comparison of engagement and emotional responses of older and younger adults interacting with 3D cultural heritage artefacts on personal devices. *Behaviour & Information Technology*, *34*(11), 1064–1078. doi:10.1080/0144929X.2015.1056548

Bolter, J. D., Engberg, M., & MacIntyre, B. (2013). Media studies, mobile augmented reality, and Interaction design. *Interaction*, *20*(1), 36–45. doi:10.1145/2405716.2405726

Bolter, J. D., & Grusin, R. (1998). *Remediation: Understanding New Media.* Cambridge, MA: MIT Press.

Brito, P. Q., & Stoyanova, J. (2018). Marker versus markerless augmented reality. Which has more impact on users? *International Journal of Human Computer Interaction*, *34*(9), 819-833. *DOI, 8.* doi:10.1080/10447318.10442017.11393974

Carmigniani, J., & Furth, B. (Eds.). (2011). *Augmented reality: An overview.* Heidelberg: Springer Verlag.

Cenfetelli, R. T. (2004). Inhibitors and enablers as dual factor concepts in technology usage. *Journal of the Association for Information Systems*, *5*(11-12), 472–492. doi:10.17705/1jais.00059

De Souza e Silva, A. (2006). From cyber to hybrid: Mobile technologies as interfaces of hybrid spaces. *Space and Culture*, *9*(3), 261–278. doi:10.1177/1206331206289022

Grasset, R., Langlotz, T., Kalkofen, D., Tatzgern, M., & Schmalstieg, D. (2012, November). Image driven view management for AR browsers. In *mixed and AR (ISMAR), 2012 IEEE International Symposium, IEEE*, 177-186.

Howe, K. B., Suharlim, C., Ueda, P., Howe, D., Kawachi, I., & Rimm, E. B. (2016). Gotta catch'em all! Pokemon GO and physical activity among young adults: Difference in differences study. *BMJ: British Medical Journal*, *355*, i6270. doi:10.1136/bmj.i6270 PMID:27965211

Kim, J. (2016). Interacting socially with the Internet of Things (IoT). *Journal of Computer-Mediated Communication*, *21*(6), 420–435. doi:10.1111/jcc4.12177

McCarthy, J., & Wright, P. (2004). *Technology as Experience.* Cambridge, MA: MIT Press.

Metz, R. (2015, May/June). Augmented advertising. *MIT's Technology Review*, *118*(3), 21.

Milgram, P., & Kishino, F. (1994). A taxonomy of mixed reality visual displays. *IEICE Transactions on Information and Systems*, *E77-D*(12), 1321–1329.

Monllos, K. (October 1, 2017). Brands are doing more experiential marketing. Here's how they're measuring whether it's working. *AdWeek,* Retrieved on November 15, 2017 from http://www.adweek.com/brand-marketing/experiential-can-create-more-meaningful-relationships-with-consumers/

Pando, A. (2017, December 15). Mixed reality will transform perceptions. *Forbes.com,* Retrieved on December 18, 2018 from https://www.forbes.com/sites/forbestechcouncil/2017/2012/2015/mixed-reality-will-transform-perceptions/#7539aff2478af

Pantano, E., Rese, A., & Baier, D. (2017). Enhancing the online decision-making process by using augmented reality: A two country comparison of youth markets. *Journal of Retailing and Consumer Services*, *38*, 81–95. doi:10.1016/j.jretconser.2017.05.011

Pavlik, J. V., & Bridges, F. (2013). The emergence of augmented reality (AR) as a storytelling medium in journalism. *Journalism & Communication Monographs*, *15*(1), 4–59. doi:10.1177/1522637912470819

Poushneh, A., & Vasquez-Parraga, A. Z. (2017). Discernible impact of augmented reality on retail customer's experience, satisfaction and willingness to buy. *Journal of Retailing and Consumer Services*, *34*, 229–234. doi:10.1016/j.jretconser.2016.10.005

Rebelo, F., Noriega, P., Duarte, E., & Soares, M. (2012, December). Using virtual reality to assess user experience. *Human Factors, 54*(6), 964-982. *DOI, 9*. doi:10.1177/0018720812465006

Rese, A., Baier, D., Geyer-Schulz, A., & Schreiber, S. (2017). How augmented reality apps are accepted by consumers: A comparative analysis using scales and opinions. *Technological Forecasting and Social Change*, *124*, 306–319. doi:10.1016/j.techfore.2016.10.010

Rizzo, A. S., Lange, B., Suma, E. A., & Bolas, M. (2011, March). Virtual reality and interactive digital game technology: New tools to address obesity and diabetes. *Journal of Diabetes Science and Technology*, *5*(2), 256–264. doi:10.1177/193229681100500209 PMID:21527091

Serino, M., Cordrey, K., McLaughlin, L., & Milanaik, R. L. (2016). Pokemon Go and augmented virtual reality games: A cautionary commentary for parents and pediatricians. *Current Opinion in Pediatrics*, *28*(5), 673–677. doi:10.1097/MOP.0000000000000409 PMID:27479151

Shapiro, A. (September 15, 2017). 6 ways marketers can get augmented reality right. *AdWeek,* Retrieved on November 15, 2017 from http://www.adweek.com/digital/2016-ways-marketers-can-get-augmented-reality-right/

Shin, D. (2018). Empathy and embodied experience in virtual environment: To what extent can virtual reality stimulate empathy and embodied experience? *Computers in Human Behavior*, *78*, 64–73. doi:10.1016/j.chb.2017.09.012

Steuer, J. (1992, December). Defining virtual reality: Dimensions determining telepresence. *Journal of Communication*, *42*(4), 73–93. doi:10.1111/j.1460-2466.1992.tb00812.x

ThinkMobiles. (2018, April). Augmented reality development companies in 2018, Retrieved on December 9, 2018 from https://thinkmobiles.com/blog/augmented-reality-companies/

Tobar-Mun~oz, H., Baldiris, S., & Fabregat, R. (2017). Augmented reality game-based learning: Enriching students' experience during reading comprehension activities. *Journal of Educational Computing*, *55*(7), 901–936. doi:10.1177/0735633116689789

Tokunaga, R. S. (2013). Engagement with novel virtual environments: The role of perceived novelty and flow in the development of the deficient self-regulation of internet use and media habits. *Human Communication Research*, *39*(3), 365–393. doi:10.1111/hcre.12008

van Krevelen, R., & Poelman, R. (2010). A survey of augmented reality technologies, applications and limitations. *International Journal of Virtual Reality*, *9*(1), 1–20.

Whipple, B. (2017, June 11). Protected: Virtual reality is becoming the next great storytelling canvas. *AdWeek,* Retrieved on November 15, 2017 from http://www.adweek.com/digital/accenture-voice/

Wisneski, C., Ishii, H., Dahley, A., Gorbet, M., Brave, S., Ullmer, B., & Yarin, P. (2008). Ambient displays: Turning architectural space into an interface between people and digital information. In *International Workshop on Cooperative Buildings (CoBuild '98)*, pp. 22–32. London: Springer.

Yang, X., & Smith, R. E. (2009). Beyond attention effects: Modeling the persuasive and emotional effects of advertising creativity. *Marketing Science*, *28*(5), 935–949. doi:10.1287/mksc.1080.0460

Yaoyuneyong, G., Foster, J., Johnson, E., & Johnson, D. (2016). Augmented reality marketing: Consumer preferences and attitudes toward hypermedia print ads. *Journal of Interactive Advertising*, *16*(1), 1630. doi:10.1080/15252019.2015.1125316

Yim, M. Y.-C., Chu, S.-C., & Sauer, P. L. (2017). Is augmented reality technology an effective tool for e-commerce? An interactivity and vividness perspective. *Journal of Interactive Marketing*, *39*, 89–103. doi:10.1016/j.intmar.2017.04.001

Zhang, B. (2017). Design of mobile augmented reality game based on image recognition. *Journal on Image and Video Processing*, 90-110.

KEY TERMS AND DEFINITIONS

Adoption Behavior: A term that studies determinants of consumers' decision-making process to adopt a new brand, a service, a technology. Depending on the adoption behavior model, the decision-making process usually involves the following five stages: product awareness, product interest, evaluation of alternatives, product trial, and adoption/divestment/rejection.

Artificial Intelligence: Also abbreviated as AI, this term refers to the ability of a computer, an IT system, or a robot to complete either ordinary or complex tasks that are previously only possible for intelligent beings (such as human beings). Some manifestations of intelligence include the ability to learn through information acquisition and interpretation, to comprehend a brand-new language, to solve problems, to reason, to develop a possible conclusion, and to generate expert insights.

Augmented Reality: Commonly abbreviated as AR is a technical term to refer to the technology that is able to create a completely artificial and virtual environment blending computer-generated audio, image, video, and even haptic information with the physical world in a real time. The term, augmented, refers to the technology-enabled augmentation of a user's real and virtual world to create a new reality.

Digital Reality: An umbrella term to cover a set of reality-creating technologies such as augmented reality, mixed reality, virtual reality, 360-degree video, and other emerging immersive technologies that are able to create a totally artificial virtual environment through computer-generated contents.

Ecosystem: A biological term that describes a community of living organisms and lifeless elements such as mineral, air, water, and soil. The term has been extended to study different players in a specific system. For example, the AR and VR ecosystem is made up for different industry sectors such as software development, 360 degree video developers, arcade, agency, education, network, university, accelerator, platform, corporate lab, tech vendor, among others.

Head/Helmet-Mounted Display: Also known as HMD, this term refers to the display device worn by users when they use digital reality applications to experience the virtual worlds through a small display in front of each eye. There are two types of HDM: monocular and binocular HDM, depending on if one or two displays are available to users.

Immersion: As a loosely-defined psychological term, this term has been used a lot to describe a unique experience when using a media or a technology. Often affiliated with virtual reality, and other "immersive" technologies, this concept refers to users' perceptions to feel a sense of presence in a non-physical world. This term often refers to a fully surrounded experiences when using HMD in a virtual space.

Internet of Things: Abbreviated as IoT. This term was first used by the digital innovation pioneer, Kevin Ashton, to refer to the speedy transmission of information between objects and devices using the Internet as the channel. IoT makes the most use of existing networking and computer technologies such as pervasive computing, communication technology, the internet of people, embedded devices.

Mixed Reality: Abbreviated as MR. This term sometimes refers to another term, hybrid reality. MR refers to the merger of both actual and virtual worlds to create an immersive virtual space where digital reality meets and coexists with physical objects to allow users to interact with reality-creating objects in real time.

New Media: A term that commonly refers to ICT-enabled distribution platforms to allow content producers to disseminate messages to end-users. Some examples of new media include digital reality technology, social networking and media, consumer-generated contents, digital out-of-home (DOOH), high-definition television, Internet, mobile phone, etc.

Nielsen: Refers to a global information company that measures viewing and usage behaviors of both traditional and new media (such as social media, mobile, and Internet media). Nielsen's Total Audience Ratings has become the industry standard to measure media consumption behaviors across different devices and platforms.

Telemedicine: A two-way, interactive, and real-time communication platform that allows the patient to interact with the physician and medical practitioners to address his or her medical problems in a remote location. Digital reality technology has facilitated the communication process by immersing the doctor into a virtual environment.

Virtual Reality: Commonly abbreviated as VR is the most well-known digital reality technologies. VR is able to create an interactive and computer-generated experience by immersing users within an artificial environment where interacting with the virtual objects are accomplished through auditory, visual, and haptic inputs.

Section 2
Emerging Themes and Practices in Digital Reality Research

The five chapters in this section deal with emerging research paradigms and practices in digital reality studies in different areas ranging from physical education and sport training, cultural industry, and higher educational context. This section is written by a panel of global experts in digital reality technologies to share their own research and implementation experiences in their individual countries, organizations, or research fields. As an emerging and converging technology, digital reality has been studied using a mixture of usability, experiment, focus group, survey, and text mining research methods demonstrating the contributions of engineering, education, humanity, and social science scholars to this burgeoning new field.

Chapter 2
Multi–User Virtual Environments for Physical Education and Sport Training

Pooya Soltani
Aix-Marseille University, France & University of Porto, Portugal

João Paulo Vilas-Boas
University of Porto, Portugal

EXECUTIVE SUMMARY

For effective learning and training, virtual environments may provide lifelike opportunities, and researchers are actively investigating their potential for educational purposes. Minimal research attention has been paid to the integration of multi-user virtual environments (MUVE) technology for teaching and practicing real sports. In this chapter, the authors reviewed the justifications, possibilities, challenges, and future directions of using MUVE systems. The authors addressed issues such as informal learning, design, engagement, collaboration, learning style, learning evaluation, motivation, and gender, followed by the identification of required elements for successful implementations. In the second part, the authors talked about exergames, the necessity of evaluation, and examples on exploring the behavior of players during playing. Finally, insights on the application of sports exergames in teaching, practicing, and encouraging real sports were discussed.

INTRODUCTION

The new generation of students is growing up in a digital world, where they can multi-task and communicate the information rapidly (Prensky, 2001). Computer games and virtual environments are visibly present in the lives of these "digital natives" from a young age. They are comfortable with digital technologies and have different attitudes, expectations, and abilities towards technology (Beck & Wade, 2006). Advanced educational technologies can enhance several skills that traditional settings cannot account for (Passig, 2015). Students' reading, writing, and communication have already been affected by the new technology, and educators are looking for possible engaging ways to increase their learning

DOI: 10.4018/978-1-5225-5912-2.ch002

capabilities (Fee, 2007; Malliarakis, Tomos, Shabalina, Mozelius, & Balan, 2015). Rather than only considering the outcome, effective teaching also focuses on context, process, and learning outcome. It also considers identity, individuality, approach, and knowledge of the learners (Kyriacou, 2009). More schools are incorporating informal techniques into their curriculum, and as a result, the boundaries of formal and informal schooling are blurring (Ketelhut & Nelson, 2016). A shift from teacher-centered environments to student-centered interventions may also increase students' motivation. Therefore, integrating technology into practice could be a viable tool for supporting different types of learners (Miyares, 2013). Debates also exist around the use of technology in sports learning and whether technology can eventually replace physical educators for promoting physical activity and health (Casey, Goodyear, & Armour, 2017).

In this book chapter, the authors talk about the integration of multi-user virtual environments (MUVE) technology for teaching and practicing sports. In the first part, the authors discuss various elements of the technology, and how virtual sports and sports exergames could be used in physical education. In the second part, the authors also characterize a swimming exergame from different aspects of biomechanics, physiology, and psychology. Based on the results of the chapter, physical education (PE) teachers and curriculum designer can decide how to use MUVE systems in their practice. Game designers could also benefit from the results of this book chapter to create more realistic and meaningful MUVE systems.

BACKGROUND

Three dimensional (3D) virtual environments resemble physical spaces and allow players to generate virtual selves (avatars) to interact with objects, virtual ambient, and other avatars. Impractical, costly, and dangerous real-life activities can be performed in virtual environments (Adams, Klowden, & Hannaford, 2001). These systems also have positive effects on learning and provide higher immersion, engagement, and motivation compared to common instruction techniques (Webster, 2016). Therefore, they may create opportunities for distance education and collaborative learning. Studies suggest that properly designed 3D virtual games may improve information retention and enable the situation to be practiced safely (Dutton, 2013). MUVE is a computer, server, or internet-based virtual environment that can be accessed by multiple users simultaneously. These systems provide low-cost and safe collaborative ambient for problem-based learning activities. They could offer similar learning outcome and satisfaction to the real-world conditions while being more pleasurable and informal compared to the stressful reality (Vrellis, Avouris, & Mikropoulos, 2016). MUVE systems provide the chance of deep learning experiences where various skills, cognitive, perceptual/motor, interpersonal, leadership, and team building could be considered at the same time (Chang & Lin, 2014; Clayton, 2017). MUVE-based interpersonal education is also easier to navigate and may fulfill pedagogical objectives (Morley et al., 2015). In recent years, there was a considerable hype around the use of virtual worlds in a variety of fields, but for efficient use of MUVE systems, some topics need to be addressed.

Various initiatives will have limited success if students are not motivated to participate actively in PE. Understanding the mechanism underlying motivation, engagement, and collaboration can optimize the system's interactions with students and increase the likelihood of realizing the potential benefits of PE participation. Gender also plays an important role in PE and overcoming traditional shortcomings (e.g., boys receiving more attention and feedback compared to girls) can ensure fair and active PE participation for everyone. In the following paragraphs, the authors will discuss these elements in MUVE systems.

Motivation

Educational and health-related virtual games can enhance players' motivation (Hamari et al., 2016). Motivation is the principal element of participation, progression, and retention in gaming environments (Konetes, 2010). According to Yee (2006), players are motivated to play games in three areas of *achievement* (progression within the game, understanding the game mechanics, and competing with others), *social* (socializing, building relationships with others, and teamwork), and *immersion* (discovering things within games, role-playing, customization, and escapism from real-life problems). Theories on need satisfaction also mention that people continue engaging in activities that satisfy motivational needs, such as competence, autonomy, or relatedness (Ryan & Deci, 2000). Different strategies can be used to create competition, cooperation, skills, role-playing, performance, and simulation (cf. Macklin & Sharp, 2016).

Each video game consists of *actions* (that players carry out to meet the game goals), *rules* (on how to play the game), *objects* (to reach the game goals), the *space* (defined by rules on which the game is played), and the *operators* (or players) of the game. To maximize the educational and health potential, virtual environments should increase players' inner desire to participate and enjoy the activity. Extrinsic motivation is also offered by the instructor or previously included rules of the game. In the academic or medical environment, extrinsic motivation is used for skill improvement or rehabilitation, through which the goal is to complete the course (Hansen, 2008). Additionally, paradigms that include both virtual and real environments might also be relevant in fostering health-related behaviors by using motivational reinforcement, personalized teaching methods, and social networking (Bordnick, Carter, & Traylor, 2011; Ershow, Peterson, Riley, Rizzo, & Wansink, 2011; Preziosa, Grassi, Gaggioli, & Riva, 2009). For example, they may clinically improve treatments of health problems such as obesity by increasing adherence through an extended sense of presence, anonymous targeted social support, and real-time feedback (Riva, Wiederhold, Mantovani, & Gaggioli, 2011).

Learning and Engagement

Teachers at all educational levels are concerned with students' engagement and learning. Although engagement might happen even without the use of technology, it can provide opportunities in ways that may otherwise be difficult to achieve (Kearsley & Shneiderman, 1998). With the recent shift in learning styles to informal and voluntary education (Clarke, Dede, & Dieterle, 2008), 3D MUVE systems could cover a broad range of educational pedagogies that extend from structured and rationalist approaches to social constructivist (Hollins & Robbins, 2009). MUVE systems may facilitate knowledge transfer from virtual to real environments in different types of participants (Freina & Canessa, 2015). Therefore, educators have many opportunities and challenges to create educational approaches with students who are familiar with these types of technologies. MUVE systems may also have the potential to increase students' engagement by offering dynamic and engaging student-centered learning environments that increase socializing, exploration, creativity, and discovery. Virtual environments such as Second Life seem to be viable learning environments because they are immersive and provide a sense of tele- and co-presence (Chen, 2016; Claman, 2015).

On the other hand, the previous adoption of learning content management systems and virtual learning environments such as Blackboard showed that such investments were mainly used for content structuring and presentation (Britain & Liber, 1999). Earlier educational MUVE systems such as Zora, SciCenter, MOOSE Crossing, and Whyville were also executed in informal settings like after-school programs, which may reflect the lack of acceptance as part of a curriculum in classrooms (Nelson & Ketelhut, 2007). Most MUVE users in informal settings may not also participate in the curriculum actively (Foley & Kobaissi, 2006). Complexity, open-ended nature, and division between formal and informal learning settings of MUVE systems may also cause students to "turn out" (Nelson & Ketelhut, 2007). In online learning environments, learners' engagement overrides learning success (Herrington, Oliver, & Reeves, 2003), and although MUVE applications may enhance communication behaviors (Tang, Lan, & Chang, 2012), lack of human interaction might be a problem in attaining proper levels of engagement (So & Brush, 2008). While students perceive virtual activities to be helpful, we should also keep in mind that the unstructuredness and informal aspects of using MUVE (as a form of self-discovery learning; Bruner, 1961) might be an obstacle in keeping learners interested in learning (Schmidt & Stewart, 2010; Hai-Jew, 2012). Bush (2009) also discussed that to keep students information-literate, educators should also be updated, learn from students, and welcome change. Other parameters such as identity conceptions, belief in the virtual world, and technical skills may also affect players' cohesion and learning within virtual worlds (deNoyelles & Kyeong-Ju Seo, 2012).

Collaborative Learning

Several studies have been performed in MUVE settings to understand the effects of games on collaboration, presence levels, team building, and teamwork (Bluemink, Hämäläinen, Manninen, & Järvelä, 2010; de Leo, Goodman, Radici, Secrhist, & Mastaglio, 2011; Ellis, Luther, Bessiere, & Kellogg, 2008; Roberts, Wolff, Otto, & Steed, 2003). Researchers have observed that increased sense of shared presence, social interaction and collaborative learning, and lower social anxiety are associated with such systems (Cook, 2009; Dede, Nelson, Ketelhut, Clarke, & Bowman, 2004). Using MUVE systems as part of collaborative team-based projects improves students' self-efficacy beliefs (Scullion, Baxter, & Stansfield, 2015). Kang et al. (2016) described the participatory design process with school teachers and suggested that a combination of physical interaction, sensing, and visualization in MUVE promote engagement, and shapes social interactions and playful experiences. By gaining collaborative experience, students increase their skill levels and feel more competent with technology (Nickerson, Corter, Esche, & Chassapis, 2007). Because of visual components of MUVE, students may also feel more connected and co-present (Leonard, Withers, & Sherblom, 2011).

The collaborative social environments may also provide opportunities to address the commitment problems. Bozanta, Kutlu, Nowlan, and Shirmohammadi (2016) mentioned that serious games are beneficial for team cohesion in MUVE environments, which could result in effective intra-group communication (Evans & Jarvis, 1980) and increased team performance (Dionne, Yammarino, Atwater, & Spangler, 2004). By using collaborative virtual environments, people can work together over networks to share experience and different tasks (Park & Kenyon, 1999). Shared virtual environments have the potential to be used for problem-solving and act as online communities (Meyers, 2009). In collaborative learning, the whole task is done by the group, and each person makes a contribution in line with the overall cognitive, interactive, and social goals. The interaction between players plays a great role in completing the task and creates an interdependence of players while developing interpersonal skills (Lorenzo, Sicilia, & Sanchez, 2012).

General guidelines (Arango, Chang, Esche, & Chassapis, 2007) for successful implementation of learning in virtual environments include: contextualizing learning in a way that makes sense to the learners, objective-based learning in which each activity should meet an objective and correctly represent the theoretical models that were previously studied by the learners, challenges that are coherent with learners' abilities, exploratory learning that allows learners to make their own decisions and see the consequences of their actions, and feedback to motivate student and enhance their performance continuously.

Design

As designers should consider interaction elements, feedback components, pedagogical, and other graphical aspects, developing a 3D MUVE environment is a complicated process (Harel & Papert, 1991). Integration factors involve pedagogical (relevance and complexity), contextual (players' prior experience, duration, and frequency of events), and logistical (usability, technical support, and hardware issues; Mayrath, Traphagan, Jarmon, Trivedi, & Resta, 2010). Pedagogical principles include curriculum content, technological content, and subject knowledge content (de Freitas & Jarvis, 2007). The flexible structure of virtual environments may cause learners to lose their attention (Ho, Rappa, & Chee, 2009). Strategies should be tailored carefully to avoid overloading players with unnecessary information and inhibiting overall learning (Ritz & Buss, 2016). Virtual worlds also increase interactivity and put students in the spatial dimension. Therefore, for better usage of these systems, users' technical skills should be improved (Petrakou, 2010). Additionally, the complexity of virtual environments that require significant computing power and high-speed internet to run smoothly are among issues that might make educators hesitate to use them. The cost of developing virtual worlds is another matter that is highly dependent on the amount of required modeling (Dutton, 2013).

Gender

Historically, gender was a good predictor of participation in virtual environments such as video games. Male and female players are different in type and duration play (Lowrie & Jorgensen, 2011). Four categories of memory task that could be affected by gender include spatial, verbal, autobiographical, and emotional. It is commonly agreed that males have better performance in spatial tasks and females in verbal tasks (Li, 2014). Additionally, male players spend more time playing video games and prefer action games compared to female players who prefer games featuring adventure, simulation, role-playing, and strategy. Moreover, males prefer games that require visual and spatial skills (e.g., dealing with maps), while females are interested in problem-solving video games. A previous study also suggests that female players are more active in virtual dance active video games and have more physical activity levels because they accept the platform as an activity consistent with their gender norms (Gao, Podlog, & Lee, 2014). Female players may also choose virtual activities that are considered as feminine, are accepted by their classmates, and are in line with their socially approved gender roles (Whitehead & Biddle, 2008). In the same way, female non-gamers tend to relate identity with physical appearance while male gamers were associating identity with personality characteristics. Moreover, female players who use virtual experimentation learn more, but male players outperform their counterparts (Ketelhut, Nelson, Clarke, & Dede, 2010). Previous research on the cognitive engagement of students also shows that male students tend to show higher levels of cognitive engagement such as self-regulation, task-focused learning, and resource management (Mandinach & Corno, 1985). On the other hand, Brom, Preuss, & Klement (2011) showed no gender differences in emotional engagement between the two genders.

VIRTUAL SPORTS FOR PHYSICAL EDUCATION

The popularity of the video game industry is ever increasing. The majority of young people own game devices and spend considerable amounts of time playing video games (Rideout, Foehr, & Roberts, 2010). Many people prefer to play video games during their leisure times than to read books or watch movies (Entertainment Software Association, 2018). Video games are usually blamed for providing aggression, violence, and making the children sedentary (Anderson et al., 2010; Lee & Peng, 2006). Insufficient physical activity (PA) which is one of the main parameters of mortality and obesity is also associated with sedentary gaming. Despite concerns regarding psychological effects of video games on the academic performance of players (Maass, Kollhorster, Riediger, MacDonald, & Lohaus, 2011), many educational researchers believe that these games could benefit the academic engagement of students, and are investigating the role of video games, their learning potential, and engagement (Young et al. 2012). These video games show reasons that might contribute to increase the quality and quantity of improved attention, executive functions, and reasoning (Neugnot-Cerioli, Gagner, & Beauchamp, 2015). Video games could also involve competition, collaboration, and might help in the development of learning communities sharing (Gee, 2008). They could also motivate players by using positive emotions to grab attention, memory, and motor skills to process information. Physical education and sports are important parts of the primary school curriculum around the world (Lindberg, Seo, & Laine, 2016). However, several reasons including instructors' lack of skills, time, and support, might contribute to reducing the quality and quantity of physical education (Lindberg, Seo, & Laine, 2016).

One exciting way of incorporating technology and teaching is by using active video games (exergames) that include visual or auditory stimulus. It provides an illusion of interacting with a virtual world and provides immediate feedback. Although it does not completely block the field of view of players, it is still capable of immersing players (Soltani, 2018). This new approach uses motion sensor technology and involves movements of body limbs during gaming. Exergames are increasingly popular as they combine gaming and exercise so that the motivation to play can encourage the individual to participate in some levels of physical activity. During the games, players have to perform active tasks such as jumping, running, dancing, virtual cycling, boxing, or tennis. Exergames might have the potential to produce more minutes of PA while being socially acceptable among both students and physical education teachers (Fogel, Miltenberger, Graves, & Koehler, 2010).

EXERGAME EVALUATION

Sports exergames are replications of real-world activities. Because they might be used for purposes such as instruction and training, they are also referred as serious games (Susi, Johannesson, & Backland, 2007). To successfully apply them in other contexts, they should be fun and provide challenges, skill, knowledge, or attitude that could be used in real-world scenarios. With various informal and voluntary learning tools and if sports exergames can improve motor skills of real sports, they might potentially facilitate familiarity with sports. To maximize their effectiveness and attractiveness, and augment their health benefits, sports exergames should be evaluated holistically. In this part, the authors analyzed a swimming exergame from different aspects of biomechanics, physiology, and psychology. The primary purpose of the biomechanical evaluation is to understand human movements better and to reveal that movements can be performed in many different ways. Another purpose of the biomechanical analysis is to increase safety. Because exergame activities involve repeated upper- and lower-limb movements, biomechanical procedures can estimate the internal loads and angles, and human-computer interaction is monitored carefully to guarantee safer experience and protect players from muscular overload.

For a realistic and meaningful experience, various design and safety considerations should also be met; especially when MUVE systems are intended to be used unsupervised and within the venerable community. Exercise physiology testing aims to understand how human systems work under different exercise conditions. Such situations might affect force production and neural control of movement pattern. Physiology also offers tools to monitor players' health via standardized tests and considers design and safety issues for unsupervised use. Finally, as motivating may ensure participation, progression, and retention in the MUVE systems, the psychological evaluation deals with players' enjoyment and motivation for playing. It also evaluates whether MUVE systems could establish a connection between virtual and real sport participation. Considering gender in this holistic framework allows tailoring various game elements carefully for both female and male players.

SWIMMING EXERGAME

Out of the water, subjects played different techniques of a swimming exergame with Microsoft Xbox and Kinect (Michael Phelps: Push the Limit, 505 Games, Italy). The game was divided into two phases of normal and fast, both controlled by visual on-screen feedback. Players had to stand in front of the Kinect sensor and bend forward (Parts B and C in Figure 1 below). With the visual command, they had to return to the standing position with arms in front (Part D in Figure 1). Afterward, they had to swim according to each technique and move the avatar inside the game (Parts E to L in Figure 1). To prevent players from swimming too slow or too fast, on-screen visual feedback indicated if the speed was moderate. In the middle of the second lap, there was a possibility of swimming as fast as possible without any limitation (Push the Limit). At the end of the event, players had to drop their upper limbs (Part M in Figure 1) and then raise one to finish the race (Part N in Figure 1). For all studies, participants were categorized based on gender, exergame experience, in-game performance, and real swimming background.

Biomechanical Evaluation

To understand the movement patterns of players, reflective markers were placed on the anatomical landmarks of the players, and their movements were captured using a 3D motion analysis system (Qualisys Track Manager, Qualisys AB, Sweden) and processed using a biomechanical analysis software (Visual3D, C-Motion Inc., U.S.A.). Due to lack of forces applied to the body from water and different body positions, kinematic differences were expectable. The evaluation showed that subjects had similar biomechanical parameters and, for better performance inside the game, they were encouraged to change their movement patterns (Table 1). Participants with real swimming background had the intention to keep their movement patterns close to real swimming, but as the device was not able to detect their precise movements, they change their patterns to just win the game (Figure 2). Additionally, experienced players were also playing the game with less effort (Soltani, Figueiredo, Fernandes, & Vilas-Boas, 2016).

The ideal goal of sports exergames would be to mimic the real-sport movements, but because of passive-playing nature of many games, players use different ways to exert. Movement patterns may vary depending on games, systems, and players' experiences. Movement comparisons show differences in

Figure 1. Body position during different phases of the game

Table 1. Biomechanical parameters of swimming exergame

Variables		Swimming Experience		Exergame Experience		Gender	
		Swimmer	Non-Swimmer	Experienced	Novice	Male	Female
Total time (s)		49.97±3.58	49.36±2.50	49.24±1.82	50.17±3.96	49.29±2.69	51.55±4.61
Number of cycle	Normal	29.20±4.73	28.82±3.57	27.82±1.70	29.86±5.35	28.11±2.82	32.27±6.90
	Fast	10.23±2.23	10.36±3.35	9.71±1.82	10.59±2.81	9.94±2.04	11.27±3.55
Hand path distance		120.51±30	120.36±19.70	117.82±25.99	122.03±29.41	117.91±28.30	128.64±26.49
Trunk rotation (°)	Normal	40.17±15.85	32.09±8.58	41.29±15.15	36.45±14.52	39.60±15.47	33.91±11.91
	Fast	36.66±13.25	29.91±11.51	36.00±14.90	34.48±12.10	35.46±13.78	33.73±10.93

Data are presented as mean±SD.

Figure 2. Movement patterns of real swimmer vs. non-swimmer during virtual swimming

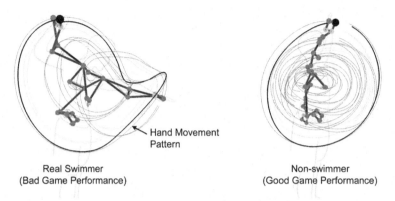

Real Swimmer
(Bad Game Performance)

Non-swimmer
(Good Game Performance)

anticipatory performance in which skilled players are more attentive to the game mechanics and such information could be interpreted as movement adaptation or learning (Soltani et al., 2016). In the game, players frequently mentioned that their real swimming movements were not applied inside the game correctly and they were encouraged to do simple movements just to win the game. Detailed biomechanical evaluation during the game design phase might help in the elimination of some of these boundaries and provide a more meaningful experience, especially if participation in real sport happens before virtual sport participation (Mueller, Agamanolis, Vetere, & Gibbs, 2009). It should be noted that there are also some modifiable and non-modifiable parameters while designing virtual sports. Non-modifiable limitations (lack of real forces from water or holding a physical object in hand) may result in differences in movement patterns and the sense of performing a real activity. Modifiable parameters are those imposed on players by the gaming platforms that affect posture and muscle loading, and might lead to cheating (Lui, Szeto, & Jones, 2011).

Physiological Evaluation

Compared to traditional methods of measuring the impacts of video games (e.g., questionnaires), physiological measurements provide more objective responses of players' experiences. While real-world sport activities may usually generate higher muscle activation compared to virtual equivalents, evaluating muscle activation during the gameplay can be used to make sports exergames closer to real activities.

Electromyography (EMG) profiling offers information in real time about the timing of muscle activities. It also allows understanding the changes in muscular activity during training and learning adaptations. With higher exergame engagement, muscle activation levels may also increase, and speed-based exergames might be used to create physical demand and to avoid boredom when players' engagements diminish (Soltani et al., 2017a). Twenty subjects played the swimming video game and activation of *biceps brachii* (BB), *triceps brachii* (TB), *upper trapezius* (UT), *latissimus dorsi* (LD), *erector spinae* (ES) muscles were monitored in two different playing velocities. Although higher muscle activation was seen in fast gameplay compared to the normal phase, after normalizing the muscle activation to the playing velocity, selective behavior was observed between the muscles (Table 2). More specifically, higher muscle activation was found in muscles that were responsible for pragmatic gameplay (swimming just to win the game). For example, during the front crawl, differences were observed between LD and ES.

Table 2. Activation of various muscles during front crawl

Event	Velocity	BB	TB	LD	UT	ES
Crawl	Normal	10.0±4.5*	17.2±14.2*	12.3±12.8*	53.9±39.6*	7.9±3.9*
	Fast	19.1±7.9	24.5±12.7	31.5±30.9	80.65±55.1	18.2±10.2
Crawl normalized	Normal	3.8±2.3	6.4±5.7	4.5±5.6*	19.8±14.3	2.9±1.7*
	Fast	4.5±2.2	5.8±3.3	7.8±9.1	19.2±13.4	4.3±2.3

*: Differences were observed between normal and fast swimming in muscles.

These two muscles are responsible for lowering the arms to start a new cycle to quickly finish the game. With this selective behavior in activating the muscles that contribute to swimming, the video game may not be used as a training device.

Heart rate, the rate of perceived exertion, and energy expenditure are other physiological parameters for measuring the intensity of exergames. These are particularly important as exergames are often promoted as means of increasing PA. Forty players played the game and oxygen uptake, and blood lactate were collected during the gameplay. From these two values, energy expenditure was measured which was also not different between performing groups. Only higher heart rate was observed in players with real swimming experience and only in the first technique. This shows that real swimmers tend to exert higher at the beginning of the gameplay, but as soon as they understood the mechanics of the game, they changed their behavior just to win the game. Each player was also filmed during the activity to measure the activity time. Total playing time, effective playing time, resting time, and effort to rest ratio were also calculated using video analysis. Recordings were tagged as total playing time (TPT), and effective playing time (EPT) in which players' movements were necessary to advance within the game. The results also showed that novice players had higher TPT and EPT compared to experienced counterparts (Table 3; Soltani et al., 2017b). This shows that novice players need more time to adapt to the game mechanics. It might also be possible that short-term positive results of an increase in PA levels are due to lack of experience of the players.

Psychological Evaluation

In the psychology part, the authors discuss both assessment of enjoyment as well as its role in changing PA and exercise intention. The concept is usually assessed by PA enjoyment scale (i.e., PACES) (Kendzierski & DeCarlo, 1991) which includes 18 items and requires respondents to select a point along a 7-point continuum between two opposite descriptors related to the enjoyment of PA (enjoy and hate, dislike and like, etc.). It is a robust predictor and correlator of PA behavior in children, youth, and older adults. The authors also used game experience questionnaire that deals with consumers' dynamic perceptions and responses of games and consists of different components including flow, a state in which there is a balance between the difficulty of the task and the skills that the performers possess (Csikszentmihalyi, 1991). With the occurrence of flow, players become immersed, ignoring the world around them (Brown & Cairns, 2004). A state of deep involvement in the game is recognized as absorption (Agarwal & Karahanna, 2000). Presence is also a psychological feeling of being in a virtual environment (Slater, Usoh, & Steed, 1994), and shows how engaged people are while playing video games (Schmierbach, Limperos, & Woolley, 2012). The System Usability Scale (SUS) is a measurement of learning, control,

Table 3. Physiological evaluation of swimming exergame

Variables		Swimming Experience		Exergame Experience		Gender	
		Swimmer	Non-Swimmer	Experienced	Novice	Male	Female
[La⁻] (mmol.l⁻¹)	[La⁻] Activity	3.0±1.4	2.3±0.8	2.4±1.0	3.0±1.3	2.7±1.2	2.1±0.5
	Crawl	3.0±3.0	2.0±0.7	2.1±1.6	3.0±2.7	2.5±2.3	2.0±0.7
	Backstroke	2.7±1.0	2.1±0.8	2.2±0.9	2.7±1.0	2.5±1.0	1.9±0.6
	Breaststroke	3.0±0.9	2.5±0.6	2.6±0.7	3.0±0.9	2.8±0.8	2.3±0.5
	Butterfly	3.3±2.1	2.7±1.4	2.6±1.4	3.5±2.1	3.1±1.9	2.4±0.8
EE (kJ)	EE_{TOTAL}	113.4±40.4	97.4±24.1	95.3±24.4	119.3±39.5	111.0±33.5	82.2±15.7
	EE_{LAC}	12.9±11.6	7.8±5.0	7.9±6.7	13.5±10.6	11.3±9.4	5.7±2.7
	EE_{AER}	100.5±32.8	89.6±23.0	87.4±22.4	105.8±32.6	99.7±28.6	76.4±14.6
	Lactic (%)	10.2±6.6	8.0±4.8	8.0±5.5	10.5±5.8	9.6±6.2	6.8±2.7
	Aerobic (%)	89.7±6.6	91.9±4.8	91.9±5.5	89.4±5.8	90.3±6.2	93.0±2.7
HR (bpm)	HR-Total	94.1±18.3	85.5±12.5	88.4±16.9	89.8±13.5	88.3±15.6	91.2±15.4
	HR-Activity	105.7±15.7	97.9±13.9	99.0±13.1	104.0±17.5	99.2±14.7	107.3±15.1
	Crawl	105.9±17.9*	96.8±11.8	100.0±15.3	101.1±15.1	98.8±15.8	106.1±11.0
	Backstroke	105.8±13.8	103.0±16.6	101.6±12.0	108.0±19.4	102.1±14.9	111.1±16.3
	Breaststroke	105.4±17.8	99.3±16.9	96.9±15.0	104.5±19.6	98.2±17.0	106.0±17.3
	Butterfly	106.0±15.8	98.2±16.9	97.8±15.5	103.7±17.0	98.3±16.3	106.4±18.8
RPE	RPE Activity	2.9±1.1	3.0±1.2	2.8±1.2	3.2±1.2	2.9±1.2	3.2±1.4
	Crawl	2.6±1.3	2.0±1.2	2.1±1.3	2.4±1.2	2.2±1.3	2.2±1.3
	Backstroke	2.8±1.0	3.0±1.6	2.6±1.3	3.4±1.5	2.7±1.3	3.6±1.5
	Breaststroke	3.0±1.4	3.2±1.5	3.0±1.5	3.3±1.5	3.0±1.4	3.5±1.6
	Butterfly	3.4±1.7	4.0±1.5	3.6±1.7	3.9±1.3	3.8±1.5	3.6±1.9
Activity profile	Active (%)	54.5±4.4	58.5±9.5	55.8±8.6	58.6±7.1	56.4±7.2	58.5±10.9
	Rest (%)	44.3±5.0	44.0±7.8	45.5±7.2	42.0±5.4	43.3±6.1	47.0±8.3
	E:R	1.2±0.2	1.3±0.4	1.2±0.3	1.4±0.3	1.3±0.3	1.2±0.2

*: Differences were observed between normal and fast swimming in muscles; EE_{LAC}: Anaerobic energy contribution; EE_{AER}: Aerobic energy contribution; Lactic: Relative anaerobic lactic percentage; Aerobic: relative aerobic percentage; HR-Total: HR from the onset of activity until the end of the last technique; HR-Activity: mean HR during the four swimming events; RPE Activity: Mean RPE during the four swimming techniques; E:R: effort to rest ratio.

and understanding a game, and offers a reliable tool for measuring usability. With ten questions of five responses (from strongly agree to strongly disagree), the game usability scale allows evaluating a wide variety of products and services. Items ask about whether the player would like to use the system frequently, if they found it unnecessarily complex, or if they need support to use the system. Additionally, the changes in intentions before and after the gameplay were monitored using the following items before and after the gameplay: "If I had a chance, I would participate in physical activity later today" and "If I had a chance to participate in physical activity, I would choose swimming."

Twenty players participated in this study and filled the questionnaires after the gameplay. Twelve participants were female. Overall, psychological parameters were not different between performing groups, but female players with real and exergame experience enjoyed the game more (Table 4). The video game also earned a good usability score with high acceptability. GEQ components were also not different between performing groups, but in general, subjects rated the absorption part lower, which might have been affected by the perceived usefulness of the game (Agarwal & Karahana, 2000). As feedback functionality affects immersion of the players (Nogueira, Torres, Rodrigues, Oliveira, & Nacke, 2016), and while the movements of different players were detected similarly, they might have immersed equally. Moreover, physical activity intentions did not change but swimming intentions increased for all subjects. A possible explanation might be that exercise intentions of those who frequently exercise may not be affected by a single session of video game playing. Another explanation is that those who do not exercise regularly might think that the benefits obtained through exergame participation are enough and there is no need for further exercising.

CONCLUSION

Physical education is emerging regarding the use of technology in classes. Virtual environments such as sports exergames might provide promising short-term results in increasing energy expenditure and physical activity levels. However, data from this study showed that as players gain experience, they might change their gameplay behavior and therefore, these games may not offer long-term maintenance of physical activity and may not be used as a teaching or training device. Instructors and users who think that virtual environments might have a place in education should understand that due to a lack of institutional resources, a lack of familiarity, and other hesitations, it may still not be practical to use such systems in practice and research sites (Johnson, 2011). Moreover, traditional methods might still be more cost-effective and more efficient and therefore, should not be fully ignored (Webster, 2016). PE teachers

Table 4. Psychological evaluation of swimming exergame

Variables		Swimming Experience		Exergame Experience		Gender	
		Swimmer	Non-Swimmer	Experienced	Novice	Male	Female
PA intention	Before	4.84±1.18	4.71±1.40	4.861.07	4.66±1.58	4.85±1.33	4.62±1.11
	After	4.82±1.07	4.63±1.61	4.78±1.18	4.66±1.56	4.81±1.37	4.52±1.20
Swim intention	Before	2.82±1.30	1.89±0.93	2.33±1.21	2.55±1.29	2.41±1.26	2.43±1.20
	After	3.53±1.60	2.63±1.62	3.25±1.53	2.93±1.88	3.17±1.76	3.05±1.39
Enjoyment		5.99±0.80	5.90±1.21	6.13±0.82	5.64±1.19	5.89±0.97	6.11±1.05
SUS%		75.53±12.32	73.67±15.25	73.28±14.47	77.14±11.95	73.92±13.38	76.87±14.48
GEQ		2.83±0.72	2.70±0.50	2.77±0.64	2.77±0.62	2.80±0.67	2.70±0.50
GEQ components	Absorption	2.21±0.74	2.21±0.66	2.15±0.66	2.32±0.76	2.23±0.71	2.17±0.68
	Flow	2.87±0.72	2.76±0.53	2.88±0.63	2.72±0.66	2.79±0.67	2.91±0.56
	Presence	3.14±0.85	3.06±0.72	3.02±0.81	3.25±0.74	3.20±0.78	2.82±0.76
	Immersion	3.38±1.26	3.14±1.04	3.10±1.22	3.57±1.03	3.35±1.18	3.05±1.14

SUS: System usability scale; GEQ: Game experience questionnaire.

should justify why and how they want to use exergames in their practice and properly design ways for their students to interact with games. A combination of techniques (virtual and traditional instruction) might provide a more effective learning experience (Webster, 2016) due to shorter training time and possible long-term retention of knowledge and skills. Future studies should also examine whether physical activity and sport participation intentions result in actual exercise participation.

RECOMMENDATIONS AND FUTURE DIRECTIONS

While evaluating players' behaviors, various parameters such as gender, ethnicity, activity levels, and exercise background should be considered. Larger sample size might increase the power of analysis, and therefore conclusions made upon the results might be more realistic. It should also be noted that acquiring biophysical data is relatively time-consuming which might not be tolerable for some participants. The novelty of exergames might also cause players to rate their psychological variables (e.g., enjoyment) higher. While the majority of studies on exergame evaluation show promising short-term results for increasing PA levels, results in this study show that even after short exposure to the sports exergames, players change the movement patterns and reduce their activity levels. Future studies should analyze players' movements and behavior over longer periods of gameplay. Other studies may also look at the possibility of using virtual sports in decreasing fear of real activity (e.g., aqua-phobia). Creating a fitness index for each game based on psycho-biophysical evaluation could be another interesting area to use exergames in PA effectively.

ACKNOWLEDGMENT

Pooya Soltani was supported by Institut Carnot STAR and Collège de France.

REFERENCES

Adams, R. J., Klowden, D., & Hannaford, B. (2001). Virtual training for a manual assembly task. *Haptics-e*, *2*(2), 1–7. Retrieved from http://hdl.handle.net/1773/34884

Agarwal, R., & Karahanna, E. (2000). Time flies when you're having fun: Cognitive absorption and beliefs about information technology usage. *Management Information Systems Quarterly*, *24*(4), 665–694. doi:10.2307/3250951

Anderson, C. A., Shibuya, A., Ihori, N., Swing, E. L., Bushman, B. J., Sakamoto, A., ... Saleem, M. (2010). Violent video game effects on aggression, empathy, and prosocial behavior in Eastern and Western countries: A meta-analytic review. *Psychological Bulletin*, *136*(2), 151–173. doi:10.1037/a0018251 PMID:20192553

Arango, F., Chang, C., Esche, S. K., & Chassapis, C. (2007). A scenario for collaborative learning in virtual engineering laboratories. In 37th Annual Frontiers in Education Conference-global Engineering: Knowledge without Borders, Opportunities Without Passports (pp. F3G-7). IEEE. doi:10.1109/FIE.2007.4417818

Beck, J. C., & Wade, M. (2006). The kids are alright: How the gamer generation is changing the workplace. Cambridge, MA: Harvard Business Review Press.

Bluemink, J., Hämäläinen, R., Manninen, T., & Järvelä, S. (2010). Group-level analysis on multiplayer game collaboration: How do the individuals shape the group interaction? *Interactive Learning Environments*, *18*(4), 365–383. doi:10.1080/10494820802602444

Bordnick, P. S., Carter, B. L., & Traylor, A. C. (2011). What virtual reality research in addictions can tell us about the future of obesity assessment and treatment. *Journal of Diabetes Science and Technology*, *5*(2), 265–271. doi:10.1177/193229681100500210 PMID:21527092

Bozanta, A., Kutlu, B., Nowlan, N., & Shirmohammadi, S. (2016). Effects of serious games on perceived team cohesiveness in a multi-user virtual environment. *Computers in Human Behavior*, *59*, 380–388. doi:10.1016/j.chb.2016.02.042

Britain, S., & Liber, O. (1999). *A framework for pedagogical evaluation of virtual learning environments*. Retrieved December 2, 2018, from http://www.leeds.ac.uk/educol/documents/00001237.htm[1]

Brom, C., Preuss, M., & Klement, D. (2011). Are educational computer micro-games engaging and effective for knowledge acquisition at high-schools? A quasi-experimental study. *Computers & Education*, *57*(3), 1971–1988. doi:10.1016/j.compedu.2011.04.007

Brown, E., & Cairns, P. (2004). *A grounded investigation of game immersion*. Paper presented at the CHI '04 Extended Abstracts on Human Factors in Computing Systems, Vienna, Austria. doi:10.1145/985921.986048

Bruner, J. S. (1961). The act of discovery. *Harvard Educational Review*, *31*, 21–32.

Bush, G. (2009). Thinking around the corner: The power of information literacy. *Phi Delta Kappan*, *90*(6), 446–447. doi:10.1177/003172170909000615

Casey, A., Goodyear, V. A., & Armour, K. M. (2017). Rethinking the relationship between pedagogy, technology and learning in health and physical education. *Sport Education and Society*, *22*(2), 288–304. doi:10.1080/13573322.2016.1226792

Chang, S. M., & Lin, S. S. (2014). Team knowledge with motivation in a successful MMORPG game team: A case study. *Computers & Education*, *73*, 129–140. doi:10.1016/j.compedu.2013.09.024

Chen, J. C. (2016). The crossroads of English language learners, task-based instruction, and 3D multi-user virtual learning in Second Life. *Computers & Education*, *102*, 152–171. doi:10.1016/j.compedu.2016.08.004

Claman, F. L. (2015). The impact of multiuser virtual environments on student engagement. *Nurse Education in Practice*, *15*(1), 13–16. doi:10.1016/j.nepr.2014.11.006 PMID:25532889

Clarke, J., Dede, C., & Dieterle, E. (2008). Emerging technologies for collaborative, mediated, immersive learning. In J. Voogt & G. Knezek (Eds.), *The international handbook of technology in primary and secondary education* (pp. 901–909). New York: Springer; doi:10.1007/978-0-387-73315-9_55

Clayton, A. S. (2017). *Multiplayer educational role playing games (MPERPGs) and the application of leadership (Ph.D.)*. Phoenix, AZ: Grand Canyon University.

Cook, A. D. (2009). *A case study of the manifestations and significance of social presence in a multi-user virtual environment (Ph.D.)*. Saskatoon, SK, Canada: University of Saskatchewan.

Csikszentmihalyi, M. (1991). *Flow: The psychology of optimal experience* (Vol. 41). New York: Harper Perennial.

de Freitas, S., & Jarvis, S. (2007). Serious games engaging training solutions: A research and development project for supporting training needs. *British Journal of Educational Technology*, *38*(3), 523–525. doi:10.1111/j.1467-8535.2007.00716.x

de Leo, G., Goodman, K. S., Radici, E., Secrhist, S. R., & Mastaglio, T. W. (2011). Level of presence in team-building activities: Gaming component in virtual environments. *The International Journal of Multimedia & Its Applications*, *3*(2), 1–10. doi:10.5121/ijma.2011.3201

Dede, C., Nelson, B., Ketelhut, D. J., Clarke, J., & Bowman, C. (2004). Design-based research strategies for studying situated learning in a multi-user virtual environment. In *Proceedings of the 6th International Conference on Learning Sciences* (pp. 158-165). Santa Monica, CA: International Society of the Learning Sciences.

deNoyelles, A., & Kyeong-Ju Seo, K. (2012). Inspiring equal contribution and opportunity in a 3D multi-user virtual environment: Bringing together men gamers and women non-gamers in Second Life®. *Computers & Education*, *58*(1), 21–29. doi:10.1016/j.compedu.2011.07.007

Dionne, S. D., Yammarino, F. J., Atwater, L. E., & Spangler, W. D. (2004). Transformational leadership and team performance. *Journal of Organizational Change Management*, *17*(2), 177–193. doi:10.1108/09534810410530601

Dutton, G. (2013). Is 3-D/virtual training dead? *Training (New York, N.Y.)*, *50*(5), 38–39.

Ellis, J. B., Luther, K., Bessiere, K., & Kellogg, W. A. (2008). Games for virtual team building. In *Proceedings of the 7th ACM Conference on Designing Interactive Systems* (pp. 295-304). ACM. 10.1145/1394445.1394477

Entertainment Software Association. (2018). *2018 essential facts about the computer and video game industry*. Retrieved December 2, 2018, from http://www.theesa.com/wp- content/uploads/2018/05/EF2018_FINAL.pdf

Ershow, A. G., Peterson, C. M., Riley, W. T., Rizzo, A. S., & Wansink, B. (2011). Virtual reality technologies for research and education in obesity and diabetes: Research needs and opportunities. *Journal of Diabetes Science and Technology*, *5*(2), 212–224. doi:10.1177/193229681100500202 PMID:21527084

Evans, N. J., & Jarvis, P. A. (1980). Group cohesion: A review and reevaluation. *Small Group Behavior*, *11*(4), 359–370. doi:10.1177/104649648001100401

Fee, K. (2007). *Delivering E-Learning*. London: Kogan Page Limited.

Fogel, V. A., Miltenberger, R. G., Graves, R., & Koehler, S. (2010). The effects of exergaming on physical activity among inactive children in a physical education classroom. *Journal of Applied Behavior Analysis*, *43*(4), 591–600. doi:10.1901/jaba.2010.43-591 PMID:21541146

Foley, B., & Kobaissi, A. (2006). *Using virtual chat to study in informal learning in online environments*. In The Annual Meeting of the American Educational Research Association, San Francisco, CA.

Freina, L., & Canessa, A. (2015). Immersive vs desktop virtual reality in game based learning. In 9th *European Conference on Games Based Learning: ECGBL2015*. Steinkjer, Norway: Academic Conferences and Publishing Limited.

Gao, Z., Podlog, L., & Lee, J. (2014). Children's situational motivation, rate of perceived exertion and physical activity levels in exergaming: Associations and gender differences. In J. Graham (Ed.), *Video games: Parents' perceptions, role of social media and effects on behavior* (pp. 17–28). Hauppauge, NY: Nova Science Publishers.

Gee, J. (2008). Learning and Games. In K. Salen (Ed.), *The ecology of games: Connecting youth, games, and learning* (pp. 21–40). Cambridge, MA: The MIT Press.

Hai-Jew, S. (2012). Addressing the "commitment problem": Driving long-term persistent. In S. L. Hai-Jew (Ed.), *Constructing self-discovery learning spaces online: Scaffolding and decision making technologies* (1st ed.). Hershey, PA: IGI Global. doi:10.4018/978-1-61350-320-1.ch013

Hamari, J., Shernoff, D. J., Rowe, E., Coller, B., Asbell-Clarke, J., & Edwards, T. (2016). Challenging games help students learn: An empirical study on engagement, flow and immersion in game- based learning. *Computers in Human Behavior*, *54*, 170–179. doi:10.1016/j.chb.2015.07.045

Hansen, M. (2008). Versatile, immersive, creative and dynamic virtual 3-D healthcare learning environments: A review of the literature. *Journal of Medical Internet Research*, *10*(3), e26. doi:10.2196/jmir.1051 PMID:18762473

Harel, I. E., & Papert, S. E. (1991). *Constructionism*. Ablex Publishing.

Herrington, J., Oliver, R., & Reeves, T. C. (2003). Patterns of engagement in authentic online learning environments. *Australasian Journal of Educational Technology*, *19*(1), 59–71. doi:10.14742/ajet.1701

Ho, C. M. L., Rappa, N. A., & Chee, Y. S. (2009). Designing and implementing virtual enactive role-play and structured argumentation: Promises and pitfalls. *Computer Assisted Language Learning*, *22*(5), 381–408. doi:10.1080/09588220903184732

Hollins, P., & Robbins, S. (2018). The educational affordances of multi user virtual environments. In D. Heider (Ed.), *Living virtually: Researching new worlds*. New York: Peter Lang Publishing.

Johnson, J. (2011). *Second Life's future in education (Ph.D.)*. Capella University.

Kang, S., Norooz, L., Oguamanam, V., Plane, A. C., Clegg, T. L., & Froehlich, J. E. (2016). SharedPhys: Live physiological sensing, whole-body interaction, and large-screen visualizations to support shared inquiry experiences. In *Proceedings of the 15th International Conference on Interaction Design and Children* (pp. 275-287). ACM. 10.1145/2930674.2930710

Kearsley, G., & Shneiderman, B. (1998). Engagement theory: A framework for technology-based teaching and learning. *Educational Technology*, *38*(5), 20–23.

Kendzierski, D., & DeCarlo, K. J. (1991). Physical activity enjoyment scale: Two validation studies. *Journal of Sport & Exercise Psychology*, *13*(1), 50–64. doi:10.1123/jsep.13.1.50

Ketelhut, D. J., & Nelson, B. C. (2016). Blending formal and informal learning environments: The case of SAVE science. In *Proceedings of the 10ᵗʰ European Conference on Games Based Learning, ECGBL 2016* (pp. 314-318). Dechema e.V.

Ketelhut, D. J., Nelson, B. C., Clarke, J., & Dede, C. (2010). A multi-user virtual environment for building and assessing higher order inquiry skills in science. *British Journal of Educational Technology*, *41*(1), 56–68. doi:10.1111/j.1467-8535.2009.01036.x

Konetes, G. D. (2010). The function of intrinsic and extrinsic motivation in educational virtual games and simulations. *Journal of Emerging Technologies in Web Intelligence*, *2*(1), 23–26. doi:10.4304/jetwi.2.1.23-26

Kyriacou, C. (2009). *Effective teaching in schools. Theory and practice*. Stanley Thornes Publishers Ltd.

Lee, K. M., & Peng, W. (2006). What do we know about social and psychological effects of computer games? A comprehensive review of the current literature. In P. Vorderer & J. Bryant (Eds.), *Playing video games: Motives, responses, and consequences* (pp. 327–345). Hillsdale, NJ: Lawrence Erlbaum Associates.

Leonard, L., Withers, L. A., & Sherblom, J. C. (2011). Collaborating virtually: Using "Second Life" to teach collaboration. *Communication Teacher*, *25*(1), 42–47. doi:10.1080/17404622.2010.527297

Li, R. (2014). Why women see differently from the way men see? A review of sex differences in cognition and sports. *Journal of Sport and Health Science*, *3*(3), 155–162. doi:10.1016/j.jshs.2014.03.012 PMID:25520851

Lindberg, R., Seo, J., & Laine, T. H. (2016). Enhancing physical education with exergames and wearable technology. *IEEE Transactions on Learning Technologies*, *9*(4), 328–341. doi:10.1109/TLT.2016.2556671

Lorenzo, C. M., Sicilia, M. Á., & Sánchez, S. (2012). Studying the effectiveness of multi-user immersive environments for collaborative evaluation tasks. *Computers & Education*, *59*(4), 1361–1376. doi:10.1016/j.compedu.2012.06.002

Lowrie, T., & Jorgensen, R. (2011). Gender differences in students' mathematics game playing. *Computers & Education*, *57*(4), 2244–2248. doi:10.1016/j.compedu.2011.06.010

Lui, D. P. Y., Szeto, G. P. Y., & Jones, A. Y. M. (2011). The pattern of electronic game use and related bodily discomfort in Hong Kong primary school children. *Computers & Education, 57*(2), 1665–1674. doi:10.1016/j.compedu.2011.03.008

Maass, A., Kollhorster, K., Riediger, A., MacDonald, V., & Lohaus, A. (2011). Effects of violent and nonviolent computer game content on memory performance in adolescents. *European Journal of Psychology of Education, 26*(3), 339–353. doi:10.100710212-010-0047-0

Macklin, C., & Sharp, J. (2016). *Games, Design and Play: A detailed approach to iterative game design.* Boston, MA: Addison-Wesley Professional.

Malliarakis, C., Tomos, F., Shabalina, O., Mozelius, P., & Balan, O. C. (2015). How to build an ineffective serious game: Worst practices in serious game design. In *9ᵗʰ European Conference on Games Based Learning: ECGBL2015* (pp. 338-345). Steinkjer, Norway: Academic Conferences and Publishing Limited.

Mandinach, E. B., & Corno, L. (1985). Cognitive engagement variations among students of different ability level and sex in a computer problem solving game. *Sex Roles, 13*(3), 241–251. doi:10.1007/BF00287914

Mayrath, M. C., Traphagan, T., Jarmon, L., Trivedi, A., & Resta, P. (2010). Teaching with virtual worlds: Factors to consider for instructional use of Second Life. *Journal of Educational Computing Research, 43*(4), 403–444. doi:10.2190/EC.43.4.a

Meyers, E. M. (2009). Tip of the iceberg: Meaning, identity, and literacy in preteen virtual worlds. *Journal of Education for Library and Information Science, 50*(4), 226–236.

Miyares, G. M. (2013). *Underachieving gifted science students and multi-user virtual environments (Ph.D.).* Fort Lauderdale, FL: Nova Southeastern University.

Morley, M., Riesen, E., Burr, A., Clendinneng, D., Ogilvie, S., & Murray, M. A. (2015). Interprofessional education for pre-licensure learners in a multi-user virtual environment: Lessons learned from students, instructors, and administrators. In *ICERI2015: 8ᵗʰ International Conference of Education, Research and Innovation* (pp. 4796-4805). Seville, Spain: Academic Press.

Mueller, F., Agamanolis, S., Vetere, F., & Gibbs, M. R. (2009). A framework for exertion interactions over a distance. In *Proceedings of the 2009 ACM SIGGRAPH Symposium on Video Games, Sandbox '09* (pp. 143-150). New Orleans, LA: ACM. 10.1145/1581073.1581096

Nelson, B. C., & Ketelhut, D. J. (2007). Scientific inquiry in educational multi-user virtual environments. *Educational Psychology Review, 19*(3), 265–283. doi:10.100710648-007-9048-1

Neugnot-Cerioli, M., Gagner, C., & Beauchamp, M. H. (2015). The use of games in pediatric cognitive intervention: A systematic review. *International Journal of Physical Medicine & Rehabilitation, 3*(4), 1000286. doi:10.4172/2329-9096.1000286

Nickerson, J. V., Corter, J. E., Esche, S. K., & Chassapis, C. (2007). A model for evaluating the effectiveness of remote engineering laboratories and simulations in education. *Computers & Education, 49*(3), 708–725. doi:10.1016/j.compedu.2005.11.019

Nogueira, P. A., Torres, V., Rodrigues, R., Oliveira, E., & Nacke, L. E. (2016). Vanishing scares: Bio-feedback modulation of affective player experiences in a procedural horror game. *Journal on Multimodal User Interfaces*, *10*(1), 31–62. doi:10.100712193-015-0208-1

Park, K. S., & Kenyon, R. V. (1999). Effects of network characteristics on human performance in a collaborative virtual environment. In Proceedings of Virtual Reality (VR) (p. 104). Houston, TX: Academic Press. doi:10.1109/VR.1999.756940

Passig, D. (2015). Revisiting the Flynn effect through 3D immersive virtual reality (IVR). *Computers & Education*, *88*, 327–342. doi:10.1016/j.compedu.2015.05.008

Petrakou, A. (2010). Interacting through avatars: Virtual world as a context for online education. *Computers & Education*, *54*(4), 1020–1027. doi:10.1016/j.compedu.2009.10.007

Prensky, M. (2001). Digital natives, digital immigrants part 1. *On the Horizon*, *9*(5), 1–6. doi:10.1108/10748120110424816

Preziosa, A., Grassi, A., Gaggioli, A., & Riva, G. (2009). Therapeutic applications of the mobile phone. *British Journal of Guidance & Counselling*, *37*(3), 313–325. doi:10.1080/03069880902957031

Rideout, V. J., Foehr, U. G., & Roberts, D. F. (2010). *Generation M²: Media in the Lives of 8- to 18-year-olds*. The Kaiser Family Foundation. Retrieved December 2, 2018, http://www.kff.org/other/event/generation-m2-media-in-the-lives-of/

Ritz, L., & Buss, A. (2016). A framework for aligning instructional design strategies with affordances of CAVE immersive virtual reality systems. *TechTrends*, *60*(6), 549–556. doi:10.100711528-016-0085-9

Riva, G., Wiederhold, B. K., Mantovani, F., & Gaggioli, A. (2011). Interreality: The experiential use of technology in the treatment of obesity. *Clinical Practice and Epidemiology in Mental Health*, *4*(7), 51–61. doi:10.2174/1745017901107010051 PMID:21559236

Roberts, D., Wolff, R., Otto, O., & Steed, A. (2003). Constructing a Gazebo: Supporting teamwork in a tightly coupled, distributed task in virtual reality. *Presence (Cambridge, Mass.)*, *12*(6), 644–657. doi:10.1162/105474603322955932

Ryan, R. M., & Deci, E. L. (2000). Self-determination theory and the facilitation of intrinsic motivation, social development, and well-being. *American Psychologist*, *55*(1), 68-78. doi:10.1037110003-066X.55.1.68

Schmidt, B., & Stewart, S. (2010). Implementing the virtual world of Second Life into community nursing theory and clinical courses. *Nurse Educator*, *35*(2), 74–78. doi:10.1097/NNE.0b013e3181ced999 PMID:20173592

Schmierbach, M., Limperos, A. M., & Woolley, J. K. (2012). Feeling the need for (personalized) speed: How natural controls and customization contribute to enjoyment of a racing game through enhanced immersion. *Cyberpsychology, Behavior, and Social Networking*, *15*(7), 364–369. doi:10.1089/cyber.2012.0025 PMID:22687145

Scullion, J., Baxter, G., & Stansfield, M. (2015). UNITE: Enhancing students' self-efficacy through the use of a 3D virtual world. *Journal of Universal Computer Science*, *21*(12), 1635–1653. doi:10.3217/jucs-021-12-1635

Slater, M., Usoh, M., & Steed, A. (1994). Depth of presence in virtual environments. *Presence (Cambridge, Mass.)*, *3*(2), 130–144. doi:10.1162/pres.1994.3.2.130

So, H. J., & Brush, T. A. (2008). Student perceptions of collaborative learning, social presence and satisfaction in a blended learning environment: Relationships and critical factors. *Computers & Education*, *51*(1), 318–336. doi:10.1016/j.compedu.2007.05.009

Soltani, P. (2018). A SWOT analysis of virtual reality (VR) for seniors. In G. Guazzaroni (Ed.), *Virtual and augmented reality in mental health treatment*. Hershey, PA: IGI Global; doi:10.4018/978-1-5225-7168-1.ch006

Soltani, P., Figueiredo, P., Fernandes, R. J., & Vilas-Boas, J. P. (2016). Do player performance, real sport experience, and gender affect movement patterns during equivalent exergame? *Computers in Human Behavior*, *63*, 1–8. doi:10.1016/j.chb.2016.05.009

Soltani, P., Figueiredo, P., Fernandes, R. J., & Vilas-Boas, J. P. (2017a). Muscle activation behavior in a swimming exergame: Differences by experience and gaming velocity. *Physiology & Behavior*, *181*, 23–28. doi:10.1016/j.physbeh.2017.09.001 PMID:28882467

Soltani, P., Figueiredo, P., Ribeiro, J., Fernandes, R. J., & Vilas-Boas, J. P. (2017b). Physiological demands of a swimming-based video game: Influence of gender, swimming background, and exergame experience. *Scientific Reports*, *7*(1), 5247. doi:10.103841598-017-05583-8 PMID:28701720

Susi, T., Johannesson, M., & Backlund, P. (2007). *Serious games: An overview* (Technical Report No. HS-IKI-TR-07-001). Skövde, Sweden: University of Skövde.

Tang, J. T., Lan, Y. J., & Chang, K. E. (2012). The influence of an online virtual situated environment on a Chinese learning community. *Knowledge Management & E-Learning: An International Journal*, *4*(1), 51-62.

Vrellis, I., Avouris, N., & Mikropoulos, T. A. (2016). Learning outcome, presence and satisfaction from a science activity in Second Life. *Australasian Journal of Educational Technology*, *32*(1), 59–77. doi:10.14742/ajet.2164

Webster, R. (2016). Declarative knowledge acquisition in immersive virtual learning environments. *Interactive Learning Environments*, *24*(6), 1319–1333. doi:10.1080/10494820.2014.994533

Whitehead, S., & Biddle, S. (2008). Adolescent girls' perceptions of physical activity: A focus group study. *European Physical Education Review*, *14*(2), 243–262. doi:10.1177/1356336X08090708

Yee, N. (2006). Motivations for play in online games. *Cyberpsychology & Behavior*, *9*(6), 772–775. doi:10.1089/cpb.2006.9.772 PMID:17201605

Young, M. F., Slota, S., Cutter, A. B., Jalette, G., Mullin, G., Lai, B., ... Yukhymenko, M. (2012). Our princess is in another castle: A review of trends in serious gaming for education. *Review of Educational Research*, *82*(1), 61–89. doi:10.3102/0034654312436980

ADDITIONAL READING

Finco, M. D., Reategui, E., Zaro, M. A., Sheehan, D. D., & Katz, L. (2015). Exergaming as an alternative for students unmotivated to participate in regular physical education classes. *International Journal of Game-Based Learning*, *5*(3), 1–10. doi:10.4018/IJGBL.2015070101

Finco, M. D., Reategui, E. B., & Zaro, M. A. (2015). Exergames lab: A complementary space for physical education classes. *Movimento*, *21*(3), 687–699. doi:10.22456/1982-8918.52435

Gibbs, B., Quennerstedt, M., & Larsson, H. (2017). Teaching dance in physical education using exergames. *European Physical Education Review*, *23*(2), 237–256. doi:10.1177/1356336X16645611

Lindberg, R., Seo, J., & Laine, T. H. (2016). Enhancing physical education with exergames and wearable technology. *IEEE Transactions on Learning Technologies*, *9*(4), 328–341. doi:10.1109/TLT.2016.2556671

Pasco, D., Roure, C., Kermarrec, G., Pope, Z., & Gao, Z. (2017). The effects of a bike active video game on players' physical activity and motivation. *Journal of Sport and Health Science*, *6*(1), 25–32. doi:10.1016/j.jshs.2016.11.007 PMID:30356595

Pedersen, S. J., Cooley, P. D., & Cruickshank, V. J. (2017). Caution regarding exergames: A skill acquisition perspective. *Physical Education and Sport Pedagogy*, *22*(3), 246–256. doi:10.1080/1740898 9.2016.1176131

Peng, W., & Hsieh, G. (2012). The influence of competition, cooperation, and player relationship in a motor performance centered computer game. *Computers in Human Behavior*, *28*(6), 2100–2106. doi:10.1016/j.chb.2012.06.014

Staiano, A. E., & Calvert, S. L. (2011). Exergames for physical education courses: Physical, social, and cognitive benefits. *Child Development Perspectives*, *5*(2), 93–98. doi:10.1111/j.1750-8606.2011.00162.x PMID:22563349

Sun, H. (2013). Impact of exergames on physical activity and motivation in elementary school students: A follow-up study. *Journal of Sport and Health Science*, *2*(3), 138–145. doi:10.1016/j.jshs.2013.02.003

Vernadakis, N., Papastergiou, M., Zetou, E., & Antoniou, P. (2015). The impact of an exergame-based intervention on children's fundamental motor skills. *Computers & Education*, *83*, 90–102. doi:10.1016/j.compedu.2015.01.001

KEY TERMS AND DEFINITIONS

Biomechanics: This term refers to the study of structure and function of the mechanical aspects of biological systems.

Collaborative Learning: An educational approach to teaching and learning that involves students working together to complete a task or to solve a problem.

Exercise Physiology: The study of the acute responses and chronic adaptations to exercise.

Exergame: A term for video games that require some degree of exercise to operate them.

MUVE: A computer-, server-, or internet-based virtual environment that can be access by multiple users simultaneously.

Physical Education: An educational course related maintaining the human body through physical exercises.

Virtual Reality: Interactive computer generated experienced that take place in simulated environments and incorporates audiovisual and sensory feedback.

ENDNOTE

[1]   All of the external links have been also saved on the Internet Archive WayBack Machine.

Chapter 3

A User Study of Virtual Reality for Visualizing Digitized Canadian Cultural Objects

Miguel Angel Garcia-Ruiz
Algoma University, Canada

Pedro Cesar Santana-Mancilla
Universidad de Colima, Mexico

Laura Sanely Gaytan-Lugo
Universidad de Colima, Mexico

EXECUTIVE SUMMARY

Algoma University holds an important collection of Canadian objects from the Anishinaabe culture dating from 1880. Some of those objects have been on display in the university's library, but most of them still remain stored in the university's archive, limiting opportunities to use them in teaching and learning activities. This chapter describes a research project focusing on digitizing and visualizing cultural artifacts using virtual reality (VR) technology, with the aim of supporting learning of Canadian heritage in cross-cultural courses. The chapter shows technical aspects of the objects' 3D digitization process and goes on to explain a user study with students watching a 3D model displayed on a low-cost VR headset. Results from the study show that visualization of the 3D model on the VR headset was effective, efficient, and satisfactory enough to use, motivating students to keep using it in further sessions. Technology integration of VR in educational settings is also analyzed and discussed.

INTRODUCTION

The digital preservation and dissemination of cultural heritage have been greatly improved over the past two decades, due to the development of technologies such as web pages, three-dimensional (3D) digitization devices, specialized 3D graphics modelling and visualization software, among other techniques (Bentkowska-Kafel & MacDonald, 2018). The web has allowed better ways of cataloging, documenting,

DOI: 10.4018/978-1-5225-5912-2.ch003

displaying and accessing cultural information. Using innovations in 3D digitization with accurate sensors allow for registering and capturing more accurate details of cultural objects, including their 3D imaging and modelling (Tsirliganis et al., 2004), and the resulting 3D graphical models can be easily displayed and consulted on websites. More recently, virtual reality (VR) technology has been proposed and researched for enhancing visualization and interaction with 3D graphical models of cultural objects (Ch'ng, Cai & Thwaites, 2018). The premise of VR is to support user's immersion (the person's perception of being physically present in a 3D virtual environment) and to use most of his/her human senses to manipulate virtual objects and perceive multisensory information from a virtual environment (Burdea & Coiffet, 2003). In VR, users generally don a VR headset that greatly facilitates visual immersion, and may use other technologies such as specialized controllers for interacting with the virtual environment (Sherman & Craig, 2002). Immersion in VR is very important for supporting engagement and motivation of users, which can also provide an enhanced learning experience (Gaitatzes, Christopoulos & Rousso, 2001). Other visualization technologies have been researched and applied in the presentation of cultural heritage such as augmented reality, where digital information such as computer graphics are superimposed on video recording from a real-world environment in real time (e.g., Pedersen et al., 2017). A detailed comparison of augmented and virtual reality technologies for cultural heritage is described by Bekele et al. (2018). However, this chapter deals with the use of VR for visualizing digitized cultural objects.

Motivations for conducting digital cultural heritage preservation include: supporting dissemination of digital media collections through websites and virtual museums, ensuring that appearance and shape of cultural objects are not damaged or lost due to natural or human-made causes or accidents, making replicas, identifying art forgery, helping analyze cultural objects (Gomes, Bellon & Silva, 2014), digital restoration and making digital archives of 3D models (Pieraccini et al., 2001) and using digitized cultural objects for learning and teaching purposes (Garcia-Ruiz, Santana-Mancilla & Gaytan-Lugo, 2017). In addition, digital heritage preservation has been used for promoting the inclusion of indigenous knowledge (Kapuire et al., 2017).

The objective of this book chapter is to describe the researchers' process of 3D digitizing Canadian cultural objects belonging to a collection from Algoma University, as part of a research project funded by Algoma University Research Fund (AURF). The chapter also explains the application of the generated 3D models in educational settings, such as Algoma University's library and in classrooms, for learning and teaching purposes. The chapter goes on to describe initial user studies, namely usability and technology acceptance studies with a 3D digital model digitized in our project, and played on a virtual reality headset in a classroom. The chapter also discusses lessons learned on the 3D digitization process and the use of virtual reality in the classroom for digital heritage learning.

BACKGROUND

The literature shows many examples and techniques for the digitization of objects, buildings and archaeological sites in 3D (Portales et al., 2017). There are a number of digital acquisition methods for capturing cultural heritage 3D data to carry out 3D reconstruction, which is the capturing of 3D digital information of a real object and constructing the object's digital shape and appearance (Gomes, Bellon & Silva, 2014). 3D digitizing methods include:

- **Digital Photogrammetry:** It is a technique for acquiring digital photographs and geometric measurements from real-world objects, buildings or sites, generating 2D and 3D graphical models based on the photographs taken with one or more digital cameras and using specialized software algorithms (Linder, 2009). Although accurate, this technique mostly takes a long time because many photographs are needed to generate an accurate 3D model (Remondino & El-Hakim, 2006).
- **Laser Scanning Techniques:** They are based on a system composed of a moving laser source emitting a laser light beam, and an optical sensor that detects the line or pattern of the laser beam projected on the cultural object. Some systems can also acquire surface color (texture) from the digitized objects. This technique generates the digitized object's geometry by applying triangulation algorithms. One advantage of laser scanners is their high accuracy (Pavlidis et al., 2007), but their cost can be high.
- **Contact Digitizing:** This technique utilizes a robotic arm with a sensor in the form of a probe or tip that is manually positioned around the object to be digitized touching its surface, and a software tool is recording its 3D position in space, generating a cloud of points which later will form a 3D model. This method has sub-millimeter accuracy but it is time consuming and it may damage the object's surface (Gomes, Bellon & Silva, 2014).
- **Shape From Structured Light:** This system projects a set of light patterns onto the object to be digitized and an optical sensor detects the distortions of the patterns formed over the object's surface. An example of this system is the Microsoft Kinect (^{TM}) sensor, a video game console motion sensor that uses an infrared pattern and acquire surface colors at a range of 30 images per second, although at low resolution. However, this technique is sensitive to the type of ambient illumination (Gomes, Bellon & Silva, 2014).

It is important to note that in some digital heritage projects both digital photogrammetry and laser scanning technologies have been successfully combined, using data fusion for digitizing historical sites and buildings, such as the work described by Guarnieri, Remondino and Vettore (2006) and Munumer & Lerma (2015).

The digitization of cultural objects in 3D has been conducted for some decades. One of the most cited works is the Digital Michelangelo Project, summarizing how a team from Stanford University digitized a number of sculptures from the Renaissance artist Michelangelo (Levoy et al., 2000), using high-end 3D scanners with a resolution of 0.125mm, digitizing the sculptures in color. Researchers found that digitizing objects with shiny and polished surfaces were one of the most challenging tasks. Moreover, The National Research Council of Canada has conducted extensive research and development on 3D scanning techniques and has digitized Canadian cultural objects for a number of years (Corcoran et al., 2002). Other cultural heritage and research institutions such as the Smithsonian Institution in the U.S. are digitizing cultural objects to make their objects' collections more easily accessible to students, researchers and scholars (Jones & Christal, 2002).

Digitizing cultural objects is not trivial, since special care must be exercised when manipulating the objects due to their fragility, and many of them have an intricate surface, which can be difficult to digitize. In addition, nearly all of the generated 3D model files are very large with millions of polygons. Efficient techniques are needed for improving the 3D object digitization and visualization (Santos et al., 2014). Once digitized, the 3D digital models can be shown on a web page and used on VR applications, supporting their analysis (Santos et al., 2014), leveraging on user's engagement, motivation, and immersion, among other characteristics that VR offers (Freina & Ott, 2015). 3D models can also be displayed along with textual or narrated descriptions of the digitized artifacts explaining how an ancient culture used the digitized object (Bustillo et al., 2015). Over the past two decades, many researchers have explored the use of VR to cultural heritage and archaeology.

As it was explained in the Introduction section, VR has been researched and applied for displaying interactive 3D virtual environments containing digitized cultural heritage sites and objects. A number of VR technologies have been used, which include the following:

- **Cave Automatic Virtual Environment (CAVE) (TM):** A CAVE is a large system where a virtual environment containing digital heritage is projected on at least two walls of the system, with the objective of covering most of the users' field of view. In it, a group of users step close to the projection and generally watch the virtual environment in stereo (a visual technique that enhances 3D projection depth) by wearing LCD (shutter) glasses, and they interact with the environment using a 3D mouse or a similar controller. This is a highly immersive system albeit expensive, taking considerable space and can be difficult to set up (Gaitatzes, Christopoulos & Roussou, 2001).

- **Immersadesk (TM):** It is a 2 x 2 meter back-projection system that can be tilted at an angle between 0 and 90 degrees. This projection can be viewed simultaneously by a group of people and they can visualize the projection in stereo by donning LCD glasses, producing high immersion (Gaitatzes, Christopoulos & Roussou, 2001). However, it is an expensive system.

- **Powerwall:** This VR technology comprises a single large projection of a virtual environment, working as a panoramic screen, where its users generally wear LCD glasses to watch the 3D environment in stereo. In addition, other stereo visualization techniques can be used, such as anaglyphs (people wear glasses with red and blue filters) and polarized glasses (Carrozzino & Bergamasco, 2010). This is a highly immersive application but it takes space and can be expensive.

- Web page or computer's software application where a 3D virtual environment can be displayed on a computer monitor. Some websites allow uploading and displaying 3D models of digitized cultural heritage, such as sketchfab.com, where its users can interact with the virtual environment using a mouse. Sketchfab and other similar websites use the Web Graphics Library (WebGL), allowing the visualization of 3D graphical models on web pages and on smartphones. WebGL also allows the visualization of the 3D model in stereo. Using web pages is a low-cost application, and digital cultural heritage can be easily displayed on a museum, a library or in a school using a stand-alone computer. Although this technology provides good interaction and can show high-resolution 3D models (Potenziani et al., 2015), it provides low immersion when played on a computer monitor without stereo projection.

- **VR Headset (Also Called Head-Mounted Display, or HMD):** It is a head-worn device that fully covers the user's field of view. A 3D virtual environment is projected in stereo inside the headset using custom-made internal screen displays, and in some types of VR headsets they are connected to a computer that generates the virtual environment and processes the user interaction. Some models such as the Oculus Go (TM) works as a self-contained system, not requiring an external computer to work. It is also possible to run a self-contained system by inserting a smartphone into some types of VR headsets and run specialized apps on them. The virtual environment then is displayed in stereo on the smartphone's screen. VR headsets detect the user's motion and is reflected this on the virtual environment by using sensors such as gyroscopes, accelerometers, proximity sensors and magnetometers. VR headset applications are highly immersive (Gonizzi

Barsanti et al., 2015). Recent computing advancements have decreased their cost and increased their efficiency and effectiveness considerably for their use in displaying digital heritage (Garcia-Ruiz, Santana-Mancilla & Gaytan-Lugo, 2017).

One of the first fully-fledged archaeological VR exhibits was developed by Gaitatzes, Christopoulos and Roussou (2001). These researchers set up a CAVE with two large immersive projections (3m x 3m) intended for a small audience, displaying a virtual world depicting reconstructions of the ancient city of Miletus (it is situated by the coast of Asia Minor) and a digital reconstruction of the Temple of Zeus at Olympia, in Greece. Users watched the projection in stereo by wearing LCD (shutter) glasses. The virtual world was interactive, where people navigated through 3D models of ancient temples by using a 3D mouse. In one activity, the VR system allowed users to reconstruct an ancient vase by putting together virtual clay pieces. Researchers found (as in other similar projects) that one of the advantages of providing VR archaeology experiences is that they transport users to other times and places that may be difficult to experience in real life.

More recently, high-end VR headsets such as the Oculus Rift (TM), which requires a powerful personal computer to operate, has been used in studies about digital heritage dissemination. For example, Gonizzi Barsanti et al. (2015) explored the use of the Oculus Rift for displaying a virtual environment containing digitized heritage about Egyptian funeral objects exhibited in the Sforza Castle in Milan, Italy. It contained responsive points of interest to facilitate navigation through the virtual environment and inspecting the digital heritage objects. The researchers also used the Leap Motion (TM), a sensor that detects hand movements in 3D, for tracking user's interaction in the virtual environment. Recent research done by Fernandez-Palacios, Morabito and Remondino (2017) utilized the Oculus Rift VR headset where digitally reconstructed heritage sites with very high resolution are displayed on it, and the Microsoft Kinect sensor was used for capturing the user's interaction with the virtual environment. The researchers point out the importance of VR applied to heritage dissemination such as fragile environments and archaeological sites with forbidden access, where users can virtually inspect their contents.

Fabola, Miller and Fawcett (2015) explored the use of the Google Cardboard (TM), a very low cost and lightweight VR headset that displays a virtual environment in stereo by running a mobile app on a smartphone that is inserted in the headset. This app uses the smartphone's sensors to adjust the viewer's position and orientation in the virtual environment, and the headset has a button that the user presses for selecting an option from a menu and navigate to a point of interest, among other actions. However, the researchers implemented in their app a hands-free interaction technique, where the app has virtual hotspots with associated events that can be triggered when the user looks towards a specific hotspot. Fabola, Miller and Fawcett (2015) developed a digital reconstruction of St. Andrews cathedral in Scotland, working as a tool for disseminating cultural heritage information. Interestingly, multimedia presentation was also presented on the 3D reconstruction, such as videos, image and audio narrations about the cathedral, providing an important context about it. Fabola, Miller and Fawcett (2015) conducted a user study of the VR application with nine people reported that the application had high usability and all the participants perceived it to have high educational value. In addition, all nine participants declared a very high immersive 3D experience. There are other research projects and applications using lightweight VR headsets for displaying digital heritage. For example, the British Museum used the Samsung Gear (TM), another type of VR headset that works with Samsung smartphones, for displaying digital heritage in one of their learning programs intended for family, teens and school visitors of the museum (Rae & Edwards, 2016). In this program, digital heritage with 3D models of artifacts and reconstruction of scenes of the Bronze Age were applied. People who used the VR application at the museum reported positive feedback and were enthusiastic about using this technology.

Casu et al. (2015) developed a VR software tool for supporting learning and teaching of art history and cultural heritage in the classroom, in particular about two digitized Michelangelo's sculptures displayed in a virtual museum. The tool offered two types of graphics rendering: In its High Fidelity Mode, students could visualize the virtual sculptures with more realism but it was computationally expensive. In its Fast Rendering Mode, the virtual sculptures were visualized at the lowest resolution but this avoided unpleasant light reflections unintentionally projected in the virtual museum. In the VR software tool, students could write textual annotations close to the virtual artworks. An early user test running the VR software tool on the Oculus Rift and on Google cardboard VR headsets found that high-school students who used the VR headsets for analyzing the virtual sculptures increased "their motivation in studying the lesson topic, in particular increasing their attention, satisfaction and the perceived relevance of the teaching material" (Casu et al., 2015, p. 83). Other research studies that used Google Cardboard for heritage site dissemination and their use in museums describe positive results (e.g. Sooai et al., 2016).

ORGANIZATION BACKGROUND

Algoma University (AlgomaU) is a teaching-oriented and student-centered educational institution located in Sault Ste. Marie, Ontario, Canada, established in 1965. It currently serves a diverse body of about 1600 regional, international students, and local indigenous students as well. AlgomaU offers professional, liberal arts and sciences degree programs, including cross-cultural courses on indigenous education.

Algoma University's Wishart Library houses an important collection of cultural objects crafted by local indigenous people from the Anishinaabe culture dating back from the 1800s. These objects belong to the Engracia de Jesus Matias Archives and Special Collections. Nearly a hundred small objects have been cataloged online, shown in Artifact collection (2018). Figure 1 shows an example of one cultural object cataloged by the Library.

However, just a very small sample of those objects have been on display at the library's main floor, mainly because of the fragility of some objects, among other reasons. Figure 2 below shows the Library's main hall and some display cases. In the authors' opinions, this may limit students' opportunities to know more about local Canadian culture.

SETTING THE STAGE

Digitizing cultural objects in 3D is not new. One of the most cited works is the Digital Michelangelo Project, summarizing how a team from Stanford University digitized a number of sculptures from the Renaissance artist Michelangelo (Levoy et al., 2000), using high-resolution 3D scanners with a resolution of 0.125mm, digitizing the sculptures in color. Researchers found that digitizing objects with shiny and polished surfaces were one of the most challenging tasks. The National Research Council of Canada has conducted extensive research and development on 3D digitizing techniques and has digitized Canadian cultural objects for a number of years (Corcoran et al., 2002).

Other cultural heritage and research institutions such as the Smithsonian Institution in the U.S. are digitizing cultural objects to make their objects' collections more easily accessible to students, researchers

Figure 1. Example of a cultural object stored in the university archives

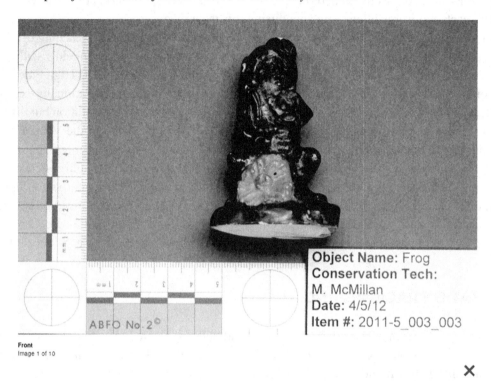

and scholars (Jones & Christal, 2002). Once digitized, the 3D digital models can be shown on a web page and used on VR applications, supporting their analysis (Santos et al., 2014) leveraging on user's immersion and engagement among other characteristics that VR offers (Freina & Ott, 2015). The 3D model can also be displayed along with a textual or narrated description of the digitized artifact explaining how an ancient culture used the digitized object (Bustillo et al., 2015). However, digitizing cultural objects is not trivial, since special care must be exercised when manipulating the objects due to their fragility, and many of them have an intricate surface, which can be difficult to digitize. In addition, nearly all of the generated 3D model files are very large with millions of polygons. Efficient techniques are needed for improving the 3D object digitization and visualization (Santos et al., 2014).

CASE DESCRIPTION

The authors are currently conducting a research project that focuses on digitizing Canadian cultural objects in 3D and use them in educational applications. Initial work has been originally described in Garcia-Ruiz et al. (2017) and was supported during its first year by the Algoma University Research Fund (AURF). The overarching aim of this project is to use the resulting objects' 3D models in courses where Canadian culture is taught. One objective is to see if the tools, methods and resulting 3D models are technically feasible for educational applications. Another objective is to carry out user studies to test and analyze the usability (ease of use) and technology acceptance of the digitized 3D models displayed on a digital library and a classroom, and using virtual reality (VR) technology such as an easy-to use VR headset.

Figure 2. The newly-renovated Arthur A. Wishart library's main floor

This should improve and support students' learning experience (Virvou and Katsionis, 2008; Zaharias, 2004, 2006), in particular about learning Canadian culture. This also supports the potential educational benefits of engagement and intrinsic motivation with the use of immersive VR (Dalgarno & Lee, 2010).

In this project, usability and technology acceptance of virtual reality technology are analyzed and studied. Usability testing analyzes how easy a computer application's user interface (UI) is to use in terms of quality components such as efficiency, effectiveness and user satisfaction in a specific context of use (Dumas & Redish, 1999; Nielsen, 2012; Rubin & Chisnell, 2008). In this project, the contexts of use were a university classroom, Algoma University's Wishart Library, and its Gaming Technology lab. This is a computer lab used by students who are taking the Bachelor of Computer Science's video game technology specialization.

Technology acceptance is a complement of usability testing. It analyzes how users of technology accept and use a particular in a specific context of use. The Technology Acceptance Model (TAM) version 2 proposes that when users are presented with a new technology, a number of factors determine their decision about when and how they will use it. The TAM version 2 questionnaire (shown in Appendix A) has been used in previous research studies for evaluating VR applications in learning and training settings (e.g., Fang et al., 2014; Fokides, 2017). In addition, the TAM analyzes user's attitudes towards technology use. This is based on two user beliefs:

- **Perceived Usefulness:** "The degree to which a person believes that using a particular system would enhance his or her job performance" (Davis, 1989, p. 320). In our case, "job performance" refers to the users' performance when using our VR system for visualizing and analyzing a digitized cultural object.
- **Perceived Ease of Use:** "The degree to which a person believes that using a particular system would be free from effort" (Davis, 1989, p. 320). This belief is related to usability, which is related to his/her preconceived notion on how easy VR will be to use for watching and interacting with a 3D model of a cultural object.

Technology Components

The authors are using in this project a Matter and Form 3D scanner (Matter and Form, 2018) for digitizing cultural objects from AlgomaU's archives. This is an affordable and easy-to-use scanner that captures detail of up to 0.43 mm in RGB color and can digitize objects with a maximum height of 25 cm and width of 18 cm, with a maximum weight of up to 3 kgs, thus it is intended for digitizing small objects. The scanner uses two laser beams to acquire 3D reference points from the object's surface and shape and uses a moving platform to rotate the object to digitize it. Digitizing (scanning) a small object takes about two hours, since it is a quite intensive and accurate process. The objects are digitized twice both in lying and upright positions for acquiring many details in 3D, from many angles. The scanner's companion software was used to merge the two obtained 3D models and their respective textures automatically. The two obtained 3D models were saved in .OBJ format, used by industry-standard computer graphics editors and 3D modelers. The Matter and Form scanner is shown in Figure 3.

The authors connected the 3D scanner to a graphics-enhanced (gaming) laptop computer with 8 GB of RAM and a solid-state hard drive (SSD). He also connected a 24" high-quality computer monitor to the laptop. This helped the 3D model visualization obtained from the digitization (shown in Figure 3). The laptop was running Windows 10 (TM) for running the 3D scanner, and the same laptop also ran Ubuntu Linux distribution, used for revising the obtained 3D models. Using Linux was a matter of preference, since the same software tools used in this project were also downloaded and ran on Windows. The graphics performance on both Linux and Windows appeared to be the same. However, the 3D scanner only offered a software tool and a driver for the Windows operating system.

It is important to note that the 3D scanner did not acquire some of the textures correctly at the time of digitizing an object. Some of them present slight imperfections and small changes in their brightness, due to the intricate objects' shape, shadows and other issues. In order to visualize, review and improve the resulting 3D models from the 3D digitizing process, the research assistants used a software tool called MeshLab (Meshlab, 2018). This tool was very useful for filling holes let by the digitization process in the 3D mesh, among other graphics operations. A student who collaborated in the project was also using Blender (Blender, 2018), another software tool used for manipulating and improving our 3D models. The student also used a powerful image editor called GIMP (GIMP, 2018) for fixing the colors of the 3D models' associated textures. All these software tools are robust, free, open source and easy to use, with a shallow learning curve.

Figure 3. The matter and form 3D scanner used in this project

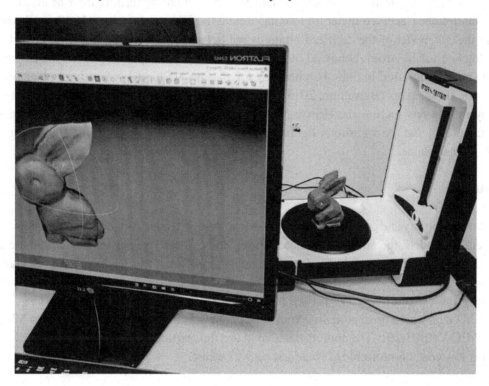

The project assistants digitized some cultural objects that were used as a proof of concept to test the VR technology used in this project, and one of them was used in our usability and technology acceptance testing sessions. They initially digitized two small wooden carved figures from the University archives, a bunny rabbit (Bunny, 2018) and a dog (Dog, 2018). The first author obtained permission from the Wishart library to use the cultural objects' 3D models and the archive's information posted online in this project.

Once the cultural objects were digitized, revised and improved, the resulting 3D models were uploaded to Sketchfab (Sketchfab, 2018). This is an easy and free-to-use web site for non-commercial applications used to share and show interactive 3D models. Sketchfab has an option to watch the models in stereo (the model is rendered twice, one graphic rendering for each eye). The 3D model is opened on a smartphone's web browser and then the smartphone is inserted into a VR headset such as Google Cardboard (Fabola et al., 2015) and similar low-cost headsets. Models uploaded to Sketchfab can be watched on a web browser from any recent mobile device (e.g. smartphones) or desktop computer that supports the WebGL 3D graphics library. Sketchfab also allows to upload and display the object's textual and metadata description, such as the digitized objects' original measurements. Sketchfab has two options for interacting with the object: "Orbit" and "First Person". When selecting the Orbit option from Sketchfab's menu, users can move the camera (panning) and zooming in or out around the 3D model. In the First Person option, users can look around the object. Both interaction options can be selected and performed using either a computer keyboard, a mouse or swiping on a touch display device such as a smartphone. Currently, however, Sketchfab does not have this capability when users visualize the object in stereo and when the smartphone is inserted into a VR headset. In addition, users can also set up the graphics rendering and lighting from Sketchfab's menu (Sketchfab Controls, 2017).

People can interact with the 3D model visualized in Sketchfab by turning their heads around, thus using the smartphones' accelerometer for looking around the 3D environment. The Sketchfab web page containing the 3D model of the digitized bunny is publicly available at: Digitized bunny (2018). The digitized dog is available from: Digitized dog (2018). Other models uploaded to the Sketchfab website have been successfully used in digital archeology for sharing 3D models of cultural objects that were acquired with 3D scanners (Barrettara, 2013). Sketchfab has also been used for disseminating cultural heritage by institutions such as the British Museum (Lloyd, 2016). Sketchfab has a very easy-to-use user interface (UI), and the website is lightweight enough for using it on almost any recent personal computer or smartphone.

User Study

To analyze the feasibility and potential applications of the proposed educational VR application displaying the obtained 3D models, the authors conducted a user study where five participants tested the usability and the technology acceptance of the Sketchfab models watched on a VR headset. The Sketchfab website was opened on the Chrome web browser from a Google Nexus 5 smartphone, shown in Figure 4. The Nexus 5 provides a resolution of 1920x1080 pixels with a diagonal size of 12.5 centimeters and a clock speed of 2.26 GHz, with a quad core processor. The phone was inserted into an EVO Next VR headset, model no. MIC-VRB03-101. The authors decided to use this particular brand and model of VR headset because it is low cost, comfortable to wear and easy to adjust.

Participants

At the beginning of the study session, participants filled out a demographic questionnaire, shown in Table 1. Five computer science students from Algoma University participated in the study. Their age average was 22 years old (4 males and 1 female). In order to evaluate the overall usability of the VR setting, the authors did not need to test it with many participants. According to Nielsen (2000), just 5 participants will report about 85% of the usability problems of an interactive computer application. None of the participants reported serious vision problems or disabilities. Some of them wore glasses, but they

Figure 4. The VR headset with the smartphone inserted in it

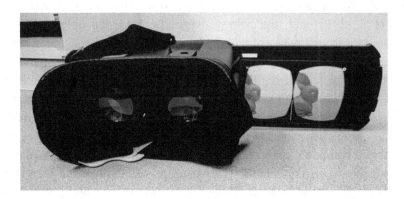

Table 1. Demographics questionnaire

These questions are used to help identify trends in responses. Please remember that your responses will be completely confidential and anonymous.
1. Gender: _____ Male _____ Female
2. Age (to the nearest year): _____
3. Have you used virtual reality (VR) equipment before (e.g. VR headset)? If yes, which one(s)? _____
_____
4. Have you taken courses where Canadian culture and/or heritage has been taught in them (Y/N) ? ___
5. Have you played 3D video games? If yes, for how long have you played video games? _____
6. What type of player are you (player skills)?:
____ Non-video game player
____ Novice player
____ Occasional player
____ Expert player
____ Frequent/hard core player

decided to remove them before they visualized the 3D model using the VR headset. Those participants reported that not wearing the glasses did not affect the model visualization, since they could successfully adjust the headset lenses.

The authors tested the VR application in three areas: Algoma University's Gaming Technology Laboratory (a computer lab), the Wishart Library, and a classroom. It is important to test the usability and analyze the VR system's technology acceptance in those places because they are natural educational settings, and the authors wanted to know how students will use the VR headset in those places. Thus, the user studies run in this project can be considered as a type of field study. Figure 5 shows a student testing the VR setting in a classroom.

The usability testing methodology applied in this user study was the Concurrent Think Aloud Protocol, or CTAP (Alshammari, Alhadreti & Mayhew, 2015). In the CTAP, usability specialists ask participants to say out loud their opinions and feelings and decisions about using a digital device's UI, while they are interacting with it. The authors consider CTAP as a practical yet powerful methodology for uncovering problems "on the fly", which may hinder learning issues in an educational application with technology. It is particularly suitable with this VR application because students can verbalize VR application's usability problems right away, when those happened, while they are visualizing the 3D model using the VR headset.

After participants completed the study tasks, they filled out the widely-used and reliable System Usability Scale (SUS) questionnaire (Brooke, 1996), shown in Table 2. This questionnaire has been previously applied in a number of studies where virtual reality environments have been evaluated (e.g. Correa et al., 2017, Garcia-Ruiz, Santana-Mancilla & Gaytan-Lugo, 2017). The SUS has ten Likert scales where participants rated each one from 1 ("strongly disagree") to 5 ("strongly agree"). They also filled out the Technology Acceptance Model version 2 (TAM2) questionnaire (Venkatesh & Davis, 2000), shown in Appendix A. The authors have successfully used both questionnaires in previous studies, yielding valuable user feedback (Garcia-Ruiz, Santana-Mancilla & Gaytan-Lugo, 2017).

Figure 5. A student wearing the VR headset

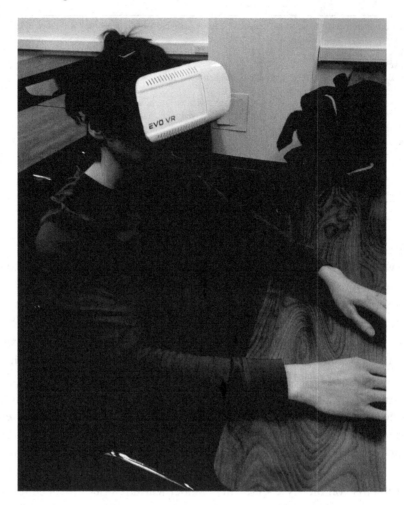

Procedure

Each participant's session lasted about 45 minutes. The participants' tasks were the following:

- Visualize a 3d model of a cultural object digitized in this project, analyzing it from any possible angle, so participants needed to "walk" around the model and turn their heads.
- Identify the type of material and estimate the real size of the digitized object.

The following describes the testing session steps, based on the usability testing steps outlined by Rubin & Chisnell (2008) and in Usability Test (2017):

- **Pre-Test Arrangement:** Prepare everything for the test. Turn the smartphone on, open the Sketchfab website on the smartphone displaying one of the digitized objects' model in 3D. Insert the smartphone in the VR headset. Make sure everything works OK.

Table 2. The SUS questionnaire

1. I think I would like to use this VR application frequently	Strongly disagree Strongly agree 1.........2........3...........4..........5
2. I found the VR application unnecessarily complex.	Strongly disagree Strongly agree 1.........2........3...........4..........5
3. I thought the VR application was easy to use.	Strongly disagree Strongly agree 1.........2........3...........4..........5
4. I think I would need the support of a technical person to be able to use this VR application.	Strongly disagree Strongly agree 1.........2........3...........4..........5
5. I found the various functions in this VR application were well integrated.	Strongly disagree Strongly agree 1.........2........3...........4..........5
6. I thought there was too much inconsistency in this VR application.	Strongly disagree Strongly agree 1.........2........3...........4..........5
7. I would imagine that most people would learn how to use this VR application very quickly.	Strongly disagree Strongly agree 1.........2........3...........4..........5
8. I found the VR application very cumbersome to use.	Strongly disagree Strongly agree 1.........2........3...........4..........5
9. I felt very confident using the VR system.	Strongly disagree Strongly agree 1.........2........3...........4..........5
10. I needed to learn a lot of things before I could get going with this VR application.	Strongly disagree Strongly agree 1.........2........3...........4..........5

- **Session Introduction:** the authors welcome the participant. They briefly explain the study objective, relevance, the TAP methodology, and the tasks. The participant reads and signs the consent form to participate in this research. The form also summarizes the instructions for the test, including the usability testing and technology acceptance objectives.
- **Testing Tasks:** the participant starts the study by wearing the VR headset and begins performing the tasks for this session, saying out loud his/her opinions, feelings and decisions about the tasks. The authors then take notes on the participant's comments. The testing continues until the all the tasks were competed or the allotted time has elapsed.
- **Post-Test Debriefing and Conclusion:** The authors ask general questions on the test. The participant fills out the SUS and TAM2 questionnaires. Finally, the authors thank the participant.

Table 3. results of the technology acceptance model (TAM2) questionnaire

Participant No.	Likert Scale (Questionnaire Item) Number (1=strongly disagree...7=strongly agree)																									
	L1	L2	L3	L4	L5	L6	L7	L8	L9	L10	L11	L12	L13	L14	L15	L16	L17	L18	L19	L20	L21	L22	L23	L24	L25	L26
P1	5	6	3	3	3	3	7	7	7	7	1	1	7	7	7	4	4	4	2	2	5	6	7	5	7	1
P2	7	7	6	6	4	4	7	7	7	7	6	4	7	7	7	4	2	2	2	3	5	6	6	6	6	4
P3	6	6	4	4	5	4	6	7	6	7	4	4	7	4	4	4	4	4	4	5	6	6	6	4	6	4
P4	6	6	5	5	5	5	7	7	7	7	4	4	7	7	7	4	4	4	4	4	6	5	6	6	6	4
P5	6	5	4	5	5	5	6	7	7	7	4	4	7	7	7	4	3	4	4	4	6	6	6	6	6	4
Median:	6	6	4	5	5	5	7	7	7	7	4	4	7	7	7	4	4	4	4	4	6	6	6	6	6	4
Mode:	6	6	4	4	5	4	7	7	7	7	4	4	7	7	7	4	4	4	4	4	6	6	6	6	6	4

RESULTS AND DISCUSSION

Most the participants reported in the CTAP that the EVO VR headset was lightweight and compact. It was easy for them to adjust the lenses' interpupillary and eyeball distances, although two of them reported that the VR headset was a little uncomfortable when sitting on the nose.

According to the results from the TAM2 questionnaire (shown in Table 3) and participants' comments made during the Concurrent Think Aloud (CTAP), it seems that the VR application motivated participants to continue using Sketchfab models displayed on a VR headset in further educational applications. In addition, this study arouses students' curiosity on how an easy-to-use VR application can be used in an educational setting. The 26 Likert scales from the TAM2 questionnaire are enlisted in Appendix A.

According to the results obtained through the participants' responses, the median for items: 3, 6, 11, 12, 16-20 and 26 was four; the median for items: 4 and 5 was five; meanwhile, the median for items: 1, 2 and 21-25 was 6; finally, the median for items: 7-10 and 14-15 was seven. Furthermore, the participants' response with the lowest median was 4,5. The second participant with the highest median was six.

Each of the SUS questionnaires (shown in Table 4) was scored according to Brooke (1996), where a usability value was obtained (a percentile) where 50=very bad usability and 100=excellent usability.

Table 4. Results of the system usability scale (SUS) questionnaire

Participant No.	Likert Scale (Questionnaire Item) Number (1=strongly disagree...5=strongly agree)										
	L1	L2	L3	L4	L5	L6	L7	L8	L9	L10	SUS Score
P1	4	1	5	2	4	1	5	1	5	1	92.5
P2	5	1	5	1	4	2	5	1	4	1	92.5
P3	4	1	4	1	3	2	4	1	4	1	82.5
P4	4	1	4	1	5	2	4	1	4	1	87.5
P5	4	2	4	1	4	2	4	1	4	1	82.5
Median and mode	4	1	4	1	4	2	4	1	4	1	

The average of the results from the five SUS questionnaires was 87.7. This score is in the 80th percentile, meaning that the VR application's usability was very high (Sauro, 2011). Individual results from the SUS' Likert scales are very favorable, although do not have excellent usability, as most of the participants rated scales 1,3,5,7 and 9 (positive usability outcomes) with a value of 4.

During the CTAP, participants were asked to estimate the real size of the digitized object visualized on the VR headset (they did not know the real size before the test). Most of the participants answered that the object's size was really big, of about one meter in height. Just one participant could correctly estimate the object's size. He mentioned in the CTAP that he was using the checkered floor from the VR environment as a reference. The real size of the digitized object is small, which is 3.2 x 7.7 x 10.2 cm. In further uses of the VR application, the authors will include reference points or other virtual objects that will help estimate the real size of digitized objects more accurately. Participants were also asked about the material the real object was made of. Three of them correctly answered that the object was made of wood. The authors think that it was due in part because of the smartphone's brightness control adjustment. Participants did not report serious usability problems. All the participants noticed a very small lag on the 3D model visualization, but it was not a big cause of concern. This can be remediated in further VR applications by using a faster smartphone and with better graphics capabilities. Each testing session was short, making it difficult to see if the VR application was engaging enough in the long term. It seems that participants experienced a "novelty effect" when they used VR technology. This is consistent with other similar studies (e.g. Merchant et al., 2014).

SOLUTIONS AND RECOMMENDATIONS

The following is a list of recommendations on the 3D digitization process and VR usage in educational settings. They are based on the authors' usability and technology acceptance study and their digitization process:

- Before starting digitizing objects in 3D you must calibrate the computer monitor(s), so your monitor(s) will show colors more closely to the digitized objects.
- The authors found that using dimmed LED lights with an opaque white filter was the best option for illuminating the digitized objects with the Matter and Form scanner. One LED light placed in front of the scanner and one in the back helped to reduce casting shadows around the object. Shadows do affect the digitization quality, and the light filters helped to decrease the object's surface shininess. The LED lights are shown in Figure 6. Compact fluorescent (CFL) light bulbs and fluorescent lights from the office ceiling were also tried with mixed and often undesirable results.
- Do not place heavy objects on the Matter and Form 3D scanner's rotating platform. If you do that you could break some of its mechanical components. That scanner can hold a weight of up to 3Kg.
- Conduct user testing of the VR equipment and its software application. Use standard usability testing and technology acceptance methodologies. The authors found in this and other studies (e.g. Garcia-Ruiz et al., 2017) that the CTAP is a very useful and practical methodology for testing VR applications, as well as using the TAM2 and SUS questionnaires.
- Run a dry test of the equipment and software before the main user study starts. Set up everything and try out the VR headset and 3D model visualizations with 1 or 2 people, to see if everything works and maybe make some final adjustments to the VR headset or the smartphone.

Figure 6. LED lights configuration

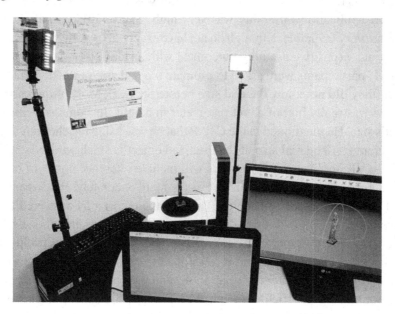

- As with most virtual reality equipment, be aware that watching the 3D models on the VR headset may cause seizures or dizziness in susceptible people. You must ask users first if it is OK if they can visualize the 3D model on the VR headset.
- Clean the smartphone screen with a special cloth prior to its usage with the VR headset. Fingerprints or dust on the smartphone's screen may make the VR visualization somewhat blurred.
- Do not forget to explain users how to adjust the lenses from the VR headset. This is a very important step, otherwise the VR application may look either blurred or distorted. Many VR headsets allow the adjustment of the lenses' interpupillary distance, which is the distance between the user's eyeballs, and the distance between the lenses and the eyeballs.
- There are actions that can be used to overcome the challenge of technology integration of VR in the classroom: having more savvy instructors who can help up other instructors (budding up), and holding hands-on information workshops with instructors, working administration staff and instructors collaborating in this endeavor (Kirkwood, 2015).

CONCLUSION

This chapter described an overview of digital preservation of cultural heritage objects in virtual reality and its importance. There are sufficient motivations to do so, including supporting dissemination of digital media collections through websites and virtual museums, ensuring that appearance and shape of cultural objects are not damaged or lost due to natural or human-made causes or accidents, identifying art forgery, and using digitized cultural objects for learning and teaching purposes. In addition, the chapter explained our research project concerning digitization of cultural objects pertaining to Algoma University, Canada, its 3D digitization process, and the visualization of digitized 3D models using VR technology. The objective of digitizing these objects is to use the obtained 3D models for supporting teaching and learning Canadian culture and heritage. The chapter also reported a user study (usability testing and technology acceptance) about interacting with the digital objects in VR. the chapter explained technical and logistic problems found in the digitization process and the use of the digitized objects. A valuable part of this chapter is the lessons learned about the 3D digitization process.

Results from the researchers' user studies indicate that low-cost VR technology can be useful and effective for supporting visualization of digital heritage objects, in particular about its use in educational settings such as in the classroom. It can become an important didactic tool which is easy to set up and use. The latter allowed us to determine the positive students' acceptance of VR technology for learning purposes. The high usability of the web site used in our study (Sketchfab) yielded high potential for further use in learning and teaching about cultural heritage. This user study also suggests that the use of the low-cost VR headset was an effective way of analyzing the graphical 3D models of cultural objects. This is in line with our previous research on educational VR (Garcia-Ruiz, Santana-Mancilla & Gaytan-Lugo, 2017).

REFERENCES

Alshammari, T., Alhadreti, O., & Mayhew, P. (2015). When to ask participants to think aloud: A comparative study of concurrent and retrospective think-aloud methods. *International Journal of Human-Computer Interaction*, *6*(3), 48–64.

Artifact Collection. (2018). Retrieved from http://archives.algomau.ca/main/node/20942

Barrettara, M. (2013). New methods for sharing and exhibiting 3D archaeology. *The Posthole*, *31*, 8–13.

Bekele, M. K., Pierdicca, R., Frontoni, E., Malinverni, E. S., & Gain, J. (2018). A Survey of Augmented, Virtual, and Mixed Reality for Cultural Heritage. *Journal on Computing and Cultural Heritage*, *11*(2), 7. doi:10.1145/3145534

Bentkowska-Kafel, A., & MacDonald, L. (Eds.). (2018). *Digital techniques for documenting and preserving cultural heritage*. Kalamazoo, MI: Arc Humanities Press.

Blender. (2018). Retrieved from: https://www.blender.org/

Brooke, J. (1996). SUS-A quick and dirty usability scale. *Usability Evaluation in Industry, 189*(194): 4-7.

Bruno, F., Bruno, S., De Sensi, G., Luchi, M. L., Mancuso, S., & Muzzupappa, M. (2010). From 3D reconstruction to virtual reality: A complete methodology for digital archaeological exhibition. *Journal of Cultural Heritage*, *11*(1), 42–49. doi:10.1016/j.culher.2009.02.006

Bunny. (2018). *Brown wooden bunny*. Retrieved from: http://archives.algomau.ca/main/node/25490

Burdea, G. C., & Coiffet, P. (2003). *Virtual reality technology*. New York, NY: John Wiley & Sons. doi:10.1162/105474603322955950

Bustillo, A., Alaguero, M., Miguel, I., Saiz, J. M., & Iglesias, L. S. (2015). A flexible platform for the creation of 3D semi-immersive environments to teach Cultural Heritage. *Digital Applications in Archaeology and Cultural Heritage*, *2*(4), 248–259. doi:10.1016/j.daach.2015.11.002

Carrozzino, M., & Bergamasco, M. (2010). Beyond virtual museums: Experiencing immersive virtual reality in real museums. *Journal of Cultural Heritage, 11*(4), 452–458. doi:10.1016/j.culher.2010.04.001

Casu, A., Spano, L. D., Sorrentino, F., & Scateni, R. (2015). RiftArt: Bringing Masterpieces in the Classroom through Immersive Virtual Reality. In *Eurographics Italian Chapter Conference* (pp. 77-84). Boston, MA: Academic Press.

Ch'ng, E., Cai, Y., & Thwaites, H. (2018). Special Issue on VR for Culture and Heritage: The Experience of Cultural Heritage with Virtual Reality: Guest Editors' Introduction. *Presence (Cambridge, Mass.), 26*(03), iii–vi. doi:10.1162/pres_e_00302

Corcoran, F., Demaine, J., Picard, M., Dicaire, L. G., & Taylor, J. (2002, April). Inuit3d: An interactive virtual 3d web exhibition. In *Proceedings of the Conference on Museums and the Web 2002*. Boston, MA: Academic Press.

Correa, A. G., Borba, E. Z., Lopes, R., Zuffo, M. K., Araujo, A., & Kopper, R. (2017, March). User experience evaluation with archaeometry interactive tools in virtual reality environment. In *Proceedings of 3D User Interfaces (3DUI), 2017 IEEE Symposium on* (pp. 217-218). IEEE.

Dalgarno, B., & Lee, M. J. (2010). What are the learning affordances of 3-D virtual environments? *British Journal of Educational Technology, 41*(1), 10–32. doi:10.1111/j.1467-8535.2009.01038.x

Davis, F. D. M. (1989, September). Perceived usefulness, perceived ease of use, and user acceptance of information technology. *Management Information Systems Quarterly, 13*(3), 319–340. doi:10.2307/249008

Digitized Bunny. (2018). *Brown wooden bunny*. Retrieved from: https://sketchfab.com/models/44ce7f 1dfdd94aeaba8ffd5951275598

Digitized Dog. (2018). *Dog*. Retrieved from: https://sketchfab.com/models/39b78840da6147599878b 1e63349f1bb

Dog. (2018). *Brown sitting dog*. Retrieved from: http://archives.algomau.ca/main/node/25489

Dumas, J. S., & Redish, J. (1999). A practical guide to usability testing. Portland, OR: Intellect Books.

Fabola, A., Miller, A., & Fawcett, R. (2015, September). Exploring the past with Google Cardboard. In *Digital Heritage, 2015* (Vol. 1, pp. 277–284). IEEE. doi:10.1109/DigitalHeritage.2015.7413882

Fang, T. Y., Wang, P. C., Liu, C. H., Su, M. C., & Yeh, S. C. (2014). Evaluation of a haptics-based virtual reality temporal bone simulator for anatomy and surgery training. *Computer Methods and Programs in Biomedicine, 113*(2), 674–681. doi:10.1016/j.cmpb.2013.11.005 PMID:24280627

Fernandez-Palacios, B. J., Morabito, D., & Remondino, F. (2017). Access to complex reality-based 3D models using virtual reality solutions. *Journal of Cultural Heritage, 23*, 40–48. doi:10.1016/j.culher.2016.09.003

Fokides, E. (2017). A model for explaining primary school students' learning outcomes when they use multi-user virtual environments. *Journal of Computers in Education, 4*(3), 225–250. doi:10.100740692-017-0080-y

Freina, L., & Ott, M. (2015). A literature review on immersive virtual reality in education: state of the art and perspectives. *eLearning & Software for Education*, (1). Retrieved from https://www.ceeol.com/search/article-detail?id=289829

Frog. (2017). *Frog – small artifact series*. Retrieved from: http://archives.algomau.ca/main/node/25494

Gaitatzes, A., Christopoulos, D., & Roussou, M. (2001, November). Reviving the past: cultural heritage meets virtual reality. In *Proceedings of the 2001 conference on Virtual reality, archeology, and cultural heritage* (pp. 103-110). ACM. 10.1145/584993.585011

Garcia-Ruiz, M. A., Santana-Mancilla, P. C., & Gaytan-Lugo, L. S. (2016). measuring technology acceptance of makey makey as an input device in a human-computer interaction class. In *Proceedings of EdMedia 2016: World Conference on Educational Media and Technology*. Association for the Advancement of Computing in Education.

Garcia-Ruiz, M. A., Santana-Mancilla, P. C., & Gaytan-Lugo, L. S. (2017). A usability study on low-cost virtual reality technology for visualizing digitized Canadian cultural objects: Implications in education. In *Proceedings of EdMedia 2017: World Conference on Educational Media and Technology*. Association for the Advancement of Computing in Education.

Gimp. (2018). Retrieved from: https://www.gimp.org/

Gomes, L., Bellon, O. R. P., & Silva, L. (2014). 3D reconstruction methods for digital preservation of cultural heritage: A survey. *Pattern Recognition Letters*, *50*, 3–14. doi:10.1016/j.patrec.2014.03.023

Gonizzi Barsanti, S., Caruso, G., Micoli, L. L., Covarrubias Rodriguez, M., & Guidi, G. (2015). 3D visualization of cultural heritage artifacts with virtual reality devices. In *25th International CIPA Symposium 2015* (*Vol. 40*, No. 5W7, pp. 165-172). Copernicus Gesellschaft mbH.

Guarnieri, A., Remondino, F., & Vettore, A. (2006). Digital photogrammetry and TLS data fusion applied to Cultural Heritage 3D modeling. *The International Archives of the Photogrammetry, Remote Sensing and Spatial Information Sciences*, *36*(5). Retrieved from http://3dom.fbk.eu/sites/3dom.fbk.eu/files/pdf/Guarnieri_etal_ISPRSV06.pdf

Jones, G., & Christal, M. (2002). *The future of virtual museums: On-line, immersive, 3D environments*. Created Realities Group. Retrieved from: http://w.created-realities.com/pdf/Virtual_Museums.pdf

Kapuire, G. K., Winschiers-Theophilus, H., Stanley, C., Maasz, D., Chamunorwa, M., Møller, R. H., & Gonzalez-Cabrero, D. (2017). Technologies to promote the inclusion of Indigenous knowledge holders in digital cultural heritage preservation. *International Conference on Culture & Computer Science*.

Kirkwood, A. (2015, June). Teaching and learning with technology in higher education: blended and distance education needs "joined-up thinking" rather than technological determinism. *Open Learning: The Journal of Open, Distance and e-Learning*, 1–16.

Kuusela, H., & Paul, P. (2000). A comparison of concurrent and retrospective verbal protocol analysis. *The American Journal of Psychology*, *113*(3), 387–404. doi:10.2307/1423365 PMID:10997234

Levoy, M., Pulli, K., Curless, B., Rusinkiewicz, S., Koller, D., Pereira, L., & Shade, J. (2000, July). The digital Michelangelo project: 3D scanning of large statues. In *Proceedings of the 27th annual conference on Computer graphics and interactive techniques* (pp. 131-144). ACM Press/Addison-Wesley Publishing Co. 10.1145/344779.344849

Linder, W. (2009). *Digital photogrammetry*. Berlin: Springer. doi:10.1007/978-3-540-92725-9

Lloyd, J. (2016, October). Contextualizing 3D Cultural Heritage. In *The Proceedings of Euro-Mediterranean Conference* (pp. 859-868). Springer International Publishing.

Matter and Form. (2018). Retrieved from: https://matterandform.net/scanner

Merchant, Z., Goetz, E. T., Cifuentes, L., Keeney-Kennicutt, W., & Davis, T. J. (2014). Effectiveness of virtual reality-based instruction on students' learning outcomes in K-12 and higher education: A meta-analysis. *Computers & Education*, *70*, 29–40. doi:10.1016/j.compedu.2013.07.033

Meshlab. (2018). Retrieved from: http://www.meshlab.net/

Munumer, E., & Lerma, J. L. (2015, September). Fusion of 3D data from different image-based and range-based sources for efficient heritage recording. In Digital Heritage, 2015 (Vol. 1, pp. 83-86). IEEE.

Nielsen, J. (2000). *Why you only need to test with 5 users*. Retrieved from: https://www.nngroup.com/articles/why-you-only-need-to-test-with-5-users/

Nielsen, J. (2012). *Usability 101: Introduction to usability*. Retrieved from: https://www.nngroup.com/articles/usability-101-introduction-to-usability/

Ott, M., & Pozzi, F. (2011). Towards a new era for Cultural Heritage Education: Discussing the role of ICT. *Computers in Human Behavior*, *27*(4), 1365–1371. doi:10.1016/j.chb.2010.07.031

Pavlidis, G., Koutsoudis, A., Arnaoutoglou, F., Tsioukas, V., & Chamzas, C. (2007). Methods for 3D digitization of Cultural Heritage. *Journal of Cultural Heritage*, *8*(1), 93–98. doi:10.1016/j.culher.2006.10.007

Pedersen, I., Gale, N., Mirza-Babaei, P., & Reid, S. (2017). More than meets the eye: The benefits of augmented reality and holographic displays for digital cultural heritage. *Journal on Computing and Cultural Heritage*, *10*(2), 11. doi:10.1145/3051480

Pieraccini, M., Guidi, G., & Atzeni, C. (2001). 3D digitizing of cultural heritage. *Journal of Cultural Heritage*, *2*(1), 63–70. doi:10.1016/S1296-2074(01)01108-6

Portales, C., Alonso-Monasterio, P., & Vinals, M. J. (2017). 3D virtual reconstruction and visualisation of the archaeological site Castellet de Bernabe (Lliria, Spain). Virtual Archaeology Review, 8(16), 75. doi:10.4995/var.2017.5890

Posey, G., Burgess, T., Eason, M., & Jones, Y. (2010, March). The Advantages and Disadvantages of the Virtual Classroom and the Role of the Teacher. In *Proceedings of Southwest Decision Sciences Institute Conference* (pp. 2-6). Decision Sciences Institute.

Potenziani, M., Callieri, M., Dellepiane, M., Corsini, M., Ponchio, F., & Scopigno, R. (2015). 3DHOP: 3D heritage online presenter. *Computers & Graphics*, *52*, 129–141. doi:10.1016/j.cag.2015.07.001

Rae, J., & Edwards, L. (2016, January). Virtual reality at the British Museum: What is the value of virtual reality environments for learning by children and young people, schools, and families? *Proceedings of MW2016: The Annual Conference Museums and the Web*.

Remondino, F., & El-Hakim, S. (2006). Image-based 3D modelling: A review. *The Photogrammetric Record, 21*(115), 269–291. doi:10.1111/j.1477-9730.2006.00383.x

Rubin, J., & Chisnell, D. (2008). *Handbook of usability testing: how to plan, design, and conduct effective tests*. Indianapolis, IN: John Wiley & Sons.

Santos, P., Pena Serna, S., Stork, A., & Fellner, D. (2014). The potential of 3D internet in the cultural heritage domain. In M. Ioannides & E. Quak (Eds.), *A Roadmap in Digital Heritage Preservation on 3D Research Challenges in Cultural Heritage (Vol. 8355)*. New York, NY: Springer-Verlag. doi:10.1007/978-3-662-44630-0_1

Sauro, J. (2011). *A Practical guide to the system usability scale: Background, benchmarks & best practices*. Denver, CO: CreateSpace.

Sherman, W. R., & Craig, A. B. (2002). *Understanding virtual reality: Interface, application, and design*. San Francisco, CA: Morgan Kauffmann/Elsevier.

Sketchfab. (2018). Retrieved from: https://sketchfab.com/

Sketchfab Controls. (2017). *Navigation and Controls*. Retrieved from: https://help.sketchfab.com/hc/en-us/articles/202509026-Navigation-and-Controls

Sooai, A. G., Sumpeno, S., & Purnomo, M. H. (2016, April). User perception on 3D stereoscopic cultural heritage ancient collection. In *Proceedings of the 2nd International Conference in HCI and UX Indonesia 2016* (pp. 112-119). ACM. 10.1145/2898459.2898476

Tsirliganis, N., Pavlidis, G., Koutsoudis, A., Papadopoulou, D., Tsompanopoulos, A., Stavroglou, K., & Chamzas, C. (2004). Archiving cultural objects in the 21st century. *Journal of Cultural Heritage, 5*(4), 379–384. doi:10.1016/j.culher.2004.04.001

Usability Test. (2017). *Running a usability test*. U.S. Department of Health & Human Services. Retrieved from: https://www.usability.gov/how-to-and-tools/methods/running-usability-tests.html

Venkatesh, V., & Davis, F. D. (2000). A theoretical extension of the technology acceptance model: Four longitudinal field studies. *Management Science, 46*(2), 186–204. doi:10.1287/mnsc.46.2.186.11926

Virvou, M., & Katsionis, G. (2008). On the usability and likeability of virtual reality games for education: The case of VR-ENGAGE. *Computers & Education, 50*(1), 154–178. doi:10.1016/j.compedu.2006.04.004

Zaharias, P.A. (2004). Usability and e-learning: the road towards integration. *eLearn Magazine, 2004*(6), 4.

Zaharias, P. A. (2006). Usability evaluation method for e-learning: Focus on motivation and learning. In *Proceedings of CHI 2006* (pp. 1571-1576), Montreal, Canada: ACM. 10.1145/1125451.1125738

ADDITIONAL READING

Donghui, C., Guanfa, L., Wensheng, Z., Qiyuan, L., Shuping, B., & Xiaokang, L. (2017). Virtual reality technology applied in digitalization of cultural heritage. *Cluster Computing.* doi:10.100710586-017-1071-5

Doulamis, N., Doulamis, A., Ioannidis, C., Klein, M., & Ioannides, M. (2017). Modelling of Static and Moving Objects: Digitizing Tangible and Intangible Cultural Heritage. In *Mixed Reality and Gamification for Cultural Heritage* (pp. 567–589). Cham: Springer International Publishing; doi:10.1007/978-3-319-49607-8_23

Guidi, G., Micoli, L. L., Gonizzi, S., Brennan, M., & Frischer, B. (2015). Image-based 3D capture of cultural heritage artifacts an experimental study about 3D data quality. In 2015 Digital Heritage (pp. 321–324). IEEE. doi:10.1109/DigitalHeritage.2015.7419514

Jiménez Fernández-Palacios, B., Morabito, D., & Remondino, F. (2017). Access to complex reality-based 3D models using virtual reality solutions. *Journal of Cultural Heritage*, *23*, 40–48. doi:10.1016/j.culher.2016.09.003

Kalay, Y. (2008). Preserving Cultural Heritage through Digital Media. In Y. Kalay, T. Kvan, & J. Afflek (Eds.), *New Heritage: New Media and Cultural Heritage* (pp. 1–10). New York: Routledge.

Kolay, S. (2016). Cultural Heritage Preservation of traditional Indian Art through virtual new-media. *Procedia: Social and Behavioral Sciences*, *225*, 309–320. doi:10.1016/j.sbspro.2016.06.030

Nagata, J. J., Garcia-Bermejo Giner, J. R., & Martinez Abad, F. (2016). virtual heritage of the territory: Design and implementation of educational resources in augmented reality and mobile pedestrian navigation. *IEEE Revista Iberoamericana de Tecnologias Del Aprendizaje*, *11*(1), 41–46. doi:10.1109/RITA.2016.2518460

Tan, B., Cai, Y., Zhang, Y., Wu, X., Chen, Y., & Yang, B. (2016). Virtual reality continuum for heritage at Haw Par Villa in Singapore. In *Proceedings of the Symposium on VR Culture and Heritage - VRCAI '16* (pp. 71–74). New York, NY: ACM Press. 10.1145/3014027.3014030

White, M., Mourkoussis, N., Darcy, J., Petridis, P., Liarokapis, F., Lister, P., ... Gaspard, F. (2004). ARCO - an architecture for digitization, management and presentation of virtual exhibitions. In *Proceedings Computer Graphics International, 2004* (pp. 622–625). IEEE; doi:10.1109/CGI.2004.1309277

KEY TERMS AND DEFINITIONS

3D Model: A 3D computer graphics object composed of polygons such as triangles or rectangles.

3D Scanner: Digital device connected to a computer used to digitize an object in 3D, capturing reference points in X, Y, and Z axes, and sometimes acquiring color from those reference points.

Anishinaabe: Autonym for a group of culturally-related indigenous peoples in Canada and northern United States including the Algonquin, Chippewa, Odawa, Ojibwe, Oji-Cree, Mississaugas, and Potawatomi peoples.

Cultural Object: An object made by people for a spiritual and/or practical purpose or activity that may have functional and/or artistic relevance.

Immersion: Psycho-physiological user perception of being physically present in a virtual environment.

Interpupillary Distance: The term refers to distance between the user's pupils, employed in virtual reality headsets and other VR-related visualization equipment.

Intrinsic Motivation: User or learner's behavior that is based on internal rewards and the motivation to engage in them. It arises from within the person because it is naturally satisfying to him/her.

Kanban Board: A workflow and work visualization chart describing activities flow within a project, originally created in the 1940s by Toyota.

Model Mesh: Collection of reference points in X, Y, and Z axes that define a graphical 3D shape with width, height, and depth.

Texture: An image that is associated to a 3D model and is generated by 3D scanners that capture color, which forms the surface ("skin") of the model.

APPENDIX

Table 5. Technology acceptance model (TAM2) questionnaire

	Strongly Disagree	Moderately Disagree	Somewhat Disagree	Neutral	Somewhat Agree	Moderately Agree	Strongly Agree
Intention to Use							
Assuming I have access to the system, I intend to use it.							
Given that I have access to the system, I predict that I would use it.							
Perceived Usefulness							
Using the system improves my performance in my activity as student.							
Using the system in my activity as student increases my productivity.							
Using the system enhances my effectiveness in my activity as student.							
I find the system to be useful in my activity as student.							
Perceived Ease of Use							
My interaction with the system is clear and understandable.							
Interacting with the system does not require a lot of my mental effort.							
I find the system to be easy to use.							
I find it easy to get the system to do what I want it to do.							
Subjective Norm							
People who influence my behavior think that I should use the system.							
People who are important to me think that I should use the system.							
Voluntariness							
My use of the system is voluntary.							
My supervisor does not require me to use the system.							
Although it might be helpful, using the system is certainly not compulsory in my activity as student.							
Image							
People in my school who use the system have more prestige than those who do not.							
People in my school who use the system have a high profile.							
Having the system is a status symbol in my school activity as student							
Relevance							
In my activity as student, usage of the system is important.							
In my activity as student, usage of the system is relevant.							
Output Quality							
The quality of the output I get from the system is high.							
I have no problem with the quality of the system's output.							
Result Demonstrability							
I have no difficulty telling others about the results of using the system.							
I believe I could communicate to others the consequences of using the system.							
The results of using the system are apparent to me.							
I would have difficulty explaining why using the system may or may not be beneficial.							

Source: Adapted from Venkatesh & Davis (2000)

Chapter 4
A Study on Visual Perturbations Effect on Balance in a VR Environment

Markus Santoso
University of Florida, USA

David Phillips
Montclair State, USA

EXECUTIVE SUMMARY

Users sometimes lost their balance or even fell down when they played virtual reality (VR) games or projects. This may be attributed to degree of content, high-rate of latency, coordination of various sensory inputs, and others. The authors investigated the effect of sudden visual perturbations on human balance in VR environment. This research used the latest VR head mounted display to present visual perturbations to disturb balance. To quantify balance, measured by double-support and single-support stance, the authors measured the subject's center of pressure (COP) using a force plate. The results indicated that visual perturbations presented in virtual reality disrupted balance control in the single support condition but not in the double support condition. Results from this study can be applied to clinical research on balance and VR environment design.

ORGANIZATION BACKGROUND

The University of Florida is a public land-grant, sea-grant and space-grant research university on a 2000-acres campus in Gainesville, Florida. It is a senior member of the State University System of Florida that traces its origins to 1853, and has operated continuously on its Gainesville campus since September 1906. The University of Florida is one of sixty-two elected member institutions of the Association of American University (AAU), the association of preeminent North American research universities, and the only AAU member university in Florida. The university is classified as a Research University with Highest Research Acticity by the Carnegie Classification of Institution of Higher Education ("The Carnegie Classification of Institution of Higher Education," n.d.). After the Florida state legislature's

DOI: 10.4018/978-1-5225-5912-2.ch004

creation of performance standards in 2013, the Florida Board of Governors designated the University of Florida as one of the three "Preeminent Universities" among the twelve universities of the State University System of Florida. For 2019, *U.S. News & World Report* ranked the University of Florida as the eighth (tied) best public university in the United States. The University of Florida is home to sixteen academic colleges and more than 150 research centers and institutes.

Montclair State University (MSU) is a public research university located in the Upper Montclair section of Montclair, at the intersection of the Great Notch area of Little Falls, and the Montclair Heights section of Clifton, in the U.S state of New Jersey. Montclair State University is the second largest university in New Jersey. As of October 2017, there were 21,013 total enrolled students: 16, 852 undergraduate students and 4,161 graduate students. The campus covers approximately 500 acres, inclusive of the New Jersey School of Conservation in Stoke State Forest ("Montclair State University," n.d.). The University attracts students from within the state, from many other states in the Northeast and elsewhere, and many foreign countries. More than 300 majors, minors and concentrations are offered. The university is a member of professional organizations such as the American Association of State Colleges and Universities, American Council on Education, Association of American Colleges and Universities and the Council of Graduate Schools. The university has consistently ranked among the top 100 public universities in the United States in the past few years. In 2017, the university was designated as a R3 Doctoral Research University ("Montclair State University," n.d.).

INTRODUCTION

People live in the three-dimensional (3D) physical world and traditional two-dimensional (2D) flat images such as photo or video are lack of the third dimension information (Geng, 2014). Almost half of human brain capacity is devoted to process visual information and the limitation of flat images and 2D displays will limit human's ability to understand the complexity of real-world objects (Geng, 2014). On the other hand, 3D display technologies improve perception and interaction with 3D scenes, and hence can make applications more effective and efficient (Mehrabi et al., 2013). Driven by the rapid improvement of computer technology, 3D display has become more powerful, affordable and comfortable. One of the 3D displays that widely adopted is stereoscopic display. Stereoscopic is recognized as one of the oldest 3D display systems and it was first proposed by C. Wheatstone in 1838. This type of display was based on stereopsis, where an observer's left and right eyes receive different perspectives separated by a stereoscopic device that the observer is wearing (Nam Kim et al., 2013). One of the stereoscopic displays is anaglyph (Image 1a in Figure 1) that use two color filtered images and glasses that usually utilize red-cyan, red-green, green-magenta and magenta-cyan colors. The other is LC shutter system or also known as active-shutter system (Image 1b in Figure 1). It is defined as a stereoscopic technique that sends the left image to the left eye while the right eye's view is blocked by the display device and user glasses, then presents the right image to the right eye while the left eye's view is blocked (Turner & Hellbaum, 1986). Stereoscopic display can also use a polarized 3D system (Image 1c in Figure 1), a technique that send polarized images to the corresponding eyes through polarization glasses (Nam Kim et al., 2013).

The other stereoscopic technique is head-mounted display (HMD). HMD is a device worn on the head, or as part of a helmet, it has a small optic display in front of each eye (Nam Kim et al., 2013). HMDs may also be equipped with additional sensors or features such as head-tracking to enable the 3 degree-of-freedom (DoF) that allow user to have 'look around' the virtual world with their head orien-

Figure 1. Stereoscopic displays

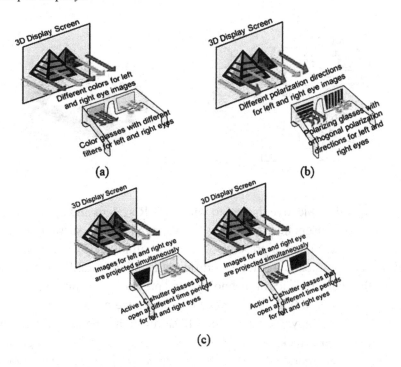

tation (Geng, 2014). In the more advance HMD setup, it has a six-axis position sensing therefore the user may move around to the respective direction. In general, there are two types of HMD based on the see-through approaches: optical (Figure 2) and video (Figure 3). HMDs are widely adopted in AR/VR field and following the rise of these fields, more and more HMD headsets have been released recently.

Virtual Reality is defined as a computer-generated digital environment that can be experienced and interacted with as if that environment was real (Jerald, 2015). Realities could take many forms with Milgram and Kishino developing a virtuality continuum that spans from the real environment to virtual environments with augmented and virtual reality in between as shown in Figure 4 (Milgram & Kishino, 1994).

Virtual reality is about psychologically being in a place different than where one is physically located. That new place could be anything, from a real world's replica to probably an imaginary world that does not, have not or even never could exist (Jerald, 2015). So, VR technology is about immersive

Figure 2. Optical see-through HMD
Source: Kiyokawa, 2007

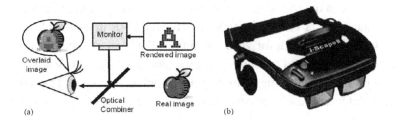

Figure 3. Video see-through HMD
Source: Kiyokawa, 2007

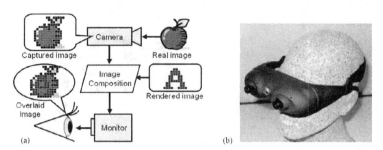

experience. Immersion is the objective degree to which a VR system and application projects stimuli onto the sensory receptors of users in a way that is extensive, matching, surrounding, vivid, interactive and plot informing. VR is also about a presence where it is simply defined as a sense of 'being there' inside a space, even when physically located in a different location (Jerald, 2015). While immersion is highly influenced by the characteristics of technology and presence is an internal psychological state of the user. Presence is a function of both the user and immersion (Jerald, 2015).

With the advance in technology, the quality of VR hardware has been significantly improved with higher screen resolution, robust tracking, faster processors, and others. Those high specification computational power able to create more immersive VR experience with higher level of presence. However, in some cases, the VR content led players or users to lose their balance and even fell down when they interacted with the VR system as shown in Figure 5. Several factors are suspected to cause this issue such as high-latency, the content, poorly-designed supporting haptic, unsafe surround environment, visual stimulation and others. VR technology is closely related with immersion and presence, and in the current VR system both aspects are heavily influenced by the visual stimulation. It is therefore important that the role of vision in VR environment be more fully analyzed. Virtual reality also presents an opportunity for clinical research to understand the role of vision in balance. How is postural stability affected by motion in virtual reality?

RESEARCH BACKGROUND

VR technology is becoming a popular platform to conduct balance training and clinical rehabilitation. In rehabilitative and motor behavioral research it is desirable to have the lab environment as close to actual conditions as possible. Physically constructing a lab to duplicate environments can be time consuming and expensive. A virtual reality environment, however, requires only space and any environment can be digitally constructed. Researchers can develop environments that can test an array of rehabilitative, motor control and learning research questions. Scientists are already recognizing that VR is a useful tool for research. In 2006, a total of 1,921 PubMed articles had the term VR in the article. Ten years later 7,701 articles are now returned when search for virtual reality in PubMed. A recent symposium on applying VR to rehabilitation outcomes aimed to identify benefits and limitations of VR as a rehabilitation tool, how VR plays a role in motor relearning following neurological trauma and how VR technology may translate into clinical and home based settings (Keshner & Fung, 2017). Most recently, human balance

Figure 4. Milgram and Kishino's virtual continuum

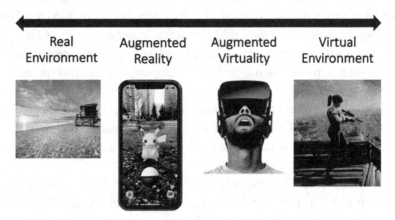

Figure 5. User falling during a VR experience

was shown to be perturbed using a smartphone based roller coaster virtual reality simulation (Rausch, Simon, Starkey, & Grooms, 2018).

Before studying balance in VR, it is important to understand how balance is controlled and measured. Humans maintain postural stability by continually monitoring the status of the environment and body position and responding to changes by sending neural signals to the musculoskeletal system. The sensory information is gathered from the visual, vestibular and proprioceptive systems (Ernst & Bülthoff, 2004; Eysel-Gosepath, McCrum, Epro, Brüggemann, & Karamanidis, 2016; Ponzo, Kirsch, Fotopoulou, & Jenkinson, 2018). Visual information is gathered through the eyes, vestibular information from the inner ear, and proprioceptive information is gathered from unique mechanical receptors located in muscles, ligaments, joints and the skin. Proprioception is often referred to as the sixth sense. This sense allows an individual to determine a limb's position without vision of the limb. For instance, you are aware that your hand is behind you back even though you cannot see. An internal representation of posture and limb position is generated using these signals (Blanke, 2012; Dijkerman & de Haan, 2007; Ehrsson, 2012; Makin, Holmes, & Ehrsson, 2008; Tsakiris, 2010).

During quiet standing, the whole body center of mass (COM) must remain within the base of support. To identify if the COM is within the base of support, the COM is projected downward onto the floor. The location of the downward projection of the COM is call the center of gravity (COG). If the COG drifts outside of the base of support, corrective action must be taken to prevent a person from falling. Corrective action without taking a step or changing the base of support, requires that the individual manipulate their center of pressure (COP). The center of pressure can be viewed as a single point within the base of support where the resultant ground reaction forces are said to act. The COP can be determined from hardware such as a force plate. The COP has been used in a multitude of studies to examine balance and postural stability (e.g., Jonsson, Seiger, & Hirschfeld, 2004; Mochizuki, Duarte, Amadio, Zatsiorsky, & Latash, 2006).

The amount of COP movement is relatively small and will always be within the base of support. Pushing the COP pressure ahead of the COG will push the COG backwards and pushing the COP behind the COG will push the COG forwards. In this way, humans can actively control the COP but the COG is passive, responding to changes in the COP or other external forces. To push the COP anterior (forwards), the platarflexors (calf muscles) are contracted. This pushes the ball of the foot into the ground. To push the COP backwards, the dorsiflexors (muscles that pull the foot upwards) are contracted. This pushes the heel of the foot into the ground. Reduced control of the COP in either the anterior-posterior or mediolateral (left/right) directions can put and individual at risk of falling. Likewise, poorly interpreting cues in the environment or changes body position can also increase this risk (Winter, 2005).

Information from the environment to maintain posture is primarily gathered by the visual system (with some from the sense of touch from the feet for instance) while internal information of body position is gathered from the vestibular system (inner ear) and proprioception. The vestibular system provides information on the orientation and acceleration experience by the head. Proprioception provides information from muscles and limbs location in space and how they are moving. Postural disturbances introduced via vision (Pavlou et al., 2011), proprioception (Eklund, 1972) and vestibular (Peterka, 2002) have been investigated previously. The integration of these sensory information is interpreted by the brain to maintain balance. While the premise that posture is maintain by integrating these systems is oversimplified, vision appears to be the most important (Goodman & Tremblay, 2018; Rossetti, Desmurget, & Prablanc, 1995).

Lee and Aronson (1974) performed an experiment on human infants' control of balance. This experiment was performed by constructing 3.6m long x 1.8m wide x 2m high room and suspending the room by four ropes. The room was not attached to the floor. This was done to allow the experimenter to control the sway of the room. While an infant was standing the experimenter would suddenly sway the room forwards or backwards. In 82% of the cases the infants would sway in the direction the room was shifted and in 33% of those cases fall in the direction of the room shift (Lee & Aronson, 1974). In later experiments on adults, the same lead author found that adults are easily able to maintain their balance on a narrow beam but all subjects failed to do so with their eyes close. They also found that when swinging the rooms sinusoidally forwards and backwards, the subjects sway in sync with the room (Lee & Lishman, 1977). More recently, a roller coaster simulation using a VR environment via a smartphone, was sufficient to increase COP movement and reduced subjects' stability (Rausch et al., 2018). However, the roller coaster simulation was not specifically designed to investigate balance or COP responses to visual perturbations. How subjects respond to discrete, sudden visual perturbations has not yet been answered. In VR environment design and clinical evaluation, quantifying the effects of different parameters (direction, velocity, displacement) of a visual perturbation on balance and COP is needed.

Creating visual distortions require the manipulation of the subject's field of view. Most of the latest VR device will fully block user's peripheral and it is expected to be sufficient to conduct a research related with visual perturbations. While there were several studies about VR in physical and exercise field, however the implementation of VR technology as visual perturbations and its impact to human balance is relatively novel. As VR is becoming an increasingly accessible tool, it is important to evaluate its possible applications to clinical research settings.

The purpose of the current research is to investigate COP responses in a VR environment specifically designed to challenge balance control. The authors further also ask how the responses are affected in different standing postures: single stance and double support. The researchers hypothesize that the COP displacement will increase immediately after a visual perturbation. In addition, we hypothesize that the response will be greater in a single stance posture. The rationale for including the single support condition comes from the Lee and Lishman (1977) experiment. Visual perturbation in double support may not be sufficient to challenge balance control. However, visual changes when balance is challenge may lead to a larger and observable effect.

A secondary objective of the study was to investigate how COP distance when subjects did not wear the HMD compared to simply standing in the VR environment with no perturbations. This is also called quiet standing. This was done simply to ensure that the simple act of being in a VR environment reduced postural stability.

RESEARCH METHODS

This research involved two important elements: presenting visual perturbations in VR using head mounted device (HMD) and Center of Pressure measurement. For the VR HMD, the latest released of Oculus Rift was used. The VR environment was developed using Unity3D game engine (Unity technologies v2017.2, San Francisco, CA). The VR environment was visualized as a virtual corridor with a width of 3 meters and a height of 2.5 meters (Figure 6). The environment was designed to suddenly move backwards or forwards a distance of 3m at 3 different velocities (1m/s, 3m/s, 5m/s). The independent variables for the

Figure 6. Virtual Corridor

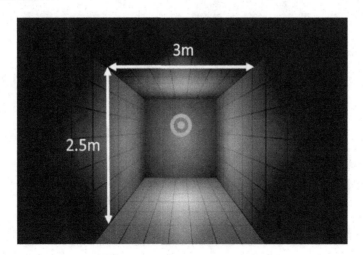

study were direction and velocity of perturbation in two different postural conditions: single support and double support. Double support has the subject standing on two feet with the feet together. Single support has the subject standing on only one foot facing forwards.

The other critical research aspect is the COP measurement. For this purpose, we use a Bertec force plate (Bertec Corporation, Columbus, OH) (Figure 7) with custom LabVIEW data collection and processing software (LabVIEW v2017, Austin, TX) (Figure 8). A force plate is able to make 6 six different measurements - forces in 3 dimensions and torques in 3 dimensions. It can be referred to as a 6 degree-of-freedom sensor. Using the different forces and moments applied onto the force plate, the location of the COP can be calculated over time in two dimensions. Clinicians would refer to these two directions as anterior-posterior (forwards and backwards) and mediolateral (left and right). In a mechanical description of the motion, COP will move in the traditional 2 dimensional x-y plane. Anterior-posterior or mediolateral movement can be along either the x axis or y axis, depending on the direction the subject is facing. In our research, movement of the COP in the *x* direction was considered anterior-posterior. The anterior-posterior distance travelled by the COP was the dependent variable in this experiment. The specific equations used to calculate COP are seen below.

$$COP_x = \frac{(-h)*(F_x) - M_y}{F_z}$$

$$COP_y = \frac{(-h)*(F_y) - M_x}{F_z}$$

where COP is center of pressure, h is the thickness of a material covering the force plate, F is a force measured by the force place, M is a torque measured by the force plate. The subscripts, *x, y* and *z,* indicate the direction. Positive *z* is upwards. In our study, COPx is the anterior-posterior direction.

Figure 7. In ground Bertec force plates for calculating center of pressure

Figure 8. VR environment and custom force plate data collection software (LabVIEW)

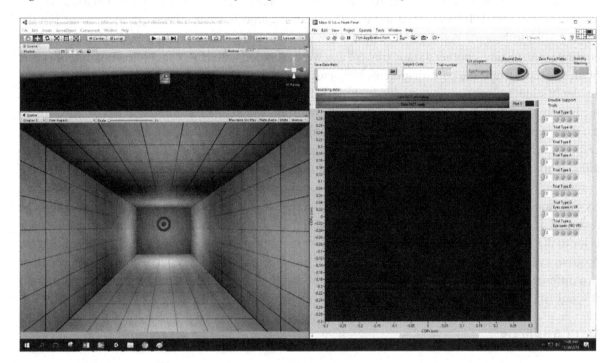

Research Participants

Eleven subjects volunteered for the study (8 males, 3 females, age: 27.6 ± 7.4 years, mass: 78.2 ± 19.3 kg, height: 174 ± 12.9 cm). Subjects were excluded if they had any neurological disorder, were taking medication or drugs that could affect their perception, aware that they were pregnant, or had any acute injuries causing pain. Subjects were briefed on the purpose and the experimental procedure prior to the start of the experiment and provided informed consent. The experiment received ethical clearance from the Internal Review Board at Montclair State University. Subjects were recruit via word of mouth and with posters place around the university campus.

Experimental Procedures

Ground reaction forces and moments were recorded using one force plate (Bertec Corp, Columbus, OH) sampling at 1000 Hz and then down-sampled to 200 Hz with custom LabVIEW software (LabVIEW v2017, Austin, TX). The virtual reality (VR) environment was presented to the subjects with a head mounted display (HMD) (Oculus VR). The VR environment consisted of a corridor with a width of 3m and a height of 2.5m. A grid pattern was used to texture all surfaces of the corridor (Figure 8). The VR environment was developed with Unity3D software (Unity Technologies v2017.2, San Francisco, CA). Subjects stood barefoot on the force plate facing a target placed on the far end of the corridor and the computer monitor in the lab.

Initially, subjects stood on the force plate without the HMD and were instructed to focus on a point drawn on a whiteboard. One trial was recorded to establish the subject's weight measure from the force plate and a further 4 static trials were recorded for 20 seconds each. Following these 4 static trials the subject put on the HMD and stood in the VR corridor. Subjects were allowed to look around in the environment to become comfortable with the device. When the subject indicated they were ready to continue with testing, another 4 static trials of 20s were recorded with HMD on. Following the collection of all the static trials, the perturbation trials began. To introduce a visual perturbation, the walls would suddenly slide 3m anterior or posterior, at three different velocities (1m/s, 3m/s or 5m/s) initiated when the researcher pressed a key. Four trials for each condition were collected for a total trial number of 24 trials presented in a preassigned random order. Subjects were not aware when a movement would occur and no warning was given. This key press was captured in the force plate data collection program to indicate the time the visual perturbation occurred in the force plate data. The subjects were instructed to remain as steady as possible but were allowed to take a step if recovery was needed. If the subject's foot did touch the ground, the trial was removed and repeated at the end of the protocol. For data to be recorded, the subject would need to be considered stable (foot position remaining static) for 5 seconds prior to the key being pressed. This was achieved by monitoring vertical ground reaction forces (in the positive z direction) for changes greater than 5% of body weight. The above procedure was repeated for two different stances in a random order: double support (Figure 9) with feet together and single support (Figure 10).

Data Analysis

Time zero ($T_0 = 0$s, the moment the key is pressed) was used to align all trials. The center of pressure (COP) in the anterior-posterior direction was calculated from ground reaction forces and moments using the previously mentioned equations. Total distance travelled by the COP was used to assess changes in balance stability. Total distance travelled was determined as $\Sigma|COP_n - COP_{n-1}|$, where n is any given anterior-posterior COP data point. For the static trials, the first and last 5 seconds of data were trimmed and total distance travelled was calculated for 10s. For the perturbation trials, total distance travelled was calculated for 5s before time zero and 5s after time zero. The average of 4 trials was calculated for each condition.

Statistical Analysis

To assess if stability is the same within the VR environment and without the HMD on, a statistical test called a paired t-test was used to compare the COP total distance travelled between the two static conditions. To assess the effect of the visual perturbation on stability, a statistical test called a 3-way repeated measures analysis of variance (ANOVA) was used to identify any effects on COP total distance travelled. The independent variables were direction of the perturbation (anterior and posterior), velocity of perturbation (1m/s, 3m/s, and 5m/s) and time (before and after perturbation). Separate ANOVAs were used to analyze single and double support. Alpha was set to 0.05 for all test and all data are reported as mean ± standard deviations. A Bonferroni adjustment was performed for all follow up comparisons if a significant effect was found.

Figure 9. Double support condition

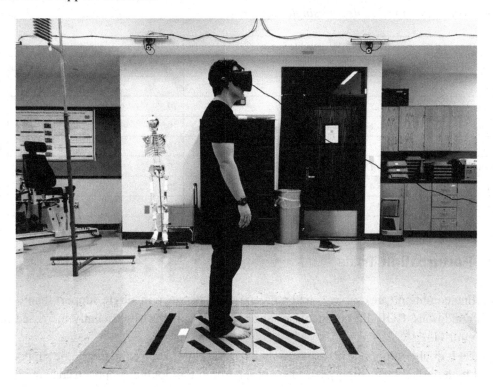

Figure 10. Single support condition

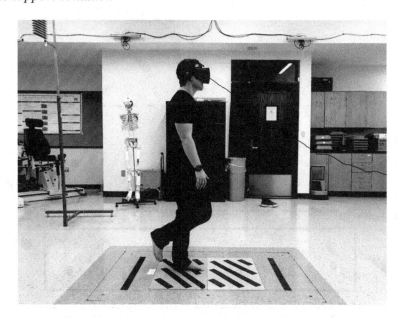

Table 1. Descriptive statistics for distance travelled (cm) by the center of pressure before (pre) and after (post) the perturbation for double and single support

Condition	Double Support				Single Support			
	PRE		Post		PRE		Post	
	M	SD	M	SD	M	SD	M	SD
1m/s Anterior	6.2	0.7	7.2	0.8	19.3	0.9	31.2	2.7
1m/s Posterior	6.1	0.6	6.3	0.4	19.7	0.9	29.4	3.2
3m/s Anterior	6.2	0.5	6.5	0.4	19.8	1.1	23.7	0.9
3m/s Posterior	6.1	0.6	5.9	0.9	20.7	2.1	28.0	2.7
5m/s Anterior	6.4	0.7	5.9	0.9	20.8	1.0	26.1	2.2
5m/s Posterior	7.5	1.4	6.4	0.7	20.3	1.4	25.3	1.0

Results: Perturbation Trials

In the baseline condition (pre) subjects had a greater COP distance in single support than double support. In all conditions, COP did not increase for double support but significantly increased for single support (Figure 11).

In Figure 11, double support trials are surrounded by a solid line box and the single support trials are surrounded by a dashed box. Simply based on observation, the double support trials are significantly more stable than the single support trials (less distance has been travelled by the COP). There is not much effect of the visual perturbations in the double support trials - the open circles (the distance travelled by the COP 5 seconds before the perturbation) are about the same as the filled circles regardless of the

Figure 11. Descriptive statistics for each perturbation type

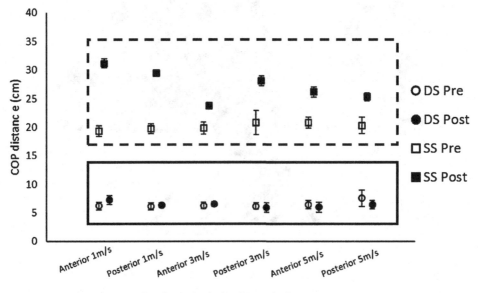

Table 2. Summarized 3-way ANOVA results for double support condition

Effect	df	F	η_p^2
Velocity	(2, 20)	15.1**	0.6
Direction	(1, 10)	0.11	0.01
Time	(1, 10)	1.1	0.1
Velocity*Time	(2, 20)	32.5**	0.77
Direction*Time	(1, 10)	3.5*	0.47
Velocity*Direction*Time	(2, 20)	1.6	0.14

Note: *$p < 0.05$, **$p < 0.001$

type of trial. However, looking at the single support trials, the COP travels a greater distance the 5 seconds after the perturbation in every condition. However, further statistical analysis is fairly complex as there are 3 independent variables. In order to simplify the analysis, we analyzed the double support and single support separately. We also decided to perform the analysis from two perspectives. The first is to look at the effect of velocity; 1m/s, 3m/s, or 5m/s (Figure 12), and the second is the effect of direction; anterior or posterior (Figure 13).

In the velocity perspective analysis for double support we see what is called in interaction effect, $p < 0.001$ (Figure 12). However, as we mentioned before for double support, when looking at the size of the effect, it is unlikely to have either a clinical or VR environment design impact. However, for the single support there is also a significant interaction between the time (5 seconds before, 5 seconds after) and the velocity. Overall, the perturbations increased the distance travelled by the COP by 36% in single support (Figure 12). More specifically, the slowest velocity, 1m/s, had the largest effect - a 55% increase! This was significantly greater than the 3m/s and 5m/s conditions. If we have a look at the analysis from the perspective of the direction; whether the perturbations were anterior or posterior, the amount of COP distance increase is approximately the same for both directions (Figure 13). This whether the environment is suddenly shifted forwards or backwards, the instability caused will be similar.

Table 3. Summarized 3-way ANOVA results for single support condition

Effect	df	F	η_p^2
Velocity	(2, 20)	86.5*	0.9
Direction	(1, 10)	5.3	0.3
Time	(1, 10)	378.8*	0.97
Velocity*Time	(2, 20)	26*	0.72
Direction*Time	(1, 10)	2	0.17
Velocity*Direction*Time	(2, 20)	11.3*	0.53

Note: *$p \leq 0.001$

Figure 12. The effect of the perturbation from the perspective of velocity
Note: Double support results are surrounded by a solid line box and the single support results are surrounded by a dashed line box. Note that since the data overlap in the conditions, the points have been offset on the x axis. DS = double support, SS = single support.

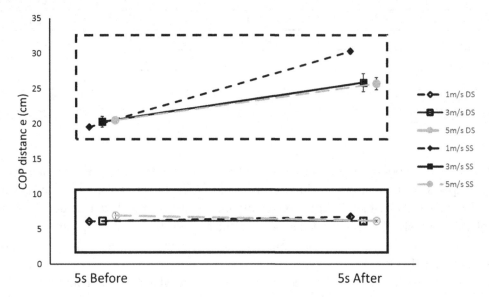

Figure 13. The effect of the perturbation from the perspective of direction

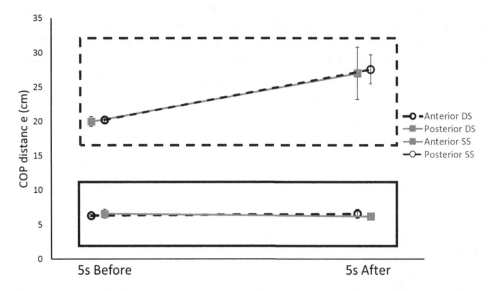

Results: Quiet Standing

The secondary objective of this study was to assess if simply being in a VR environment affected the distance travelled by the COP. The COP distance was less when subjects were standing without the HMD for double support (DS), $p < 0.05$. The difference in double support is likely not important. The difference between the means was only 2.7cm (Figure 14). While there is a statistical difference between the two

Figure 14. COP travelled in the two stances when subjects are not wearing the HMD and when Wearing the HMD viewing the VR environment

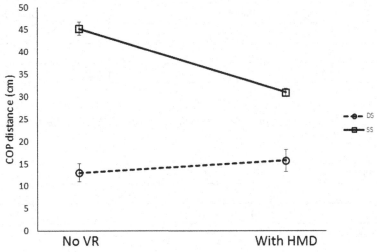

conditions, this is unlikely to be a destabilizing factor when subjects are standing in VR because it is so small. However, we observed that subjects standing on one foot in VR (with the HMD on) were more stable, $p < 0.001$. This likely has to do with a practice effect. Since the testing order was always to test the no VR condition first, subjects had some practice standing on one leg. Double support was, unsurprisingly, significantly more stable (less COP distance travelled) compared to single support, $p < 0.001$.

DISCUSSION

The aim of this pilot research is to investigate the COP response to discrete, visual perturbations. A brief summary of the results follows. Anterior-posterior visual perturbations in virtual reality do not make subjects less stable in a double support but this is not true in single support. In single support subjects, users, or patients may be vulnerable to falls if they do not have two feet on the ground. This decreased stability is particularly apparent when the perturbation in the environment is slow.

Prior to discussing the perturbation response, the simple comparison balance of wearing the HMD, (and being in the VR) and standing without the HMD in the lab environment needs to be discussed. In double support, there was no difference in the COP distance whether the subjects did or did not wear the HMD. This is a good indication that simply wearing the HMD is not changing how subjects maintain their balance in VR compared to real world circumstances. However, in single support, the results indicate that subjects were better at balance, ie. had a decreased COP distance, wearing the HMD (standing in the VR environment) compared to standing on one foot in real world circumstances (Figure 14). This result could be due to two possible reasons. Either subjects are better at standing in VR or there is a practice effect. The order for this was not randomized - the trials without the HMD were always recorded first and the trials with the HMD recorded second. If the data in table 4 is examined, the open squares (single support COP distance 5 seconds before the perturbation) average 20.1 cm. As this is for only 5 seconds and in Figure 14 is the COP distance travelled for 10 seconds, we can double this number to 40.2 cm as

Table 4. Descriptive statistics for distance travelled (cm) by COP while standing without the HMD and standing wearing the HMD in VR

Condition	Double Support		Single Support	
	M	*SD*	*M*	*SD*
No VR	13.0	2.0	45.3	1.5
With VR	15.7	2.4	30.9	0.9

Table 5. Summary table for T-tests comparing standing without VR and with the HMD in the VR environment

Condition	*df*	*t*	Cohen's d
Double Support	10	-2.4*	0.73
Single Support	10	35**	10.5

Note: *$p < 0.05$, **$p < 0.001$

a reference value. If this value had been closer to 30 cm, we would expect the VR environment to be having an effect. Given this interpretation, it is most likely a practice effect rather than a VR related effect.

Single leg balance is naturally more difficult than when standing on two feet. Postural stability and balance is determined by five factors: size of the base of support; height of the COM; location of the COG within the base of support; body mass; and friction (Whiting & Rugg, 2006). Single leg support will more than half the base of support making the task more challenging. In addition, there is also less musculature to make any balance related corrections. This means that the COM may move more from a stable position and more corrections need to be made - ie. the distance travelled by the COP will increase. This can be clearly see from our results that simply standing on one foot is more difficult than standing on 2 feet (Figures 11, 12, 13, & 14). There is both an increased physical demand and attention to sensory information to maintain balance (Lajoie, Teasdale, Bard, & Fleury, 1993). As vision is considered the dominant sense, more weight is placed on it, possibly sparring cognitive resources from focusing on other cues like proprioception. The increased emphasis on vision as the primary feedback means that the system is more vulnerable to perturbations in the visual field.

During double support, the nervous system is able to detect that the visual information from the perturbation is not congruent with the proprioceptive and vestibular sensory information. However, because of the increased reliance on vision during the single support, the visual perturbation results in a disturbance to balance and postural control. If all the single support trials are taken together, there was a 36% increase in the distance the COP travelled due to the visual perturbation. This is an increase above what is seen when simply maintaining single support balance. There is also the magnitude response for different velocities to consider. The largest response was observed during the 1m/s perturbation in single support. There could be 2 possible reasons for this. The first is that because the displacement was kept constant at 3m, therefore the 1m/s condition had the longest perturbation exposure time - 3 seconds. While the 3m/s trial type had a 1 second exposure time and the 5m/s trial type had a 0.6 second exposure time. The second is that the expected proprioceptive and vestibular information was below the threshold detection level. This means that the central nervous system would not expect the vestibular and proprioceptive system to be stimulated due to the observed visual perturbation. Therefore, the system only responded to the visual information.

The fact that with different postural supports there are different responses is an important observation for clinicians and VR environment designers. All the subjects in this study were healthy, with no neurological disorders or any acute injuries causing pain. Clinicians can exploit the lack of response in double support to evaluate neurological disorders. For example, concussions are a common traumatic brain injury of which disturbed balance is a common symptom. However, as patients recover and return to sport, balance disturbances remain (Powers, Kalmar, & Cinelli, 2014) but can only be detected using a force plate or laboratory motion capture equipment (D. R. Howell, Osternig, & Chou, 2015). A force plate and motion capture cameras are expensive and generally inaccessible pieces of equipment to clinicians. An accelerometer (a common sensor found in smartphones) could be paired with VR visual perturbations to track recovery similar to what has previously been done in walking research (D. Howell, Osternig, & Chou, 2015). However, concussion researchers may be concerned about the increased sensitivity to light after a concussion (Laker, 2015). If researchers plan to use VR as research tool in concussion research, dim environments should be considered.

As this experiment is perturbing balance, the protocol may also be useful in identifying individuals at risk of falls. Falls are a significant economic and health issue. An estimated $31 billion is spent annually treating fall related injuries (Burns, Stevens, & Lee, 2016). This study focused on a healthy population but balance deteriorates with age. Young, healthy individuals were non-responders in double support. However, an older individual with reduced muscle mass and reaction times would rely more extensively on vision. If an individual responds to the visual perturbations (COP distance increases), it would likely indicate that the person is at a higher risk of a fall. If VR technology is useful in identifying individuals at a high risk of falling, it may also be a potential treatment tool. This could be accomplished by exposing high fall risk individuals to visual circumstances leading to a fall within VR. The individuals can be trained to recognize what visual cues may place them at risk of falling and take corrective measure before they fall.

Virtual environments, particularly gaming environments, can have many sudden shifts in the visual field. It is also common to have users move to different location in the virtual environment requiring locomotion. Walking requires that a subject be in a single support position 40% of the time. Sudden shifts in the environment, single support, and focus on external tasks (such as shoot in first person shooter games) mean that significant cognitive resources are being used. This research show that even without external distractions, the virtual environment alone can challenge balance control. A poorly designed virtual environment could place a user at an unnecessary risk of falling. This is of particular concern if the user is an older adult.

This study has examined balance responses to discrete visual perturbations. It is important to keep in mind that this is unpublished pilot data and additional data should continue to be collected and the research reproduced.

CONCLUSION AND FUTURE WORK

From the experiments that conducted in this paper, both the double-support support during pilot study and the single-support condition, it showed an evidence that the visual perturbations using in VR head mounted displays may challenge the subject's stability. This is only true when healthy subjects experience the visual perturbation when standing on one foot. The observed increase in COP distance travelled, and greatest disturbance to balance, was greatest in the 1m/s trial type. This information can be leveraged in the clinic to study visual perturbations responses and fall risk in different populations. This is also valuable information in VR environment design. VR environment designers can more safely 'translate' a user about an environment as long as they have both feet on the ground. If an environment requires a subject to move around or perform tasks standing on one leg, or any that decreases balance control, sudden translations could place the user at risk of falling. This is particularly important in an older population who are already at an increased risk of falling.

Theoretical Implications

Virtual reality technology is becoming a more affordable technology. Given the observations made in this research, VR may be very useful to balance and fall researchers who wish to study the role of vision in falls. Creating VR environments reducing the space requirements to conduct fall screening and even perform clinical treatment to prevent falls. This clinical treatment can be in the form of exposure therapy. Users are exposed an environment that could lead to a fall. Users could either train a more appropriate response or take corrective action upon recognizing a high risk visual environment. [Editor's note: consider expanding and adding this sub-section]

Practical Implications

The outcomes of this research have important implications for VR environment design. Gaming environments consistently ask users to move around in physical space to move in the VR environment. The research demonstrates that using only vision, a user's posture stability can put at risk and cause possible injury. Environments where a user will always be on two feet are low risk. However, sudden shifts when a user is on a single foot, can place them at risk of falling. Single support occurs for approximately 60% of the walking cycle (Whittle, 2014). This phenomenon can also be useful to VR environmental designs where the goal is to specifically disorientate or destabilize the user.

REFERENCES

Blanke, O. (2012). Multisensory brain mechanisms of bodily self-consciousness. *Nature Reviews. Neuroscience, 13*(8), 556–571. doi:10.1038/nrn3292 PMID:22805909

Burns, E. R., Stevens, J. A., & Lee, R. (2016). The direct costs of fatal and non-fatal falls among older adults— United States. *Journal of Safety Research, 58*, 99–103. doi:10.1016/j.jsr.2016.05.001 PMID:27620939

Dijkerman, H. C., & de Haan, E. H. F. (2007). Somatosensory process subserving perception and action. *Behavioral and Brain Sciences, 30*(02), 189–239. doi:10.1017/S0140525X07001392 PMID:17705910

Ehrsson, H. H. (2012). The concept of body ownership and its relation to multisensory integration. In B. Stein (Ed.), *In The New Handbook of Multisensory Processes* (pp. 775–792). Cambridge, MA: MIT Press.

Eklund, G. (1972). Position sense and state of contraction; the effects of vibration. *Journal of Neurology, Neurosurgery, and Psychiatry, 35*(5), 606–611. doi:10.1136/jnnp.35.5.606

Ernst, M. O., & Bülthoff, H. H. (2004). Merging the senses into a robust percept. *Trends in Cognitive Sciences, 8*(4), 162–169. doi:10.1016/j.tics.2004.02.002 PMID:15050512

Eysel-Gosepath, K., McCrum, C., Epro, G., Brüggemann, G. P., & Karamanidis, K. (2016). Visual and proprioceptive contributions to postural control of upright stance in unilateral vestibulopathy. *Somatosensory & Motor Research, 33*(2), 72–78. doi:10.1080/08990220.2016.1178635 PMID:27166786

Geng, J. (2013). Three-dimensional display technologies. *Advances in Optics and Photonics, 5*(4), 456–535. doi:10.1364/AOP.5.000456 PMID:25530827

Goodman, R., & Tremblay, L. (2018). Using proprioception to control ongoing actions: Dominance of vision or altered proprioceptive weighing? *Experimental Brain Research, 236*(7), 1–14. doi:10.100700221-018-5258-7 PMID:29696313

Howell, D., Osternig, L., & Chou, L. (2015). Monitoring recovery of gait balance control following concussion using an accelerometer. *Journal of Biomechanics, 48*(12), 3364–3368. doi:10.1016/j.jbiomech.2015.06.014 PMID:26152463

Howell, D. R., Osternig, L. R., & Chou, L. S. (2015). Return to activity after concussion affects dual-task gait balance control recovery. *Medicine and Science in Sports and Exercise, 47*(4), 673–680. doi:10.1249/MSS.0000000000000462 PMID:25100340

Jerald, J. (2015). *The VR Book: Human-Centered Design for Virtual Reality* (T. Ozsu, Ed.). New York, NY: ACM Books. doi:10.1145/2792790

Jonsson, E., Seiger, Å., & Hirschfeld, H. (2004). One-leg stance in healthy young and elderly adults: A measure of postural steadiness? *Clinical Biomechanics (Bristol, Avon), 19*(7), 688–694. doi:10.1016/j.clinbiomech.2004.04.002 PMID:15288454

Keshner, E. A., & Fung, J. (2017). The quest to apply VR technology to rehabilitation: Tribulations and treasures. *Journal of Vestibular Research: Equilibrium and Orientation, 27*(1), 1–5. doi:10.3233/VES-170610 PMID:28387695

Kim, N., Phan, A. H., Erdenebat, M. U., Alam, A., Kwon, K. C., Piao, M. L., & Lee, J. H. (2013). 3D Display Technology. *Display and Imaging, 1*, 73–95.

Kiyokawa, K. (2007). An Introduction to Head Mounted Display for Augmented Reality. In M. Haller, M. Billinghurst, & B. Thomas (Eds.), *Emerging Technologies of Augmented Reality: Interfaces and Design* (pp. 43–63). Hershey, PA: Idea Group Publishing. doi:10.4018/978-1-59904-066-0.ch003

Lajoie, Y., Teasdale, N., Bard, C., & Fleury, M. (1993). Attentional demands for static and dynamic equilibrium. *Experimental Brain Research, 97*(1), 139–144. doi:10.1007/BF00228824 PMID:8131825

Laker, S. R. (2015). Sports-Related Concussion. *Concussion and Head Injury, 19*(41), 8–11. PMID:26122533

Lee, D., & Aronson, E. (1974). Visual propriceptive control of standing in human infants. *Perception & Psychophysics, 15*(3), 529–532. doi:10.3758/BF03199297

Lee, D., & Lishman, L. (1977). Vision - the most efficient source of proprioceptive information for balance control. *Agressologie: Revue Internationale de Physio-Biologie et de Pharmacologie Appliquees Aux Effets de l'Agression, 18*, 83–94. PMID:22251

Makin, T. R., Holmes, N. P., & Ehrsson, H. H. (2008). On the other hand: Dummy hands and peripersonal space. *Behavioural Brain Research, 191*(1), 1–10. doi:10.1016/j.bbr.2008.02.041 PMID:18423906

Mehrabi, M., Peek, E. M., Wuensche, B. C., & Lutteroth, C. (2013). Conferences in Research and Practice in Information Technology: Vol. 139. *Making 3D Work: A Classification of Visual Depth Cues, 3D Display Technologies and Their Applications*. Adelaide, Australia: CRPIT.

Mochizuki, L., Duarte, M., Amadio, A. C., Zatsiorsky, V. M., & Latash, M. L. (2006). Changes in postural sway and its fractions in conditions of postural instability. *Journal of Applied Biomechanics, 22*(1), 51–60. doi:10.1123/jab.22.1.51 PMID:16760567

Montclair State University. (n.d.). Retrieved from https://www.montclair.edu/

Pavlou, M., Quinn, C., Murray, K., Spyridakou, C., Faldon, M., & Bronstein, A. M. (2011). The effect of repeated visual motion stimuli on visual dependence and postural control in normal subjects. *Gait & Posture, 33*(1), 113–118. doi:10.1016/j.gaitpost.2010.10.085 PMID:21144753

Peterka, R. J. (2002). Sensorimotor Integration in Human Postural Control. *Journal of Neurophysiology, 88*(3), 1097–1118. doi:10.1152/jn.2002.88.3.1097 PMID:12205132

Ponzo, S., Kirsch, L. P., Fotopoulou, A., & Jenkinson, P. M. (2018, March). Balancing body ownership: Visual capture of proprioception and affectivity during vestibular stimulation. *Neuropsychologia, 117*, 311–321. doi:10.1016/j.neuropsychologia.2018.06.020 PMID:29940194

Powers, K. C., Kalmar, J. M., & Cinelli, M. E. (2014). Recovery of static stability following a concussion. *Gait & Posture*, *39*(1), 611–614. doi:10.1016/j.gaitpost.2013.05.026 PMID:23810088

Rausch, M., Simon, J. E., Starkey, C., & Grooms, D. R. (2018). Smartphone virtual reality to increase clinical balance assessment responsiveness. *Physical Therapy in Sport*, *32*, 207–211. doi:10.1016/j.ptsp.2018.05.017 PMID:29803943

Rossetti, Y., Desmurget, M., & Prablanc, C. (1995). Vectorial coding of movement: Vision, proprioception, or both? *Journal of Neurophysiology*, *74*(1), 457–463. doi:10.1152/jn.1995.74.1.457 PMID:7472347

Slater, M., & Wilbur, S. (1997). A Framework for Immersive Virtual Environments (FIVE): Speculation on the Role of Presence in Virtual Environments. *Presence (Cambridge, Mass.)*, *6*(6), 603–616. doi:10.1162/pres.1997.6.6.603

Tsakiris, M. (2010). My body in the brain: A neurocognitive model of body-ownership. *Neuropsychologia*, *48*(3), 703–712. doi:10.1016/j.neuropsychologia.2009.09.034 PMID:19819247

Turner, T. L., & Hellbaum, R. F. (1986). LC shutter glasses provide 3-D display for simulated flight. *Information Display*, *2*(9), 22–24.

Whiting, C., & Rugg, S. (2006). *Dynatomy: Dynamic human anatomy*. Champaign, IL: Human Kinetics.

Whittle, M. (2014). *Gait Analysis: An Introduction* (4th ed.). Burlington, VT: Elsevier Science.

Winter, D. (2005). *Biomechanics and motor control of human movement* (3rd ed.). Hoboken, NJ: John Wiley & Sons, Inc.

ADDITIONAL READING

Azuma, R., Baillot, Y., Behringer, R., Feiner, W., Julier, S., & MacIntyre, B. (2001). Recent Advances in Augmented Reality. *IEEE Computer Graphics and Applications*, *21*(6), 34–47. doi:10.1109/38.963459

Keshner, E. A., Kenyon, R. V., & Langston, J. (2004). Postural responses exhibit multisensory dependencies with discordant visual and support surface motion. *Journal of Vestibular Research*, *14*, 307–319. PMID:15328445

Palmieri, R. M., Ingersoll, C. D., Stone, M. B., & Krause, B. A. (2002). Center-of-Pressure Parameters Used in the Assessment of Postural Control. *Journal of Sport Rehabilitation*, *11*(1), 51–66. doi:10.1123/jsr.11.1.51

Zanier, E. R., Zoerle, T., Di Lernia, D., & Riva, G. (2018, May). Virtual reality for traumatic brain injury. *Frontiers in Neurology*, *9*, 1–4. doi:10.3389/fneur.2018.00345 PMID:29867748

KEY TERMS AND DEFINITIONS

Center of Gravity (COG): The vertical projection of the COM onto the floor.

Center of Mass (COM): The net location of all mass represented in 3D space.

Center of Pressure (COP): The point on the force plate where the net ground reaction forces act or the point of application of the ground reaction force vector.

Double Support: Standing with both feet on the ground.

Force: A push or a pull on an object.

Head Mounted Display: A display that is more or less rigidly attached to the head.

Human Balance: Maintaining the center of gravity within the base of support.

Immersive Technology: Technology that blurs the line between the physical world and digital or simulated world, thereby creating a sense of immersion.

Single Support: Balancing on one foot with the other in the air.

Torque: The rotational effect due to a force.

Virtual Reality: A computer-generated digital environment that can be experienced and interacted with as if that environment was a real.

Visual Perturbations: A sudden change in the visual field.

Chapter 5
Lectures and Discussions in Semi–Immersive Virtual Reality Learning Environments:
The Effect of Communication Modality on Learner Satisfaction and Mental Effort

Natalie Nussli
https://orcid.org/0000-0002-2411-0023
University of Applied Sciences and Arts Northwestern Switzerland, Switzerland

Kevin Oh
University of San Francisco, USA

Nicole Cuadro
University of San Francisco, USA

Melisa Kaye
University of San Francisco, USA

EXECUTIVE SUMMARY

This chapter describes a study that was conducted in a semi-immersive desktop virtual reality environment. The study investigated teacher trainees' perceptions of their mental effort in Second Life, their satisfaction with the communication modalities, and their perceived social behavioral changes. In the first event, only the instructor (host) used voice to communicate while all participants as well as the in-text facilitator (co-host) used text chat only. In the second event, not only did both hosts use voice, but the participants also had the option to use voice rather than text. The majority of teacher trainees appreciated the freedom to choose either modality. The integration of voice was perceived as humanizing the discussion, increasing the flow, and making the conversation more engaging. However, the addition of multiple voices was believed to increase their mental effort. While some teacher trainees felt more relaxed and more open in a virtual discussion, others reported a lack of attention and honesty as well as a tendency to ignore social conventions.

DOI: 10.4018/978-1-5225-5912-2.ch005

INTRODUCTION

Participants who are engaging in a virtual reality learning environment (VRLE) for the first time may experience cognitive stress as they negotiate an unfamiliar educational resource. Although there is ample research with regard to the challenges of using semi-immersive virtual worlds in education, there is limited research with regard to the successful implementation of lecture events and discussion groups set in such virtual environments. In the present study, one of the goals was to develop a better understanding how online educators may address potential challenges hindering students' effective participation in a virtual lecture and discussion event. These challenges include a variety of factors that may put the success of a learning event in a VRLE at risk. For example, individuals may be frustrated over communicative challenges that prevent them from fully participating in a virtual lecture and discussion event.

The goals of this study were to gain a better understanding of the role that the communication modalities play during a lecture and group discussion set in Second Life, a 3D virtual world. The participants' mental effort expended during this event, their satisfaction with the communication modalities (text chat and voice), and their perceived behavioral changes were explored.

BACKGROUND

Semi-Immersive Desktop Virtual Reality

Desktop virtual reality (VR) runs on low-cost personal computers and enables multiple users to work collaboratively in a game, simulation or virtual world (Lee & Wong, 2014). Although desktop VR is less immersive than fully immersive, augmented, and mixed VR (Huang, Rauch, & Liaw, 2010), users of desktop VR still experience a sense of presence and immersion, depending on the degree of representational fidelity and the degree of interaction among users (Dalgarno, Hedberg, & Harper, 2002).

The use of desktop-based VR technologies for educational purposes is widespread. 3D virtual worlds are categorized as semi-immersive VR systems (Virtual Reality Society, 2018) and offer partial immersion without the need for VR gear, such as data gloves or head-mounted displays. The results of a meta-analysis suggest that semi-immersive virtual reality-based instruction is an effective means of enhancing learning outcomes (Merchant, Goetz, Cifuentes, Keeney-Kennicutt, & Davis, 2014). A total of 69 studies was categorized into three forms of desktop-based virtual reality technologies, namely, simulations, games, and virtual worlds. Real-time visualization and interaction emerged as the key factors that make 3D virtual worlds, such as Second Life, a valid alternative to fully immersive VR (Huang et al., 2010; Merchant et al., 2014), without experiencing the potential caveats of motion sickness, nausea, headaches, and fatigue commonly associated with true immersive VR (Herold & Molnar, 2018; Tax'en & Naeve, 2002).

The authors carefully considered which virtual world might be best to host the learning events described in this study. Conrad (2011) suggested evaluating virtual worlds against four dimensions, namely, their contexts, the immersion level, cost, and their persistence. The participants' level of digital literacy, the available computer equipment, and the participants' bandwidth needed to be taken into account. As a result, the authors chose to conduct the lecture and discussion events in Second Life due to its popularity among educators and its easy and free access. A review of over 100 articles on educational uses of virtual worlds (Duncan, Miller, & Jiang, 2012) indicates an overwhelming use of Second Life because it is relatively easy to set up and use and allows simulating a real world context in which the users are primarily in control of their interactions with other users and the environment (Richards & Taylor, 2015).

Fully immersive VR systems, in contrast, need a virtual-reality package. Although fully immersive VR has begun to make inroads in education, the educational value of fully immersive VR is not clear. More research is needed to justify why schools should invest in these technologies because "the field has suffered from a dearth of content that has clear educational value beyond simply engaging students" (Herold & Molnar, 2018, p. 10). There are also concerns with regard to the long-term impact on users' emotions, which is why some equipment, such as Samsung's GearVR viewer, should not be used by children younger than 13 (Herold & Molnar, 2018).

Using Desktop VR for Lectures and Group Discussions

Compared to 2D platforms, semi-immersive VRLEs offer unique capabilities. Specifically, the simultaneousness of visual, spoken, and written communication may help to reduce potential misunderstandings that would be more likely to happen in email exchanges or during conference calls (Wigert, de Vreede, Boughzala, & Bououd, 2012).

This chapter revolves around the use of semi-immersive desktop VR for lecture and discussion purposes and explores various factors that may influence the participants' sense of satisfaction with the virtual communication space. Factors influencing mental effort include the users' processing capabilities of mixed multi-modal messages, the potential humanization of virtual communication by adding voice to text chat, the concepts of synchronicity and immediacy and their potential connection to flow (Prude, 2013) as well as the concept of social presence.

Reported benefits of participating in a virtual discussion include convenience, an increased sense of privacy and anonymity, higher levels of focused interaction and reduced stressors, group empathy, increased honesty, and an absence of social pressure (Barak & Grohol, 2011; Changrani et al., 2008; Gilbert, Murphy, & Avalos, 2011; Green-Hamann, Campbell Eichhorn, & Sherblom, 2011; Nussli & Oh, 2017, 2018). VRLEs are the most successful when the learner is immersed and engaged in the event (Mount, Chambers, Weaver, & Priestnall, 2009).

Immersion and Social Presence in VRLEs

Immersion is considered the degree to which an individual feels engaged or engrossed in a virtual environment (Slater, 2009). Both the level of immersion and interaction with other individuals are influential factors in determining the degree of presence. Accordingly, a higher degree of presence is associated with greater engagement (Slater, 2009). The notions of immersion, presence, and engagement are highly correlated although their relationship is not easily disentangled (Mount et al., 2009).

Social presence is the ability to feel social cohesion within a community, to develop interpersonal relationships, and to communicate purposefully in a trusting environment (Garrison, 2009). Indicators of social presence in VRLEs include virtual sharing acts (e.g., sharing chocolate during a virtual discussion); communicating synchronously to support immediacy; spending time with each other; observing real-life social norms; showing politeness, such as apologizing for interrupting; showing social emotionality; using humor; using emoticons and emotes; using voice for humanized communication; and conveying intonation in writing (Nussli & Oh, 2017, 2018).

Higher levels of social presence in computer-mediated environments have been associated with significantly higher learning performance, possibly because a higher sense of social cohesion enriches communication (Hostetter & Busch, 2013; Lambert & Fisher, 2013). One of the factors influencing the degree of perceived social presence is immediacy, which has been defined as the directness of interaction with others (Wei, Chen, & Kinshuk, 2012). In the present study, the synchronous communication mode via text and voice chat maximized opportunities for immediate feedback, thus supporting social presence.

MAIN FOCUS OF THE CHAPTER

Communication Modalities

The communication modalities are among the most widely reported challenges (Bailenson, Yee, Blascovich, Beall, Lundblad, & Jin, 2008; Girvan & Savage, 2013; McVey, 2008; Wang, Anstadt, Goldman & Lefaiver, 2014). Examples of communicative challenges include: missing the humanization factor; missing social cues, gestures, and intonation; being untrained in virtual discussion; being unfamiliar with the use of abbreviations commonly used by expert communicators; a lack of time to process information; and a limited ability to integrate a mix of multi-modal input (Nussli & Oh, 2017, 2018). A combination of these factors may result in cognitive overload (Chandler & Sweller, 1992; Sweller, 1988, 1999, 2005) as one of the key challenges hindering effective participation in virtual discussions.

Cognitive Load in a VRLE

Cognitive load theory is a psychological framework that explains the learning process as a result of both the capabilities and limitations of human cognitive architecture (Plass, Moreno, & Brünken, 2010). Following Paas and Van Merriënboer's (1994) model, cognitive load can be measured by assessing mental load, mental effort, and performance (Brünken, Seufert, & Paas, 2010; Paas & Van Merriënboer, 1993; Paas, Tuovinen, Tabbers, & Van Gerven, 2003; Sweller, Ayres, & Kalyuga, 2011).

The present study focuses on the notion of mental effort. Defined as the amount of controlled cognitive processing necessary for effective learning, mental effort varies in intensity and can be either a boon or a hindrance to the learning process (Paas, 1992; Sweller, 1988, 1999, 2005). Processing difficulties arise when the working memory is overloaded with the amount of incoming information.

Mayer and Moreno (2003) have proposed a number of multimedia principles and recommendations how to address cognitive overload scenarios by effectively organizing and presenting visual and verbal information. In a virtual discussion where both text chat and voice are used simultaneously, there is a great risk that the visual and auditory channels are being overloaded. In addition to handling the communicative challenges, a learner needs to process the content, manage navigation, and handle general stress, which may depend on a variety of individual learner characteristics (e.g., technology background, attitude toward VRLE, experience with online communication). For example, auditory learners participating in a virtual discussion are likely to prefer voice to text and may experience cognitive overload when attempting to process the text channel.

Split Attention

The split-attention effect occurs when separate sources of information need to be mentally integrated. Input types may include voice chat, group text chat, private text chat, and/or visual material (e.g. lecture slides). The auditory split attention effect and the visual split-attention effect (Ayres & Sweller, 2014; Chandler & Sweller, 1992; Moreno & Mayer, 2000) are scenarios central to an effective facilitation of virtual lectures and discussions. In a VRLE, learners are immersed in an environment rich with visual and auditory information, thus increasing the risk of split attention (Nelson & Erlandson, 2008). Text chat, for example, moves fast in a medium-to-large group due to the number of posts. It may often be unclear which comment refers to which statement due to linearity of the text chat. There may be an entirely different dialogue in-between someone's question and someone else's answer requiring the reader to scan the text chat channel in an attempt to identify which segments refer to each other (Nussli & Oh, 2017, 2018). The visually rich background in a VRLE as well as moving avatars may distract learners even further.

Design Approaches

The relevance of cognitive overload scenarios is the focus of a study by Nelson and Erlandson (2008) who recommend a number of redesign approaches for multi-user virtual environments (MUVEs). One of these redesign approaches is particularly relevant to the present research, namely, that offloading printed text to the verbal channel may reduce cognitive overload and, as a result, decrease the split attention effect. In an investigation of students' cognitive load while completing a science curriculum in an educational MUVE, it was found that using voice resulted in lower levels of cognitive load than did the exclusive use of text (Erlandson, Nelson, & Savenye, 2010).

Using voice and text in parallel, however, might further complicate the situation for some learners, as illustrated in the following scenario: In a learning session involving a host, a co-host, and a group of 20 learners in a VRLE, the host uses voice to introduce a discussion question. The participants need to respond immediately, although they may still be busy processing their peers' posts to the text chat as well as the in-text facilitator's (co-host's) questions for clarification. This dual mode (voice and text) may split the students' attention due to an inability to reconcile the three incoming streams of information (i.e., host voice, co-host text, and peer text) simultaneously. While they can go back to the text chat and reread a section they missed, they cannot listen to the host's question again unless they explicitly ask for repetition. By the time they have realized this gap, the conversation has likely already moved on.

This example illustrates one of many ways in which cognitive overload may occur during virtual lecture and discussion events. When participants experience split attention, the resulting feelings of frustration and disengagement impede the learning process. Thus, two of the five research questions revolve around the communication modalities and the mental effort associated with these modalities. Further areas of investigation include behavioral changes in online communication, teachers' perceptions of the value and caveats of group discussions set in desktop VR, and their perceptions of their levels of social presence.

Purpose and Research Questions

The authors have proposed the following five research questions to guide this study:

Research Question #1: How does the behavior of teacher trainees participating in a lecture and discussion group set in desktop VR change compared to their real-life behavior?

Research Question #2: What are teacher trainees' perceptions of the educational benefits and challenges of participating in a discussion group set in desktop VR?

Research Question #3: How does using both voice and text chat affect student communication in desktop VR?

Research Question #4: How does desktop VR affect the mental effort needed for students to access educational content and participate in an online discussion effectively?

Research Question #5: What are teacher trainees' perceptions of their social presence while participating in a discussion group set in desktop VR?

METHODOLOGY

Method Selection

To capture the perceptions of a small sample of participants (N=16), the authors decided that two different approaches would generate the richest data. Thus, it was determined to use the online survey method for individual data gathering immediately after the virtual experiences and the face-to-face focus group approach for collective data gathering two weeks after the virtual experiences.

Participants

Sixteen participants (college age adults) were recruited from a technology class for learning specialists. Of the sixteen participants, 13 (81%) were female and three (19%) male. This intervention was part of their regularly scheduled curriculum for the course. The instructor informed students of the individual steps involved in the project. If students wished to opt out, they needed to contact the instructor for alternative assignments. Students were informed in writing that completion of the first survey constituted implied consent to participate in this project. None of the students opted out.

The lecture and discussion events were an integral part of the coursework. Therefore, the instructor was aware of the participants' identity (avatar names) at all times. The participants were also aware of their peers' identities, although some confusion arose due to the fact that several participants happened to choose the same avatar, that is, up to four avatars, including the instructor, looked exactly the same.

Data Collection and Development of Rating Scales

Paas et al. (2003) emphasized that rating scales presume the respondents' ability to self-report the amount of mental effort expended in a given process, which assumes that people are able reflect on their cognitive processes. Findings by Gopher and Braune (1984) suggest that people are, indeed, capable of estimating their perceived mental burden. Thus, two nine-point rating scales were included in the second survey that would allow participants to self-report their mental effort and satisfaction with the communication modalities.

The scale measuring mental effort was adopted from Paas' (1992) subjective rating scale. The numerical labels and values assigned to the categories ranged from *very, very low* mental effort (1) to *very, very high* mental effort (9). This scale pertained to the participants' perceived *overall* mental effort required to process and manage content, communication, navigation, and general stress (Erlandson et al., 2010).

The second scale measured participant satisfaction with the communication modalities on a nine-point rating scale, ranging from *extremely unsatisfied* (1) to *very satisfied* (9). Due to the fact that the two scales were single-item ratings, reliability was not established. While such single-item ratings are commonly used in education, they are often associated with inadequate psychometric properties (Ginns & Barrie, 2004). Test-retest reliability could have been measured if the scales had been administered more than once. In this study, the scales were only administered once after the second lecture and discussion event. Although reliability of single-item scales can also be estimated either using the correction for attenuation formula or factor analysis (Ginns & Barrie, 2004), a much larger sample size would have been needed in this case.

Survey 1

The first survey (Appendix 1) was adopted from Nussli (2014) and was administered after the first lecture and discussion. The survey inquired about the participants' technology background (Rogers, 1962) and experience with virtual worlds. It included open-ended questions inquiring about the participants' location during the lecture and discussion as well as the aspects that they liked or disliked about this experience.

Survey 2

The second survey (Appendix 2) was administered after the second lecture and discussion and was designed to measure the participants' satisfaction with the communication modality, their comfort level using voice and text, and the mental effort expended during the second lecture and discussion. Two questions explored social behavior in virtual worlds. The participants were asked whether they had noticed any differences in their behavior compared to a face-to-face class meeting. The final question required the respondents to compare the first lecture and discussion event with the second event.

Figure 1 shows the communication modalities used in the two events. In the first event, only the host used voice while the co-host and all participants used text chat exclusively. In the second lecture and

Figure 1. Communication modalities

Roles	Second Life Lecture & Discussion #1		Second Life Lecture & Discussion #2	
	Voice	Group Text Chat	Voice	Group Text Chat
1 Host	✔	-	✔	-
1 Co-host	-	✔	✔	✔
8 Participants	-	✔	✔	✔

discussion, however, both the host and co-host used voice in parallel. The participants used text chat to answer the host's initial questions. To answer the host and co-host's follow-up questions, they were encouraged to use voice although they were free to use text chat if they felt uncomfortable using voice.

Focus Group

The focus group (three groups of five to six participants, 30 minutes each) was held in a face-to-face setting. It was semi-structured and led by the co-host. The questions (Appendix 3) were designed to provide an opportunity for a collaborative review of participants' experiences and to dig deeper into a number of issues that had emerged from the participants' responses given in the second survey. Thus, an initial version of the questions was revised and extended after the second survey.

Ad hoc Interventions

After the introductory fieldtrip (i.e., prior to the first discussion and lecture), it became evident that the level of excitement coming from the participants regarding Second Life tended to be low. The participants shared some concerns and communicated their strong resistance to the virtual world. Many of them felt frustrated and uncomfortable with the flying and mobility aspect of Second Life ("I really hope we don't have to fly to our lecture location"). Some were concerned about a lack of safety ("There are too many creepy people in Second Life") or had difficulty in using SL ("I have never felt more frustrated in my life with technology"). As an immediate intervention measure designed to curb the participants' lack of buy-in and hesitation to use Second Life, the instructor sent an email to the participants prior to the first lecture and discussion assuring them that the Second Life experience was going to be held in a safe Second Life island specifically designed for educational purposes, namely, *Science Circle.* To address the participants' concern about a lack of relevance for their own instruction, the instructor highlighted that the purpose of the study was to explore ways to make online educational experiences more interactive by moving away from asynchronous discussion boards and learning management systems to more synchronous contexts.

A second intervention was required after the first discussion and lecture event. Due to a lack of interactivity and engagement, the authors decided on the following four modifications: (a) both the host (i.e., the instructor) and the co-host would use voice in the second event, (b) the co-host was assigned a much more engaging role than in the first event where the co-host's sole responsibility was to facilitate the text chat; (c) the host would pick a few contributions posted to the text chat and ask all of the students to comment on these specific contributions either by using voice or text chat in order to enhance participation; and (d) seats would need to be rearranged so that the participants would be able to look at each other while still being able to read the lecture slides.

PROCEDURES

Step-by-Step

Consent to conduct this study was obtained from the university's IRB Review Board. The participants met in person (regular class meetings on campus) for the Second Life introduction, orientation field trip, and the focus group. They met virtually (preferably from home) for the two events. Participants were asked to download Second Life prior to the introductory fieldtrip, to create an account, to choose an avatar, and to share their Second Life identity/name with the instructor. The instructor emailed the students the Second Life URLs, known as *SLurls*, for the specific venues of the introductory fieldtrip, the lecture and discussion group activities, and the links to the surveys. The participants were also advised that they should have a stable internet connection (hard-wired, if possible) to allow for an uninterrupted remote participation in the discussion group activities. They were advised against using a network heavily guarded by a firewall. They were also informed that using their cell phone as a hotspot would result in an extremely unstable connection, which would most likely prevent them from participating. They were asked to be in a quiet environment so that they would be able to hear the host's lecture. Finally, the participants were informed that the use of a mouse would facilitate navigation and camera control. With regard to learning basic navigation and communication skills in Second Life, it was decided to train the following set of skills: how to walk/run/fly, sit, post something to the group or private chat, enable audio (e.g., hearing the sound of dolphins and whales in *Science Circle*), set audio preferences in order to hear the host's voice, and teleport to a specific location.

The study began with an in-class introduction and orientation demonstration to the Second Life virtual environment. Then, over the following four weeks, two lessons were held online as part of the regularly scheduled curriculum. Each of the online sessions lasted for 45 minutes, that is, approximately 20 minutes for lecture and 25 minutes for discussion. There were two sessions available for students to join. The two groups, Group A and Group B, consisted of eight participants each. Each of the groups participated in two online sessions. Following the first session, participants completed the first survey. Following the second session, participants completed the second survey. Two weeks after the completion of the intervention, all participants participated in a focus group (small groups of five to six participants each) to gain additional insights into the use of 3D virtual worlds in education. Table 1 displays the step-by-step procedure.

Table 1. Overview of steps

Steps	Duration	Location
All Participants: Second Life (SL) Introduction, Orientation Fieldtrip	30 minutes	On Campus
Group A: First SL-Lecture & Discussion, Survey 1	45 minutes	Online Access
Group B: First SL-Lecture & Discussion, Survey 1	45 minutes	Online Access
Group A: Second SL-Lecture & Discussion, Survey 2	45 minutes	Online Access
Group B: Second SL-Lecture & Discussion, Survey 2	45 minutes	Online Access
All Participants: Focus Group	30 minutes	On Campus

Selection of Virtual Destinations

For the introductory fieldtrip, the authors decided to visit two educational regions emphasizing two commonly cited affordances of virtual worlds, namely, 'hands-on experimentation' allowing visitors to 'observe an outcome'. The specific locations chosen for the fieldtrip were *Genome Island* and *Sploland*, whereas the lecture and discussion group activities were conducted in a sandbox in *Science Circle*. Figure 2 shows the two different seating arrangements used in the first and second event, respectively.

Second Life remains one of the better-known social virtual worlds (Gallego, Bueno, & Noyes, 2016), although the educational community has begun using OpenSim-based alternatives, such as Reaction Grid (Conrad, Hassan, Koshy, Kanamgotov, & Christopoulos, 2017). Considering that there are hundreds of Open-Sim based grids (http://opensimulator.org/wiki/Grid_List), it might be challenging for online educators to identify those grids with educational value.

DATA ANALYSIS

Multiple data streams were used as triangulation tools. The qualitative data emerged from the focus groups and the open-ended items of both the first survey and the second survey. Two nine-point rating scales used in the second survey complemented the qualitative data. Several items in both surveys provided descriptive data. Rereading of the raw qualitative data allowed identifying recurring themes through open-coding. Overlapping codes were combined into recurring themes and organized around the research questions.

It was ensured that the categories constructed during data analysis meet certain criteria, namely, that they are responsive to the purpose of the research; exhaustive; mutually exclusive; as sensitive to the data as possible; and, conceptually congruent, that is, the categories should be at the same level of abstraction (Merriam, 2009).

After manual coding and agreement by all authors through an interrater reliability process, the codes were entered into MaxQDA for the purpose of coding comparisons and generating frequencies. Max-QDA determined the frequency with which codes were applied. The most common codes were retained for further analysis, whereas moderately used codes were collapsed and rarely used codes eliminated.

Figure 2. Seating arrangement first event (left) vs. seating arrangement second event (right)

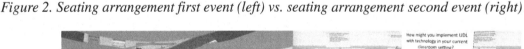

Reliability

Interrater reliability was calculated to demonstrate consistency among the ratings provided by multiple coders (Hallgren, 2012). At two interrater meetings, all four authors individually rated a subset of 60 units (23% out of a total of 256 units) by applying and validating five themes encompassing 42 codes identified by the lead author. For each of the 60 units, the four raters had to select a suitable code out of 42 codes. Each of the five themes was represented by a similar number of units to be coded. To facilitate the coding process, they received matrices indicating which one or two themes to focus on. For each of the units, percent agreement (pair-wise agreement among the four raters) was calculated. If the interrater agreement was below 75% for anyone unit, the codes were reconsidered. As a result of the interrater meeting, 18 changes were implemented (i.e., eliminating or merging codes, moving codes to a different theme) and resulted in a revised code chart. The lead author coded the remaining 196 response items using the revised code chart. The observed percentage agreement across all five themes was 86% (theme 1: 85%, theme 2: 95%, theme 3: 81%, theme 4: 79%, theme 5: 92%). The five themes were reported under "Major Themes" in the next section.

RESULTS

Participants' Technology Background

Table 2 shows the results of the first survey, which gathered information about the participants' technology background.

Table 2a. Participants' technology background (N=16): (1) How much virtual worlds experience do you have?

Response Choice	%	Count
No experience	56.2	9
Inexperienced	25.0	4
Some experience	6.25	1
Experienced	12.5	2
Very experienced	0.00	0

Table 2b. Participants' technology background (N=16): (2) How tech-savvy would you describe yourself on a rating scale from 1-10? (1=I dislike technology and I don't feel comfortable using it. 10= I love technology)

Scale	1 (Dislike)	2	3	4	5	6	7	8	9 (Love it)
%	0.00	0.00	6.25	12.50	25.00	18.75	12.50	6.25	0.00
Count	0	0	1	2	4	3	2	1	0

Table 2c. Participants' technology background (N=16): (3) Please take a look at the four technology adoption categories (Rogers, 1962). How would you describe yourself?

Response Choice	%	Count
Innovator	0.00	0
Early adopter	56.25	9
Early majority	31.25	5
Laggard	12.50	2

Major Themes

The codes were organized around five major themes, namely, behavioral changes, affordances, challenges, communication modalities, and mental effort. Only the most common codes will be reported and discussed. The key findings are summarized in Table 3.

Behavioral Changes Using a Desktop VR

In the second survey, participants were asked if they had noticed any changes in their behavior compared with how they would typically behave in a face-to-face discussion, for example, if they had been more honest in the virtual environment than they would have been in a real-life conversation. Sixty-nine percent reported noticing changes in their behavior compared with how they would typically behave. They provided numerous examples of behavioral changes. On the positive side, several participants expressed that the virtual environment was a more relaxed environment than a real classroom, that they felt more comfortable to contribute to the discussion, were less shy to say hello to new people online, and were more open than in a face-to-face (f2f) discussion.

I feel like I was more comfortable saying what I wanted. I always tend to let other people speak in conversations/discussions and I take a backseat, just listening and thinking/reflecting in my head. Being able to type as other people speak/type let's me share what's on my mind without feeling like I'm interrupting or being put on the spot. For example, when M. was expanding on what she had typed, I could continue typing my expansion of what I had typed.

A number of verbal learners felt it was easier for them to contribute to the virtual discussion than to a f2f discussion. The slower pace and the text chat played an important role.

Yes, I think it is easier for me to participate in discussion. Because we have to type out a response, it helps me gather my thoughts. When I am in a classroom discussion it is much harder for me to participate and convey those thoughts verbally.

Table 3. Themes and most common codes

Themes	Code Descriptions	Count
Absence of Behavioral Changes	Same or similar social behavior as in real life (e.g., avatar would apologize if he/she bumped into another avatar; asking a friend how their day was prior to the start of the virtual lecture) and same or similar level of honesty.	10
Presence of Behavioral changes	Potentially compromising effects: • Less likely to be honest (e.g., less likely to disagree because text chat does not capture tone and meaning, may sound impolite). • Less likely to apologize (e.g., if one's avatar bumped into someone else's avatar). • More likely to be rude due to the impersonal environment (e.g., standing up and leaving if there were no repercussions, ignoring the instructor's question). • Avoiding humor for fear of misinterpretation. • Less likely to elaborate on one's answer (e.g., not enough time; text chat allows less room for errors; no elaborate answers; not user-friendly). • Second-guessing one's responses in text chat more than in RL (permanent record). • Less likely to engage in a casual conversation. Positive Effects: • More likely to feel relaxed (e.g., contribute via text chat whenever one wants, feeling more comfortable saying what one wants). • More honest and open (e.g., being less shy, saying hello to new people more easily)	44
Affordances	• Appreciation for the privacy and convenience of participating from home. • Text chat is an easy-to-use think-and-share platform; appreciation for instant feedback and individual pace (e.g., having sufficient think time before responding).	29
Challenges	• Technical issues (e.g., slow connection resulting in lag, log-in problems, several applications open simultaneously leading to SL crashing, voice/text chat slows down computer and one's speed in responding). • Resistance to virtual environments, strong preference for face-to-face. • Distraction (e.g., by animal sounds, camera noise, or visuals in the background). • Ineffective pacing (e.g., dead air time, awkward silence, speaking over each other). • Inauthentic interaction (e.g., feels impersonal, lacks components of real discussion, limited peer interaction).	42
Communication Modalities	Positive aspects of the integration of voice and text: • accommodates auditory and visual learners. • increases flow. • freedom to choose communication modality. • everyone can participate using text chat, even in the absence of voice (whether voluntary or due to technical issues). Unique affordances of adding voice were identified as: • making event more engaging, more conversational and more personal. • easy to use. • allows elaborating on written comments. • voice preferable because typing too slow. • allows people's voices to be heard, yet they do not have to be seen (anonymity).	41
Lowered Mental Effort	Mental effort lowered due to: • disengagement (e.g., disinterest in the use of online platforms for learning, concerns about SL as a platform for learning and its classroom applicability). • frustration and/or sense of wasted time (e.g., topic repetition; inability to navigate avatar into the discussion circle resulting in feeling left out; classroom applicability questionable).	19
Increased Mental Effort	Mental effort increased: • processing two communication modalities (voice and text) simultaneously. • processing multiple voices (hosts and peers) • multitasking (i.e., simultaneously processing lecture and slides; processing and addressing the host's and co-host's questions, typing up contributions immediately, and responding to peer contributions). • difficulty interpreting questions, unable to ask for clarification or answer a question.	34

On the negative side, a lack of attention, an inability to express oneself fully, a lack of honesty, and an "unreal" feeling were often mentioned as obstacles to contributing meaningfully and authentically.

I paid a lot less attention this way. I would be more honest if there was a social piece involved because I would be more connected to what was going on. I don't learn this way so it is too easy to check out.

Another topic that emerged was that of a reduced likelihood to be honest. Especially, there was concern about the act of disagreeing because they felt they could not do so in an appropriate manner in an online conversation. Even if they used voice to express themselves rather than text chat, some participants believed that they would still be unable to incorporate non-verbal clues.

I'm less likely to type out my disagreement. I feel more comfortable disagreeing with someone face-to-face because I can do it politely. I can monitor my tone and use specific body language. Disagreeing with someone online can easily be mistaken for aggression or indifference.

In addition, they reported avoiding humor for fear of misinterpretation. The inability to express oneself fully emerged as a frequent point of criticism.

I did notice changes in my behavior because I felt like I was not able to eleborate [sic] my responses as I would have in a face-to-face discussion. I was still honest with my responses but I felt like I was not able to express myself fully.

The participants were asked to provide examples of their social behavior that may or may not have been different from the real world, such as: Would they have dared to stand up in the middle of the discussion and disappear? Or if they bumped into an avatar, would they apologize? Again, responses were mixed. Some participants reported feeling less bound by social conventions, as in, "I didn't respond to something the co-host typed back to me, which is something I probably couldn't get away with in real life." It was frequently mentioned that they were more likely to be rude due to the impersonal environment.

I feel like I can be just as honest in real life as in Second Life. The main difference is, for me personally, I don't have to wait my turn, read other people's expressions, decide if it's the right time/place for me to speak in the virtual world - I can just type whatever I want - because it's so impersonal and I can be a little "rude," but I can also just be honest and blunt and not hesitiate [sic].

A minority of participants, however, demonstrated stronger adherence to real-life conventions.

No I definitely wouldn't have stood up as an avatar and move around during the discussion. I would not be able to see the presentation or hear what people were saying. I could also block others' view of the presentation. However, I would stand up in person to disappear if it is for the bathroom. I think virtual lectures are nice because there a [sic] minimal distractions, such as people leaving.

This minority also reported feeling comfortable communicating and was more likely to engage in casual conversation.

As I probably would in real life I did personally talk to a friend in the room before the lecture started without talking to everyone in the room. I used it to ask a friend how their day was. I did not bump into anyone, but I certainly would have apologized if I had. If social behavior was the same in both the virtual and real world I believe society would be a lot better off.

Participants' Satisfaction with the Communication Modalities

To capture the participants' satisfaction with the communication modalities, data were amalgamated from the rating scale and open and closed questions from the second survey. The scale reported on the degree to which they were satisfied with the communication modalities used during the Second Life lecture and discussion. It consisted of nine reply options (1= "extremely dissatisfied" to 9= "extremely satisfied"). Results indicated that 50% of the participants were unsatisfied with the communication modalities of voice and chat (ratings 1-4). The other half of the participants expressed satisfaction with the communication modalities (ratings 6-8). None of the participants expressed neutrality about the communication modalities. The mean was rather low at 4.5 on a nine-point rating scale. The results are shown in Table 4.

When asked if they found the virtual discussion a pleasant way to communicate with others, half of the participants agreed, whereas the other half either perceived it as unpleasant or considered the question irrelevant. When asked how easy or difficult it had been to express what they wanted to communicate, forty-four percent rated this way of communication as "easy", six percent as "average", whereas thirty-one percent of participants found it to be difficult or even very difficult. Nineteen percent of the participants considered the question irrelevant. Some participants' responses reflected mixed emotions, such as anxiety with regard to the pace and the use of voice, yet also an appreciation for being able to hear their peers' and hosts' voices.

Yes, having multiple options to communicate gave everyone a chance to participate. I was [sic] little nervous about using the microphone however and almost chose to use it. Also it can be hard to tell if I should speak right after another person or wait for permission. I did appreciate hearing other people speak, it does help to enrich the discussion.

Conversely, the reactions of a number of participants were invariably negative. The following participant expressed dissatisfaction with a variety of factors, such as the sound quality, the text chat format, an inadequate pace preventing the participant from contributing to the discussion, and the anonymity of avatar names.

I did not find it a pleasant way to cominucate [sic] with others it was hard to hear sometimes. I did not know when to share out or if I wanted to comment on a person's post it had moved up and I had to go

Table 4. Participants' satisfaction with the communication modalities

Scale	1 Extremely Dissatisfied	2	3	4	5	6	7	8	9 Extremely Satisfied
%	12.50	25.00	0.00	12.50	0.00	18.75	25.00	6.25	0.00
Count	2	4	0	2	0	3	4	1	0

find it. It is very hard to keep track of the conversation in the chat box it is very small. If I wanted to respond, agree, or comment to someone's post sometimes I did not know who it was because all we see is the avatar name. At one point I wanted to share out using the speaker but did not want to cut off C.. Once C. was done someone else jumped in and I was not able to add to C.'s comment.

A majority of participants, however, reported appreciating the text chat and perceived it as bringing the discussion forward while allowing everyone to contribute at their own pace. One participant noted, "I like that I can add to the discussion at any point and not worry about interrupting anyone. I also like receiving feedback. This time around, I felt we also provided more feedback to each other as classmates." Many participants emphasized the integration of both communication modalities.

Today's lecture seemed to go more smoothly because it integrated both voice & chat. People were using whichever modality suited them (I didn't want to talk so I used chat) and so there were kind of two conversations going on at once. I felt this helped the conversation to flow more quickly. However, it could be hard to concentrate on both at times.

Freedom to choose either modality emerged as a key affordance of a virtual discussion. A participant commented,

I think it's good to practice the whole giving students a choice in how they express knowledge, understanding, and comprehension, but making sure they can do both. For myself, I don't really find too many occasions where I feel like I NEED to speak out my responses, as I feel like typing my answers would be adequate. However, there are times I know I need to speak to someone about a topic because typing back and forth would not be adequate.

Although not a major trend, a few participants expressed full satisfaction with the online discussion. Factors included the ease of contributing to the discussion, expertise in online communication, an appreciation for interaction, yet a preference for written communication.

I felt it was easy for me to express what I wanted to communicate in the virtual discussion. I grew up using AIM (AOL Instant Messenger) and online discussion boards, so I'm really comfortable communicating in an online setting like this. I also prefer to write my thoughts down rather than speak them. However, I also like interacting with people in person, so I feel like I'm in a good place where I'm flexible in how and where I communicate.

Participants' Integration of Voice

Benefits of Integrating Voice

The participants frequently mentioned that they were afraid of being asked to respond using voice rather than text. All participants in the first lecture and discussion voluntarily responded to each discussion question via the text chat function. During the second event, when the host called on some participants and asked them to use voice, there were more involuntary voice responses than voluntary voice responses.

Several students emphasized that although they appreciated having the choice of using either voice or text, they still had a strong preference for text. However, it was frequently mentioned that they enjoyed hearing their peers' voices because it made the discussion more personal and conversational than using text only, as evidenced by the following contribution:

I am more satisfied because this made the lecture more engaging. Instead of having to just receive information and give comments, we were able to be more included. This time around class felt more like a conversation. Compared to last time this lecture is a step up for me.

A few participants specifically highlighted the practical implementation of Universal Learning Design (UDL), which was the topic of the first learning event. In addition, they also expressed appreciation for the scaffolding with regard to the use of technology.

I was satisfied with the combination because it allows access for visual and auditory learners. This is the idea of UDL. I appreciate that this form of class was not introduced as both a voice and text chat. I liked how they were introduce [sic] to us slowly so I didn't get overwhelmed.

Meeting the needs of both visual and auditory learners also clearly emerged as one of the key affordances of having a virtual discussion.

I could see how it is satisfying because it gives people the opportunity to talk during a discussion if they may get nervous with in person discussions. It allows people's voices to be heard, yet they don't have to be seen. On the other hand, if a person did not have speech, they would also be able to participate in a discussion without them feeling behind.

Although a majority of the participants valued the integration of voice, they also identified a number of challenges.

Challenges of Integrating Voice

Three key challenges were associated with the integration of voice: a lack of authenticity, an awkward pace, and reduced attention. For example, the interaction was often described as unrealistic and inauthentic, as in:

Maybe, after asking the question we need to respond to, provide examples or keep talking while we have a chance to respond. The interaction is not realistic. We wouldn't sit in class, staring at each other while each students [sic] comes up with a response.

Perceptions as to the pace of the discussion were also mixed. Some participants had difficulties getting used to the silence while everybody was typing up their responses, whereas other participants appreciated having sufficient think time to formulate their responses, especially those who realized that the text chat was going to be a permanent record. One participant, who expressed his preference for text over voice, emphasized his fear that the use of two communication channels might reduce attention.

I enjoy the discussion through the text box rather than providing a voice response. I feel that people are more likely to look at my written response because they have to write in the same box. If people are talking and another is typing, I feel that the person typing is less likely to pay attention to what was verbally said. I know as a visual learner, I was looking at the written responses and taking in that information, than the information that was said over the voice chat.

Several participants highlighted a strong preference for face-to-face communication, potentially lacking a sense of immersion and social presence in a virtual environment.

However, there is something about live interaction, person-to-person, being in the same physical room. As someone who has tried online graduate level work, I know I am someone who does not learn best in that environment.

As opposed to a number of participants who reported a strong preference for brick-and-mortar classrooms, there were several participants who were in favor of online learning, but not in a virtual world. "I think the combination of both is more helpful then [sic] just text. However, I would much rather just follow along a video chat."

Mental Effort Expended

The second rating scale included in the second survey inquired about the participants' perceived mental effort expended during the lecture and discussion. Results showed that approximately one third of participants each rated their mental effort in the low, neutral, and high ranges. As shown in Table 5, 38% reported varying degrees of "low" mental effort (ratings 1-4), 31% reported neither low nor high mental effort, and 31% reported relatively high mental effort (ratings 6+7). The mean was rather low at 4.25 on a nine-point rating scale.

At the conclusion of the lectures and discussions, participants were asked to reflect on their emotional state following the experiences. Results show that many of the participants were "relieved" at the conclusion of the Second Life experiences. Other more frequent responses included "satisfied" (15.40%), "exhausted" (11.50%), and "frustrated" (15.40%). Table 6 details the response options provided and the frequency of those responses.

Table 5. Participants' mental effort expended during the lecture and discussion

Scale	1 Very, Very Low	2 Very Low	3 Low	4 Rather Low	5 Neither Low nor High	6 Rather High	7 High	8 Very High	9 Very, Very High
%	18.75	6.25	6.25	6.25	31.25	25.00	6.25	0.00	0.00
Count	2	4	0	2	0	3	4	1	0

Table 6. Participants' self-reported emotional state following two Second Life events

Response Option	%	Count
"Stimulated"	7.70	2
"Inspired"	3.85	1
"Energized"	3.85	1
"Satisfied"	15.40	4
"Relieved"	34.60	9
"Overwhelmed"	7.70	2
"Exhausted "	11.50	3
"Frustrated"	15.40	4

Note: Participants were instructed to choose all response options that apply.

Mental Effort Increased Due to Multiple Sources of Input

Overall, the majority of participants reported increased mental effort due to the integration of two communication modalities (text and chat). The mental effort was further intensified due to the addition of the co-host's voice in the second event and due to the fact that the host called on several participants to elaborate on their written posts using voice, which some of them did involuntarily. Several visual learners experienced difficulties with the integration of voice and chat.

My mental effort for tonight's class [sic] rather high. Although I liked this class because we got to speak, I still struggled to sit a [sic] listen during the lecture. I am not an auditory learner and I have ADD. In order for me to not move on to watching something else I had to look at the slides and the pictures in the back.

Whereas some participants perceived the silent periods as awkward, other participants would have preferred more think time. Their mental effort seemed to increase whenever they failed to have enough time for reflection.

I expended more mental effort this time around. The questions were a little more engaging and so it felt more like a conversation than just a question, answer, and move on. There were some good questions posed. However, I still would have felt more comfortable given time to think things over in person (I did feel like I had to give rushed answers at time [sic]).

The virtual experience was often perceived as challenging because "everything was moving too fast, which made it difficult to keep track of the conversation in the chat box and the conversation I was hearing". Especially when two different questions were asked (one by the host and one by the co-host), the participants found it challenging to process and answer the questions. Diverted attention emerged as another frequently mentioned issue associated with increased mental effort. Due to the multiple sources of input and output, some participants expressed that they felt like falling behind because "I am so focused on what I am going to say instead of hearing/seeing what everyone else has to say".

Mental Effort Increased by the Addition of Voice

The participants' feelings about both hosts using voice and asking questions were ambivalent. On the one hand, integration of voice humanized the discussion and made it more personal, informal, and engaging, as in, "It was nice having multiple voices to feel more like an in person discussion". On the other hand, the event was perceived as being more confusing. Hearing multiple voices made it "difficult to keep track of everyone talking and of the conversation". Most participants reported an increased mental effort during the second lecture and discussion not only due to the processing of multiple sources of input, but also because of the co-host's increased involvement. In the first event, the co-host was only tasked with occasional in-text facilitation, whereas in the second event the co-host was actively engaged in the discussion, using voice and text chat simultaneously.

I did not like the co-host using her voice to speak. It opened up too many questions and I could not handle it. Meaning, there was no way to respond to everything she was asking. I was barely able to answer the professor's questions in a meaningful way.

The host's questions were often followed by the co-host's efforts to dig deeper, which some students recognized as making the conversation more interactive on the one hand. On the other hand, these follow-up questions resulted in some participants feeling overwhelmed.

Unlike last time there were two people talking which made it hard for me because both of you were asking questions. I think if questions were to be asked one at a time and maybe by one person they would be more clear.

Focus Groups: Insights

To further examine participant experiences, focus groups were conducted after the two lectures and discussions. Each session had a duration of 30 minutes and consisted of a moderator and five to six participants. The sessions were video and audio recorded, and analysis of the focus group recordings yielded four main themes including challenges of Second Life, suggested improvements to future virtual world learning experiences, comparison between 2D and 3D virtual experiences, and potential application of the Second Life environment to other educational contexts.

Challenges of SL

The focus group participants raised a number of issues with the Second Life world. Difficulties with the chat functionality were common. Complaints included the slowness of the process, the difficulty reading and posting simultaneously, and the lack of visual cues to increase clarity. One participant expressed confusion and frustration about her experience by asking, "When do I jump in? Is this person done? Are you cutting people off? If we can look at each other, it's easier". Other participants discussed on the learning curve necessary in Second Life, and one commented,

Getting to the place, zooming in, that it took me 20 minutes sitting down in a chair. Couldn't get a better view of the slides, frustrating. Didn't know which slide to focus on, took me another 10 minutes to figure out. In the second lecture, I clicked on something, great, I am in another world, didn't where [sic], took me 10 minutes to figure out how to get back.

Another participant, who was 30 years old, lamented, "We're a generation too soon for something like this. Kids who grow up with this will love this. It's always been a struggle for me". Finally, participants were challenged by the seeming mismatch between the lecture and discussion format and having an avatar present in the virtual world. One participant noted, "If we're going to be avatars, I don't want to just sit. I want to have brain breaks. I wanted to move around".

Improving Virtual World Learning Experiences

A second theme focused on how to improve future virtual world learning experiences. Participants noted a number of strategies including a variety of small group activities (e.g., "think-pair-share") and increasing active engagement opportunities in the virtual environment and interaction between participants. Ideas included field trips, virtual tours, interactive videos, and scavenger hunts. Participants tended not to view either lecture or structured discussion as the best use of the Second Life environment. One participant indicated, "[it was] very hard for me to just sit and listen. If there were more things to do in a virtual world, I would think, yeah, I can totally get into this". Another participant recommended, "go on a virtual tour of what the lecture was about so that we're interacting and engaging. [I] would have liked a lot more interaction".

Comparing 2D and 3D Virtual World Learning Experiences

In regard to 3D versus 2D learning environments, participants tended to prefer 2D contexts. They suggested that seeing a real person rather than an avatar would be preferred. By seeing their classmates and instructor, they could better read non-verbal cues and glean information from others' eye contact and expressions. Some wanted to take it a step further and attend only live classes. One participant noted, "For me it felt a bit less personal than if you used Skype where you can see each other. Even if the avatar had looked like me, I would still have preferred to see the real person".

Application of Second Life to Other Educational Contexts

Most of the participants are working as special education teachers. Although some thought that Second Life would be a good vehicle for virtual tours of content and active learning station activities, there was a significant amount of pushback to the idea of using Second Life with their pupils. The lack of policing of the site (and thus, the potential of stumbling onto adult content or users who are not "G" rated) and the potential for social media problems were frequently sited. One participant said,

With my middle schoolers, we have a lot of social media issues, we would definitely not use this for them. Stranger danger. Get themselves in weird situations. A lot of my students hide behind their virtual identities and say negative things about their peers. If I'm getting bullied, I'm going to bully this random person.

DISCUSSION

The social behavioral changes were dominated by potentially compromising effects, such as decreased honesty, which contradicts previous findings (Green-Hamann et al., 2011; Nussli & Oh, 2017, 2018), and a decreased chance of social politeness (e.g., less likely to apologize). The impersonal environment encouraged some participants to act more inconsiderately than they would have in real life. Some participants feared being misinterpreted, which caused them to avoid humor and minimize their contributions. Again, the virtual environment had a different impact on different learners. Some learners were appreciative of the virtual environment in that they reported feeling more relaxed, more honest, and more open to casual conversations.

The participants' perceptions of the affordances and challenges they experienced during the lectures and discussions were full of tensions. On the one hand, their appreciation for the affordances of virtual interactions confirms previous research, such as the privacy and convenience of participating from home, the use of text chat as an easy-to-use think-and-share, platform highly focused interaction on account of instant feedback, and the individual pace allowing for sufficient think time before responding (Barak & Grohol, 2011; Changrani et al., 2008; Green-Hamann et al., 2011).

On the other hand, their challenges went beyond the scope of typically reported issues, such as technical problems, the skepticism toward using virtual environments for educational purposes, and the distraction due to the background sounds and the rich visual environment (Cheal, 2009; Inman, 2010; Jarmon, Traphagan, Mayrath, & Trivedi, 2009; Storey & Wolf, 2010; Wimpenny, Savin-Baden, Mawer, Steils, & Tomb, 2012). In addition, ineffective pacing (e.g., dead air time, awkward moments of silence, and speaking over each other) and the perception of a virtual discussion as inauthentic interaction were repeatedly mentioned. These concerns may be addressed by redesigning the lecture and discussion format. Rather than providing a teacher-led lecture with incremental discussions, participants might benefit from an exploratory fieldtrip in a VRLE capitalizing the affordances of 3D spaces, followed by a student-led discussion group that takes advantage of the unique 3D communication capabilities.

In studies where communication was limited to text, such as in Green-Hamann et al. (2011), the possibility to write and edit messages before posting them was highly appreciated, which has also been confirmed by the participants in this study. The participants in Green-Hamann et al. (2011) also expressed an appreciation for the nearly synchronous text-chat because these instant messages allow for immediate responses and feedback, which, in turn, potentially increases a sense of presence, cohesion, and engagement (Mount et al., 2009).

The majority of the participants in the present study perceived the mix of multi-modal input from multiple sources with ambivalence, which broadly concurs with the communicative challenges previously reported (Bailenson et al., 2008; Girvan & Savage, 2013; McVey, 2008; Wang et al., 2014). However, this study does not confirm previous research where virtual environments were associated with reduced stressors (Gilbert et al., 2011). In fact, many participants reported feeling increased stress due to the mix of multi-modal input and the open nature of the host's and co-host's questions, similar to what students experienced in a study by Morgan (2013). While some participants reported "feeling like I'm drowning in the ocean", other participants repeatedly expressed their appreciation for being given a choice of communication modalities and apparently used them with relative ease.

The integration of voice clearly emerged as a controversial issue. On the one hand, the simultaneous use of voice and text was perceived as increasing flow, accommodating various learner preferences, making the event more engaging and personal, and allowing for further elaborations that would have gone beyond the limited capabilities of text chat. On the other hand, the integration of voice resulted in increased mental effort due to the need for multitasking and the processing of multiple input channels from multiple speakers. If subtle gestures, such as the visual cues to indicate who is going to speak next, could be mediated in a VRLE, the interaction could be paced more naturally, thus increasing a sense of authenticity and alleviating disengagement and frustration. Konstantinidis, Thrasyvoulos, Theodouli, and Pomportsis (2010), for example, used a tool indicating the current speaker by displaying a circle over the speaker's head. Such a strategy might have helped to address the issue of ineffective pacing.

Repeated practice sessions during which the participants are exposed to multi-modal input as well as introductory activities to help develop a greater awareness of the affordances of using VRLEs for educational purposes might help to address the issues revolving around facilitating a lecture and discussion session in a VRLE.

Limitations

The intervention had several limitations. No comparison was made of the use of SL versus an alternative, such as other semi-immersive desktop VRs (e.g., Active Worlds, OpenSim, ReactionGrid) or a fully immersive VR platform (e.g., OculusRift). Depending on the participants' bandwidth and computer graphic card, technical issues may have arisen that were detrimental to the participants' virtual experience. The results are only true for the 16 participants investigated in this study. As already discussed in the methodology section, reliability was not established for the two single-item rating scales. Finally, due to the short duration of the virtual events, the results of our analyses should be treated with caution. Results might have been quite different if participants had engaged in a series of virtual lecture and discussion events over an extended period of time.

CONCLUSION

In this study, the researchers have explored the participants' perceived behavioral changes experienced during a lecture and discussion set in a desktop VR, the participants' level of satisfaction with a mix of multi-modal input, and their self-reported mental effort. The participants' experiences in this study indicate that in preparing a learning event in a VRLE, educators need to carefully explore the issues that the activity presents for learner engagement (or a lack thereof). While some issues are related to the individual characteristics of the learners, such as a preference for f2f learning or a preference for visual input, other issues are determined by the capabilities of the VRLE (Mount et al., 2009). Educators need to take such issues into account to determine the appropriateness of using a VRLE for a given learning task. For example, developing a clear rationale as to the choice of communication modalities is recommended.

The setup of a virtual discussion should be carefully aligned with the participants' needs and skills. Designing pre-training opportunities for the VRLE interface and processes (Nelson & Erlandson, 2008) helps to acquire a set of critical skills in order to participate effectively in a virtual lecture and discussion. These skills include navigating (e.g., moving one's avatar into the discussion circle), being skilled at using the text chat box (e.g., typing fast, keeping track of incoming posts), using voice with ease, being trained in switching from text to voice, developing the ability to process a mix of multi-modal messages with speed, and developing a sense of social presence. If the notions of synchronicity and immediacy had been emphasized more in the present study, participants might have developed a greater appreciation for the affordances of virtual reality. Lecture slides with limited opportunities for interaction might not be the best use of this technology. A VRLE is better suited for exploration and inquiry. The instructor could move around to different parts of the virtual environment and provide information instead of lecturing in a virtual auditorium.

FUTURE RESEARCH DIRECTIONS

This research has raised many questions in need of further examination. The field of social behavioral changes, for instance, offers an abundance of avenues for future research. It can also be assumed that a discussion group setting in a fully immersive VRLE would reveal different results. To further this research, the authors are planning to explore the impact that the frequency and duration of virtual discussion groups over an extended period of time has on the participants' sense of cohesion, mental effort, and satisfaction. In a similar vein, the participants' experience with virtual reality-based communication and how it affects their satisfaction with the communication modalities could be examined. It is also unclear if it takes expert communicators to make a virtual discussion successful or if repeated exposure would be sufficient to increase the participants' skills and level of satisfaction with an ongoing discussion group. Future studies could target the question whether an exploratory element is crucial to the success of a virtual encounter, such as a fieldtrip to various destinations or a collaborative task requiring avatars to move around and negotiate with each other, or whether a discussion group event can "stand by itself".

In a similar vein, instructional designers and educators need to develop educational content for truly immersive VR platforms. It can be anticipated that an increasing number of schools will be equipped with sophisticated VR kits in the near future. Facebook, for example, has started distributing VR kits to high schools in Arkansas, U.S. (Herold & Molnar, 2018). But educators will be hesitant to buy in to the use of true VR until researchers and practitioners endorse these new technologies for educational use. The use of semi-immersive desktop VR could be a stepping-stone to helping students and instructors become more familiar with the different types of VR systems. Immersion into true VR right away might be too overwhelming for both the participants and instructors.

In conclusion, the prospect of being able to use virtual environments, whether semi- or fully immersive, for educational, collaborative gatherings serves as a continuous incentive for future research.

ACKNOWLEDGMENT

The authors are grateful to Prof. Hajime Nishimura for his kind permission to let the research team use *Science Circle* for the virtual lectures and discussions.

REFERENCES

Ayres, P., & Sweller, J. (2014). The split-attention principle in multimedia learning. In R. E. Mayer (Ed.), *The Cambridge Handbook of Multimedia Learning* (2nd ed.). Cambridge, UK: Cambridge University Press. doi:10.1017/CBO9781139547369.011

Bailenson, J., Yee, N., Blascovich, J., Beall, A., Lundblad, N., & Jin, M. (2008). The use of immersive virtual reality in the learning sciences: Digital transformations of teachers, students, and social context. *Journal of the Learning Sciences*, *17*(1), 102–141. doi:10.1080/10508400701793141

Barak, A., & Grohol, J. M. (2011). Current and future trends in Internet-supported mental health interventions. *Journal of Technology in Human Services*, *29*(3), 155–196. doi:10.1080/15228835.2011.616939

Brünken, R., Seufert, T., & Paas, F. (2010). Measuring cognitive load. In J. L. Plass, R. Moreno, & R. Brünken (Eds.), *Cognitive load theory* (pp. 181–202). Cambridge, UK: Cambridge University Press. doi:10.1017/CBO9780511844744.011

Chandler, P., & Sweller, J. (1992). The split-attention effect as a factor in the design of instruction. *The British Journal of Educational Psychology*, *62*(2), 233–246. doi:10.1111/j.2044-8279.1992.tb01017.x

Changrani, J., Lieberman, M., Golant, M., Rios, P., Damman, J., & Gany, F. (2008). Online cancer support groups: Experiences with underserved immigrant Latinos. *Primary Psychiatry*, *15*(10), 55–62.

Cheal, C. (2009). Student perceptions of a course taught in Second Life. *Innovate: Journal of Online Education, 5*(5), Article 2. Retrieved https://nsuworks.nova.edu/innovate/vol5/iss5/2

Conrad, M. (2011). Leaving the lindens: Teaching in virtual worlds of other providers. In *Proceedings of Researching Learning in Immersive Virtual Environments (ReLIVE): 28*. Milton Keynes, UK: Open University.

Conrad, M., Hassan, A., Koshy, L., Kanamgotov, A., & Christopoulos, A. (2017). Strategies and challenges to facilitate situated learning in virtual worlds post-second life. *Computers in Entertainment, 15*(1). 1–9. doi:10.1145/3010078

Dalgarno, B., Hedberg, J., & Harper, B. (2002). *The contribution of 3D environments to conceptual understanding*. Paper presented at the ASCILITE 2002, Auckland, New Zealand.

Duncan, I. A., Miller, A., & Jiang, S. (2012). A taxonomy of virtual worlds usage in education. *British Journal of Educational Technology*, *43*(6), 949–964. doi:10.1111/j.1467-8535.2011.01263.x

Erlandson, B. E., Nelson, B. C., & Savenye, W. C. (2010). Collaboration modality, cognitive load, and science inquiry learning in virtual inquiry environments. *Educational Technology Research and Development*, *58*(6), 693–710. doi:10.100711423-010-9152-7

Gallego, M. D., Bueno, S., & Noyes, J. (2015). Second Life adoption in education: A motivational model based on uses and gratifications theory. *Computers & Education*, *100*, 81–93. doi:10.1016/j.compedu.2016.05.001

Garrison, D. R. (2009). Communities of inquiry in online learning. In P. L. Rogers (Ed.), *Encyclopedia of distance learning* (2nd ed.; pp. 352–355). Hershey, PA: IGI Global. doi:10.4018/978-1-60566-198-8.ch052

Genome Island in Second Life. (n.d.). Retrieved from http://maps.secondlife.com/secondlife/Genome/128/128/48

Gilbert, R. L., Murphy, N. A., & Avalos, M. C. (2011). Communication patterns and satisfaction levels in three-dimensional versus real-life intimate relationships. *Cyberpsychology, Behavior, and Social Networking*, *14*(10), 585–589. doi:10.1089/cyber.2010.0468 PMID:21381970

Ginns, P., & Barrie, S. (2004). Reliability of single-item ratings of quality in higher education: A replication. *Psychological Reports*, *95*(3), 1023–1030. doi:10.2466/pr0.95.3.1023-1030 PMID:15666951

Girvan, C., & Savage, T. (2013). Guidelines for conducting text based interviews in virtual worlds. In *Understanding learning in virtual worlds* (pp. 21-40). London, UK: Springer-Verlag. doi:10.1007/978-1-4471-5370-2_2

Gopher, D., & Braune, R. (1984). On the psychophysics of workload: Why bother with subjective measures? *Human Factors*, *26*(5), 519–532. doi:10.1177/001872088402600504

Green-Hamann, S., Campbell Eichhorn, K., & Sherblom, J. C. (2011). An exploration of why people participate in Second Life social support groups. *Journal of Computer-Mediated Communication*, *16*(4), 465–491. doi:10.1111/j.1083-6101.2011.01543.x

Hallgren, K. A. (2012). Computing inter-rater reliability for observational data: An overview and tutorial. *Tutorials in Quantitative Methods for Psychology*, *8*(1), 23–24. doi:10.20982/tqmp.08.1.p023 PMID:22833776

Herold, B., & Molnar, M. (2018). Virtual reality for learning raises high hopes and serious concerns. *Education Week*, *37*(20), 10.

Hostetter, C., & Busch, M. (2013). Community matters: Social presence and learning outcomes. *The Journal of Scholarship of Teaching and Learning*, *13*(1), 77–86.

Huang, H.-M., Rauch, U., & Liaw, S.-S. (2010). Investigating learners' attitudes toward virtual reality learning environments: Based on a constructivist approach. *Computers & Education*, *55*(3), 1171–1182. doi:10.1016/j.compedu.2010.05.014

Inman, C. (2010). *Pre-service teachers in Second Life: Are digital natives prepared for a Web 2.0 experience?* (Doctoral Dissertation). Retrieved from ProQuest Dissertation Database.

Jarmon, L., Traphagan, T., Mayrath, M., & Trivedi, A. (2009). Virtual world teaching, experiential learning, and assessment: An interdisciplinary communication course in Second Life. *Computers & Education*, *53*(1), 169–182. doi:10.1016/j.compedu.2009.01.010

Konstantinidis, A., Thrasyvoulos, T., Theodouli, T., & Pomportsis, A. (2010). Fostering collaborative learning in Second Life: Metaphors and affordances. *Computers & Education*, *55*(2), 603–615. doi:10.1016/j.compedu.2010.02.021

Lambert, J. L., & Fisher, J. L. (2013). Community of inquiry framework: Establishing community in an online course. *Journal of Interactive Online Learning, 12*(1), 1–16.

Lee, E. A.-L., & Wong, K. W. (2014). Learning with desktop virtual reality: Low spatial ability learners are more positively affected. *Computers & Education, 79,* 49–58. doi:10.1016/j.compedu.2014.07.010

Mayer, R. E., & Moreno, R. (2003). Nine ways to reduce cognitive load in multimedia learning. *Educational Psychologist, 38*(1), 43–52. doi:10.1207/S15326985EP3801_6

McVey, M. H. (2008). Observations of expert communicators in immersive virtual worlds: Implications for synchronous discussion. *ALT-J. Research in Learning Technology, 16*(3), 173–180. doi:10.3402/rlt. v16i3.10896

Merchant, Z., Goetz, E. T., Cifuentes, L., Keeney-Kennicutt, W., & Davis, T. J. (2014). Effectiveness of virtual reality-based instruction on students' learning outcomes in K-12 and higher education: A meta-analysis. *Computers & Education, 70,* 29–40. doi:10.1016/j.compedu.2013.07.033

Merriam, S. B. (2009). *Qualitative research: A guide to design and implementation.* San Francisco, CA: Jossey-Bass.

Moreno, R., & Mayer, R. E. (2000). A coherence effect in multimedia learning: The case for minimizing irrelevant sounds in the design of multimedia instructional messages. *Journal of Education & Psychology, 92*(1), 117–125. doi:10.1037/0022-0663.92.1.117

Morgan, E. J. (2013). Virtual worlds: Integrating Second Life into the history classroom. *The History Teacher, 46*(4), 547–559.

Mount, N. J., Chambers, C., Weaver, D., & Priestnall, G. (2009). Learner immersion engagement in the 3D virtual world: Principles emerging from the DELVE project. *Innovation in Teaching and Learning in Information and Computer Sciences, 8*(3), 40–55. doi:10.11120/ital.2009.08030040

Nelson, B. C., & Erlandson, B. E. (2008). Managing cognitive load in educational multi-user virtual environments: Reflection on design practice. *Educational Technology Research and Development, 56*(5-6), 619–641. doi:10.100711423-007-9082-1

Nussli, N. (2014). *An investigation of special education teachers' perceptions of the effectiveness of a systematic 7-Step virtual worlds teacher training workshop for increasing social skills (Unpublished doctoral dissertation).* University of San Francisco. Retrieved from http://repository.usfca.edu/diss/113

Nussli, N., & Oh, K. (2017). Field research in Second Life: Strategies for discussion group facilitation and benefits of participation. In G. Panconesi & M. Guida (Eds.), *Handbook of Research on Collaborative Teaching Practice in Virtual Learning Environments* (pp. 348–373). Hershey, PA: IGI Global. doi:10.4018/978-1-5225-2426-7.ch018

Nussli, N., & Oh, K. (2018). Avatar-based group discussions in virtual worlds: Facilitation, communication modalities, & benefits of participation (Book Chapter Enhancement). *International Journal of Virtual and Personal Learning Environments, 8*(1), 1–14. doi:10.4018/IJVPLE.2018010101

Open Simulator. (2018). *Grid list.* Retrieved November 16, 2018 from: http://opensimulator.org/wiki/Grid_List

Paas, F. (1992). Training strategies for attaining transfer of problem-solving skill in statistics: A cognitive load approach. *Journal of Educational Psychology, 84*(4), 429–434. doi:10.1037/0022-0663.84.4.429

Paas, F. G. W. C., Tuovinen, J. E., Tabbers, H., & Van Gerven, P. W. M. (2003). Cognitive load measurement as a means to advance cognitive load theory. *Educational Psychologist, 38*(1), 63–71. doi:10.1207/S15326985EP3801_8

Paas, F. G. W. C., & Van Merriënboer, J. J. G. (1993). The efficiency of instructional conditions: An approach to combine mental-effort and performance measures. *Human Factors, 35*(4), 737–743. doi:10.1177/001872089303500412

Paas, F. G. W. C., & Van Merriënboer, J. J. G. (1994). Variability of worked examples and transfer of geometrical problem solving skills: A cognitive-load approach. *Journal of Educational Psychology, 86*(1), 122–133. doi:10.1037/0022-0663.86.1.122

Plass, J. L., Moreno, R., & Brünken, R. (Eds.). (2010). *Cognitive load theory.* Cambridge, UK: Cambridge University Press. doi:10.1017/CBO9780511844744

Prude, M. A. (2013). A classroom of bunnies, blimps, and werewolves. *ASIANetwork Exchange, 20*(2), 1–12.

Richards, D., & Taylor, M. (2015). A comparison of learning gains when using a 2D simulation tool versus a 3D virtual world: An experiment to find the right representation involving the marginal value theorem. *Computers & Education, 86*, 157–171. doi:10.1016/j.compedu.2015.03.009

Rogers, E. (1967). *Diffusion of innovations.* New York, NY: Free Press.

Science Circle in Second Life. (n.d.). Retrieved from http://maps.secondlife.com/secondlife/The%20Science%20Circle/188/64/56

Slater, M. (2009). Place illusion and plausibility can lead to realistic behaviour in immersive virtual environments. *Philosophical Transactions of the Royal Society of London. Series B, Biological Sciences, 364*(1535), 3549–3557. doi:10.1098/rstb.2009.0138 PMID:19884149

Sploland in Second Life. (n.d.). Retrieved from http://maps.secondlife.com/secondlife/sploland/128/128/28

Storey, V. A., & Wolf, A. A. (2010). Utilizing the platform of Second Life to teach future educators. *International Journal of Technology in Teaching and Learning, 6*(1), 58–70.

Sweller, J. (1988). Cognitive load during problem solving: Effects on learning. *Cognitive Science, 12*(2), 257–285. doi:10.120715516709cog1202_4

Sweller, J. (1999). *Instructional design in technical areas.* Camberwell, Australia: ACER Press.

Sweller, J. (2005). Implications of cognitive load theory for multimedia learning. In R. E. Mayer (Ed.), *The Cambridge handbook of multimedia learning* (pp. 19–30). New York, NY: Cambridge University Press. doi:10.1017/CBO9780511816819.003

Sweller, J., Ayres, P., & Kalyuga, S. (2011). *Cognitive load theory*. New York, NY: Springer. doi:10.1007/978-1-4419-8126-4

Tax'en, G., & Naeve, A. (2002). A system for exploring open issues in VR-based education. *Computers & Graphics*, *26*(4), 593–598. doi:10.1016/S0097-8493(02)00112-7

Virtual Reality Society. (2018). *Semi-immersive virtual reality environments*. Retrieved Nov. 15, 2018 from: https://www.vrs.org.uk/virtual-reality-environments/semi-immersive.html

Wang, C. X., Anstadt, S., Goldman, J., & Lefaiver, M. L. M. (2014). Facilitating group discussions in Second Life. *MERLOT Journal of Online Learning and Teaching*, *10*(1), 139–152.

Wei, C.-W., Chen, N.-S., & Kinshuk, S. (2012). A model for social presence in online classrooms. *Educational Technology Research and Development*, *60*(3), 529–545. doi:10.100711423-012-9234-9

Wigert, B., de Vreede, G., Boughzala, I., & Bououd, I. (2012). The role of the facilitator in virtual world collaboration. *Journal of Virtual Worlds Research*, *5*(2), 1–18. doi:10.4101/jvwr.v5i2.6225

Wimpenny, K., Savin-Baden, M., Mawer, M., Steils, N., & Tombs, G. (2012). Unpacking frames of reference to inform the design of virtual world learning in higher education. *Australasian Journal of Educational Technology*, *28*(3), 522–545. doi:10.14742/ajet.848

ADDITIONAL READING

Brünken, R., Plass, J. L., & Leutner, D. (2003). Direct measurement of cognitive load in multimedia learning. *Educational Psychologist*, *38*(1), 53–61. doi:10.1207/S15326985EP3801_7

Gadalla, E., Abosag, I., & Keeling, K. (2016). Second Life as a research environment: Avatar-based focus groups (AFG). *Qualitative Market Research*, *19*(1), 101–114. doi:10.1108/QMR-08-2015-0070

Galley, R., Conole, G., & Alevizou, P. (2014). Community indicators: A framework for observing and supporting community activity on Cloudworks. *Interactive Learning Environments*, *22*(3), 373–395. doi:10.1080/10494820.2012.680965

Grinberg, A. M., Careaga, J. S., Mehl, M. R., & O'Connor, M. F. (2014). Social engagement and user immersion in a socially based virtual world. *Computers in Human Behavior*, *36*, 479–486. doi:10.1016/j.chb.2014.04.008

Hürst, W. O., & Nunez, H. C. (2013). Touch me, tilt me - comparing interaction modalities for navigation in 2D and 3D worlds on mobiles. *Advances in Computer Entertainment -. Lecture Notes in Computer Science*, *8253*, 93–108. doi:10.1007/978-3-319-03161-3_7

Kantanen, H., & Manninen, J. (2016). Hazy boundaries: Virtual communities and research ethics. *Media and Communication*, *4*(4), 86–96. doi:10.17645/mac.v4i4.576

Kawulich, B. B., & D'Alba, A. (2018). Teaching qualitative research methods with Second Life, a 3-dimensional online virtual environment. *Virtual Reality (Waltham Cross)*, 1–10. doi:10.100710055-018-0353-4

Konstantinidis, A. (2017). Using SmallWorlds to enhance social presence, group cohesion, and group identity in an online postgraduate course. In G. Panconesi & M. Guida (Eds.), *Handbook of Research on Collaborative Teaching Practice in Virtual Learning Environments* (pp. 92–110). IGI Global. doi:10.4018/978-1-5225-2426-7.ch005

Konstantinidis, A., & Goria, C. (2016). Cultivating a community of learners in a distance learning post-graduate course for language professionals. In Papadima-Sophocleous, S., Bradley, L., & Thouësny, S. (Eds), CALL communities and culture – short papers from EUROCALL 2016 (pp. 230-236). Research-publishing.net. doi:10.14705/rpnet.2016.eurocall2016.567

Mikropoulos, T. A., & Natsis, A. (2011). Educational virtual environments: A ten-year review of empirical research (1999–2009). *Computers & Education, 56*(3), 769–780. https://doi:10.1016/j.compedu.2010.10.020

Murgado-Armenteros, E. M., Torres-Ruiz, F. J., & Vega-Zamora, M. (2012). Differences between on-line and face to face focus groups, viewed through two approaches. *Journal of Theoretical and Applied Electronic Commerce Research, 7*(2), 73–86. doi:10.4067/S0718-18762012000200008

Nagel, L., Blignaut, A. S., & Cronjé, J. C. (2009). Read-only participants: A case for student communication in online classes. *Interactive Learning Environments, 17*(1), 37–51. doi:10.1080/10494820701501028

Panconesi, G., & Guida, M. (2017). *Handbook of Research on Collaborative Teaching Practice in Virtual Learning Environments* (pp. 1–637). Hershey, PA: IGI Global; doi:10.4018/978-1-5225-2426-7

Ren, Y., Harper, F. M., Drenner, S., Terveen, L., Kiesler, S., Riedl, J., & Kraut, R. E. (2012). Building member attachment in online communities: Applying theories of group identity and interpersonal bonds. *Management Information Systems Quarterly, 36*(3), 841–864. doi:10.2307/41703483

Ridings, C., & Wasko, M. (2010). Online discussion group sustainability: Investigating the interplay between structural dynamics and social dynamics over time. *Journal of the Association for Information Systems, 11*(2), 95–121. doi:10.17705/1jais.00220

Siriaraya, P., & Ang, C. S. (2012). Age differences in the perception of social presence in the use of 3D virtual world for social interaction. *Interacting with Computers, 24*(4), 280–291. doi:10.1016/j.intcom.2012.03.003

Traphagan, T. W., Chiang, Y. V., Chang, H. M., Wattanawaha, B., Lee, H., Mayrath, M. C., ... Resta, P. E. (2010). Cognitive, social and teaching presence in a virtual world and a text chat. *Computers & Education, 55*(3), 923–936. doi:10.1016/j.compedu.2010.04.003

Van Merriënboer, J. J. G., & Sweller, J. (2005). Cognitive load theory and complex learning: Recent developments and future directions. *Educational Psychology Review, 17*(2), 147–171. doi:10.100710648-005-3951-0

Wang, F., & Burton, J. K. (2013). Second Life in education: A review of publications from its launch to 2011. *British Journal of Educational Technology, 44*(3), 357–371. doi:10.1111/j.1467-8535.2012.01334.x

Wigham, C. R., & Chanier, T. (2013). A study of verbal and nonverbal communication in Second Life – the ARCHI21 experience. *ReCALL, 25*(1), 63–84. doi:10.1017/S0958344012000250

Wigham, C. R., & Chanier, T. (2015). Interactions between text chat and audio modalities for L2 communication and feedback in the synthetic world Second Life. *Computer Assisted Language Learning, 28*(3), 260–283. doi:10.1080/09588221.2013.851702

Wilkes, S. F. (2016). Communication modality, learning, and Second Life. In S. Gregory, M. J. W. Lee, B. Dalgarno, & B. Tynan (Eds.), *Learning in virtual worlds: Research and applications* (pp. 43–65). Edmonton, Canada: Athabasca University Press.

KEY TERMS AND DEFINITIONS

Asynchronous: Asynchronous communication happens at different times. A typical example of asynchronous communication and interaction is a discussion board where users contribute their posts at different times.

Communication Modality: Refers to the communication channel in a virtual environment.

Social Cues: Social cues include anything that may humanize communication, that is, make a conversation or discussion more personal and more authentic. Social cues may include smiles, laughs, touch, gestures of politeness, acts of sharing, signs of empathy, etc. Expert communicators are skilled at mediating social cues even in a computer-mediated environment.

Social Presence: Experiencing a sense of presence involves feeling immersed in a computer-mediated environment. The concept of social presence has been associated with satisfaction and a sense of achievement in a virtual learning environment.

Synchronous: An example of synchronous communication is a live online group discussion or a video conference where participants either communicate simultaneously or take turns.

Virtual Discussions in 3D: Individuals gather in a virtual environment for the purposes of discussion. Benefits of participating include, for example, a sense of community, the opportunity to gather with like-minded people regardless of their geographical location, a sense of anonymity, and an increased sense of honesty. Potential limitations involve communicative challenges.

APPENDIX 1: SURVEY 1

Figure 3.

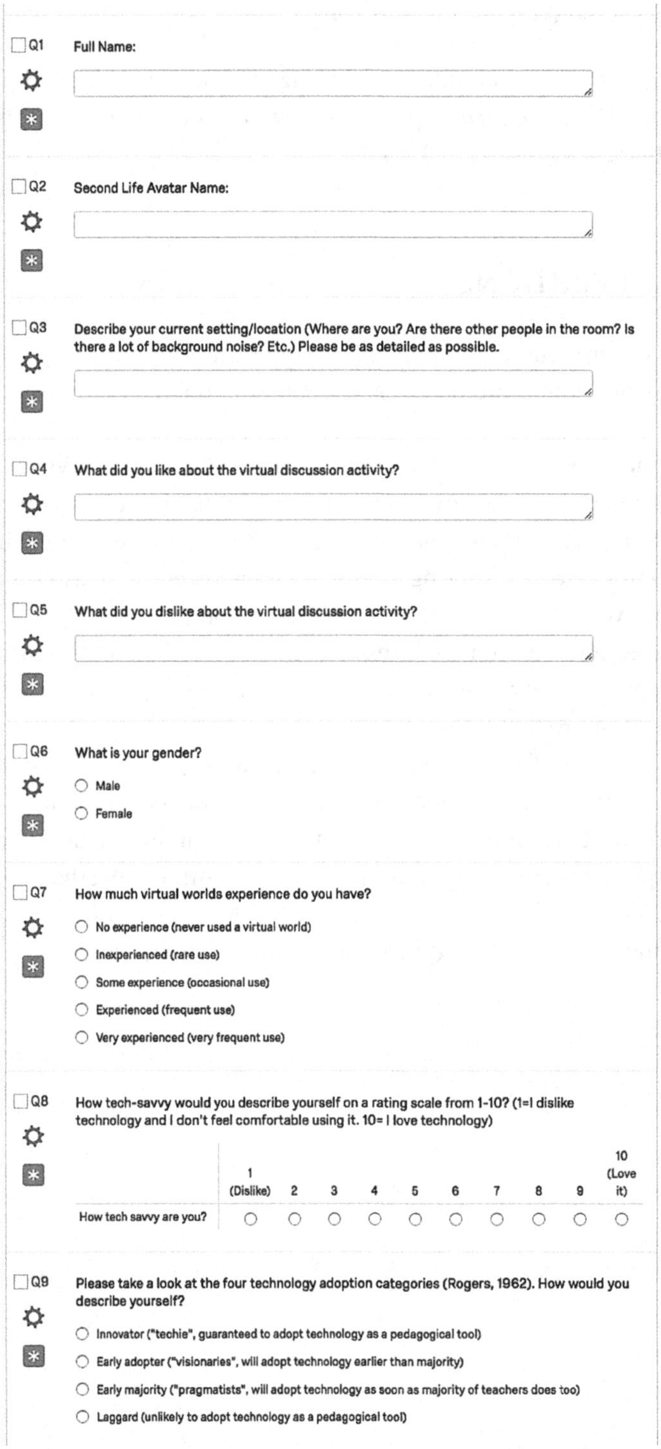

☐ Q1   Full Name:

☐ Q2   Second Life Avatar Name:

☐ Q3   Describe your current setting/location (Where are you? Are there other people in the room? Is there a lot of background noise? Etc.) Please be as detailed as possible.

☐ Q4   What did you like about the virtual discussion activity?

☐ Q5   What did you dislike about the virtual discussion activity?

☐ Q6   What is your gender?
   ○ Male
   ○ Female

☐ Q7   How much virtual worlds experience do you have?
   ○ No experience (never used a virtual world)
   ○ Inexperienced (rare use)
   ○ Some experience (occasional use)
   ○ Experienced (frequent use)
   ○ Very experienced (very frequent use)

☐ Q8   How tech-savvy would you describe yourself on a rating scale from 1-10? (1=I dislike technology and I don't feel comfortable using it. 10= I love technology)

	1 (Dislike)	2	3	4	5	6	7	8	9	10 (Love it)
How tech savvy are you?	○	○	○	○	○	○	○	○	○	○

☐ Q9   Please take a look at the four technology adoption categories (Rogers, 1962). How would you describe yourself?
   ○ Innovator ("techie", guaranteed to adopt technology as a pedagogical tool)
   ○ Early adopter ("visionaries", will adopt technology earlier than majority)
   ○ Early majority ("pragmatists", will adopt technology as soon as majority of teachers does too)
   ○ Laggard (unlikely to adopt technology as a pedagogical tool)

APPENDIX 2: SURVEY 2

Figure 4.

Full Name:

Second Life Avatar Name:

Describe your current setting/location (Where are you? Are there other people in the room? Is there a lot of background noise? Etc.) Please be as detailed as possible.

To which degree were you satisfied with the communication modality in Second Life, that is, the combination of voice and chat?

Extremely Unsatisfied ○ ○ ○ ○ ○ ○ ○ ○ ○ Very Satisfied

Please add your comments about what satisfied or dissatisfied you about the combination of voice and text chat during your time in Second Life. (Response must be at least 4 sentences)

How much mental effort have you expended during the discussion group activity in Second Life?

	Very, very low	Very low	Low	Rather low	Neither low nor high	Rather high	High	Very high	Very, Very high
Mental Effort	○	○	○	○	○	○	○	○	○

Please add your comments about the mental effort you expended during your discussion group activity in Second Life. (Response must be at least 4 sentences)

How did you feel when the discussions were over? (Check all that apply)

- ☐ Stimulated
- ☐ Inspired
- ☐ Overwhelmed
- ☐ Energized

- ☐ Relieved
- ☐ Frustrated
- ☐ Satisfied
- ☐ Exhausted

Figure 5.

Was the discussion a pleasant way to communicate with others? Please explain and provide specific examples. (Response must be at least 4 sentences)

Was it easy or difficult to express in the virtual discussion what you wanted to communicate? Please explain and provide specific examples. (Response must be at least 4 sentences)

Did you notice any changes in your behavior compared with how you would typically behave in a face-to-face discussion? (For example, were you more honest than you would have been in real-life conversation where people know who you are?) Please explain and give examples. (Response must be at least 4 sentences)

Please give examples of your social behavior that may or may not have been different from the real world. (For example, would you have dared to stand up in the middle of the discussion and disappear? Or if you bumped into an avatar, did you apologize, as you would have in real life? Or did you pay someone a compliment?) (Response must be at least 4 sentences)

Please compare the first lecture/discussion event with today's second lecture/discussion event. For example, did it make any difference to you that not only the instructor but also the co-host was using voice today? Did the option of using voice and/or text chat during the discussion make any difference to you? To which extent did today's new seating arrangement influence your interaction with your colleagues, if at all? (Response must be at least 4 sentences)

APPENDIX 3: FOCUS GROUP PROMPTS

Main Prompts

1. What impact did the 3D setting have on your experience compared to a regular two-dimensional text-based discussion forum?

2. How would you use the two communication modalities (voice and text chat) if you were facilitating a discussion in a virtual world?

3.   How could this event be modified in order to make it feel more like a "conversation"? How could it be modified to feel more authentic, inclusive, and engaging?

4.   What was the impact of using an avatar and being heard but not seen in the second discussion/lecture event?

5.   How could the discussion group format in a 3D virtual world be used to support learning, if at all?

6.   If you were designing a synchronous virtual learning environment, what would you include (or exclude) to optimize the experience for learners? Think both about lecture and discussion activities.

7.   What were the factors that affected your comfort level while participating in the virtual discussions? Please explain.

Prompts to Clarify or Elicit Greater Depth of Discussion

8.   Why was the experience hard/easy, frustrating/satisfying/etc.?

9.   What could be done differently next time?

10.   How might you adapt this experience for use with your own students?

11.   What could have made the experience more engaging/successful/effective/interactive/authentic/conversational/etc.?

12.   If you were the instructional designer for a lesson like the ones you participated in, how would you create the activities and what might they include?

13.   Was the difficulty/benefit more due to the learning curve or the whole experience/etc.?

14.   Would more training/experience in virtual world navigation have helped? If so, what and how?

Chapter 6

To Move or Not to Move?
The Challenge of Including Believable Self–Motion Cues in Virtual Reality Applications – Understanding Motion Cueing Generation in Virtual Reality

Sergio Casas
https://orcid.org/0000-0002-0396-4628
Universitat de València, Spain

Cristina Portalés
Universitat de València, Spain

Marcos Fernández
Universitat de València, Spain

EXECUTIVE SUMMARY

This chapter deals with the problem of including motion cues in VR applications. From the challenges of this technology to the latest trends in the field, the authors discuss the benefits and problems of including these particular perceptual cues. First, readers will know how motion cues are usually generated in simulators and VR applications in general. Then, the authors list the major problems of this process and the reasons why its development has not followed the pace of the rest of VR elements (mainly the display technology), reviewing the motion vs. no-motion question from several perspectives. The general answer to this discussion is that motion cues are necessary in VR applications—mostly vehicle simulators—that rely on motion, although, unlike audio-visual cues, there can be specific considerations for each particular solution that may suggest otherwise. Therefore, it is of the utmost importance to analyze the requirements of each VR application before deciding upon this question.

DOI: 10.4018/978-1-5225-5912-2.ch006

INTRODUCTION

Virtual Reality (VR) could be defined as the process, means and technologies by which one or several individuals experience the sensation of belonging to an alternative reality that is not the one they are actually living in (Casas, Portalés, Vera, & Riera, 2019). This alternative synthetic reality needs to be believable enough so that suitable deceptions of reality are created and accepted as real by the participants. As a complete recreation is sometimes impossible – or even undesirable because the simulated actions could be in some occasions harmful -, it is often acceptable that the perception of belonging to the virtual world be only partial. Nevertheless, although it is not necessary that the recreated virtual reality be indistinguishable from the real one, it is sensible to think that the more perceptual cues are generated by the VR application - generated to deceive the human senses - the better for the sense of immersion.

Therefore, VR applications need to deceive human senses by generating visual, sound, haptic, tactile, and even olfactive or gustatory perceptual cues (Casas, Portalés, García-Pereira, & Fernández, 2017). However, humans have a sixth sense that is often neglected: the capacity to perceive our own motion, which is called kinaesthesia and is mostly (but not exclusively!) captured by the vestibular human system (the whole perception mechanism is not completely understood). This perceptual cue is very important in many VR applications, such as vehicle simulators, but it is, more often than not, forgotten in VR solutions for a variety of reasons. Motion cues are introduced in VR as a way to make the user perceive self-motion that is compatible with their navigation within the virtual world. This is usually accomplished by means of robotic devices that are synchronized with the rest of the VR application software. These devices physically move the VR users so that their experience is consistent with the virtual world depiction. In the case of vehicle simulators, which are, by far, the most commonly use case for motion-based VR applications, these robotic devices consist of motion platforms that move the user's seat according to the movement of the virtual vehicle they are controlling in the virtual world (Reymond & Kemeny, 2000). Treadmills and walking simulators are a different type of device, since they do not move the user but allow them to move somehow freely, so that their navigation is more natural. Unlike motion platforms, which have been used for decades, these virtual walking devices represent a new and interesting research area that is also worth studying.

Contrary to what most people think, VR is not a new technology. There are records of primitive flight simulators as early as 1910 (Allerton, 2009; Page, 2000), although the consideration of these early devices as VR applications is arguable. Only after microcomputers started to be used to create synthetic virtual environments – during the 1970s and 1980s - could these applications be considered true VR systems.

Indeed, the development of VR applications in the last twenty years has been magnificent, especially due to the rapid development of visual techniques and display hardware, such as cheap graphic cards with parallel GPU-based processing power, real-time realistic visualization software, VR-glasses, projectors, stereographic systems, realistic vehicle models, etc. (Boletsis, 2017; Garrett & Best, 2010). Unfortunately, motion generation systems have not followed this pace. Despite of a huge reduction in the price and cost of robotic motion platforms in the last decades, the algorithms, the methods and the problems have not changed much since the first motion-based VR applications were developed in the 1960s and 1970s (Casas, Coma, Riera, & Fernández, 2015) and the motion cueing problem remains the subject of much discussion (Garrett & Best, 2010). The reasons for this apparent relative lack of substantial progress have prompted the proposal of this chapter.

This chapter has three major goals. First, the authors will briefly explain how to generate self-motion cues in VR applications. Second, the chapter will analyse the factors that lead many VR systems to neglect the necessity of this kind of perceptual cues. Finally, the motion versus no-motion question will be discussed, trying to offer a broad perspective of the situation.

The first goal includes explaining the process by which motion cues are generated, emphasizing the points that pose challenges and problems: cost increase, physical space, the high complexity of the algorithms that are designed to control this process, motion sickness, parameter tuning and the difficulty of assessing the effectiveness of the solution, either objectively or subjectively.

The second goal deals with the apparent contradiction by which many certification standards require motion-based systems for some training simulators (DNV, 2011; ICAO, 2009), but many VR applications refuse to include these solutions. The reasons are thought to be mainly economic but a deeper analysis also reveals other reasons such as the impossibility to clearly know if the inclusion of these motion cues is beneficial for the objectives of the VR application being developed.

Finally, and related with the previous issue, the chapter will discuss and review some research works that have tried to clarify if motion-based VR applications are a better option than fixed-based VR applications. This obviously depends on the particular goal the application is targeted at, but there are a number of broad considerations that can be taken into account. Some researchers have studied the problem for some different case studies, and the chapter will try to analyse this topic, so that readers, practitioners and future researchers know the advantages and disadvantages of this technology and can identify if motion cueing is a valid option for a particular VR case study.

BACKGROUND

Motion Cueing Generation

There are many types of VR applications with different purposes and objectives. Therefore, the different set-ups of a VR application can be very dissimilar. However, one key aspect of VR is the ability of the user (or users) to interact with the virtual world and move freely inside this synthetic world (Boletsis, 2017). In this regard, it is perfectly understandable that a well-designed VR system needs to make the user feel the sense of motion if the user decides to move. However, motion can be generated in several ways and therefore two main scenarios can be identified depending on how the user moves through the virtual world.

When motion is simultaneously performed *in situ* and *in silico* (in the real and in the virtual world), like in a VR setup with a head-mounted display where the user is actually moving in the real world (usually by walking), the challenge is to translate this motion *in situ* to the virtual world, so that the visual perception of motion is consistent with the actual motion (Boletsis, 2017). This problem does not pose a significant challenge with state-of-the-art technology, which is capable of performing accurate tracking of a person's movements. The only (important) limitation is that the available workspace is usually small due to wire length, wireless signal power constraints and actual physical space in the simulator facilities. In recent years, a number of creative locomotion solutions have been proposed to overcome this limitation. Treadmills and walk-through simulators (Anthes, García-Hernández, Wiedemann, & Kranzlmüller, 2016; Callaghan, Eguíluz, McLaughlin, & McShane, 2015; Infinadeck, 2017; Janeh et al., 2017; Virtuix, 2017) are getting more and more important, since natural interfaces are much more immersive than a joystick or a mouse. The ability to move around the virtual world just as you would do it in the real world creates a compelling sensation that enhances realism and makes VR applications reach a higher level of immersion. In this type of VR application, no additional self-motion cues need to be generated since the user is actually moving in the real world and would feel his/her own motion.

On the contrary, when motion is performed *in silico* but not *in situ*, like in a vehicle simulator where the user actuates pedals, levers or steering wheels but they do not actually move in the real world, the VR system needs to find a way to deceive human senses so that the brain believes that actual motion is happening. This problem represents the opposite situation compared with the former idea: motion has to be first recreated in the virtual world (simulating the effects of the user's actions in the virtual vehicle, for instance) and later translated from the virtual world to the real world. Of course, the creation of actual motion (or at least actual motion cues) is much more complicated than the creation of virtual motion *in silico*. Therefore, this problem is much more challenging. The process by which this motion cueing generation is implemented can be summarized in Figure 1. This diagram shows how to generate self-motion cues in vehicle simulators. This kind of simulators represent the most common VR set-up in which motion cues are required. Although this scheme could be varied and this is just a possible approximation, a brief survey over the state-of-the-art reflects that this, with small variations, is the process that vehicle simulators use to generate motion cues.

The centre of the process is, of course, the user (also known as pilot, driver or vehicle operator depending on the type of vehicle). The user controls the virtual motion by actually moving the vehicle controls located in a reproduction of the vehicle cockpit. The cockpit serves also to provide information about this virtual motion by means of real or virtual gauges that communicate several aspects of the state of

Figure 1. Scheme for the generation of motion cues in vehicle simulators

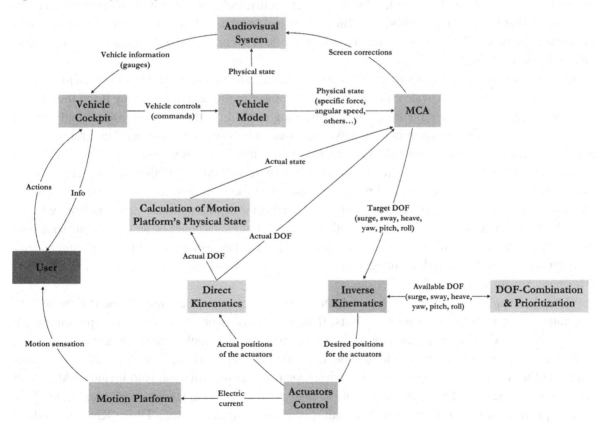

the vehicle (speedometer, revolution counter, fuel indicator, etc.). The actions of the user feed a vehicle model, which reproduces *in silico* the behaviour of the vehicle. In other words, this model simulates the motion of the vehicle by solving numerically the differential equations of the laws of physics (Witkin & Baraff, 1997), as explained in previous research (Casas et al., 2012; Filipczuk & Nikiel, 2008). This data is used to update the visual information and also to create sound cues that are consistent with this motion.

Up to this point, no *in situ* motion has been generated in the real world. Motion is only virtual and its perception is purely audio-visual. Therefore, these three modules represent the most basic setup where only audio-visual information is generated. Most vehicle simulators choose to stick with this setup because it is simple, relatively cheap and most of the perceptual cues are generated by means of audio-visual content.

However, if motion cues have to be included in the simulator, additional modules are needed (depicted in blue in Figure 1). First, a Motion Cueing Algorithm (MCA) is needed. This algorithm takes the physical state of the simulated vehicle (acceleration, speed, specific force, angular speed, etc.) and uses this information to calculate the pose (position plus orientation) of the motion device (the motion platform). In most of the motion systems, the pose of the motion platform needs to be translated to actual displacement of the actuators that control its motion. Therefore, the Inverse Kinematics (IK) problem (Casas, Coma, Portalés, & Fernández, 2017) needs to be solved to convert these desired poses (DOF) into linear or angular displacements of the actuators. This step depends much on the particular shape, type and construction of the motion platform. In fact, in some designs, the desired DOF may not be reachable and need to be limited or combined so they can fit into the physical constraints of the motion platform. This is represented by the "DOF-Combination and Prioritization" module. The literature of the problem does not usually consider this module explicitly, but in some way or another, it has to be included so that the actuators do not reach their limits and break out. Several mitigation strategies can be applied (Schwarz, 2007), although the most simple rule is to combine the different DOF proportionally to the desired value.

Once the desired positions of the actuators are calculated, a low-level control layer is used to perform the final step, which is to provide enough mechanical power to the actuators so they reach their target positions quickly but at the same time without suffering instability. The control system finally makes the motion platform move, which in turn, makes the user feel self-motion. Low-level control strategies are of the utmost importance, since they represent the layer upon everything else is applied. As control problems have been thoroughly studied for decades and there are several solutions to correctly solve it, this module is often neglected in motion cueing studies that focus on high-level strategies (the MCA). However, there are researchers that acknowledge that treating the control module as a separate one without considering possible complex interactions with higher-level modules could be an oversimplification of the problem. The same can be applied to the software and hardware elements, which are usually dealt with separately. In this regard, an integrated design of the software and hardware has been proposed (Hosman, Advani, & Haeck, 2002).

Other VR applications different than vehicle simulators can also use this scheme if they need to generate motion cues from the user's actions. If no vehicle is involved, the module representing the vehicle cockpit would be eliminated or replaced, but the rest of modules could be perfectly suitable. In this regard, this pipeline of modules can be, of course, modified, although it serves as a good reference point for the generation of self-motion cues. One possible modification is to include a MCA that not only takes the virtual physical state of the vehicle as input, but also the actual physical state of the motion platform *in situ*. This is rarely done, but it is a possibility. To do so, a Direct Kinematics (DK) module is necessary to convert actuators' motion into the actual pose of the motion platform expressed as actual DOF. This pose allows to calculate the actual physical state of the motion platform, which might be used by the MCA to slow down motion if the limits of the device are expected to be reached (Casas, Olanda, & Dey, 2017).

However, as aforementioned, MCA are usually oblivious not only of the state of the motion platform, but also of the type and parameters of this physical device. There are good reasons to separate the motion algorithms (MCA) from the motion devices (motion platform hardware). This decision makes MCA more general, universal (usable with any motion platform), easier to understand, implement and design but also harder to optimally tune them for each particular situation, since it is impossible for the MCA to enforce physical limits that are unknown for the algorithm (Colombet et al., 2008).

Motion Cueing Algorithms

There are many MCA in the literature. The objective of this chapter, however, is not to review them in detail. Good literature reviews on the topic can be found in other research papers (Casas, Olanda et al., 2017; Garrett & Best, 2010; Stahl, Abdulsamad, Leimbach, & Vershinin, 2014). In short, most of these MCA are designed upon three basic principles (Reid & Nahon, 1985; Reymond & Kemeny, 2000). The first idea is actually very simple. As actual movement *in situ* is usually not feasible (due to lack of power by the actuators, not enough physical space in the simulator facilities, etc.) and sometimes even undesirable (unexpected sharp motion could be harmful or dangerous in certain situations), the most natural solution is to downscale the motion signals by a factor lower than unity. For rotational motion, this strategy could be enough, since some vehicles have physical limits that make large rotations impossible or very unlikely (think about a car, which is not expected to roll or pitch more than a few tens of degrees unless it overturns). The rationale behind this strategy is that it is expected that the human motion perception system would accept motion that is correlated with the rest of the perceptual inputs (mostly visual inputs) even if the scale of this motion does not completely match in the different perceptual channels. The amount of downscale that can be successfully applied (i.e. without making the brain aware of this difference) is unknown, but recent experiments suggest that correlation is one of the main indicators of properly generated motion (Casas et al., 2015).

However, translational motion cannot be handled with just this scaling strategy, as the virtual vehicle could move several orders of magnitude further than the actual *in situ* available space. Therefore, the second idea is to eliminate the acceleration signals that lead to sustainable displacements. This is usually accomplished by applying high-pass filters to the acceleration signals. This way, low-frequency accelerations, which are responsible for sustainable motion, are removed. Of course, this reduces the *physical validity* of the resulting self-motion cues (Reymond & Kemeny, 2000), but increases the chances that the *perceptual validity* is improved given the physical constraints of the problem. In order to increase this perceptual validity, in an attempt to restore the perception of the low-frequency accelerations removed earlier, most MCA make use of the so-called *tilt-coordination* technique (Groen & Bles, 2004). Tilt-coordination is a deception method by which a small and slow tilt is performed on the motion platform to induce the perception of sustainable motion (low-frequency accelerations). It is based on the fact that the brain can sometimes confuse a small tilt by a sustainable acceleration. This is called the *somatogravic illusion* (Berger, Schulte-Pelkum, & Bülthoff, 2010; MacNeilage, Banks, Berger, & Bulthoff, 2007) and allows to increase the perceptual validity of the simulator without compromising the physical limits of the motion platform. MCA usually apply this technique by mean of low-pass filters that identify possible sustainable movements that are going to be eliminated by the high-pass filters. These low-pass filters feed a tilt-coordination solver that adds the result directly to the pitch and roll DOF of the motion platform (this idea cannot be applied to yaw motion since the trick uses gravity to confuse the user and yaw motion is applied on an axis parallel to gravity).

One of the effects of these filters is that they make the motion platform go back to the neutral/central position once motion input is zero. This effect is known as *washout*. Hence, those MCA that perform these operations are usually known as *washout filters* (Reid & Nahon, 1985). Although not all the MCA use all these three ideas, most of them do. Therefore the term washout filter and MCA are usually confused, which is not correct since there are MCA that do not rely on washout filters. Examples of MCA are the classical washout algorithm, the adaptive algorithm, the optimal control algorithm, and the Model Predictive Control (MPC) algorithm (Dagdelen, Reymond, Kemeny, Bordier, & Maizi, 2009; Nahon & Reid, 1990; Nahon, Reid, & Kirdeikis, 1992; Salisbury & Limebeer, 2016). These four strategies are the most commonly used in motion cueing. MPC represents the latest trend in the field (Bruschetta, Maran, & Beghi, 2017; Mohammadi, Asadi, Mohamed, Nelson, & Nahavandi, 2016), and although some researchers claim that the algorithm outperforms the others, this is something that it has been stated for almost of the solutions that have been proposed.

The Classical Washout

Figure 2 shows the operation of the classical washout algorithm as depicted in (Reid & Nahon, 1985, 1986a, 1986b). Despite being a thirty-year old reference, this is the *de facto* standard scheme in the field,

Figure 2. Scheme of the classical washout algorithm

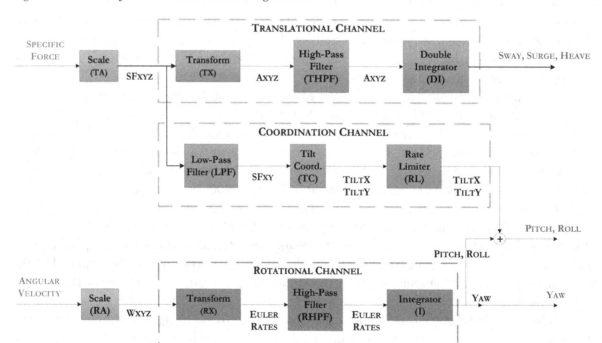

since it is fairly easy to implement and tune for a human expert. The algorithm works by means of three separate motion channels: a translation channel, a tilt coordination channel and a rotational channel. The inputs to the classical washout are the linear specific force and the angular velocity of the virtual vehicle (in body frame). The output is the desired 6-component pose {sway, surge, heave, yaw, pitch, roll} for the motion platform.

The translational channel implements the high-pass filtering. It is composed of a translational amplifier (TA), which downscales the input; a translational transformation (TX), which is used to convert the input to a world-frame reference system; a high pass-filter (THPF) and a double integrator (DI) to provide X, Y, Z displacements (Casas, Coma, Portalés, & Fernández, 2016).

The coordination channel implements the tilt-coordination technique. The process is composed of the same downscale module (TA) as in the previous channel; a low-pass filter (LPF) in order to remove high-frequency components that would have been fed to the previous channel; a tilt coordination (TC) module, which converts acceleration into pitch and roll tilt; and a rate-limiter (RL) to smooth the output.

The rotational channel works like the translational channel but operates with angular velocities instead of specific forces and accelerations (that explains why the integrator is not a double integrator in this channel). The pitch and roll output is combined with the output of the tilt-coordination channel, while yaw is directly an output of the MCA. With the exception of the MPC that uses a different approach, the rest of the MCA follow most of the principles shown here, using filters and signal reducers.

MAIN FOCUS OF THIS CHAPTER

Research Questions and Research Methods

As aforementioned, one of the goals of this chapter is to perform a critical review of the works in the literature that deal with the question of identifying evidences that support or refuse the idea of introducing motion cueing devices and motion cueing algorithms in vehicle simulators and VR applications in general. First, the authors will identify the problems and challenges of motion cueing, which cause that these solutions be absent in some VR setups, and then the motion versus no motion question will be reviewed and discussed. The research question is thus: Are motion cues necessary in VR applications?

The review will be critical because it does not only mention the different works that have analysed this problem but tries to offer also answers and explanations to the different issues in this matter, given the different results observed in the literature of this area.

The methodology relies on a targeted review with a non-systematic in-depth approach to this specific research question. The authors have gathered all the research papers they have found dealing with the following terms: "motion cueing", "motion drive algorithm", "washout filter", "motion fidelity", "motion-based simulation", "motion simulator" and "simulation delay", discarding those that do not discuss about the suitability of using this kind of techniques in VR applications or that do not allow to discuss about the problems and challenges that are sometimes used to justify why some VR designers do not include motion cues in their systems. Since the research question is rather general and involves multiple aspects (simulator sickness, motion hardware, delays, tuning, perception, presence, motion fidelity, etc.) the authors have relied on a knowledgeable selection of high-quality papers, rather than using a systematic literature review process in which all manuscripts are considered equally valuable.

Challenges of Motion Cueing

There are several factors that could hinder and sometimes make it impossible to generate suitable motion cues in VR applications. This section describes the problems and challenges that are used to justify (sometimes faithfully, sometimes not) why some VR designers "forget" about motion cues.

The first one is obvious: virtual motion is unbounded - since it only takes to change a mathematical model - but actual motion has physical limits, since the simulator needs a particular facility with a limited physical space. This space is sometimes several orders of magnitude smaller than the actual motion (depending on the simulated entity and the simulation facility) (Hosman, 1999) and therefore simulators need to find a way to map unbounded virtual motion into constrained real motion. As readers may understand, there is no easy solution for this issue and, as a general rule, any solution that can be proposed should be considered suboptimal since a perfect match between virtual and real motion is impossible.

The second problem is that virtual accelerations can be as high as needed. On the contrary, actual motion devices have a limited power, more often than not much smaller than the entity being simulated, and therefore it is sometimes impossible to match the virtual motion reproduced by the VR application. However, even if the accelerations could be physically reproduced, they may not always be desirable since they could be dangerous (as in a collision). A key aspect in simulation is to keep users safer than in a real experiment. Therefore, in some occasions it is preferable not to fully recreate the effects of a real accident, for instance.

The third problem is related with the perception of motion. As a one-to-one motion reproduction is not feasible or desirable, motion-based VR systems are usually designed to create motion that is perceptually equivalent to the simulated one (or at least close to it). This is referred to as perceptual validity in the literature as opposed to physical validity, which is both generally unfeasible and occasionally undesirable as explained earlier, and to *behavioural validity* (Reymond & Kemeny, 2000), which could be important for pilot control behaviour in vehicle simulators where the goal is to train pilots/drivers for a particular task. The problem is that perception mechanisms are both not completely known and suffer from inter-individual differences. In addition, there are certain persons that get sick when they experiment a motion-based VR application (Kolasinski, 1995). Simulator sickness is a common problem in vehicle simulators. Although it is widely believed that motion-based simulators decrease the possibility of people suffering simulator sickness, some researchers suggest that this is not true (Wentink, Valente Pais, Mayrhofer, Feenstra, & Bles, 2008) while others report a decrease in simulator sickness (Curry, Artz, Cathey, Grant, & Greenberg, 2002; Klüver, Herrigel, Preuß, Schöner, & Hecht, 2015). A sensible conclusion is that the inclusion of motion cues should reduce the discrepancies between the different human perception systems (visual, vestibular, tactile, etc.) if they are properly generated. However, it is not unreasonable to think that false motion cues (caused by poor motion cueing) increase the possibility of motion sickness. As false motion cues may be related with small cheap and not powerful motion devices, the economic aspects could be crucial.

Fourth, motion platforms are expensive devices. Therefore, their use needs to be fully justified because they can raise the cost of a VR system by a great amount (Casas, Fernández, & Riera, 2017). This is probably the main reason why many VR applications do not include motion cueing in their setups. Working with simulated motion platforms (Casas, Olanda, Fernandez, & Riera, 2012) could help reducing costs by identifying potential mistakes and optimizing the device prior to its construction, but the final device needs to be physically built and could be unaffordable depending on the requirements of the device.

Finally, the algorithms that control these processes are hard to implement and tune. They require expert technicians and it is still unknown which algorithm is the best one. This is a consequence of the subjectivity of the problem that makes this task hard to assess. Some automatic tuning systems have been proposed recently (Asadi, Mohamed, Rahim Zadeh, & Nahavandi, 2015; Asadi et al., 2016; Casas et al., 2016; Casas, Portalés, Coma, & Fernández, 2017; Mohammadi et al., 2016), but they rely on objective motion fidelity indicators that are not universally accepted. Nevertheless, objective motion cueing metrics are gaining importance with several works trying to provide a standard way to assess these algorithms (Advani, Hosman, & Potter, 2007; Hosman & Advani, 2016; ICAO, 2009; Stroosma, Van Paassen, Mulder, Hosman, & Advani, 2013). Most of these works are focused on flight simulation but recent approaches have tried to incorporate these techniques also to other vehicle simulators (Fischer, Seefried, & Seehof, 2016). This objective assessment method seems to represent a promising trend in the field.

In addition, there are several things in the scheme depicted in Figure 1 that can go wrong when generating motion cues in VR:

- The vehicle model could be inaccurate. Therefore, the user may notice that the generated motion does not correspond with the expected one. In this case, as the visual perception of motion would be inaccurate too, only expert users could be able to tell the difference.
- IK could have indeterminate forms and singular points where the solution is unusable. Therefore, it is important to be sure that this formulation is properly solved so that it can be known for sure the correspondence between DOF and actuators displacements.
- Most motion platforms rely on parallel designs due to its superior payload (Küçük, 2012). However, parallel robots have limited workspaces. Therefore, DOF combination often results in a downscale of the DOF petition. Even a clever implementation of the DOF combination module could not be enough to tackle this problem. Thus, physical and perceptual validity could be severely compromised depending on the type of motion platform used.
- The actuators' control algorithms are not always prepared for varying situations. The tuning of the control algorithms are often performed with some set of predefined signals and it is not easy to make them behave properly for different uses.
- The MCA itself may be underusing the workspace of the motion platform or may be badly tuned and make the hardware reach its limits creating false cues.
- Finally, the motion platform itself may not be appropriate for the application. Most of them are heavy machines with large inertias. Therefore, the delay between visual and actual motion could be high. Some researchers have tried to identify a maximum limit for motion delays so that perception, pilot control behaviour, performance and training transference are properly achieved (Bailey, Knotts, Horowitz, & Malone, 1987; Frank, Casali, & Wierwille, 1988).

All these causes, and some others, have reduced the availability of motion generation systems in VR applications. However, the main concern is usually the price. Most of these systems are very expensive. Therefore, if there are not strong evidences supporting that the inclusion of motion cues is decisive and budget restrictions are a factor (and they usually are), simulator designers leave them aside. However, although the economic aspects hinder the widespread use of this technology, if a universally accepted solution were found, the economic issue would play a much more minor role. If a technology is expensive but effective, the market usually finds a way to make it mainstream. On the contrary, if it is expensive but suffers from the aforementioned problems, its deployment could be much slower.

However, several organizations and standards require that (mostly training) simulators include proper motion cues for them to apply for an official certification (DNV, 2011; ICAO, 2009). This poses an apparent contradiction: certification requires motion-based systems but most simulators are not motion-based. This just reflects the current situation of VR systems with respect to this issue: motion cues are considered necessary but the cost of recreating them properly could be so high that it does not sometimes pay off in terms of investment-reward ratio. The chapter dive into this question in the next section.

To Move or Not to Move? That Is the Question

The fact that many VR applications that may benefit from motion cueing do not include this kind of perceptual cue raises an immediate question. Are they really necessary?

Of course, the answer really depends on what motion cues are needed for. From a purely perceptual point of view, the answer is undoubtedly yes. If the VR application wants to reach the maximum perceptual validity (it is assumed that physical validity is impossible to achieve in a general case because of the inherent physical restrictions of the simulator), these perceptual cues have to be included one way or another, since they are present in a real situation.

However, from different – more pragmatic - points of view the answer could be not as clear, or can be even a no. Motion generation systems are expensive. In some situations, they can be as expensive as the rest of elements in the simulator (Casas, Fernández et al., 2017). Low-cost solutions exist and are an alternative, but for some simulators this may not be an option. It is important to take into account that even 6-DOF systems do not offer solutions that can be considered physically valid. Therefore, reduced-DOF solutions could have an even more limited performance. The literature in this point is controversial, since the 6-DOF Stewart-Gough hexapod is considered the *de facto* solution, but some works have shown that limited-DOF solutions could provide a similar performance at a fraction of a cost (Casas et al., 2015; Pouliot, Gosselin, & Nahon, 1998), reaching a seeming contradiction. If limited-DOF solutions are by definition less powerful than 6-DOF solutions, but they do not behave significantly worse than 6-DOF solutions, there are two possible explanations: either the elimination of DOF is not critical (which seems quite counterintuitive), or perhaps 6-DOF are not performing well and the difference between the different solutions is small because they are both underperforming. The authors believe that this second idea explains the results of some experiments that compare limited-DOF solutions versus the reference 6-DOF solution, such as (Pouliot et al., 1998).

The motion versus not motion question has been analysed in the past by several researchers (Bertollini, Glase, Szczerba, & Wagner, 2014; Colombet et al., 2008; Reid & Nahon, 1988; Watson, 2000). These studies try to establish, among several other issues, if motion-based simulators provide significant advantages over fixed-base simulators, so that the cost of the motion generation system pays off. Of course, to answer this question it is necessary first to define a criterion by which motion cueing is considered useful.

From a perceptual point of view, the general answer is yes, users prefer verbally motion-based simulators and simulator fidelity rates increase with the inclusion of motion (Bertollini et al., 2014; Grant, Yam, Hosman, & Schroeder, 2006; Hall, 1989; Reid & Nahon, 1988). It is therefore generally accepted that perceived realism is enhanced when motion cues are properly included in a simulator. However, it is important to emphasize that these works do not generally analyse the conditions under which motion-based simulators are preferred over fixed-based simulators. Since the performance of motion platforms and MCA could be very different for different vehicles, virtual environments and motion platforms, it would be necessary to perform a deeper analysis varying these conditions (Casas & Rueda, 2018).

From the point of view of simulator sickness, the answer is inconclusive (Bertollini et al., 2014). There is a general consensus that simulator sickness comes from a mismatch between different channels of our perception sensors. In this regard, visual-only VR applications should induce simulator sickness and motion-based VR applications should reduce it, since in visual-only VR applications the visual perception of motion is inconsistent with a vestibular perception of absence of motion. However, even the most advanced motion platforms have noticeable delays between the visual flow and their corresponding motion. Therefore, absence of motion could be better than a delayed motion that confuses our senses. The explanation is that false cues (those which are in the opposite direction to that of the vehicle or that occur when no cue was expected) are considered more harmful for perception than the absence of cues. The delay threshold is still a matter of debate (Hosman, 1999; Hosman & Advani, 2013).

From a training point of view, it seems reasonable to think that replicating in a simulator the conditions of real situations as much as possible should provide benefits. This, of course, includes motion. The question was so recurrent a few decades ago that it was the matter of several meta-analyses studying the issue by analysing previous research (Hays, Jacobs, Prince, & Salas, 1992; Jacobs, Prince, Hays, & Salas, 1990). Now it is the generally accepted that training skills improve with the inclusion of motion. The majority of the conducted research shows that the inclusion of motion cues is beneficial for VR training applications (Bauer, 2005; Pool, Harder, & van Paassen, 2016). This explains why certification organizations require motion devices to certify that actual training can be substituted by virtual training.

From a performance and task-oriented point of view, it is generally accepted that the addition of motion cues helps performing tasks that provide motion feedback in real environments (Grant et al., 2006; Reymond, Kemeny, Droulez, & Berthoz, 2001). As pilots/drivers are accustomed to feeling particular vestibular cues when performing particular tasks, the absence of motion in the simulator could make them underperform. This explains why the majority of the research points in favour of motion-based simulators with respect to performance. However, some researchers have suggested that for some tasks, such as car following or curve negotiation at constant velocity, motion-based systems are not effective (Colombet et al., 2008; Damveld, Wentink, van Leeuwen, & Happee, 2012). Indeed, it is not unreasonable to think that motion could play no role (or even hinder) the realization of some particular tasks, even if motion is present in a real condition. Then, if motion is eliminated in these cases, the task could be performed more easily. These situations are more likely to occur when there are important visual cues that are sufficient to complete the task. Driving simulators, for instance, provide many visual cues to the drivers, whereas inertial cues are decisive when using a flight simulator where visual references are scarce.

Another important factor in not opting to generate motion cues is the difficulty of tuning these MCA. Some researchers have studied the influence of tuning in the performance of MCA (Bruenger-Koch, 2005; Bruenger-Koch, Briest, & Vollrath, 2006; Gouverneur, Mulder, van Paassen, Stroosma, & Field, 2003; Nahon et al., 1992; Reid & Nahon, 1988) or have tried to propose a systematic mechanism to perform this task (Grant, 1996; Grant & Reid, 1997a, 1997b). However, most of these studies are limited to some fixed set of parameters or do not provide a non-subjective procedure. Therefore, few conclusions can be drawn. Nevertheless, it is clear that the performance of these algorithms can be significantly improved (but also degraded) by performing a parameter-tuning (Casas, Portales, Riera, & Fernandez, 2017). In this regard, it would be very interesting to study how the perception, training, task performance or simulator sickness vary as the parameters of the MCA are modified.

RECOMMENDATIONS, LIMITATIONS, AND FUTURE DIRECTIONS

Motion platforms have been used in VR applications for a very long time. However, the question of how to optimally simulate self-motion using motion cueing devices is a matter of much debate. Despite this debate, current simulation standards require that vehicle simulators under regulation include motion cueing systems. The situation is of course different for other (mostly unregulated) areas, such as entertainment with vehicle simulators, where motion cueing is considered important but not necessary. Generally, those vehicle simulators involving skill learning or training (military training is one important area in this field) should benefit from motion cues. Other areas of VR different from vehicle simulation, such as virtual heritage, telepresence, virtual medicine, etc. should not generally need to consider the inclusion of this kind of systems, since either little or no motion is generated in these applications, or motion does not play a relevant factor in the objectives of these VR-based tools.

Having reviewed the motion versus no motion question in vehicle simulators, it seems clear that significant research in this area is still necessary and that a review of existing works is insufficient to conquer new milestones in this area. On the one hand, it seems clear that the physical features of the motion cueing mechanisms (reachable workspace, power of the actuators, physical limitations, etc.) have a decisive influence in the result. On the other hand, given the lack of standardized assessment methods, the tuning of MCA emerges as a very important, and at the same time, complex task. However, several questions are still unclear. For instance, is power more important that physical workspace? How much influence does the number of DOF of the robotic mechanism have in the resulting motion cues? How much influence does the tuning procedure have in the final result?

Ideally, these questions should be answered by performing experiments with real expert users and several motion platforms, building them with different features and sizes. This task would, of course, require a very significant amount of effort. For this reason, the authors believe that researchers in this field should try to answer these questions with simulated motion platforms and perception models or objective motion fidelity indicators, such as OMCT (Hosman & Advani, 2012, 2016). This way, it would be possible to perform massive and fair comparisons of different devices with different physical properties, and establish standardized limits to define when (and when not) motion cueing devices are effective in VR applications, and at the same time answer the aforementioned research questions.

CONCLUSION

In order to advance in the VR field, not only audio-visual cues need to be properly generated. The rest of the perceptual cues have to be rendered in a realistic way so that VR applications really offer believable virtual environments. Therefore, it is of the utmost importance to analyse the challenges of motion-based systems so it can be invested in improving them. At the same time, understanding the strengths and weaknesses of these solutions, VR designers can have more information about how and when to include motion cues in VR applications.

In this chapter, the authors have explained how to include motion cues in VR applications and have also analysed the challenges and problems of including these perceptual cues. The authors conclude that the field is far from an ideal situation and it is still not mature enough, since several (and sometimes contradictory) studies can be found with respect to the effectiveness of motion cues in simulators. This issue, the difficulty of properly generating these motion cues, and the fact that motion devices are usually quite expensive explain why most VR applications that need motion cueing do not include this kind of perceptual feedback.

Although it is true that no consensus has been found about how to properly generate motion cues in VR applications, the majority of the research points in the positive direction: motion cues are necessary and effective. Then, the general answer should be yes, motion cues need to be included in simulators. However, there are shades of grey and situations where the amount of benefit is too small to invest in this type of solutions. Practitioners and designers should be able to identify these situations, and the chapter has provided some ground to do so.

The reasons that explain why some studies favour motion cues and some others do not, are just speculative, but as the number of parameters and possible set-ups to perform motion cueing are so big and their differences so evident, it is hard to compare different studies. A possible explanation is that the line between bad and good motion cueing is so thin and the difference (in effectiveness) between a no-motion solution and a bad solution may be in some occasions so small, that crossing the line is too easy. This may explain the differences in the results.

In any case, as standard and regulatory organizations demand motion-based solutions when VR applications are used to substitute real training, the inclusion of these systems should become more popular, overcoming the resistance of some simulator designers. The improvement of these motion-based simulators is, nevertheless, a necessity, and should come along with a standardized way to assess the solutions, so that different proposals could be compared in an objective way, and tuning could be automated, avoiding the non-systematic tuning and assessment methods that have been used in the field. As perception is subjective, this is, of course, no easy task.

REFERENCES

Advani, S., Hosman, R., & Potter, M. (2007). *Objective motion fidelity qualification in flight training simulators.* Paper presented at the AIAA Modeling and Simulation Technologies Conference and Exhibit, Hilton Head, SC. 10.2514/6.2007-6802

Allerton, D. (2009). *Principles of flight simulation* (1st ed.). Chichester, UK: Wiley.

Anthes, C., García-Hernández, R. J., Wiedemann, M., & Kranzlmüller, D. (2016). *State of the art of virtual reality technology.* Paper presented at the Aerospace Conference. 10.1109/AERO.2016.7500674

Asadi, H., Mohamed, S., Rahim Zadeh, D., & Nahavandi, S. (2015). Optimisation of nonlinear motion cueing algorithm based on genetic algorithm. *Vehicle System Dynamics, 53*(4), 526–545. doi:10.1080/00423114.2014.1003948

Asadi, H., Mohammadi, A., Mohamed, S., Lim, C. P., Khatami, A., Khosravi, A., & Nahavandi, S. (2016). *A Particle Swarm Optimization-based washout filter for improving simulator motion fidelity.* Paper presented at the Systems, Man, and Cybernetics (SMC), 2016 IEEE International Conference. 10.1109/SMC.2016.7844527

Bailey, R., Knotts, L., Horowitz, S., & Malone, I. H. (1987). *Effect of time delay on manual flight control and flying qualities during in-flight and ground-based simulation.* Paper presented at the Flight Simulation Technologies Conference. 10.2514/6.1987-2370

Bauer, M. (2005). *Evaluating the effectiveness of training system approaches for highly complex flight training* (Doctoral Dissertation). University of Central Florida, Orlando, FL.

Berger, D. R., Schulte-Pelkum, J., & Bülthoff, H. H. (2010). Simulating believable forward accelerations on a Stewart motion platform. *ACM Transactions on Applied Perception, 7*(1), 5:1-5:27. Doi:10.1145/1658349.1658354

Bertollini, G., Glase, Y., Szczerba, J., & Wagner, R. (2014). *The effect of motion cueing on simulator comfort, perceived realism, and driver performance during low speed turning.* Paper presented at the Proceedings of the Driving Simulator Conference, Paris, France.

Boletsis, C. (2017). The new era of Virtual Reality locomotion: A systematic literature review of techniques and a proposed typology. *Multimodal Technologies and Interaction, 1*(4), 24. doi:10.3390/mti1040024

Bruenger-Koch, M. (2005). *Motion parameter tuning and evaluation for the DLR automotive simulator.* Paper presented at the Driving Simulation Conference North America (DSC-NA), Orlando, FL.

Bruenger-Koch, M., Briest, S., & Vollrath, M. (2006). *Do you feel the difference? A motion assessment study.* Paper presented at the Driving Simulation Conference Asia/Pacific, Tsukuba, Japan.

Bruschetta, M., Maran, F., & Beghi, A. (2017). A fast implementation of MPC-based motion cueing algorithms for mid-size road vehicle motion simulators. *Vehicle System Dynamics*, 1–25.

Callaghan, M., Eguíluz, A. G., McLaughlin, G., & McShane, N. (2015). *Opportunities and challenges in virtual reality for remote and virtual laboratories.* Paper presented at the Remote Engineering and Virtual Instrumentation (REV), 2015 12th International Conference. 10.1109/REV.2015.7087298

Casas, S., Coma, I., Portalés, C., & Fernández, M. (2016). Towards a simulation-based tuning of motion cueing algorithms. *Simulation Modelling Practice and Theory, 67*, 137–154. doi:10.1016/j.simpat.2016.06.002

Casas, S., Coma, I., Portalés, C., & Fernández, M. (2017). Optimization of 3-DOF parallel motion devices for low-cost vehicle simulators. *Journal of Advanced Mechanical Design, Systems, and Manufacturing, 11*(2).

Casas, S., Coma, I., Riera, J. V., & Fernández, M. (2015). Motion-cuing algorithms: Characterization of users' perception. *Human Factors: The Journal of the Human Factors and Ergonomics Society, 57*(1), 144–162. doi:10.1177/0018720814538281 PMID:25790575

Casas, S., Fernández, M., & Riera, J. V. (2017). Four different multimodal setups for non-aerial vehicle simulations - A case study with a speedboat simulator. *Multimodal Technologies and Interaction, 1*(2,10), 1-17.

Casas, S., Olanda, R., & Dey, N. (2017). Motion cueing algorithms: A review - Algorithms, evaluation and tuning. *International Journal of Virtual and Augmented Reality*, *1*(1), 90–106. doi:10.4018/IJVAR.2017010107

Casas, S., Olanda, R., Fernandez, M., & Riera, J. V. (2012). *A faster than real-time simulator of motion platforms*. Paper presented at the CMMSE, Murcia, Spain.

Casas, S., Portalés, C., Coma, I., & Fernández, M. (2017). Applying particle swarm optimization to the motion-cueing-algorithm tuning problem. *Proceedings of the Genetic and Evolutionary Computation Conference Companion*. 10.1145/3067695.3075990

Casas, S., Portalés, C., García-Pereira, I., & Fernández, M. (2017). On a first evaluation of ROMOT -a RObotic 3D MOvie Theatre - for driving safety awareness. *Multimodal Technologies and Interaction*, *1*(2,6), 1-13.

Casas, S., Portales, C., Riera, J. V., & Fernandez, M. (2017). Heuristics for solving the parameter tuning problem in motion cueing algorithms. *Revista Iberoamericana de Automática e Informática Industrial*, *14*(2), 193–204. doi:10.1016/j.riai.2016.09.011

Casas, S., Portalés, C., Vera, L., & Riera, J. V. (2019). Virtual and augmented reality mirrors for mental health treatment: analysis and future directions. In G. Guazzaroni (Ed.), Virtual and Augmented Reality in Mental Health Treatment (pp. 95-117). Hersey, PA: IGI Global. doi:10.4018/978-1-5225-7168-1.ch007

Casas, S., & Rueda, S. (2018). Lessons learned from the design and development of vehicle simulators: A case study with three different simulators. *International Journal of Virtual and Augmented Reality*, *2*(1), 59–80. doi:10.4018/IJVAR.2018010105

Casas, S., Rueda, S., Riera, J. V., & Fernández, M. (2012). *On the real-time physics simulation of a speed-boat motion*. Paper presented at the GRAPP/IVAPP.

Colombet, F., Dagdelen, M., Reymond, G., Pere, C., Merienne, F., & Kemeny, A. (2008). *Motion cueing: what's the impact on the driver's behaviour?* Paper presented at the Driving Simulator Conference, Monte-Carlo, Monaco.

Curry, R., Artz, B., Cathey, L., Grant, P., & Greenberg, J. (2002). Kennedy ssq results: fixed-vs motion-based FORD simulators. *Proceedings of DSC*.

Dagdelen, M., Reymond, G., Kemeny, A., Bordier, M., & Maizi, N. (2009). Model-based predictive motion cueing strategy for vehicle driving simulators. *Control Engineering Practice*, *17*(19), 995–1003. doi:10.1016/j.conengprac.2009.03.002

Damveld, H. J., Wentink, M., van Leeuwen, P. M., & Happee, R. (2012). Effects of motion cueing on curve driving. *Proceedings of the Driving Simulation Conference 2012*.

DNV. (2011). *Standard for certification of maritime simulator systems No. 2.14*. Retrieved from https://rules.dnvgl.com/docs/pdf/DNV/stdcert/2011-01/Standard2-14.pdf

Filipczuk, P., & Nikiel, S. (2008). *Real-time simulation of a sailboat*. Paper presented at the Human System Interactions, 2008 Conference. 10.1109/HSI.2008.4581575

Fischer, M., Seefried, A., & Seehof, C. (2016). Objective motion cueing test for driving simulators. *Proceedings of the DSC 2016 Europe*, 41-50.

Frank, L. H., Casali, J. G., & Wierwille, W. W. (1988). Effects of visual display and motion system delays on operator performance and uneasiness in a driving simulator. *Human Factors*, *30*(2), 201–217. doi:10.1177/001872088803000207 PMID:3384446

Garrett, N. J. I., & Best, M. C. (2010). Driving simulator motion cueing algorithms – A survey of the state of the art. *Proceedings of the 10th International Symposium on Advanced Vehicle Control (AVEC)*.

Gouverneur, B., Mulder, J. A., van Paassen, M. M., Stroosma, O., & Field, E. J. (2003). *Optimisation of the Simona research simulator's motion filter settings for handling qualities experiments*. Paper presented at the AIAA Modeling and Simulation Technologies Conference and Exhibit, Austin, TX. 10.2514/6.2003-5679

Grant, P. R. (1996). *The development of a tuning paradigm for flight simulator motion drive algorithms (Ph.D)*. Toronto, ON, Canada: University of Toronto.

Grant, P. R., & Reid, L. D. (1997a). Motion washout filter tuning: Rules and requirements. *Journal of Aircraft*, *34*(2), 145–151. doi:10.2514/2.2158

Grant, P. R., & Reid, L. D. (1997b). PROTEST: An expert system for tuning simulator washout filters. *Journal of Aircraft*, *34*(2), 152–159. doi:10.2514/2.2166

Grant, P. R., Yam, B., Hosman, R., & Schroeder, J. A. (2006). Effect of simulator motion on pilot behavior and perception. *Journal of Aircraft*, *43*(6), 1914–1924. doi:10.2514/1.21900

Groen, E. L., & Bles, W. (2004). How to use body tilt for the simulation of linear self motion. *Journal of Vestibular Research*, *14*(5), 375–385. PMID:15598992

Hall, J. R. (1989). *The need for platform motion in modern piloted flight training simulators (Vol. FM35)*. Bedford, UK: Royal Aerospace Establishment.

Hays, R. T., Jacobs, J. W., Prince, C., & Salas, E. (1992). *Flight simulator training effectiveness: A meta-analysis*. Mahwah, NJ: Lawrence Erlbaum.

Hosman, R. (1999). *Are criteria for motion cueing and time delays possible?* Paper presented at the AIAA Modeling and Simulation Technologies Conference, Portland, OR. 10.2514/6.1999-4028

Hosman, R., & Advani, S. (2012). Status of the ICAO Objective Motion Cueing Test. *New Frontiers Conference Proceedings*.

Hosman, R., & Advani, S. (2013). *Are criteria for motion cueing and time delays possible? Part 2*. Paper presented at the AIAA Modeling and Simulation Technologies Conference, Boston, MA. 10.2514/6.2013-4833

Hosman, R., & Advani, S. (2016). Design and evaluation of the objective motion cueing test and criterion. *Aeronautical Journal*, *120*(1227), 873–891. doi:10.1017/aer.2016.35

Hosman, R., Advani, S., & Haeck, N. (2002). *Integrated design of flight simulator motion cueing systems*. Paper presented at the Royal Aeronautical Society Conference on Flight Simulation, London, UK.

ICAO. (2009). Manual of criteria for the qualification of flight simulation training devices: Vol. 1. Aeroplanes (3rd ed.). International Civil Aviation Organization.

Infinadeck. (2017). *Infinadeck, the world's first true commercially viable omnidirectional treadmill*. Retrieved 01/10/2018, 2018, from http://www.infinadeck.com/

Jacobs, J. W., Prince, C., Hays, R. T., & Salas, E. (1990). *A meta-analysis of the flight simulator training research*. Orlando, FL: Naval Training Systems Center. doi:10.21236/ADA228733

Janeh, O., Langbehn, E., Steinicke, F., Bruder, G., Gulberti, A., & Poetter-Nerger, M. (2017). Walking in Virtual Reality: Effects of manipulated visual self-Motion on walking biomechanics. *ACM Transactions on Applied Perception*, *14*(2), 12. doi:10.1145/3022731

Klüver, M., Herrigel, C., Preuß, S., Schöner, H. P., & Hecht, H. (2015). Comparing the incidence of simulator sickness in five different driving simulators. *Proceedings of Driving Simulation Conference*.

Kolasinski, E. M. (1995). *Simulator sickness in virtual environments*. Technical Report 1027. U.S. Army Research Institute for Behavioral and Social Sciences.

Küçük, S. (Ed.). (2012). *Serial and parallel robot manipulators - Kinematics, dynamics, control and optimization*. London, UK: InTech. doi:10.5772/2301

MacNeilage, P. R., Banks, M. S., Berger, D. R., & Bulthoff, H. H. (2007). A Bayesian model of the disambiguation of gravitoinertial force by visual cues. *Experimental Brain Research*, *179*(2), 263–290. doi:10.100700221-006-0792-0 PMID:17136526

Mohammadi, A., Asadi, H., Mohamed, S., Nelson, K., & Nahavandi, S. (2016). *MPC-based motion cueing algorithm with short prediction horizon using exponential weighting*. Paper presented at the Systems, Man, and Cybernetics (SMC), 2016 IEEE International Conference on. 10.1109/SMC.2016.7844292

Nahon, M. A., & Reid, L. D. (1990). Simulator motion-drive algorithms - A designer's perspective. *Journal of Guidance, Control, and Dynamics*, *13*(2), 356–362. doi:10.2514/3.20557

Nahon, M. A., Reid, L. D., & Kirdeikis, J. (1992). Adaptive simulator motion software with supervisory control. *Journal of Guidance, Control, and Dynamics*, *15*(2), 376–383. doi:10.2514/3.20846

Page, L. R. (2000). *Brief history of flight simulation*. Paper presented at the SimTecT 2000 Proceedings, Sydney, NSW, Australia.

Pool, D., Harder, G., & van Paassen, M. (2016). Effects of simulator motion feedback on training of skill-based control behavior. *Journal of Guidance, Control, and Dynamics*, *39*(4), 889–902. doi:10.2514/1.G001603

Pouliot, N. A., Gosselin, C. M., & Nahon, M. A. (1998). Motion simulation capabilities of three-degree-of-freedom flight simulators. *Journal of Aircraft*, *35*(1), 9–17. doi:10.2514/2.2283

Reid, L. D., & Nahon, M. A. (1985). *Flight simulation motion-base drive algorithms: Part 1 - Developing and testing the equations* (Vol. 296). University of Toronto: UTIAS.

Reid, L. D., & Nahon, M. A. (1986a). *Flight simulation motion-base drive algorithms: Part 2 - Selecting the system parameters* (Vol. 307). University of Toronto: UTIAS.

Reid, L. D., & Nahon, M. A. (1986b). *Flight simulation motion-base drive algorithms: Part 3 - Pilot evaluations*. University of Toronto: UTIAS.

Reid, L. D., & Nahon, M. A. (1988). Response of airline pilots to variations in flight simulator motion algorithms. *Journal of Aircraft*, *25*(7), 639–646. doi:10.2514/3.45635

Reymond, G., & Kemeny, A. (2000). Motion cueing in the Renault driving simulator. *Vehicle System Dynamics: International Journal of Vehicle Mechanics and Mobility*, *34*(4), 249–259. doi:10.1076/vesd.34.4.249.2059

Reymond, G., Kemeny, A., Droulez, J., & Berthoz, A. (2001). Role of lateral acceleration in curve driving: Driver model and experiments on a real vehicle and a driving simulator. *Human Factors*, *43*(3), 483–495. doi:10.1518/001872001775898188 PMID:11866202

Salisbury, I. G., & Limebeer, D. J. (2016). Optimal motion cueing for race cars. *IEEE Transactions on Control Systems Technology*, *24*(1), 200–215. doi:10.1109/TCST.2015.2424161

Schwarz, C. W. (2007). Two mitigation strategies for motion system limits in driving and flight simulators. *IEEE Transactions on Systems, Man, and Cybernetics. Part A, Systems and Humans*, *37*(4), 562–568. doi:10.1109/TSMCA.2007.897590

Stahl, K., Abdulsamad, G., Leimbach, K., & Vershinin, Y. A. (2014). *State of the art and simulation of motion cueing algorithms for a six degree of freedom driving simulator*. Paper presented at the 17th International Conference on Intelligent Transportation Systems (ITSC), Qingdao, China. 10.1109/ITSC.2014.6957745

Stroosma, O., Van Paassen, M. M., Mulder, M., Hosman, R., & Advani, S. (2013). *Applying the objective motion cueing test to a classical washout algorithm*. Paper presented at the AIAA Modeling and Simulation Technologies (MST) Conference, Boston, MA.

Virtuix. (2018). *Virtuix Omni Platform*. Retrieved 01/10/2018, 2018, from http://www.virtuix.com/product/omni-platform/

Watson, G. (2000). A synthesis of simulator sickness studies conducted in a high-fidelity driving simulator. In *Proceedings of Driving Simulation Conference* (pp. 69-78). Paris, France: Driving Simulation Association.

Wentink, M., Valente Pais, R., Mayrhofer, M., Feenstra, P., & Bles, W. (2008). First curve driving experiments in the Desdemona simulator. *DSC Europe 08*.

Witkin, A., & Baraff, D. (1997). Physically based modeling: principles and practice. *SIGGRAPH '97 Course notes*. Retrieved 01/10/2018, 2018, from https://www.cs.cmu.edu/~baraff/sigcourse/

ADDITIONAL READING

Asadi, H., Mohamed, S., Nelson, K., Nahavandi, S., & Zadeh, D. R. (2015). *Human perception-based washout filtering using genetic algorithm*. Paper presented at the International Conference on Neural Information Processing. 10.1007/978-3-319-26535-3_46

Avizzano, C. A., Barbagli, F., & Bergamasco, M. (2000). *Washout filter design for a motorcycle simulator*. Paper presented at the Proceedings of the IEEE Conference on Systems, Man, and Cybernetics, Nashville, TN, USA. 10.1109/ICSMC.2000.885980

Casas, S., Portalés, C., Gimeno, J., & Fernández, M. (2018). Simulation of parallel mechanisms for motion cueing generation in vehicle simulators using AM-FM bi-modulated signals. *Mechatronics, 53*, 251–261. doi:10.1016/j.mechatronics.2018.06.008

Cleij, D., Venrooij, J., Pretto, P., Pool, D. M., Mulder, M., & Bülthoff, H. H. (2018). Continuous subjective rating of perceived motion incongruence during driving simulation. *IEEE Transactions on Human-Machine Systems, 48*(1), 17–29. doi:10.1109/THMS.2017.2717884

De Ridder, K., & Roza, M. (2015). *Automatic optimization of motion drive algorithms using OMCT*. Paper presented at the AIAA Modeling and Simulation Technologies Conference. 10.2514/6.2015-1139

Le Bouthillier, J., Liang, Y., & Allard, P. (2012). Pilot evaluation of a low cost 3 degree-of-freedom flight simulator driven by the classical washout filter algorithm. *The Online Journal on Computer Science and Technology, 2*(1), 102–106.

Onur, C., Türe, U., & Zengin, U. (2017). *Pilot perception and control behavior models as a tool to assess motion-cueing algorithms*. Paper presented at the AIAA Modeling and Simulation Technologies Conference. 10.2514/6.2017-3475

Pool, D. M. (2012). *Objective evaluation of flight simulator motion cueing fidelity through a cybernetic approach*. (PhD Thesis), Delft University, The Netherlands.

Roza, M., Meiland, R., & Field, J. (2013). *Experiences and perspectives in using OMCT for testing and optimizing motion drive algorithms*. Paper presented at the AIAA Modeling and Simulation Technologies (MST) Conference. 10.2514/6.2013-4835

Shirley, R. S., & Young, L. R. (1968). Motion cues in man-vehicle control - Effects of roll-motion cues on human operator's behavior in compensatory systems with disturbance inputs. *Man-Machine Systems. IEEE Transactions on, 9*(4), 121–128. doi:10.1109/TMMS.1968.300016

Young, L. R. (1967). Some effects of motion cues on manual tracking. *Journal of Spacecraft and Rockets, 4*(10), 1300–1303. doi:10.2514/3.29075

KEY TERMS AND DEFINITIONS

Interaction: A kind of action that occurs as two or more objects have an effect upon one another.

Motion Cueing Algorithm: Control algorithm that transforms simulated vehicle dynamics into realizable motion commands for a motion platform so that suitable motion cues are generated for a simulated vehicle.

Motion Cues: Perceptual mechanism by which humans sense the motion of our own body with respect to the surrounding environment.

Motion Fidelity: A measure of the extent to which human perception of self-motion in a vehicle simulator is similar to a real situation.

Motion Platform: A robotic mechanism, usually electro-mechanic, designed to convert motions of one or several bodies into constrained motions of other bodies. They are used in VR applications to generate perceptually believable motion on the user of the simulator.

Motion Sickness: A condition in which a disagreement exists between the perception of motion by one or more of the human perception mechanisms, leading to dizziness, fatigue, or nausea.

Simulator Sickness: A type of motion sickness that is typically experienced by pilots who use a vehicle simulator.

Vehicle Simulator: A VR application by which the operation and control of a real vehicle is replicated in a controlled environment. They have countless applications in driving safety, research, vehicle design, road design, psychology, etc.

Virtual Reality (VR): A technology that allows replacing the real world by a synthetic one, making the user believe that she/he is in another realm.

Section 3
Applications and Best Practices in Digital Reality

The six chapters in Section 3 demonstrate the applications and best practices of digital reality technologies. The pervasive applications of digital reality platforms have been seen in the marketing, creative cultural industries, higher education institutes, and formal and informal learning contexts, including special education for people with autism using an integrated approach to combine AR, MR, and VR technologies with other emerging platforms such as game and online learning platforms.

Chapter 7
Edutainment With Flipped IDEAS

Norita Ahmad

(iD) https://orcid.org/0000-0001-5129-1133

American University of Sharjah, UAE

Kevin Rose Dias
American University of Sharjah, UAE

EXECUTIVE SUMMARY

Virtual learning environments are receiving a growing interest due to exponential advancements in technology alongside the millennial users' preference for more modern rather than traditional means of studying. This chapter narrows down on optimizing edutainment in the classroom by strategically using the methods of flipped classroom, team-based learning, and the IDEAS method. The study provides an explained framework that highlights what needs to be implemented on behalf of the instructor and what outcomes can be expected as a result. An experimental study was conducted on students within a course at the graduate level in the United Arab Emirates (UAE). The main objective is to study the effect of virtual learning environment that incorporates the use of flipped classroom, Team-based learning and IDEAS methods on students' academic performance.

INTRODUCTION

Several technologies exist that take advantage of immersive learning environments directly in its usage; however, there lacks an efficient framework that utilizes such technologies in optimizing the extent of knowledge obtained within the limited time students can afford (Bergmann & Sams, 2015). While virtual reality, augmented reality, and mixed reality have made swift strides in educational advancements, a lack of focus on systematically implementing them in the classroom can cause it to be redundant in its purpose. Present day research has been expanding these advancements to educational technology (Dalgarno & Lee, 2010; Fowler, 2015), but little research is conducted on implementation and hence there is a need for an adaptive classroom setup that allows both students and teachers to integrate technology in optimizing the immersive educational experience. One specific branch under the virtual

DOI: 10.4018/978-1-5225-5912-2.ch007

learning umbrella is 'edutainment' which stems from the marriage of the pros of entertainment with the benefits of education (Aksakal, 2015). There is a distinct similarity between virtual learning and immersive virtual reality (VR). VR is the portrayal of an artificially created environment that replaces a user's real-world surroundings that is convincing enough that it is able to suspend disbelief and fully engage with the created environment. Similarly, a well-designed virtual learning environment includes curriculum mapping, student tracking, and online support that allow individuals to be fully immersive in the learning process (Fowler, 2015). Education practitioners and researchers can reap the benefits of better user engagement, motivation, productivity, memory and stress management that were exclusive only to entertainment through gaming (Stein, 2014). Gamification in edutainment has five main principles for it to be successful ("Gamification in eLearning," 2015). They are to boost motivation, build learner engagement, increase learning retention, performance feedback and enhance productivity ("Gamification in eLearning," 2015). It is necessary to properly define these principles first in the context of edutainment, in order to propose a methodology of achieving them. Motivation can be boosted through gamification simply by adding a reward system in the form of giveaways to incentivize students to perform better (Pirker, Riffnaller-Schiefer, & Gütl, 2014). Learner engagement is a practice that is often thought to be the most difficult to build on. The purpose of gamification is that learners often spend more time than usual on academic material without realizing that they are in fact 'studying' (Pirker, Riffnaller-Schiefer, & Gütl, 2014). Long-term learning retention can be enforced when students are involved in fun, immersive learning (Stein, 2014). Adding elements of gaming to examination and/or projects can enhance the quality of output (Pirker, Riffnaller-Schiefer, & Gütl, 2014). Gamification demands students to be more efficient, time-sensitive and collaborative in their assignments; therefore, enhancing overall productivity (Bergmann & Sams, 2015).

BACKGROUND

As will be highlighted, this book chapter will initially contribute to the field by aligning all the fields of research that are relevant to immersive education. The proposed framework from the preliminary research was introduced and later supported by experimental evidence. Ultimately, based on this field research, the chapter justifies a unified solution to these predicted problems by proposing a disruptive edutainment model.

A virtual learning environment (VLE) is a framework of teaching and learning methods created to improve a student's learning experience by introducing computers and the Internet into the learning process. Similarly, immersive virtual reality (VR) is the portrayal of an artificially created environment that replaces a user's real-world surroundings that is convincing enough for the user to be fully engaged with the created environment. The proposed model employed in this book chapter is a flipped classroom approach integrated with team-based learning (TBL) and the IDEAS method (Stein, 2014). The flipped classroom approach to education is a product of blended learning strategies wherein the focus is on students' individual application of conceptual knowledge through purposeful activities rather than traditional transfer of information ("What is the 'Flipped Classroom'?," 2018). TBL incorporates team building as a necessary activity for collaborative learning and includes structured approaches for in-class learning activities (Michaelsen & Sweet, 2008). The IDEAS method illustrates how the virtues of 'improvise', 'design', 'experiment', 'aesthetics' and 'strengths' should be pinpointed in an ideal learning experience

(Ahmad & Abu Hasan, 2017). Flipped classroom strategies generally exist with technology integrated within it and TBL includes a process for students to provide constructive feedback on team contribution to other team members (Bergmann & Sams, 2015). Hence incorporating the IDEAS methodology with the two methods would give birth to an ideally-blended learning environment. In line with the elements that define virtual environment applications that includes continuity of surroundings, conformance to human vision, freedom of movement, physical interaction, physical feedback and narrative engagement.

As a simple example, the application can be as straightforward as a combination of face-to-face learning and web-based online learning that is structured based on the IDEAS method. It is completely different from the traditional self-studying approach to learning and can be effectively used in encouraging engagement between both teachers and learners across different levels of learning (Bull, 2013). This integrative approach consists of experimental engagement that involves activities, game stimulation interactions, and competitive rewarding component (Ahmad & Abu Hasan, 2017). The leaderboard system and prizes, when organized and executed in the right way, can stimulate active learning before, during and even after class time ("Active Ingredients For The Flipped Classroom Infographic," 2013). Overall, the backbone of the model is a chain consisting of learning, feedback, and use of appropriate and updated technology.

Virtual Learning and Virtual Reality

As early as in the 1990's, research from the Washington Technology Center in the University of Washington compared attributes of VR environments to educational theory and pedagogical practice (Bricken, 1991). It dictates that VR is experiential and actively inhabit a spatial multi-sensory environment. In contrast to traditional oral presentations, VR proposes a three dimensional environment that delivers to verbal, logical, auditory, kinesthetic, interpersonal and intrapersonal natures of human intelligence. It also shows that VR enables natural human interaction with information as the technology is designed to fit human architecture as the environment creates a world that encourages one to talk, move, gesture and even manipulate objects and systems, using the same skills as one would in the real world. Hence, one would not necessarily required to be technically skilled in programming to be able to manipulate and process data to make it meaningful. Pan et al. (2006) justify the application of virtual reality in learning environments as a developing technique based on the perspectives of general architecture, human computer interaction, synthetic characters, storytelling, psychology and physiology factors and learning with entertainment. The research supports the list of criteria through real-world implications in education. Two specific examples are sports simulation where virtual rehearsal system of group calisthenics that enabled a mass number of gymnasts to train and practice prior to the 2008 Olympics and storytelling where a 'magic story cube' technology is a mixed AR/VR concept where a user uses a head mounted display (HMD) with a camera mounted to manipulate a 3D story in front of them using two-hand interactions. Another early success in immersive virtual learning environment research is the narrative-based, immersive, constructionist/collaborative environments (NICE) project (Roussos, Johnson, Moher, & Leigh, 2006). NICE is a virtual learning environment that utilizes a constructivist approach to learning, collaboration and narrative development. It is designed to combine the strengths of VR: immersion, telepresence, immediate visual feedback and interactivity under the belief that the best learning takes place on interaction with an object or system. The environment was a success and its limitations can be tackled by ensuring that the learning goal of future projects are important to people, hard and challenging, distinctly valuable with VR technology integration and up to date with current research milestones. The constructivist approach for VR learning environments is further studied by Huang et. al (2010) who suggest five learning strategies namely situated learning (learning in immersive real-life situations), role-playing, cooperative/collaborative learning, problem-based learning and creative learning.

Edutainment

Edutainment is defined in several different perspectives, one of which establishes it as "combining education and entertainment and increasing learners' excitement and enthusiasm to teach them subject and information that is hard to learn" (Aksakal, 2015, p. 1233). The relevance of edutainment to this chapter is that if applied effectively, the results from a study session should indicate an increase in knowledge through a two-way communication in which students actively seek answers about limitations, concepts and information (Ahmad & Abu Hasan, 2017). Most common approaches in edutainment include but are not limited to taking a role in interaction, dramatization, simulations and an educator-classroom atmosphere (Aksakal, 2015). Having the opportunity to switch roles with the educator in class activities allows students to participate in 'active learning' that is known for positive results in memory retention and overall increase in interest (Ahmad & Abu Hasan, 2017). Educational drama or performing is effective in learning as it allows students to reflect on their feelings and thoughts to allow the motivation to come from themselves (Aksakal, 2015,). Simulation and narration allow students to feel responsible for study contents as if case studies were a part of real-life events. The traditional classroom environment is often enhanced with more interaction between educator and students using activities and technologies.

Team-based Learning

Team-Based Learning (TBL) was developed in the early 1970s and is a teaching method where students learn material in advance of a teaching session (Michaelsen et. al, 2004). TBL is a structured form of group learning that requires student preparation prior to classroom activities, while applying what was learnt in class (Brame, 2018). Firstly, team-based learning is a means by which learners in groups interact amongst each other to promote learning by sharing personal experiences and perspectives while the teacher serves as just a facilitator (Michaelsen et. al, 2004). Secondly, it is a system that mandates a fair grading approach to all independent members of the team (Michaelsen et. al, 2004). Grading is based on both individual and group participation that thus holds each student accountable for his or her contribution (Brame, 2018). Additionally, students are aware that there will be a peer evaluation of their team-members that will impact their individual overall score (Brame, 2018). Team building is important with TBL because team skills are critical in solving a variety of complex problems seen in many fields such as entrepreneurship, engineering and medicine (Michaelsen & Sweet, 2008). In TBL, teams are brought together to achieve a goal that could not have been successfully accomplished individually.

Flipped Classroom

The flipped classroom approach is more than just a single model; it is the concept to flip the conventional lecture-based classroom instruction and utilize pre-assigned visual, audio content and reading assignments prior to class (Green, Banas, & Perkins, 2017). The flipped classroom allows educators to support students as they implement and share the concepts that they have independently worked on in a structured, interactive classroom setting; essentially allowing students to become the educators themselves (Green, Banas, & Perkins, 2017). As will be further elaborated in the chapter, the flipped classroom approach is beneficial however it also poses several concerns if implemented. Implementing a flipped classroom/immerse environment setting means that extra costs will have to be incurred by students (TeachThoughtStaff, 2018). It relies on a trust that students will deliver from their end, and it encourages more time spent in front of screens rather than with people and places (Green, Banas, & Perkins, 2017). Effectively carrying out a flipped classroom approach poses an additional burden on educators to properly prepare concise, presentable content for their students' activities (TeachThoughtStaff, 2018). Furthermore, flipped classrooms do not follow the model of teaching to improve the traditional test scores as they do not prepare students for tests that they are still mandated to take.

IDEAS Method

The IDEAS method is a learning framework that advocates the key elements of improvise, design, experiment, aesthetics and strengths that are an essential personality focus of any learning process to at the individual level, followed by at the team level (Ahmad & Abu Hasan, 2017). Improvisation is a skill that would allow a student to make efficient real-time decisions in unchartered and novel situations using existing information and appropriate routines or patterns (Stein, 2014). Design is a creative behavior that one would have if they were able to see and build an object or process that meets set criteria/goals of a consumer or recipient (Stein, 2014). Experimentation is the ability to decide between different contrasting goals, perspectives or courses of actions by being able to rank them based on effective criteria (Stein, 2014). Aesthetics is the ability to discriminate between sensory inputs to recognize the feelings and thoughts invoked from a design from both a creator and observer point of view (Stein, 2014). Strengths refer to the multiple intelligences that people possess that if realized, can be focused on to result in best productivity and output (Stein, 2014). The IDEAS method promotes learning through individual active interpretation of experience and sharing that experience with others to help create better understanding of the materials (Ahmad & Abu Hasan, 2017).

MAIN FOCUS OF THE CHAPTER

There are a few distinct similarities between virtual learning and immersive virtual reality as an application that allow virtual learning to be a branch within the field of immersive VR. A well-designed VLE includes curriculum mapping, student tracking, online support for both teacher and student, electronic communication and other virtual links to additional learning resources. The VLE proposed in this chapter is one where a student is paired with other student (groups) and paired with a teacher (classroom), sharing and building motivation (a principle of TBL) to execute tasks before, during and after a classroom (based on flipped classroom method) - the commonality between the student tracking and online support elements of VLE and the physical feedback and narrative engagement elements of immersive VR. Over the duration of the semester, in order to expedite these tasks, the relationships are matured digitally through virtual communications, shared online documents, presentations and other prepared/impromptu activities and assignments that ensure continuity of surroundings element of VR. Thus, the students complete the course having experienced a constant learning environment inside and outside of the classroom that is distinct from the traditional classroom setup - a type of immersive virtual reality application.

The main focus of this chapter is therefore to study the effect of virtual learning environment that incorporates the use of flipped classroom, TBL and IDEAS methods on students' academic performance. Specifically, the research questions that this chapter aims to answer were:

- Does virtual learning environment that incorporates the use of flipped classroom, TBL and IDEAS methods impact students' in-class engagement, teamwork and self-directed ability?
- Does virtual learning environment that incorporates the use of flipped classroom, TBL and IDEAS methods affect students' academic performance?

METHODOLOGY

The Selection of an Experiment Research

In order to apply the concepts described above, a posttest only experiment with the intervention of VLE that incorporates the use of flipped classroom, TBL and IDEAS methods is used to measure students' prior course knowledge and learning at the end of the semester. In this design, students were divided into two groups. The first group was the experimental group and the second group was the control group.

Given the main objective of this study was to assess the impact of VLE that incorporates the use of flipped classroom, TBL and IDEAS on students' academic performance, a posttest only design is deemed appropriate (Campbell & Stanley, 1963). In addition, prior to the admission to the program, students had to sit for the qualifying exam and if needed, they had to go through a preparatory course prior to their matriculation to the program. As such, it is safe to assume that students in the two groups started at equal levels of attitudes, knowledge, and skills (Schumann, Anderson, Scott, & Lawton, 2014). The first group was given the intervention of VLE that incorporates the use of flipped classroom, TBL, and IDEAS methods in their learning instructions while the second group was taught using traditional method. At the end of the semester, a test was given to both groups (the posttest) and results from the two groups were then compared in order to see the effect of the intervention.

Sampling Method and Sample Characteristics

Participants in this study were students of the 'Management Decision Analysis' MBA course at an AACSB accredited business school at a major global university in the United Arab Emirates (UAE). The course examines analytical tools and methods used to effectively make management-level decisions. It introduces the concepts of decision and process analysis, design and capacity management. Techniques studied include decision trees, value stream mapping, process modeling, spreadsheet simulations and dynamic modeling. It is taught at the graduate level of the university and educates students on effective managerial level decision-making and management, team-building and self-understanding concepts that support it.

A total of 40 students participated and were formed into groups based on equal dispersion of varying academic background, work experience, age and gender across all groups at the beginning of the semester. The control group consisted of a total of 17 students, which was further divided into a group of 4-5 people. The experimental group consisted of 23 students, which was also divided into a group of 4-5 students. Table 1 shows the demographic background of the students. The control group attended a traditional lecture designed coursework while the experimental group participated in the VLE of the same course. Both groups successfully completed the courses in the same time frame presented by the same instructor. The experiment covers the entire duration of the academic semester (14 weeks) and the lecture topics of this specific course make it particularly effective in evaluating the effectiveness of the proposed approach.

The traditional method was a lecture-based course that included lectures, case discussion, and video presentation in the same sequence as the VLE method. All the learning objectives were designed the same for both groups. The only difference was the teaching method. The core principle of the VLE with edutainment approach draws from team-based learning (TBL) that encourages group learning through student preparation out of class and application of the knowledge in class (Brame, 2018). The instructor assigned before-classroom tasks such as reading articles, watching videos, and scouting relevant websites to prepare for the during-classroom activity which includes team-based competition, role-play, simulation, case-analysis and impromptu presentation. Furthermore, the instructor used a grading scheme that allowed the students to after class reflect upon their approach, content depth, understanding and creativity when tackling their given assignment. These grading criteria solved an additional purpose that is to support how successful this experiment was in justifying the model. Expected outcomes of this holistic approach to learning, apart from excellent performance, are that students learn at both the independent, individual level as well as through peer mentoring. The following sections describe the different class exercises and assignments that were assigned to the experimental (VLE) students throughout the semester.

Experimental Procedures

This experimental research was made of several class activities as described below.

Table 1. Participants' demographic

Demographic Categories	Range	Percentage
Gender	Male Female	45.0% 55.0%
Age	21-25 26-30 Above 30	45.0% 27.5% 27.5%
Major	Finance/Accounting Management Economics Marketing Engineering	30.0% 20.0% 5.0% 20.0% 10.0%
Work Experience	Other 1-2 years 3-5 years 5-10 years	15.0% 25.0% 45.0% 30.0%

Class Activity 1

The first activity was an introduction to team-based learning as well as setting up the semester-long teams in the classroom. Teams were built based on an equal dispersion in academic background, gender, work experience and even age wherever relevant. Based on the group development theory by Dr. Bruce Tuckman (Ryder, 2017) this lecture revolves around the first stage of 'forming, storming, norming and performing'. 'Forming' as a stage essentially comprises of two parts: understanding what skills each team member brings to the table and establishing emotional connections. Both stages gave the team a boosted productivity, allowing them to smoothly transition through the remaining three stages throughout the semester.

- **In-Class Activity:** In the classroom, this was accomplished by giving the teams time to reflect upon a team name, assigning roles and what is needed at both an individual and team levels to learn effectively in the course. In order for the instructor to get to know the students better and to help students ease through the first day of class, the instructor asked the following questions: 1) Your earliest memory 2) Your most treasured possession 3) Your lifetime goal 4) If you could spend a day with anyone, who would it be and why? 5) If you could know how to do anything, what would it be?
- **Take-Home Activity:** All students were assigned the task of completing the online questionnaires on personality type and multiple intelligences (MI) strengths. The reports from these are to be submitted to the instructor to establish better understanding in course delivery and to be used within the team to assign more specific roles and responsibilities to the members. This exercise further allows students to reflect upon the completed class activity.

Class Activity 2

This class activity consisted of three different parts that challenged creativity, team collaboration, time-constrained decision-making and an understanding of trade-offs and conflicting objectives in decision-making.

- **In-Class Activity:** Part A was a team design exercise. First, all students were given a 10-minute assignment to go around the campus and take pictures of 2 small balls (provided) as a test of perception and seeing. Then the students were asked to return to their teams and spend 25 minutes forming their team members' roles based on their previously assessed multiple intelligences. Then they were given 5 minutes with the actual task, which was to create a product/story using all the combined pictures.

Part B was a time sensitive process design exercise that simulated real-time pressures of product development teams. The case study was first given to the students who took some time to read it. Following that, the 35-minute assignment began where the teams were asked to allocate timelines and task durations for each role in the development team of the case company. The 35 minutes replicated the development phase up until the launch of the product. The instructor introduced "press releases" that simulated market/competitor behavior at different points during the assignment duration that may force students to re-evaluate their answers such as consumers' interest in cross-platform gaming, competitors' strategy, product features and the availability of the games on both Windows and Mac platforms.

Part C was based on a Harvard business review case study that students were asked to read prior to the class. This activity involved making a choice when each option has trade-offs. The case involved a job seeker who had 4 different job offers with 3 factors: growth, work hours and annual salary with which they were compared. Students were introduced to and carried out 3 different procedures to choose the best job. The first procedure involved comparing the first two jobs on the list and comparing the winner of the two with the next on the list and so on. The second procedure was to rank each option by factor and average the factors to have an average rank for each option. The third procedure gave points to each factor based on the value of that factor to the decision-maker and these points were computed/ aggregated across the three factors to give a total score for each option.

In all these activities, student teams worked on the same significant problem that required making a specific choice, and where they simultaneously reported their choices. Each team needed to arrive at a consensus on the most appropriate answer or solution, and then had a dialogue with the whole class on their solution. As such, the activities created a motivational framework that encouraged team interactions and productive teamwork.

- **Take-Home Activity:** Students were provided feedback in class and were graded on the creativity and content of their presentations. Students were then asked to reflect on the activities and provide detail feedback on the group performance and each individual team members including themselves.

Class Activity 3

The third activity was a strategy simulation exercise. It involved the negotiator's dilemma as a key concept to understand any real-time decision-making scenario. This concept helped students to understand how interactions could present difficult strategic choices and how one must consider different possible responses by counterparts. Probing a counterpart's strategy is crucial however it could pose possible risks along with the benefits. Negotiation was another key concept that requires students to realize that it is a dynamic and ongoing process of learning, adapting and influencing as events unfold in the decision-making scenario.

- **In-Class Activity:** Students were divided into groups of four, engaging in a moderated online game activity. The four participants engaged in ten rounds of 'competing' versus 'cooperating' choices that resulted in earnings or losses as pay-offs. If all four compete, everyone loses 1 point and if all four cooperate, everyone earns 1 point. At the end of the activity, students were asked to analyze the outcomes and imagine if they were going to play the game again, with three different people. What would their first strategy be: cooperate or compete? Students were also asked to critique the process and to suggest any other factors that would have significant impact to the game. Additionally, students also explored the concept of trust in decision-making.
- **Take-Home Activity:** Based on the results and feedback of the game activity, students were able to reflect upon how negotiation involves real-time learning, adapting and influencing in a strategic environment. In addition, they were able to realize that counterparts might have one strategy or a

combination of several strategies that were difficult to anticipate. The exercise also allowed students to explore the concept of trust especially in the virtual environment where body languages were completely missing.

Class Activity 4

After being introduced to the IDEAS method in class, students were then assigned to work with their group members in exploring the concepts further. Specifically in order to understand the concepts of improvisation and design, they were asked to watch "Sully", a movie about Captain Sullenberger who landed US Airways Flight 1549 safely in the Hudson River, a few series of "Whose Line is it Anyway", and top TV advertisements and radio jingles. In order to explore the concepts of experiment and aesthetics, they were asked to study companies such as Apple, Burberry, IKEA and Nike. Finally, in order to understand the concept of strengths, they were asked to watch "Rocky Balboa" movie and search for other common sources of strengths such as songs, poems, or artworks.

Prior to Class Activity 4, students were asked to read articles relevant to corporate social responsibility (CSR) and philanthropy. The class activity was then outlined in two parts: a time constrained research phase and a team design exercise. During the first 20 minutes of class, the founder for a Non-Government Organization (NGO) gave a brief introduction of her organization and the most recent initiative that she was working on. Students were then given 10 minutes to ask any related questions to the guest speaker. Once the questions and answers session was over, students were asked to design an advertisement to represent either how another business could participate as a customer or as a competitor to the initiative.

- **In-Class Activity:** The first part required teams to decide on either a customer or a competitor role towards the NGO. Depending on the role, students should consider whether they should participate (as a customer) or compete (as a competitor) with the initiative and the impact of their decision on their company's overall image and success. The teams were to do preliminary research that involved identifying what is known and what needs to be known to decide on their strategic move. Students would then prepare a presentation on how the team established this decision. The second part involved the team advertisement design exercise that was based on the role decided. The advertisement should contain picture(s) appropriate for the initiative and advertising copy of at least 50 words or catchy slogan to motivate and support the initiative. Students had exactly 1 hour to work on the entire task. At the end of the presentation, students were provided feedback in class and were graded on the creativity and content of their presentations.
- **Take-Home Activity:** Students were asked to reflect on the activities and provide detail feedback on the group performance and each individual team members including themselves. Additionally, they were asked to provide any specific changes that they would make to their overall in-class presentation if they were given more time or a chance to redo the entire presentation.

Assignment 1

In class, students were introduced to the concept of both critical and creative problem solving. For critical problem solving, the focus was on Socratic questioning technique where students were shown clips from the Paper Chase, and Legally Blond movies before a long discussion of the subject were carried

Table 2. Grading rubric

Criteria	Excellent (15 points)	Good (12 points)	Fair (10 points)	Beginner (7)
Critical Thinking • Identify & analyze real or potential problems	Formulate a clear description of the problem or concept and specify its major components to be examined.	Describe the problem and its components.	List or recognize a variety of components related to the concept or problem.	Recognize that there is a problem or concept that needs to be solved.
• Research, categorize, organize, and prioritize information.	Select and prioritize information appropriate to solving the problem or concept.	Examine, categorize and organize research information.	Gather research information.	List areas in general.
• Establish criteria and propose solutions.	Construct exemplary proposed solutions consistent with the proposed criteria.	Prioritize the criteria and propose at least one possible solution consistent with the proposed criteria.	Evaluate the criteria and propose a solution.	Propose a solution that is not well aligned with the proposed criteria.
• Implement and evaluate solutions	Select and justify the final solution to the problem.	Analyze and evaluate all assessment/information.	Gather information about the implemented proposed solution(s).	Implement at least one proposed solution
Creative Thinking • Solve real-world problems in a way that demonstrates imagination and invention	Able to identify and define creative solutions.	Identify and define some creative solutions.	Effort in identifying and defining creative solutions.	Unable to identify and define creative solution.
• Transfer of knowledge and skills to a new context	Go beyond solving the problem at hand to optimizing the process in a new environment or situation.	Be able to see problem or challenge in a wider context.	Identify what the final solution should determine.	Unable to connect to a new context.
Personal Assessment (10%)				
Personal Development • Realizes how much he or she can learn from others;	Appreciates people whose values, lifestyles or culture are different from his or her own.	Understands the factors that make people different.	Tolerant of people whose values, lifestyles or cultures are different.	Believes he or she has little to learn from others.

out. As for creative problem solving, a few in-class activities were done including building the tallest building in the world using a single piece of an A4 paper. They were then asked to read a case study from Harvard Business Review, titled "Gen Y in the Workforce" by Tamara J Erickson.

- **Out of Class Assignment:** The assignment involved implementing the Socratic methodology and to use a reflective problem-solution map to identify the problem. Furthermore, students were required to take the opinion of different individuals on the case study and revisit the problem-solution map with an enhanced perspective. Students were tested on their critical thinking ability, creativity and personal development (see Table 2 for details). In terms of critical thinking, students should be able to analyze real or potential problems; research, categorize, organize and prioritize information; establish criteria and propose solutions; and implement and evaluate solution. As for creativity, they should be able to solve real-world problems in a way that demonstrates imagination and invention, and transfer knowledge and skills to a new context. In terms of personal development, students should be able to demonstrate how much he or she can learn from others.

- **In-Class Activity:** Students were asked to grade their peers' assignment and provide detail feedback (names of both the writers and graders were kept confidential). To ensure that students do not take this task lightly, the instructor would then grade their grading and feedback as well. By being the grader, students were exposed to a new set of thinking and were able to learn to be more critical of their own work.

Assignment 2

Students were introduced to an in-depth Harvard Business Review Case Analysis study as an assignment. The case revolves around Toyota and an individual by the name of Jack Smith who joins as a new recruit. The case was chosen in order to help the students understand how to develop organization capability, the role of managers in promoting problem solving and innovations, and the importance of developing people at all levels of the organization.

- **Out of Class Assignment:** The assignment included several questions on Jack Smith's and his supervisors' decision-making throughout the story of the text. It allowed students an opportunity to reflect on the decisions made by the characters as well as relate to the experiences with their own. Students were also asked to compare their view of a manager to what they perceived from the case in the first assignment to what was illustrated in this assignment. Students were encouraged to apply the methods that they did in Assignment 1 (i.e. Socratic questioning and interviews) in exploring this case further.
- **In-Class Activity:** Students were introduced to the concept of "Gemba" and "the three actuals", i.e. "go to the actual place, talk to the actual people and do the actual work." The class discussion evolved around the role of managers in creating work systems in which problem solving, improvement and creativity are built at all levels in the organization.

COURSE OUTCOMES/RESULTS

In order to answer the first research question, *"Does virtual learning environment that incorporates the use of flipped classroom, TBL and IDEAS methods impact students' in-class engagement, teamwork and self-directed ability?"* the following survey questions (Table 3) were distributed to all the 40 participants. The questions that measure participants' in-class engagement were adapted from Burch, Heller, Burch, Freed, & Steed (2015) while questions related to self-directed ability teamwork were adapted from Orr, Feret, Lemay, Cohen, Mac Donnell, Seeram, & Hume (2015). All questions use a five-point Likert scale that is scored from 1 (strongly disagree) to 5 (strongly agree). A higher score indicates a higher degree of in-class engagement, self-directed ability or greater agreement about the value of teamwork.

As shown in Table 3, virtual learning environment that incorporates the use of flipped classroom, TBL and IDEAS methods significantly influenced the students' in-class engagement, self-directed ability and teamwork. In terms of in-class engagement, the experimental group indicated that they were very enthusiastic about the course (mean = 4.8) and they also exerted full efforts toward the course (mean = 4.8). When it comes to self-directed ability, the experimental group indicated that they were fully prepared for the course ahead of time (mean = 4.8) compared to the control group (mean = 2.75). One reasonable explanation for this behavior could be due to the concept of flipped classroom enforced in

Table 3. In-class engagement, self-directed ability and teamwork results

In-Class Engagement	Control Group (Mean)	Experimental Group (Mean)
I feel energetic when I am in this class/course.	3.75	4.4
I am interested in material I learn in this class/course.	3.5	3.8
I am excited about coming to this class/course.	3.75	4.6
When I am in the classroom for this class/course, I pay a lot of attention to class discussion and activities.	3.75	4.8
I am enthusiastic about this class/course.	3.75	4.4
I exert my full efforts toward this class/course.	3.5	4.8
Self-Directed Ability		
I prepare for class ahead of time	2.75	4.8
I have developed an effective process to gather necessary information	3.25	4.6
I feel learning from mistakes helps me better retain information	2.75	4.4
I am aware of language and cultural barriers that exist with communication and have developed skills to work with others of diverse backgrounds	3.25	4.6
Teamwork		
I work well as a participant in small team	3.5	4.2
I have positive attitude about working in a team	3	3.8
I learn better when working with a team as opposed to studying alone	2.5	4.2
I believe that working with a team improves problem-solving skills	3.25	4.8
I contributed meaningfully to my team in this course	3.75	3.8
I am comfortable being assessed by my peers	2.5	3.6
I am comfortable assessing my peers	2.5	3.6
I have an approach to resolving conflicts that arise between myself and others	3	4.2
I feel immediate feedback helps me better retain information	3.25	4.6

the experimental group where students were expected to be well prepared when attending classes. On the other hand, students in the control group were expecting to learn from the class lecture itself. As for teamwork, the experimental group felt very strongly that working with a team help to improve their problem solving skills (mean = 4.8). However, they did not feel highly comfortable being assessed by their peers (mean = 3.6) or assessing their peers (mean = 3.6).

In order to answer the second research question, "*Does virtual learning environment that incorporates the use of flipped classroom, TBL and IDEAS methods affect students' academic performance?*" the actual class activities' scores, assignments scores, term project score and final exam score were compared between the control and experimental groups. As shown in Table 4, the average score for all assessments were significantly higher for the experimental group compared to the control group. The average score for the final exam for the experimental group was an A- (93.04) while the average score for the control group was only B- (81.8). The results indicated that the use of virtual learning environment that incorporates the use of flipped classroom, TBL and IDEAS methods had a strong influence on the students' academic performance.

Table 4. Comparison of test scores

	Control Group (Mean)	Experimental Group (Mean)
Class Activity 1	77.1	88.84
Class Activity 2	86.9	92.92
Class Activity 3	89.7	94.7
Class Activity 4	90.65	95.96
Assignment 1	73.85	85.44
Assignment 2	84.425	94.92
Class Project	85.075	93.42
Final Exam	81.8	93.054

FUTURE RESEARCH DIRECTIONS

The scope of gamification in education is boundless and technology innovation is moving exponentially. Five years from now, classrooms worldwide will have some form of technology integrated into them. However, with the rapid technological advancements comes a similar rapid demand for expertise. The problem that will arise is that by the time students graduate with a four-year college degree for example, their technical knowledge would have become obsolete (Banerjee & Belson, 2015). To reduce unemployment due to this phenomenon, education systems will need to work towards a means to regularly update their academic material (Ahmad & Abu Hasan, 2017). This can be made easier with the help of advancements in digitization and automation. Furthermore, the flipped classroom approach should be further explored with regards to better personalize the learning, so students can receive a return on investment that meets their growing expectations. As found in this study, the effects of teamwork on students' in-class engagement and learning behavior were significant, however, most students were not very comfortable in being assessed by their peers or assessing their peers. As such, future research on teamwork should pay more attention to peer assessments. Lastly, a promising topic to be explored is innovation in career goals. Though innovation and creativity are fundamental to the IDEAS and flipped classroom combined approach, years from now with the discovery of new fields of study, students could be encouraged to create new career paths and jobs in the market. As the branch of virtual learning environments is an exponentially advancing field, the solutions to the problems mentioned will be based on novel research and be added back into further optimizing the proposed model.

This study has a few limitations related to methodology and teams assignment. First, it was carried out with a small number of students in only one specific course. Future research should be conducted with a larger sample size in different courses and at different levels. Second, the posttest design is limited in scope and may pose assignment bias. Even though necessary actions were taken to reduce assignment bias, some teams may have had students with more work experience affecting the subsequent learning and teamwork dynamic. Future study could use a more robust design such as pretest-posttest designs to ensure a strong level of internal validity.

CONCLUSION

Teaching methods including the flipped classroom and TBL require students to pre-learn course materials before a teaching session, where exercises rely on students using self-gained knowledge. This could be challenging because it is the reverse to "traditional" teaching when course materials are presented during a lecture, and students are assessed on that material during another session at a later stage. As such, it is important for the instructor to have an introductory orientation class session that prepares and engages students to successfully participate in courses requiring pre-learning. Learning takes place in a variety of ways. The role of educators should be to enriched and not restricted to teaching basic fundamentals only. The IDEAs method promotes a constructivist approach to learning where learners are not simply passively waiting for information to be given to them. In addition, it encourages students to realize that creativity is not just for artists, musicians and writers – everyone is creative in their own way.

Practical Implications for Virtual Reality Applications in Education

Virtual reality already has large applications in education; to name a few: virtual field trips, language immersion, skills training, philosophical theories, architecture and design, special education, distance learning, improved collaboration, game-based learning and even virtual campus visits (Stenger, 2017). From this list itself, it is easy to see that virtual reality not only aids in making current learning methods more effective, but also opens the doors to learning for special people as well as the opportunities for all to learn certain topics that were previously inaccessible through traditional means. Several classes can easily be substituted by more effective virtual reality counterparts. History and geography lessons can be optimized through virtual field trips seen from the lens of an Oculus Rift headset and language classes can be more effective through language immersion that simulates interaction with native speakers in the native environment. Technical skills such as transportation, medicine and military training can be cost-effectively practiced through virtual skills training (Christou, 2010). Astronomy or classes for students with disabilities can be enhanced through third-person virtual reality allowing the user the freedom to do break through physical limitations. Additionally, virtual reality is more popularly used for game-based learning to add a challenging and competitive nature to learning. The concept of game-based learning is a core concept influencing the "flipped ideas" framework as not only does it stimulate a competitive motivation to excel, but also because it is game-based, it is more memorable due to the visual and kinesthetic experience in learning.

Theoretical Implications for Virtual Reality Applications in Education

In 2002, Yale University School of medicine practitioners researched virtual reality used in surgical simulation for training (Seymour, et al., 2002). Sixteen surgical residents were randomly assigned, eight each to either VR training or control non-VR training. While no differences were seen in baseline assessments, gallbladder dissection was 29% faster for VR-trained surgical residents. Non-VR trained surgical residents were studied to be nine times more likely to transiently fail to make progress and five times more likely to injure the gallbladder or burn non-target tissue. Furthermore, surgical errors were almost six times less likely to occur in VR-trained groups. Today, VR can be used to showcase products that would otherwise require physical presence and interaction to understand. Additionally, a virtual environment that replicates the perks of a showroom would minimize business costs. A study was made using both a Unity3D game-engine to create a virtual furniture room that allows real-time furniture customization and also 3D furniture content projection on different walls of a real showroom (VR Projection, 2017). The former caters to the need for interaction and customization while the latter allows for a real-life immersive experience of a tangible product. In the mining industry, insufficient training leads to fatalities on a daily basis. Reality based training tools using VR can provide repetitive exposure to such extreme situations in a safe environment that would otherwise not be possible in an industry such as mining (van Wyk & de Villiers, 2009). In the tourism industry, virtual reality has a revolutionizing role in replacing several manual and costly projects through its positive impact on virtual sales and promotions, virtual theme parks and even artificial tourism (Williams & Hobson, 1995).

REFERENCES

Active Ingredients For The Flipped Classroom Infographic. (2013, December 24). Retrieved from E-Learning: https://elearninginfographics.com/active-ingredients-for-the-flipped-classroom-infographic/

Ahmad, N., & Abu Hasan, J. (2017). Making tomorrow's leaders today: Bringing the real world into the classroom. *Infonomics Society*, 8(1), 2497–2505.

Aksakal, N. (2015). Theoretical view to the approach of the edutainment. *Procedia - Social and Behavioral Sciences, 186*, 1232-1239.

Banerjee, P. M., & Belson, G. (2015, January 26). *Digital education 2.0: From content to connections*. Retrieved from Deloitte Insights: https://www2.deloitte.com/insights/us/en/deloitte-review/issue-16/future-digital-education-technology.html

Bergmann, J., & Sams, A. (2015, November 25). *Infographic: 4 learning strategies for flipped learning*. Retrieved from ISTE: https://www.iste.org/explore/articleDetail?articleid=14

Brame, C. (2018). *Team-based learning*. Retrieved from Vanderbilt University: https://cft.vanderbilt.edu/guides-sub-pages/team-based-learning/

Bricken, M. (1991). Virtual reality learning environments: Potentials and challenges. *Computer Graphics*, 25(3), 178–184. doi:10.1145/126640.126657

Bull, B. (2013, February 21). *A Flipped Classroom Primer*. Retrieved from Etale: http://etale.org/main/2013/02/21/a-flipped-classroom-primer/

Burch, G. F., Heller, N. A., Burch, J. J., Freed, R., & Steed, S. A. (2015). Student engagement: Developing a conceptual framework and survey instrument. *Journal of Education for Business*, 90(4), 224–229. doi:10.1080/08832323.2015.1019821

Campbell, D. T., & Stanley, J. C. (1963). *Experimental and Quasi-Experimental Designs for Research*. Chicago: Rand McNally.

Christou, C. (2010). Virtual Reality in Education. *Affective, Interactive and Cognitive Methods for E-Learning Design: Creating an Optimal Education Experience*, 228-243.

Dalgarno, B., & Lee, M. (2010). What are the learning affordances of 3-D virtual environments? *British Journal of Educational Technology, 41*(1), 10–32. doi:10.1111/j.1467-8535.2009.01038.x

Fowler, C. (2015). Virtual reality and learning: Where is the pedagogy? *British Journal of Educational Technology, 46*(2), 412–422. doi:10.1111/bjet.12135

Gamification in eLearning. (2015). Retrieved from Litmos: https://www.litmos.com/lp/gamification-elearning/

Green, L. S., Banas, J. R., & Perkins, R. A. (2017). *The Flipped College Classroom Conceptualized and Re-conceptualized*. Springer International Publishing. doi:10.1007/978-3-319-41855-1

Huang, H.-M., Rauch, U., & Liaw, S.-S. (2010). Investigating learners' attitudes toward virtual reality learning environments: Based on a constructivist approach. *Computers & Education, 55*(3), 1171–1182. doi:10.1016/j.compedu.2010.05.014

Michaelsen, L. K., Knight, A. B., & Fink, L. D. (2004). *Team-Based Learning: A Transformative Use of Small Groups in College Teaching*. Sterling, VA: Stylus.

Michaelsen, L. K., & Sweet, M. (2008). The essential elements of team-based learning. *New Directions for Teaching and Learning, 2008*(116), 7–27. doi:10.1002/tl.330

Orr, K. K., Feret, B. M., Lemay, V. A., Cohen, L. B., Mac Donnell, C. P., Seeram, N., & Hume, A. L. (2015). Assessment of a hybrid team-based learning (TBL) format in a required self-care course. *Currents in Pharmacy Teaching and Learning, 7*(4), 470–475. doi:10.1016/j.cptl.2015.04.016

Pan, Z., Cheok, A. D., Yang, H., Zhu, J., & Shi, J. (2006). Virtual reality and mixed reality for virtual learning. *Computers & Graphics, 30*(1), 20–28. doi:10.1016/j.cag.2005.10.004

Pirker, J., Riffnaller-Schiefer, M., & Gütl, C. (2014). Motivational active learning: Engaging university students in computer science education. In *Proceedings of 19th Annual Conference on Innovation and Technology in Computer Science Education (ITiCSE '14)* (pp. 297–302). Uppsala, Sweden: ACM. 10.1145/2591708.2591750

Roussos, M., Johnson, A., Moher, T., Leigh, J., Vasilakis, C., & Barnes, C. (2006). Learning and building together in an immersive virtual world. *Presence (Cambridge, Mass.), 8*(3), 247–263. doi:10.1162/105474699566215

Ryder, L. (2017, June 5). *Storm to perform: The 4 stages of team productivity*. Retrieved from Trello: https://blog.trello.com/form-storm-norm-perform-stages-of-team-productivity

Schumann, P. L., Anderson, P. H., Scott, T. W., & Lawton, L. (2014, March). A framework for evaluating simulations as educational tools. In *Developments in Business Simulation and Experiential Learning: Proceedings of the Annual ABSEL conference* (*Vol. 28*). Academic Press.

Seymour, N., Gallagher, A., Roman, S., O'Brien, M., Bansal, V., Andersen, D., & Satava, R. (2002). Virtual reality training improves operating room performance - Results of a randomized, double-blinded study. *Annals of Surgery, 236*(4), 458–464. doi:10.1097/00000658-200210000-00008 PMID:12368674

Stein, E. W. (2014). *Designing Creative High Power Teams and Organizations: Beyond Leadership*. New York: Business Expert Press.

Stenger, M. (2017). *10 Ways Virtual Reality is Already Being used in Education*. InformEd. Retrieved from: https://www.opencolleges.edu.au/informed/edtech-integration/10-ways-virtual-reality-already-used-education/

TeachThoughtStaff. (2018, January 8). *10 Pros and Cons of a Flipped Classroom*. Retrieved from TeachThought: https://www.teachthought.com/learning/10-pros-cons-flipped-classroom/

van Wyk, E., & de Villiers, R. (2009). Virtual reality training applications for the mining industry. *6th International Conference on Computer Graphics, Virtual Reality, Visualisation and Interaction in Africa*, (pp. 53-63). Academic Press. 10.1145/1503454.1503465

What is the 'Flipped Classroom'? (2018). Retrieved from The University of Queensland: http://www.uq.edu.au/teach/flipped-classroom/what-is-fc.html

Williams, P., & Hobson, J. (1995). Virtual reality and tourism: Fact or fantasy? *Tourism Management*, *16*(6), 423–427. doi:10.1016/0261-5177(95)00050-X

ADDITIONAL READING

Ahmad, N., & Abdulkarim, H. (2018). The impact of flow experience and personality type on the intention to use virtual world. *International Journal of Human-Computer Interaction*, 1–12. doi:10.1080/10447318.2018.1509500

Ahmad, S. Z., Bakar, A. R. A., & Ahmad, N. (2018). An evaluation of teaching methods of entrepreneurship in hospitality and tourism programs. *International Journal of Management Education*, *16*(1), 14–25. doi:10.1016/j.ijme.2017.11.002

Glen, R., Suciu, C., & Baughn, C. (2014). The need for design thinking in business schools. *Academy of Management Learning & Education*, *13*(4), 653–667. doi:10.5465/amle.2012.0308

Mayo, M. J. (2009). Video games: A route to large-scale STEM education? *Science*, *323*(5910), 79–82. doi:10.1126cience.1166900 PMID:19119223

Miller, D. I., & Halpern, D. F. (2013). Can spatial training improve long-term outcomes for gifted STEM undergraduates? *Learning and Individual Differences*, *26*, 141–152. doi:10.1016/j.lindif.2012.03.012

Okan, Z. (2003). Edutainment: Is learning at risk? *British Journal of Educational Technology*, *34*(3), 255–264. doi:10.1111/1467-8535.00325

Osborn, A. F. (1953/1979). *Applied imagination: Principles and procedures of creative problem-solving*. New York: Scribner's.

Parmelee, D. X., & Michaelsen, L. K. (2010). Twelve tips for doing effective team-based learning (TBL). *Medical Teacher*, *32*(2), 118–122. doi:10.3109/01421590903548562 PMID:20163226

Puccio, G. J., Murdock, M. C., & Mance, M. (2007). *Creative leadership: Skills that drive change.* Thousand Oaks, CA: Sage Publications.

Tucker, B. (2012). The flipped classroom. *Education Next*, *12*(1), 82–83.

KEY TERMS AND DEFINITIONS

Aesthetic: The feelings and thoughts invoked of certain criteria such as beauty.

Augmented Reality: Interactive computer-generated experience that occurs in a simulated environment that makes the experience closer to the real world. It adds graphics, sounds, haptic feedback, and smell to the natural world as it exists.

Creativity: Looking at the same thing as everyone else and thinking something different.

Critical Thinking: The skill of thinking about your thinking. It requires the mental control for situational assessment and context.

Design: The ability to envision and construct an object or process that meets the goals and requirements of a particular user.

Experiment: The ability to decide between two competing goals, courses of action or viewpoints by designing a process that yields sufficient information to rank each choice according to certain criteria.

Immersive: A digital technology or images or activities that actively engage one's senses and may create an altered mental state to make one fully engaged with the environment.

Improvisation: The ability to make effective real-time decisions in new and complex situations.

Strength: The multiple intelligences possessed by all people that can be targeted for development and creative expression.

Virtual Reality: Interactive computer-generated experience that occurs in a simulated environment.

Chapter 8
Multiliteracies Performance Assessment Zones (MPAZ):
A New Tool to Explore Multimodal Interactions for Virtual Learning

Stefania Savva
Cyprus University of Technology, Cyprus

EXECUTIVE SUMMARY

Recognition of the dramatically changing nature of what it means to be literate in the so-called "information age" has resulted in an increasing interest among the educational research community around the importance of students developing "multiliteracy" skills and engaging in multimodal learning. Nevertheless, for such learning to be meaningful, requires to reconceptualize delivery strategies and assessment of multimodally mediated experiences. The aim of this chapter is dual: First to introduce an alternative framework for formative assessment of multimodal interactions for learning. Secondly, the intention is to uncover the story of culturally and linguistically diverse students' multimodal experiences, resulting from engagement in the creation of a student-generated virtual museum during a design-based research implementation. Drawing from the literature, analysis, and evaluation using the framework explained, it is evident that virtual museum-based multiliteracies engagement, benefits pupils' multimodal awareness, meaning making, and development as active designers of their learning.

INTRODUCTION

Today's emerging technological achievements seem to be moving towards the realisation of ubiquitous learning as described by Weiser (1991). Nevertheless, ubiquitous learning is not preconceived or a priori; the number of possibilities offered by such learning can only happen through strategies and practices that re-conceptualize the content, processes and human relationships of teaching and learning. Part of the more widespread use of the Internet in the context of digital heritage, was the rise of text-based and online image collections (Terras, 2015), in the form of virtual museums, as information repositories by physical museums.

DOI: 10.4018/978-1-5225-5912-2.ch008

This chapter introduces an alternative framework for formative assessment of multimodal interactions through engagement in a virtual museum environment. Drawing on the findings from an empirical doctoral investigation into technology-enhanced multiliteracies engagement (Savva, 2016a), a formative assessment educational tool called Multiliteracies Performance Assessment Zones (MPAZ) is developed and elaborated. The intention is to explore impacts upon pupils' multimodal awareness and self-regulation, to determine the extent to which the instructional design framework designed and implemented, could support agile virtual learning pathways in the modern classroom.

BACKGROUND

Multimodal Literacy in Education

Teaching and learning in the 21st century have been characterized by a constant process of change. It is undeniable that the new millennium has introduced new tools for communication and it is the educators' responsibility to determine the value of these tools and how the curricula is affected. It is critical to question, therefore, what kind of pedagogies are appropriate for the 21st century (Scott, 2015) and how much traditional approaches appeal to today's learner. What do we need to change and how feasible is it? It is within this evolving context of learning that educators need to expand their pedagogical repertoires to nurture 21st century competencies and skills (Saavedra & Opfer, 2012; Scott, 2015; Smith & Hu, 2013). McCoog (2008) in addressing this issue, suggests that educators have a new charge: teaching the new three r's - "rigor" "relevance" and "real world skills".

It becomes apparent that the learning demands and needs of students are challenged in an increasingly digitally-mediated reality (Fleming, 2005, p. 114). In this context, a traditional view of literacy as reading and writing skills (Fleming, 2005, p. 114), becomes obsolete. The nature of literacy pedagogy, research and practice has shifted to embrace the idea of literacy as more of a plurality, discussing about various 'literacies' (Liddicoat, 2007, p. 15). This reshaped notion of literacy is aligned with "the exponential growth and adoption of new media and information and communication technologies (ICTs)" (Day & Lau, 2010, p. 111). The latter involve not only spoken and written words, but also images and symbols of all kinds, sounds and music, bodily gestures and movement (all kinds of semiotic resources), and physical and virtual objects. This conceptualization in literacy terms, is defined as multimodal literacies (Jewitt & Kress, 2003; Kress, 2003, 2010; Walsh, 2009). The term refers to the proliferation of multimodal texts and the significance of all the semiotic resources and modalities in meaning making. Human beings communicate not only in linguistic modes, but also visual, spatial, gestural, and audio. Multimodal literacy or literacies acknowledges that all these systems equally contribute to meaning making rather than be ancillary to language. Kress (1999) argues that language "is necessarily a temporally, sequentially organized mode... the visual by contrast is a spatially and simultaneously organized mode" (p. 79). Norris (2004) observes that "[a]ll movements, all noises, and all material objects carry interactional meanings as soon as they are perceived by a person" (p. 2). In this sense, all interaction is multimodal, including teaching and learning. As O'Toole (1994) observes, "we 'read' people in everyday life: facial features and expression, stance, gesture, typical actions and clothing" (p. 15). Hence, there is a need to understand how the lesson experience is constructed by exploring the functional affordances and constraints of these semiotic resources and modalities as well as how they are co-deployed in the orchestration of the lesson which may lead to more effective teaching and learning in the classroom (Lim, O' Halloran, & Podlasov, 2012).

MULTILITERACIES PEDAGOGY AS A MEANS TO EXPLORE MULTIMODAL LITERACY

Research recommends explicit teaching of multimodal literacy so that students understand how various modes can be used to develop dynamic multidimensional texts that effectively communicate messages to different audiences (Callow, 2008; Hassett & Curwood, 2009). Multiliteracies pedagogy is such a framework for teaching and learning proposed by the New London Group (1996) and Cope and Kalantzis (2000). In its essence, the term, multiliteracies, immediately shifts us from the dominant written print text, to acknowledge the complexities of practices, modes, technologies and languages which literate people need to engage in the contemporary world. Multiliteracies as "new basics" (Kalantzis, Cope, & Harvey, 2003, p. 16) -contrasted with the "old basics" of traditional literacy- are understood as the metalinguistic ability to understand and apply the multimodal grammar and social uses of emerging technologies and modes combined with print texts (De Lissovoy, 2008; Luke, 2000, p. 82;). As such, the term, multiliteracies, is often used interchangeably with new literacies, digital literacies, or media literacies, although in this chapter the use of multiliteracies is preferred due to the theoretical framework that informs the research. The reason being that, the multiliteracies framework, or schema, which has its roots in a sociolinguistic approach to pedagogy and education, seeks to make visible the discourses of power, economics, and technology that shape students, educators and reorder notions of just what counts for literacy. The emphasis in multiliteracies is on "multiple discourses", "multiple designs", and "multiple metalanguages" to support students and educators as they navigate through changes in their 'lifeworlds' (Clark, 2007, p. 35).

Attention is increasingly paid to these competencies and multimodal literacy practices that students need to acquire and utilize in various contexts in order to succeed in the postmodern world (Savva, 2016b). From the policy makers' and educators' perspective, it is their responsibility to design and enact a curriculum that engages students in experiences that prepare them for this multicultural, multimedia-based world. Yet, contrary to this pervasive need, research has consistently shown that print literacy reading and writing activities still dominate mainstream learning contexts (Winch, Ross-Johnston, Holliday, Ljungdahl, & March, 2004).

Virtual Museums and Multimodal Interaction

This followed a generic appellation of the term 'virtual museum' to be applied to these digital reflections of physical exhibitions (Karp, 2014). A virtual museum is considered as a means to bring together similar objects physically distant in reality (Cilasun, 2012, p. 3). Djindjian (2007, p. 9) suggests that:

The virtual museum is dematerializing the object for the benefit of providing much more information on the object: the image in all its manifestations (2D, 3D, details, physico-chemical analyses, facsimiles, etc.) and the knowledge of the image.

Therefore, "a virtual museum dematerializes the museum itself by making possible a "remote visit" (Djindjian, 2007, p. 9). Virtual museums "apart from effective exhibition of objects serve issues of accessibility" (Cilasun, 2012, p. 2); they "facilitate dialogue among people sharing the same virtual space (same context)" (Wazlawick et al., 2001, p. 15). In particular with the proliferation of technologies, "online virtual museums are becoming more immersive and interactive, promoting richer visitor experiences – with scenarios, characters, and objects - with their collections using the latest in multimedia innovations" (Payne, Cole, Simon, Goodmaster, & Limp, 2009, p. 292). Based fundamentally on the principles of multimodal design, in which "information (is) presented in multiple modes such as visual and auditory" (Chen & Fu, 2003, p. 350), as well as written modes, virtual museums fit naturally in a multiliteracies-driven framework as they offer a concrete instantiation of New Literacies, allowing instructional elements to be presented in more than one sensory mode (visual, aural, written).

Virtual museums have been used widely in learning settings in recent years. Virtual reality (VR) and mixed reality (MR) are seen as potentially enhancing experiences in museum spaces, while also acting transformative in terms of the way people interact with each other (Sylaiou, Kasapakis, & Dzardanova, 2018). Maintaining a virtual museum is considered a manifestation of digital cultural heritage as part of using technological innovations to aid the long-term preservation of cultural heritage and to promote new models of public engagement (Museums Computer Group, 2011). It is considered that developing community-based digital archives (Tait et al., 2013) therefore is a win-win situation (Stevens, Flinn, & Shepherd, 2010).

Within the last three decades, interest in Computer Supported Cooperative Work (CSCW) applications using virtual reality has been growing, resulting in the development of "Collaborative Virtual Environments (CVEs)" (Wazlawick et al., 2001, p. 3). Further to this, the technology has also been used to support learning, as for example in the "*museuVirtual*" project (Wazlawick et al., 2001) and Ho, Nelson and Müeller-Wittig's study (2011). Based on these fundamental understandings, the concept of a virtual museum is used throughout this chapter to denote a virtual platform which presents the attributes of a museum specialising in the exhibition of digital material (Karp, 2014), in this case objects, research in text-based form and multimodal and any other artwork in the form of exhibits that was student-generated. In relation to the multimodal and interactive nature of virtual museums, it is considered that these materials may lead learners to perceive that it is easier to learn and improve attention, thus leading to improved learning performance and facilitate understanding (Moreno, 2002) in particular for lower-achieving students (Chen & Fu, 2003; Moreno & Mayer, 2007; Zywno, 2003) such as culturally and linguistically diverse students.

Fadel (2008, p. 13) found that, "students engaged in learning that incorporates multimodal designs, on average, outperform students who learn using traditional approaches with single modes". In addition, this sort of work could be undertaken in the form of informal, inquiry-driven learning (Dewey, 1938, 1991; Kuhn, Black, Kesselman, & Kaplan, 2000; Vavoula, Sharples, Rudman, Meek, & Lonsdale, 2009) through active participant engagement. Finally, it was hypothesized that creating a multimodal learning environment would enable collaborative learning (Dillenbourg, 1999). The latter can "take place within environments such as a virtual one which allow communication, exchange of ideas, and decision making" (Wazlawick et al., 2001, p. 14). This sort of interactivity, "motivates a wide range of students to learn and carry out tasks due to its social potential" (Wazlawick et al., 2001, p. 14). This characteristic was a definite element towards utilizing virtual museums to respond to the research questions addressed in this research. The intention is to address a lack of scholarship on how to capitalize on these opportunities for multiliteracies pedagogy afforded by the museum environment (Savva, 2013). Given the philosophical standing of this research, evaluating students' performance in particular through their literacy engagement and transformations was an essential part of the learning process (Kalantzis and Cope, 2005). In this respect, findings in this chapter answer the research questions:

Research Question 1: What would be a formative tool of assessment of students' multimodal literacy engagement?
Research Question 2: How does the virtual museum intervention developed, affect students' literacy practices and performance?

DESIGN OF THE LEARNING UNIT

The Conceptual Framework of the Research

Bearing the previous in mind, i.e. the premises of the ubiquitous multimodal learning agenda as explained above, a particular framework, the Museum Multiliteracies Practice (MMP) framework presented in Figure 1, was developed and tested during an intervention in a primary school. The conceptual backdrop draws from the field of New Literacy Studies, and involves a creative overlap of the multiliteracies pedagogy of the New London Group, multimodal literacies, and the Learning by Design (LbD) Model proposed by Kalantzis and Cope (2000, 2005). Learning by Design refers to the variant life experiences

Figure 1. The pedagogies interacting in the museum multiliteracies practice framework

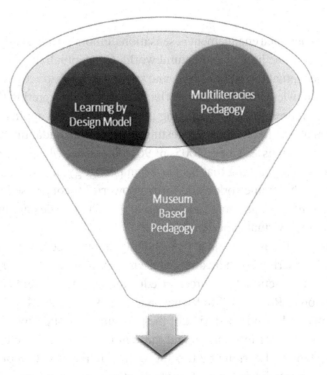

Museum Multiliteracies Practice (MMP)

and interests each student brings to classroom (Kalantzis & Cope, 2012), while also acknowledging that learners are not on the same page at the same time (Kalantzis & Cope, 2005).

LbD involves four core knowledge processes – experiencing, conceptualizing, analyzing and applying. These follow Kolb's (1984), and Bernice McCarthy's (1987) 4MAT model. The original model moved through four distinct phases of the learning cycle using both right and left-brain strategies for knowing. It was constructed along two continua, namely perceiving and processing. Perceiving occurs in an infinite variety of ways that range from experiencing to conceptualizing, while processing occurs in ways that extend from analyzing to applying. The four ways of knowing have been expanded by Kalantzis and Cope (2005) to include eight subcategories, and are intended to correlate to each of the four curriculum orientations of the multiliteracies pedagogy discussed above (Kalantzis & Cope, 2005, p. 72):

1. **Experiencing:**
   a. the known, and
   b. the new;
2. **Conceptualizing:**
   a. naming concepts, and
   b. theorizing;
3. **Analyzing:**
   a. functionally, and
   b. critically;
4. **Applying:**
   a. appropriately, and
   b. creatively;

Experiencing involves personal engagement in sensations, emotions, physical memories, involvement of the self, and immersion in the human and natural world. Conceptualizing is the translation and synthesis of experiences, conceptual forms, language, and symbols into abstract generalizations. Analyzing is the transformation of knowledge by ordering, reflecting on, and interpreting the underlying rationale for particular designs and representations. Applying is "the experiential application of internal thought processes to external situations in the world by testing the world and adapting knowledge to multiple, ambiguous situations" (Kalantzis & Cope, 2005, p. 96). These knowledge processes are intended to enable teachers to analyses the learning that occurs when pedagogy of multiliteracies is implemented. The anticipation is that, such a framework could form a powerful theory-based, and empirically-driven pedagogical tool that can inform a growing field of research on how to design, implement, and evaluate students' multimodal literacy virtual experiences.

To carry out the program, it was essential to plan and implement a specific instructional development/ design. This procedure is described by educational researchers in general as a process that involves the design and evaluation of instructional resources or educational packs (Heinich, Molenda, Russell, & Smaldino, 2002; Kimpston & Rogers, 1986; Richey, Klein, & Wayne, 2004; Richey & Klein, 2007). In addition, the overall thinking behind the design of the museum-school partnership was consistent with Anstey's and Bull's guidelines for teaching in and through multiliteracies pedagogy (2006). In accordance with Cope and Kalantzis' Learning by Design Approach, the selection of multiliteracy texts and resources was undertaken through a balance of paper, electronic and live texts, semiotic systems, genre, and delivery platforms, while ensuring engagement with all four practices.

Rationale for the Development of a Student-Generated Virtual Museum

The decision was made for the purposes of this research that educational virtual museums could be an appropriate approach to transfer the developed learning framework into practice. Regarding the educational uses of VR technology, Youngblut (1998) classifies existing tools to support learning features into three categories summarized in terms of their objectives, and the age and characteristics of the users (the students). The first category refers to the students' use of pre-developed virtual worlds without any collaboration. The second category concerns the development of virtual worlds by the students. Students have the opportunity to participate in a more effective way by creating, or extending simple virtual worlds that they consider interesting (Youngblut, 1998). The third category of tools concerns multi-user, distributed world where students physically placed around the world and connected by the Internet to learn about a subject that is of group interest (Youngblut, 1998).

In this research, the decision was to opt for a student-generated virtual museum which is situated in the second category; the basic planning for the museum would be initiated by the principal researcher, though the students themselves would decide the topic of the museum and construct the space through minimal guidance. This perspective encompasses a recent trend concerning museum visitors' expectations: the interactivity feature, while also responds and tests the elements of the theoretical framework and pedagogical scenarios pursued in this research. Importantly, there is a scarcity of research on educational contexts that reports to predominantly student-generated design and content for virtual museums; and these studies involve relatively older participants and served different research purposes (Ho et al., 2011). In addition, theory-based engagement in virtual museum making practice as proposed in this research is even more limited.

More specifically, a stated objective was for students to expand their repertoires of literacy practices through multimodal engagement in the construction of the virtual museum and researching for sources, including a wide range of genres and semiotic systems (fine art, advertisements, photography, TV programs, films, etc.). As Pena-Shaffa and Nicholls (2004) contend, engaging students in the construction of a virtual museum could trigger the development of a metalanguage for dealing with multimodal texts, thus sharpening the processes of inquiry and learning. Furthermore, according to Hwang, Wu, Tseng and Huang (2011) the process for the construction of the virtual museum might enhance participant collaboration and exchange (El-Bishouty, Ogata, & Yano, 2008) which are critical to constructing a learning design for the MMP framework which builds on the idea of inquiry driven learning. Students could develop their imaginative, creative skills and overall adaptive capacities for designing meaning on their own and extend their competencies in critical literacy and higher order thinking to understand the impact of multimodal texts on their literacy identities.

In addition to these, the expectation through the use of the platform (the virtual museum) was that it would allow the teaching or reinforcement of cross-curricular content by having students linking ideas, taking inspiration from different subjects. The multimodal character of virtual museums could also offer a form of visual and kinesthetic learning that is favorable for visual learners (Keeler, 2009), encourages writing and allows for differentiated instruction/learning for culturally and linguistically diverse students; which is of particular importance in this research.

The intention was for the MMP framework to be cultivated in such a way that it would provide other students and adults "outside" the group (including teachers and school administrators) with better insights into their language and literacy capabilities, including those of culturally and linguistically diverse students. The premise was that this multimodal learning environment would allow the students to acknowledge their common experiences, therefore solidifying group identities and memberships while enhancing group dynamics.

The impression was that this sort of computer-based learning environment could be motivational for all students involved in the research, as it promotes meaningful opportunities to integrate technology through interactive and engaging learning (Higgins, 2003). In this sense, the virtual museum could be utilized to enable ways to infuse 21st-century skills into traditional learning to align with students' contemporary needs and interests. Drawing on these conceptualizations, the various stages of the intervention were separated in three layers of work: selecting the topic and designing the relevant activities, designing the materials for the construction of the virtual museum, and incorporating these into a coherent instructional resource for students to work with.

Research Methods

To test the feasibility of the framework in a real life setting, a design-based research (DBR) methodology was utilised to undertake the research using both qualitative and quantitative data collection methods and analysis. DBR is a pragmatic paradigm of a framework for educational enquiry that aspires to merge design and research as a more seamless activity (e.g., Brown, 1992; Cobb, 2001). To succeed so, the aim is to engage in teaching and learning innovations or the systematic design and study of instructional strategies and tools (Barab & Squire, 2004; Brown, 1992; Collins, 1992; Dede, 2004). The research unfolded in three phases: the preliminary stage, the prototyping stage and the implementation and evaluation stage. In particular, an intervention was designed, implemented and evaluated in a primary school with a group of students coming from various cultural and linguistic backgrounds. The focus is on the experiences of 4 schoolteachers, 2 museum educators and 17 primary students aged 10-12 years old in the island of Cyprus. The students engaged in multimodal design of a virtual museum from March until May 2012 in Limassol, Cyprus.

An array of data was collected to cross-reference interpretations (Yin, 2012) including:

1. Researcher-facilitator observations of interactions reported in field notes;
2. Questionnaires with teachers and students;
3. Semi-structured interviews with teachers prior and after the field study;
4. Focus group interviews with students;
5. Bloom's Digital Taxonomy Activity Analysis Tool;
6. Multiliteracies Performance Assessment Zones (MPAZ); and
7. Artefact collection, including samples of students' work both print and online.

To assist interpretation, a hybrid methodology of qualitative methods of thematic analysis-identification of emerging themes (Daly, Kellehear & Gliksman, 1997) - incorporating both inductive (data-driven) and deductive (a priori template of codes) methods was employed. In this DBR research, the qualitative and quantitative data utilized were analyzed separately to answer the three main research questions. These were later merged to facilitate a deeper and more holistic interpretation in order to gain an in-depth understanding (Creswell & PlanoClark, 2007). This approach complemented the research questions: the tenets of qualitative research were integral to the process of deductive thematic analysis, while allowed for themes to emerge directly from the data using inductive coding.

Table 1. The research sample and data collection instruments

The Main Phases of Research and Duration	Research Activities	Participants				Data Collection Instruments
		Teachers	Museum Educators	Students	Experts	
Preliminary analysis	Context analysis and literature review	2	2	17	2	Documents Semi-structured classroom observations Focus group interviews Field notes
Prototyping	Experts' review	-	-	-	2	Guiding questions
	Users' review	1	1	7	-	Open ended questionnaires
	Pilot with teachers and students	2	1	12	1	Observation checklists Semi-structured interviews Evaluation forms Focus group interviews Researcher journal
Final Implementation and evaluation	LMP programme implementation and evaluation (school sessions, workshop and museum visit)	2	-	17	1	Classroom observation checklists Semi-structured interviews Evaluation forms Focus group interviews Researcher journal Evaluation rubrics

Source: Savva, 2016a, p. 66

Developing an Assessment Tool for Multimodal Virtual Learning

Pollard (2002) argues strongly that teachers should involve students in evaluation and assessment by giving them opportunities to review their own learning and determine what they have learned. This is of the most prominent modern assessment practices in the 21st century. Based on the above conceptualizations of assessment, this research adopted an ongoing evaluation of the programme implemented. It was significant to make this clear to students, as they were used to a specific form of assessment (memorization tasks and measured scores) which affected the way they approached the learning process. Cope and Kalantzis (2005) note in their Learning by Design Model that assessment should not consider the 'right' answer or one correct way to do things, but rather address comparable performance in relation to standards. In other words, the multiliteracies framework of thought argues that there are different ways for different learners to do things and thus different ways to evaluate their performance (New London Group, 1996). This research addressed particularly the evaluation of the knowledge processes by focusing on a schema proposed by Cope and Kalantzis which can be incorporated into planned learning experiences. Essentially, this chapter aims to analyse the changes over time on students' knowledge processes as the implementation of the MMP evolved during the intervention described above. To assess how each student meets the criteria in each of the knowledge processes and define their level of performance, the Multiliteracies Performance Assessment Zones (MPAZ) tool of evaluation was developed and tested.

The mix of Knowledge Processes in the Learning by Design model is of most relevance to the development of the MPAZ tool, as it allows different emphases and activity types as appropriate to students' different 'learning orientations' (Kalantzis & Cope, 2005, p.97). All the Knowledge Processes also change direction of the knowledge flows and the balance of responsibility for learning toward a more active view of learning-as-engagement; in this context, learner identities and subjectivities become more manifest. Learning is conceived as a journey, in a transformational (rather than static) view of diversity in which neither the world nor the learner is quite the same as they were at the beginning by the time their journey finishes. Kalantzis et al. (2005, p. 87) clarify how the knowledge processes are "not a sequence to be followed". They refer to it instead as a kind of meta-pedagogy, a schema against which any pedagogy can be mapped" (p. 87). In this sense the Knowledge Process framework, as "an analytical, diagnostic lens" (Kalantzis & Cope, 2005, p. 148) becomes a tool for a knowledge process analysis/ evaluation for teachers to perform a diagnostic assessment of language and literacy programmes. These conceptualisations were taken into consideration in this research.

The MPAZ incorporates the following schemes of formative assessment. The schema primarily draws on the 'Learning by Design Criteria for Measuring Learning' (Kalantzis et al., 2005, pp. 95-97), an assessment schema using a teacher rating sheet (TRS) in an attempt to gauge the effectiveness of the MMP framework in the virtual museum making practice. The different levels of knowledge are addressed in Table 2, namely demonstration of experiential knowledge, conceptual knowledge, analytical knowledge and applied knowledge, as well as the multiliteracies experience of students. Kalantzis and Cope (2005) posit that the TRS is an effective tool to evaluate changes in students' repertoires of literacy and this was confirmed in this research as it allowed to track students' performance in each of the knowledge processes.

In regards to each of the knowledge processes, three levels of performance exist that define how a student moves from the competence to think and act with assistance, to the competence to think and act independently, and finally the competence to perform collaboratively. These are presented in Figure 1 and reflect: 1) assisted competence, 2) autonomous competence and 3) collaborative competence, with the former being considered the most difficult and higher order level to achieve. Therefore, the schema enables a follow up of how well a learner transitions from "[t]he competence to think and act with assistance", to "[t]he competence to think and act independently", and "[t]he competence to perform collaboratively". As it appears from the schema, the most difficult and higher order form of competence relates to collaborative thinking, as it involves communication, negotiation and sensitivity apart from solid subject matter knowledge. Figure 2 provides a description of each of these levels of performance.

Table 2. Assessment criteria in the teacher rating sheet (TRS)

Assessment Criterion The student demonstrates that he/she can:	Evidence
Demonstrate Experiential Knowledge Students' ability to use their previous and new knowledge to interpret the virtual museum topic	• Experiencing: The Known • Experiencing: The New
Demonstrate Conceptual Knowledge Students' ability to understand the requirements of the topic after researching	• Conceptualising: By Naming • Conceptualising: By Theorising
Demonstrate Analytical Knowledge Students' ability to select appropriate ideas in relation to the topic after researching	• Analysing: Functionally • Analysing: Critically
Demonstrate Applied Knowledge Students' ability to construct museum wings, fill in the different rooms and enrich them with supporting details and fulfil the requirements of the writing genre	• Applying: Appropriately • Applying: Creatively
Multimodal representations Museum Multiliteracies Students' ability to integrate multimodal meanings in their various presentations; graphics, gestures, spatial, linguistic, visual and audio	• Linguistic • Visual • Audio • Gestural and Spatial

Source: Adapted from Kalantzis and Cope, 2005

Figure 2. Literacy performance levels

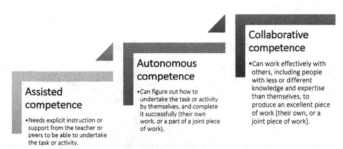

To explore the four interrelated dimensions of multiliteracies and the exhibited level of performance, the researchers pertained also to the work of Hill (2005), who proposes the use of an analytical tool called a Multiliteracies Map. This tool was based on the renowned Four Resources Model adapted by Luke and Freebody (1990) involving namely: the functional dimension, the meaning making dimension, the critical dimension and the transformative dimension. These are explained in Table 3. These dimensions correspond respectively to each of the knowledge processes on the Assessment Schema by Cope and Kalantzis, and together reflect a zone of multiliteracies competence.

The proposition is that each of these dimensions combined with the knowledge processes reflect a zone of multiliteracies competence. The elements of the MPAZ are shown in Figure 3.

Table 3. The four resources model elements

Practices Used to Complete Task With Text	Resources Needed to Engage in Practice	
	What Students Need to Know (Knowing What to Do)	**What Students Need to Be Able to Do (Knowing How to Do It)**
Code breaker Identify and use semiotic systems in texts. Make sense of marks, gestures, is the resource knowledge of all semiotic systems, how texts work.		
Meaning maker Context is important. Exploring the meaning making resources, from which a major resource is the person's literacy identity (all previous literacy social, cultural technological experiences). Different groups have different literacy identities and thus different meaning.		
Text user Use of texts in real life situations. Instructions, negotiations, working collaboratively. Multiple modes exist (listening, speaking, viewing, writing) use multiple semiotic systems, multiple types of texts.		
Text analyst Critical analysis of literacy activities and the text used to make informed decisions on texts. Understanding how texts potentially shape people's perception of the world, how they live, how they participate, how texts are constructed and produced. Resources This leads to an active and informed citizen.		

Figure 3. The multiliteracies performance assessment zones (MPAZ)

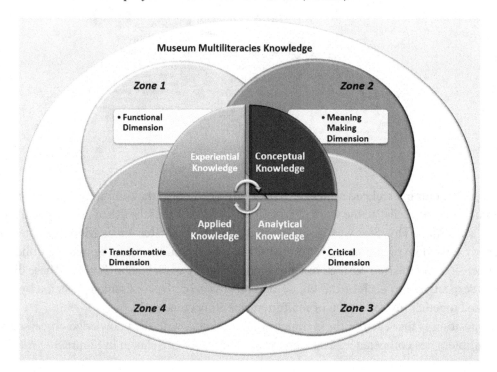

Sample and Sample Characteristics

The target group for this study comprised primary aged students drawn from two classrooms, namely Grade Five and Six. A total of seventeen students, nine boys and eight girls comprised the student group involved in the final implementation of the intervention. This section provides a brief outline of the profiles of the student participants in this investigation, coming from culturally and linguistically diverse backgrounds with varied learning levels and difficulties. The sample and sample characteristics are displayed in Table 4.

Demographic data are also presented in Table 5, for the two schoolteachers whose classes' participated in the research (Teacher Participant #1 and #2).

Findings on Students' Literacy Performances

This part highlights findings from each of the four categories of performance in which students exhibited a range of abilities and possibilities of expressing and representing their knowledge, exhibiting complex literacy practices. Since literacy practices are realized in particular events, the unit of analysis through means of the MPAZ, were the major literacy events within the virtual museum making practice. This was intended to elicit insights into the students' literacy performances within the Multiliteracies Zones. The focus is on the extent to which the students were able to manage the basic codes of reading and writing, their capacities to understand the meaning making systems behind texts they read and write, their abilities to use texts across a range of social purposes including an understanding of the relationships between the forms and functions of different text-types and genres; and their capacity to think critically in the analysis of how texts build up their meanings, and the consequences of different choices that authors make in the construction of texts (Alloway, Freebody, Gilbert, & Muspratt, 2002). Intersected in the narrative are quotations, analysis and interpretation, with the emphasis being on interpretation over analysis.

Demonstrations of Experiential Knowledge

The evaluation of the qualitative content analysis of data from the observations and interviews with students suggested that the majority of them exhibited improved performance in regards to the demonstrated experiential knowledge drawing on the LbD Model developed by Kalantzis and Cope (2000, 2005). In particular, findings derived using the MPAZ tool as shown in Figure 4, suggested that fifteen of the seventeen students moved to a higher level of performance in regards to their experience of the known and the new but existed at different levels: Ten students who were at the assisted competence level in need of explicit instruction or support from the teacher or peers to be able to undertake the task or activity moved to the autonomous level. At this level of performance, students could figure out how to undertake the task or activity by themselves, and complete it successfully; whether it is their own work, or a part of a joint piece of work. In addition, five students who were at the autonomous level moved to the collaborative competence level where they were able to work effectively with others, including people with less or different knowledge and expertise than themselves, to produce an excellent piece of work (their own, or a joint piece of work). Finally, two students remained at the same level, one at the assisted competence level and one at the autonomous competence level. The following paragraphs describe students' literacy repertoires in relation to each level of performance to show how these expanded or not.

Students' Literacy Repertoires

As Figure 3 demonstrates, the majority of the students (10) prior to the enactment of the museum-school partnership were graded at the assisted competence level (Rating: 0-5). Following the intervention, according the assessment schema, these students exhibited an improvement in their performance in both experiencing the known and the new reaching at the autonomous competence level (Rating: 3-7). In regards to *experiencing the known*, while previously they needed prompts from the teacher or peers to make a connection between their everyday life experience and the learning task, it was evident that the museum multiliteracies approach benefited them as they were able to figure out for themselves the connection between their own everyday life experience and the learning task.

Moreover, these students improved in *experiencing the new*. Whereas before the intervention they needed scaffolds by the teacher or peers to make sense of an unfamiliar text, place, activity or group of people, following the intervention, they were able to make enough sense on their own of an unfamiliar text, place, activity or group setting to be able to understand its general gist. In other words, students' assessed demonstrated autonomous competence was profound in their ability to figure out for themselves the relevance between their personal experiences and using those experiences to relate to the virtual museum topic while simultaneously connecting new ideas relevantly to the thesis statements, topic sentences and supporting details.

Five students were graded at the autonomous competence level during the preliminary context analysis of this research (Rating: 3-7). Following the implementation of the final prototype, these students showed a significant improvement in terms of their literacy practices. In particular, they were graded at the collaborative level (Rating: 5-10), the highest performance level in relation to the assessment criteria

Table 4. Participants and characteristics

Male Participants
Participant #1: Grade: Six / Background: Bulgarian / Speaks: Greek, Bulgarian Characteristics: Reads with difficulty, writes with difficulty, communicates arguments well, able to solve complex problems, works with ease in a team.
Participant #2: Grade: Six / Background: Russian / Speaks: Greek, Russian Characteristics: Reads with ease, writes with ease, communicates arguments appropriately, good with complex problems, works well in a team.
Participant #3: Grade: Six / Background: Cypriot / Speaks: Greek, English Characteristics: Reads with ease, writes fluently, communicates arguments well, good with complex problems, works excellent in a team.
Participant #4: Grade: Six / Background: Russian / Speaks: Russian Characteristics: Reads with difficulty, writes with difficulty, communicates arguments with difficulty, analyses and solves complex problems, works well in a team.
Participant #5: Grade: Six / Background: Cypriot / Speaks: Greek, English Characteristics: Reads fluently, writes fluently, communicates arguments excellent, difficulty with complex problems, works well in a team.
Participant #6: Grade: Six / Background: Cypriot / Speaks: Greek Characteristics: Reads fluently, writes well, communicates arguments with difficulty, solves complex problems with difficulty/ timid to work in a team.
Participant #7: Grade: Six / Background: Cypriot-English / Speaks: Greek, English Characteristics: Reads fluently, writes fluently, has extreme difficulty to communicate arguments, difficulty with complex problems, difficulty working in a team.
Participant #8: Grade: Five / Background: Cypriot / Speaks: Greek Characteristics: Reads fluently, writes with difficulty, communicates arguments appropriately, difficulty with complex problems, leadership in a team.
Participant #9: Grade: Five / Background: Russian / Speaks: Greek, Russian, English Characteristics: Reads fluently, writes fluently, communicates arguments with difficulty, has difficulty solving complex problems, has difficulty working in a team.
Female Participants
Participant #1: Grade: Six Background: Cypriot Speaks: Greek, English Characteristics: Reads fluently, writes fluently, difficulty to communicate arguments, difficulty with complex problems, timid in a team.
Participant #2: Grade: Six Background: Cypriot-English Speaks: Greek, English Reads with difficulty, writes with difficulty, communicates arguments well, Characteristics: difficulty with complex problems, works excellent in a team.
Participant #3: Grade: Six Background: Cypriot-Russian Speaks: Greek, English, Russian Characteristics: Reads with difficulty, writes with difficulty, communicates arguments appropriately, difficulty with complex problems, timid in a team.
Participant #4: Grade: Six Background: Persian Speaks: Greek, English, Arabic Characteristics: Reads fluently, writes fluently, communicates arguments well, copes excellent with complex problems, leadership role in a team.
Participant #5: Grade: Five Z Background: English Speaks: English Characteristics: Reads with difficulty, writes well, communicates with ease, difficulty with complex problems, works excellent in a team.
Participant #6: Grade: Five Background: Greek Speaks: Greek Characteristics: Reads fluently, writes fluently, communicates arguments excellent, solves problem task easily, works excellent in a team.
Participant #7 / Grade: Five Background: Russian / Speaks: Russian Does not read, does not write, communicates arguments average, difficulty Characteristics: with complex problems, works well in a team.
Participant #8: Grade: Five Background: Russian Speaks: Russian Characteristics: Reads with difficulty, writes with difficulty, communicates arguments well, solves problem tasks easily, works well in a team.

Table 5. Characteristics of schoolteacher participants in the research

	Teacher Participant #1	Teacher Participant #2
Gender	Female	Male
Class	Grade Five	Grade Six
Years of experience	15	4
Education	BA Primary Education MA in Music Education	BA Primary Education MA in Science Education

Figure 4. Zone 1: students' performance level in experiential knowledge following the intervention (n=17)

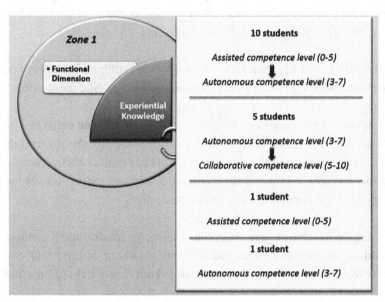

proposed by Kalantzis and Cope (2005). This level in terms of *experiencing the known* meant that the students were able to demonstrate to others the connections between the learning task at hand, and their own or the other person's everyday life experience.

The assessment of students' performance indicated improvements in their conceptualizations during *experiencing the new* process. Students' advanced competencies were observed as they were able to function beyond making enough sense on their own of an unfamiliar text, place, activity or group setting to be able to understand its general gist, to engaging in and with this text, place, activity, or group in such a way that they actively interact with it or add meaning based on their own perspective, knowledge and experience. These students were therefore able to use their previous knowledge to engage with the different activities from the WebQuest and concurrently engage with the main ideas interactively based on their research. In addition, students in the groups reaching the collaborative level could showcase their ability to use previous and new knowledge to discuss during the debate activity on different statements, classification of species and supporting details in relation to these categories. Two students maintained the same level of performance despite the new approach. In particular, one student remained at the assisted competence level and the second one at the autonomous competence level.

Findings from the reflective interviews with teachers revealed how the instructional approach during the intervention facilitated students' existing knowledge while also encouraged students to research ideas that were relevant to the virtual museum making practice. According to Teacher Participant #2:

Normally, the lesson plan is such that will leave little room for engaging in activities that are relevant to the students' lives and personal literacy experiences. The approach within the intervention was such that it enabled to connect their experiences and stimulate their interest. Culturally relevant themes during the induction session of the project made a huge difference. I felt that it helped some of my students to evolve as autonomous learners without as much need for scaffolding as they would have needed... I could see how they took a step further using both previous and new knowledge to interpret the topic for the virtual museum and especially some students were able to reach at the collaborative level during the debate activity. (Teacher Participant #2, from Grade Six)

Similar to Teacher Participant #1, from Grade Five affirmed students' improved performance during the situated practice stage which addresses experiential knowledge. She mentioned:

I could sense that most of my students were gradually immersed into the activities stemming from their own experiences. Although this was not the case for all of them, for those working previously as assisted learners, they seemed to not explicitly need prompts to connect their everyday experiences and the learning task provided. This enhanced their confidence in writing in concrete ways as the Web of Life activity showed. (Teacher Participant #1, from Grade Five)

It was evident that students were engaged in collaboration, discussion and listening during the situated practice stages. Building on their own ideas and listening to others' in the group and how to use them through *experiencing the known and the new*, students did not 'leave behind their individual attributes.

Demonstrations of Conceptual Knowledge

Another level of analysis of the impact of the implementation of the intervention, was with regards to the conceptual knowledge process. The analysis shown in Figure 5, indicated that twelve of the seventeen students demonstrated an increased level of performance with regards to *conceptualising by naming* and *by theorising*: Nine students who were at the assisted competence level moved to the autonomous level. Another three students who were at the autonomous level moved to the collaborative competence level. The remaining five students maintained the same level of performance, which was four at the assisted competence level and one at the autonomous level. The paragraphs that follow describe the students' literacy repertoires in relation to each level of performance to show how these expanded or not.

Students' Literacy Repertoires

The majority of the students (9) were graded at the assisted competence level prior to the enactment of the museum-school partnership (Rating: 0-5). Following the intervention, these students exhibited an improvement in their performance derived from the assessment schema in both conceptualising by naming and by theorising reaching to the autonomous competence level (Rating: 3-7). In regards to *con-*

Figure 5. Zone 1: students' performance level in conceptual knowledge following the intervention (n=17)

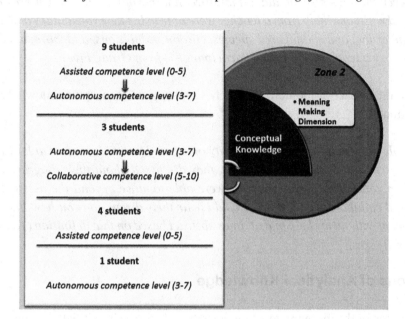

ceptualising by naming, once explained to them, the students were able to use a concept appropriately in context, and generalise effectively using this concept. It was evident that the museum multiliteracies approach enhanced this understanding as they were able to work out for themselves the meaning of a concept from the context of its use or by looking up its meaning, and then use that concept to make an abstraction. Further to this, these students improved in their conceptualising by theorising. Whereas before the intervention they could see the connection between two or more concepts once this was pointed out to them, following the program implemented, they were able to work out for themselves the connections between concepts in a theory.

Three students were graded at the autonomous competence level in regards to conceptual knowledge during the preliminary context analysis of this research (Rating: 3-7). Following the implementation of the final prototype, these students showed a significant improvement in terms of their literacy repertoires. In particular, they were graded at the collaborative level (Rating: 5-10), the highest performance level in relation to the assessment criteria proposed by Kalantzis and Cope (2005). This level in terms of *conceptualising by naming* meant that the students were able to put concepts together in a theory and explain that theory to another person.

As the data using the MPAZ tool indicated, these three students' performance was evidently improved during *conceptualising by theorising* similar to the other knowledge processes. Students' advanced competencies were observed as they were able to function beyond working out for themselves the connections between concepts in a theory, and being able to put concepts together in a theory and explain that theory to another person. Five students maintained the same level of performance despite the new approach. Four students remained at the assisted competence level and one at the autonomous competence level.

Findings from teachers' reflective interviews following completion of the TRS suggested both teachers found the knowledge and skills gained from participation in the partnership as facilitating to expanding their students' literacy performance. As indicated by Teacher Participant #1:

I could see how even the students who did not improve in terms of the TRS were more actively engaged in the activities and with some help from a teacher were able to list new vocabulary and define key terms such as ecosystem, extinct and endangered species, curator, exhibitions, and more, although they could not explain the theory adequately (Teacher Participant #1, from Grade Five)

Discussing on the impact of the new approaches on students' conceptual knowledge, Teacher Participant #2, mentioned:

I found a noticeable difference in the vast majority of my students with respect to how they engaged in exploration and discussion of concepts. The way they discussed about their diagram and categorized types of animals in concept maps showed they were able to move beyond the assisted level to acting as autonomous and collaborative learners. I could hear their discussions on how they figured out the meaning of a concept without my help and at times abstract based on that definition (Teacher Participant #2, from Grade Six)

Demonstrations of Analytical Knowledge

In the implementation of the museum multiliteracies-based approach, critical framing is the component that relates to analytical knowledge. The analysis of the MPAZ tool demonstrated in Figure 6, together with the interviews and observation checklists, suggested that nine of the seventeen student participants in the research demonstrated an increased level of performance with regards to *analysing functionally* and *critically*: Six students who were at the assisted competence level moved to the autonomous level. Another three students who were at the autonomous level moved to the collaborative competence level. The remaining eight students maintained the same level of performance, which was the assisted competence level for five of them and the autonomous level for the remaining three. What follows is discussion of students' literacy repertoires in relation to each level of performance to show how these expanded or not.

Students' Literacy Repertoires

Six of the seventeen students prior to the enactment of the museum-school partnership were graded at the assisted competence level (Rating: 0-5) using the MPAZ tool. The analysis derived from the data of the research suggested that these students improved in their performance reaching to the autonomous competence level (Rating: 3-7) in both *analysing functionally* and to a certain extent at analysing critically. In regards to *analysing functionally*, previously they were able to understand, once pointed out to them, the general function or purpose of a piece of knowledge, text or human activity, or causal connections. Following the intervention, it was evident that they benefited as they were able to analyse causal connections for themselves.

In addition, these students improved in *analysing critically* although not at the expected degree. Whereas before the intervention they could comprehend, once explained to them, some of the obvious human interests and agendas behind a text, action or piece of knowledge, following the program implemented, they could construct a plausible interpretation of the underlying motives, agendas and interests driving a text, action or piece of knowledge.

Three students were graded at the autonomous competence level in regards to analytical knowledge during the preliminary context analysis of this research (Rating: 3-7). After the implementation of the

Figure 6. Zone 1: students' performance level in analytical knowledge following the intervention (n=17)

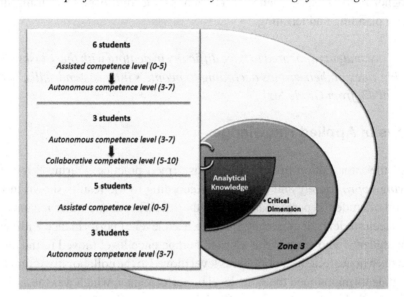

final prototype, these students improved and were assessed at the collaborative level (Rating: 5-10), the highest performance level in relation to the assessment criteria proposed by Kalantzis and Cope (2005). This level in terms of *analysing functionally* meant that the students were able to work with others to figure out and demonstrate the way they see causal connections to people who may not see them the same way. Assessment using the MPAZ tool demonstrated that these three students' performance was evidently improved during *analysing critically*. Students' advanced competencies were observed as they were able to work with their group members to demonstrate collaborative competence. Students were able to effectively select appropriate ideas and make causal connections, corroborate ideas from multiple sources and analyse ideas.

From the rest of the group, five students were graded at the assisted competence level during the preliminary context analysis of this research (Rating: 0-5). Following the implementation of the final prototype, there was no difference noted in their performance. Still they needed scaffolding in under-standing causal relations pertaining to the virtual museum topic, and their understanding was checked through the relevance of ideas selected and presented during the various activities.

Another three students who were reported as belonging to the autonomous competence level of performance, also maintained the same level of performance.

Teachers in their interviews revealed how some of their students successfully undertook both functional and critical analysis demonstrating an improved performance in terms of their analytical knowledge. Teacher Participant #1 stated:

It was profound how some of these students, including the ones exhibiting low performance during normal school routine, could uptake the task of exhibition designers and this activated their agency and promoted task ownership. Those showing to operate within the autonomous level, could plan the next activities into manageable tasks while making causal connections, and analysed ideas without scaffold-ing. (Teacher Participant #1, from Grade Five)

Likewise, Teacher Participant #2 identified challenges and improvements in his students' literacy performance due to planning and teaching:

I would say some of my students appeared to have difficulty in dealing with these tasks, yet they delivered the task of assigning roles in their groups according to people's interests and skills, without much help (Teacher Participant #2, from Grade Six)

Demonstrations of Applied Knowledge

The final stage of the intervention involved the transformed practice. During this stage students are engaged in *applying appropriately* and *creatively*. According to the results shown in Figure 7, drawn from the evaluation of students' performance using the MPAZ tool and other means of interpretation, ten out of the seventeen students demonstrated an increased level of performance with regards to applied knowledge: Eight students who were at the assisted competence level moved to the autonomous level. Another two students who were at the autonomous level moved to the collaborative competence level. The remaining seven students maintained the same level of performance, which was the assisted competence level for three of them and at the autonomous level for the remaining four. The paragraphs that follow students' literacy repertoires in relation to each level of performance to show how these expanded or not.

Students' Literacy Repertoires

Context analysis prior to the enactment of the museum-school partnership indicated that eight students were graded at the assisted competence level (Rating: 0-5). Following the intervention, according the MPAZ assessment schema, these students exhibited an improvement in their performance in both *apply-*

Figure 7. Zone 1: students' performance level in applied knowledge following the intervention (n=17)

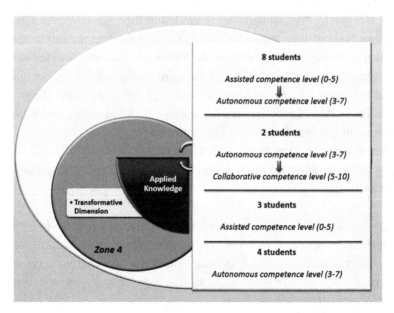

ing appropriately and *creatively* reaching to the autonomous competence level (Rating: 3-7). In regards to *applying appropriately*, while previously they were able in a supportive and structured environment, to communicate or act in ways which conform to conventions or textual genres, it was evident that the museum multiliteracies approach benefited them as they were able to progress and independently and without explicit scaffolds or instructions, communicate or act in ways which conform to conventions or textual genres.

Further to this, these students improved in *applying creatively* as the LbD describes this step of the knowledge processes. Whereas before the intervention they were able, in a supportive and structured environment, to put together in a meaningful way, two or more conventional forms of communication or action, following the intervention, they were able to independently and without explicit scaffolds or instructions, put together in a meaningful way, two or more conventional forms of communication or action, fulfilling the requirements of the various genres through the construction of the wings and rooms of the virtual museum satisfactorily.

Two students who were at the autonomous level moved to the collaborative competence level, indicating a significant improvement in terms of their literacy practices. In particular, in terms of *applying appropriately* this meant that the students were able to master a convention or a genre to the point where they become fully-fledged members of a new community of practice.

The students' performance was evidently improved also during the *applying creatively* as the data indicated. Students' advanced competencies were observed as they were able to progress beyond putting together in a meaningful way, two or more conventional forms of communication or action, independently and without explicit scaffolds or instructions, to creating a hybrid text, action, or group environment which involves a genuinely original combination of knowledge, actions and ways of communicating. This level of group work reflects students' ability in mastering the requirements of each genre and their creativity in outlining the framework of their rooms. The remaining seven students maintained the same level of performance, which was the assisted competence level for three of them, and for four of them the autonomous level. For the students in the assisted level of observed group work, it was obvious that they needed scaffolding in enhancing their understanding of particular genres and construction of the virtual museum.

Results from the reflective interviews revealed that the two teachers participating in the partnership found various skills were acquired by the students during the transformed practice stage that related to applied knowledge. According to Teacher Participant #1:

It was evident that students exhibited creative skills through the writing up of the newspaper articles for the news room. As autonomous and collaborative learners, my students could show coherence and unity in each paragraph and I could see this during the drafting stage of their essays. The different activities prior, while and after writing helped to become more creative (Teacher Participant #1, from Grade Five)

Further findings from the interviews confirmed results from the TRS completed by the two teachers and myself. It was evident that the average and weaker students gained confidence and improved their style of writing. The sessions during the transformed practice using the MMP framework were found as facilitating for students to create hybrid texts such as the virtual museum galleries and video rooms. This comment by Teacher Participant #2 was characteristic:

It was not easy to complete all wings of the museum. Some groups struggled and needed scaffolding, which belonged to the assisted level. On the other hand, the knowledge processes in the intervention made a great difference for other groups since students, mostly as autonomous learners mastered the requirements of each genre and their creativity in developing the layout and writing the stories for the 'News stand' of the virtual rooms. (Teacher Participant #2, from Grade Six)

Demonstrations of Museum Multiliteracies Knowledge

The final evaluation criterion in the MPAZ involved assessing in particular students' museum multiliteracies knowledge. During this stage, students were rated in their participation during group work in communicating meaning using multiple modes of meaning which encompass the linguistic, visual, audio, gestural and spatial aspects of the sessions. According to the results from the evaluation of students' performance illustrated in Figure 8, the analysis pointed out that eleven of the seventeen students participating in the multiliteracies activities were given an excellent rating by both teachers and myself (collaborative level). Another four students' work was rated as good (autonomous level) and one student's work was deemed as being average, thereby considered as an assisted learner.

Students' Literacy Repertoires

When the two teachers (Teacher Participant #1 and #2) where probed to comment on how they perceived the use of technology and engagement in multiliteracies influenced students' performance, both pointed explicitly to the benefits including learning outcomes gained from multimedia, and multimodal activities during the program.

Figure 8. Students' performance level in multiliteracies knowledge following the intervention (n=17)

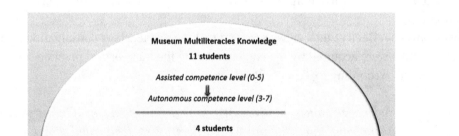

186

It was evident that students benefited from the multiliteracy nature of the activities for the virtual museum making practice. I always knew they could benefit from using ICT in my teaching, yet I was timid to try new things and perhaps disappointed overall by their attitude. Yet I would say the most important benefit came in terms of their improvement in their writing performance (Teacher Participant #2, from Grade Six)

Students were enthusiastic about using the WebQuest and writing on the computer. I was very impressed by their creativity of researching ideas which helped you to achieve the writing outcomes. (Teacher Participant #1, from Grade Five)

A common observation among the teachers was that attempting to improve literacy outcomes by expanding repertoires could be achieved even for the weaker students since new technologies and multimodal activities stimulated students' interest. Teacher Participant #2 stated:

While at times I get demotivated myself when I see my students inattentive and not willing to engage in any activity, when you introduced multiliteracies activities for the museum, my students were delighted and excited so much that kept working even during recess. (Teacher Participant #2, from Grade Six)

An indicative statement from Teacher Participant #2 was:

Obviously, using ICT and multimodal modes of literacy made an impact in many ways, especially in terms of students' motivation to write. Their engagement level was high and resulted in working as autonomous and collaborative learners which surprised me in a positive way (Teacher Participant #2, from Grade Six)

Both teachers identified that they and their students had limited access to new technologies, particularly those that would encourage the development of newer forms of multimodal literate practices due to lack of resources yet it was necessary to undertake such initiatives that would supplement such multiliteracies teaching to engage in potentially transformative pedagogies.

Museum multiliteracies is one way of making literacy 'relevant' to students.

Obviously they are exposed to multiliteracies outside school yet I have not being using it systematically in my teaching. This will change. (Teacher Participant #1, from Grade Five)

Now that I've seen first-hand the improvement in their performance, especially in terms of using visual, audio and gestural aspects such as through the videos, images and role play activities, I shall implement it in my teaching (Teacher Participant #2, from Grade Six)

DISCUSSION

The MPAZ was integrated in the DBR as a research instrument to gauge possible improvements in terms of the students' literacy performances. Based on the evaluation from the combined TRS, and teacher interviews, as it is displayed in Figure 3 (Experiential knowledge), Figure 4 (Conceptual knowledge),

Figure 5 (Analytical knowledge), Figure 6 (Applied knowledge) and Figure 7 (Museum Multiliteracies knowledge), it was obvious that students in their majority benefited from engagement in the partnership. Effective pedagogy should take into account students' knowledge or else their background knowledge, and this was pertinent in planning and advocating the pedagogical practice in this research (Kalantzis & Cope, 2005). Indeed the evaluation using the MPAZ suggested a significant proportion of students benefited from using relevant experiences to their lives as they moved to a level where they could act with little or no scaffolding (autonomous and collaborative levels).

In some cases, the collaborative activities suggested the program, and in particular digitally mediated activities through the WebQuest achieved the impact of promoting a positive learning environment where the average and weak students gained self-esteem which in turn enhanced their literacy performance in particular in writing and multimodal tasks. Kellough and Kellough (2008) make the point that teachers should use effective teaching approaches which can lead to a positive classroom environment. It was evident that the various activities in the intervention, paved the way for students to research ideas, act creatively and perform better using the five aspects of multiliteracies through the computer as a medium and to later present their work.

The MPAZ tool was developed drawing on theoretical insights to inform evaluation of students' literacy performance in relation to the knowledge processes of the LbD Model. Importantly, through the MPAZ tool it was able to communicate about learning to teachers who were able to gain a deeper level of understanding regarding the knowledge processes and how these could be practically used to plan explicit instruction and assessment. The four zones had different focus in each drawing on the components of multiliteracies pedagogy and Luke and Freebody's (1990) Model of literacy practice:

- The functional user or operational skills;
- How students make sense or meaning from the text;
- The critical aspects to using technology; the cultural perspectives; power and positioning;
- The transformative aspects of the computer: how students have taken their new learning and used this in other ways.

What the evaluation suggested is, that students' repertoires of literacy practice did expand during the program implemented. Different indicators of students' learning in relation to the knowledge processes were presented in this chapter drawing on the MPAZ tool. It was evident that, despite their differences in terms of their literacy performance and background, the participating students were able to perform well together and improved from the levels they were prior to the enactment of the program. These findings supplemented by the evaluation of student work samples, as well as the rest of the ratings using the MPAZ tool indicated transformation of all the students through the knowledge processes of Learning by Design implemented through the MMP. Standardized testing could not show the extent of learner transformation since it is one dimensional and does not address diversity or capture the learning that students can demonstrate (van Haren, 2010). An increasing body of research studies affirm on the need to use authentic assessment and measurement of achievement against starting points instead of state averages to address diversity (Comber & Kamler, 2004; Black & Wiliam, 2009; Hayes, Mills, Christie, & Lingard, 2006; Newmann, 1996; Strong, Silver, & Robinson, 2001).

FUTURE RESEARCH DIRECTIONS

Limitations of the Research

An important challenge with regards to a DBR approach relates to the most relevant indicators of quality, success, and the impact of interventions. In this research, this was dealt with in part with the more specific assessment criteria for exploring the impact on students' literacy performance derived from the Multiliteracies Performance Assessment Zones (MPAZ) tool. A key methodological concern as the research is conducted in a naturalistic setting, relates to the extent to which it is possible to generalize findings, or in other words whether the findings are transferable in other settings (Lincoln & Guba, 1985).

Although it could be that the findings of this research are generalized in situations in other settings, to increase the 'adaptability' in these new settings, "it is essential to provide with guidance on how to apply the findings of this research" (Wang & Hannafin, 2005, p.12). Nevertheless, it should be also noted that given the nature of data collection in DBR, in particular during the formative evaluation stage, "the samples selected are often limited to small figures" (Van der Akker, 2013, p. 67).

In this respect, intended users should look "to make their own attempts to explore the potential transfer of the research findings to theoretical propositions" relevant to their own settings (van der Akker, 2013, p. 68). It is possible to reach the previous goal through the task of 'analogy reasoning', utilizing the clearly defined design principles applied as they are described in reports of DBR, and by reflection on the results afterwards. These design principles should entail therefore information on both the (substantive) what and (methodological) how of the intended interventions, but also offer theoretical explanations for the research carried out and the innovation (van der Akker, 2013).

Recommendations

Based on the insights provided by the use of the MPAZ tool for this research, it is suggested that:

The practitioners and curriculum developers in the field of multimodal virtual learning, should reconsider the role of multimodally-driven tools for assessing 21st -century virtual teaching and learning. Although there are challenges to adopt virtual museum learning principles, still the museum multiliteracies-based approach offers a framework of practice that could lead to beneficial outcomes. Using the MPAZ tool to replace existing traditional assessment strategies, will help improve students' knowledge processes and multimodal engagement and participation.

The formative assessment tools used for exploring multimodal virtual learning, should be based on teachers' and students' identified needs which relate to the curriculum and personal interests and backgrounds. It is crucial that a clear understanding of the context of learning, realistic goals of teachers, students' needs and appropriate theoretical literature should guide the design and implementation of effective formative assessment strategies for multimodal student encounters.

It is essential based on evidence from this research that a high level of facilitation and scaffolding is pursued. A culture of dialogue should be cultivated (AAM, 1984; Hirzy, 1996; Sheppard, 1993) among the key persons involved in the learning process and reflective meetings should take place on an ongoing basis. Such strategies should be embedded in the school agenda by both Ministry's providers and curriculum makers to support students' learning and update of instructional practices.

CONCLUSION

The aim of this research was to demonstrate how (rather than why) these students used the semiotic resources available to them (van Leeuwen, 2000, p. 303) in their multimodal virtual meaning making practice. To address the effectiveness of the intervention in terms of its contribution to expanding CLD students' repertoires of literacy practices, the Multiliteracies Performance Assessment Zones (MPAZ) was developed. The tool was primarily based on the Assessment Schema proposed by Kalantzis and Cope (2005) and Luke and Freebody's Four Resources Model (1990) which was incorporated into the planned intervention. The MPAZ allowed to track students' performance in each of the knowledge processes, namely demonstration of experiential knowledge, conceptual knowledge, analytical knowledge and applied knowledge with respect to three levels of competence (assisted competence, autonomous competence, and collaborative competence).

Evidence from the MPAZ, interviews, and in-depth observations of focal students' group suggested overall that the majority of the students exhibited improved literacy performance. In particular with regards to the demonstrated experiential knowledge, findings suggested that fifteen of the seventeen students moved to a higher level of performance in terms of *experiencing the known* and *the new*. Further to these, five students who were at the autonomous level moved to the collaborative competence level where they were able to work effectively with others, including people with less or different knowledge and expertise than themselves, to produce an excellent piece of work. Finally, two students remained at the same level, one at the assisted competence level and one at the autonomous competence level.

Another level of analysis of the impact on students' repertoires of literacy was with regards to the conceptual knowledge process. Findings indicated that twelve of the seventeen students demonstrated an increased level of performance with regards to *conceptualizing by naming* and *by theorizing*: Nine students moved to the autonomous level and three more moved to the collaborative competence level. The remaining five students maintained the same level of performance.

The third stage of the museum multiliteracies-based approach involves critical framing which relates to analytical knowledge. The analysis showed that nine of the seventeen student participants in the research demonstrated an increased level of performance with regards to *analyzing functionally* and *critically*: Six students moved to the autonomous level while another three moved to the collaborative competence level. The remaining eight students maintained the same level of performance (the assisted competence level for five of them and the autonomous level for the remaining three).

The final stage of the intervention involved the transformed practice. According to the results from the evaluation of students' performance, the analysis pointed out that ten out of the seventeen students demonstrated an increased level of performance with regards to applied knowledge: Eight students moved to the autonomous level and a further two students who were at the autonomous level moved to the collaborative competence level. The remaining seven students maintained the same level of performance (the assisted competence level for three of them and at the autonomous level for the remaining four).

This research contributes to an underexplored area of theory-based museum practice on how virtual museum learning can be evaluated. More specifically, the research informs a growing field of study on theory, research and practice of assessment tools for multimodal engagement and participation, focusing on students' multimodal literacy practices. Evidence from this investigation in line with other studies indicate that the characteristics of the design and approaches adopted within the theoretical framework implemented, can support diversity and multiliteracies-based virtual learning and assessment for the 21st century. In particular, the evaluation of the MMP using the MPAZ tool, suggested that it can potentially expand culturally and linguistically diverse students' repertoires of literacy through active self-directed learning and multimodal meaning making and awareness. The MPAZ elicited significant insights into students' improved performance over time, informing current and future methods of assessment of students' multimodal virtual learning.

REFERENCES

Alloway, N., Freebody, P., Gilbert, P., & Muspratt, S. (2002). *Boys, literacy and schooling: Expanding the repertoires of practice.* Melbourne: Curriculum 426 Wayne Martino and Michael Kehler Corporation. Retrieved September 3, 2016, from http://www.dest.gov.au/sectors/school_education/publications_resources/profiles/boys_literacy_ schooling.htm

American Association of Museums (AAM). (1984). *Museum for a new century.* Washington, DC: American Association of Museums.

Anstey, M., & Bull, G. (2006). *Teaching and Learning Multiliteracies.* International Reading Association.

Barab, S. A., & Squire, K. (2004). Design-based research: Putting a stake in the ground. *Journal of the Learning Sciences*, *13*(1), 1–14. doi:10.120715327809jls1301_1

Black, P., & Wiliam, D. (2009). Developing the theory of formative assessment. *Educational Assessment, Evaluation and Accountability*, *21*(1), 5, https://doi.org/10.1007/s11092-008-9068-5

Brown, A. (1992). Design experiments: Theoretical and methodological challenges in creating complex interventions in classroom settings. *Journal of the Learning Sciences*, *2*(2), 141–178. doi:10.120715327809jls0202_2

Callow, J. (2006). Images, politics and multiliteracies: Using a visual metalanguage! *Australian Journal of Language and Literacy*, *29*(1), 7–23.

Chen, G., & Fu, X. (2003). Effects of multimodal information on learning performance and judgment of learning. *Journal of Educational Computing Research*, *29*(3), 349–362. doi:10.2190/J54F-B24D-THN7-H9PH

Cilasun, A. (2012). *Virtual Museum and Review of Virtual Museums in Turkey.* Paper presented at 5T A New Affair: Design History and Digital Design Museum, At İzmir.

Clark, K. R. (2007). *Charting transformative practice: Critical multiliteracies via informal learning design.* UC San Diego Electronic Theses and Dissertations.

Cloonan, A. (2007). *The Professional Learning of Teachers, a Case Study of Multiliteracies Teaching in the Early Years of Schooling* (Unpublished Thesis). School of Education Design and Social Context Portfolio.

Cobb, P. (2001). Supporting the improvement of learning and teaching in social and 456 institutional context. In S. Carver & D. Klahr (Eds.), *Cognition and Instruction: 25 Years of Progress* (pp. 455–478). Mahwah, NJ: Lawrence Erlbaum Associates, Inc.

Collins, A. (1992). Towards a design science of education. In E. Scanlon & T. O'Shea (Eds.), *New Directions In Educational Technology* (pp. 15–22). Berlin: Springer. doi:10.1007/978-3-642-77750-9_2

Comber, B., & Kamler, B. (2004). Getting Out of Deficit: Pedagogies of reconnection. *Teaching Education*, *15*(3), 293–310. doi:10.1080/1047621042000257225

Cope, B., & Kalantzis, M. (2000). Designs for social futures. In B. Cope & M. Kalantzis (Eds.), *Multiliteracies: Literacy Learning and the Design of Social Futures* (pp. 203–234). London: Routledge.

Creswell, J. W., & Planoclark, V. (2007). *Designing and Conducting Mixed Methods Research*. London: Sage.

Daly, J., Kellehear, A., & Gliksman, M. (1997). *The Public Health Researcher: A Methodological Approach*. Melbourne, Australia: Oxford University Press.

Day, R. E., & Lau, A. J. (2010). Psychoanalysis as Critique in the Works of Freud, Lacan, and Deleuze and Guattari. In G. J. Leckie, L. M. Given, & J. E. Buschman (Eds.), *Critical Theory for Library and Information Science: Exploring the Social from across the Discipline* (pp. 101–119). Santa Barbara, CA: Libraries Unlimited.

De Lissovoy, N. (2008). Conceptualising oppression in educational theory: Toward a compound standpoint. *Cultural Studies, Critical Methodologies*, *8*(1), 82–105. doi:10.1177/1532708607310794

Dede, C. (2004). Enabling distributed-learning communities via emerging technologies. In *Proceedings of the 2004 Conference of the Society for Information Technology in Teacher Education* (pp. 3-12). Charlottesville, VA: American Association for Computers in Education.

Dewey, J. (1991). Logic: The theory of inquiry. In J. A. Boydston (Ed.), John Dewey: The Later Works, 1925—1953. Carbondale, IL: SIU Press. (Original work published 1938)

Dewey, J. (1991). *The Child and The Curriculum*. Chicago: University of Chicago Press.

Djindijian, F. (2007). The Virtual Museum: An Introduction. *Archeologia e Calcolatori Supplemento*, *1*, 9–14.

El-Bishouty, M. M., Ogata, H., & Yano, Y. (2008). A Model of Personalized Collaborative Computer Support Ubiquitous Learning Environment. *Proceedings of the 2008 Eighth IEEE International Conference on Advanced Learning Technologies (ICALT08)*, 97-101. 10.1109/ICALT.2008.55

Fadel, C. (2008). *Multimodal Learning Through Media: What the Research Says*. San Jose, CA: Cisco Systems.

Fleming, D. (2005). *Managing change in museums*. Paper presented at the Museum and Change International Conference, Prague, Czech Republic.

Hassett, D. D., & Curwood, J. S. (2009). Theories and practices of multimodal education: Semiotics and the instructional dynamics of new literacies. Presented at the *American Education Research Association conference*, San Diego, CA.

Hayes, D., Mills, M., Christie, P., & Lingard, B. (2006). *Teachers and Schooling Making a Difference*. Crows Nest, New South Wales: Allen & Unwin.

Heinich, R., Molenda, M., Russell, J. D., & Smaldino, S. E. (2002). *Instructional Media and Technologies for Learning*. Upper Saddle River, NJ: Pearson Education.

Higgins, S. (2003). *Does ICT improve learning and teaching in schools?* Newcastle University.

Hill, S. (2005). *Mapping Multiliteracies: Children of the New Millennium Report of the Research Project 2002–2004*. University of South Australia and South Australian Department of Education and Children's Services.

Hirzy, E. C. (1996). *True Needs, True Partners: Museums and Schools Transforming Education*. Washington, DC: Institute of Museum Services.

Ho, C. M. L., Nelson, M. E., & Müeller-Wittig, W. (2011). Design and implementation of a student-generated virtual museum in a language curriculum to enhance collaborative multimodal meaning-making. *Computers & Education*, *57*(1), 1083–1097. doi:10.1016/j.compedu.2010.12.003

Hwang, G. J., Wu, C. H., Tseng, J. C. R., & Huang, I. (2011). Development of a ubiquitous learning platform based on a real-time help-seeking mechanism. *British Journal of Educational Technology*, *42*(6), 992–1002. doi:10.1111/j.1467-8535.2010.01123.x

Jewitt, C., & Kress, G. (Eds.). (2003). *Multimodal Literacy*. New York: Peter Lang.

Kalantzis, M., & Cope, B. (2005). *Learning by Design*. Melbourne, VIC: Victorian Schools Innovation Commission and Common Ground.

Kalantzis, M., & Cope, B. (2005). *Learning by Design*. Melbourne: Victorian Schools Innovation Commission and Common Ground.

Kalantzis, M., & Cope, B. (2012). *Literacies*. Cambridge, UK: Cambridge University Press. doi:10.1017/CBO9781139196581

Kalantzis, M., Cope, B., & Harvey, A. (2003). Assessing multiliteracies and the new basics. *Assessment in Education: Principles, Policy & Practice*, *10*(1), 15–26. doi:10.1080/09695940301692

Karp, C. (2014). Digital Heritage in Digital Museums. *Museum*, *66*(1-4), 157–162. doi:10.1111/muse.12069

Keeler, C. (2009). *Educational Virtual Museums Developed Using PowerPoint*. Retrieved July 14, 2016 from http://christykeeler.com/EducationalVirtualMuseums.html

Kellough, R. D., & Kellough, N. G. (2008). *Teaching Young Adolescents: Methods and Resources for Middle Grades Teaching* (5th ed.). Upper Saddle River, NJ: Pearson Merrill Prentice Hall.

Kimpston, R. R., & Rogers, K. B. (1986). *A Framework for Curriculum Research*. Ontario Institute For Studies In Education/University of Toronto. Retrieved November 10, 2016, from Http://Www.Jstor.Org/Stable/1179432

Kolb, D. A. (1984). *Experiential Learning: Experience as the Source of Learning And Development*. Prentice-Hall.

Kress, G. (1999). "English" at the crossroads: Rethinking curricula of communication in the context of the turn to the visual. In G. E. Hawisher & C. L. Selfe (Eds.), *Passions, Pedagogies, and 21ˢᵗ Century Technologies* (pp. 66–88). Logan, UT: Utah State University. doi:10.2307/j.ctt46nrfk.7

Kress, G. (2003). *Literacy in the New Media Age.* London: Routledge.

Kress, G. (2009). What is a mode? In C. Jewitt (Ed.), *The Routledge Handbook of Multimodal Analysis* (pp. 54–67). Abingdon, UK: Routledge.

Kress, G. (2010). *Multimodality: A Social Semiotic Approach to Contemporary Communication.* London: Routledge.

Kress, G. R., & Van Leeuween, T. (1996). Reading images: The Grammar of Visual Design. New York: Routledge.

Kuhn, D., Black, J. B., Kesselman, A., & Kaplan, D. (2000). The development of cognitive skills to support inquiry learning. *Cognition and Instruction, 18*(4), 495–523. doi:10.1207/S1532690XCI1804_3

Liddicoat, A. (2007). *Language Planning and Policy: Issues in Language Planning and Literacy.* Cromwell Press. doi:10.21832/9781853599781

Lim, F. V., O'Halloran, K. L., & Podlasov, A. (2012). Spatial pedagogy: Mapping meanings in the use of classroom space. *Cambridge Journal of Education, 42*(2), 235–251. doi:10.1080/0305764X.2012.676629

Lincoln, Y. S., & Guba, E. G. (1985). *Naturalistic Inquiry.* Beverly Hills, CA: Sage Publications, Inc. doi:10.1016/0147-1767(85)90062-8

Luke, A., & Freebody, B. (1990). Literacies programs: Debates and demands in cultural context. *Prospect: Australian Journal of TESOL, 5*(7), 7–16.

Luke, C. (2000). Cyber-schooling and technological change: Multiliteracies for new times. In B. Cope & M. Kalantzis (Eds.), *Multiliteracies: Literacy Learning and the Design of Social Futures* (pp. 69–91). London: Routledge.

McCarthy, B. (1987). *The 4MAT System: Teaching to Learning Styles with Right/left Mode Techniques.* Barrington, IL: Excel.

McCoog, I. (2008). *21st Century teaching and learning.* Retrieved November 2, 2018, from http://www.eric.ed.gov/ERICWebPortal/recordDetail?accno=ED502607

Moreno, R. (2002). *Who Learns With Multiple Representation? Cognitive Theory of Ed-Media.* The World Conference On Educational Media And Hypermedia And Communications, Denver, CO.

Moreno, R., & Mayer, R. (2007). Interactive multimodal learning environments. *Educational Psychology Review, 19*(3), 309–325. doi:10.100710648-007-9047-2

Museums Computer Group. (2011). *Homepage.* Retrieved August 13, 2018, from http://museumscomputergroup.org.uk/

New London Group. (1996). A pedagogy of multiliteracies: Designing social futures. *Harvard Educational Review, 66*(1), 60–92. doi:10.17763/haer.66.1.17370n67v22j160u

Newmann, F. M. (1996). *Authentic Achievement: Restructuring Schools for Intellectual Quality*. San Francisco, CA: Jossey-Bass.

Norris, S. (2004). Multimodal Discourse Analysis: A conceptual framework. In P. Levine & R. Scollon (Eds.), *Discourse & Technology* (pp. 101–115). Washington, DC: Georgetown University Press.

O'Toole, M. (1994/2010). *The Language of Displayed Art* (2nd ed.). London: Routledge.

Payne, A., Cole, K., Simon, K., Goodmaster, C., & Limp, F. (2009). *Designing the Next Generation Virtual Museum: Making 3D Artifacts Available for Viewing and Download. Center for Advanced Spatial Technologies, University of Arkansas*. GeoMarine, Inc.

Pena-Shaffa, J. B., & Nicholls, C. (2004). Analysing student interactions and meaning construction in computer bulletin board discussions. *Computers & Education*, *42*(3), 243–265. doi:10.1016/j.compedu.2003.08.003

Pollard, A. (2002). *Reflective Teaching: Effective and Research-based Professional Practice*. London: Continuum.

Richey, R. C., & Klein, J. D. (2007). *Design and Development Research: Methods, Strategies, and Issues*. Lawrence Erlbraum Associates, Inc.

Richey, R. C., Klein, J. D., & Nelson, W. A. (2004). *Developmental Research: Studies on Instructional Design and Development*. Retrieved September 21, 2018, from http://www.aect.org/edtech/41.pdf

Saavedra, A., & Opfer, V. (2012). *Teaching and Learning 21st Century Skills: Lessons from the Learning Sciences*. A Global Cities Education Network Report. New York: Asia Society. Retrieved August 13, 2018, from http://asiasociety.org/files/rand-0512report.pdf

Savva, S. (2013). Museum-based Multiliteracies and Learning for 21st Century Skills: A Preliminary Study. *The International Journal of the Inclusive Museum*, *6*(2), 117–130. doi:10.18848/1835-2014/CGP/v06i02/44444

Savva, S. (2016a). *The potential of a museum-school partnership to support diversity and multiliteracies based pedagogy for the 21st century* (Unpublished PhD thesis). University of Leicester, UK.

Savva, S. (2016b). Re-imagining schooling: weaving the picture of school as an affinity space for 21st century through a multiliteracies lens. In Reimagining the Purpose of Schools and Educational Organisations (pp. 49-64). Springer Publishing.

Scheweibenz, W. (2004). Virtual Museums. *ICOM News*, *3*, 1.

Scott, C. L. (2015). *The Futures Of Learning 3: What Kind Of Pedagogies For The 21st Century? Education Research and Foresight*. Working Papers. United Nations Educational, Scientific and Cultural Organisation.

Sheppard, B. (1993). *Building Museum and School Partnerships*. Washington, DC: The American Museum Association.

Smith, J., & Hu, R. (2013). Rethinking Teacher Education: Synchronizing Eastern and Western Views of Teaching and Learning to Promote 21st Century Skills and Global Perspectives. *Education Research and Perspectives, 40*, 86–108.

Stevens, M., Flinn, A., & Shepherd, E. (2010). New frameworks for community engagement in the archive sector: From handing over to handing on. *Journal of Heritage Studies, 16*(1/2), 59–76. doi:10.1080/13527250903441770

Strong, R. W., Silver, H. F., & Robinson, A. (1995). What do students want (and what really motivates them)? *Educational Leadership, 53*(1), 8–12.

Sylaiou, S., Kasapakis, V., & Dzardanova, E. (2018). Leveraging Mixed Reality Technologies to Enhance Museum Visitor Experiences. *International Conference on Intelligent Systems (IS)*, Madeira, Portugal.

Tait, E., MacLeod, M., Beel, D., Wallace, C., Mellish, C., & Taylor, S. (2013). Linking to the past: An analysis of community digital heritage initiatives. *Aslib Proceedings, 65*(6), 564–580. doi:10.1108/AP-05-2013-0039

Terras, M. (2015). So you want to reuse digital heritage content in a creative context? Good luck with that. *Art Libraries Journal, 40*(4), 33–37. doi:10.1017/S0307472200020502

Van der Akker, J. (2013). Curricular Development Research as a Specimen of Educational Design Research. In T. Plomp & N. Nieveen (Eds.), *Educational design research – part A: An introduction* (pp. 52–71). Enschede, The Netherlands: SLO.

Van Haren, R. (2010). Engaging Learner Diversity through Learning by Design. *E-Learning and Digital Media, 7*(3), 258–271. doi:10.2304/elea.2010.7.3.258

Van Leeuwen, T. (2000). It was just like magic – a multimodal analysis of children's writing. *Linguistics and Education, 10*(3), 273–305. doi:10.1016/S0898-5898(99)00010-8

Vavoula, G., Sharples, M., Rudman, P., Meek, J., & Lonsdale, P. (2009). Myartspace: Design and evaluation of support for learning with multimedia phones between classrooms and museums. *Computers & Education, 53*(2), 286–299. doi:10.1016/j.compedu.2009.02.007

Walsh, M. (2009). Pedagogic potentials of multimodal literacy. In W. H. L. Tan & R. Subramanian (Eds.), *Handbook of Research on New Media Literacy at the K-12 Level: Issues and Challenges.* Hershey, PA: IGI Global. doi:10.4018/978-1-60566-120-9.ch003

Wang, F., & Hannafin, M. J. (2005). Design-based research and technology-enhanced learning environments. *Educational Technology Research and Development, 53*(4), 5–23. doi:10.1007/BF02504682

Wazlawick, R. S., Rosatelli, M. C., Ramos, E. M. F., Cybis, W., Storb, B. H., Schuhmacher, V. R. N., … Fagundes, L. C. (2001). Providing More Interactivity to Virtual Museums: A Proposal for a VR Authoring Tool. *Presence: Teleoperators and Virtual Environments, 10*(6), 647-656

Weiser, M. (1991). The Computer for the 21st Century. *Scientific American, 265*(3), 66–75. doi:10.103 8cientificamerican0991-94 PMID:1754874

Winch, G., Ross-Johnston, R., Holliday, M., Ljungdahl, L., & March, P. (2006). *Literacy* (3rd ed.). New York: Oxford University Press.

Yin, R. K. (2003). *Case Study Research: Design and Methods*. Thousand Oaks, CA: Sage Publications.

Youngblut, C. (1998). *Educational Uses of Virtual Reality Technology*. Technical Report D2128. Institute for Defense Analysis, Alexandria, VA.

Zwyno, M. S. (2003). Hypermedia instruction and learning outcomes at different levels of Bloom's taxonomy of cognitive domain. *Global Journal of Engineering Education, 7*(1), 59–70.

ADDITIONAL READING

Anstey, M., & Bull, G. (2004). *The Literacy Labyrinth* (2nd ed.). Sydney, Australia: Pearson.

Callow, J. (2006). Images, politics and multiliteracies: Using a visual metalanguage! *Australian Journal of Language and Literacy, 29*(1), 7–23.

Carr, M. (2001). *Assessment in early childhood settings: Learning stories*. London: Paul Chapman.

Christal, M., Kreipe de Montano, M., Resta, P., & Roy, L. (2001). *Virtual museums from four direction: An emerging model for school museum collaboration. Reports–Research*. Speeches/Meeting Papers.

Jewitt, C. (2008). Multimodality and literacy in school classrooms. *Review of Research in Education, 1*(1), 241–267. doi:10.3102/0091732X07310586

Jewitt, C. (2009). An introduction to multimodality. In C. Jewitt (Ed.), *The Routledge Handbook of Multimodal Analysis* (pp. 14–27). New York: Routledge.

Kalantzis, M., & Cope, B. (2016). Multiliteracies. Encyclopedia of Educational Philosophy and Theory, 1-8.

Kress, G. (2000). Multimodality. In B. Cope & M. Kalantzis (Eds.), *Multiliteracies: Literacy learning and the design of social futures* (pp. 182–202). Melbourne: Macmillan.

Leu, D. J. Jr, & Kinzer, C. K. (2000). The convergence of literacy instruction with networked technologies for information, communication, and education. *Reading Research Quarterly, 35*(1), 108–127. doi:10.1598/RRQ.35.1.8

Luke, A., & Freebody, B. (1999). A map of possible practices. Further notes to the four resources model. *Practically Primary, 4*(2), 5–8.

Luke, A., & Freebody, P. (2000). *Literate futures: Report of the Literacy Review for Queensland State Schools*. Brisbane: Queensland Government Printer.

Sheppard, B. (2010). Insistent Questions in Our Learning Age. *Journal of Museum Education, 35*(3), 217–227. doi:10.1080/10598650.2010.11510669

Ventola, E., & Guijarro, A. J. M. (Eds.). (2009). *The World Told and the World Shown: Multisemiotic issues*. Hampshire: Palgrave Macmillan. doi:10.1057/9780230245341

Walsh, M. (2011). *Multimodal Literacy: Researching Classroom Practice*. Sydney, Australia: Primary English Teaching Association.

Zammit, K., & Downes, T. (2002). New learning environments and the multiliterate individuals: A framework for educators. *Australian Journal of Language and Literacy*, *25*(2), 24–36.

KEY TERMS AND DEFINITIONS

Learning by Design Model (LbD): The pedagogy of learning by design represents an inclusive approach to learner diversity, adhering to an understanding that not every learner will bring the same lifeworld experiences and interests to learning; therefore, it is not assumed that every learner has to be on the same page at the same time.

Multiliteracies: The concept of "multiliteracies" refers to a broad and inclusive model of literacy that accounts for the complex and rapidly changing modes of meaning making within our diverse society.

Multiliteracies Performance Assessment Zones (MPAZ): A formative assessment tool for exploring multimodal interactions for learning, incorporating understanding of knowledge processes and the learning by design criteria of demonstration of experiential knowledge, conceptual knowledge, analytical knowledge, and applied knowledge. These dimensions are evaluated based on autonomous, assisted, and collaborative levels of performance exhibited by students.

Multimodal Literacies: The term refers to the proliferation of multimodal texts and the significance of all the semiotic resources and modalities in meaning making. Incorporated in the concept, is the acknowledgement that we communicate not only in linguistic modes, but also through visual, spatial, gestural, and audio.

Multimodality: Multimodality has a twofold meaning: first it refers to the way in which a text has been designed, and second, it refers to the process involved during design. The intention is to tackle the deeper process of transition between written, oral, visual, audio, tactile, gestural and spatial modes, when a learner tries to make meaning from a particular text.

Museum Multiliteracies Practice (MMP) Framework: The conceptual backdrop for this research draws from the field of new literacy studies, where different pedagogies and theories overlap to form the proposed framework: multiliteracies pedagogy of the New London Group, the learning by design model adapted from Cope and Kalantzis and Schwartz's museum-based pedagogy, inform a multiliteracies-driven approach to teaching and learning practice.

Virtual Museums: The term virtual museum broadly speaking, refers to a collection of digital objects in a coherent and logic order, following taxonomy and it can include variant media. Due to the nature of the virtual environment, it can be easily accessible and remotely connect people, regardless of place and space.

Chapter 9
Techniques on Multiplatform Movement and Interaction Systems in a Virtual Reality Context for Games

Konstantinos Ntokos
Solent University of Southampton, UK

EXECUTIVE SUMMARY

When a student works on a VR game design project, the input scheme is often bypassed because it is considered to be one of the easiest things to implement. But should design affect the inputs, or the other way around? The author attempts to solve this with the creation of a unified communication tool among students, academics, and developers. This proposed tool will define which movement and/or interaction technique is best suited, depending on the following factors: platform, constraints, context, physique, space, immersion, and user experience. The game design framework will be described, discussed, and presented in a table format to address all of the above when working on VR games. This chapter will also include a section that will define what the player can do and how.

ORGANIZATION BACKGROUND

Solent has become a university since July 2005, but it has a long and complex educational history. Incorporated as an independent higher education institution in 1989, the University's origins can be traced back to a private School of Art founded in 1856. Mergers between Southampton College of Art, the College of Technology and the College of Nautical Studies at Warsash has laid the foundations for what is now Southampton Solent University. Since becoming a university, Southampton Solent has helped nearly fifty thousand students from all walks of life to make the most of their potential. Guided by three Vice-Chancellors in turn, the University has changed dramatically over the past ten years – from campus improvements to the state-of-the-art facilities (Solent University, 2018).

DOI: 10.4018/978-1-5225-5912-2.ch009

INTRODUCTION

There is an urgent need to differentiate all the possible movement and interaction systems game development students would have at their disposal to develop a VR game project. That is especially important when students specialized in game development are in the process of completing their Final Major Project (FMP) that intends to define what a game would be, after considering all types of inputs in the design process. Both movement and interaction systems available to game developers would define whether a game could be built as a mobile or a desktop/console game. Those considerations would greatly affect the game design foundation, and, in turn, affect the nature and quantity of features or mechanics in a game design product. The author has been assigned the task by *PacktPub* to develop two online courses to teach VR Development using Unreal Engine (Ntokos & Eleutheriou, 2017). *PacktPub* is a publisher of technology- or developer-oriented technical textbooks. *PacktPub* also develops online courses that require a careful study of system movements and interactions.

BACKGROUND

As part of the Solent University's curriculum, students will be required to complete a final year project at their last semester of study. Some of them opt to do a VR project which often involves issues of great technical and academic importance. Technically speaking, a significant question is which platform students could choose from to develop their game design project. Academically, the VR project itself could bring a new layer of learning experiences for students that need special consideration before delving into game design or code in the areas of movement and input constraints. These issues as mentioned above are likely to pose many challenges for students, which warrants the proposition of a pedagogical framework to define how a game should be made or constrained by game developers.

Technological Concerns

The technical concerns to justify this pedagogical chapter to teach game design principles is that the game design process needs a principle-based framework that can be used for a multi-platform context. Depending on the type of game project that students want to complete, there would be several VR techniques needed for each of these game platforms. Students may also need a full access to PC and/ or mobile headsets, and even subsequently adjust their own game design projects because of these technological limitations. For example, it might not be practical for students to design a VR game for mobile platforms, with the expectation that all end users always have a mobile-friendly gamepad for interactions. Furthermore, mobile headsets are different from each other. In the mobile context, game developers have frequently relied on *Google Cardboard* (Google, 2014) and *Fibrum* headset (Fibrum Limited, 2017). *Fibrum* headset does not have the hole on the upper right corner to allow a finger to be inserted to tap on the screen. On the other hand, *Google Cardboard* is the cheapest solution for mobile VR and it also allows tapping on screen through a hole.

Academic Concerns

The educational concerns are of higher importance as to developing a pedagogical framework to teach VR or game design that might directly impacts on the learning outcomes of the final year project. Furthermore, it could affect students' understanding that both movement and interaction techniques are core aspects of any VR experience. This book chapter summarizes a list of design principles from a series of observation of existing game products on the marketplace. This chapter aims to develop a student-friendly framework that is used during the development of a VR design project or, possibly. any game design project. The framework itself, should be used as a common language among those who are interested in developing a VR project. Furthermore, this pedagogical framework should also be used to either define game design or be constrained by game design itself, depending on the chosen design approach by the game developer. This pedagogical framework itself should be able to differentiate between both movement and interaction systems, for both PC and mobile platforms, or even any applicable game genres in any platforms. Additionally, this descriptive framework could also help students to narrow down their own design choices in the process of completing their own final year project.

Current Challenges Facing the Organization

The challenge experienced by the author at Solent University is that there is no single framework to define which types of movement or interaction systems students could use for their VR design projects. As a result, at Solent University, there is a need to develop a pedagogical framework with a list of clearly-defined techniques and principles for both students and instructors to follow when teaching game design. This framework to teach game design would be used to communicate how the final year project should be structured, particularly on the components of both movement and interaction techniques. The main challenge experienced by many educators teaching the final project is that the student would focus on game design and gameplay elements in their final VR project, but fail to consider as much on how the player would move or interact during gameplay. The best way to demonstrate their knowledge and skills in learning movement and interaction logic in their code is to look at how other commercially successful games have been developed in the past and learn by imitating the relevant design techniques in their project.

Research Questions

On the basis of the above background, this book chapter aims to provide answers to the following three research qestions:

Research Question 1: What design techniques are used by existing video games to implement movement?
Research Question 2: What design techniques are used by existing video games to implement interaction?
Research Question 3: What will be the most efficient combinations of movement and interaction techniques when developing the most natural VR experiences?

MAIN FOCUS OF THE CHAPTER

Movement Techniques

The solution to the problems above is the creation of a pedagogical framework that would define the ways various controlled characters would move around in a VR game. This is based on several technical limitations the game developer would have on any chosen platform. The first thing to consider will be a differentiation on a plethora of easily perceptible techniques. Two factors need to be taken into consideration. First, game developers need to consider which technique to use (no matter whether they are movement or interaction). Secondly, what will be the best platform (desktop or mobile) to choose from? The author analyzes these techniques as well as the platforms to discuss their superiority and to explain if there are any other technical limitations that might hinder the usage of these techniques in an actual design project.

The starting point is to define what constitute the types of movement techniques a game developer may use. In the context of VR, the primary goal of a movement technique is to avoid motion sickness that users may experience. The secondary goal is to increase the immersion of the player by using a realistic movement pattern significant in a given context.

The context of a digital game is very important to define which movement and interaction techniques will be applicable. For example, when a player controls a car, a movement technique using a steering wheel will provide more immersion and realism. When a player controls an Iron-Man-like character who is seeing the world through a suit's user interface, then the best technique would be *LookAt*, which is analyzed further below.

The first, also the most common technique, for VR games on the market is the *Classic* technique. This technique involves any type of input device in the hands of the player, such as a touch device, a game controller, a keyboard & mouse setup, or a mobile-friendly gamepad. The *Classic* technique is the easiest implementation, as the developer only needs to bind the button presses and axis to a specific in-game movement by the character. An example of the games using this technique is *Resident Evil 7* (Capcom, 2017).

While movement may seem to be a trivial task, it really isn't, because it is not just the translation of an object in a 3D space, but it is also the rotation of that object. Consequently, since players are looking through the eyes of a character in a VR game, it is important that a developer needs to think of a user-friendly way of turning around. Problems can arise if a player wants to make a 180-degree turn. It is certain that players will get motion sickness, if turning and rotating are not implemented properly (Harmony Studios Limited, 2018). Turning players' head around and changing the orientation of the camera with this movement is something that is natural when playing a VR game.

The best solution is assigning a button or axis (like the analog/thumb stick – depending on the controller) to a slight but quick turn in degrees (Mason, 2015). As soon as the player tilts the analog stick to any direction, a very slight rotation would occur, within such a very short timeframe, to allow the player even to notice it. The ideal timeframe needs to be adjusted by the developer is likely to be between 0.1 to 0.3 seconds, which might make the change in rotation almost unnoticeable to players. Another factor that needs to be considered is the angle of rotation to be made. Rotating in increments of 5 degrees around the range of 15-30 degrees seems to be ideal, but it is subject to further experimentation to confirm its applicability when designing a game.

The second technique is the *LookAt* technique. With this technique, the developers could design their characters as stationary objects. These characters would make a move only when the player is looking at a specific object within the game world. That can be executed by having the player look at an object while instantly making a move. Additionally, by adding the parameter of duration, the player can keep staring at the object for a specified amount of time, considered to be meaningful for the game context. An example of using the *LookAt* movement technique would be on flight games where the players always move forward, based on where they are looking at. An example of this type of games is *Froggy VR* (FIBRUM, 2017).

As a movement technique, *LookAt* is very easy to implement, and the way the character moves is going to be scripted in a way that prevents motion sickness. *LookAt* may also be one of the few available options, especially when the developers are constrained by inputs available to them. This specific movement technique only uses the selected headset's stereoscopic movements. It is further implemented with a single raycast from the middle of the screen towards the forward-facing axis of the player's head orientation within a specified or infinite range. Another possible drawback is that the movement does not seem to be realistic or immersive as the player cannot directly control the character's actual movement.

The third movement technique that developers can use in VR games is called *Toggled*. By using this technique, the character is always moving forward at a pre-defined speed, based on the forward-facing vector of the player's head orientation. However, this technique would mean that, unless the players want the character to always move forward, there needs to be a mechanism that toggles the character movement. Constantly moving forward is both unrealistic, not immersive, to say the least, and may be a sign of faulty game design. That is the reason the author comes up with the term *Toggled* as this movement needs to be toggled on and off to optimize players' experiences. A plethora of games that use *Google Cardboard* on mobile devices tends to heavily rely on this technique. One of them is *House of Terror VR* for the *PlayStore* (Lakento, 2018).

This technique can be implemented as follows. Firstly, it can be implemented via as simple as a key on a gamepad. The execution can also be done with a simple tap on the touch screen of a mobile device (provided there is a way for a finger to access the touch screen through the headset). Another implementation method would be to design a specific sprite that, when looked at, the player will stop moving. An example would be a sprite that states "STOP". The same sprite would then be used to make the character moving again. That specific sprite needs to follow the player character around and be placed either high up or on the ground, so it does not interfere with the game environment. However, that sprite is lowering the immersion and can get tiring for the user and not as good for motion-sensitive people. A third implementing approach of the toggling would be to ignore the sprite and have a specific angle-threshold that the player will need to raise his or her head above (or below). This could cause the angle between his or her forward-facing vector to be greater (or lower) than the threshold and toggle the movement. That may also be tiring for the player but at least there is not an immersion-breaking graphic. This type of movement technique is more suitable for mobile game platforms since there are input constraints for VR games in that platform.

The above specific movement technique at first glance seems to be more immersive than *LookAt* technique discussed above since the player has a more active role regarding when he or she wants to move. However, with a bit of consideration, that immersion may be easily broken, especially when toggling happens with head tilting or looking at a sprite. Toggling the movement using a gamepad or a simple tap on a mobile device seems to be the most simple and straightforward method. However, three questions may be brought up: "Is that realistic?"; "Can the mobile headset accommodate the tap?"; and "Is this movement type viable for games that can support gamepads, keyboard, mouse and other types of input?"

The answers to these important questions would come after testing those inputs in an actual game, and the short answers to these questions are often "No", "It depends", and "No", in that order. "No" for the first question because it just does not make sense in a game context to tilt one's head to toggle movement. "It depends" for the second question bcause the type of headset one may have (mobile ones specifically, because some headsets do not allow tapping with any available holes in the headset. Finally, "No" for the third question, as if the developers are having other types of input, they should probably use those instead.

The next movement technique is called "Locomotion". With this technique, the character in a VR game moves if quick changes in the acceleration of the VR headset are identified. This involves the real player making fast movements with his or her VR headset, which is achieved by running (so his/her head is moving up and down). Technically, this measures the acceleration of the headset during specific time intervals, and if those changes in acceleration are present, then the character is moving. This is achieved through either the headset's built-in accelerometer, or the phone's accelerometer in a mobile game.

The main drawback of this movement technique, even if it seems natural and realistic, is that it is not as immersive, as the player is not actually running, but is running in-place, which may seem confusing. Consequently, even though it may be realistic, it is not as immersive. However, that is not the case when the technique is used in conjunction with GPS Sensors of the phone, so movement only happens when acceleration and actual GPS updates occur. Another problem with this technique is that there are also no ways of clearly differentiating the acceleration from different speeds. Finally, the most important factor that will make this technique less favorable is that the player needs to be constantly moving when he or she wants the character to move as well. In addition to that, the technique requires a lot of physical stamina for the player who may not be as fit as the game would require. After all, what needs to be considered is that when a video game is created, the focus is to entertain the player and not exhaust him or her during gameplay. However, that is not the case when the game is focused on fitness, which is a great idea of implementing VR in fitness games or apps together.

The *Locomotion* technique may be more realistic than both *LookAt* and *Toggled* techniques that have been discussed above. After repetitive and excessive testing, it seems that this technique does not cause motion sickness as much as the other two techniques. The player's physical movements and excitement do not allow the player to feel that the movement is any different interacting with the game. It seems conclusive that the *Locomotion* technique could allow the player to have the most active control over the character's actual movement. However, this is the most arduous technique for the player in terms of the requirement for physical stamina and fitness. Finally, this technique is recommended to be used with mobile VR games since the actual headset does not require any cabling around it, so the player can run and jump around freely and without any physical restraint. Being a physically-demanding movement, this technique is greatly paired with fitness VR apps and *exergaming* in general. A game example of integrating this movement technique would be the *BitGym* game for a mobile platform (Active Theory Inc, 2018).

The fifth technique the author has explored in this book chapter is the *Rail* technique. It is assumed that the player has no control over his or her movement and only follows a designated path. This movement technique works on the assumption that the player is either mounting a self-driven vehicle that follows a specific pre-scripted trail (such as a mine cart, a jeep, a boat or an airplane). The game design needs to clearly point out that the player will not have any control over that vehicle. For example, where the vehicle is controlled by some other player such as an NPC (i.e., Non-Player Character) driver or gravity and other means. The *Rail* technique has been mostly used in the *Rail Shooter* game genre that are known for their automatic movement during gameplay, and the only concern of the player should be on pointing his/her gun at something before shooting it. An example of a game using *Rail* technique would be *Zombie Shooter VR* (FIBRUM, 2017) for mobile or *Until Dawn: Rush of Blood* (Supermassive Games, 2016). The *Rail* technique is an excellent design choice when the developer does not want the player to have any control over his or her movement to just "enjoy the ride". The occasion could be a rail shooter where the player character walks on his or her own or when he or she is mounting another vehicle. If the designer uses this technique, the players instantly lose any control over their own movement during gameplay. When this occurs, the only focus of the game design is about the actual interaction with in-game design element in the game world. It is apparent that this technique is only immersive when the character is mounted, and it is a good fit for the mobile devices and platofrms. As an added value, it relieves the game developers of the stress due to input constraints, so they only focus on interaction during gameplay. Technically, the only thing that the developers would implement will be the scripted path that the characters would take.

The sixth movement technique, *Teleport*, is the first technique that requires special touch input devices (i.e., haptic sensors), such as *Oculus Touch, Vive Touchpad, PlayStation Move*, etc. The game developers can assume they cannot use this technique on mobile devices. When this technique is implemented, the players are able to move around when they point with their touch controllers to a specific point in space. When this becomes a *Candidate Teleportation Position*, the players need to have a visual indicator that can show them exactly where the position is located at. Following this graphical indication, the players need to use one of the buttons on the touch control to confirm the teleportation.

A very important note to cover is that, whenever a player uses the teleportation mechanic, the developer must fade the screen in and out instantaneously, so the quick movement is obscured from the player. As a result, the player will not have a strong sense of disorientation or motion sickness. Another drawback of this technique is its lack of immersive or realistic feeling in any way, since these characters are constantly blinking from space to space or doing a scripted movement (such as a well-calculated jump using a trajectory). The only challenging part of this technique is to make the actual movement meaningful to players in the game. The *Teleport* technique is also slightly more complex to implement than the other techniques mentioned above, though it is also constrained to be used to either PC or console platforms due to input limitations. The input scheme also has many known variations like *Teleport by Projection, Teleport by Point, Teleport by Throwing Object* (Carbotte, 2018). An example of Teleportation movement in VR game would be *Doom VFR* (id Software, 2017).

The *Rope* technique is characterized by the way the movement is executed within the game context. Like *Teleport*, *Rope* also requires touch input devices. This technique also uses the depth from a VR camera sensor to see when users' hands are completely stretched forward and backward. Technically, players need to stretch out their arms and close the grip of their hands by pressing a relevant button on the touchpad. Afterwards, the players keep the button pressed and as they move the arm back in its original position, the character keeps moving forward based on the delta position of their hands. The above description explains the design philosophy behind this technique and to demonstrate why *Rope* refers to the movement made by the hands to resemble the physical movement of pulling a rope. Summing up, the players need to stretch out their arms, close their grip firmly (simulated with a button press) and then move the hand backwards toward the direction of the players. *Vindicta* game uses the *Rope* technique (Game Cooks, 2017).

While that movement technique is constrained on PC and console VR platforms, it still may not be as realistic or immersive, unless the actual game involves hand stretching or, rope pulling. *Rope*, as a design technique, also does not lead to motion sickness because the player may sometimes "pull the rope" harder or softer than usual. On the other hand, the player may feel the need to have more control over the movement of the character.

The eighth technique refers to a very specialized design principle and can only be used in games where the player controls something through a steering wheel from a car, a robot, a go-kart, even a pirate ship as the name *Wheel* has implied. This technique requires a steering wheel controller or a gamepad which includes an accelerometer. Examples of digital game using this design technique are *the DualShock 4* or *the Xbox 360/One/One X controller*. Unless the player has access to a special mobile device, which supports such a controller, this technique is exclusive to PC and console game. However, this limitation has a very positive effect on the player's immersive experiences and thus, ideal for a racing genre or a game genre that simulates a driving experience when the player is sitting down. The way this technique works is that based on the rotation of the steering wheel, the player will be able to turn around, and accelerate or brake as needed. Furthermore, there is a good chance that extra buttons will be on the steering wheel to allow players to gain extra control. This control scheme also appears in non-VR games which have to do with racing that support a racing wheel.

Racing games are a natural extension of this design technique. Even though the immersion level might be maxed out, this design technique may cause disorientation and motion sickness. This is true, as some people are not able to handle great speeds in a virtual environment. It is also natural that players will experience gameplay at a high velocity and, in that case, may cause some players to be susceptible to motion sickness or not.

Another game design technique in the proposed framework is called *Scripted* because the game developer are not able to really use any of the above techniques. It is very constrained based on the input devices available, or the game does not really evolve around move at all. The technique closest to *Scripted* is the *Rail* technique, since the player does not really have direct access over his or her character's movements and rather focuses on interaction during gameplay. *Scripted* and *Rail* are different as explained below. Using the *Rail* technique, the character in the game is constantly following a pre-scripted path, while the *Scripted* technique will only allow the player to move once during a specific number of events when conditions are met or triggered. This movement is accomplished through a path, blinking teleportation, or any other way.

In a zombie shooting game that is implemented by the *Rail* movement technique, the character would keep on walking no matter what, and the player would need to shoot as many zombies as possible. In the *Scripted* technique, the character would be standing still, and all zombie enemies may need to be defeated or a specific timeframe must pass to trigger subsequent movement.

Several *scripted* techniques are also used in puzzle or escape room games, where the character is constrained on a chair and cannot really do much besides looking around at objects in the virtual environment. This technique also gives the game developers the freedom to design for either a mobile, a desktop, or a console platform that does not require any input from the user directly. As such, the main conditions required to trigger the transition are facilitated through player's own interaction with the virtual environment.

The game design framework is further enhanced with two other techniques to supplement both the movement and interaction techniques discussed in this book chapter. The context and implementation change, in the end, will be at the discretion of the game developers as to how to use two supplementary techniques properly: *Voice* and *Kinetic*. The *Voice* technique requires that the player has full access to a microphone of a mobile device, a USB or condenser microphone for a PC/Console, or the *PlayStation* VR headset with a built-in microphone. The player can control the way his or her character moves using either specific voice commands (voice recognition) or just the pitch or volume of his or her own voice. An example of how these techniques have been used can be found in *Star Trek: Bridge Crew* (Red Storm Entertainment, 2017). The way movement is executed is like the *Scripted* technique, but the actual condition that needs to be met is the voice command or pitch/volume itself.

Technically, the *Voice* technique is also one of the hardest things to implement, especially if one is considering using solely voice commands. The *Voice* technique needs an underlying voice recognition software or algorithm to understand simple words at first, and complex sentences at a later stage. However, this is a very immersive movement technique which may also be the only movement technique to move AI-controlled NPCs within a game context. For example, a character may be tied to a chair, may be handicapped, or may even be completely paralyzed. The only method of moving other NPCs is through the character's own voice as a control mechanism. That would be ideal if the character is sitting in a monitor room, observing other NPCs through the CCTV cameras, as they advance in a game environment infested with zombies where voice is the only way to command them.

The final movement technique is the *Kinetic* technique that could enable player's movement to be completed whenever the player is moving specific body parts using the depth sensor of a VR camera. This movement technique is appropriate for the design of *exergaming* and fitness games. Like the *Locomotion* and *Rope* techniques, the *Kinetic* technique will require a great amount of player stamina as the movement process may get strenuous after a while. The actual movement, like *Voice*, resembles the *Scripted* technique, as the player does not control his or her movement directly, but the body movements actually trigger this transition. This technique can be also expressed as *Superman Locomotion* where a player must hold his or her hands towards a direction he or she wants to move. The *Superman Locomotion* is often experienced by a player in *Weightless* (Schubert, 2016), which uses Leap Motion Technology that involves a hand-tracking technology to develop VR games and applications.

The above discussions review different types of movement techniques that are commonly used in game design circle and students majoring in game design. These techniques with a short explanation are summarized in Table 1.

To conclude this section, it is also worth noting here that a movement technique should not be associated with the way a camera is set. There are 3rd Person Platformers for VR that use a *floating head* camera following the character, but the actual movement is done through the *Classic* technique. This movement happens since the game character moves around using axis and button presses from a gamepad.

Interaction Techniques

Moving around can influence the game design and the mechanics to be built or the platform that will be chosen in the design process. Interaction on its own has the same amount of influence in defining game design and platform choice, which becomes important when a movement technique combines with other interaction techniques.

The first interaction technique is *Haptic* that enables the player to use the touch sensors to interact with the environment mainly through gripping. The player in the game can interact with the environment by grabbing objects, throwing them around, and using his or her hands to press buttons or to fire weapons during gameplay. A multitude of game genres has used this interaction technique when the

Table 1. Types of movement techniques

Movement Techniques						
Technique	**Recommended Platform**	**Player Immersion**	**Motion Sickness**	**Ease of Control**	**Extra Hardware**	**Recommended Context**
Classic	PC/Console	Medium	Varied	High	Mobile gamepad if possible.	Most VR contexts with complex inputs.
LookAt	Mobile	Low	Medium	Medium	-	Mobile games with input constraints and simple mechanics.
Toggled	Mobile	Low	Medium	Low	-	Mobile games with simple interaction and three toggle modes: toggle via tap, via angle and via look at. Not all headsets support holes for tapping on screen.
Locomotion	Mobile	Medium	Low	Varied by Physique	-	Fitness Game, powered by GPS
Rail	All	High	Low	High	-	Simulate a character that is mounted on something or sits on the passenger's seat.
Teleport	PC/Console	Medium	Low	Medium	Touch Controls, Depth Sensor	Any context that blinking/ teleporting/ jumping on specific spots make sense.
Rope	PC/Console	Medium	Medium	Medium	Touch Controls	Simulate mountain climbing or when hand-stretching is required like controlling a robot monitor
Wheel	All	High	Varied	High	Steering Wheel	Racing or Driving game or simulator. Ideal for simulating cockpits of all types.
Scripted	Mobile	High	Low	High	-	Puzzle or Escape room game, with a focus on interaction input.
Voice	All	Medium	Low	High	Microphone	Games where the player acts as an overlord, tasking the AI with actions or where the character has no legs or hands.
Kinetic	PC/Console	High	Low	Varied by Physique	Depth Sensor	Exergaming or other fitness-related apps/ games.

character can use two objects at the same time with the environment. A demonstration of this technique in a game would be *Skyrim VR edition* that allows a player to control a melee weapon on one hand and a spell on the other. Additionally, the player can hold a bow with one hand and load & shoot an arrow with the other (Bethesda Softworks, 2017). *Haptic* is also based on grabbing and gripping mechanics, and as such, the game features should involve those game mechanics. This technique is very similar to *Rope* and *Teleport* movement techniques, which can be used along with the *Kinetic* interaction technique. This technique is by far the most immersive control scheme of all possible interaction techniques, because it is the only technique that uses the touch sense to its full potential. The most challenging part when selecting a *Haptic* interaction technique is to choose a right movement technique to allow game developers to provide the best possible experience for its end user. The *Haptic* interaction technique, however, is not suitable for mobile devices.

The second interaction technique is straightforward and is a counterpart of the *Classic* movement technique. Thus, the *Classic* interaction technique involves controls through a mainstream input controller, such as a gamepad, or mouse & keyboard. Interaction through these devices is achieved through a simple button and a key press, axis manipulation, and a mouse button click. This technique is applicable for PC and Console games, but this technique for mobile devices can be implemented through tapping the touch screen.

In terms of realism, the *Classic* interaction technique seems to be a straightforward choice, and while it may not be as immersive as *Haptic*, it is the most comfortable choice for the end users. Whenever developers want to favor ease of use and user experience over realism and immersion, the *Classic* interaction technique is the definite choice, while *Haptic* will sacrifice some comfort for immersion. The game developers also need to make sure that whenever the *Classic* interaction technique is used for mobile devices, they need to ensure that the mobile headset allows for users to tap on the touch screen.

The third interaction technique is yet another counterpart of the *LookAt* technique. In the context of interaction, it is not only irrelevant of how the character moves, but also the character interacts with his or her environment by looking at the character. More specifically, just as looking at objects for a short period of time, a specific movement would occur for the the *LookAt* movement technique. So, if the player's forward-facing axis is directed towards a usable object, then the character would examine or interact with the virtual object in a way that makes sense for the game the players are currently playing.

The *LookAt* interaction technique is better used in mobile VR games, and is best suited when the players do not have a gamepad or equivalent for input. It is one of the few resources developers can leverage if players do not have any other means of input that could have an impact on the realism and immersion. An example of using the *LookAt* interaction technique would be when a gun always shooting forward after a specific time interval, because there is not a way of manually firing automatically.

The fourth interaction technique is called *VR Gun* that requires a very special sensor to be used an actual gamepad-like gun to be connected to a PC or a console via a USB cable, using a simple Wi-Fi connection. This technique is exclusive for a PC or console platform since it requires that special type of input. The *VR Gun* technique works like the *Classic* interaction technique, though the *VR Gun* can be used to point at objects within the game context based on its own orientation. As the gun comes with an assortment of buttons, the player can easily reload, shoot and perform other types of interaction as well. A game example that has used this technique in its design is *Farpoint* (Impulse Gear, 2017).

The main drawback of this interaction technique is the difficulty in reaching a larger pool of audience, since it requires a very specific input device in the interaction process. Another limitation of this technique is the constraint related to only a few game genres besides FPS and action-oriented games can actually accommodate such a device. On the other hand, the level of immersion is very high. The feeling of control and absolute autonomy will affect the user to enjoy this VR game.

The fifth interaction technique is *Voice* which functions the same way as it does in other movement techniques. The player can interact with the virtual environment using the voice pitch and/or volume as well as voice commands, which relies on a voice recognition algorithm. A microphone will be needed to use *Voice* to interact with the game. If the character is not disabled in any way, then using *Voice* as a secondary interacting tool will increase a sense of immersion. On the other hand, if this is the only way of interacting when the game character is not disabled or constrained to voice only, this will reduce the level of immersion, no matter how simple this technique will be used in designing a VR game.

One final note for the *Voice* technique, whether it is being used as a movement or interaction technique, is that it is the only technique that requires an audio input, which means that the player needs to reply on voice cues in the virtual space. This technical requirement could make the game unappealing or even, unplayable for the player that cannot make any sound in the environment.

The sixth interaction technique is *Kinetic* which shares similarities with the movement technique using the same label. This technique allows the player to interact with the environment via the depth sensor of the VR camera, and thus is only viable for PC/Console VR games. The player can move his or her whole body or individual body parts (depending on the type of VR games) to interact with the environment, such as waving hello or goodbye to someone, or any other real-time gestures. This interaction technique is ideal for action-demanding *exergaming*, fitness games, or VR games which require very specific movements incorporated into the game design mechanic. However, *Kinetic* is the only technique that could be more demanding than all others, in terms of adding realism and immersion.

The seventh and final interaction technique is called *Automatic* which is the only interaction technique used as a fallback when any other technique is not available. This technique is characterized by its automatic interaction because it needs the player to move into a trigger area to execute a specific interaction. Because interaction is done automatically, this technique cannot be used with *Scripted* or *Rail* movement technique, because either technique needs to be directly controlled and influenced by the player and contradicts what *Automatic* means. The *Automatic* technique can be easily implemented through trigger points and trigger areas in the virtual environment and is very simple to use. Also, both mobile and PC/Console VR games can leverage the *Automatic* technique, but is more recommended for mobile devices when inputs are a big constraint. On the other hand, a big disadvantage of this technique is that it is not so realistic or immersive to directly influence the environment. It should be mentioned that it is a necessary sacrifice to simplify interaction with the virtual environment. Furthermore, there are tricks that a developer can use to reduce a sense of removed realism and immersion. Intentionally, placing the character to only investigating and examining objects as part of core gameplay will be likely to address this problem because it is then only action the character can take. Table 2 summarizes the above discussions.

Table 2. Types of interaction techniques

Interaction Techniques					
Technique	**Recommended Platform**	**Player Immersion**	**Ease of Control**	**Extra Hardware**	**Recommended Context**
Haptic	PC/Console	High	High	Touch Controls, Depth Sensor	VR Games with dual-object wielding or grip mechanics, like a carnival-simulation game.
Classic	PC/Console	Medium	High	Mobile Gamepad if supported	Most VR contexts with complex inputs.
LookAt	Mobile	Low	Medium	-	Mobile games with input constraints and simple mechanics.
VR Gun	PC/Console	High	High	Special VR Gun	First Person Shooter and heavy action-packed games.
Voice	All	High	High	-	Games where the player acts as an overlord, tasking the AI with actions or where the character has no legs or hands.
Kinetic	PC/Console	Medium	Varied by Physique	Touch Controls, Depth Sensor	Exergaming or other fitness-related apps/games.
Automatic	Mobile	Low	High	-	Mobile games with a lot of input constraints where the character ideally is performing simple tasks that are environmental context-aware.

Matching Movement With Interaction Techniques in Game Design

After discussing all the movement and interaction techniques, the author has identified all possible and feasible combinations among these techniques in the design process. Furthermore, these movement and interaction techniques have been mapped out on two tables (PC/Console, mobile context), which are also used as reference points to assist future game developers, students and academics on VR projects. Table 3 and Table 4 present the movement and interaction techniques mapped out on a matrix to guide

Table 3. Combination of techniques to maximize efficiency for pc/console platforms

Technique Combination Efficiency Matrix (PC/ Console)							
Techniques	**Haptic**	**Classic**	**LookAt**	**VR Gun**	**Voice**	**Kinetic**	**Automatic**
Classic	High	High	Medium	N/A	Medium	Low	Low
LookAt	Medium	Low	Low	Low	Medium	Low	Medium
Toggled	Low	Low	Low	Low	Low	Low	Medium
Locomotion	High	Low	Medium	High	Low	High	Medium
Rail	High	High	Medium	High	Medium	Low	N/A
Teleport	High	Low	High	N/A	Medium	Low	Medium
Rope	High	Low	Medium	N/A	Medium	Low	Medium
Wheel	N/A	High	N/A	N/A	N/A	N/A	N/A
Scripted	High	Low	Low	High	Low	Low	N/A
Voice	Medium	Medium	Low	Medium	Medium	Medium	Low
Kinetic	High	N/A	Low	N/A	Medium	High	Medium

Table 4. Combination of techniques to maximize for mobile platforms

Technique Combination Efficiency Matrix (Mobile)							
Techniques	**Haptic**	**Classic**	**LookAt**	**VR Gun**	**Voice**	**Kinetic**	**Automatic**
Classic	N/A	High (if mobile gamepad is supported or headset can support tapping)	Medium	N/A	Medium	N/A	Medium
LookAt	N/A	Medium	High	N/A	Medium	N/A	High
Toggled	N/A	Low	High	N/A	Medium	N/A	High
Locomotion	N/A	Low	Medium	N/A	Low	N/A	Medium
Rail	N/A	Medium	High	N/A	Low	N/A	N/A
Teleport	N/A	N/A	N/A	N/A	N/A	N/A	N/A
Rope	N/A	N/A	N/A	N/A	N/A	N/A	N/A
Wheel	N/A	N/A	N/A	N/A	N/A	N/A	N/A
Scripted	N/A	High (if mobile gamepad is supported or headset can support tapping)	High	N/A	High	N/A	N/A
Voice	N/A	Low	Medium	N/A	High	N/A	Low
Kinetic	N/A	N/A	N/A	N/A	N/A	N/A	N/A

both professional and beginning game designers to determine how efficiently each of those techniques can be combined for either a PC or console context. All interaction techniques have been placed in the columns horizontally, and all movement techniques have been placed in the rows vertically as shown in Table 3 and Table 4.

These two tables offer game designers a useful tool to determine which techniques should be chosen. For example, when it comes to PC or console games that the player has more input choices, the best choices for interaction techniques would be *Haptic* or *Classic*. *Classic* is working best when combined with either *Classic* movement (since both techniques use the same gamepad or keyboard). The *Wheel* technique will be great because, playing VR racing games, the wheel itself has buttons, making it a great combination of different design principles. The *Haptic* technique can also be best combined with the *Classic* movement technique since there are bound to be buttons on the touch sensors and both can help the developer to use an alternative technique. Another stunning combination is *VR Gun* that is designed with *Rail*, *Scripted* or *Locomotion* movement techniques to address the interactions that involve the player running around and shooting virtual objects common in most games. Finally, the *Kinetic* interaction technique seems to be best used with its counterpart, *Kinetic* movement technique, or with the *Locomotion* technique. Both technique are able to keep input consistent by using physical movements of the body. *Voice* is not a definite way of working on platforms with many other inputs, but it could be a great secondary or supplementary technique for movement or interaction.

The combinations of different techniques presented in Table 3 and Table 4 are the most useful design considerations, and thus the more powerful when used together. The process of game design depends on what the developers want, what is designed to be done beforehand, and what type of experience the developers attempt to create for users. When game developers are designing for idle/sitting players in front of a computer desk or a TV, an obvious choice for input would be a gamepad or a wheel. When the players are expected to stand and/or have space between them and a depth sensor, then haptics, dual-wielded grips are the obvious choices. Designing a VR game needs to balance both immersion and comfort at the same time.

RESEARCH METHOD

These tables to provide a list of movement and interaction techniques and are based on observations after collecting and analyzing at a sample of 100 VR games using either mobile, PC, or console platforms. The benefits of researching existing digital games are because their input schemes have already based on the developers' perspective. The summary list of techniques is based on actual game examples.

CONCLUSION

Future Research Directions

One of the main constraints when working on input schemes for movement and interaction with VR is the fact that the player needs to use a heavy headset connected to a PC, usually through a cable. Facebook has announced that the company will be publishing the world's first wireless VR headset for PC, with its latest *Oculus Quest* technology. *Oculus Quest* can be a game-changer for VR development as it will be consumer friendly as the headset will be working standalone. (Facebook Technologies, LLC, 2018). The new headset can influence and improve players' overall VR experiences previously constrained by a small environment and will drastically reduce the environmental hazards. Furthermore, this innovation has the potential to release the developers' creative freedom to experiment with more design techniques. This is especially true regarding movement that can be added on the identified movement technique table in the future.

Practical Implications for PC and Console Game

While mobile devices have more input-limitations compared with a PC / console platform, it requires expensive hardware to develop and is not easy for developers and/or students alike. This situation should not be taken for granted that everyone, especially for students, to purchase entire VR headsets with motion sensors and camera setups on expensive PCs to run VR software. The situation is even worse for *PSVR* (Sony Interactive Entertainment, 2016) that demand users to acquire a *PSVR Kit*, a compatible powerful PC and hard-to-get *PlayStation 4 Dev Kit*. This constraint will probably be solved in the future with more accessible VR headsets, such as *Oculus Quest*.

Practical Implications Mobile Platforms

The biggest drawback for mobile devices, besides the reduction in frame rate, the lower-quality graphics, and the constraint in input, is that some devices do not have a depth sensor. However, mobile devices vary with this capability (Wagner, 2018) when this feature is still not "mainstream" and easily accessible. Furthermore, when *VR Gun*, *haptics* or *kinetic* movement techniques are not supported, everything needs to be designed around the player looking at things. However, because mobile devices are not cabled, the player can play any VR game with the constraints of equipment. For mobile VR game, developers cannot provide complex inputs because not everyone will have a mobile VR headset for tapping. Furthermore, not everyone has a mobile-compliant gamepad. A combination of the two *LookAt* techniques seems to be appropriate to ask players to interact by staring at virtual objects. That can be further supported by having either *LookAt* for movement and *Automatic* for interaction, or combining *LookAt* for interaction and *Scripted* for movement in that scenario. For most cases, besides *LookAt*, *Scripted*, or *Automatic* techniques, game developers can have one less layer of difficulty in integrating input in game design.

The design decision to choose the best input mechanism really depends on the development needs of the game designer. The developers need to consider the inputs before designing a game. Furthermore, the platform where the VR game will be played can define the path they can follow and what technique to use. This will immediately result in some gains or losses in terms of possible input hardware available to the end users. A mobile game will require the mobile VR headset and whether it supports tapping on screen. Another possible consideration would be the genre of the game or the experience intended with the game. Finally, some games require a specific physique or physical setup to be experienced adequately by the player, and thus those requirements must be specified for players to be seated or how to deal with disabled player to interact with the virtual environment. The proposed unified game-design framework hopes to provide answers to these requirements, after it tackles all possible cases, multi-platform issues as well as suggests solutions for movement and interaction systems. The framework is also a good starting point that can possibly bridge the knowledge gap for students, academics and developers alike.

REFERENCES

Active Theory Inc. (2018, September 5). BitGym: Virtual Cardio Tours. Google PlayStore.

Bethesda Softworks (2017, November 17). The Elder Scrolls V: Skyrim VR. Bethesda Softworks.

Capcom. (2017, January 24). Resident Evil 7: Biohazard. Worldwide: Capcom.

Carbotte, K. (2018, March 10). *Do the Locomotion: The 19 Ways you walk and run in VR Games*. Retrieved from https://www.tomshardware.co.uk/picturestory/230-virtual-reality-games-locomotion-methods.html

Facebook TechnologiesL. L. C. (2018). Retrieved https://www.oculus.com/quest/

FIBRUM. (2017a, April 11). Froggy VR. Google PlayStore.

FIBRUM. (2017b, May 17). Zombie Shooter VR. Google PlayStore.

Fibrum Limited. (2017). *Fibrum VR*. Retrieved from https://fibrum.com/

Game Cooks (2017, June 20). Vindicta. Game Cooks.

Google. (2014). Retrieved from Google Cardboard: https://vr.google.com/cardboard/

Harmony Studios Limited. (2018). *VR Sickness: What it is and how to stop it*. Retrieved from https://www.harmony.co.uk/vr-motion-sickness/

id Software. (2017, December 1). Doom VFR. Bethesda Softworks.

Impulse Gear. (2017, May 16). Farpoint. Sony Interactive Entertainment.

Lakento. (2018, October 18). House of Terror VR 360 Cardboard Horror Game. Google PlayStore.

Mason, W. (2015, November 16). *Five Ways to Reduce Motion Sickness in VR*. Retrieved from https://uploadvr.com/five-ways-to-reduce-motion-sickness-in-vr/

Ntokos, K., & Eletheriou, O. (2017b). *Exploring Unreal Engine 4 VR Editor and Essentials of VR*. BirPacktPub.

Ntokos, K., & Eleutheriou, O. (2017a). *Creating a VR Shooter Game Using Optimized Techniques*. Birmingham, AL: PacktPub.

Red Storm Entertainment. (2017, May 30). Star Trek: Bridge Crew. Ubisoft.

Schubert, M. (2016, March 10). Weightless. Itch.Io.

Solent University. (2018). Retrieved from https://www.solent.ac.uk/about/our-history

Sony Interactive Entertainment. (2016, October 13). *PlayStation VR*. Retrieved from https://www.playstation.com/en-gb/explore/playstation-vr/

Supermassive Games. (2016, October 13). Until Dawn: Rush of Blood. Sony Interactive Entertainment.

Wagner, D. (2018). Retrieved from https://medium.com/@DAQRI/depth-cameras-for-mobile-ar-from-iphones-to-wearables-and-beyond-ea29758ec280

ADDITIONAL READING

Harmony Studios Limited. (2018). *VR Sickness: What it is and how to stop it*. Retrieved from Harmony Studios: https://www.harmony.co.uk/vr-motion-sickness/

Lee, J., Kim, M., & Kim, J. (2017). A study on immersion and VR sickness in walking interaction for immersive virtual reality applications. *Symmetry*, *9*(5), 78. doi:10.3390ym9050078

Mason, W. (2015). *Five ways to reduce motion sickness in VR*. Retrieved from Upload VR Website: https://uploadvr.com/five-ways-to-reduce-motion-sickness-in-vr/

Ntokos, K., & Eleutheriou, O. (2017). *Creating a VR Shooter Game Using Optimized Techniques*. Birmingham: PacktPub.

Ntokos, K., & Orfeas, E. (2017). Exploring Unreal Engine 4 VR Editor and Essentials of VR. Birmingham: PacktPub.

University of Waterloo. (2018). *Virtual reality motion sickness may be predicted and counteracted*. *ScienceDaily*. Retrieved from www.sciencedaily.com/releases/2018/09/180927083336.htm

Upload (2018). *The Best way to interact within VR*. Retrieved from Upload: https://uploadvr.com/the-best-way-to-interact-within-vr/

Wagner, D. (2018). Depth Cameras for Mobile AR: From Iphones to Wearables and Beyond. Retrieved from https://medium.com/@DAQRI/depth-cameras-for-mobile- ar-from-iphones-to-wearables-and-beyond-ea29758ec280

Wareable (2018). *A new wave of VR motion sickness solutions is here*. Retrieved from https://www.wareable.com/vr/new-wave-vr-motion-sickness-solutions

KEY TERMS AND DEFINITIONS

FMP: Abbreviation of final major project, also known as dissertation or thesis. This is the final project students work on when reaching the final year and complete before graduating.

HMD: Head-mounted display. Refers to the headsets players wear on their heads to experience VR games, apps, and VR-experiences in general, for example, the Oculus Rift, the HTC Vive, and the Steam VR.

Leap Motion: Technology focused in hand-tracking for VR applications.

LookAt: Interaction or movement technique that has the VR player look towards a specific point in 3D space for several seconds to "confirm" movement or interaction. This is used instead of the conventional controllers or motion sensors.

NPC: Non-player character. Usually refers to other characters within a game world that are controlled by the AI.

Unreal Engine: Industry-standard game engine, primarily used in AAA 3D games. Some games created with Unreal Engine include *Bioshock, Mass Effect, Deus Ex, Batman: Arkham City, XCOM: Enemy Unknown*, and the well-known *Fortnite*.

VR: Abbreviation for virtual reality. Refers to the computer-generated simulation of a 3D world, usually in a gaming or non-gaming context, where the user immerses himself/herself.

Chapter 10
Augmented, Mixed, and Virtual Reality Applications in Cause-Related Marketing (CRM)

Kenneth C. C. Yang
The University of Texas at El Paso, USA

Yowei Kang
National Taiwan Ocean University, Taiwan

EXECUTIVE SUMMARY

This chapter deals with emerging augmented, mixed, and virtual reality platforms and their applications in cause-related marketing (CRM) campaigns. This chapter provides definitions and examples of augmented, mixed, and virtual realities and explains their importance CRM professionals. Compared with traditional marketing platforms, reality-creating technologies are characterized with their capabilities to interact with marketing contents through their geolocation specificity, mobility, and synchronization of virtuality and reality. These technological characteristics have made reality-creating technologies very promising for many cause-related marketing (CRM) campaigns. This chapter surveys current discussions in the existing literature and ends with three cause-related marketing (CRM) campaigns. The study concludes with an overview of emerging issues, future directions, and professional best practice recommendations.

INTRODUCTION

The Emergence of Augmented, Mixed, and Virtual Reality

Using digital information to generate a sense of immersive reality is commonly referred to digital reality technologies that include "an amalgamation of augmented reality (AR), virtual reality (VR), mixed reality, 360°, and immersive technologies" (Cook, Jones, Raghavan, & Saif, 2017, n.p.). A recent research report by ResearchAndMarkets.com (2018) predicts that the global revenue for both augmented reality

DOI: 10.4018/978-1-5225-5912-2.ch010

(AR) and virtual reality (VR) applications will reach $94.4 billion by 2023. International Data Corporation (IDC) (2017) similarly forecasts a rosy prediction that these reality-creating technologies and their applications will reach $13.9 billion in 2017. The compound annual growth of AR and VR is expected to reach $143.3 billion in 2020 (IDC, 2017). Separately, AR is predicted to generate $120 billion in revenue by 2020, according to *Forbes* (Gaudiosi, 2015). The forecast of the "disruptive" mixed reality (MR) is even more astonishing as the technology is said to affect the $2 trillion entertainment market (Rizzotto, 2016). These technologies are expected to diffuse to other industry sectors in society, ranging from education, financial services, real estate, and retailing industries (Cook et al., 2017). Citing smartphone penetration as a main driver of these technologies due to its ubiquitous presence in people's lives, it is projected that consumer applications in entertainment, gaming, and media will account for 30% of the revenue in 2017 (ResearchAndMarkets.com, 2018). The popularity of *Pokémon Go* location-sensitive AR game in 2016 is an excellent example of the convergence applications, which has earned over $1.2 billion worldwide (Suciu, 2018). ResearchAndMarkets.com (2018) also estimates that the Asia-Pacific Region will see the fastest growth.

The applications of digital reality technologies could be traced back to 1990s. As early as 2010, HarperCollins Publishers experimented with AR to promote Cecelia Athern's book, *The Book of Tomorrow*, in its campaign (everydayismagical.com) (Shields, 2010; Yang & Kang, 2018). Ford's UK VR campaign (https://www.youtube.com/watch?v=bl8T9oYO5vY) allowed young mobile phone users to view images superimposed virtually onto another picture to promote its *Ka* model (Clifford-Marsh, 2009). Ford campaign also employs an interactive kiosk inside a shopping mall to deliver the immersive digital reality experiences by allowing users to virtually interact with different Ford models (https://www.youtube.com/watch?v=bl8T9oYO5vY).

Interest in technology-driven marketing activities such as customer acquisition, customer nurturing, brand affinity, and point of sale in both consumer-to-consumer or business-to-business electronic commerce has led to their growing applications in almost all industry sectors (Marketo, n.d.). A survey of agency clients reported that 67% of media buyers and planners are interested in incorporating AR and VR into their digital marketing campaigns (Martin, 2017). The survey also found that VR (67%) was favored over AR (17%) in their media buy (Martin, 2017). Due to their popularity, AR and VR marketing campaigns have gradually been recognized in major professional awards (e.g., the Auggie Awards, the Emmy Awards, or the Webby Awards) (Giardina, 2017). Interactive Advertising Bureau (IAB) expects these reality technologies will ultimately become major advertising media in the next five years because of their immersive storytelling and emotion-eliciting benefits that can influence consumer brain at its neocortex, limbic system, and reptilian brain (Klie, 2016; Marketo, n.d.). Trade publications and conferences avidly advocate the coming of VR, and other reality technologies, as one of the noteworthy trends (Alcántara, 2018; Braiker, 2018; Burritt, 2017b; Higham, 2018). For example, a VR campaign by McCann Erickson (2016) allows kids to experience what it is like and how people feel to be bullied (https://www.youtube.com/watch?v=NKln3HNkwIU). The campaign also won the best CRM campaign, The 2017 Webby Awards (The Webby Awards, 2017). Similarly, Expedia, the online travel site, collaborates with its agency, *180LA*, to develop an immersive VR campaign, *St Jude Dream Adventures* (https://www.youtube.com/playlist?list=PLdgCSoJzrmKHooMkCbpL00HE0EB-OPCP), to allow sick children to travel virtually to their dream destinations (Dias, 2016). This award-winning CRM campaign has successfully created awareness and driven donations to St. Jude Children Research Hospital (The Shorty Social Good Awards, 2016). The impacts of these digital reality technologies are far more important to other aspects of contemporary human experiences, ranging from medical diagnoses by doctors in a distant location, promotion of box office movies and HBO's *Game of Thrones*, and visualization of customers' home improvement projects by Lowes (Marketo, n.d.).

Objectives of the Study

This book chapter offers a thorough description of AR, MR, and VR technologies and their applications in CRM campaigns. This chapter also provides definitions and examples of AR, MR, and VR and explains their importance for CRM practitioners in terms of generating campaign awareness and brand affinity (Marketo, n.d.). Compared with more traditional marketing platforms, reality-creating technologies offer a great potential because of its innovative ways to interact with commercially relevant contents (Javornik 2016; Yang & Kang, 2018). Reality-creating technologies are characterized with their "interactivity, virtuality (presence of elements of virtual reality), geolocation feature/location specificity, mobility (in terms of portability and wearability) and synchronization of virtual and physical/real (augmentation)" (Javornik, 2016, p. 253). Characteristics such as the above have made these technologies promising for many CRM practitioners because they represent a "fundamental shift" as to how communication contents will be experienced and presented (Walker, 2017, n.p.). This book chapter surveys what has been discussed in the existing literature and then ends with two best practice CRM campaigns to better engage consumers to support a company's social causes. The objectives of this chapter aim to provide CRM professionals with an understanding of the emergence of AR, MR, and VR platforms by focusing on several key areas to affect the success of reality-creating technologies in the planning and deployment of CRM campaigns. The authors conclude this chapter by examining two best practice CRM campaigns to demonstrate how these reality-creating technologies could enhance campaign effectiveness and help to accomplish the campaign objectives. This book chapter attempts to answer the following two research questions through a combination of case study and literature review method:

Research Question 1: What is the current state of AR, MR, and VR technologies in relation to CRM campaigns and practitioners?

Research Question 2: What are the contemporary practices, potential impacts, opportunities, and challenges of reality-creating technologies when it comes to the planning and executing of CRM campaigns?

BACKGROUND

AR, MR, and VR as Reality-Creating Technologies

AR, MR, and VR can be grouped into an emerging set of technological innovations commonly known as *reality* (or *reality-creating*) (http://www.realitytechnologies.com/companies) or *digital reality* technologies (Cook et al., 2017). A reality technology system is generally composed of 1) a graphic rendering system; 2) gloves, trackers, and user interface to detect and input users' movements; 3) output devices to facilitate aural, haptic, and visual interactions in a virtual environment; 4) a software to model virtual objectives and to construct databases; 5) a system to deliver sensory stimuli such as visual display technology to offer users interactive and immersive experiences (Claudio & Maddalena, 2014; Yang & Kang, 2018). For specific applications such as *Pokémon Go* AR game/app, location-sensitive geo-information also becomes part of the technical system to overlay computer-generated images with those from the physical context (Gortari, 2018). Players of *Pokémon Go* are required to walk around their surroundings to capture AR-generated characters unique to a specific location.

In relation to CRM campaigns, VR applications have been reported in both advertising (Bazilian, 2017a, 2017b; Baek, Yoo, & Yoon, 2015; Johnson, 2017a, 2017b, 2017c, 2017d) and marketing literatures because of their widespread applications (Ballings, McCullough, & Bharadwaj, 2018; Heine, 2017; Javornik, 2016). VR refers to a computer-generated and simulated virtual world where users are immersed in a virtual environment to experience the presence of other objects or realities through interaction with them (Heim, 1998; Hsu, 2017; Kerrebroeck, Brengman, & Willems, 2017; Pan & Hamilton, 2018; Shin, 2017; Yang & Kang, 2018). VR is often characterized with three key technological attributes; that is, "immersion, interactivity, and information intensity" (Claudio & Maddalena, 2014, pp. 2-3). In terms of its technological attributes that might influence what consumers experience with these technologies, Shin (2017) similarly identifies immersion and presence as two main characteristics of VR. Immersion, or perceived immersion (Slater, 2018), is an important aspect of VR (or any reality-creating technologies) that makes users feel surrounded by the virtually-created objects and the environment. In addition, Shin (2017) introduces the concept of affordance (e.g., technological and affective) to refer to what users have experienced in a VR environment.

VR applications are often emphasized by CRM practitioners for their ability to engage consumers through immersive storytelling (Lafayette, 2017). Best spoken by Pamela Park, Toyota Motor North America, after integrating Discovery VR app in a 38-episode TRVLR campaign below:

VR offers an opportunity to connect with consumers through an immersive storytelling format. Viewers of VR content often tend to be engaged and receptive to experiences that transport them to environments that may be out of reach in real life. Further, VR is authentic and aspirational and that aligns well with the Toyota brand values. (Lafayette, 2017, p. 46)

AR is a branch of VR because both integrate virtual digital information into a 3D real environment in real time (Chen, Peng, Li, & Yang, 2016; Yang & Kang, 2018). Praised as a smart technology (Çeltek, 2015), AR also allows consumers to interact with virtually-created digital graphics, imagery, and objects that are made up of both computer-generated virtual and real world data to enable real-time interactions, with the illusion of co-existing in the same space (Rese, Baier, Geyer-Schulz, & Schreiber, 2017; van Krevelen & Poleman, 2010; Williams, 2009; Yang & Kang, 2018). However, it is different from VR on whether users' physical environment is enhanced (as in AR) or completely replaced (as in VR) (Baek, Yoo, & Yoon, 2018; Huang & Liao, 2015). To sum up, AR is characterized by its "interactivity, virtuality (presence of elements of virtual reality), geo-location feature/location specificity, mobility (in terms of portability and wearability) and synchronization of virtual and physical/real (augmentation)" (Javornik, 2016, p. 253). Like VR, AR also "imposes computer-generated information such as images and sounds on a user's real-world view" (Baek et al., 2018, p. 422). This description is echoed by Zhang (2017) that AR is conceptualized as "a three-dimensional scene where virtual objects are superimposed on a real scene" (p. 1).

Marketers have been attracted to AR because consumers are able to virtually try and "dynamically engage with" the product before making any purchase decision (Das, 2018; Hilken, de Ruyster, Chylinski, Mahr, & Keeling, 2017). For example, demonstration of Samsung's AR gear in its flagship stores allows consumers to virtually experience its product attributes by immersing themselves in several virtual adventures (Marketo, n.d.). AR also helps increase awareness, obtain product information, and make consumers' shopping experiences enjoyable (Çeltek, 2015; Huang & Liao, 2015). Olsson and Salo (2012) collect and analyze experiential narratives from 84 users of AR technologies (such as *Junaio*, *Layar*, and *Google Goggles*) and conclude the following themes from their experiential narratives: *amazement*, *empowerment*, *fascination*, *immersion*, *novelty*, *positive surprise*, and *social connectivity*. For example, Ben & Jerry uses Facebook's augmented reality platform (http://www.benjerry.com/flavors/special-stash) to promote its new marshmallow-flavored ice cream (Johnson, 2017d; Loop, 2017). This AR campaign also includes both game and mobile phone platforms to allow consumers to catch marshmallows falling from the sky. Consumers will continue the AR game if they do not miss more than five marshmallows (Johnson, 2017d). With the exponential growth of smartphone, many have predicted that the advent of mobile AR campaigns is likely to generate the maximum influence on AR applications in the future (Szymczyk, 2009; Yang & Kang, 2018). The capabilities of AR will allow consumers to personalize their own immersive mobile AR experiences when interacting with a CRM campaign.

The recent surge of MR is claimed to become "the 21st century's passport to an ethereal world of endless possibilities" (Pando, 2017, p. 2). The concept was first introduced by Milgram, Takemura, Utsumi, and Kishino (1994) and is also known as *hybrid reality* (https://rubygarage.org/blog/difference-between-ar-vr-mr) which enables users to experience a different kind of reality when data or images are overlaid onto physical items to create virtual objects (Higham, 2018). MR employs cutting-edge sensors to capture users' gestures and location to integrate users' physical environment with digitally-generated contents where real and virtual environments coexist (Cook et al., 2017). Like other reality technologies and their marketing applications, MR also reinvents the storytelling process about the product and allows consumers to interact with marketing contents, content designers, and other users (Pando, 2017). For example, *Amazon* released its *Sumerian* software to allow e-retailers to create MR experiences for online shoppers (Burritt, 2017a). Microsoft (2018) derives from human-computer interaction research and conceptualizes MR as an intersection of computer processing, human input, environmental input (See Figure 1).

To conclude this section, Rizzotto (2016) best explains the differences between AR, MR, and VR. VR is a technology that creates digital environments shutting out the real world, while MR allows digital contents to interact with user's real world and AR superimposes digital contents on top of user's real

Figure 1. Mixed reality as conceptualized by Microsoft

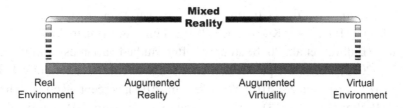

Figure 2. A Continuum of reality-creating technologies (or known as reality-virtuality continuum)

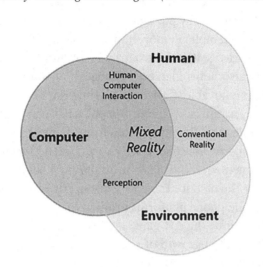

world (Rizzotto, 2016). Similarly, Milgram et al. (1994) proposes their well-known *Reality-Virtuality Continuum* that visually describes MR is a combination of both real- and virtual-world objects into a single display (See Figure 2). Figure 2 best explains the distinction between various reality-creating technologies.

Technology-Driven CRM Campaigns

Cause-related marketing (henceforth, CRM) refers to "an offer from the firm CRM refers to "an offer from the firm to contribute a specified amount to a designated cause when customers engage in revenue-providing exchanges that satisfy organizational and individual objectives" (Varadarajan & Menon, 1988, p. 60, cited in Ballings et al., 2018, p. 235). CRM promotes both social causes and a company's marketing objectives to achieve its own financial goals (Melero & Montaner, 2016). Some has estimated that CRM activities have influenced around 75% of U.S. adult population (Mintel, 2014 cited in Hamby & Bringer, 2018). In practice, CRM often takes the form of donation by contributing a certain percentage of sales to the sponsored social causes or organizations (Melero & Montaner, 2016). As a result, CRM has been claimed to offer a mutually beneficial situation for companies, non-profit organizations, and the public (Chang & Chen, 2017). An extensive review of CRM literature has confirmed that CRM campaigns could enhance brand awareness, change attitude toward the cause, the brand and the firm, increase purchase intention and willingness to pay, modify consumer behaviors, among others (See Ballings et al., 2018 for review).

Existing CRM literature often draws from theories and variables in advertising (Chang & Chen, 2017), consumer behavior (Bae, 2017; Kuo & Rice, 2015; Hamby & Bringer, 2018; Melero & Montaner, 2016), and marketing (Ballings et al., 2018) studies. Often studied variables from these research areas include culture (Bae, 2017), consumer persuasion knowledge about CRM (Hamby & Bringer, 2018), product involvement (Lucke & Heinze, 2015; Youn & Kim, 2018), perceptual congruence (Kuo & Rice, 2015), profitability (Ballings et al., 2018), self-construal (Youn & Kim, 2018), a firm's credibility and motive (Kim, Lee, & Kim, 2017), etc. For example, Ballings et al. (2018) provides empirical evidence to support that Yoplait's CRM activities contribute to the brand profitability (2.7%), while damaging Dannon's profitability by -13.31%. Chang and Chen (2017), on the other hand, employs an eye-tracking experiment to study whether product type, cause-focus, and consumer characteristics play any role in affecting CRM campaign effectiveness, and observe that a cause-focused vs. product-oriented image influences CRM advertising messages differently. Similarly, Melero and Montaner (2016) uses a 2 by 2 between-subject experimental design to examine whether product types (i.e., utilitarian vs. hedonic) and perceived fit (i.e., high vs. low) might affect consumers' brand attitude and purchase intention. Their findings confirm that consumers' brand attitude is influenced more by the hedonic product type, while the utilitarian product type generates higher purchase intention.

Despite the ample amount of research in CRM, a less investigated area is how different CRM platforms may play a role in influencing its campaign effectiveness. Existing studies on the integration of social media into CRM campaigns do not vary the selection of platforms (Kim et al., 2017; Lou & Alhabash, 2018). Therefore, it is not possible to empirically test whether different platforms may interact with message, source, and consumer factors. Nevertheless, platform choice has been an important topic because many marketing campaigns are now integrated through multi-platforms (Yang, 2018). For example, AT&T's successful *It Can Wait* anti-texting CRM employs a variety of advertising platforms, including traditional media and emerging mobile apps (http://about.att.com/sites/it_can_wait_drivemode) and VR (http://about.att.com/newsroom/your_attention_please.html) to alter teenagers' text and driving behaviors after demonstrating the danger of distracted driving. Users of its VR campaign site can virtually drive a car and experience how important it is to be fully concentrated and not been distracted by sending out texts.

Studying technological impacts on CRM campaigns is increasingly important because emerging media such as social media (Kim et al., 2017; Lou & Alhabash, 2018) are likely to affect how CRM campaigns will be planned and deployed. Although extant literature has not discussed the relationship between technologies and CRM campaign effectiveness, studies have examined variables that might help practitioners to speculate. For example, social media (such as Facebook) are beneficial to many CRM practitioners because of their low-cost and easy access (Lou & Alhabash, 2018). Because of their technical characteristics of sharing, liking, and networking, new effectiveness metrics (such as *Viral Behavioral Intention*, VBI) (Lou & Alhabash, 2018) have been proposed to measure advertising and marketing campaigns on social media. Shin (2017) studies the application of VR in the educational setting and confirms the affordance in a VR environment to allow users to interact with numerous virtual objects leads to favorable user experience and learning benefits. Rauschanbel (2018) borrows from uses and gratifications (U&G) theory and empirically confirms that utilitarian, hedonic, social, sensual, and symbolic gratifications (sought from using augmented reality smart glasses) affect people's usage behaviors in public and private. It is likely that the emergence of AR, MR, and VR might generate similar, if not greater, impacts on CRM campaigns. To better understand how CRM practitioners, envision the forthcoming influence of these reality-creating technologies, the authors examine and discuss the current state, potential impacts, challenges and opportunities of AR, MR, and VR technologies.

MAIN FOCUS OF THE CHAPTER

In this book chapter, the following sections will develop an analytical framework to help the analysis of reality-creating technologies and their applications in CRM campaigns.

Analytical Framework

Reality-creating technologies, as viable advertising and marketing platforms, are often approached by examining their technological attributes to articulate how they will contribute to the creation of a successful CRM campaign. Adapted from Javornik (2016, p. 254), Table 1 offers a good summary of major technical benefits of AR, MR, and VR, and their relevance to the CRM industry. These seven technological characteristics are *interactivity, hypertextuality, modality, connectivity, location-specificity, mobility, and virtuality.* A detailed list of definitions of these characteristics is explained in Table 1.

These technological attributes play an important role in affecting how CRM practitioners decide to employ reality technologies in the campaigns (O'Mahony, 2015). Therefore, the authors propose to include these attributes in a decision-making model adapted from O'Mahony's (2015) model. The proposed model below describes to what extent the attributes of reality technologies could affect CRM campaigns at both decision-making and deployment stages. The authors revise and extend the framework (Figure 3) to analyze two CRM campaigns in the discussion below. While consumers' responses could play a key role in determining the success of any CRM campaign, this book chapter is limited due to the inability to obtain relevant data. Using a case study method, this book chapter is also not able to empirically obtain consumer response data through experimental manipulation of a variety of variables.

Table 1. Technical characteristics of reality-creating technologies

Media Characteristics	Definition
Interactivity	Machine and personal interactivity, feature-based or perceived, composed of control, responsiveness and two-way communication
Hypertextuality	Potentially high number of linked sources
Modality	Diversity of content representation
Connectivity	Technological capability of expanding and sustaining a model of network, where many users can be connected among themselves
Location-Specificity	Specificity with which a technology and its user can be targeted based on the precise geolocation
Mobility	Portability and wearability that allow a mobile use
Virtuality	Combination of virtual elements that causes immersion in an environment constructed with computer graphics and digital video

Figure 3. Analytical framework to examine the role of reality technologies in crm campaign planning and deployment

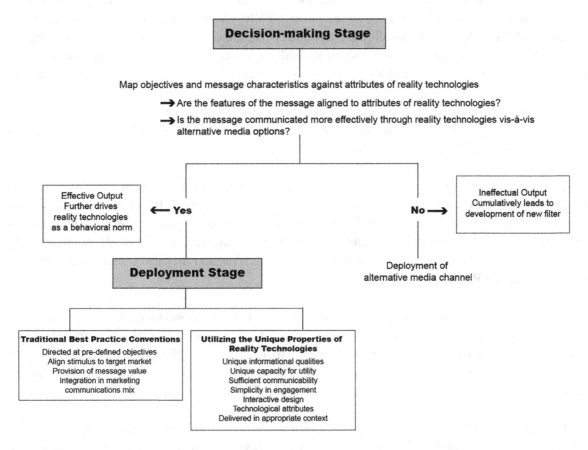

Best Practice CRM Campaigns

TOMS' "Walk in Their Shoes" VR Campaign (2016)

In collaboration with AT&T, TOMS' develops this CRM campaign (https://www.youtube.com/watch?v=sr-pWI0Y-_A)

to show consumers that their participation in TOMS' *One-for-One* CRM campaigns in the past does create impacts on people (Beer, 2016; CONE, 2016). Using a 360-degree video, consumers can interact with the video to virtually experience what it feels like when one of the donor's travels to Columbia to see how his good-will helps children in that country (CONE, 2016). TOMS also gives away 100,000 Google Cardboard VR viewers to customers who purchase TOMS' shoes (CONE, 2016). The use of VR in this campaign makes the best use of two technological attributes of VR; that is, *interactivity* and *virtuality*. According to Javornik (2016), interactivity of this 360-degree video refers to the interaction between viewers and the video through a navigation panel on the upper left-hand side of the screen. By choosing up, down, left, or right buttons in the top left hand corner of the video, viewers can control the video contents in order to have a more immersive and personalized experience. Furthermore, the all-encompassing 360-degree video creates a sense of immersion with the location where the donor visits to experience how children benefit from the donated shoes. Creating a sense of immersion in an environment corresponds to Javornik's (2016) *virtuality* dimension of VR. This campaign aims to communicate the mission of TOMS' *One-for-One* by allowing consumers to take a virtual journey to an isolated village to learn about the impacts of giving out free shoes to children (Marketo, n.d.). As spoken by AT&T's brand marketing manager, the *virtuality* of VR technology greatly enhances the effectiveness of the campaign:

What we love about this is that it's a really immersive way to experience the impact that buying one pair of Toms shoes can have, in this case on one boy in Colombia...... It's a powerful way to show how to make a difference in the world. (Beer, 2016, n.p.)

The technological attributes of VR clearly have been taken into consideration when planning and deploying this CRM campaign based on the proposed model (See Figure 3). For example, in considering whether VR should be included in a CRM campaign, it is vital to think about whether medium attributes are able to enhance the message and its effectiveness. The following statement by TOMS' founder, Blake Mycoskie, demonstrates the ability to map campaign objectives and message characteristics through the utilization of VR:

VR is the greatest technology I've seen to create empathy... Ultimately, whether you're a nonprofit or a social enterprise like Toms, the most important thing is for our customers and donors to understand the real impact they can have. It's amazing when people experience and see things first-hand. We know this because we've seen it when we take people on giving trips over the years. Obviously, that's not scalable, but a VR experience is infinitely scalable. (Beer, 2016, n.p.)

The integration of VR into TOMS' CRM campaign has created an opportunity for its customers to experience the benefits of their donation, not only from the perspectives of children, but the donors themselves. The immersive multi-perspective story-telling is best represented through a 360-degree video that allows viewers to determine their own experience by navigating the video in their own ways. Traditional marketing platforms are less likely to generate the same level of experiential marketing effects as VR and other reality-creating technologies. The capabilities of VR to engage consumers through its interactive contents will "create entirely new, shocking, eye-opening and honest immersive experiences – bringing consumers along on the cause journey like never before" (CONE, 2016, n.p.). Empirical research has supported that the use of immersive VR video leads to more favorable results. For example, Vibrant studies a large number of advertising and marketing campaigns used either VR and 360-degree video or traditional 2D video and observes that better marketing effects are generated in terms of interaction rates (600%), content recall (700%), brand recall (2,700%), and product intent (200%) (Martin, 2017).

WWF and Coca-Cola Arctic Home Campaign AR Campaign (2013)

Launched on January 17, 2013 at Science Museum in London, this AR campaign (https://www.youtube.com/watch?v=h2Jg8ryVk1k) is a collaboration between Coca-Cola and World Wildlife Fund (WWF) to protect polar bear home in the Arctic (The Coca-Cola Company, 2011). The campaign is multi-platform and integrated in nature because other marketing communication activities (such as packaging, mobile texting donation, traditional media, 3D video, etc) are used in addition to the AR component (The Coca-

Cola Company, 2013). The objectives of this technology-enabled CRM campaign are to raise awareness and fund from the public to help WWF's conservation efforts to protect polar bear home (The Coca-Cola Company UK, 2013). The creation of an AR campaign as part of its public relations activity also matches the overall objectives of creating awareness by allowing museum visitors to see how climate changes will destroy polar bear habitat through its AR demonstration.

As demonstrated in the campaign video (https://www.youtube.com/watch?v=h2Jg8ryVk1k), this CRM campaign employs three technological attributes made possible by AR: *interactivity*, *mobility*, and *virtuality* (Javornik, 2016). This AR campaign is accessible through a portable mobile device that allow museum-goers to experience the cracking of iceberg and possible impacts on polar bear home. By virtually immersing users in the Arctic, they will experience what could happen to polar bears when their habit is destroyed by global warming. The design of the AR campaign is based on a combination of computer-generated graphics and videos to create an enhanced environment to simulate the negative impacts of climate change in the Arctic. The Arctic Home AR campaign is able "to create an enhanced experience to reach existing goals" (Crawley, 2018). The proposed analytical model has also confirmed that its success is based on the maximization of AR's properties to create consumer engagement, empathy, and action (Crawley, 2018). As part of an integrated campaign, the AR component makes best use of its technological attributes to communicate the global warming problems effectively, when compared with other traditional marketing platforms. At the campaign deployment stage, AR also allows WWF to demonstrate the climate change impacts by fully immersing users in a computer-enhanced environment where WWF's conversation efforts are experienced, not just told. This CRM campaign is another good example to show when message and campaign objectives influence WWF's decision to use AR due to its *interactivity*, *mobility*, and *virtuality* (Javornik, 2016).

CONCLUSION

This book chapter was written to address the gap in the existing reality-creating technology literature and to provide a preliminary assessment of the current state, impacts, challenges, and opportunities of AR, MR, and VR in relation to the creation and planning of CRM campaigns by practitioners. The authors pay attention to how these reality-creating technologies will influence the planning and deployment of CRM campaigns. The integration of AR, MR, and VR technologies into CRM campaigns has opened many opportunities for advertisers and marketers (CONE, 2016). For example, as demonstrated in the above CRM campaigns, practitioners have adopted these technologies to allow consumers to interact and engage with CRM campaign messages. The reality-creating technologies function as a vital component to demonstrate negative ecological impacts on the environment through immersing users in the virtually-created world. These technological attributes have been found in past advertising and marketing literature to generate better consumer engagement (Lafayette, 2017; Monllos, 2017; Scholz & Smith, 2016), to avoid future ad blocking behaviors (Martin, 2017), to build better brand awareness (Martin, 2017), to connect consumers to the product through a self-referencing effect (Baek et al., 2015), to make people better attached to a brand sponsoring these social causes, and to have more engaging storytelling (Johnson, 2018).

Despite the hyperbole, the feasibility and profitability of these technologies remains to be a concern since their early introduction (Williams, 2009). Scholars have pointed out that, to allow the full potential of these reality-creating technologies in marketing applications, information-intensive AR, MR, or VR will need fast streaming speeds to communicate data to consumers' devices (Laposky, 2017). Other industry pundits also point out that cost could be an important factor (Baumgartner, 2016). As reality can be manipulated through these reality-creating technologies, practitioners and researchers are concerned whether the trust, privacy, and surveillance could be some emerging issues that need to be properly address (Rizzotto, 2016). Other pertinent issues related to these reality-creating technologies include addition (Bordnick, Carter, & Taylor, 2011), educational applications (Bujak, Radu, Catrambone, MacIntyre, & Zheng, 2013), advertising applications (Kassaye, 2007; Metz, 2015a, b), health promotion (*Marketing Week*, 2006), consumer behavior research (Pantano, Rese, & Baier, 2017). There needs to be more programmatic research to investigate issues related to consumer-, system-, message-, and product-related factors in relation to CRM campaigns to explore both their practical and theoretical implications (Yang & Kang, 2018).

REFERENCES

Alcántara, A.-M. (2018, March). Brands are finally embracing augmented reality, but not without speed bumps. *AdWeek*. Retrieved on August 4, 2018 from https://www.adweek.com/digital/brands-are-finally-embracing-augmented-reality-but-with-speed-bumps-along-the-way/

Bae, M. (2017). Matching cause-related marketing campaign to culture. *Asian Journal of Communication, 27*(4), 415-432. doi:10.1080/01292986.01292017.01280064

Baek, T. H., Yoo, C. Y., & Yoon, S. (2015). *The impact of augmented reality on self-brand connections and purchase intentions*. Paper presented at the Academy of American Advertising, Chicago, IL.

Baek, T. H., Yoo, C. Y., & Yoon, S. (2018). Augment yourself through virtual mirror: The impact of self-viewing and narcissism on consumer responses. *International Journal of Advertising, 37*(3), 421-439. doi:10.1080/02650487.02652016.01244887

Ballings, M., McCullough, H., & Bharadwaj, N. (2018). Cause marketing and customer profitability. *Journal of the Academy of Marketing Science, 46*(2), 234–251. doi:10.100711747-017-0571-4

Baumgartner, J. (2016, January 23-30). Top VR adoption challenge: Cost. *Broadcasting & Cable, 12*.

Bazilian, E. (2017a, April 23). Infographic: What consumers really think about VR. *AdWeek*. Retrieved on November 15, 2017 from http://www.adweek.com/digital/infographic-what-consumers-really-think-about-vr/

Bazilian, E. (2017b, May 1). Time Inc.'s VR guru is forging a new path through immersive storytelling. *AdWeek*. Retrieved on November 15, 2017 from http://www.adweek.com/digital/time-inc-s-vr-guru-is-forging-a-new-path-through-immersive-storytelling/

Beer, J. (2016, May 6). Why TOMS shoes and AT&T are taking a virtual reality trip to Colombia. *Fast Company*. Retrieved on August 6, 2018 from https://www.fastcompany.com/3059526/why-toms-shoes-and-att-are-taking-a-virtual-reality-trip-to-colombia

Bordnick, P. S., Carter, B. L., & Traylor, A. C. (2011, March). What virtual reality research in addictions can tell us about the future of obesity assessment and treatment? *Journal of Diabetes Science and Technology, 5*(2), 265–271. doi:10.1177/193229681100500210 PMID:21527092

Braiker, B. (2018, March 5). Four things we learned at mobile world congress. *Advertising Age, 89*, 6.

Bujak, K. R., Radu, I., Catrambone, R., MacIntyre, B., Zheng, R., & Golubski, G. (2013). A psychological perspective on augmented reality in the mathematics classroom. *Computers & Education, 68*, 536–544. doi:10.1016/j.compedu.2013.02.017

Burritt, M. (2017a, November 6-12). AI, mixed reality spawn top tech trends for 2018. *Furniture/Today,* 18-20.

Burritt, M. (2017b, December 11-24). Experts: Amazon's mixed reality software is a tool, not a solution. *Furniture/Today,* 6.

Çeltek, E. (2015, September 30). Smart technologies: Augmented reality applications in tourism marketing. *Mobile Computing and Wireless Networks: Concepts, Methodologies, Tools, and Applications, 2-4*, 876–892.

Chang, C.-T., & Chen, P.-C. (2017). Cause-related marketing ads in the eye tracker: It depends on how you present, who sees the ad, and what you promote. *International Journal of Advertising, 36*(2), 336-355. doi:10.1080/02650487.02652015.01100698

Chen, P., Peng, Z., Li, D., & Yang, L. (2016). An improved augmented reality system based on Andar. *J. Visual Communication Image Research, 37*, 63–69. doi:10.1016/j.jvcir.2015.06.016

Claudio, P., & Maddalena, P. (2014, January). Overview: Virtual reality in medicine. *Journal of Virtual Worlds Research, 7*(1), 1–34.

Clifford-Marsh, E. (2009, February). Ford KA's augmented reality check. *Revolution (Staten Island, N.Y.),* 19.

CONE. (2016, May 13). *Toms and AT&T help consumers take a "walk in their shoes".* Retrieved on August 6, 2018 from http://www.conecomm.com/insights-blog/toms-att-walk-in-their-shoes-vr

Cook, A. V., Jones, R., Raghavan, A., & Saif, I. (2017, December 5). Digital reality: The focus shifts from technology to opportunity. *TechTrends,* Wired, Retrieved on October 10, 2018 from https://www.wired.com/brandlab/2018/02/digital-reality-focus-shifts-technology-opportunity/.

Crawley, C. (2018, April 17). *Augmented reality for good.* Retrieved on August 7, 2018 from https://www.forbes.com/sites/forbescommunicationscouncil/2018/2004/2017/augmented-reality-for-good/#2752c2090abad2011b

Das, S. (2018, January 2). 5 tech trends that will rule digital platforms in 2018. *Communication World Magazine,* 1-3.

Dias, A.-C. (2016, March 21). Expedia takes sick children on thrilling real-time adventures-- without leaving the hospital. *AdAge.* Retrieved on August 3, 2018 from http://adage.com/article/behind-the-work/expedia-takes-sick-children-thrilling-real-time-adventures-leaving-hospital/303218/

Gaudiosi, J. (2015, April 25). How augmented reality and virtual reality will generate $150 billion in revenue by 2020. *Fortune.* Retrieved on December 23, 2017 from http://fortune.com/2015/2004/2025/augmented-reality-virtual-reality/

Giardina, C. (2017, September 6). Tux? Check. Virtual reality goggles? Got 'em. *The Hollywood Reporter,* p. 70.

Gortari, A. B. O. (2018). Empirical study on game transfer phenomena in a location-based augmented reality game. *Telematics and Informatics, 35*(2), 382–396. doi:10.1016/j.tele.2017.12.015

Hamby, A., & Bringberg, D. (2018, Summer). Cause-related marketing persuasion knowledge: Measuring consumers' knowledge and ability to interpret CRM promotions. *The Journal of Consumer Affairs,* 373-392. doi:10.1111/joca.12167

Heim, M. (1998). *Virtual realism.* New York: Oxford University Press.

Heine, C., & Kapko, M. (2017, August 20). Facebook and apple are about to take AR mainstream. Here's how marketers are gearing up. *AdWeek.* Retrieved on November 15, 2017 from http://www.adweek.com/digital/facebook-and-apple-are-about-to-take-ar-mainstream-heres-how-marketers-are-gearing-up/

Higham, W. (2018). 10 consumer trends to watch in 2018. *Director,* 9–10.

Hilken, T., Ruyter, K. D., Chylinski, M., Mahr, D., & Keeling, D. I. (2017). Augmenting the eye of the beholder: Exploring the strategic potential of augmented reality to enhance online service experiences. *Journal of the Academy of Marketing Science, 45*(6), 884–905. doi:10.100711747-017-0541-x

Hsu, W.-Y. (2017). Brain-computer interface connected to telemedicine and telecommunication in virtual reality applications. *Telematics and Informatics, 34*(4), 224–238. doi:10.1016/j.tele.2016.01.003

Huang, T.-L., & Liao, S. (2015). A model of acceptance of augmented-reality interactive technology: The moderating role of cognitive innovativeness. *Electronic Commerce Research, 15*(2), 268–295. doi:10.100710660-014-9163-2

IDC. (2017, February 27). *Worldwide spending on augmented and virtual reality forecast to reach $13.9 billion in 2017, according to IDC.* Retrieved on November 19, 2017 from https://www.idc.com/getdoc.jsp?containerId=prUS42331217)

Javornik, A. (2016). Augmented reality: Research agenda for studying the impact of its media characteristics on consumer behaviour. *Journal of Retailing and Consumer Services, 30,* 252–261. doi:10.1016/j.jretconser.2016.02.004

Johnson, B. (2018, May). The new reality. Augmented and virtual reality offer new ways to engage with customers. *SCT,* 80-82.

Johnson, L. (2017a, November 15). This horror movies campaign shows how VR can affect your body. *AdWeek.* Retrieved on November 15, 2017 from http://www.adweek.com/digital/this-horror-movies-campaign-shows-how-vr-can-affect-your-body/

Johnson, L. (2017b, July 26). Why brands like L'Oréal and Acura are betting big on augmented reality. *AdWeek*. Retrieved on November 15, 2017 from http://www.adweek.com/digital/why-brands-like-loreal-and-acura-are-betting-big-on-augmented-reality/

Johnson, L. (2017c, November 15). This horror movies campaign shows how VR can affect your body. *AdWeek*. Retrieved on November 15, 2017 from http://www.adweek.com/digital/this-horror-movies-campaign-shows-how-vr-can-affect-your-body/

Johnson, L. (2017d, June 23). Björk's real-time music video wins digital craft grand prix for breaking new ground with VR. *AdWeek*. Retrieved on November 15, 2017 from http://www.adweek.com/digital/bjorks-real-time-music-video-wins-digital-craft-grand-prix-for-breaking-new-ground-with-vr/

Kassaye, W. W. (2007). Virtual reality as source of advertising. *Journal of Website Promotion*, 2(3/4), 103–124. doi:10.1080/15533610802174979

Kerrebroeck, H. V., Brengman, M., & Willems, K. (2017). Escaping the crowd: An experimental study on the impact of a virtual reality experience in a shopping mall. *Computers in Human Behavior*, 77, 437–450. doi:10.1016/j.chb.2017.07.019

Kim, J., Lee, J., & Kim, S. (2017). The efficacy of cause-related marketing within a social network: The effects of congruency, corporate credibility, familiarity of cause brands, and perceived altruistic motive. *Journal of Marketing Communications*, 23(5), 429-455. doi:10.1080/13527

Klie, L. (2016, December 1). Virtual reality to become a true reality. *Destination CRM*. Retrieved on August 3, 2018 from https://www.destinationcrm.com/Articles/ReadArticle.aspx?ArticleID=115061

Kuo, A., & Rice, D. H. (2015). The impact of perceptual congruence on the effectiveness of cause-related marketing campaigns. *Journal of Consumer Psychology*, 25(1), 78–88. doi:10.1016/j.jcps.2014.06.002

Lafayette, J. (2017, October 16). Toyota revs up virtual reality efforts by sponsoring discovery's TRVLR. *Broadcasting & Cable*, p. 46.

Laposky, J. (2017, August 21). A virtual reality data crunch is coming. *Twice*, p. 8.

Loop, E. (2017, November 5). *Catch marshmallows with Ben & Jerry's new Facebook AR filter!* Retrieved on November 19, 2017 from http://redtri.com/catch-marshmallows-with-ben-jerrys-new-facebook-ar-filter/)

Lou, C., & Alhabash, S. (2018). Understanding non-profit and for-profit social marketing on social media: The case of anti-texting while driving. *Journal of Promotion Management*, 24(4), 484-510. doi:10.1080/10496491.10492017.11380109

Lucke, S., & Heinze, J. (2015). The role of choice in cause-related marketing investigating the underlying mechanisms of cause and product involvement. *Procedia: Social and Behavioral Sciences*, 213, 647–653. doi:10.1016/j.sbspro.2015.11.466

Marketing Week. (2016, May 26). NHS launches first ever augmented reality billboard campaign to show power of blood donations. *Marketing Week*, p. 6.

Marketo. (n.d.). *Virtual reality: A fresh perspective for marketers.* Retrieved on November 24, 2018 from https://www.marketo.com/infographics/virtual-reality-a-fresh-perspective-for-marketers/

Martin, E. J. (2017, May/June). How virtual and augmented reality ads improve consumer engagement. *EContent (Wilton, Conn.), 5,* 8.

Melero, I., & Montaner, T. (2016). Cause-related marketing: An experimental study about how the product type and the perceived fit may influence the consumer response. *European Journal of Management and Business Economics, 25*(3), 161–167. doi:10.1016/j.redeen.2016.07.001

Metz, R. (2015a, May/June). Augmented advertising. *MIT's Technology Review, 118*(3), 21.

Metz, R. (2015b, March 18). Virtual reality advertisements get in your face. *MIT Technology Review.* Retrieved on November 13, 2017 from https://www.technologyreview.com/s/535556/virtual-reality-advertisements-get-in-your-face/

Microsoft. (2018, March 20). *What is mixed reality?* Retrieved on August 6, 2018 from https://docs.microsoft.com/en-us/windows/mixed-reality/mixed-reality

Milgram, P., Takemura, H., Utsumi, A., & Kishino, F. (1994). *Augmented reality: A class of displays on the reality-virtuality continuum.* Paper presented at the Telemanipulator and Telepresence Technologies. Boston, M.A

Monllos, K. (October 1, 2017). Brands are doing more experiential marketing. Here's how they're measuring whether it's working. *AdWeek.* Retrieved on November 15, 2017 from http://www.adweek.com/brand-marketing/experiential-can-create-more-meaningful-relationships-with-consumers/

O'Mahony, S. (2015). A proposed model for the approach to augmented reality deployment in marketing communications. *Procedia: Social and Behavioral Sciences, 175,* 227–235. doi:10.1016/j.sbspro.2015.01.1195

Olsson, T., & Salo, M. (2012). Narratives of satisfying and unsatisfying experiences of current mobile augmented reality applications. *Conference on Human Factors in Computing Systems Proceedings.* 10.1145/2207676.2208677

Pan, X., & Hamilton, A. F. C. (2018). Why and how to use virtual reality to study human social interaction: The challenges of exploring a new research landscape. *British Journal of Psychology, 109*(3), 395–417. doi:10.1111/bjop.12290 PMID:29504117

Pando, A. (2017, December 15). *Mixed reality will transform perceptions.* Retrieved on December 18, 2017 from https://www.forbes.com/sites/forbestechcouncil/2017/2012/2015/mixed-reality-will-transform-perceptions/#7539aff2478af

Pantano, E., Rese, A., & Baier, D. (2017). Enhancing the online decision-making process by using augmented reality: A two country comparison of youth markets. *Journal of Retailing and Consumer Services, 38,* 81–95. doi:10.1016/j.jretconser.2017.05.011

Rauschnabel, P. A. (2018). Virtually enhancing the real world with holograms: An exploration of expected gratifications of using augmented reality smart glasses. *Psychology and Marketing*, *35*(8), 557–572. doi:10.1002/mar.21106

Rese, A., Baier, D., Geyer-Schulz, A., & Schreiber, S. (2017). How augmented reality apps are accepted by consumers: A comparative analysis using scales and opinions. *Technological Forecasting and Social Change*, *124*, 306–319. doi:10.1016/j.techfore.2016.10.010

ResearchAndMarkets.com. (2018, July 30). *Global augmented reality (AR) & virtual reality (VR) market outlook to 2023 by devices, component, application and geography*. Retrieved on August 2, 2018 from https://www.businesswire.com/news/home/20180730005663/en/

Rizzotto, L. (2016, November 29). *The mixed reality revolution is here, and it'll change your world forever*. Retrieved on August 7, 2018 from https://medium.com/futurepi/the-mixed-reality-revolution-is-here-and-itll-change-your-world-forever-177b06dac792

Scholz, J., & Smith, A. N. (2016). Augmented reality: Designing immersive experiences that maximize consumer engagement. *Business Horizons*, *59*(2), 149–161. doi:10.1016/j.bushor.2015.10.003

Shields, R. (2010, October 7). HarperCollins uses augmented reality to promote authors. *New Media Age*, 6.

Shin, D. (2018). Empathy and embodied experience in virtual environment: To what extent can virtual reality stimulate empathy and embodied experience? *Computers in Human Behavior*, *78*, 64–73. doi:10.1016/j.chb.2017.09.012

Slater, M. (2018). Immersion and the illusion of presence in virtual reality. *British Journal of Psychology*, *109*(3), 431–433. doi:10.1111/bjop.12305 PMID:29781508

Suciu, P. (2018, April). A new perception: Augmented reality is changing how newspapers (and readers) are seeing things. *Editor & Publisher (E&P)*, 37-43.

Szymczyk, M. (2009, December 28). 2010: The year of augmented reality? *AdWeek*. Retrieved November 15, 2017 from http://www.adweek.com/brand-marketing/2010-year-augmented-reality-101138/

The Coca-Cola Company. (2011, November 18). *Arctic home campaign fact sheet*. Retrieved on August 7, 2018 from https://www.coca-colacompany.com/stories/arctic-home-campaign-fact-sheet

The Coca-Cola Company (UK). (2013, January 17). *Coca-Cola Great Britain and WWF announce new arctic home campaign*. Retrieved on August 7, 2018 from https://www.coca-cola.co.uk/newsroom/press-releases/coca-cola-and-wwf-announce-new-arctic-home-campaign

The Shorty Social Good Awards. (2016). *Expedia dream adventures (winner in hospitality and travel)*. Retrieved on August 3, 2018 from http://shortyawards.com/1st-socialgood/expedia-dream-adventures

The Webby Awards. (2017). Bullying in virtual reality. *The Webby Awards*. Retrieved on August 3, 2018 from https://www.webbyawards.com/winners/2017/advertising-media-pr/campaigns/best-cause-related-campaign/bullying-in-virtual-reality/

van Krevelen, R., & Poelman, R. (2010). A survey of augmented reality technologies, applications and limitations. *International Journal of Virtual Reality, 9*(1), 1–20.

Walker, J. (2017, July 14). Virtual reality to create an 'internet of experience' by 2030. *Digital Journal.* Retrieved on August 3, 2018 from http://www.digitaljournal.com/tech-and-science/technology/virtual-reality-to-create-an-internet-of-experience-by-2030/article/497608

Williams, M. (2009, July 10). Advertisers test alimented reality's durability. *Campaign,* p. 9.

Yang, K. C. C. (Ed.). (2018). Multi-platform advertising strategies in the global marketplace. Hershey, PA: IGI-Global Publisher. doi:10.4018/978-1-5225-3114-2

Yang, K. C. C., & Kang, Y. W. (2018). Integrating virtual reality and augmented reality into advertising campaigns: History, technology, and future trends. In N. Lee, X.-M. Wu, & A. El Rhalibi (Eds.), *Encyclopedia of computer graphics and games.* New York, NY: Springer. doi:10.1007/978-3-319-08234-9_132-1

Youn, S., & Kim, H. (2018). Temporal duration and attribution process of cause-related marketing: Moderating roles of self-construal and product involvement. *International Journal of Advertising, 37*(2), 217-235. doi:10.1080/02650487.02652016.01225332

Zhang, B. (2017). Design of mobile augmented reality game based on image recognition. *Journal on Image and Video Processing,* 90-110.

ADDITIONAL READING

Armitage, A., & Keeble-Allen, D. (2008, November). Undertaking a structured literature review or structuring a literature review: Tales from the field. *Electronic Journal of Business Research Methods, 6*(2), 123–216.

Bacon, J. (2016, March). How to launch new tech. *Marketing Week,* pp. 24-25.

Bailey, J. O., & Bailenson, J. N. (2017). Considering virtual reality in children's lives. *Journal of Children and Media, 11*(1), 107–113. doi:10.1080/17482798.2016.1268779

Barone, M. J., Norman, A. T., & Miyazaki, A. D. (2000). The influence of cause-related marketing on customer choice: Does one good turn deserve another? *Journal of the Academy of Marketing Science, 28*(2), 248–262. doi:10.1177/0092070300282006

Beltrone, G. (September 22, 2017). Patrón's snazzy new AR app lets you visit a hacienda and chat with a bartender. *AdWeek,* Retrieved on November 15, 2017 from http://www.adweek.com/creativity/patrons-snazzy-new-ar-app-lets-you-visit-a-hacienda-and-chat-with-a-bartender/

Brito, P. Q., & Stoyanova, J. (2018). Marker versus markerless augmented reality. Which has more impact on users? *International Journal of Human Computer Interaction, 34*(9), 819-833. *DOI, 8.* doi:10.1080/10447318.10442017.11393974

Bulearca, M., & Tamarjan, D. (2012). Augmented reality: A sustainable marketing tool? *Global Business and Management Research: An International Journal, 2*(2 &3), 237–252.

Burrows, C. N., & Blanton, H. (2016). Real-world persuasion from virtual-world campaigns: How transportation into virtual worlds moderates in-game influence. *Communication Research, 43*(4), 542–570. doi:10.1177/0093650215619215

Carmigniani, J., & Furth, B. (Eds.). (2011). *Augmented reality: An overview* (pp. 3–46). Heidelberg: Springer Verlag.

Chahal, M. (2016, January 28). Bringing brands virtually to life. *Marketing Week,* pp. 29-31.

Chung, N., Lee, H., Kim, J.-Y., & Koo, C. (2017). The role of augmented reality for experience-influenced environments: The case of cultural heritage tourism in Korea. *Journal of Travel Research,* 1–17.

Cohen, D. (2016, May 10). Twitter brings augmented reality to 'the voice'. *AdWeek.com,* Retrieved on December 18, 2017 from http://www.adweek.com/digital/twitter-augmented-reality-the-voice/

Cohen, D. (July 12, 2017). The Facebook spaces beta VR app now supports Facebook live. *AdWeek,* Retrieved on November 15, 2017 from http://www.adweek.com/digital/facebook-spaces-facebook-live/

Cohen, D. (June 16, 2017). YouTube is letting creators see what's heating up their 360-degree and VR videos. *AdWeek,* Retrieved on November 15, 2017 from http://www.adweek.com/digital/youtube-heatmaps-2360-degree-vr-videos/

Cohen, D. (March 29, 2017). Oculus revealed the release date for the new gear VR and the gear VR controller. *AdWeek,* Retrieved on November 15, 2017 from http://www.adweek.com/digital/oculus-new-gear-vr-gear-vr-controller-platform-updates/

Conway, R. (2017, April). The future of online advertising. *NZB,* pp. 40-41.

Cox, A. M., Cromer, K. W., Guzman, I., & Bagui, S. (2017, May). Virtual worlds, virtual reality, and augmented reality: Differences in purchase intentions based on types, users, and sex. *Journal of Virtual Worlds Research, 10*(1), 1–21. doi:10.4101/jvwr.v10i1.7247

Cox, A. M., Guzman, I., Cromer, K. W., & Bagui, S. (2017, May). Virtual worlds, virtual reality, and augmented reality: Differences in purchase intentions based on types, users, and sex. *Journal of Virtual Worlds Research, 10*(1), 1–20. doi:10.4101/jvwr.v10i1.7247

Craig, A. B. (2013). *Understanding augmented reality.* The Netherlands: Elsvier, Morgan Kaufmann.

Dacko, S. G. (2017). Enabling smart retail settings via mobile augmented reality shopping apps. *Technological Forecasting and Social Change, 124,* 243–256. doi:10.1016/j.techfore.2016.09.032

Damala, A., Schuchert, T., Rodriguez, I., Moragues, J., Gilleade, K., & Stojanovic, N. (2013). Exploring the affective museum visiting experience: Adaptive augmented reality (A2R) and cultural heritage. *International Journal of Heritage in the Digital Era, 2*(1), 117–142. doi:10.1260/2047-4970.2.1.117

Engberg, M., & Bolter, J. D. (2014). Cultural expression in augmented and mixed reality. *Convergence (London)*, *20*(1), 3–9. doi:10.1177/1354856513516250

Gartner. (2010, October 7). *Gartner's 2010 hype cycle special report evaluates maturity of 1,800 technologies*. Stamford, C.T.: Gartner.

Gottlieb, U., & Bianchi, C. (2017). Virtual trade shows: Exhibitors' perspectives on virtual marketing capability requirements. *Electronic Commerce Research and Applications*, *21*, 17–26. doi:10.1016/j.elerap.2016.12.004

Granquist, C., Stromberg, F., & Seilen, K. S. (2015). Games as a marketing channel - the impact on games as a marketing channel - the impact on players and spectators. *International Journal of Electronic Business Management*, *13*, 57–65.

Gualeni, S. (2016, December). The experience machine: Existential reflections on virtual worlds. *Journal of Virtual Worlds Research*, *9*(3), 1–10. doi:10.4101/jvwr.v9i3.7229

Hofmann, S., & Mosemghvdlishvili, L. (2014). Perceiving spaces through digital augmentation: An exploratory study of navigational augmented reality apps. *Mobile Media & Communication*, *2*(3), 265–280. doi:10.1177/2050157914530700

Hopp, T., & Gangadharbatla, H. (2016). Novelty effects in augmented reality advertising environments: The influence of exposure time and self-efficacy. *Journal of Current Issues and Research in Advertising*, *37*(2), 113–130. doi:10.1080/10641734.2016.1171179

Howie, K. M., Yang, L., Vitell, S. J., Bush, V., & Vorhies, D. (2018). Consumer participation in cause-related marketing: An examination of effort demands and defensive denial. *Journal of Business Ethics*, *147*(3), 679–692. doi:10.100710551-015-2961-1

Javornik, A. (2016). Augmented reality: Researchagenda forstudying the impact of its media characteristics on consumer behavior. *Journal of Retailing and Consumer Services*, *30*, 252–261. doi:10.1016/j.jretconser.2016.02.004

Jin, S.-A. A. (2009). Modality effects in second life: The mediating role of social presence and the moderating role of product involvement. *Cyberpsychology & Behavior*, *12*(6), 717–721. doi:10.1089/cpb.2008.0273 PMID:19522681

Jin, S.-A. A., & Bolebruch, J. (2009, Fall). Avatar-based advertising in second life: The role of presence and attractiveness of virtual spokespersons. *Journal of Interactive Advertising*, *10*(1), 51–60. doi:10.1080/15252019.2009.10722162

Jin, S.-A. A., & Sung, Y. (2010). The roles of spokes-avatars' personalities in brand communication in 3D virtual environments. *Journal of Brand Management*, *17*(5), 317–327. doi:10.1057/bm.2009.18

Jorner, J. (2017, November 10). How augmented reality is creating a new target market on social media. *AdWeek,* Retrieved on November 15, 2017 from http://www.adweek.com/digital/james-jorner-effective-inbound-marketing-guest-post-augmented-reality/

Kari, T. (2017). Pokémon Go 2016: Exploring situational contexts of critical incidents in augmented reality. *Journal of Virtual Worlds Research, 9*(3), 1–12.

Kassaye, W. W. (2007). Virtual reality as source of advertising. *Journal of Website Promotion, 2*(3/4), 103–124. doi:10.1080/15533610802174979

Kim, K., Hwang, J., Zo, H., & Lee, H. (2016). Understanding users' continuance intention toward smartphone augmented reality applications. *Information Development, 32*(2), 161–174. doi:10.1177/0266666914535119

Kourouthanassis, P., Boletsis, C., Bardaki, C., & Chasanidou, D. (2015). Tourists responses to mobile augmented reality travel guides: The role of emotions on adoption behavior. *Pervasive and Mobile Computing, 18*, 71–87. doi:10.1016/j.pmcj.2014.08.009

Krishen, A. S., Hardin, A. M., & LaTour, M. S. (2013). Virtual world experiential promotion. *Journal of Current Issues and Research in Advertising, 34*(2), 263–281. doi:10.1080/10641734.2013.788386

Laine, T. H., & Suk, H. J. (2016). Designing mobile augmented reality exergames. *Games and Culture, 11*(5), 548–580. doi:10.1177/1555412015572006

LaVecchia, G. (2017, August 4). Why location intelligence is mobile marketing's AR opportunity. *AdWeek,* Retrieved on November 15, 2017 from http://www.adweek.com/digital/why-location-intelligence-is-mobile-marketings-ar-opportunity/

Liao, T. (2015). Augmented or admented reality? The influence of marketing on augmented reality technologies. *Information, Communication & Society, 18*(3), 310-326. *DOI, 3*. doi:10.1080/136911 8X.1362014.1989252

Liao, T. (2018). Mobile versus headworn augmented reality: How visions of the future shape, contest, and stabilize an emerging technology. *New Media & Society, 20*(2), 796–814. doi:10.1177/1461444816672019

Liarokapis, F. (2006). December). An exploration from virtual to augmented reality gaming. *Simulation & Gaming, 37*(4), 507–533. doi:10.1177/1046878106293684

Lin, J.-H. T. (2017). Fear in virtual reality (VR): Fear elements, coping reactions, immediate and next-day fright responses toward a survival horror zombie virtual reality game. *Computers in Human Behavior, 72*, 350–361. doi:10.1016/j.chb.2017.02.057

CRM Magazine. (2016, December). Virtual reality to become a true reality. *Customer Relationship Management,* p. 14.

Martin-Gutierrez, J., Guinters, E., & Perez-Lopez, D. (2012). Improving strategy of self-learning in engineering: Laboratories with augmented reality. *Procedia: Social and Behavioral Sciences, 51*, 832–839. doi:10.1016/j.sbspro.2012.08.249

Meißner, M., Pfeiffer, J., Pfeiffer, T., & Oppewal, H. (2017, September). Combining virtual reality and mobile eye tracking to provide a naturalistic experimental environment for shopper research. *Journal of Business Research.* doi:10.1016/j.jbusres.2017.09.028

Milgram, P., & Kishino, F. (1994). A taxonomy of mixed reality visual displays. *IEICE Transactions on Information and Systems, E77-D*(12), 1321–1329.

Mota, J., Ruiz-Rube, I., Dodero, J., & Arnedillo-Sánchez, I. (2017). Augmented reality mobile app development for all. *Computers & Electrical Engineering*, 1–11.

Natividad, A. (October 6, 2017). KLM gave VR headsets to budget airline passengers, so they'd feel like they're on klm. *AdWeek*, Retrieved on November 15, 2017 from http://www.adweek.com/creativity/klm-gave-vr-headsets-to-budget-airline-passengers-so-theyd-feel-like-theyre-on-klm/

O'Shea, C. (2016, October 10). Elle cover uses augmented reality. *AdWeek.com*, Retrieved on December 18, 2017 from http://www.adweek.com/digital/elle-cover-uses-augmented-reality/

Pagés, R., Amplianitis, K., Monaghan, D., Ondřej, J., & Smolić, A. (2018). Affordable content creation for free-viewpoint video and vr/ar applications. *Journal of Visual Communication and Image Representation, 53*, 192–201. doi:10.1016/j.jvcir.2018.03.012

Papagiannis, H. (2014). Working towards defining an aesthetics of augmented reality: A medium in transition. *Convergence (London), 20*(1), 33–40. doi:10.1177/1354856513514333

Pavlik, J. V., & Bridges, F. (2013). The emergence of augmented reality (AR) as a storytelling medium in journalism. *Journalism & Communication Monographs, 15*(1), 4–59. doi:10.1177/1522637912470819

Persaud, A., & Azhar, I. (2012). Innovative mobile marketing via smartphones: Are consumers ready? *Marketing Intelligence & Planning, 30*(4), 418–443. doi:10.1108/02634501211231883

Petersen, N., & Stricker, D. (2015). Cognitive augmented reality. *Computers & Graphics, 53*, 82–91. doi:10.1016/j.cag.2015.08.009

Poushneh, A., & Vasquez-Parraga, A. Z. (2017). Discernible impact of augmented reality on retail customer's experience, satisfaction and willingness to buy. *Journal of Retailing and Consumer Services, 34*, 229–234. doi:10.1016/j.jretconser.2016.10.005

Rauschnabel, P. A., Rossmann, A., & Dieck, M. C. (2017). An adoption framework for mobile augmented reality games: The case of Pokemon go. *Computers in Human Behavior, 76*, 276–286. doi:10.1016/j.chb.2017.07.030

Rebelo, F., Noriega, P., Duarte, E., & Soares, M. (2012, December). Using virtual reality to assess user experience. *Human Factors, 54*(6), 964-982. *DOI, 9*. doi:10.1177/0018720812465006

Richards, K. (2017, August 31). American express built a game that lets you play tennis against an AI opponent at the U.S. Open. *AdWeek*, Retrieved on November 15, 2017 from http://www.adweek.com/brand-marketing/american-express-built-a-game-that-lets-you-play-tennis-against-an-ai-opponent-at-the-u-s-open/

Richards, K. (2017, September 19). Ikea and 72andsunny Amsterdam share how they worked together to launch AR app IKEA place. *AdWeek*, Retrieved on November 15, 2017 from http://www.adweek.com/brand-marketing/ikea-and-2072andsunny-amsterdam-share-how-they-worked-together-to-launch-ar-app-ikea-place/

Rizzo, A. S., Lange, B., Suma, E. A., & Bolas, M. (2011, March). Virtual reality and interactive digital game technology: New tools to address obesity and diabetes. *Journal of Diabetes Science and Technology, 5*(2), 256–264. doi:10.1177/193229681100500209 PMID:21527091

Rothman, A. (2015. May 25). Advertisers looking for new opportunities in virtual and augmented spaces. Retrieved 15 November 2017 from https://subwayfold.com/tag/augmented-reality-advertising/

Rowe, S. D. (2017, November). Seeing the realities of augmented reality. *Customer Relationship Management,* pp. 22-26.

Schimelpfenig, E. (2017, September). Virtual and augmented reality. *Kitchen & Bath Design News*, 26-27.

Scholz, J., & Smith, A. N. (2016). Augmented reality: Designing immersive experiences that maximize consumer engagement. *Business Horizons, 59*(2), 149–161. doi:10.1016/j.bushor.2015.10.003

Schultz, E. J. (2015, September 16). Gatorade lets viewers step up to bat with virtual reality campaign. *AdAge.com,* Retrieved on December 18, 2017 from http://adage.com/article/digital/gatorade-puts-viewers-bat-virtual-reality-campaign/300384/

Search, P. (2016). Information design opportunities with augmented reality applications. *Information Design Journal, 22*(3), 237–246. doi:10.1075/idj.22.3.04sea

Seitz, P. (2018, January 29). Augmented reality glasses still 23 years from consumer market. *Investors Business Daily*, n.p.

Shapiro, A. (September 15, 2017). 6 ways marketers can get augmented reality right. *AdWeek,* Retrieved on November 15, 2017 from http://www.adweek.com/digital/2016-ways-marketers-can-get-augmented-reality-right/

Shaul, B. (2014, March 27). Disneynature explore: Interact with animals in this augmented reality app. *AdWeek.com,* Retrieved on December 18, 2017 from http://www.adweek.com/digital/disneynature-explore-interact-with-animals-in-this-augmented-reality-app/

Stein, J. (2015, August 17). Inside the box. *Time*, 40–49.

Steuer, J. (1992, December). Defining virtual reality: Dimensions determining telepresence. *Journal of Communication, 42*(4), 73–93. doi:10.1111/j.1460-2466.1992.tb00812.x

Suciu, P. (2018, April). A new perception: Augmented reality is changing how newspapers (and readers) are seeing things. *Editor & Publisher (E&P),* pp. 37-43.

Swant, M. (2017, August 25). KFC created a wacky, creepy virtual-reality escape game to train new cooks. *AdWeek,* Retrieved on November 15, 2017 from http://www.adweek.com/digital/kfc-created-a-wacky-creepy-virtual-reality-escape-game-to-train-new-cooks/

Swant, M. (20017, April 21). Developers see endless possibilities and pitfalls with social VR after testing facebook spaces. *AdWeek,* Retrieved on November 15, 2017 from http://www.adweek.com/digital/developers-see-endless-possibilities-and-pitfalls-with-social-vr-after-testing-facebook-spaces/

Tobar-Mun~oz, H., Baldiris, S., & Fabregat, R. (2017). Augmented reality game-based learning: Enriching students' experience during reading comprehension activities. *Journal of Educational Computing*, *55*(7), 901–936. doi:10.1177/0735633116689789

Vanian, J. (2018, July 10). Facebook is testing augmented reality ads in news feed. *Fortune.com*, Retrieved on September 1, 2018 from http://fortune.com/2018/07/10/facebook-augmented-reality-news-feed/

Webb, A. (2016, November). Virtually convincing. *INC*, p. 72.

Yaoyuneyong, G., Foster, J., Johnson, E., & Johnson, D. (2016). Augmented reality marketing: Consumer preferences and attitudes toward hypermedia print ads. *Journal of Interactive Advertising*, *16*(1), 1630. doi:10.1080/15252019.2015.1125316

KEY TERMS AND DEFINITIONS

Augmented Reality: The term refers to a simulated, but enhanced, reality that combines both computer-generated virtual and real-world data to enable users to perform real-time interactions with computer-generated graphics, imagery, and objects, in a seamless way and with an illusion of these layers of information coexisting in the same space.

Best Practice: Refers to a method, procedure, or technique that has demonstrable evidence through research or practice to generate the maximum results and become a benchmark or a standard to widespread adoption by the industry.

Cause-Related Marketing (CRM): A sub-set of marketing activities that is related to a company's social responsibility programs (CSR). CRM focuses on linking a company's sale (usually a percentage of sale) with the amount to be donated to non-profit organizations to support their social causes.

Digital Advertising: An umbrella term to refer to emerging advertising practices (such as internet, social, mobile, reality technologies, etc.).

Mixed Reality: A term that refers to the computer-generated reality when the physical world blends with the digital world through environmental input, spatial sound, and location.

Reality (Reality-Creating) Technology: An umbrella term when referring to technologies that can create simulated realities using computer-generated images, videos, interactions. Usually, the term refers to augmented reality, mixed reality, and virtual reality technologies.

Virtual Reality: Refers to an assembly of technologies that provides immersive, interactive, and information-rich virtual experiences through a computerized, simulated, real-time 3D virtual environment.

Chapter 11
Virtual Reality (VR) Applications in Learning:
"Living Autism"

Vanessa Camilleri
University of Malta, Malta

Foaad Haddod
University of Malta, Malta

Matthew Montebello
University of Malta, Malta

Joseph C. Camilleri
Saint Martin's Institute of Higher Education, Malta

Alexiei Dingli
University of Malta, Malta

Vince Briffa
University of Malta, Malta

EXECUTIVE SUMMARY

This chapter illustrates the use of VR applications in professional development and introduces an application used to assist teachers, learning support assistants (LSAs), and teaching assistants (TAs) to better understand autistic children's behaviors while in the classroom. One of the challenges faced in classrooms is how to understand the autistic children's behaviors and empathize with them. The proposed VR application repurposes a different form of narrative of the world of a child on the autism spectrum in an immersive environment designed for educators. The VR application in this chapter uses recorded footage through 360-degree cameras and special effects powered by Unity. In a context where integration is a key to today's learning and education, the researchers believe that the use of VR to assist the teachers in empathizing with their learners' traits and conditions may be of great benefit to the learners' school experiences.

DOI: 10.4018/978-1-5225-5912-2.ch011

INTRODUCTION

The simplest definition of empathy can be given as one's ability to tune in to someone else's thoughts or feelings. However, empathy becomes quite complex when humans try to understand physical or emotional pain which they cannot associate to or with through their own differing experiences (Baron-Cohen & Wheelwright, 2004). The way human beings empathise with others, is through our past observations, experiences, associated memories or reasoning. But when the situation is beyond anything which the researchers have ever encountered or observed mindfully, it becomes increasingly difficult to put ourselves in others' shoes. The two primary components of empathy that have been identified include the affective component and the cognitive one (Decety & Ickes, 2011). Although in an empathic individual both components work in synchrony, the researchers believe that the latter can be supported through the development of one's mental capacities to take the other's perspectives. The researchers note as well, that very frequently empathy manifests itself as a shared representation of what one observes.

Thus, when facing a person who is expressing some form of emotion, whether this is sadness or happiness people tend to share those feelings with that person. When a person is for example discussing an illness, one tends to try and remember an experience in which the researchers have felt sick – this is referred to as embodied cognition. By manifesting such behaviour, one can put himself or herself in a better position to empathise with that person. However, when that representation involves some disorder, disability or impairment it becomes increasingly difficult for us to transfer those perceptions to an embodied cognition.

When the disorder is in itself as multifaceted as the autism spectrum, then the complexity becomes even more pronounced. Individuals exhibit different traits and properties, but one common point of agreement between the various communities working with the autism spectrum disorder is that research in autism should adopt a person-centred approach, focusing on the individual needs and differences of people affected by autism rather than focus on its definitions (Kenny, et al., 2015). The reason for this, is that many individuals affected by autism most often manifest behavioural traits in different ways. Autism Europe defines autism as a "lifelong disability… People on the autism spectrum experience persistent difficulties with social communication and social interaction, and might display restricted and repetitive patterns of behaviours, activities or interests." This is a rather broad definition of autism. In fact, many people affected describe it in terms of the ways in which it affects their life experiences. Through a series of classroom observations, it was noted that around 80% of all children diagnosed as being on the autism spectrum exhibit sensory hyperactivity that may lead them to feeling distraught at the various sounds, touch or even movement (Case-Smith, Weaver, & Fristad, 2015). Although there are a number of documented sensory intervention methods used with children with autism spectrum disorder (ASD), when these children are in class with their teachers and their classmates, the situation changes.

This brings back to the initial argument that empathising with people in these challenging contexts, becomes extremely difficult unless one goes through their life experiences. A teacher or a learning support assistant in a class environment may not always be aware of what may affect a child diagnosed with ASD, and some actions, often overlooked as trivial or taken for granted may indeed prove to be disturbing for the child.

Virtual Reality (VR) technology has the potential to exploit sensory stimulation which can evoke in people different emotions, such as fear, sadness, happiness (Cho et al., 2016). It can cause people to attempt to run, move and touch the virtual objects as though these were real. Most of these responses are due to the perception which is generated through associations within the human brain where an illusion of presence; of 'being there' is generated in a way that the mind believes that it is really placed in the virtual context. Research in VR shows that people's reactions when immersed in a virtual environment change to reflect the virtual context in which they are placed. For example, people who have tried the VR elevator experience, where they are taken up 40 storeys via a virtual elevator and then asked to walk a plank hanging out in mid-air, to save a kitten, report feeling extreme fear that is also often manifested by physical reactions, including dilated pupils, increased heart beat and sweat secretion (Bailey, Bailenson, & Casasanto, 2016).

For these reasons, VR has increasingly seen its use in therapeutic and medical contexts by immersing patients into a realistically simulated scenario, whilst at the same time monitoring the psychophysiological reactions (Won et al., 2017). The benefits of this form of exposure therapy is that the environment can be adjusted to accommodate to individual needs and psychophysiological responses.

On the other hand, Autism is very often defined as very diverse in its traits and characteristics. This poses quite some challenges when attempting to produce a VR experience, without being too generalised in the approach. Literature as well as parents of children diagnosed with ASD, indicate that children may experience dizziness when they feel uncomfortable with the surrounding noise. Some of the children may start humming or may try to indicate their discomfort using other means.

In this chapter, the researchers describe another form of context which can benefit from the use of VR and its empathic potential. The researchers propose a VR environment as a professional development platform for educators working with children diagnosed with ASD.

Professional Development and VR

One of the attributes of a professional person is a life-long pledge to maintain the highest levels of associated knowledge and skills through education. Continuous Professional Development (CPD) is one systematic way of providing such education and is essential for any professional who seeks to excel and remain abreast of contemporary information, tools, techniques or methodologies within the field of that same profession. As the field of expertise evolves and rapidly moves ahead, the need and necessity for a professional to follow CPD activities does not cease, in an effort to assist the same professional in diligently perform current duties and enhance career progression opportunities. CPD can take different forms and shapes, be formal or informal, as long as it is relevant to the field of work and focusses on career needs and objectives. Pierke Bosschieter (2016) points out that CPD can be a combination of various approaches, ideas and techniques that assist in learning and growing as a professional. She argues that the main focus should be on the end product, namely the benefits yielded in real practical terms. Every professional should be responsible and consciously recognise the need to maintain the highest level of standards in one's vocation to voluntarily seek and feel the need of continuous career development. The use of technologies and digital applications assist and facilitate the CPD process as hand-held devices, apps, and multi-media methodologies allow professionals to access, experience and appreciate such educational materials. The potential of new media plays a crucial part in CPD (Bosschieter, 2016).

The teaching profession is no exception and the need for seasoned educators to pursue their training to ensure they are on their game is always on. Ross and Morrison (2004) claims that teachers are required to meet the needs of an ever-evolving audience, and thereby they are compelled to regularly practice CPD. However, a variety of factors around educators are continuously changing as Day and Leitch (2007) list administrative issues like legislation, regulations and teaching conditions, as well as academic matters like curricula, teaching approaches and aids, apart from other broader external factors like environmental, socio-economical, and cultural. The researchers identify the development of the system, the educator and the learner as three closely-related purposes why CPD for teachers are instrumental. Yet, if the researchers had to focus specifically on the development of the teacher in isolation then ulterior purposes can emerge, from classroom practical needs to the changing role of the teacher, from evolving school-wide needs to novel government educational policies, apart from personal and professional needs as each educator progresses in life. Bev Jones (2017) picks on the first of these purposes as she investigates the challenges teachers encounter when coming in contact with digital and technological tools. She reports that less than 3% of further education institutions in UK had the majority of their academics competent in the use of learning technologies, while 70% of the teacher population confessed that they have a lack of confidence in the use of digital applications. Use of technology should not be done just for the sake of being different, novel or trendy, but educators need to appreciate and comprehend that a particular technology is relevant within the specific contextual circumstances that fit in with the planned lesson and the expected academic objectives and outcomes. Richard Walker et al., (2014) conclude in their TEL survey report that teachers will only employ a particular technology only if they envisage it to enhance their current practice as a beneficial academic aid to the educator and student alike.

To overcome such obstacles and in an attempt to encourage teachers to experiment and experience the benefits of employing different technologies training agencies and CPD providers have reverted to Virtual Reality (VR). Researchers at the University at Buffalo in the state of New York have been employing VR to introduce new technologies to educators in an attempt to create a middle-ground safe space whereby educators can freely practice, explore and experiment with what it is like to employ different technologies with non-real kids (Anzalone, 2017). The up-and-close experience, that the designers compare to a "flight simulator for teachers", employs images of real students recorded inside a classroom with the help of 360-degree high definition cameras, creating a three-dimensional seamless and immersive environment. Teachers are able to enjoy the full capabilities that VR has to offer in other domains like gaming, medicine, automobile industry, tourism and modelling, whereby users can experience incredible events that would either be impossible in real life. Some examples include walking through a building that has not been built yet, switch genders and enter someone's body, drive a Formula 1 car, free fall from the sky, dive around the Titanic, and visit numerous museums and places of interest from your living room. The sensation is so real, maximising the use of one's senses, that users go through a series of emotional phases that researchers are exploiting to understand the role of context on learning, memory, and emotion while maintaining experimental control (Kroes, Dunsmoor, Mackey, McClay, & Phelps, 2017).

The quality and intensity of the VR experience when compared with other simulation technologies employed in education renders this immersive technology more than suitable for teachers' CPD (Bambury, 2017). A number of companies have developed virtual environments in an attempt to replicate and simulate the classroom environment and what a teacher experiences in reality (Loewus, 2017). A combination of animation-like surroundings and cartoon-like avatar characters tend to denigrate the intense experience an educator goes through when facing a class, as a consequence the comparison of a virtual environment to a VR-generated ambient is unfair and yet they are too far apart. The use of real video combined by the natural movement of one's head to inspect the entire classroom and the students around you embodies an authentic experience that comes as close to the factual thing as one can possibly can. It provides a visceral sensation that no video on a flat screen can inflict on one's emotional experience. Liana Loewus (2017) reports empirical results from a research project managed by a neuro-cognition scientist, Richard Lamb, who analysed data collected from numerous VR users through heart rate monitors, sphygmomanometers to measure the blood pressure, electrodermal readers to determine the galvanised skin response, and neuroimaging apparatus to picture brain activity. The results were compared to respective data collected when person experience real life situations, and what emerged was that the body in both cases responded in a similar way. His conclusions showed no difference whatsoever between a teacher delivering within a real class and delivering a session through the VR-enabled experience.

The VR technology is still evolving to further enhance the user experience by closing the gap between a real-life occurrence and the VR-generated one. Crosswater Digital Media (Crosswater, 2017) are adding functionality to their 360/VR experience by enabling VR users to move and interact with individual students as they comprehensively collect video data from within a real classroom. Movements include stepping in any direction, kneeling and verbally addressing persons within the video itself. This will eventually render the VR experience even more realistic and genuinely faithful to classroom settings. Teachers can experience their anxieties, challenges and novel situations through a controlled VR recreation session during their CPD in order to master and muscle memorise their response actions when they come across and experience that same stressful pedagogical event.

VR Experience Design

VR design is mostly about how to create the right communication interface between the technology and the user. It is also about recreating the right perceptual conditions for the user to be able to live through the experience as though it was part of her reality. Perception can be defined as a user process that collates sensory information from the environment and interprets this in a way that is reflected from the user's own past experiences or associations. Most often perceptions are quite subjective. VR can package all the sensory information for the user and present it to her. In this way the user's brain can process sensory information, derived from auditory and visual stimuli whilst the user's brain reacts as though these stimuli are quite real (Sanchez-Vives & Slater, 2005).

In this view, the researchers also make the distinction between presence and immersion in VR. Whilst VR can be characterised by three main features acting in synchrony which include immersion, interaction and involvement (Piovesan, Passerino, & Pereira, 2012), the sense of *being there* through presence is achieved when the user responds to the virtual place and events in that place as though the user's own body is part of that virtual place. Immersion is in itself defined by the fidelity of the features that are inserted in the VR – therefore the researchers refer to the extent of the field of view, the sensory systems it stimulates, and the realism of the images displayed (Sanchez-Vives & Slater, 2005). What makes VR stand out from other technologies is however its affordance in making a near-real life experience repeatable in a safe controlled environment (Kandalaft et al., 2013). This makes it quite unique for therapeutic purposes.

In a recent study by Gehlbach et al (2015) about social perspective taking by individuals, the researchers argue that when people take on others' perspectives the overall quality of life improves. This reflects the definition of empathy as "an emotional response that stems from another's emotional state or condition and is congruent with the other's emotional state or condition" (Eisenberg et al., 2014). As part of their study, the researchers involve participants in different roles inside a virtual environment. The results obtained from this study indicate that even with a low level of immersion, users could experience the different perspectives of people in different roles in a way which they wouldn't have been able to during passive learning (Gehlbach, et al., 2015). Yet the researchers report that with more detail added to the virtual environment script, the users' brain can quickly replicate the rich virtual experience as though it is quite real. Although the experience they presented was not a VR, the researchers believe that with the increased realism and with the right scripting the researchers can help individuals experience another person's emotion with the aim of raising awareness of the other's perspectives. The following subsections describe in detail the methodology, film and audio as well as the technology which was developed for the creation of the 'Living Autism' project.

METHODOLOGY

The methodology for the design of the VR experience is to focus on presenting an immersive reality arising from different sensory modalities such as visuals and audio, combining surroundings in the field of view and spatial audio with a strong narrative to render a more vivid imaging of the unfolding sequence of events.

Research Method Selection

Educational psychology research is most often characterised by a number of methods that include experimental research. The experimental method of research shows how the changing environmental conditions of learning, through various experimental designs, may impinge on the participant's cognitive state. In this specific example, the researchers carried out an experiment whereby the researchers developed an immersive reality app specifically designed for educators working with children diagnosed with ASD. In this instance, the researchers have hypothesised that through the designed VR, whereby users are immersed into a first-hand experience of a child on the Autistic Spectrum at primary school, their empathic awareness increases. For this reason, the researchers have adopted the empathy quotient tool devised and validated by Spreng et al., (2009) to create a pre- and post- experience tool for the participants in the study. The scope of this tool was to give an indication of any change, if at all, in the participants' sense of empathy towards the children's sensory response to the stimuli in everyday class practice.

Research Framework

The researchers make use of an embodied cognition (EC) framework to understand how mental representations are manifested through the individuals' behaviour. People generate mental representations through situated actions, and states involving physical actions. So, when a person's mental models are triggered by a stimulus (which can vary from printed text to an interactive digital medium), that person's actions start reflecting the mental models generated. The embodied cognition framework may be described as what goes on in someone's head as one goes through an experience which is pre-constructed and which is heavily dependent on the environment that is presented (Bailey, Bailenson, & Casasanto, 2016). The embodied cognition framework presupposes that the body plays an important role in the perceptual and cognitive processes during an interaction within a situated context which may include interactive art experiences (Bilda, Candy, & Edmonds, 2007) and of course VR (Bailey, Bailenson, & Casasanto, 2016).

Experimental Stimuli Development

The context of the VR experience is built using data for the construction of the case scenarios which the researchers obtained from a number of sources. The relevant literature about autism and autistic traits was overlaid to the responses from direct interviews with teachers, learning support assistants, and parents of children diagnosed on the autism spectrum. The interviews were coded in terms of the actions and behaviours of children on the autism spectrum. A number of general stimuli that might cause discomfort in children on the ASD were then identified and compared to the literature. These general stimuli included sounds of shouting and general chaos in the classroom, people swarming together, disturbing repetitive noises, etc. The overlapping causes of possible negative reactions in people on the autism spectrum were then inserted into the script of the case scenarios unfolding over a typical day at primary school. This includes classroom sessions as well as lunch breaks and walking in corridors.

Using Interactive Narratives in VR Research

The role of the viewer changes in the prospect of interactive narrative. Interactive narrative is a form of digital interactive experience in which users influence a dramatic storyline through actions by assuming the role of a character in a fictional virtual world. It can be used for serious applications such as education and training as in the case of this research project. The most common form of interactive narrative involves the user taking on the role of the protagonist in an unfolding storyline. If the right techniques are not employed in an amalgamated manner the user can become a disembodied observer as if watching a movie. The goal of interactive narrative is thus to immerse the user in a virtual world such that he or she believes that they are an integral part of an unfolding story and that their actions have meaningful consequences as per the embodied cognition framework.

Taking into context the main scope of using VR to foster empathy a decision was taken to focus the VR experience around a child's negative responses to set stimuli in a class scenario. To do this, the researchers used a voice (which as indicated previously in filming it is often referred to as God's voice), to attempt to reveal insights into the children's thoughts by communicating them in voice. Although the researchers are aware that most children with ASD have difficulty in communicating their thoughts the researchers needed to consciously move away from what happens in reality to help users build embodied cognition which can lead them to recognise the children's responses as a consequence of external environmental factors. Thus, in this way the researchers are helping users create forms of associations that would help them become more aware of the responses they might trigger in a child with ASD, when they take certain decisions or behave in set ways.

Even so, these voiced-thoughts are not without any grounding. Two different sources were used as a base to develop the appropriate thoughts when reacting to the identified situations in the VR environment. Fleischmann (2012) reveals the real story of a child with ASD, highlighting the challenges she had when communicating in her social environment. The researchers reveal insights, thoughts and reactions in various situations and contexts, and these, together from real experiences gathered from teachers, LSAs and parents of children with ASD, became our grounding to create the overall narrative.

Using Film and Audio for Stimuli Development

Chris Milk (2015) in a TED talk entitled, 'How virtual reality can create the ultimate empathy machine', describes film as a group of rectangles which can be played in a sequence. This can be demonstrated quite visually through the work of early film makers such Eadweard Muybridge (1830-1904) (Muybridge, 1878)and Guy-Blaché (1896-1906) among others. Claire Bishop (2012) describes the notion of *dérive*. This is described as a tool in 'psychogeography', which studies the effects of a given environment on the emotions and behaviour of individuals. The notion of *dérive* acts as a mode of increasing one's awareness of urban surroundings. In the case of Situationist 'unitary urbanism', *dérive* enabled an undoing of the dehumanising effect of modernist forms of contemporary urban high-rise living (Bishop, 2012).

Virtual reality filming reuses these concepts, through the implementation of an experience which will attempt to isolate instances in a human's existence and portray the reality that extends beyond the visual through the provoking of empathetic situations in the individual's life. Unlike games, where players can take their time to play, VR filmmakers need to tell their stories in minutes. Compared to traditional filmmaking, VR filming needs to be rethought on a new level. This would mean the application of existing techniques from traditional filmmaking to new techniques, born through the adaptation of this new means of narrative technology (Gardner, 2016; Riedl & Bulitko, 2012; Riedl & Young, 2006). Given that the viewer has the ability to look around, a director cannot simply change shots, this would create the possibility of getting the viewer to lose the sense of where he or she is. Filmmakers cannot use conventional strategies and methods to film a scene, as the scene is a whole bubble with no beginning and no end, says Simon Robinson from the software firm, The Foundry. The immersion created once a headset is donned would be broken once any flaws in filming are sensed (2016).

Figures 1 and 2 demonstrate visually, how technology had an important role in the increase of immersion, or as Maurice Merleau-Ponty calls it - the Chiasm (The Visible and the Invisible, 1968). According to Mark Billinghurst (2016) in his keynote speech given at the '22nd International Conference on Virtual Systems & Multimedia, VSMM', realism has increased with the passage of time *and* the invention of new technologies which allowed the viewer to partake more in the experience. With the arrival of 360° video, and the involvement of an actual constructed 3D space in the 2000s, reality kept on soaring upwards as it attained a more virtual application. With time, more physical and psychological reactions have been employed through the engagement of new technologies which invited the use of such physical and psychological responses, such as gesture, emotion and thought. Would Billinghurst then be saying that prior to the 2000s, the viewer was not employing gesture, emotion and thought whilst experiencing paintings and/or film? The truth is that it is difficult to word the difference between; immersion in, for example a High Renaissance or Baroque painting and immersion in a painting done wholly using technological and virtual means, like the Tilt Brush for HTC Vive and recently also adapted for Oculus Rift (Google, 2017), and immersion in the direction of a film projected entirely in VR. All three have factors of immersion which are similar and will continue being similar, as these are the factors which are intrinsic in all art of a particular aptitude. Other factors of immersion would be singular to the medium being used for that specific artwork.

'Living Autism' delves into the elements which can be borrowed from traditional filming, techniques and how these elements can be tested and experimented with to try to understand and establish what captures a viewer's attention and how this attention, once captured, be retained, and how can this same attention, be manipulated to guide the viewer through the VR film. As 2D movies have captured the hearts

Figure 1. The role of technology in developing content capture approaches

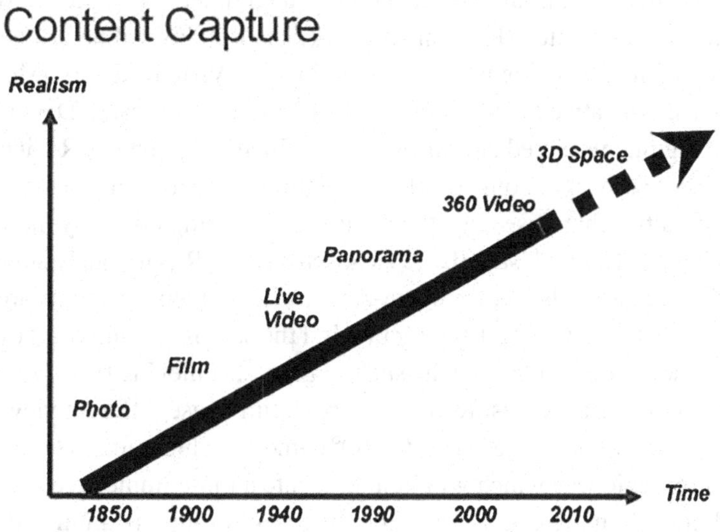

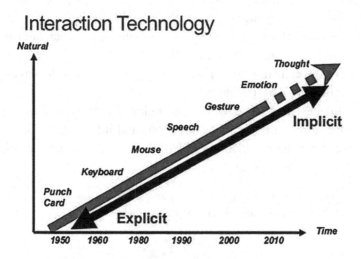

Figure 2. The development of interaction technology since 1950s

and minds of millions and led them through narratives which evoked fear, tears and laughter, over the last one hundred years, this project has been created as an experiment with attention capture and retention.

Kevin Brooks, comments thus with regards to such factors that need to be implemented in the practice of VR filming and other VR applications,

By experiencing a good story well told, we create our own immersive environments, with details unrivalled by electronic media. We are able to see the anxiety in faces, we can hear the excitement in voices, we can smell the food in kitchens, we can feel the hairs on the back of our neck react to scary situations. Technological additions should complement the immersion already present in the human system. (2003, p. 4).

It is hence of great importance, to analyse traditional artistic forms of film making, and establishing what had been used and evolved through the years, to create immersion in the viewer, and subsequently transpose these same elements into VR. John Bucher (2016), in his online article about the basics of shooting film in VR and his upcoming book, 'Storytelling for Virtual Reality: Methods and Principles for Crafting Immersive Narratives' (2017) as well as Michael Naimark, David Larence and James McKee have tackled arguments aimed at improving VR cinematography (VR Cinematography Studies for Google, 2016). These authors not only tackle the methods needed to create a narrative in VR filming but recognise the difficulties that arise once the filming is not being done any more for a 2D screen but for a 360-degree ambience. Naimark says that, "Headset-based VR is uniquely suited for experiences in the nearfield" (2016), what he calls the, 'intimate-zone', where video and sound are within arm's reach, hence as close as possible to the viewer, keeping in mind the stitching limitations of the camera. He also concludes that VR made for computer models, such as games, achieving the right point-of-view (POV) is trivial, "but when the material comes from cameras, getting these different viewpoints is much more challenging" (2016). Here Naimark is referring to 360° cameras, which similar to traditional filming need to be positioned in a strategic way which will help to create a more immersive narrative for the viewer. The director in traditional filming can cut between diverse close-up, medium and long shots, which is not possible in 360° filming, yet other aspects like low and high shots are applicable for both styles of filming. The viewing of people is greatly affected by the relationship between the height of the subject and height of the camera. This is commonly referred to as the 'eye line', which translates roughly to the point-of-view of the viewer vis-à-vis the subject matter.

During filming, it was found that a camera placed at a minimum of 20cm above the microphone and green chroma screen gave results that are more effective.

Figure 3 below shows the camera position relative to the scene and the environment in which the user (portrayed as the child with ASD) is placed.

As figure 4 shows, the designed VR environment included four main VR environment scenes and four auxiliary scenes that aim to provide more directions and information about the experience: The user menu, development team, an introductory video, the corridor scene, two classroom scenes, the playground scene, and the closing message.

Figure 3. Camera's position representing the autistic

Figure 4. Scenes creation, combining, and transitioning

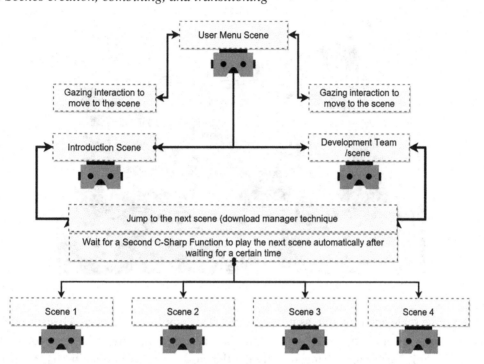

In the case of the 'Living Autism' project, great attention was given to the placement of the rig to keep the camera at an eye-level with the rest of the children who surrounded the camera, sitting at their desks. The camera simulated the user's point of view and this was in turn reflected back to the user through filming and audio from the perspective of a child. Hence, the positioning of the camera proved to be an important factor to take into consideration in such a way that the relative height made sense in the context of the surroundings. The viewer had to find himself/herself, looking at other children but also at the LSA which was at a different height, thus strengthening the embodied cognition that the user is now under the illusion of being a child.

When filming on the outside, in the playground, the same attention was given to the placement of the camera. This scene required that the autistic child, being represented by the rig, would be seated amongst the other children waiting to be chosen for a game in the playground, during break-time. The camera was placed at a lower level than it had been positioned in the classroom scenes. This scene was intended in a way were the child was to be 'sitting down on the floor', as opposed to the classroom scenes, where the child had been 'sitting down on a chair', hence the eye level would have been higher in the classroom than in the playground. Placing the camera so low in the playground also helped to give the viewer to feel in a less privileged position. A shot taken from a low-angle in 360° filming would require the viewer to tilt his/her head up, unlike traditional film. The tilting is thus used to provoke a sense of *feeling small* in the viewer, supporting the embodied cognition being created in the user. Figure 5 illustrates a scene when the used camera was set up.

When the camera is below the eye line, the subject looks 'privileged', on the other hand, when the camera is above the eye line, the viewer feels privileged (Naimark, Lawrence, & McKee, 2016). Orthoscopy refers to the science of placing an image in context. An image is orthoscopically correct when it

Figure 5. Setting up video and audio hardware in the classroom scene

appears at the same scale and direction as it was filmed. This amplification occurs because viewing VR images requires the viewer to physically pan and tilt their head accordingly, to be 'embodied', hence the possible increase of immersion, which is usually not the case in screen-based cinema. Traditional film audiences viewing a close-up in the centre of a movie screen look at the centre of the movie screen, regardless of the eye line from which she was shot. Because of this, eye line and camera height seem much more critical in VR than in screen-based media (2016). Figure 6 shows a process of adjusting the best camera height experience.

'Living Autism' attempts to shed light on possible feelings in the child's consciousness and recreate them as a spoken consciousness to be experienced by the viewer, thus placing the viewer into a position where that consciousness is reflecting the projected visuals. Sound and audio thus become key components in supporting the sense of presence and the illusion of embodiment in a VR experience. Recording sound offers another challenge that needs to be planned and tackled before the recording actually starts. Sound is also used as one of the methods that can guide the viewer's gaze, and that can be done through the use of omnidirectional microphones or binaural microphones, which can be either placed together with the 360° camera.

For the project, and at it is shown in figures 7 and 8, the researchers utilised a SR3D microphone positioned beneath the camera to further enhance the possibility of capturing pristine binaural/directional/3D sound. The sound quality from this microphone was tested, to compare with other binaural microphones, like the 3Dio, on multiple human subjects.

Using Unity for VR

There are different techniques to design and create VR surrounding environments. For this project, and as it is presented in figure 9, Unity engine was used to develop a 6D environment that plays 360° videos.

Like any interactive VR environment, the users need to find a way how to interact with it. Users are introduced to a menu to allow users to choose between the two options; start the application or read

Figure 6. Filming a scene

Figure 7. The SR3D binaural microphone (shown front and rear here) is as clear and directional in recording as the 3Dio, but comes at a lower price range

more about the team of researchers involved. To interact with the different options, a cursor was added to the scene and a gazing interaction was also provided.

'Living Autism' was piloted using Android OS on Samsung Galaxy S7 and a Samsung Gear VR. Filming was carried out using a Canon 750D camera for 2D shooting and a Samsung Gear 360° for 3D (no depth) filming (see figure 10 for the used camera). The footage was edited using Adobe Suite tools such as Adobe After Effects CC, Adobe Premiere Pro CC and Adobe Photoshop CC. The Samsung Gear VR has been the prequel of its 2017 counterpart release; the Samsung Gear VR V2. The first camera was a mid-range 360° camera, just shy of 4K resolution at 3840x1920 at 30fps. The front and rear lenses, of the gear 360, each capture 180° horizontally and vertically, creating a near-seamless and complete 360° field of view (FOV). It can be easily mounted on any kind of mount, including monopods and tripods of any size. Hence, it can be positioned in a very unobtrusive way in the centre of the area of filming, providing very little interference with the actors and the ambience. The small size of this camera goes a

Figure 8. Testing three-dimensional sound. The SR3D was attached to a tascam to capture pure unaltered sound in WAV format. These files could then be edited using audacity sound editing software.

Figure 9. Steps taken for the creation of VR

Figure 10. Samsung gear 360 attached to SR3D binaural microphone separated by green felt for post-production chroma keying

long way to merge seamlessly with the scene wherein the filming is occurring, making it a great choice, especially during the filming of this project and the inclusion of child actors. Children's' attention can be easily diverted to anything which tends to interest them. The small size of this camera helped in making this problem minimal during the shooting.

With regards to filming, the 'nadir hole' is another challenge that needs to be tackled in concept before filming starts. The 'nadir hole' is the region at the bottom of the panoramic sphere where either the camera rig can't see, or if it did, saw the tripod (Naimark, Lawrence, & McKee, 2016). The idea in this project was to use green coloured material to hide the binaural microphone. This green coloured material would serve as a 'green screen' for later removal through Chroma-key compositing. Chroma keying allows media technicians to easily separate green screens and panels from the people standing in front of them and replace those backgrounds with other assets.

One of the major challenges in creating VR is that of limiting the sense of motion sickness that users might experience. The researchers tried to reduce motion sickness by attaching the camera to a selfie-stick which was then in turn attached to a tracker with rubber wheels (for shock minimisation). Another factor, which needs to be kept in mind during the whole of the filming process is that due to the two fish-eye lenses in use on the camera, which create an element of distortion if subject is close by, and the fact that the footage from each of these cameras needs to 'meet' and stitch with the other, there must be a distance of not less than 60cm in radius, around the camera, an area where there should be no moving subjects or objects. With regards to stationary objects or subjects, the distance is not as important than when the subject or objects on shot are moving, yet there will be, what is called a 'stitching' line, which might interrupt with the flow of the video. This can be later amended, during editing. Figures 11 and 12 show snapshots for editing some of the scenes in the used 360° videos.

Unity engine offers a number of image and video effects and one of the commonly used effects in games and cinema is the blur effect. Blur effect has been used to mimic characters' dizziness when they are tired or get shot in games. A motion blur effect was used in this project to simulate when the child panics and gets nervous.

Moreover, the image blur effect was added to the scene and was played through a code to control when it starts and stops. In addition to the blur, a humming sound clip was also used to emphasise the need for comfort during set contexts and scenarios.

Figure 13 shows the different approaches to support embodied cognition, thus possibly leading to a more empathic response to ASD.

Sound was one of the key components that were used to build a strong sense of presence in the VR experience. Children with ASD are very sensitive to sounds among other stimuli, and high/low pitch sound may cause a disturbing effect on them. A number of sound clips were recorded to mimic different scenarios e.g. when the child complains about the LSA's perfume smell, when the child gets annoyed by the different noises in the classroom, or when the child gets asked many questions at the same time. All the recorded 3D sound clips were combined with the VR environment through using audio source objects. In addition, to synchronising those studio sources with 360° videos, A C-sharp code was used to control on when start and stop playing every single sound clip. Although the 3D sound clips worked well and achieved a high level of interaction, one main challenge that needs to be overcome is to record high quality sounds. Using recorded sounds in the real classroom environment does not always yield high quality outputs.

Figure 11. Adobe premiere pro is one choice for video post-editing

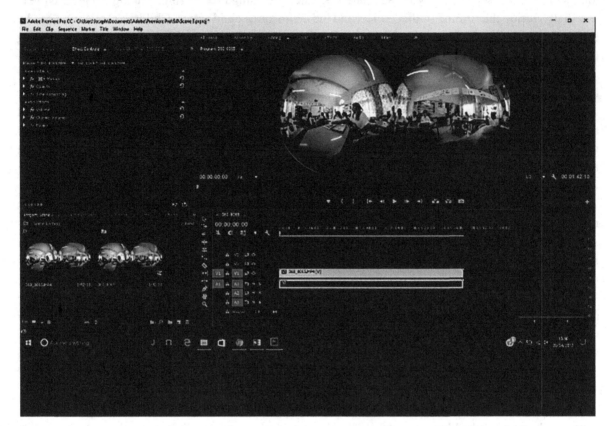

Figure 12. Adobe after effects, import of raw stitched footage in post-production

Figure 13. Approaches involving 360 filming, 3D sound, and motion blur effects to simulate some negative responses in children with ASD

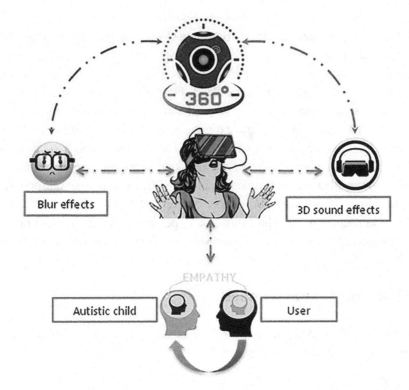

As 3D sound moves through space, different HRTFs and attenuation functions may become active, potentially introducing discontinuities at audio buffer boundaries (Corey & Wakefield, 1999). These discontinuities will often manifest as clicks, pops or ripples. They may be masked to some extent by reducing the speed of traveling sounds and by ensuring that the sounds have broad spectral content. While latency affects all aspects of VR, it is often viewed as a graphical issue. However, audio latency can be disruptive and immersion-breaking as well. Depending on the speed of the host system and the underlying audio layer, the latency from buffer submission to audible output may be as short as 2ms in high performance PCs using high end, low-latency audio interfaces, or, in the worst case, as long as hundreds of milliseconds. High system latency becomes an issue as the relative speed between an audio source and the listener's head increases. In a relatively static scene with a slow-moving viewer, audio latency is harder to detect. In the real world, sound takes time to travel, so there is often a noticeable delay between seeing and hearing something. For example, you would see the muzzle flash from a rifle fired at you 100 meters away roughly 330ms before you would hear it. Modelling propagation time incurs some additional complexity and may paradoxically make things seem less realistic, as the researchers are conditioned by popular media to believe that loud distance actions are immediately audible. Not all sounds need to be spatialized. Plenty of sounds are static or head relative, such as:

- User interface elements, such as button clicks, bleeps, transitions, and other cues
- Background music

- Narration
- Body sounds, such as breathing or heart beats

Such sounds should be segregated during authoring as they will probably be in stereo. Some sounds may not benefit from spatialization even if placed in 3D in the world (Murphy & Pitt, 2003). For example, the class bell played in the last scene could be played as a standard stereo sound with some panning and attenuation (Oculus, 2016). The VR experience being built had two completely diverse settings. The main one was the school setting, that is class scenes and a playground scene, whilst the other setting was termed as God's voice. The voice-over for the experience was to be imported into the main sequence, during the class scenes to emulate the voice of the autistic child. There was no spatialization applied to this narrative sequence as this voice had to source from inside the head of the viewer and not from around the viewer's head, as in the other voices and sounds captured by the binaural microphone. In addition to recorded sounds, this project made use of a number of free audio clips integrated to the scenes to play real sounds in the background e.g. fan, chair movement, pen dropping, door knocking ...etc.

Figure 14 better illustrates how different sound sources were used in one scene and combined with the 360° VR environment.

Sampling and Sample Characteristics

The target audience for 'Living Autism' includes adults working in close collaboration with children and more specifically those on the autism spectrum.

Experimental Procedures

The VR experience is designed, developed and evaluated with a group of teachers chosen by convenience sampling. During the VR experience, users get a first-person perspective of a child going through the motions of a typical school day at a local school in Malta. The user is briefed that the child, through whose eyes, she will be viewing the VR world, has been diagnosed with ASD. Throughout the experience the user is surrounded by a cacophony of sounds and visual stimuli, accompanying her through the various scenes as the school day unfolds and she is flanked by a learning support assistant. This experience is meant to replicate the confusion, and the uncertainty that a child diagnosed with ASD may feel.

The VR pilot app was tested and evaluated in a lab environment, with 63 participants who were recruited by convenience sampling from teachers' continuous professional development sessions, parental meetings and two educator conferences held across the country. Out of these, 26.2% of the participants were male, whilst 73.8% of the participants were female. 42.2% of the participants were in the 25-34 age range, whilst 29.7% were in the 35-44 age range. Each participant was asked to go through the VR experience using a head-mounted display and participate in a pre- and post-experience survey, giving a measure of a) their self-presence in the environment and b) their perceptions about autism. While users test the VR application, observations about their reactions were captured – figure 15 shows an example of this process. This was also followed by a more in-depth qualitative analysis of the self-reported perceptions, and the level of self-reported empathy through recorded observations and interviews.

The pre- and post- experience measured primarily the variables of empathy.

Figure 14. Combining 3D sound clips with 360-degree VR environment

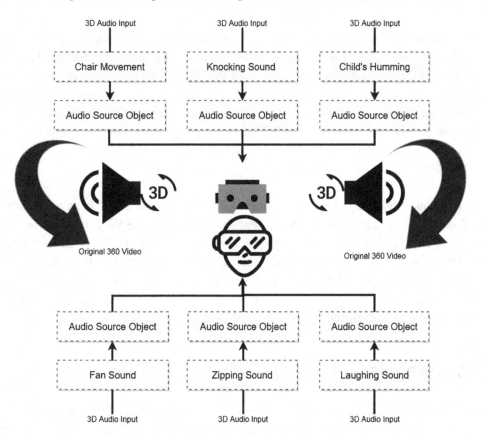

Figure 15. Trying the VR autism experience

Questionnaire Development

The surveys were adopted and adapted from the empathy measures developed by the Research Collaboration Lab (Gaumer et al. 2016) and the Toronto Empathy Questionnaire (Spreng et al., 2009). The surveys developed focus on empathy as a measure of the efforts that any given person would make to understand others, as well as the ability of a person to communicate her understanding of somebody's personal situation. For both pre- and post-VR survey, the researchers used 11 empathy items (see Table 1) measured using a 5-point Likert Scale from 1 (strongly disagree) to 5 (strongly agree).

Participant Observation

In addition to the questionnaire, researchers were assigned to observe users' behaviour during the VR experience. Codes were used to discern various user behaviour during the VR experience session for each participant. These included changes in Facial Expressions (F), Sighing (S), Heavy Breathing (B), Crying (C), Visible Emotion (E), Impassivity (I), and Smiling (Sm). Although the observations provide only a superficial level of the impact of the VR experience and do not give a direct measure of the quantity of the levels of empathy, these give an indication of how the experience affected the users through the manifestation of their outwardly behaviour.

RESEARCH FINDINGS

The results from this study indicate that the VR experience had an impact on the participants and emerge from the statistical paired sample *t*-test. This is a statistical procedure used to determine whether the mean difference between two sets of observations is zero. Since the researchers use the pre- and post- experience survey the researchers measure each empathy quotient twice thus the researchers obtain pairs of observations following the participants' self-reported empathy levels, before and after the VR experience. Table 2 shows the findings after comparing the pre- and post- values following the VR experience. A paired samples t-test was run on the participants to determine whether there was a statistically significant mean difference in their empathy levels before and after the VR experience.

Interestingly, all the items listed as having had a significant statistical change refer to projected perceptions of another human being in a specific situation as compared to the other items in the questionnaire

Table 1. Empathy quotient items

T1	I see others' point of view
T2	When I don't understand someone's point of view I ask questions to learn more
T3	When I disagree with someone it's hard for me to see their perspective
T4	I consider people's circumstances when talking with me
T5	I try to imagine how I would feel in someone else's situation
T6	When someone is upset I try to remember a situation when I felt the same way
T7	When I am reading a book or watching a movie I think about how I would react if I were one of the characters
T8	Sometimes I wonder how it would feel like if I were a student in a classroom
T9	When I see one of my students upset I try to talk to them
T10	I easily feel sad when people around me are sad
T11	I get upset when I see someone being treated disrespectfully

Table 2. Paired samples t-test for the pre- and post- empathy questionnaire

T-Test	Pre		Post		Paired Samples test			
	Mean	Std. Dev.	Mean	Std. Dev.	95% Confidence Interval	Std. Dev.	t	Sig. (2-tailed)
T1	4.440	0.562	4.460	0.618	-.2, .168	0.729	-0.173	0.863
T2	4.333	0.539	4.365	0.679	-.23387, .17038	0.803	-0.314	0.755
T3	2.540	0.930	2.810	1.216	-.55666, .01697	1.139	-1.881	0.065
T4	4.267	0.578	4.200	0.819	-.12279, .25612	0.733	0.704	0.484
T5	4.318	0.563	4.587	0.558	-.45194, -.08775	0.723	-2.962	0.004
T6	4.191	0.692	4.492	0.564	-.49154, -.11164	0.754	-3.174	0.002
T7	4.079	0.885	4.365	0.848	-.55112, -.02031	1.054	-2.152	0.035
T8	4.127	0.852	4.635	0.517	-.70958, -.30629	0.801	-5.035	0.000
T9	4.254	0.740	4.349	0.765	-.34181, .15133	0.979	-0.772	0.443
T10	4.095	0.756	4.413	0.710	-.56449, -.07043	0.981	-2.569	0.013
T11	4.677	0.696	4.532	0.503	-.05447, .34479	0.786	1.454	0.151

N=63, df=62, p<.05

tool that refer to the individual's own personality traits. This means that the VR experience has in no significant way affected the participants' personality, but it has affected the way they think about other human beings in possibly difficult circumstances. Figure 16 shows the observations related to the following reactions: Facial Expressions (F), Sighing (S), Heavy Breathing (B), Crying (C), Visible Emotion (E), Impassivity (I), and Smiling (Sm).

During the visual observation method, participants displayed visible emotion throughout the VR experience. This included body language displays that showed a degree of agitation. Some of the participants expressed additional emotions such as crying and changes in facial expressions and examples of these emotions can be seen in figure 17.

Moreover, participants explained that they felt in another dimension and that their bodies felt as though trapped within the scenario presented. Some reported as feeling the chaos surrounding them as overwhelming whilst some reported that they went back to feeling like a child in class.

Figure 16. Visible observations of participants during VR

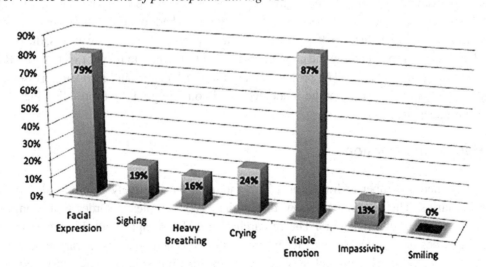

Figure 17. Examples of reactions when trying the VR application

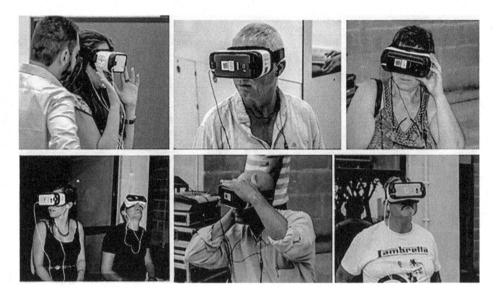

FUTURE RESEARCH DIRECTIONS

Research Limitations

A number of technical challenges have been encountered during the design and development process of this VR experience including filming in 360°, 3D audio recording, 6D environment design, prototype design, and the extraction of the developed VR application on mobile devices. These included redundant vibration noises resulting from the motion of the camera, catching unwanted scene objects during the 360 filming, low quality sound capture and post-filming stitching and other editing challenges. Some of these challenges can be overcome with the use of more expensive hardware, but some pertain to the design of the VR experience itself, and because it was filmed entirely in a realistic location.

Although creating the 6D environment gave us good results on the Unity platform, it was not supported on Android platforms, which meant that the researchers had to work a different way around the approach towards developing the app. It is suggested that for projects as extensive as this, the professional edition of Unity is used to overcome the challenges related to the movie player assets and VR application extraction on mobile devices. The professional edition of Unity would also support the facility of extracting a full .apk toolkit so it can be made accessible on Google Play Store allowing any user to install and run the application.

Future Research Directions

The study itself had a number of limitations. This included the relatively generalised autism-related classroom scenarios. The researchers know that autism is a complex disorder that manifests itself across a wide spectrum of behaviours. The researchers could not capture all the behaviours because every individual person can tend to react to different situations and contexts in various ways and thus this cannot be generalised. The researchers were aware of this limitation from the start, and the project in fact is presented as a pilot to understand the future directions that development in this area can take. Despite another limitation of sample size, the findings are promising, and they show there is potential for further development to help raise awareness within the context of autism and how as fellow human beings, small changes in our own behaviour can improve the quality of life of other human beings that the researchers know are on the autism spectrum disorder. Although the researchers took the context of a classroom, this can be easily scaled to the workplace or any other community space.

The virtual embodiment presented in this VR experience does not give an in-depth measure of how the users' attitude towards children diagnosed on the autism spectrum disorder has been affected nor how this will impinge on their behaviour in class. The researchers also do not know how deeply this experience has affected the participants and whether the effects will be felt over a period of time. A longitudinal follow up study is part of our future work in the area to try and understand whether the self-reported changes in empathy would still be significant after a period of time.

Furthermore, it is difficult to precisely gauge the level of user's empathy as they experienced the VR environment. For this pilot case study, the researchers relied on two approaches to measure this through the use of surveys/interviews and observing physical reactions. However, it is necessary to find a better way to achieve more accurate measurement of the level of empathy.

For example, external devices can be connected to the VR application (e.g., smart watches or special mobile apps) that give a measure of physiological data, such as heart beat rate or sweat secretion. Connecting an app to a smart watch and coding it to collect data at determinate times during the experience will allow us to understand at which point during the experience the user is reaching an emotional peak. Through this, the researchers can also discover any design flaws to improve the effectiveness of this VR experience. Neuroscience is another scientific field which is also gathering more popularity as it merges with VR. The merging of neuroscience and psychology would help us understand more which scenes and narratives would most likely trigger empathy and if the addition of more advanced VR interactive techniques, such as control, navigation and decision making, would increase empathy levels. A person finds it more difficult to empathise with another human who is suffering or is in a difficult situation (Bergland, 2013). At this moment, there does not seem to be any direct evidence on how empathy can be mediated but if the researchers can, through neuroscientific research demonstrate that VR can indeed support the development of empathy in people, it would bring great promise to the field of research in VR and human behaviour. Future work is however needed to merge the users' experience, their changes in perceptions, attitudes, and neuroscientific research to be able to target the section of the brain that can facilitate empathic behaviour. Such small steps can indeed take us towards an improved human altruism resulting in the exploitation of VR technology to help make the world a better place.

CONCLUSION

This chapter gives an overview of the project that was carried out at the University of Malta, using VR as a medium for creating a first-person narrative of the daily classroom life of a child on the Autistic Spectrum. The scope for the project was to investigate the effect, if any, of the VR experience on the empathy skills of educators partaking in the project in particular those working with children on the Autistic Spectrum. The chapter outlines the methods for the development of the narrative and the stimuli which have been used in the VR experience, and the challenges, issues and limitations posed by the technologies. An experimental research method using a pre- and post-experience empathy questionnaire tool, together with participant observation, have indicated that the VR experience has had an impact on the educators. The findings indicate that participants report an increased empathic quotient with children in their classroom who may be affected with autism. This chapter highlights a number of theoretical implications for the design of VWs that support empathic behaviour including the narrative structure, as well as the film and audio capture. In terms of practical implications, this chapter has emphasised how such an application may impinge on the behaviour of educators towards children on the Autistic Spectrum in their classrooms and schools, which in turn may affect the lives of the children who may respond negatively to certain stimuli. With increased awareness and empathy towards stimuli that may be kept under control or in check, the quality of school life of children on the Autistic Spectrum may improve considerably thus helping them achieve a more successful education experience.

REFERENCES

Anzalone, C. (2017). *UB's virtual reality expertise creates simulated classroom environment for aspiring teachers.* Retrieved from https://www.buffalo.edu/ubnow/stories/2017/06/vr-teacher-training.html

Autism Europe. (2018). *About Autism.* Retrieved October 2017, from http://www.autismeurope.org/about-autism/

Bailey, J. O., Bailenson, J., & Casasanto, D. (2016). When Does Virtual Embodiment Change Our Minds? *PRESENCE: Teleoperators and Virtual Environments.*

BamburyS. (2017). *CPD in VR.* Retrieved from https://www.virtualiteach.com/cpd-in-vr

Baron-Cohen, S., & Wheelwright, S. (2004). The Empathy quotient: An investigation of adults with Asperger Syndrome or High Functioning Autism, and normal sex differences. *Journal of Autism and Developmental Disorders, 34*(2), 163–175. doi:10.1023/B:JADD.0000022607.19833.00 PMID:15162935

Bergland, C. (2013). *The neuroscience of empathy.* Retrieved from https://www.psychologytoday.com/blog/the-athletes-way/201310/the-neuroscience-empathy

Bilda, Z., Candy, L., & Edmonds, E. (2007). An embodied cognition framework for interactive experience. *CoDesign, 3*(2), 123–137. doi:10.1080/15710880701251443

Billinghurst, M. (2016). *VSMM 2016 Keynote: Using AR and VR to create empathic experiences.* VSMM 2016 Conference, Kuala Lumpur, Malaysia. Retrieved November, 2016, from http://www.slideshare.net/marknb00/vsmm-2016-keynote-using-ar-and-vr-to-create-empathic-experiences

Bishop, C. (2012). *Artificial Hells: Participatory Art and the Politics of Spectatorship.* London: Verso.

Bosschieter, P. (2016). Continuing professional development (CPD) and the potential of new media. *The Indexer, 34*(3), 71–74. doi:10.3828/indexer.2016.20

Brooks, K. (2003). *There is nothing virtual about immersion: Narrative immersion for VR and other interfaces.* Retrieved September, 2016, from MIT Media Lab, http://alumni.media.mit.edu/~brooks/storybiz/immersiveNotVirtual.pdf

Bucher, J. (2016). *How to shoot virtual reality: seven basics to launch you toward virtual virtuosity.* Retrieved March, 2017, from MovieMaker: http://www.moviemaker.com/archives/summer2016/how-to-shoot-virtual-reality-seven- basics/

Case-Smith, J., Weaver, L. L., & Fristad, M. A. (2015). A systematic review of sensory processing interventions for children with autism spectrum disorders. *Autism, 19*(2), 133–148. doi:10.1177/1362361313517762 PMID:24477447

Cho, J., Lee, T. H., Ogden, J., Stewart, A., Tsai, T. Y., Chen, J., & Vituccio, R. (2016, July). Imago: presence and emotion in virtual reality. In ACM SIGGRAPH 2016 VR Village (p. 6). ACM. doi:10.1145/2929490.2931000

Corey, C. I., & Wakefield, G. H. (1999). Introduction to head-related transfer functions (HRTFs): Representations of HRTFs in time, frequency, and space. *Audio Engineering Society Convention, 107.*

Crosswater. (2017). *VR/360.* Retrieved from https://crosswater.net/

Day, C., & Leach, R. (2007). The continuing professional development of teachers: Issues of coherence, cohesion and effectiveness. In T. Townsend (Ed.), *International Handbook of School Effectiveness and Improvement* (pp. 707–726). Dordrecht: Springer. doi:10.1007/978-1-4020-5747-2_38

Decety, J., & Ickes, W. (2011). The Social Neuroscience of Empathy. Cambridge, MA: The MIT Press.

Gardner, K. (2016). *Virtual reality storytelling: How is virtual reality (VR) changing the future of storytelling? TEDxPrincetonU.* Princeton, NJ: TEDx. Retrieved November 2016, from https://www.youtube.com/watch?v=7LNEkmcR4BM&t=2s

Google. (2017). *Painting from a New Perspective.* Retrieved October 2017, from Tilt Brush by Google: https://www.tiltbrush.com/

Jones, B. (2017). *To raise teaching standards we must first improve the use of technology in the classroom.* Retrieved October, 2017, from The Telegraph Education section: http://www.telegraph.co.uk/education/2017/02/01/raise-teaching-standards-must-first- improve-use-technology-classroom/

Kenny, L., Hattersley, C., Molins, B., Buckley, C., Povey, C., & Pellicano, E. (2015). Which terms should be used to describe autism? Perspectives from the UK autism community. *Autism, 20*(4), 442–462. doi:10.1177/1362361315588200 PMID:26134030

Kroes, M., Dunsmoor, J., Mackey, W., McClay, M., & Phelps, E. (2017). Context conditioning in humans using commercially available immersive Virtual Reality. *Scientific Reports, 7*(1), 8640. doi:10.103841598-017-08184-7 PMID:28819155

Loewus, L. (2017). How virtual reality is helping. *Education Week, 37*(3), 1–2.

Merleau-Ponty, M. (1968). The Visible and the Invisible (C. Lefort, J. Wild, J. M. Edie, Eds., & A. Lingis, Trans.). Evanston, IL: Northwestern University Press.

Milk, C. (2015). *How virtual reality can create the ultimate empathy machine. TED Talks: Chris Milk: How virtual reality can create the ultimate empathy machine.* TED Talks. Retrieved November 2016, from https://www.youtube.com/watch?v=iXHil1TPxvA

Morrison McGill, R. (2013). *Professional development for teachers: how can we take it to the next level?* Retrieved from https://www.theguardian.com/teacher-network/teacher-blog/2013/jan/29/professional-development-teacher-training-needs

Murphy, D., & Pitt, I. (2003). Spatial sound enhancing virtual story telling. In O. Balet, G. Subsol, & P. Torguet (Eds.), *Virtual Storytelling: Using Virtual Reality Technologies for Storytelling* (pp. 20–29). Avignon: Springer.

Muybridge, E. (Director). (1878). *Sallie Gardner at a Gallop/The Horse in Motion* [Motion Picture]. Retrieved November 2016, from https://www.youtube.com/watch?v=IEqccPhsqgA

Naimark, M., Lawrence, D., & McKee, J. (2016, June 22). *VR Cinematography Studies for Google.* Retrieved January 2017, from Medium: https://medium.com/@michaelnaimark/vr- cinematography-studies-for-google-8a2681317b3

Oculus, V. R. (2016). *Oculus Story Studio.* Retrieved September 2016, from Story Studio, https://storystudio.oculus.com/en-us/

Oculus. (2017). *Oculus / Developers.* Retrieved April 1, 2016, from https://developer3.oculus.com/documentation/audiosdk/0.10/concepts/audio-intro-mixing/

Riedl, M., & Bulitko, V. (2012). Interactive narrative: An intelligent systems approach. *AI Magazine*, *34*(1), 67. doi:10.1609/aimag.v34i1.2449

Riedl, M. O., & Young, R. (2006). From linear story generation to branching story graphs. *IEEE Computer Graphics and Applications*, *26*(3), 23–31. doi:10.1109/MCG.2006.56 PMID:16711214

Ross, S. M., & Morrison, G. R. (2004). Experimental research methods. Handbook of Research on Educational Communications and Technology, 2, 1021-43.

Spreng, R. N., McKinnon, M. C., Mar, R. A., & Levine, B. (2009). The Toronto empathy questionnaire: Scale development and initial validation of a factor-analytic solution to multiple empathy measures. *Journal of Personality Assessment*, *91*(1), 62–71. doi:10.1080/00223890802484381 PMID:19085285

Walker, R., Voce, J., Nicholls, J., Swift, E., Ahmed, J., Horrigan, S., & Vincent, P. (2014). *2014 Survey of Technology Enhanced Learning for Higher Education in the UK.* Oxford, UK: UCISA.

Won, A., Bailey, J., Bailenson, J., Tataru, C., Yoon, I., & Golianu, B. (2017). Immersive Virtual Reality for Pediatric Pain. *Children*, *4*(7), 52. doi:10.3390/children4070052 PMID:28644422

ADDITIONAL READING

Bailenson, J. (2018). *Experience on Demand: What Virtual Reality Is, how it Works, and what it Can Do*. New York, N.Y.: W.W. Norton & Company.

Carey, K., Saltz, E., Rosenbloom, J., Micheli, M., Choi, J. O., & Hammer, J. (2017, October). Toward measuring empathy in virtual reality. In *(missing editor's info) Extended Abstracts Publication of the Annual Symposium on Computer-Human Interaction in Play* (pp. 551-559). ACM. 10.1145/3130859.3131325

Cummings, J. J., & Bailenson, J. N. (2016). How immersive is enough? A meta-analysis of the effect of immersive technology on user presence. *Media Psychology*, *19*(2), 272–309. doi:10.1080/1521326 9.2015.1015740

Herrera, F., Bailenson, J., Weisz, E., Ogle, E., & Zaki, J. (2018). Building long-term empathy: A large-scale comparison of traditional and virtual reality perspective-taking. *PLoS One*, *13*(10), e0204494. doi:10.1371/journal.pone.0204494 PMID:30332407

Lorenz, M., Busch, M., Rentzos, L., Tscheligi, M., Klimant, P., & Fröhlich, P. (2015, March). I'm There! The influence of virtual reality and mixed reality environments combined with two different navigation methods on presence. *Virtual Reality (VR), 2015 IEEE* (pp. 223-224).

Oh, S. Y., & Bailenson, J. (2017). *Virtual and augmented reality* (pp. 1–16). The International Encyclopaedia of Media Effects.

Ohta, Y., & Tamura, H. (2014). *Mixed reality: merging real and virtual worlds*. New York, N.Y.: Springer Publishing Company, Incorporated.

Shin, D. (2018). Empathy and embodied experience in virtual environment: To what extent can virtual reality stimulate empathy and embodied experience? *Computers in Human Behavior*, *78*, 64–73. doi:10.1016/j.chb.2017.09.012

Tham, J., Duin, A. H., Gee, L., Ernst, N., Abdelqader, B., & McGrath, M. (2018). Understanding virtual reality: Presence, embodiment, and professional practice. *IEEE Transactions on Professional Communication*, *61*(2), 178–195. doi:10.1109/TPC.2018.2804238

van Loon, A., Bailenson, J., Zaki, J., Bostick, J., & Willer, R. (2018). Virtual reality perspective-taking increases cognitive empathy for specific others. *PLoS One*, *13*(8), e0202442. doi:10.1371/journal.pone.0202442 PMID:30161144

KEY TERMS AND DEFINITIONS

3D Audio: Achieved through the use of omnidirectional or binaural microphones for creating a 3-D stereo sound sensation for the listener to feel as if he/she is surrounded by different sounds and presence.

3D Film: A method or process of filming for the VR environment.

ASD: Autism spectrum disorder; a disorder that may affect individual social, communication, and behavioral responses to external stimuli.

Empathy: The ability to understand and share the feelings and experiences of others, also referred to as the ability to walk in someone else's shoes.

Experimental Research Method: A method used in psychology and education-based research whereby a group of participants go through an experience with changing environmental variables to test a hypothesis that is often related to a change in behavior.

Interactive Narratives: Telling stories with the aid of technology-based media which offer interactive features that can be adapted to emerging user behavior.

Professional Development: An ongoing learning process often carried out at or as an extension to the workplace.

VR: Virtual reality; an immersive 360-degree computer generated interactive environment that offers users a simulated experience incorporating auditory, visual, and at times tactile feedback.

Chapter 12

The Applications of Digital Reality in Creative and Oceanic Cultural Industries:
The Case of Taiwan

Yowei Kang
National Taiwan Ocean University, Taiwan

EXECUTIVE SUMMARY

Digital reality technologies have become a key component of promoting creative and cultural industries in Taiwan. In 2016, Taiwan's Ministry of Culture funded 45 projects to promote creative and cultural industries in this island country. A total of USD$25.6 million dollars have been granted to this project. Among these projects, the applications of virtual reality (VR) and augmented reality (AR) technologies have been found to be the latest trend in Taiwan's creative and cultural industries. This chapter employs a case study approach to survey the current state of digital reality technology applications particularly in the area of creative and oceanic cultural industries in Taiwan. Using a detailed description of these best practices among creative and cultural industries to promote Taiwanese oceanic culture, this chapter aims to provide a detailed examination of digital reality applications in the creative and cultural industry sectors in a non-Western context.

INTRODUCTION

Defining Creative and Cultural Industry

The term, cultural industry, can find its historical root in the Frankfurtian school (Abruzzese & Borrelli, 2000). This concept often refers to industries "which combine the creation, production and commercialization of creative contents which are intangible and cultural in nature" (Mariani, 2018, n.p.). Cultural industries often include a wide variety of information-intensive and –dependent economic sectors that produce artifacts through advertising, marketing, journalism, publication, public relations,

DOI: 10.4018/978-1-5225-5912-2.ch012

etc (Hesmondhalgh, 2002, cited in Deuze, 2007). According to Mariani (2018), industry sectors such as audiovisual, cinematographic productions, crafts and design, phonographic contents, printing and publication, multimedia, among others are also considered to be part of the cultural industry ecosystem. More specific categorization of the creative and cultural industries includes advertising, architecture, arts, design and fashion, film and TV, music, and culture, as well as IT, software, and digital game (UK Creative Industries, 2018).

With the emergence of knowledge-based economy, this term increasingly appears with a more recent term, creative industry, which carries less critical cultural connotations, but with more economic benefits these particular activities can bring to a country (Ministry of Culture, 2015). Both terms refer to similar categories of economic activities, but creative industries place more emphasis on "the product or service contains a substantial element of artistic or creative endeavour and include activities such as architecture and advertising" (Mariani, 2018, n.p.). The merger of mass production of culture and individual creative activities has led to the interchangeable use of "creative industry" and "cultural industry" (Deuze, 2007) and sometimes with a newly coined term, "creative cultural industry" (UK Creative Industries, 2018). The original definition of "creative industries" refers to "those industries which have their origin in individual creativity, skill and talent and which have a potential for wealth and job creation through the generation and exploitation of intellectual property" (Yoshimoto, 2003, p. 1).

The emergence of several digital technologies has posed new challenges and opportunities to the cultural and creative industries (Dueze, 2007). For example, the advent of multi-platforms has allowed cultural and creative production to be simplified and their contents to be disseminated to consumers (Dueze, 2007) through both the traditional print media and more contemporary social, mobile, and reality-creating technologies. Furthermore, these emerging digital platforms often influences how information will be commented, shared, and produced among users (Deuze, 2007). Some noteworthy examples will be the rise of Twitter, YouTube, and other social media platforms as the channels to share and comment on these creative and cultural contents.

The popularity of creative and cultural industries has attracted a lot of enthusiasm around the world (Fung, 2016; Ministry of Culture, 2015; UK Creative Industries, 2018). For example, Fung (2016) examines the growth of creative industries in China and argues that its development has been affected by two factors: global reliance and ideological control. As a rising economic powerhouse, China's cultural and creative industries have been relying on international capital, management, and foreign talents (mainly from Taiwan, and Hong-Kong) (Fung, 2016). Furthermore, despite its apparent contradiction with the core value of creative industries that emphasize individual creativity, the ruling Chinese Communist Party government has exerted stringent control over its media industry to control and generate cultural contents that "could easily sway, mobilize, or narcotize the public" (Fung, 2016, p. 3007).

However, the approach to take advantage of the economic potential of creative and cultural industries is varied among countries. As one of the foremost countries to promote creative and cultural industries as a potential economic sector, their size, as measured by the *Gross Value Added* (GVA) is estimated to reach £101.5 billion in U.K. in the year of 2017 (UK Creative Industries, 2018). The rapid rise of creative and cultural industries in UK can be demonstrated by its 53.1% increase of these sectors, when compared with 29.7% growth among other economic sectors in UK (UK Creative Industries, 2018). However, despite the economy of Japan is three times of that of U.K., the creative industry sectors in Japan are still in their nascent state in terms of the total revenue generated and the total number of employment related to creative and/or cultural industries (Yoshimoto, 2003). In Japan, about 3.2% of its workforce (1,878,000 persons) is employed in creative industries, according to the 2001 statistics (Yoshimoto,

2003). The number is 4.6% of its total workforce, equivalent of 1,300,000 persons (Yoshimoto, 2003). Compared with other Asian countries, 3.6% of its workforce (about 337,000 persons) is employed in creative and cultural industries, while the percentage in Hong Kong is 5.3% (about 170,000 persons) and Singapore (3.4%, or 72,000) (Yoshimoto, 2003).

The following figure provides the best descriptive categories of what creative and cultural industries encompass (Mariani, 2018, n.p.). As shown in Figure 1 below, these economic sectors generally include broadcasting, electronic or digital media and films, cultural goods manufacturing and sales, environmental heritage, design, fashion, library and archives, literature and print media, museums, music composition and publishing, visual arts and crafts, performing arts, etc. (Mariani, 2018, n.p.).

Although the framework and categories to define what constitutes creative and cultural industries, most of the discussions follow the original 1998 classification by U.K. *Department for Culture, Media and Sport* that define thirteen creative industries as "(1) advertising, (2) architecture, (3) art & antiques market, (4) crafts, (5) design, (6) designer fashion, (7) film & video, (8) interactive leisure software, (9) music, (10) performing arts, (11) publishing, (12) software and computer services, and (13) television and radio" (Yoshimoto, 2003, p. 1). In Hong Kong and Japan, the categories are reduced to eleven, but cover similar sectors in the creative and cultural industries: "(1) advertising, (2) architecture, (3) art, antiques and crafts, (4) design, (5) digital entertainment, (6) film and video, (7) music, (8) performing arts, (9) publishing, (10) software & computing, and (11) television and radio" (Yoshimoto, 2003, p. 2). This book chapter will focus on the applications of AR, MR, and VR technologies in the context of museums to exhibit, disseminate, and promote creative and cultural contents (such as art & antiques [3], crafts [4]) in Taiwan.

BACKGROUND

Taiwan: Country Profile

Taiwan, an island republic, is off China's eastern coast and has enjoyed its reputation as one of the Asia's big traders (BBC News, 2018; Central Intelligence Agency, n.d.; Library of Congress, 2005) and one of the four Asian Tigers (Central Intelligence Agency, n.d.) during the Asian economic boom in the late 80's.

Figure 1. Types of creative and cultural industries

However, its uncertain political status and tense relationships with China since 1949 has made Taiwan Strait that separates Taiwan from China one of the most volatile flashpoint in the global geo-politics (BBC News, 2018; Tweed & Leung, 2018). Along with similarly tense locations in Asia (such as North Korea, South China Sea, East China Sea, and Xinjiang (Tweed & Leung, 2018), the battle ground in Taiwan can be easily ignited when U.S. and China is undergoing their trade war.

Geographically, Taiwan is made up of its main island and several of its neighboring isles, such as Pescadores, Matsu, Quemoy islands and Green Island (Central Intelligence Agency, n.d.). The country covers a total landmass of 32,260 square km and its size ranks about 139 in the world (Central Intelligence Agency, n.d.). As a democratic republic, Taiwan has regular national and local elections and has experienced major political reshuffling in the past 20 years, allowing the ruling *Nationalist Party (KMT)* to rotate its control of central and local governments with the *Democratic Progressive Party (DPP)* (BBC News, 2018).

Relevant to the adoption of AR, MR, and VR is Taiwan's technology infrastructure. Internet penetration is high with 88% of the island population (about 20.601 million) has uncensored access to the Internet and this statistics ranks the country No. 32 in the world (Central Intelligence Agency, n.d.). According to *eMarketer.com* (2016), Taiwan also ranks as the most mobile country in the world. The penetration rate of mobile phone has increased from 84.1% in 2015, to 84.5% in 2016, to 84.8% in 2017, to 85% in 2018, and is expected to grow to 85.5% in 2020 (*eMarketer.com*, 2016). The use of smartphone has seen similarly astonishing growth from 69.9% in 2015 to 77.6% in 2018. The penetration is expected to reach about 80% in 2020 (*eMarketer.com*, 2016). The rapid diffusion of smartphone is particularly instrumental to the integration of augmented reality into a wide variety of applications in creative and cultural industries in Taiwan.

The Rise of Creative and Oceanic Cultural Industries in Taiwan

The term, *oceanic culture*, has recently been introduced into Taiwan to refer to a unique cultural experience and subsequent production of cultural artefacts and contents by past and current residents of the island country. The claim that Taiwan's culture is unique and different from that of Mainland China, has its anthropological foundation (Trejaut et al., 2005). The first human settlement in Taiwan can be dated as far as at least 15,000 years, equivalent of the Paleolithic age (Library of Congress, 2005). The island was originally inhabited by Austronesian people (Central Intelligence Agency, n.d.). After multiple waves of immigration from China at different periods during the 18th to 20th century, the current demographic composition of Taiwan include the *Minnan* (73.5%), *Hakka* (17.5%), and nine aboriginal Taiwanese tribes that can be broadly divided into *Rukai* and *Paiwan* in the South, *Atayal* and *Saisiat* in the North, and *Amis, Bunun, Tsou, Puyuma,* and *Yami* in the central and mountainous areas of Taiwan (Library of Congress, 2005; Trejaut et al., 2005). In spite of their small number, inter-group marriage has allowed the spread of aborigines' gene among current Taiwanese population. Genetically speaking, research by Trejaut et al. (2005) have found that *HVS-I motif 16189–16217–16261*, that has been classified within *haplogroup B4a* is shared between Polynesian and Taiwanese populations (Trejaut et al., 2005). Trejaut and his colleagues (2015) also found that three specific mutations in their *mtDNA* are shared among the indigenous Melanesian, Polynesian, and Taiwanese populations, a phenomenon not found among other mainland or East Asian populations. The sharing of a common ancestral link between Taiwanese and its Polynesian relatives provides support to Taiwanese culture as oceanic in nature (*PLos Biol*, 2005).

This genetic discovery has contributed to the growing awareness among many Taiwanese people to feel proud of their own culture.

In addition to the anthropological and genetic evidences, the strategic geo-political location of Taiwan has also made it an important island during *the Age of Discovery* (Exploration) in the 17th century (Library of Congress, 2005) and subsequent historical events when European powers began to invade China for their economic benefits in the 18th and 19th century. As seen on the welcome page of *Yang-Ming Oceanic Culture & Art Museum* (https://keelung-for-a-walk.com/en/culture/keelung-port-ym-oceanic-culture-art-museum/), the unique experiences of Taiwanese as a juncture for land and sea powers is documented below:

The window of Keelung is always facing the ocean, and over the past few centuries the oceanic culture of the region has accumulated rich and diverse imprints and experiences. In the mid-nineteenth century (1863), Keelung Port opened, and it served an important role in the strategy and trade that attracted attention overseas. During the Japanese colonial period, Keelung Port was the closest gateway to Japan and, on May 4, 1915, the original building of Yangming Oceanic Culture & Art Museum was first completed. It was originally named Nippon Yusen Kaisha (Japan Mailboat Steamship Line) and was the Keelung branch office. Since the liberation of Taiwan, it has been operated by the Yang Ming Marine Transport Corporation.

To build Taiwan as a creative and cultural hub in the Asia-Pacific Region, the government has heavily invested on creative and cultural industry sectors in recent years (Liu, 2015). As early as 2009, the creative and cultural industries have been promoted by the government as "emerging industries" (Liu, 2015). The emphasis on creative and cultural industries is not purely economic. It can be argued that the promotion of Taiwan's oceanic culture is a natural development from Taiwanese's search for national identification (Dittmer, 2004), nation building (Chen, Yen, Wang, & Hioe, 2017), and a demonstration of these awakening and nation-building processes. Daniel Lynch of the University of Southern California has argued that "DPP efforts at collective identity construction as a self-conscious project of nation-building" (Dittmer, 2004, p. 479). Recent national identity shift to *Taiwanese*, rather than *Chinese*, is likely to further lend strong support to promotion of its unique culture (Zhong, 2016). A series of longitudinal surveys by *The Election Study Center* at Taiwan's *National Chengchi University (NCCU)* have noted that those who identify themselves as *Taiwanese* have increased to 40% (in the 1990s) to 60% (in 2014) (Zhong, 2016). During the same period, self-identification as *Chinese* has dropped to less than 10% (Zhong, 2016).

This historical and political context helps explain the multiple purposes of promoting creative and cultural industries in Taiwan. On the basis of *The 2015 Taiwan Cultural and Creative Industries Annual Report*, the overall creative and cultural industries are made up of 15 industry sectors and 62,264 companies and is estimated to have a value of USD$25.55 billion (Australian Trade and Investment Commission, 2018). A more recent statistics have shown that the number of companies has grown to 63,339 and has grown to USD$26.19 billion in 2016 (Ministry of Culture, 2017). The total sale includes 11.47% of foreign export of these creative and cultural products (Ministry of Culture, 2017).

Table 1 below provides an overview of the types of creative and cultural industries and their growth (in terms of the number of companies and growth rate) from 2013 to the 1st half of 2018 (Ministry of Culture, 2017). There was a total of 30,718 companies specialized in creative and cultural industries

Table 1. Current state of creative and cultural industries in Taiwan

Industry Sectors		2013	2014	2015	2016	2017	2018 (1st Half)
Audio-Visual Contents	# of Companies	2,454	2,455	2,458	2,429	2,442	2,290
	Growth Rate		0.04%	0.12%	-1.18%	0.54%	-6.22%
Music and Performing Arts	# of Companies	2,465	2,809	3,160	3,442	3,843	4,072
	Growth Rate		13.96%	12.50%	8.92%	11.65%	5.96%
Cultural Heritage, Exhibits, and Facilities	# of Companies	125	155	173	185	206	83
	Growth Rate		24.00%	11.61%	6.94%	11.35%	-59.71%
Crafts	# of Companies	10,846	10,958	11,031	10,898	10,841	10,799
	Growth Rate		1.03%	0.67%	-1.21%	-0.52%	-0.39%
Film	# of Companies	1,550	1,554	1,622	1,752	1,907	2,003
	Growth Rate		0.26%	4.38%	8.01%	8.85%	5.03%
Radio and TV Broadcasting	# of Companies	1,501	1,488	1,649	1,696	1,776	1,827
	Growth Rate		-0.87%	10.82%	2.85%	4.72%	2.87%
Printing and Publication	# of Companies	8,282	8,042	7,908	7,801	7,690	7,688
	Growth Rate		-2.90%	-1.67%	-1.35%	-1.42%	-0.03%
Popular Music	# of Companies	3,495	3,511	3,516	3,510	3,524	3,531
	Growth Rate		0.46%	0.14%	-0.17%	0.40%	0.20%
Total	# of Companies	30,718	30,972	31,517	31,713	32,229	32,293
	Growth Rate		0.83%	1.76%	0.62%	1.63%	0.20%

in 2013. The number of companies has since grown from 30,718 (in 2013), to 30,972 (in 2014), to 31,713 (in 2016), to 32,229 (in 2017), and 32,293 (in 2018) (Refer to Table 1). The greatest number of companies falls under the crafts sector at 10,958 (in 2013), but grew to 10,958 in 2014, then to 10,799 in the first half of 2018 (Refer to Table 1). Printing and publication sector is the 2nd largest creative and cultural industry, shrinking from 8,282 (in 2013), to 8,042 (in 2014), to 7,908 (in 2015), to 7,801 (in 2016), to 7,688 (in 2018), indicating the demise of printing and publication sector (Refer to Table 1). Most relevant to this book chapter is the cultural heritage, exhibits, and facilities sector, where a rapid growth rate of 24% has been recorded, growing from 125 (in 2013) to 155 (in 2014). The growth trend continues to the year of 2017, increasing from 173 (in 2015), to 185 (in 2016), to 206 (in 2017), but has seen dramatic decrease in 83 (a 56.71% reduction in the first half of 2018 alone) (Refer to Table 1).

Table 2 provides another overview of the creative and cultural industries in Taiwan by examining the market size of each industry sector (Ministry of Culture, 2017). The total economic contribution of these industries have grown from NTD$431,737,217 (in 2013, about USD$1.40 million), to NTD$439,652,82 (in 2014, USD$1.42 million), but shrunk to NTD$200,956,36 (in 2018, about USD$0.65 million) (Refer to Table 2). Among these creative and cultural industries, the cultural heritage, exhibits, and facilities sectors have seen an irregular growth or decline trend between 2013 and 2018. These sectors first grow 29.49% from 2013 to 2014, but begin to decline from 2016 (-4.44%), but increase in 2017 (10.23%), but decline significantly in the first half of 2018 (-43.19%) (Refer to Table 2).

The creative and cultural industries are facing many problems. One of the them is the strong competition from South Korea where Taiwan's creative and cultural industry outputs trail far behind its former

Table 2. market size of current state of creative and cultural industries in Taiwan

Industry Sectors		2013	2014	2015	2016	2017	2018 (1ˢᵗ half)
Audio-Visual Contents	$[a]	6,329,525	6,836,538	5,763,841	5,729,669	5,976,115	2,928,758
	Change		8.01%	-15.69%	-0.59%	4.30%	-0.86%
Music and Performing Arts	$	13,312,214	14,493,846	18,200,515	17,207,253	21,775,728	11,256,408
	Change		8.88%	25.57%	-5.46%	26.55%	13.71%
Cultural Heritage, Exhibits, and Facilities	$	962,229	1,246,037	1,623,191	1,551,082	1,709,700	457,756
	Change	-	29.49%	30.27%	-4.44%	10.23%	-43.19%
Crafts	$	101,913,194	112,190,553	109,828,953	91,976,276	81,052,188	42,569,484
	Change	-	10.08%	-2.10%	-16.25%	-11.88%	11.55%
Film	$	28,667,002	29,380,770	32,203,909	29,482,122	29,591,121	13,808,899
	Change	-	2.49%	9.61%	-8.45%	0.37%	-8.57%
Radio and TV Broadcasting	$	142,925,382	139,412,045	127,282,599	146,514,192	148,024,584	67,517,315
	Change	-	-2.46%	-8.70%	15.11%	1.03%	-1.32%
Printing and Publication	$	108,835,358	107,234,899	105,357,550	103,802,341	99,988,398	47,368,153
	Change	-	-1.47%	-1.75%	-1.48%	-3.67%	0.04%
Popular Music	$	28,792,437	28,858,132	28,992,998	30,329,560	30,722,760	15,049,588
	Change		0.23%	0.47%	4.61%	1.30%	-0.87%
Total	$	431,737,271	439,652,82	429,253,556	426,592,495	418,840,594	200,956,361
	Change	-	1.83%	-2.37%	-0.62%	-1.82%	1.56%

Note:
[a]: in NTD (about 1 USD=30.50 NTD)

competitor (Taiwan Soft Power, n.d.). For example, the printing and publication, as well as film and popular music, sectors in South Korea about 6 times larger than those of Taiwan (Taiwan Soft Power, n.d.). One the other hand, the advertising and broadcasting sectors in South Korea is about 3 times larger than those of Taiwan (Taiwan Soft Power, n.d.). Citing the report from *The China Times* (2017, August 15), the lack of competitiveness among Taiwan's creative and cultural industries has been attributed to the lack of laws and policy (Taiwan Soft Power, n.d.).

Integrating Digital Reality Technologies Into Taiwan's Creative and Cultural Industries

Ryan and Hearn (2010) note that several media technological trends have begun to impact on the production and dissemination of creative and cultural industries. For example, they argue that the convergence of multiple media platforms has led to the possibilities of creating multi-media contents that some film makers have eagerly embraced to allow audience to consumer film contents via multiple platforms (such as the Internet or mobile devices) (Ryan & Hearn, 2010). Because film industry belongs to one of the creative and cultural industries, it is likely the same impact can be observed and felt by other sectors in these industries.

New digital technologies have the benefits of lowering of distribution cost through digital platforms for the filmmaking industry, as eloquently described by Ryan and Hearn (2010, p. 135) below:

Digital distribution, the rapidly increasing availability of high-quality, low-cost digital video production and editing equipment, and the rise of online content aggregators, among other factors, are both lowering barriers to aspiring filmmakers and creating possibilities for screen production to bypass traditional distribution avenues.

Digital reality technologies have the great potential to generate new contents that can contribute to users' interactions with contents and products of creative and cultural industries (Ministry of Culture, 2017). For example, Cannes Film Festival (2017) and Venice Film Festival (2017) have both included new award categories for VR-based short films, television dramas, and movies (Longwell, 2018; Ministry of Culture, 2017). For example, the film, *Awavena*, by Lynette Wallworth, employs VR technology to allow viewers to virtually visit the Amazon forest with the first female shaman of the local *Yawanawa* tribe (Longwell, 2018).

In addition to these applications in the film sector, digital reality technologies have begun to spread to other creative and cultural industry sectors such as audio-visual and design, popular music, and museum and art exhibition sectors (Ministry of Culture, 2017). Other creative and cultural industry sectors have similarly eager to embrace the potentialities of digital reality technologies. Particularly, in the context of museum and art exhibitions that this book chapter aims to focus on, Ministry of Culture (2017) in Taiwan has encouraged and invested on the convergence of arts and technologies to enable digital and Internet technologies to be used in a variety of museum and art exhibitions. Adopting VR technologies to promote cultural heritage, Bruno, Bruno, De Sensi, Luchi, Mancuso, and Muzzupappa (2010) propose a VR-based *Virtual Exhibition System* that will enable archeological museums to transform their archeological finds into more immersive creative and cultural contents to lay persons. Applications such as *ARCHEOGUIDE, ARCO,* and *3D-MURALE* have allowed museum-goers to access archeological artefacts and sites remotely without visiting the museums (Bruno et al., 2010). Digital reality technologies (such as VR) have the great potential to promote creative and cultural industry contents, because of their interactivity, realism, and visualization (cited in Bruno et al., 2010).

Integration of AR, MR, and VR technologies into digital games, television broadcasting, design, and intelligent devices has been aggressively launched since 2016, claimed to be the Year of VR by Taiwanese government (Ministry of Culture, 2017). Innovative projects have been developed for *National Museum for Prehistory* (Taitung, Taiwan) to immerse visitors into *Peinan* tribal life in the pre-historical Taiwan (Ministry of Culture, 2017). Archeological finds are reconstructed using 3D modeling and animation to recreate what it is like to live among the earliest settlers of Taiwan. An estimate of USD$20 million has been invested in three major projects that involve the construction of a national culture memory bank to promote its contents through digital technologies, the production of HDTV contents, and multiplatform media content production (Ministry of Culture, 2017). These projects are meant to promote the use of digital reality technologies such as AR and VR to develop original cultural contents that tell stories about Taiwan (Ministry of Culture, 2017).

MAIN FOCUS OF THE CHAPTER

Research Objectives and Research Questions

This book chapter employs a case study approach to survey the current state of digital reality technology applications in the area of creative and oceanic cultural industries in Taiwan. This study focuses on how AR, MR, and VR technologies has been used in one of the most pertinent creative and cultural industry sector to promote oceanic cultural contents for domestic and international visitors in the museum and exhibition environment. After an extensive literature review, the author has found that AR, MR, and VR applications in museums and exhibitions as part of the creative and cultural industry sectors offer the most promising area as demonstrated by many museums around the world. For example, *Darwin Centre of the Natural History Museum* (NHM) has adopted augmented reality to allow museum-goers to experience a "virtual journey into the revolutionary past" (p. 5). Using a detailed description of these best practices among creative cultural industries, this book chapter also aims to provide a detailed examination of digital reality applications in the creative cultural industry sectors in a non-Western context.

This book chapter aims to answer the following three research questions:

Research Question #1: What is the current state of augmented (AR), mixed (MR), or virtual reality (VR) applications in the creative and oceanic cultural industry sectors in Taiwan?

Research Question #2: What insights can be generated after analyzing best practice examples in AR, MR, and VR roles in promoting museums and exhibitions to deliver creative and oceanic cultural industry contents in Taiwan?

Research Question #3: What are the opportunities and challenges by museums and exhibitions when taking advantage of this emerging trend in Taiwan?

Research Methodology: A Case Study Approach

Case study has been a widely used research method in business and other social scientific disciplines to analyze a phenomenon of significant interest to the researchers within a specific context (Mills & Duprepos, 2013; Research Methodology, n.d.). The objective of using a case study method is to provide "the intense focus on a single phenomenon" (Mills, Duprepos, & Wiebe, 2010, n.p.) by recording, analyzing, and interpreting facts and statistics related to the phenomenon.

There are two types of case study methods: exploratory and descriptive case study (Mills et al., 2010; Research Methodology, n.d.). Using an explanatory case study method will require the researchers to provide very accurate account of facts, statistics, and other relevant information about a phenomenon to provide a reliable explanation consistent with these factual materials (Mills et al., 2010). On the other hand, a descriptive case study aims to "assess a sample in detail and in depth" to generate a descriptive theory after "mining for abstract interpretations of data and theory development" (Mills et al., 2010).

The case study method has been used in previous research in creative and cultural industries (Deuze, 2007). For example, Deuze (2007) provides a very thorough study of digital games, advertising, and other creative and cultural industries to examine the interactions between media companies and cultural convergence. As an exploratory study, this book chapter employs an explanatory case study to demonstrate what have been accomplished through the integration of AR, MR, and VR in the context of museums and exhibitions of creative and oceanic cultural contents (such as literature, history, archeological discoveries, traditional culture, and marine ecology).

Existing AR, MR, and VR Applications in the Creative and Cultural Industries

AR, MR, and VR applications have shown their most productive applications by art exhibitions, art galleries, and museums to deliver creative and cultural contents to promote art, crafts, literature, music, among others (Chang, Chang, Hou, Sung, Chao, & Lee, 2014; Iyer, 2015/2016). For example, Iyer (2015/2016) and *nextplayground guardian* (2015) describe the AR art gallery, *Martell AiR Gallery*, in Singapore as the first of its kind to integrate augmented reality into contemporary art exhibition. Choi and Kim (2017) have argued that the implementation of digital technologies (such as head-mounted display devices and beacons) for museum exhibitors is likely to increase museum visitors' overall experiences by telling a compelling stories about artefacts. On the other hand, Chang et al. (2014) employ a quasi experiment design to examine the effects of an AR-guided, audio-guided, and non-guided device in an art appreciation context among 135 college participants. Their empirical results confirm the superiority of AR technology to positively enhance exhibition visitors' learning effectiveness, result in better flow experience, generate higher engagement in their gallery experience, and increase the amount of time visitors spent on the paintings (Chang et al., 2014).

According to Taiwan's Ministry of Culture (2017), the cultural asset and performance industry sectors include four sub-sectors that show different growth potential. For example, the theater, theater management, and social education facility sub-sector has grown from NTD$18,494,000 (in 2011, about USD$0.6 million), to NTD$166,649,000 (in 2016, about USD$5.4 million), even though there are growth variations each year (Refer to Table 3). Most relevant to this book chapter is the museums, historical sites, and other similar institutions that have been the second most important area in this creative and cultural industry division (Ministry of Culture, 2017). The total economic contribution of this sub-sector has grown from NTD$253,831,000 (in 2011, about USD$8.23 million), to NTD$297,618,000 (in 2016, about USD$9.64 million) (Refer to Table 3).

Table 3. Market Size of museums, art exhibitions, performing arts sectors in Taiwan

Industry Sectors		2011	2012	2013	2014	2015	2016
Theater, Theater Management, Social Education Facilities	$[a, b]	18,494	11,013	46,882	18,801	33.942	166,649
	Change	-	-40.45%	325.68%	-59.90%	80.53%	390.98%
Music Halls, Musical Performing Centers	$	824,792	641,811	487,649	690,009	647,714	678,748
	Change	-	-22.19%	-24.02%	41.50%	-6.13%	4.79%
Other Art Performance Facilities	$	90,171	105,892	125,501	294,330	664,680	589,146
	Change	-	17.43%	18.52%	134.52%	125.83%	-11.36%
Museums, Historical Sites, and Similar Institutions	$	253.831	267,373	289,090	348,799	314,666	297,618
	Change	-	5.33%	8.12%	20.65%	-9.79%	-5.42%

Note:
[a]: in NTD (about 1 USD=30.50 NTD)
[b]: in 1,000 NTD

To attract more museum-goers, this creative and cultural industry sector is the most avid adopters of digital reality technologies. For example, in their study of AR museum guide in a gallery, Chang et al. (2014) conclude that "AR not only retains the advantages of the digital guide, but also allows visitors to see the supplementary explication above a painting through a camera lens, bringing the guide information and the artwork together within the user's range of vision" (p. 186). A similar experience-enhancement application can be found in *National Museum of Natural Science* in Taichung, Taiwan where AR, VR, and other immersive technologies are used to allow museum visitors to experience running with dinosaurs in a virtually-created world (Ministry of Culture, 2017; Su, 2017) (Refer to Figure 2 from Liberty Times). A treasure hunt App is also developed for develop for mobile platforms to further engage visitors of the museum (Ministry of Culture, 2017; Su, 2017).

In the same way, *Mobile Museum of Taiwan Literature* (http://enmobilemuseum.cmtestgo.com/) by *National Museum of Taiwan Literature* has launched a mobile outdoor exhibition campaign to deliver Taiwan literature contents to the general public (Central News Agency, 2017; National Education Radio, 2017). The 40-foot long container truck makes its first stop at National Taitung University to bring the unique cultural experiences to people living in Taitung County (Central News Agency, 2017). QR code App is employed to allow smartphone users to experience masterpieces in Taiwan literature through immersive audio-visual experiences (Central News Agency, 2017). Those who attend this event can also access AR cultural contents after scanning the pictures outside the truck (Central News Agency, 2017) (Refer to Figure 3 from ETNews).

Best Practice Example #1: HTC VIVELAND Theme Park

HTC, a major VR equipment maker in Taiwan, opened its first Vive branded VR cafe in Shenzhen, China (Nafarrete, 2016). A similar 3,500 square foot installation, called *VIVELAND*, was launched in Taiwan around 2016 to allow users of the theme park to access more than 20 different types of VR experiences (Nafarrete, 2016). The arcade allows users to experience VR contents through HTC's VIVE headset with

Figure 2. The 5D dinosaur park, national museum of natural science, Taichung, Taiwan

Figure 3. Mobile museum of Taiwan literature, Taitung, Taiwan

a minimal fee (Nafarrete, 2016). Admission is about USD$12 for 30 minutes in a closed booth, while USD$6 is charged for a 15-minute session in an open booth (Nafarrete, 2016).

Some of these VR experiences include *Everest VR, Fruit Ninja VR, Zombie Camp, Project Cars, Front Defense, Cloudlands, VR Minigolf, Audio Arena, Pierhead Arcade*, and *The Walk* (Nafarrete, 2016). Working closely with the burgeoning digital game industry in Taiwan, *Bounty VR in 4D* will allow users to battle with aliens and to drive spaceships in a haptic seat (Nafarrete, 2016). In Figure 4 and Figure 5, both screenshots demonstrate what users are able to see inside VIVELAND's immersive environment. Particularly in Figure 5, where the player is immersed in a temple scene, shows a potential usage in promoting creative and cultural contents. For example, this AR application can allow users to experience a virtual journey in a historical site, an archeological excavation, or a sea journey from Mainland China to relive what their ancestors had experienced 300 hundred years ago.

Best Practice Example #2: National Museum of Prehistory (Taitung, Taiwan)

Digital reality technology is able to transform static and information-intensive museum exhibitions to be more emotionally-charged and experiential. Chang et al. (2014) summarize previous studies in the area and conclude that past studies have found the benefits of AR in offering museum- and exhibition-goers "interesting, fun, and challenging experiences, as well as immersive sensations" (p. 185). *National Museum of Prehistory* has been a pioneer in exploring how 3D animation and other digital reality technologies can transform visitors' experiences (Chen, 2012). The AR application developed by *Next Animation Studio* (2017) through its AR and 3D animation technologies is able to provide a best practice example to demonstrate how the archeological remains at the *Peinan Site* can be turned into interactive and authentic experiences for museum visitors of *Beinan Cultural Park*, as part of *National Museum of Prehistory* (www.nmp.gov.tw). An interactive game is also developed to allow visitors to virtually participate in the excavation process, through learning about the *Peinan* people from 3,000 years ago,

Figure 4. HTC's VIVELAND VR theme park

Figure 5. HTC's VIVELAND VR theme park: Temple

living inside the pre-historical settlement, and uncovering archeological objects with the explorers (Chen, 2012; Next Animation Studio, 2017).

This best practice example shows that digital reality technology has the capabilities to add more values to creative and cultural contents by engaging visitors with the archeological artefacts with more attractive narratives and immersive experiences, as empirically tested by many scholars (Bruno et al., 2010; Chang et al., 2014). As shown in Figure 6 below, museum visitors are now able to see what *Peinan* people look like and how they live their lives 3,000 years ago. The AR reconstruction of the *Peinan Site* allows users to overlay computer-generated image of this pre-historical settlement above the archeological remains to feel what it is like to walk around the settlement (Refer to Figure 7).

Figure 6. 3D animation of Peinan people

Figure 7. AR application in Peinan archeological remains

Digital reality technology has helped develop and implement the museum's promotion of creative and oceanic cultural contents through its other on-going projects, such as *The Digital Project for the Education and Promotion of Taiwan's Prehistory Cultures, The Peinan Site and Peinan Culture*, to develop a virtual museum and exhibition hall of indigenous peoples in Taiwan through "a virtual reality for interactive reconstruction of archaeological discoveries" (Chen, 2012, n.p.). The capabilities to integrate both the physical archeological artefacts, or other creative and cultural contents, with digitally-generated information have been empirically tested to trigger curiosity and encourage intention to explore the museum space (Chatzidimitris, Kavakli, Economou, & Gavalas, 2013).

Best Practice Example #3: Dream Ocean Project, Main Library, National Taiwan Ocean University (Keelung, Taiwan)

One of the most enticing features of digital reality technology is that its implementation can be small-scale and financially feasible. The *Dream Ocean Project*, developed by the Main Library at National Taiwan Ocean University, is a good best practice to demonstrate the flexibility of the technology in the development and implementation processes. After interviewing the librarian, the author is told that total equipment and software cost is about USD$2,000. The VR headset, VIVE, is manufactured by Taiwan's own HTC. Located on the 3rd floor of the Main Library, the VR component is part of *The Dream Ocean Project* (http://lib.ntou.edu.tw/readers/space/index.php) that also include a special topic book collection section on oceanic culture, multimedia contents appreciation section, and data retrieval division (http://lib.ntou.edu.tw/readers/space/index.php). The following Figure 8 and Figure 9 show what the VR Experience Site can offer to users, free of charge, to bother students and staff to virtually immerse in three types of marine ecology.

Figure 8. VR equipment for the dream ocean project, National Taiwan Ocean University

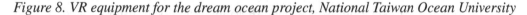

Best Practice Example #5: National Taiwan Museum (Taipei, Taiwan)

Even without a large-scale and cost-inhibitive implementation, digital reality technology can enrich visitors' overall experiences with creative and cultural contents in a multi-platform campaign. The 5th best practice example by *National Taiwan Museum* demonstrates the flexibility of these technologies to integrate with more conventional platforms (i.e., poster) to promote creative and oceanic cultural contents in an innovative manners. As an island country, Taiwan's rich marine ecological systems have become an essential part of people's experiences. To promote the beauty of this part of creative and oceanic cultural contents, the *Underwater Photographic Exhibition* was launched in 2017 by *National Taiwan Museum*. VR technology is used as part of the photography exhibition to allow visitors to experience the beautiful underwater environment through a VR headset (National Taiwan Museum n.d., https://www.ntm. gov.tw/exhibition_188_900.html). This VR installation in the photographic exhibition has transformed traditionally 2D experience with photographs into an immersive and surrounded experience in a virtual journey the Green Island to better promote what it would feel like underwater or personally visit The Green Island National Park in the eastern part of Taiwan (National Taiwan Museum n.d., https://www. ntm.gov.tw/exhibition_188_900.html).

Best Practice Example #5: Reliving the Time of George Leslie MacKay

George Leslie MacKay was a Canadian Presbyterian minister in the 19th century and he had offered his medical expertise to help then deprived and poor Taiwanese people in the *Tamsui* region in northern Taiwan. Targeting at children as the exhibition's main audience, this AR and VR project lacks government-backed funding, but still has taken advantage of the potential digital reality technology could provide through an immersive storytelling about the history of Taiwan (Yang, 2018). Supported by Aletheia University, formerly founded by Minister MacKay himself as Oxford University College, *Reliving the Time of George Leslie MacKay Project* employs VR and AR to integrate local historical and cultural facts into a more engaging cultural experience that children to experience the time of Minister MacKay in the 19th century Taiwan (Yang, 2018, November 18). As shown in Figure 11, despite the lack of fancy technical installation, users can access the rich historical cultural contents through a HMD to immerse

Figure 9. VR equipment for the dream ocean project, national Taiwan Ocean University

Figure 10. Ad flyer of the underwater photographic exhibitions – the marine life

in the time of MacKay and to learn about his great contribution to the local residents. Old photos are experientially enhanced by integrating with audio and visual information to make people's journey through the historical *Tamsui* to be more engaging.

Discussions

Among many creative and cultural industries, advertising, publishing, museums, and other cultural insitutions are among the most enthusiastic adopters of these digital reality technologies (Bruno et al., 2010; Chang et al., 2014; Chatzidimitris et al., 2013; GearBrain, 2018; Zastrow, 2016). For example, the virtual *Ancient Egyptian Collections Project*, also known as *Met's Met360*, (https://www.youtube.com/watch?time_continue=20&v=h9OTCFAmbmA) exhibition at *The Metropolitan Museum of Art*

Figure 11. Reliving the life of George Leslie MacKay

and *The British Museum* has created a virtual exhibition to allow visitors to experience a virtual through either a *Google Cardboard* or any VR headset (such as Samsung Gear VR headset) (GearBrain, 2018). This VR and 360 degree video project allows users to experience *The Temple of Dendur* that was built around 15 B.C. when Egypt was ruled by the Roman Emperor Augustus (The Met, 2017, https://www.youtube.com/watch?time_continue=20&v=h9OTCFAmbmA).

Museums around the world are now increasingly offering new methods of engaging and educating their visitors by means of human–computer interaction (HCI) systems (Alelis, Bobrowicz, & Ang, 2015; Bruno et al., 2010; Chang et al., 2014; Chatzidimitris et al., 2013). For example, Bruno et al., (2010) employ 3D reconstruction of archeological finds to transform a museum into a virtual institution and remotely available to any interested visitors. Chang et al. (2014) and Chatzidimitris et al. (2013) boh explore the potential of mobile or smartphone devices on enhancing visitors' engagement, learning effectiveness, and behavioral intention of cultural heritage, which is an essential part of creative and cultural industries. Many of these applications have the potentialities to transform conventional cultural institutions (such as museums, art exhibit halls, performance arts centers, galleries, among others) into becoming virtual to allow traditional visitors to stay at home to experience their huge amount of archeological, cultural, or artistic collections. Past academic research that examines the integration of digital reality technologies into museum and art exhibitions has often investigated the following three major areas of research.

First, Capuano, Gaeta, Guarino, Miranda, & Tomasiello (2016) have studied the effects of using narratives to overlay with artefacts to enrich and enhance museum visitors overall experiences. Capuano et al. (2016) employ AR with semantic techniques to create digital stories tied to traditional museum artefacts. The conventional statistic cultural artefacts are augmented through AR to enhance their presentation and meaning to visitors. Sensory inputs, such as 3D animations, sound, video, and even haptic, have the benefits of enriching people's experiences with media contents (including creative and oceanic cultural contents in this context) (Capuano et al., 2016). These types of multi-platform narratives in digital reality technology have been proven beneficial to the promotion and dissemination of oceanic creative and cultural contents as discussed above.

Following this line of research, Collin-Lachaud and Passebois (2008) employed a qualitative interview method to conduct about 25 in-depth inquiry with 21 participants and museum visitors. Their study has identified several important aspects of visitors' experiential narratives that may lend support to the importance of overlaying narrative information with the static creative and cultural artefacts such as archeological finds (Bruno et al., 2010), artistic objects (Chang et al., 2014), and cultural heritage (Chatzidimitris et al., 2013). Immersive technologies such as AR, MR, and VR are conductive to enhancing museum visitors' cognitive, play, and functional values as manifested in the experiential narratives of 21 participants of this study.

Secondly, another important line of research explores the effects of communication modality (such as those provided by digital reality technologies) on consumer emotional or cognitive responses (Alelis, Bobrowicz, & Ang, 2015; Jarrier & Bourgeon-Renault, 2012). The diffusion of digital reality technology not only poses challenges to the conventional manner of disseminating creative and cultural contents, but also are likely to transform museums, music halls, performance arts centers, as the physically present institutions to disseminate these contents. With the advent of these digital reality technologies, many museums (e.g., *The Ancient Egyptian Collection Project* by *The Metropolitan Museum of Art* and *The British Museum*) have ventured to develop an immersive and virtual museum experiences for potential visitors. Other best practice examples discussed in this book chapter also demonstrate a similar trend of virtualization of these long-existing cultural institutions (Alelis et al., 2015). Alelis et al. (2015) point out the wide availability of cutting-edge computer software and hardware is likely to allow cultural institutions such as museums to become digital and virtual to share and store their artefacts. A website, called *Virtual Tours* (http://www.virtualfreesites.com/museums.museums.html), claims to offer "over 300 Museums, Exhibits, Points of Special Interest and Real-Time journeys which offer online multimedia guided tours on the Web. Most of the following offer text and pictures, others in addition transmit sound and an occasional movie" around the clock (*Virtual Tours*, n.d., http://www.virtualfreesites.com/museums.museums.html)

An important question is asked by Alelis et al. (2015) to examine whether different age groups of museum visitors will experience and respond to the presentations of museum artefacts in a traditional/ physical or interactive/3D model manner. Their findings observe that viewing digitalized artefacts outside a museum can generate emotional responses among both older and young visitors (Alelis et al., 2015). It would be intriguing to study how various demographic attributes of museum visitors, as well as their technological literacy with these digital reality technologies, might play any role in predicting and explaining the relationships among many variables investigated in the literature (Alelis et al., 2015; Bruno et al., 2010; Capuano et al., 2016; Chang et al., 2014).

Thirdly, other scholars on the topic of AR, MR, and VR applications in museums and exhibitions have explored whether the (communication/media) modalities to access the creative and cultural contents in a museum could have any effects on visitors' overall experiences (Jarrier & Bourgeon-Renault, 2012). Chang et al.'s (2014) study of AR-guided, audio-guided, and no-guided devices in their art gallery study may offer some insights into the potential modality effects. However, the modality effects of creative and cultural contents warrant more programmatic study to uncover any variations with people's museum experiences through either quantitative (Jarrier & Bourgeon-Renault, 2012) or qualitative (Collin-Lachaud & Passebois, 2008) research. Along this line of research, scholars aim to examine if contents delivered through audio guides, AR presentation, interactive terminals, smartphone, or touch-screen tablets) might lead to different behavioral intention to revisit and different museum experiences (such as cognitive-rhetorical, praxeological, temporal, or hedonic-sensorial dimensions) (Refer to Jarrier & Bourgeon-Renault, 2012 for detailed description of these experiential dimensions).

RECOMMENDATIONS, LIMITATIONS, AND FUTURE DIRECTIONS

Recommendations

On the basis of the above detailed case studies and extensive literature review about the current state of AR, MR, and VR applications in creative and oceanic cultural industries in Taiwan, the following recommendations are provided to practitioners:

Recommendation #1: Enticing creative and oceanic cultural contents remains to be critical to the successful adoption and diffusion of AR, MR, and VR integration in Taiwan.

Recommendation #2: Developing talented content-producers to transform Taiwan's oceanic cultural elements through storytelling is likely to influence the success of using AR, MR, and VR.

Recommendation #3: There has been a lack of research in how Taiwanese audience will respond to contents created using these digital reality technologies. Research in the areas of interface design, modality effects, and users' characteristics should be useful to offer practical insights into planning, developing, and implementing more effective AR, MR, and VR applications in the context of creative and oceanic cultural industries.

Study Limitations

In spite of the attempt to include as many best practice examples as possible, this book chapter is limited by its length to fully explore the potentialities of AR, MR, VR, and other immersive technologies (such as 360 degree video) in promoting creative and oceanic cultural contents. Nevertheless, this study has provided an initial attempt to examine the possible impacts of emerging digital reality technologies on the production and dissemination of creative and oceanic cultural industry contents in Taiwan. Written as a case study for practitioners, future research directions are not the main focus of this book chapter. However, scholars of digital reality technologies are likely to pursue issues related to the design of an AR, MR, and VR system in the context of museums and exhibitions, or broadly for creative and cultural industry sectors. Issues related to system design, modality effects, consumer responses, and content development issues are likely to generate interesting insights into how these digital reality technologies will enhance the transformation of creative and oceanic cultural industries and the promotion of cultural contents to a wide audience.

REFERENCES

Alelis, G., Bobrowicz, A., & Ang, C. S. (2015). Comparison of engagement and emotional responses of older and younger adults interacting with 3D cultural heritage artefacts on personal devices. *Behaviour & Information Technology*, *34*(11), 1064–1078. doi:10.1080/0144929X.2015.1056548

Australian Trade and Investment Commission. (2018). *Creative industries to Taiwan: Trends and opportunities*. Taipei, Taiwan: Australian Trade and Investment Commission. Retrieved on December 13, 2018 from https://www.austrade.gov.au/Australian/Export/Export-markets/Countries/Taiwan/Industries/Creative-industries

BBC News. (2018, January 9). Taiwan country profile. *BBC News*. Retrieved on December 15, 2018 from https://www.bbc.com/news/world-asia-16164639

Biggs, M., & Buchler, D. (2008). Eight criteria for practice-based research in the creative and cultural industries. *Art. Design & Communication in Higher Education*, *7*(1), 5–18. doi:10.1386/adch.7.1.5_1

Bruno, F., Bruno, S., De Sensi, G., Luchi, M., Mancuso, S., & Muzzupappa, M. (2010). From 3D reconstruction to virtual reality: A complete methodology for digital archaeological exhibition. *Journal of Cultural Heritage*, *11*(1), 42–49. doi:10.1016/j.culher.2009.02.006

Capuano, N., Gaeta, A., Guarino, G., Miranda, S., & Tomasiello, S. (2016). Enhancing augmented reality with cognitive and knowledge perspectives: A case study in museum exhibitions. *Behaviour & Information Technology*, *35*(11), 968–979. doi:10.1080/0144929X.2016.1208774

Central Intelligence Agency (CIA). (n.d.). *The World Factbook*. Langley, MD: Central Intelligence Agency (CIA). Retrieved on December 15, 2018 from https://www.cia.gov/library/publications/the-world-factbook/geos/tw.html

Central News Agency (CNA). (2017, May 16). First of its kind. An outdoor AR experience with mobile museum of taiwan literature. *Central News Agency (CNA)*. Retrieved on December 16, 2018 from https://www.cna.com.tw/postwrite/Detail/213656.aspx#.XBc213650t213652hKjIU

Chang, K.-E., Chang, C.-T., Hou, H.-T., Sung, Y.-T., Chao, H.-L., & Lee, C.-M. (2014). Development and behavioral pattern analysis of a mobile guide system with augmented reality for painting appreciation instruction in an art museum. *Computers & Education*, *71*, 185–197. doi:10.1016/j.compedu.2013.09.022

Chatzidimitris, T., Kavakli, E., Economou, M., & Gavalas, D. (2013). Mobile augmented reality edutainment applications for cultural institutions. In *2013 Fourth International Conference on Information, Intelligence, Systems and Applications (IISA)* (pp. 1-4). Piraeus: IEEE. 10.1109/IISA.2013.6623726

Chen, F.-Y., Yen, W.-T., Wang, A. H.-E., & Hioe, B. (2017, January 2). The Taiwanese see themselves as Taiwanese, not as Chinese. *The Washington Post*. Retrieved on December 15, 2018 from https://www.washingtonpost.com/news/monkey-cage/wp/2017/2001/2002/yes-taiwan-wants-one-china-but-which-china-does-it-want/?noredirect=on&utm_term=.2017b04375117bb

Choi, H.-S., & Kim, S.-H. (2017, February). A content service deployment plan for metaverse museum exhibitions-centering on the combination of beacons and HMDs. *International Journal of Information Management, 37*(11b), 1519–1527. doi:10.1016/j.ijinfomgt.2016.04.017

Collin-Lachaud, I., & Passebois, J. (2008). Do immersive technologies add value to the museumgoing experience? An exploratory study conducted at France's Paléosite. *International Journal of Arts Management, 11*(1), 60–71.

Colombo, F. (2018). Reviewing the cultural industry: From creative industries to digital platforms. *Communicatio Socialis, 31*(4), 135–146.

Crown. (2018). *Industrial strategy: Creative industries sector deal*. London: HM Government.

Damala, A., Schuchert, T., Rodriguez, I., Moragues, J., Gilleade, K., & Stojanovic, N. (2013). Exploring the affective museum visiting experience: Adaptive augmented reality (a2r) and cultural heritage. *International Journal of Heritage in the Digital Era, 2*(1), 117–142. doi:10.1260/2047-4970.2.1.117

Deuze, M. (2007, June 1). Convergence culture in the creative industries. *International Journal of Cultural Studies, 10*(2), 243–263. doi:10.1177/1367877907076793

Dittmer, L. (2004, July/August). Taiwan and the issue of national identity. *Asian Survey, 44*(4), 475–483. doi:10.1525/as.2004.44.4.475

eMarketer.com. (2016, December 16). *Mobile Taiwan: A look at a highly mobile market*. Retrieved on December 16, 2018 from https://www.emarketer.com/Article/Mobile-Taiwan-Look-Highly-Mobile-Market/1014877

Fung, A. (2016). Strategizing for creative industries in China: Contradictions and tension in nation branding. *International Journal of Communication, 10*, 3004–3021.

GearBrain(GB). (2018, June 4). The 5 best museum AR/VR experiences this summer. *GearBrain (GB)*. Retrieved on December 15, 2018 from https://www.gearbrain.com/virtual-reality-museum-art-summer-2577767924.html

Hesmondhalgh, D. (2002). *The cultural industries*. London: Sage.

Iyer, B. (2015, December). Augmented-reality gallery enhances Singapore sights. *Campaign Asia-Pacific,* p. 31.

Jarrier, E., & Bourgeon-Renault, D. (2012, Fall). Impact of mediation devices on the museum visit experience and on visitors' behavioural intentions. *International Journal of Arts Management, 15*(1), 18–29.

Library of Congress-Federal Research Division. (2005, March). *Country profile: Taiwan*. Washington, DC: Library of Congress-Federal Research Division. Retrieved on December 15, 2018 from https://www.loc.gov/rr/frd/cs/profiles/Taiwan-new.pdf

Liu, P. (2015, December 14). Cultural and creative businesses thriving in Taiwan. *Taiwanese Business Topics*. Retrieved on December 13, 2018 from https://topics.amcham.com.tw/2015/2012/cultural-and-creative-businesses-thriving-in-taiwan/

Longwell, T. (2018, September 4). Creative forces in VR at Venice Festival learn from the past. *Variety*. Retrieved on December 16, 2018 from https://variety.com/2018/film/festivals/creative-forces-in-vr-at-venice-festival-learn-from-the-past-1202926218/

Magazine, A. V. (2011, January). NHM turns to augmented reality. *AV Magazine (London)*, 5.

Mariani, G. (2018). The cultural and creative industries. *Guillaume Mariani*. Retrieved on December 13, 2018 from https://www.guillaume-mariani.com/creative-industries/

Mills, A. J., & Durepos, G. (2013). *Case study methods in business research* (Vols. 1–4). Thousand Oaks, CA: Sage Publications Ltd. doi:10.4135/9781446286166

Mills, A. J., Durepos, G., & Wiebe, E. (2010). Explanatory case study. In Encyclopedia of case study research. Thousand Oaks, CA: Sage. doi:10.4135/9781412957397.n138

Ministry of Culture (Taiwan). (2015, September 16). *Contents and scope of cultural creative industries*. Taipei, Taiwan: Ministry of Culture. Retrieved on December 13, 2018 from https://www.moc.gov.tw/information_311_20450.html

Ministry of Culture Taiwan. (2017). *2017 Taiwan cultural & creative industries annual report*. Taipei, Taiwan: Ministry of Culture. Retrieved on December 13, 2018 from http://cci.culture.tw/upload/cht/attachment/b131e555ec34a192be359838c9a4eb07.pdf

Nafarrete, J. (2016, November 1). HTC opens VIVELAND VR theme park in Taiwan. *Virtual Reality Pulse*. Retrieved on December 13, 2018 from http://www.virtualrealitypulse.com/taiwan/?open-article-id=5764515&article-title=htc-opens-viveland-vr-theme-park-in-taiwan&blog-domain=vrscout.com&blog-title=vrscout

National Education Radio. (2017, May 16). Mobile museum of Taiwan literature truck stops by national Taitung University with outdoor AR experiences. *Yahoo.News*. Retrieved on December 16, 2018 from https://tw.news.yahoo.com/%E2016%2096%2087%E2015%AD%B2018%E2018%A2011%2018C%E2015%2018B%2095%E2015%2018D%2019A%E2017%2089%A2019%E2019%A2014%A2018%E2015%2081%2019C%E2019%2019D%A2010%E2016%2019D%B2011%E2015%A2014%A2017-%E2019%A2016%2096%E2015%2089%B2015%E2018%BB%2018A%E2019%AB%2094%E2015%A2014%2096%E2017%2018E%A2019ar-113100831.html

National Taiwan Museum. (n.d.). *Images of the ocean: An exhibition of marine ecology photos with VR experiences*. Taipei, Taiwan: National Taiwan Museum. Retrieved on December 15, 2018 from https://event.culture.tw/NTM/portal/Registration/C0103MAction?useLanguage=tw&actId=70004

Next Animation Studio. (2017, March 5). *Next Animation Studio partners with national museum of prehistory*. Retrieved on December 15, 2018 from https://eprnews.com/next-animation-studio-partners-with-national-museum-of-prehistory-87380/

Nextplayground guardian. (2015, November 3). Martell Singapore: Experience Martell air gallery. *Nextplayground Guardian*. Retrieved on December 16, 2018 from https://nextplayground.net/campaigns/martell-singapore-experience-martell-air-gallery/

PLoS Biol. (2005). Mitochondrial DNA provides a link between Polynesians and indigenous Taiwanese. *PLoS Biol, 3*(8), e281. Retrieved on December 13, 2018 from https://www.ncbi.nlm.nih.gov/pmc/articles/PMC1166355/

Research Methodology. (n.d.). *Case study*. Research Methodology. Retrieved on December 16, 2018 from https://research-methodology.net/research-methods/qualitative-research/case-studies/

Ryan, M. D., & Hearn, G. (2010, August). Next-generation "filmmaking": New markets, new methods and new business models. *Media International Australia, 136*(1), 133–145. doi:10.1177/1329878X1013600115

Su, M. J. (2017, November 7). Engaging audience through VR and AR technology in the national museum of natural science. *The Liberty Times*. Retrieved on December 16, 2018 from http://news.ltn.com.tw/news/life/breakingnews/2246155

Taiwan Cultural Creative Industries. (2018, August). *Cultural industries bimonthly: Information and trend analysis*. Taipei, Taiwan: Taiwan Cultural Creative Industries, Ministry of Culture. Retrieved on December 13, 2018 from http://cci.culture.tw/upload/cht/attachment/fed2d8ce1f2daae065f0155709146006.pdf

Taiwan Soft Power. (n.d.). Taiwan cultural & creative industry. *Taiwan Soft Power*. Retrieved on December 16, 2018 from http://www.humanrights.fi/TaiwanCulturalCreativeIndustries.htm

Trejaut, J. A., Kivisild, T., Loo, J. H., Lee, C. L., He, C. L., Hsu, C. J., & ... . (2005, August). Traces of archaic mitochondrial lineages persist in Austronesian-speaking Formosan populations. *PLoS Biol, 38*, e247. doi:10.1371/journal.pbio.0030247

Tsang, C.-H. (2012). *The development of digitalizationat the national museum of prehistory, Taitung, Taiwan*. Taitung, Taiwan, Republic of China: National Museum of Prehistory. Retrieved on December 15, 2018 http://pnclink.org/annual/annual2003/programe/presenpdf/110727.pdf

Tweed, D., & Leung, A. (2018, September 17). Five Asia flashpoints to watch as U.S.-China trade war heats up. *Bloomberg*. Retrieved on December 1, 2018 from https://www.bloomberg.com/news/articles/2018-2009-2018/five-asia-flashpoints-to-watch-as-u-s-china-trade-war-heats-up

UK Creative Industry Council (CIC). (2018, November). UK creative industries -value. *UK Creative Industry Council (CIC)*. Retrieved on December 13, 2018 from http://www.thecreativeindustries.co.uk/resources/infographics

Yang, M. J. (2018, November 17). Experiencing MacKay's daily life in Taiwan through VR and AR. *The Liberty Times*. Retrieved on December 15, 2018 from http://m.ltn.com.tw/news/life/breakingnews/2615715?utm_medium=M&utm_campaign=SHARE&utm_s

Yoshimoto, M. (2003, December). The status of creative industries in Japan and policy recommendations for their promotion. *NLI Research*, 1-9.

Zastrow, J. (2016, December). Gamification meets meaningful play: An inside look. *Computers in Libraries*, 12–15.

Zhong, Y. (2016). Explaining national identity shift in Taiwan. *Journal of Contemporary China, 25*(99), 336-352. doi:10.1080/10670564.10672015.11104866

ADDITIONAL READING

Adval, R., & Wyer, R. Jr. (1998). The role of narratives in consumer information processing. *Journal of Consumer Psychology, 7*(3), 207–245. doi:10.120715327663jcp0703_01

Baumgartner, J. (2016, January 23-30). Top VR adoption challenge: Cost. *Broadcasting & Cable,* p.12.

Bazilian, E. (April 23, 2017). Infographic: What consumers really think about VR. *AdWeek,* Retrieved on November 15, 2017 from http://www.adweek.com/digital/infographic-what-consumers-really-think-about-vr/

Bazilian, E. (May 1, 2017). Time Inc.'s VR guru is forging a new path through immersive storytelling. *AdWeek,* Retrieved on November 15, 2017 from http://www.adweek.com/digital/time-inc-s-vr-guru-is-forging-a-new-path-through-immersive-storytelling/

Bordnick, P. S., Carter, B. L., & Traylor, A. C. (2011, March). What virtual reality research in addictions can tell us about the future of obesity assessment and treatment. *Journal of Diabetes Science and Technology, 5*(2), 265–271. doi:10.1177/193229681100500210 PMID:21527092

Bulearca, M., & Tamarjan, D. (2012). Augmented reality: A sustainable marketing tool? *Global Business and Management Research: An International Journal, 2*(2 &3), 237–252.

Chahal, M. (2016, January 28). Bringing brands virtually to life. *Marketing Week,* 29-31.

Chen, S., Yusuf, P., Chek Tien, T., & Songjia, S. (2017). An initial understanding of how game users explore virtual environments. *Entertainment Computing, 19,* 13–27. doi:10.1016/j.entcom.2016.11.003

Chung, N., Lee, H., Kim, J.-Y., & Koo, C. (2017). The role of augmented reality for experience-influenced environments: The case of cultural heritage tourism in Korea. *Journal of Travel Research,* 1–17.

Claudio, P., & Maddalena, P. (2014, January). Overview: Virtual reality in medicine. *Journal of Virtual Worlds Research, 7*(1), 1–34.

Conway, R. (2017, April). The future of online advertising. *NZB,* 40-41.

Cox, A. M., Cromer, K. W., Guzman, I., & Bagui, S. (2017, May). Virtual worlds, virtual reality, and augmented reality: Differences in purchase intentions based on types, users, and sex. *Journal of Virtual Worlds Research, 10*(1), 1–21. doi:10.4101/jvwr.v10i1.7247

Dacko, S. G. (2017). Enabling smart retail settings via mobile augmented reality shopping apps. *Technological Forecasting and Social Change, 124,* 243–256. doi:10.1016/j.techfore.2016.09.032

Damala, A., Cubaud, P., Bationo, A., Houlier, P., & Marchal, I. (2008). Bridging the gap between the digital and the physical: design and evaluation of a mobile augmented reality guide for the museum visit. In S. Tsekeridou, A. D. Cheok, K. Giannakis, & J. Karigiannis (Eds.), *The Third International Conference on Digital Interactive Media in Entertainment and Arts* (pp. 120–127). Athens: ACM. 10.1145/1413634.1413660

Engberg, M., & Bolter, J. D. (2014). Cultural expression in augmented and mixed reality. *Convergence (London)*, *20*(1), 3–9. doi:10.1177/1354856513516250

Haenlein, M., & Kaplan, A. M. (2009). Flagship brand stores within virtual worlds: The impact of virtual store exposure on real-life attitude toward the brand and purchase intent. *Recherche et Applications en Marketing*, *24*(3), 57–79. doi:10.1177/076737010902400304

Hofmann, S., & Mosemghvdlishvili, L. (2014). Perceiving spaces through digital augmentation: An exploratory study of navigational augmented reality apps. *Mobile Media & Communication*, *2*(3), 265–280. doi:10.1177/2050157914530700

IDC. (2017, February 27). Worldwide spending on augmented and virtual reality forecast to reach $13.9 billion in 2017, according to IDC. Retrieved on November 19, 2017 from https://www.idc.com/getdoc.jsp?containerId=prUS42331217)

Javornik, A. (2016). Augmented reality: Research agenda for studying the impact of its media characteristics on consumer behaviour. *Journal of Retailing and Consumer Services*, *30*, 252–261. doi:10.1016/j.jretconser.2016.02.004

Jennett, C., Cox, A. L., Cairns, P., Dhoparee, S., Epps, A., Tijs, T., & Walton, A. (2008). Measuring and defining the experience of immersion in games. *International Journal of Human-Computer Studies*, *66*(9), 641–661. doi:10.1016/j.ijhcs.2008.04.004

Jin, S.-A. A. (2009). Modality effects in second life: The mediating role of social presence and the moderating role of product involvement. *Cyberpsychology & Behavior*, *12*(6), 717–721. doi:10.1089/cpb.2008.0273 PMID:19522681

Jin, S.-A. A., & Sung, Y. (2010). The roles of spokes-avatars' personalities in brand communication in 3d virtual environments. *Journal of Brand Management*, *17*(5), 317–327. doi:10.1057/bm.2009.18

Kelly, L., & Groundwater-Smith, S. (2009). Revisioning the physical and on-line museum. *Journal of Museum Education*, *34*(1), 55–68. doi:10.1080/10598650.2009.11510619

Liarokapis, F. (2006). December). An exploration from virtual to augmented reality gaming. *Simulation & Gaming*, *37*(4), 507–533. doi:10.1177/1046878106293684

Mahony, S. O. (2015). A proposed model for the approach to augmented reality deployment in marketing communications. *Procedia: Social and Behavioral Sciences*, *175*, 227–235. doi:10.1016/j.sbspro.2015.01.1195

Metz, R. (2015, March 18). Virtual reality advertisements get in your face. *MIT Technology Review*, Retrieved on November 13, 2017 from https://www.technologyreview.com/s/535556/virtual-reality-advertisements-get-in-your-face/

Olson, K. E., O'Brien, M. A., Rogers, W. A., & Charness, N. (2011). Diffusion of technology: Frequency of use for younger and older adults. *Ageing International*, *36*(1), 123–145. doi:10.100712126-010-9077-9 PMID:22685360

Pallud, J., & Monod, E. (2010). User experience of museum technologies: The phenomenological scales. *European Journal of Information Systems*, *19*(5), 562–580. doi:10.1057/ejis.2010.37

Petridis, P., White, M., Mourkousis, N., Liarokapis, F., Sifniotis, M., Basu, A., & Gatzidis, C. (2005). Exploring and interacting with virtual museums. In A. Figueiredo & G. A. Velho (Eds.), *Proceedings of Computer Applications and Quantitative Methods in Archaeology*. Tomar: CAA.

Styliani, S., Fotis, L., Kostas, K., & Petros, P. (2009). Virtual museums, a survey and some issues for consideration. *Journal of Cultural Heritage*, *10*(4), 520–528. doi:10.1016/j.culher.2009.03.003

Sylaiou, S., Mania, K., Karoulis, A., & White, M. (2010). Exploring the relationship between presence and enjoyment in a virtual museum. *International Journal of Human-Computer Studies*, *68*(5), 243–253. doi:10.1016/j.ijhcs.2009.11.002

Tallon, L., & Walker, K. (2008). Digital Technologies and the Museum Experience: Handheld Guides and Other Media. Lanham, M.D. AltaMira Press.

Wojciechowski, R. (2012). Modeling interactive augmented reality environments. In *Interactive 3D Multimedia Content* (pp. 137–170). London: Springer. doi:10.1007/978-1-4471-2497-9_6

KEY TERMS AND DEFINITIONS

Austronesian: A historical and anthropological term to refer to the peoples originated from the prehistorical Taiwan and speak Austronesian languages such as Filipino, Malay, Iulocano, Javanese, Malagasy, and other Polynesian languages.

Behavioral Intention: A concept that is derived from the theory of planned action to define the subjective probability that a person will engage in a given behavior as determined by, for example, a marketer.

Best Practice: A term that refers to a method or a procedure that can generate the optimal result when compared with other alternatives.

Case Study Approach: Refers to a social scientific research method that provides detailed and thorough description of an issue, an objective, a phenomenon, or a situation of interest as a case object.

Creative Industry: A term to refer to a set of knowledge-based and generating economic sectors, ranging from advertising, broadcasting, crafts, film, graphic design, music, publishing, tourism, etc.

Cultural Industry: A term that originated from Marxist philosophy and was coined by Theodor Adorno and Max Horkheimer to describe the production and marketing of culture as a branch of the industry. It often covers a wide variety of industries, such as architecture, craft, film and television production, music, publication, etc.

Digital Reality Technology: A term that covers augmented, mixed, and virtual reality technologies to offer users an immersive and engaging experiences with their actual physical environment through the integration of computer-generated contents.

Engagement: A term to describe the process or outcome to encourage a company's customers to interact and share their experiences with the contents, the advertised brand, or the company (i.e., advertiser) in an advertising or marketing campaign.

Indigenous Taiwanese People: An anthropological term to refer to aboriginal people in Taiwan. Also, known as Taiwanese aborigines, Formosan People, Austroneisa Taiwanese, or High-Mountain Tribal People (i.e., *Gaoshan* tribes). They account for about 2.3% of the population of 23 million in the island republic of Taiwan.

Museum: Refers to an establishment that conserves, restores, and exhibits a collection of artistic, cultural, historical, scientific objects that are of importance to human experiences.

Oceanic Culture: Refers to a type of culture that is developed by people that depends on ocean and its ecological system.

Prehistoric: A term refers to historical events that occurred before the written history.

Compilation of References

Active Ingredients For The Flipped Classroom Infographic. (2013, December 24). Retrieved from E-Learning: https://elearninginfographics.com/active-ingredients-for-the-flipped-classroom-infographic/

Active Theory Inc. (2018, September 5). BitGym: Virtual Cardio Tours. Google PlayStore.

Adams, R. J., Klowden, D., & Hannaford, B. (2001). Virtual training for a manual assembly task. *Haptics-e*, *2*(2), 1–7. Retrieved from http://hdl.handle.net/1773/34884

Advani, S., Hosman, R., & Potter, M. (2007). *Objective motion fidelity qualification in flight training simulators*. Paper presented at the AIAA Modeling and Simulation Technologies Conference and Exhibit, Hilton Head, SC. 10.2514/6.2007-6802

Agarwal, R., & Karahanna, E. (2000). Time flies when you're having fun: Cognitive absorption and beliefs about information technology usage. *Management Information Systems Quarterly*, *24*(4), 665–694. doi:10.2307/3250951

Ahmad, N., & Abu Hasan, J. (2017). Making tomorrow's leaders today: Bringing the real world into the classroom. *Infonomics Society*, *8*(1), 2497–2505.

Aksakal, N. (2015). Theoretical view to the approach of the edutainment. *Procedia - Social and Behavioral Sciences*, *186*, 1232-1239.

Alcántara, A.-M. (2018, March). Brands are finally embracing augmented reality, but not without speed bumps. *AdWeek*. Retrieved on August 4, 2018 from https://www.adweek.com/digital/brands-are-finally-embracing-augmented-reality-but-with-speed-bumps-along-the-way/

Alelis, G., Bobrowicz, A., & Ang, C. S. (2015). Comparison of engagement and emotional responses of older and younger adults interacting with 3D cultural heritage artefacts on personal devices. *Behaviour & Information Technology*, *34*(11), 1064–1078. doi:10.1080/0144929X.2015.1056548

Allerton, D. (2009). *Principles of flight simulation* (1st ed.). Chichester, UK: Wiley.

Alloway, N., Freebody, P., Gilbert, P., & Muspratt, S. (2002). *Boys, literacy and schooling: Expanding the repertoires of practice*. Melbourne: Curriculum 426 Wayne Martino and Michael Kehler Corporation. Retrieved September 3, 2016, from http://www.dest.gov.au/sectors/school_education/publications_resources/profiles/boys_literacy_ schooling.htm

Alshammari, T., Alhadreti, O., & Mayhew, P. (2015). When to ask participants to think aloud: A comparative study of concurrent and retrospective think-aloud methods. *International Journal of Human-Computer Interaction*, *6*(3), 48–64.

American Association of Museums (AAM). (1984). *Museum for a new century*. Washington, DC: American Association of Museums.

Anderson, C. A., Shibuya, A., Ihori, N., Swing, E. L., Bushman, B. J., Sakamoto, A., ... Saleem, M. (2010). Violent video game effects on aggression, empathy, and prosocial behavior in Eastern and Western countries: A meta-analytic review. *Psychological Bulletin, 136*(2), 151–173. doi:10.1037/a0018251 PMID:20192553

Anstey, M., & Bull, G. (2006). *Teaching and Learning Multiliteracies.* International Reading Association.

Anthes, C., García-Hernández, R. J., Wiedemann, M., & Kranzlmüller, D. (2016). *State of the art of virtual reality technology.* Paper presented at the Aerospace Conference. 10.1109/AERO.2016.7500674

Anzalone, C. (2017). *UB's virtual reality expertise creates simulated classroom environment for aspiring teachers.* Retrieved from https://www.buffalo.edu/ubnow/stories/2017/06/vr-teacher-training.html

Arango, F., Chang, C., Esche, S. K., & Chassapis, C. (2007). A scenario for collaborative learning in virtual engineering laboratories. In 37th Annual Frontiers in Education Conference-global Engineering: Knowledge without Borders, Opportunities Without Passports (pp. F3G-7). IEEE. doi:10.1109/FIE.2007.4417818

Arena, R. (2018, August 17). *Mixed reality not a reality for most companies, at least for now.* Retrieved on December 18, 2018 from https://www.emarketer.com/content/mixed-reality-tbd

Artifact Collection. (2018). Retrieved from http://archives.algomau.ca/main/node/20942

Asadi, H., Mohammadi, A., Mohamed, S., Lim, C. P., Khatami, A., Khosravi, A., & Nahavandi, S. (2016). *A Particle Swarm Optimization-based washout filter for improving simulator motion fidelity.* Paper presented at the Systems, Man, and Cybernetics (SMC), 2016 IEEE International Conference. 10.1109/SMC.2016.7844527

Asadi, H., Mohamed, S., Rahim Zadeh, D., & Nahavandi, S. (2015). Optimisation of nonlinear motion cueing algorithm based on genetic algorithm. *Vehicle System Dynamics, 53*(4), 526–545. doi:10.1080/00423114.2014.1003948

Australian Trade and Investment Commission. (2018). *Creative industries to Taiwan: Trends and opportunities.* Taipei, Taiwan: Australian Trade and Investment Commission. Retrieved on December 13, 2018 from https://www.austrade. gov.au/Australian/Export/Export-markets/Countries/Taiwan/Industries/Creative-industries

Autism Europe. (2018). *About Autism.* Retrieved October 2017, from http://www.autismeurope.org/about-autism/

Ayres, P., & Sweller, J. (2014). The split-attention principle in multimedia learning. In R. E. Mayer (Ed.), *The Cambridge Handbook of Multimedia Learning* (2nd ed.). Cambridge, UK: Cambridge University Press. doi:10.1017/CBO9781139547369.011

Baek, T. H., Yoo, C. Y., & Yoon, S. (2015). *The impact of augmented reality on self-brand connections and purchase intentions.* Paper presented at the Academy of American Advertising, Chicago, IL.

Baek, T. H., Yoo, C. Y., & Yoon, S. (2018). Augment yourself through virtual mirror: The impact of self-viewing and narcissism on consumer responses. *International Journal of Advertising, 37*(3), 421-439. doi:10.1080/02650487.0265 2016.01244887

Bae, M. (2017). Matching cause-related marketing campaign to culture. *Asian Journal of Communication, 27*(4), 415-432. doi:10.1080/01292986.01292017.01280064

Bailenson, J., Yee, N., Blascovich, J., Beall, A., Lundblad, N., & Jin, M. (2008). The use of immersive virtual reality in the learning sciences: Digital transformations of teachers, students, and social context. *Journal of the Learning Sciences, 17*(1), 102–141. doi:10.1080/10508400701793141

Bailey, J. O., Bailenson, J., & Casasanto, D. (2016). When Does Virtual Embodiment Change Our Minds? *PRESENCE: Teleoperators and Virtual Environments.*

Bailey, R., Knotts, L., Horowitz, S., & Malone, I. H. (1987). *Effect of time delay on manual flight control and flying qualities during in-flight and ground-based simulation.* Paper presented at the Flight Simulation Technologies Conference. 10.2514/6.1987-2370

Ballings, M., McCullough, H., & Bharadwaj, N. (2018). Cause marketing and customer profitability. *Journal of the Academy of Marketing Science, 46*(2), 234–251. doi:10.100711747-017-0571-4

BamburyS. (2017). *CPD in VR.* Retrieved from https://www.virtualiteach.com/cpd-in-vr

Banerjee, P. M., & Belson, G. (2015, January 26). *Digital education 2.0: From content to connections.* Retrieved from Deloitte Insights: https://www2.deloitte.com/insights/us/en/deloitte-review/issue-16/future-digital-education-technology.html

Barab, S. A., & Squire, K. (2004). Design-based research: Putting a stake in the ground. *Journal of the Learning Sciences, 13*(1), 1–14. doi:10.120715327809jls1301_1

Barak, A., & Grohol, J. M. (2011). Current and future trends in Internet-supported mental health interventions. *Journal of Technology in Human Services, 29*(3), 155–196. doi:10.1080/15228835.2011.616939

Barker, K. (2016). Virtual spaces and virtual layers - governing the ungovernable? *Information & Communications Technology Law, 25*(1), 62–70. doi:10.1080/13600834.2015.1134146

Baron-Cohen, S., & Wheelwright, S. (2004). The Empathy quotient: An investigation of adults with Asperger Syndrome or High Functioning Autism, and normal sex differences. *Journal of Autism and Developmental Disorders, 34*(2), 163–175. doi:10.1023/B:JADD.0000022607.19833.00 PMID:15162935

Barrettara, M. (2013). New methods for sharing and exhibiting 3D archaeology. *The Posthole, 31*, 8–13.

Bauer, M. (2005). *Evaluating the effectiveness of training system approaches for highly complex flight training* (Doctoral Dissertation). University of Central Florida, Orlando, FL.

Baumgartner, J. (2016, January 23-30). Top VR adoption challenge: Cost. *Broadcasting & Cable, 12.*

Bazilian, E. (2017a, April 23). Infographic: What consumers really think about VR. *AdWeek.* Retrieved on November 15, 2017 from http://www.adweek.com/digital/infographic-what-consumers-really-think-about-vr/

Bazilian, E. (2017b, May 1). Time Inc.'s VR guru is forging a new path through immersive storytelling. *AdWeek.* Retrieved on November 15, 2017 from http://www.adweek.com/digital/time-inc-s-vr-guru-is-forging-a-new-path-through-immersive-storytelling/

BBC News. (2018, January 9). Taiwan country profile. *BBC News.* Retrieved on December 15, 2018 from https://www.bbc.com/news/world-asia-16164639

Beck, J. C., & Wade, M. (2006). The kids are alright: How the gamer generation is changing the workplace. Cambridge, MA: Harvard Business Review Press.

Beer, J. (2016, May 6). Why TOMS shoes and AT&T are taking a virtual reality trip to Colombia. *Fast Company.* Retrieved on August 6, 2018 from https://www.fastcompany.com/3059526/why-toms-shoes-and-att-are-taking-a-virtual-reality-trip-to-colombia

Bekele, M. K., Pierdicca, R., Frontoni, E., Malinverni, E. S., & Gain, J. (2018). A Survey of Augmented, Virtual, and Mixed Reality for Cultural Heritage. *Journal on Computing and Cultural Heritage, 11*(2), 7. doi:10.1145/3145534

Benes, R. (2018, October 11). *Five charts: How marketers use AI: Automated ad targeting is on the rise.* Retrieved on December 1, 2018 from https://content-na2011.emarketer.com/five-charts-how-marketers-use-ai

Bentkowska-Kafel, A., & MacDonald, L. (Eds.). (2018). *Digital techniques for documenting and preserving cultural heritage*. Kalamazoo, MI: Arc Humanities Press.

Berger, D. R., Schulte-Pelkum, J., & Bülthoff, H. H. (2010). Simulating believable forward accelerations on a Stewart motion platform. *ACM Transactions on Applied Perception, 7*(1), 5:1-5:27. Doi:10.1145/1658349.1658354

Bergland, C. (2013). *The neuroscience of empathy*. Retrieved from https://www.psychologytoday.com/blog/the-athletes-way/201310/the-neuroscience-empathy

Bergmann, J., & Sams, A. (2015, November 25). *Infographic: 4 learning strategies for flipped learning*. Retrieved from ISTE: https://www.iste.org/explore/articleDetail?articleid=14

Bertollini, G., Glase, Y., Szczerba, J., & Wagner, R. (2014). *The effect of motion cueing on simulator comfort, perceived realism, and driver performance during low speed turning*. Paper presented at the Proceedings of the Driving Simulator Conference, Paris, France.

Bethesda Softworks (2017, November 17). The Elder Scrolls V: Skyrim VR. Bethesda Softworks.

Biggs, M., & Buchler, D. (2008). Eight criteria for practice-based research in the creative and cultural industries. *Art. Design & Communication in Higher Education, 7*(1), 5–18. doi:10.1386/adch.7.1.5_1

Bilda, Z., Candy, L., & Edmonds, E. (2007). An embodied cognition framework for interactive experience. *CoDesign, 3*(2), 123–137. doi:10.1080/15710880701251443

Billinghurst, M. (2016). *VSMM 2016 Keynote: Using AR and VR to create empathic experiences*. VSMM 2016 Conference, Kuala Lumpur, Malaysia. Retrieved November, 2016, from http://www.slideshare.net/marknb00/vsmm-2016-keynote-using-ar-and-vr-to-create-empathic-experiences

Bishop, C. (2012). *Artificial Hells: Participatory Art and the Politics of Spectatorship*. London: Verso.

Black, P., & Wiliam, D. (2009). Developing the theory of formative assessment. *Educational Assessment, Evaluation and Accountability, 21*(1), 5, https://doi.org/10.1007/s11092-008-9068-5

Blanke, O. (2012). Multisensory brain mechanisms of bodily self-consciousness. *Nature Reviews. Neuroscience, 13*(8), 556–571. doi:10.1038/nrn3292 PMID:22805909

Blender. (2018). Retrieved from: https://www.blender.org/

Bluemink, J., Hämäläinen, R., Manninen, T., & Järvelä, S. (2010). Group-level analysis on multiplayer game collaboration: How do the individuals shape the group interaction? *Interactive Learning Environments, 18*(4), 365–383. doi:10.1080/10494820802602444

Boletsis, C. (2017). The new era of Virtual Reality locomotion: A systematic literature review of techniques and a proposed typology. *Multimodal Technologies and Interaction, 1*(4), 24. doi:10.3390/mti1040024

Bordnick, P. S., Carter, B. L., & Traylor, A. C. (2011). What virtual reality research in addictions can tell us about the future of obesity assessment and treatment. *Journal of Diabetes Science and Technology, 5*(2), 265–271. doi:10.1177/193229681100500210 PMID:21527092

Bosschieter, P. (2016). Continuing professional development (CPD) and the potential of new media. *The Indexer, 34*(3), 71–74. doi:10.3828/indexer.2016.20

Bozanta, A., Kutlu, B., Nowlan, N., & Shirmohammadi, S. (2016). Effects of serious games on perceived team cohesiveness in a multi-user virtual environment. *Computers in Human Behavior, 59*, 380–388. doi:10.1016/j.chb.2016.02.042

Braiker, B. (2018, March 5). Four things we learned at mobile world congress. *Advertising Age, 89*, 6.

Brame, C. (2018). *Team-based learning*. Retrieved from Vanderbilt University: https://cft.vanderbilt.edu/guides-sub-pages/team-based-learning/

Bricken, M. (1991). Virtual reality learning environments: Potentials and challenges. *Computer Graphics, 25*(3), 178–184. doi:10.1145/126640.126657

Britain, S., & Liber, O. (1999). *A framework for pedagogical evaluation of virtual learning environments*. Retrieved December 2, 2018, from http://www.leeds.ac.uk/educol/documents/00001237.htm[1]

Brom, C., Preuss, M., & Klement, D. (2011). Are educational computer micro-games engaging and effective for knowledge acquisition at high-schools? A quasi-experimental study. *Computers & Education, 57*(3), 1971–1988. doi:10.1016/j.compedu.2011.04.007

Brooke, J. (1996). SUS-A quick and dirty usability scale. *Usability Evaluation in Industry, 189*(194): 4-7.

Brooks, K. (2003). *There is nothing virtual about immersion: Narrative immersion for VR and other interfaces*. Retrieved September, 2016, from MIT Media Lab, http://alumni.media.mit.edu/~brooks/storybiz/immersiveNotVirtual.pdf

Brown, E., & Cairns, P. (2004). *A grounded investigation of game immersion*. Paper presented at the CHI '04 Extended Abstracts on Human Factors in Computing Systems, Vienna, Austria. doi: 10.1145/985921.986048

Brown, A. (1992). Design experiments: Theoretical and methodological challenges in creating complex interventions in classroom settings. *Journal of the Learning Sciences, 2*(2), 141–178. doi:10.120715327809jls0202_2

Bruenger-Koch, M. (2005). *Motion parameter tuning and evaluation for the DLR automotive simulator*. Paper presented at the Driving Simulation Conference North America (DSC-NA), Orlando, FL.

Bruenger-Koch, M., Briest, S., & Vollrath, M. (2006). *Do you feel the difference? A motion assessment study*. Paper presented at the Driving Simulation Conference Asia/Pacific, Tsukuba, Japan.

Bruner, J. S. (1961). The act of discovery. *Harvard Educational Review, 31*, 21–32.

Brünken, R., Seufert, T., & Paas, F. (2010). Measuring cognitive load. In J. L. Plass, R. Moreno, & R. Brünken (Eds.), *Cognitive load theory* (pp. 181–202). Cambridge, UK: Cambridge University Press. doi:10.1017/CBO9780511844744.011

Bruno, F., Bruno, S., De Sensi, G., Luchi, M. L., Mancuso, S., & Muzzupappa, M. (2010). From 3D reconstruction to virtual reality: A complete methodology for digital archaeological exhibition. *Journal of Cultural Heritage, 11*(1), 42–49. doi:10.1016/j.culher.2009.02.006

Bruschetta, M., Maran, F., & Beghi, A. (2017). A fast implementation of MPC-based motion cueing algorithms for mid-size road vehicle motion simulators. *Vehicle System Dynamics*, 1–25.

Bucher, J. (2016). *How to shoot virtual reality: seven basics to launch you toward virtual virtuosity*. Retrieved March, 2017, from MovieMaker: http://www.moviemaker.com/archives/summer2016/how-to-shoot-virtual-reality-seven-basics/

Bujak, K. R., Radu, I., Catrambone, R., MacIntyre, B., Zheng, R., & Golubski, G. (2013). A psychological perspective on augmented reality in the mathematics classroom. *Computers & Education, 68*, 536–544. doi:10.1016/j.compedu.2013.02.017

Bull, B. (2013, February 21). *A Flipped Classroom Primer*. Retrieved from Etale: http://etale.org/main/2013/02/21/a-flipped-classroom-primer/

Bunny. (2018). *Brown wooden bunny*. Retrieved from: http://archives.algomau.ca/main/node/25490

Burch, G. F., Heller, N. A., Burch, J. J., Freed, R., & Steed, S. A. (2015). Student engagement: Developing a conceptual framework and survey instrument. *Journal of Education for Business, 90*(4), 224–229. doi:10.1080/08832323.2015.1019821

Burdea, G. C., & Coiffet, P. (2003). *Virtual reality technology.* New York, NY: John Wiley & Sons. doi:10.1162/105474603322955950

Burns, E. R., Stevens, J. A., & Lee, R. (2016). The direct costs of fatal and non-fatal falls among older adults— United States. *Journal of Safety Research, 58*, 99–103. doi:10.1016/j.jsr.2016.05.001 PMID:27620939

Burritt, M. (2017, December 11-24). Experts: Amazon's mixed reality software is a tool, not a solution. *Furniture/Today, 6.*

Burritt, M. (2017a, November 6-12). AI, mixed reality spawn top tech trends for 2018. *Furniture/Today,* 18-20.

Burritt, M. (2017b, December 11-24). Experts: Amazon's mixed reality software is a tool, not a solution. *Furniture/Today, 6.*

Bush, G. (2009). Thinking around the corner: The power of information literacy. *Phi Delta Kappan, 90*(6), 446–447. doi:10.1177/003172170909000615

Business Wire. (2018, November 28). Global virtual reality (VR) market analysis & forecast to 2027 - increasing adoption of head-mounted displays (HMD) in the gaming & entertainment sector - researchandmarkets.Com. *Business Wire.* Retrieved on December 1, 2018 from https://www.businesswire.com/news/home/20181128005629/en/

Bustillo, A., Alaguero, M., Miguel, I., Saiz, J. M., & Iglesias, L. S. (2015). A flexible platform for the creation of 3D semi-immersive environments to teach Cultural Heritage. *Digital Applications in Archaeology and Cultural Heritage, 2*(4), 248–259. doi:10.1016/j.daach.2015.11.002

Butnaru, T., & Girbacia, F. (2009). *Collaborative pre-surgery planning in a tele-immersive environment using VR technology.* Paper presented at the FMBE Proceedings of International Conference on Advancements of Medicine and Health Care through *Technology.*

Callaghan, M., Eguíluz, A. G., McLaughlin, G., & McShane, N. (2015). *Opportunities and challenges in virtual reality for remote and virtual laboratories.* Paper presented at the Remote Engineering and Virtual Instrumentation (REV), 2015 12th International Conference. 10.1109/REV.2015.7087298

Callow, J. (2006). Images, politics and multiliteracies: Using a visual metalanguage! *Australian Journal of Language and Literacy, 29*(1), 7–23.

Campbell, D. T., & Stanley, J. C. (1963). *Experimental and Quasi-Experimental Designs for Research.* Chicago: Rand McNally.

Capcom. (2017, January 24). Resident Evil 7: Biohazard. Worldwide: Capcom.

Capuano, N., Gaeta, A., Guarino, G., Miranda, S., & Tomasiello, S. (2016). Enhancing augmented reality with cognitive and knowledge perspectives: A case study in museum exhibitions. *Behaviour & Information Technology, 35*(11), 968–979. doi:10.1080/0144929X.2016.1208774

Carbotte, K. (2018, March 10). *Do the Locomotion: The 19 Ways you walk and run in VR Games.* Retrieved from https://www.tomshardware.co.uk/picturestory/230-virtual-reality-games-locomotion-methods.html

Carrozzino, M., & Bergamasco, M. (2010). Beyond virtual museums: Experiencing immersive virtual reality in real museums. *Journal of Cultural Heritage, 11*(4), 452–458. doi:10.1016/j.culher.2010.04.001

Casas, S., Coma, I., Portalés, C., & Fernández, M. (2017). Optimization of 3-DOF parallel motion devices for low-cost vehicle simulators. *Journal of Advanced Mechanical Design, Systems, and Manufacturing, 11*(2).

Casas, S., Fernández, M., & Riera, J. V. (2017). Four different multimodal setups for non-aerial vehicle simulations - A case study with a speedboat simulator. *Multimodal Technologies and Interaction, 1*(2,10), 1-17.

Casas, S., Olanda, R., Fernandez, M., & Riera, J. V. (2012). *A faster than real-time simulator of motion platforms.* Paper presented at the CMMSE, Murcia, Spain.

Casas, S., Portalés, C., García-Pereira, I., & Fernández, M. (2017). On a first evaluation of ROMOT -a RObotic 3D MOvie Theatre - for driving safety awareness. *Multimodal Technologies and Interaction, 1*(2,6), 1-13.

Casas, S., Portalés, C., Vera, L., & Riera, J. V. (2019). Virtual and augmented reality mirrors for mental health treatment: analysis and future directions. In G. Guazzaroni (Ed.), Virtual and Augmented Reality in Mental Health Treatment (pp. 95-117). Hersey, PA: IGI Global. doi:10.4018/978-1-5225-7168-1.ch007

Casas, S., Rueda, S., Riera, J. V., & Fernández, M. (2012). *On the real-time physics simulation of a speed-boat motion.* Paper presented at the GRAPP/IVAPP.

Casas, S., Coma, I., Portalés, C., & Fernández, M. (2016). Towards a simulation-based tuning of motion cueing algorithms. *Simulation Modelling Practice and Theory, 67*, 137–154. doi:10.1016/j.simpat.2016.06.002

Casas, S., Coma, I., Riera, J. V., & Fernández, M. (2015). Motion-cuing algorithms: Characterization of users' perception. *Human Factors: The Journal of the Human Factors and Ergonomics Society, 57*(1), 144–162. doi:10.1177/0018720814538281 PMID:25790575

Casas, S., Olanda, R., & Dey, N. (2017). Motion cueing algorithms: A review - Algorithms, evaluation and tuning. *International Journal of Virtual and Augmented Reality, 1*(1), 90–106. doi:10.4018/IJVAR.2017010107

Casas, S., Portalés, C., Coma, I., & Fernández, M. (2017). Applying particle swarm optimization to the motion-cueing-algorithm tuning problem. *Proceedings of the Genetic and Evolutionary Computation Conference Companion.* 10.1145/3067695.3075990

Casas, S., Portales, C., Riera, J. V., & Fernandez, M. (2017). Heuristics for solving the parameter tuning problem in motion cueing algorithms. *Revista Iberoamericana de Automática e Informática Industrial, 14*(2), 193–204. doi:10.1016/j.riai.2016.09.011

Casas, S., & Rueda, S. (2018). Lessons learned from the design and development of vehicle simulators: A case study with three different simulators. *International Journal of Virtual and Augmented Reality, 2*(1), 59–80. doi:10.4018/IJVAR.2018010105

Case-Smith, J., Weaver, L. L., & Fristad, M. A. (2015). A systematic review of sensory processing interventions for children with autism spectrum disorders. *Autism, 19*(2), 133–148. doi:10.1177/1362361313517762 PMID:24477447

Casey, A., Goodyear, V. A., & Armour, K. M. (2017). Rethinking the relationship between pedagogy, technology and learning in health and physical education. *Sport Education and Society, 22*(2), 288–304. doi:10.1080/13573322.2016.1226792

Casu, A., Spano, L. D., Sorrentino, F., & Scateni, R. (2015). RiftArt: Bringing Masterpieces in the Classroom through Immersive Virtual Reality. In *Eurographics Italian Chapter Conference* (pp. 77-84). Boston, MA: Academic Press.

Çeltek, E. (2015, September 30). Smart technologies: Augmented reality applications in tourism marketing. *Mobile Computing and Wireless Networks: Concepts, Methodologies, Tools, and Applications, 2-4*, 876–892.

Central Intelligence Agency (CIA). (n.d.). *The World Factbook.* Langley, MD: Central Intelligence Agency (CIA). Retrieved on December 15, 2018 from https://www.cia.gov/library/publications/the-world-factbook/geos/tw.html

Central News Agency (CNA). (2017, May 16). First of its kind. An outdoor AR experience with mobile museum of taiwan literature. *Central News Agency (CNA)*. Retrieved on December 16, 2018 from https://www.cna.com.tw/postwrite/Detail/213656.aspx#.XBc213650t213652hKjIU

Ch'ng, E., Cai, Y., & Thwaites, H. (2018). Special Issue on VR for Culture and Heritage: The Experience of Cultural Heritage with Virtual Reality: Guest Editors' Introduction. *Presence (Cambridge, Mass.)*, *26*(03), iii–vi. doi:10.1162/pres_e_00302

Chandler, P., & Sweller, J. (1992). The split-attention effect as a factor in the design of instruction. *The British Journal of Educational Psychology*, *62*(2), 233–246. doi:10.1111/j.2044-8279.1992.tb01017.x

Chang, C.-T., & Chen, P.-C. (2017). Cause-related marketing ads in the eye tracker: It depends on how you present, who sees the ad, and what you promote. *International Journal of Advertising*, *36*(2), 336-355. doi:10.1080/02650487.0265 2015.01100698

Chang, K.-E., Chang, C.-T., Hou, H.-T., Sung, Y.-T., Chao, H.-L., & Lee, C.-M. (2014). Development and behavioral pattern analysis of a mobile guide system with augmented reality for painting appreciation instruction in an art museum. *Computers & Education*, *71*, 185–197. doi:10.1016/j.compedu.2013.09.022

Changrani, J., Lieberman, M., Golant, M., Rios, P., Damman, J., & Gany, F. (2008). Online cancer support groups: Experiences with underserved immigrant Latinos. *Primary Psychiatry*, *15*(10), 55–62.

Chang, S. M., & Lin, S. S. (2014). Team knowledge with motivation in a successful MMORPG game team: A case study. *Computers & Education*, *73*, 129–140. doi:10.1016/j.compedu.2013.09.024

Chatzidimitris, T., Kavakli, E., Economou, M., & Gavalas, D. (2013). Mobile augmented reality edutainment applications for cultural institutions. In *2013 Fourth International Conference on Information, Intelligence, Systems and Applications (IISA)* (pp. 1-4). Piraeus: IEEE. 10.1109/IISA.2013.6623726

Cheal, C. (2009). Student perceptions of a course taught in Second Life. *Innovate: Journal of Online Education*, *5*(5), Article 2. Retrieved https://nsuworks.nova.edu/innovate/vol5/iss5/2

Chen, F.-Y., Yen, W.-T., Wang, A. H.-E., & Hioe, B. (2017, January 2). The Taiwanese see themselves as Taiwanese, not as Chinese. *The Washington Post*. Retrieved on December 15, 2018 from https://www.washingtonpost.com/news/monkey-cage/wp/2017/2001/2002/yes-taiwan-wants-one-china-but-which-china-does-it-want/?noredirect=on&utm_term=.2017b04375117bb

Chen, G., & Fu, X. (2003). Effects of multimodal information on learning performance and judgment of learning. *Journal of Educational Computing Research*, *29*(3), 349–362. doi:10.2190/J54F-B24D-THN7-H9PH

Chen, J. C. (2016). The crossroads of English language learners, task-based instruction, and 3D multi-user virtual learning in Second Life. *Computers & Education*, *102*, 152–171. doi:10.1016/j.compedu.2016.08.004

Chen, P., Peng, Z., Li, D., & Yang, L. (2016). An improved augmented reality system based on Andar. *J. Visual Communication Image Research*, *37*, 63–69. doi:10.1016/j.jvcir.2015.06.016

Cho, J., Lee, T. H., Ogden, J., Stewart, A., Tsai, T. Y., Chen, J., & Vituccio, R. (2016, July). Imago: presence and emotion in virtual reality. In ACM SIGGRAPH 2016 VR Village (p. 6). ACM. doi:10.1145/2929490.2931000

Choi, H.-S., & Kim, S.-H. (2017, February). A content service deployment plan for metaverse museum exhibitions-centering on the combination of beacons and HMDs. *International Journal of Information Management*, *37*(11b), 1519–1527. doi:10.1016/j.ijinfomgt.2016.04.017

Christou, C. (2010). Virtual Reality in Education. *Affective, Interactive and Cognitive Methods for E-Learning Design: Creating an Optimal Education Experience*, 228-243.

Chung, N., Lee, H., Kim, J.-Y., & Koo, C. (2017). The role of augmented reality for experience-influenced environments: The case of cultural heritage tourism in Korea. *Journal of Travel Research*, 1–17.

Cilasun, A. (2012). *Virtual Museum and Review of Virtual Museums in Turkey.* Paper presented at 5T A New Affair: Design History and Digital Design Museum, At İzmir.

Claman, F. L. (2015). The impact of multiuser virtual environments on student engagement. *Nurse Education in Practice*, *15*(1), 13–16. doi:10.1016/j.nepr.2014.11.006 PMID:25532889

Clarke, J., Dede, C., & Dieterle, E. (2008). Emerging technologies for collaborative, mediated, immersive learning. In J. Voogt & G. Knezek (Eds.), *The international handbook of technology in primary and secondary education* (pp. 901–909). New York: Springer; doi:10.1007/978-0-387-73315-9_55

Clark, K. R. (2007). *Charting transformative practice: Critical multiliteracies via informal learning design.* UC San Diego Electronic Theses and Dissertations.

Claudio, P., & Maddalena, P. (2014, January). Overview: Virtual reality in medicine. *Journal of Virtual Worlds Research*, *7*(1), 1–34.

Clayton, A. S. (2017). *Multiplayer educational role playing games (MPERPGs) and the application of leadership (Ph.D.).* Phoenix, AZ: Grand Canyon University.

Clemmons, N. (2017, June 8). Analyzing the false dichotomy of AR vs. VR. *Gamasutra.* Retrieved on December 1, 2018 from https://www.gamasutra.com/blogs/NolanClemmons/20170608/20299550/Analyzing_the_False_Dichotomy_of_AR_vs_VR.php

Clifford-Marsh, E. (2009, February). Ford KA's augmented reality check. *Revolution (Staten Island, N.Y.)*, 19.

Cloonan, A. (2007). *The Professional Learning of Teachers, a Case Study of Multiliteracies Teaching in the Early Years of Schooling* (Unpublished Thesis). School of Education Design and Social Context Portfolio.

Cobb, P. (2001). Supporting the improvement of learning and teaching in social and 456 institutional context. In S. Carver & D. Klahr (Eds.), *Cognition and Instruction: 25 Years of Progress* (pp. 455–478). Mahwah, NJ: Lawrence Erlbaum Associates, Inc.

Collet, A., Chuang, M., Sweeney, P., Gillett, D., Evseev, D., & Calabrese, D. (n.d.). *High-quality streamable free-viewpoint video.* Redmond, WA: Microsoft. Retrieved on December 1, 2018 from http://hhoppe.com/fvv.pdf

Collin-Lachaud, I., & Passebois, J. (2008). Do immersive technologies add value to the museumgoing experience? An exploratory study conducted at France's Paléosite. *International Journal of Arts Management*, *11*(1), 60–71.

Collins, A. (1992). Towards a design science of education. In E. Scanlon & T. O'Shea (Eds.), *New Directions In Educational Technology* (pp. 15–22). Berlin: Springer. doi:10.1007/978-3-642-77750-9_2

Colombet, F., Dagdelen, M., Reymond, G., Pere, C., Merienne, F., & Kemeny, A. (2008). *Motion cueing: what's the impact on the driver's behaviour?* Paper presented at the Driving Simulator Conference, Monte-Carlo, Monaco.

Colombo, F. (2018). Reviewing the cultural industry: From creative industries to digital platforms. *Communicatio Socialis*, *31*(4), 135–146.

Comber, B., & Kamler, B. (2004). Getting Out of Deficit: Pedagogies of reconnection. *Teaching Education, 15*(3), 293–310. doi:10.1080/1047621042000257225

CONE. (2016, May 13). *Toms and AT&T help consumers take a "walk in their shoes".* Retrieved on August 6, 2018 from http://www.conecomm.com/insights-blog/toms-att-walk-in-their-shoes-vr

Conrad, M. (2011). Leaving the lindens: Teaching in virtual worlds of other providers. In *Proceedings of Researching Learning in Immersive Virtual Environments (ReLIVE): 28.* Milton Keynes, UK: Open University.

Conrad, M., Hassan, A., Koshy, L., Kanamgotov, A., & Christopoulos, A. (2017). Strategies and challenges to facilitate situated learning in virtual worlds post-second life. *Computers in Entertainment, 15*(1). 1–9. doi:10.1145/3010078

Cook, A. D. (2009). *A case study of the manifestations and significance of social presence in a multi-user virtual environment (Ph.D.).* Saskatoon, SK, Canada: University of Saskatchewan.

Cook, A. V., Jones, R., Raghavan, A., & Saif, I. (2017, December 5). Digital reality: The focus shifts from technology to opportunity. *TechTrends*, Wired, Retrieved on October 10, 2018 from https://www.wired.com/brandlab/2018/02/digital-reality-focus-shifts-technology-opportunity/.

Cope, B., & Kalantzis, M. (2000). Designs for social futures. In B. Cope & M. Kalantzis (Eds.), *Multiliteracies: Literacy Learning and the Design of Social Futures* (pp. 203–234). London: Routledge.

Corcoran, F., Demaine, J., Picard, M., Dicaire, L. G., & Taylor, J. (2002, April). Inuit3d: An interactive virtual 3d web exhibition. In *Proceedings of the Conference on Museums and the Web 2002.* Boston, MA: Academic Press.

Corey, C. I., & Wakefield, G. H. (1999). Introduction to head-related transfer functions (HRTFs): Representations of HRTFs in time, frequency, and space. *Audio Engineering Society Convention, 107.*

Correa, A. G., Borba, E. Z., Lopes, R., Zuffo, M. K., Araujo, A., & Kopper, R. (2017, March). User experience evaluation with archaeometry interactive tools in virtual reality environment. In *Proceedings of 3D User Interfaces (3DUI), 2017 IEEE Symposium on* (pp. 217-218). IEEE.

Crawley, C. (2018, April 17). *Augmented reality for good.* Retrieved on August 7, 2018 from https://www.forbes.com/sites/forbescommunicationscouncil/2018/2004/2017/augmented-reality-for-good/#2752c2090abad2011b

Creswell, J. W., & Planoclark, V. (2007). *Designing and Conducting Mixed Methods Research.* London: Sage.

Crosswater. (2017). *VR/360.* Retrieved from https://crosswater.net/

Crown. (2018). *Industrial strategy: Creative industries sector deal.* London: HM Government.

Csikszentmihalyi, M. (1991). *Flow: The psychology of optimal experience* (Vol. 41). New York: Harper Perennial.

Curry, R., Artz, B., Cathey, L., Grant, P., & Greenberg, J. (2002). Kennedy ssq results: fixed-vs motion-based FORD simulators. *Proceedings of DSC.*

Curtis, B., & Curtis, C. (2011). *Social research: A practical introduction.* Thousand Oaks, CA: Sage Publications. doi:10.4135/9781526435415

Dagdelen, M., Reymond, G., Kemeny, A., Bordier, M., & Maizi, N. (2009). Model-based predictive motion cueing strategy for vehicle driving simulators. *Control Engineering Practice, 17*(19), 995–1003. doi:10.1016/j.conengprac.2009.03.002

Dalgarno, B., Hedberg, J., & Harper, B. (2002). *The contribution of 3D environments to conceptual understanding.* Paper presented at the ASCILITE 2002, Auckland, New Zealand.

Dalgarno, B., & Lee, M. J. (2010). What are the learning affordances of 3-D virtual environments? *British Journal of Educational Technology*, *41*(1), 10–32. doi:10.1111/j.1467-8535.2009.01038.x

Daly, J., Kellehear, A., & Gliksman, M. (1997). *The Public Health Researcher: A Methodological Approach*. Melbourne, Australia: Oxford University Press.

Damala, A., Schuchert, T., Rodriguez, I., Moragues, J., Gilleade, K., & Stojanovic, N. (2013). Exploring the affective museum visiting experience: Adaptive augmented reality (a2r) and cultural heritage. *International Journal of Heritage in the Digital Era*, *2*(1), 117–142. doi:10.1260/2047-4970.2.1.117

Damveld, H. J., Wentink, M., van Leeuwen, P. M., & Happee, R. (2012). Effects of motion cueing on curve driving. *Proceedings of the Driving Simulation Conference 2012*.

Das, S. (2018, January 2). 5 tech trends that will rule digital platforms in 2018. *Communication World Magazine*, 1-3.

Davis, F. D. (1989). Perceived usefulness, perceived ease of use and user acceptance of information technology. *Management Information Systems Quarterly*, *13*(3), 319–340. doi:10.2307/249008

Davis, F. D., Bagozzi, P. R., & Warshaw, P. R. (1989). User acceptance of computer technology: A comparison of two theoretical models. *Management Science*, *35*(8), 982–1003. doi:10.1287/mnsc.35.8.982

Day, C., & Leach, R. (2007). The continuing professional development of teachers: Issues of coherence, cohesion and effectiveness. In T. Townsend (Ed.), *International Handbook of School Effectiveness and Improvement* (pp. 707–726). Dordrecht: Springer. doi:10.1007/978-1-4020-5747-2_38

Day, R. E., & Lau, A. J. (2010). Psychoanalysis as Critique in the Works of Freud, Lacan, and Deleuze and Guattari. In G. J. Leckie, L. M. Given, & J. E. Buschman (Eds.), *Critical Theory for Library and Information Science: Exploring the Social from across the Discipline* (pp. 101–119). Santa Barbara, CA: Libraries Unlimited.

de Freitas, S., & Jarvis, S. (2007). Serious games engaging training solutions: A research and development project for supporting training needs. *British Journal of Educational Technology*, *38*(3), 523–525. doi:10.1111/j.1467-8535.2007.00716.x

de Gortari, A. B. O. (2018). Empirical study on game transfer phenomena in a location-based augmented reality game. *Telematics and Informatics*, *35*(2), 382–396. doi:10.1016/j.tele.2017.12.015

de Leo, G., Goodman, K. S., Radici, E., Secrhist, S. R., & Mastaglio, T. W. (2011). Level of presence in team-building activities: Gaming component in virtual environments. *The International Journal of Multimedia & Its Applications*, *3*(2), 1–10. doi:10.5121/ijma.2011.3201

De Lissovoy, N. (2008). Conceptualising oppression in educational theory: Toward a compound standpoint. *Cultural Studies, Critical Methodologies*, *8*(1), 82–105. doi:10.1177/1532708607310794

Decety, J., & Ickes, W. (2011). The Social Neuroscience of Empathy. Cambridge, MA: The MIT Press.

Dede, C. (2004). Enabling distributed-learning communities via emerging technologies. In *Proceedings of the 2004 Conference of the Society for Information Technology in Teacher Education* (pp. 3-12). Charlottesville, VA: American Association for Computers in Education.

Dede, C., Nelson, B., Ketelhut, D. J., Clarke, J., & Bowman, C. (2004). Design-based research strategies for studying situated learning in a multi-user virtual environment. In *Proceedings of the 6th International Conference on Learning Sciences* (pp. 158-165). Santa Monica, CA: International Society of the Learning Sciences.

Deloitte Consulting LLP & Consumer Technology Association. (2018, February 8). *Digital reality. A technical primer.* Deloitte Consulting LLP & Consumer Technology Association. Retrieved on December 8, 2018 from https://www2.deloitte.com/insights/us/en/topics/emerging-technologies/digital-reality-technical-primer.html

deNoyelles, A., & Kyeong-Ju Seo, K. (2012). Inspiring equal contribution and opportunity in a 3D multi- user virtual environment: Bringing together men gamers and women non-gamers in Second Life®. *Computers & Education, 58*(1), 21–29. doi:10.1016/j.compedu.2011.07.007

Deuze, M. (2007, June 1). Convergence culture in the creative industries. *International Journal of Cultural Studies, 10*(2), 243–263. doi:10.1177/1367877907076793

Dewey, J. (1991). Logic: The theory of inquiry. In J. A. Boydston (Ed.), John Dewey: The Later Works, 1925—1953. Carbondale, IL: SIU Press. (Original work published 1938)

Dewey, J. (1991). *The Child and The Curriculum.* Chicago: University of Chicago Press.

Dias, A.-C. (2016, March 21). Expedia takes sick children on thrilling real-time adventures-- without leaving the hospital. *AdAge.* Retrieved on August 3, 2018 from http://adage.com/article/behind-the-work/expedia-takes-sick-children-thrilling-real-time-adventures-leaving-hospital/303218/

Digitized Bunny. (2018). *Brown wooden bunny.* Retrieved from: https://sketchfab.com/models/44ce7f1dfdd94aeaba8ffd5951275598

Digitized Dog. (2018). *Dog.* Retrieved from: https://sketchfab.com/models/39b78840da6147599878b1e63349f1bb

Dijkerman, H. C., & de Haan, E. H. F. (2007). Somatosensory process subserving perception and action. *Behavioral and Brain Sciences, 30*(02), 189–239. doi:10.1017/S0140525X07001392 PMID:17705910

Dionne, S. D., Yammarino, F. J., Atwater, L. E., & Spangler, W. D. (2004). Transformational leadership and team performance. *Journal of Organizational Change Management, 17*(2), 177–193. doi:10.1108/09534810410530601

Dittmer, L. (2004, July/August). Taiwan and the issue of national identity. *Asian Survey, 44*(4), 475–483. doi:10.1525/as.2004.44.4.475

Djindijian, F. (2007). The Virtual Museum: An Introduction. *Archeologia e Calcolatori Supplemento, 1,* 9–14.

DNV. (2011). *Standard for certification of maritime simulator systems No. 2.14.* Retrieved from https://rules.dnvgl.com/docs/pdf/DNV/stdcert/2011-01/Standard2-14.pdf

Dog. (2018). *Brown sitting dog.* Retrieved from: http://archives.algomau.ca/main/node/25489

Dumas, J. S., & Redish, J. (1999). A practical guide to usability testing. Portland, OR: Intellect Books.

Duncan, I. A., Miller, A., & Jiang, S. (2012). A taxonomy of virtual worlds usage in education. *British Journal of Educational Technology, 43*(6), 949–964. doi:10.1111/j.1467-8535.2011.01263.x

Dutton, G. (2013). Is 3-D/virtual training dead? *Training (New York, N.Y.), 50*(5), 38–39.

Ehrsson, H. H. (2012). The concept of body ownership and its relation to multisensory integration. In B. Stein (Ed.), *In The New Handbook of Multisensory Processes* (pp. 775–792). Cambridge, MA: MIT Press.

Eklund, G. (1972). Position sense and state of contraction; the effects of vibration. *Journal of Neurology, Neurosurgery, and Psychiatry, 35*(5), 606–611. doi:10.1136/jnnp.35.5.606

El-Bishouty, M. M., Ogata, H., & Yano, Y. (2008). A Model of Personalized Collaborative Computer Support Ubiquitous Learning Environment. *Proceedings of the 2008 Eighth IEEE International Conference on Advanced Learning Technologies (ICALT08)*, 97-101. 10.1109/ICALT.2008.55

Ellis, J. B., Luther, K., Bessiere, K., & Kellogg, W. A. (2008). Games for virtual team building. In *Proceedings of the 7th ACM Conference on Designing Interactive Systems* (pp. 295-304). ACM. 10.1145/1394445.1394477

eMarketer.com. (2016, December 16). *Mobile Taiwan: A look at a highly mobile market.* Retrieved on December 16, 2018 from https://www.emarketer.com/Article/Mobile-Taiwan-Look-Highly-Mobile-Market/1014877

eMarketer.com. (2016, February 1). *Virtual reality is an immersive medium for marketers.* Retrieved on December 9, 2018 from https://www.emarketer.com/Article/Virtual-Reality-Immersive-Medium-Marketers/1013526

eMarketer.com. (2017, December 4). *Planned change in spending on mobile content among smartphone users worldwide*, by content type, Nov. 2017 (% of respondents).* Retrieved on December 1, 2018 from http://totalaccess.emarketer.com/chart.aspx?r=215051

eMarketer.com. (2018a, April 9). *Chart: Virtual and augmented reality device shipment and sales share worldwide, by device type, 2022 (% of total).* Retrieved on Dec. 1, 2018 from http://totalaccess.emarketer.com/chart.aspx?r=219212

eMarketer.com. (2018b, April 24). *Chart: UK smartphone users who prefer using smart glasses vs. Smartphone for select augmented reality activities, April 2018 (% of respondents).* Retrieved on December 1, 2018 from http://totalaccess.emarketer.com/chart.aspx?r=220210

eMarketer.com. (2018c, April 5). *Industries in which augmented reality users in select countries in Western Europe have used AR, Nov. 2017 (% of respondents).* Retrieved on December 1, 2018 from http://totalaccess.emarketer.com/chart.aspx?r=219349

eMarketer.com. (2018d, November 12). *Ownership of VR headsets among US internet users, July 2014-Aug 2018 (% of respondents).* Retrieved on December 1, 2018 from, http://totalaccess.emarketer.com/chart.aspx?r=224365

eMarketer.com. (2018e, September 7). *Executives in select countries whose companies are experimenting with vs. Implementing AR & VR for industrial use, by country (% of respondents, June 2018).* Retrieved on December 19, 2018 from http://totalaccess.emarketer.com/chart.aspx?r=222816

eMarketer.com. (2018f, April 5). *Usage and awareness of augmented reality among internet users in select countries in Western Europe, Nov 2017 (% of respondents).* Retrieved on December 1, 2018 from http://totalaccess.emarketer.com/chart.aspx?r=219347

eMarketer.com. (2018g, March 13). *Types of content in which marketers in select countries will invest in 2018 (% of respondents).* Retrieved on December 1, 2018 from http://totalaccess.emarketer.com/chart.aspx?r=217368

eMarketer.com. (2018h, September 24). *Which emerging technologies are agencies and brands in Europe using in their marketing strategy? (% of respondents, July 2018).* Retrieved on December 1, 2018 from http://totalaccess.emarketer.com/chart.aspx?r=222826

eMarketer.com. (2018i, March 15). *Demographic profile of us mobile augmented reality users, jan 2018 (% of total).* Retrieved on December 1, 2018 from http://totalaccess.emarketer.com/chart.aspx?r=219053

eMarkter Editors. (2018, April 24). *Marketers' roundtable: Why the healthcare industry is embracing virtual reality and how organizations can get started.* Retrieved on December 1, 2018 from https://content-na2011.emarketer.com/why-the-healthcare-industry-is-embracing-virtual-reality

Emma-Ogbangwo, C., Cope, N., Behringer, R., & Fabri, M. (2014). *Enhancing user immersion and virtual presence in interactive multiuser virtual environments through the development and integration of a gesture-centric natural user interface developed from existing virtual reality technologies.* Paper presented at the International Conference, HCI International 2014. 10.1007/978-3-319-07857-1_72

Entertainment Software Association. (2018). *2018 essential facts about the computer and video game industry.* Retrieved December 2, 2018, from http://www.theesa.com/wp- content/uploads/2018/05/EF2018_FINAL.pdf

Erlandson, B. E., Nelson, B. C., & Savenye, W. C. (2010). Collaboration modality, cognitive load, and science inquiry learning in virtual inquiry environments. *Educational Technology Research and Development, 58*(6), 693–710. doi:10.100711423-010-9152-7

Ernst, M. O., & Bülthoff, H. H. (2004). Merging the senses into a robust percept. *Trends in Cognitive Sciences, 8*(4), 162–169. doi:10.1016/j.tics.2004.02.002 PMID:15050512

Ershow, A. G., Peterson, C. M., Riley, W. T., Rizzo, A. S., & Wansink, B. (2011). Virtual reality technologies for research and education in obesity and diabetes: Research needs and opportunities. *Journal of Diabetes Science and Technology, 5*(2), 212–224. doi:10.1177/193229681100500202 PMID:21527084

Evans, N. J., & Jarvis, P. A. (1980). Group cohesion: A review and reevaluation. *Small Group Behavior, 11*(4), 359–370. doi:10.1177/104649648001100401

Eysel-Gosepath, K., McCrum, C., Epro, G., Brüggemann, G. P., & Karamanidis, K. (2016). Visual and proprioceptive contributions to postural control of upright stance in unilateral vestibulopathy. *Somatosensory & Motor Research, 33*(2), 72–78. doi:10.1080/08990220.2016.1178635 PMID:27166786

Fabola, A., Miller, A., & Fawcett, R. (2015, September). Exploring the past with Google Cardboard. In *Digital Heritage, 2015* (Vol. 1, pp. 277–284). IEEE. doi:10.1109/DigitalHeritage.2015.7413882

Facebook TechnologiesL. L. C. (2018). Retrieved https://www.oculus.com/quest/

Fadel, C. (2008). *Multimodal Learning Through Media: What the Research Says.* San Jose, CA: Cisco Systems.

Fang, T. Y., Wang, P. C., Liu, C. H., Su, M. C., & Yeh, S. C. (2014). Evaluation of a haptics-based virtual reality temporal bone simulator for anatomy and surgery training. *Computer Methods and Programs in Biomedicine, 113*(2), 674–681. doi:10.1016/j.cmpb.2013.11.005 PMID:24280627

Fee, K. (2007). *Delivering E-Learning.* London: Kogan Page Limited.

Fernandez-Palacios, B. J., Morabito, D., & Remondino, F. (2017). Access to complex reality-based 3D models using virtual reality solutions. *Journal of Cultural Heritage, 23*, 40–48. doi:10.1016/j.culher.2016.09.003

Fibrum Limited. (2017). *Fibrum VR.* Retrieved from https://fibrum.com/

FIBRUM. (2017a, April 11). Froggy VR. Google PlayStore.

FIBRUM. (2017b, May 17). Zombie Shooter VR. Google PlayStore.

Filipczuk, P., & Nikiel, S. (2008). *Real-time simulation of a sailboat.* Paper presented at the Human System Interactions, 2008 Conference. 10.1109/HSI.2008.4581575

Fink, C. (2017, December 13). Why consumer adoption of VR and AR will be slow. *Forbes.* Retrieved on December 8, 2018 from https://www.forbes.com/sites/charliefink/2017/2012/2013/why-consumer-adoption-of-vr-ar-will-be-slow/#2011f2783f28359f

Fischer, M., Seefried, A., & Seehof, C. (2016). Objective motion cueing test for driving simulators. *Proceedings of the DSC 2016 Europe*, 41-50.

Fleming, D. (2005). *Managing change in museums.* Paper presented at the Museum and Change International Conference, Prague, Czech Republic.

Fogel, V. A., Miltenberger, R. G., Graves, R., & Koehler, S. (2010). The effects of exergaming on physical activity among inactive children in a physical education classroom. *Journal of Applied Behavior Analysis, 43*(4), 591–600. doi:10.1901/jaba.2010.43-591 PMID:21541146

Fokides, E. (2017). A model for explaining primary school students' learning outcomes when they use multi-user virtual environments. *Journal of Computers in Education, 4*(3), 225–250. doi:10.100740692-017-0080-y

Foley, B., & Kobaissi, A. (2006). *Using virtual chat to study in informal learning in online environments.* In The Annual Meeting of the American Educational Research Association, San Francisco, CA.

Forbes, T., Kinnell, P., & Goh, M. (2018, August 17). *A study into the influence of visual prototyping methods and immersive technologies on the perception of abstract product properties.* Paper presented at the NordDesign: Design in the Era of Digitalization, NordDesign 2018.

Fowler, C. (2015). Virtual reality and learning: Where is the pedagogy? *British Journal of Educational Technology, 46*(2), 412–422. doi:10.1111/bjet.12135

Frank, L. H., Casali, J. G., & Wierwille, W. W. (1988). Effects of visual display and motion system delays on operator performance and uneasiness in a driving simulator. *Human Factors, 30*(2), 201–217. doi:10.1177/001872088803000207 PMID:3384446

Freina, L., & Canessa, A. (2015). Immersive vs desktop virtual reality in game based learning. In *9th European Conference on Games Based Learning: ECGBL2015.* Steinkjer, Norway: Academic Conferences and Publishing Limited.

Freina, L., & Ott, M. (2015). A literature review on immersive virtual reality in education: state of the art and perspectives. *eLearning & Software for Education*, (1). Retrieved from https://www.ceeol.com/search/article-detail?id=289829

Frog. (2017). *Frog – small artifact series.* Retrieved from: http://archives.algomau.ca/main/node/25494

Fung, A. (2016). Strategizing for creative industries in China: Contradictions and tension in nation branding. *International Journal of Communication, 10*, 3004–3021.

Gagliordi, N. (2017, March 16). VR, AR headset shipments will increase tenfold by 2021: IDC. *ZDNet.* Retrieved on December 1, 2018 from https://www.zdnet.com/article/vr-ar-headset-shipments-will-increase-tenfold-by-2021-idc/

Gaitatzes, A., Christopoulos, D., & Roussou, M. (2001, November). Reviving the past: cultural heritage meets virtual reality. In *Proceedings of the 2001 conference on Virtual reality, archeology, and cultural heritage* (pp. 103-110). ACM. 10.1145/584993.585011

Gallego, M. D., Bueno, S., & Noyes, J. (2015). Second Life adoption in education: A motivational model based on uses and gratifications theory. *Computers & Education, 100*, 81–93. doi:10.1016/j.compedu.2016.05.001

Game Cooks (2017, June 20). Vindicta. Game Cooks.

Gamification in eLearning. (2015). Retrieved from Litmos: https://www.litmos.com/lp/gamification-elearning/

Gao, Z., Podlog, L., & Lee, J. (2014). Children's situational motivation, rate of perceived exertion and physical activity levels in exergaming: Associations and gender differences. In J. Graham (Ed.), *Video games: Parents' perceptions, role of social media and effects on behavior* (pp. 17–28). Hauppauge, NY: Nova Science Publishers.

Garcia-Ruiz, M. A., Santana-Mancilla, P. C., & Gaytan-Lugo, L. S. (2016). measuring technology acceptance of makey makey as an input device in a human-computer interaction class. In *Proceedings of EdMedia 2016: World Conference on Educational Media and Technology*. Association for the Advancement of Computing in Education.

Garcia-Ruiz, M. A., Santana-Mancilla, P. C., & Gaytan-Lugo, L. S. (2017). A usability study on low-cost virtual reality technology for visualizing digitized Canadian cultural objects: Implications in education. In *Proceedings of EdMedia 2017: World Conference on Educational Media and Technology*. Association for the Advancement of Computing in Education.

Gardner, K. (2016). *Virtual reality storytelling: How is virtual reality (VR) changing the future of storytelling? TEDxPrincetonU*. Princeton, NJ: TEDx. Retrieved November 2016, from https://www.youtube.com/watch?v=7LNEkmcR4BM&t=2s

Garrett, N. J. I., & Best, M. C. (2010). Driving simulator motion cueing algorithms – A survey of the state of the art. *Proceedings of the 10th International Symposium on Advanced Vehicle Control (AVEC)*.

Garrison, D. R. (2009). Communities of inquiry in online learning. In P. L. Rogers (Ed.), *Encyclopedia of distance learning* (2nd ed.; pp. 352–355). Hershey, PA: IGI Global. doi:10.4018/978-1-60566-198-8.ch052

Gaudiosi, J. (2015, April 25). How augmented reality and virtual reality will generate $150 billion in revenue by 2020. *Fortune*. Retrieved on December 23, 2017 from http://fortune.com/2015/2004/2025/augmented-reality-virtual-reality/

GearBrain(GB). (2018, June 4). The 5 best museum AR/VR experiences this summer. *GearBrain (GB)*. Retrieved on December 15, 2018 from https://www.gearbrain.com/virtual-reality-museum-art-summer-2577767924.html

Gee, J. (2008). Learning and Games. In K. Salen (Ed.), *The ecology of games: Connecting youth, games, and learning* (pp. 21–40). Cambridge, MA: The MIT Press.

Geng, J. (2013). Three-dimensional display technologies. *Advances in Optics and Photonics*, *5*(4), 456–535. doi:10.1364/AOP.5.000456 PMID:25530827

Genome Island in Second Life. (n.d.). Retrieved from http://maps.secondlife.com/secondlife/Genome/128/128/48

Giardina, C. (2017, September 6). Tux? Check. Virtual reality goggles? Got 'em. *The Hollywood Reporter*, p. 70.

Gilbert, R. L., Murphy, N. A., & Avalos, M. C. (2011). Communication patterns and satisfaction levels in three-dimensional versus real-life intimate relationships. *Cyberpsychology, Behavior, and Social Networking*, *14*(10), 585–589. doi:10.1089/cyber.2010.0468 PMID:21381970

Gimp. (2018). Retrieved from: https://www.gimp.org/

Ginns, P., & Barrie, S. (2004). Reliability of single-item ratings of quality in higher education: A replication. *Psychological Reports*, *95*(3), 1023–1030. doi:10.2466/pr0.95.3.1023-1030 PMID:15666951

Girvan, C., & Savage, T. (2013). Guidelines for conducting text based interviews in virtual worlds. In Understanding learning in virtual worlds (pp. 21-40). London, UK: Springer-Verlag. doi:10.1007/978-1-4471-5370-2_2

Gomes, L., Bellon, O. R. P., & Silva, L. (2014). 3D reconstruction methods for digital preservation of cultural heritage: A survey. *Pattern Recognition Letters*, *50*, 3–14. doi:10.1016/j.patrec.2014.03.023

Gonizzi Barsanti, S., Caruso, G., Micoli, L. L., Covarrubias Rodriguez, M., & Guidi, G. (2015). 3D visualization of cultural heritage artifacts with virtual reality devices. In *25th International CIPA Symposium 2015* (*Vol. 40*, No. 5W7, pp. 165-172). Copernicus Gesellschaft mbH.

Goodman, K. (2016). *Ethical considerations in the use of virtual reality*. Paper presented at the Home Ethics in Investigational & Interventional Uses of Immersive Virtual Reality (e3iVR).

Goodman, R., & Tremblay, L. (2018). Using proprioception to control ongoing actions: Dominance of vision or altered proprioceptive weighing? *Experimental Brain Research*, *236*(7), 1–14. doi:10.100700221-018-5258-7 PMID:29696313

Google. (2014). Retrieved from Google Cardboard: https://vr.google.com/cardboard/

Google. (2017). *Painting from a New Perspective*. Retrieved October 2017, from Tilt Brush by Google: https://www.tiltbrush.com/

Gopher, D., & Braune, R. (1984). On the psychophysics of workload: Why bother with subjective measures? *Human Factors*, *26*(5), 519–532. doi:10.1177/001872088402600504

Gouverneur, B., Mulder, J. A., van Paassen, M. M., Stroosma, O., & Field, E. J. (2003). *Optimisation of the Simona research simulator's motion filter settings for handling qualities experiments*. Paper presented at the AIAA Modeling and Simulation Technologies Conference and Exhibit, Austin, TX. 10.2514/6.2003-5679

Grant, P. R. (1996). *The development of a tuning paradigm for flight simulator motion drive algorithms (Ph.D)*. Toronto, ON, Canada: University of Toronto.

Grant, P. R., & Reid, L. D. (1997a). Motion washout filter tuning: Rules and requirements. *Journal of Aircraft*, *34*(2), 145–151. doi:10.2514/2.2158

Grant, P. R., & Reid, L. D. (1997b). PROTEST: An expert system for tuning simulator washout filters. *Journal of Aircraft*, *34*(2), 152–159. doi:10.2514/2.2166

Grant, P. R., Yam, B., Hosman, R., & Schroeder, J. A. (2006). Effect of simulator motion on pilot behavior and perception. *Journal of Aircraft*, *43*(6), 1914–1924. doi:10.2514/1.21900

Green-Hamann, S., Campbell Eichhorn, K., & Sherblom, J. C. (2011). An exploration of why people participate in Second Life social support groups. *Journal of Computer-Mediated Communication*, *16*(4), 465–491. doi:10.1111/j.1083-6101.2011.01543.x

Green, L. S., Banas, J. R., & Perkins, R. A. (2017). *The Flipped College Classroom Conceptualized and Re-conceptualized*. Springer International Publishing. doi:10.1007/978-3-319-41855-1

Groen, E. L., & Bles, W. (2004). How to use body tilt for the simulation of linear self motion. *Journal of Vestibular Research*, *14*(5), 375–385. PMID:15598992

Grubb, J. (2015, July 10). 7 factors that will make virtual reality and augmented reality worth $150b. *VB*. Retrieved on December 8, 2018 from https://venturebeat.com/2015/2007/2010/2017-factors-that-will-make-virtual-reality-and-augmented-reality-worth-2150b/

Guarnieri, A., Remondino, F., & Vettore, A. (2006). Digital photogrammetry and TLS data fusion applied to Cultural Heritage 3D modeling. *The International Archives of the Photogrammetry, Remote Sensing and Spatial Information Sciences*, *36*(5). Retrieved from http://3dom.fbk.eu/sites/3dom.fbk.eu/files/pdf/Guarnieri_etal_ISPRSV06.pdf

Gunkel, D., & Hawhee, D. (2003). Virtual alterity and the reformating of ethics. *Journal of Mass Media Ethics*, *18*(3&4), 173–193. doi:10.1207/S15327728JMME1803&4_3

Hai-Jew, S. (2012). Addressing the "commitment problem": Driving long-term persistent. In S. L. Hai-Jew (Ed.), *Constructing self-discovery learning spaces online: Scaffolding and decision making technologies* (1st ed.). Hershey, PA: IGI Global. doi:10.4018/978-1-61350-320-1.ch013

Hallgren, K. A. (2012). Computing inter-rater reliability for observational data: An overview and tutorial. *Tutorials in Quantitative Methods for Psychology*, *8*(1), 23–24. doi:10.20982/tqmp.08.1.p023 PMID:22833776

Hall, J. R. (1989). *The need for platform motion in modern piloted flight training simulators (Vol. FM35)*. Bedford, UK: Royal Aerospace Establishment.

Hamari, J., Shernoff, D. J., Rowe, E., Coller, B., Asbell-Clarke, J., & Edwards, T. (2016). Challenging games help students learn: An empirical study on engagement, flow and immersion in game- based learning. *Computers in Human Behavior*, *54*, 170–179. doi:10.1016/j.chb.2015.07.045

Hamby, A., & Bringberg, D. (2018, Summer). Cause-related marketing persuasion knowledge: Measuring consumers' knowledge and ability to interpret CRM promotions. *The Journal of Consumer Affairs*, 373-392. doi:10.1111/joca.12167

Hansen, M. (2008). Versatile, immersive, creative and dynamic virtual 3-D healthcare learning environments: A review of the literature. *Journal of Medical Internet Research*, *10*(3), e26. doi:10.2196/jmir.1051 PMID:18762473

Harel, I. E., & Papert, S. E. (1991). *Constructionism*. Ablex Publishing.

Harmony Studios Limited. (2018). *VR Sickness: What it is and how to stop it*. Retrieved from https://www.harmony.co.uk/vr-motion-sickness/

Hassett, D. D., & Curwood, J. S. (2009). Theories and practices of multimodal education: Semiotics and the instructional dynamics of new literacies. Presented at the *American Education Research Association conference*, San Diego, CA.

Hayes, D., Mills, M., Christie, P., & Lingard, B. (2006). *Teachers and Schooling Making a Difference*. Crows Nest, New South Wales: Allen & Unwin.

Hays, R. T., Jacobs, J. W., Prince, C., & Salas, E. (1992). *Flight simulator training effectiveness: A meta-analysis*. Mahwah, NJ: Lawrence Erlbaum.

Heim, M. (1998). *Virtual realism*. New York: Oxford University Press.

Heine, C., & Kapko, M. (2017, August 20). Facebook and apple are about to take AR mainstream. Here's how marketers are gearing up. *AdWeek*. Retrieved on November 15, 2017 from http://www.adweek.com/digital/facebook-and-apple-are-about-to-take-ar-mainstream-heres-how-marketers-are-gearing-up/

Heinich, R., Molenda, M., Russell, J. D., & Smaldino, S. E. (2002). *Instructional Media and Technologies for Learning*. Upper Saddle River, NJ: Pearson Education.

Herold, B., & Molnar, M. (2018). Virtual reality for learning raises high hopes and serious concerns. *Education Week*, *37*(20), 10.

Herrington, J., Oliver, R., & Reeves, T. C. (2003). Patterns of engagement in authentic online learning environments. *Australasian Journal of Educational Technology*, *19*(1), 59–71. doi:10.14742/ajet.1701

Herschman, N. (2017, October 23). How AR/VR can create a "wow" experience at retail. *TWICE*, p. 14.

Hesmondhalgh, D. (2002). *The cultural industries*. London: Sage.

Higgins, S. (2003). *Does ICT improve learning and teaching in schools?* Newcastle University.

Higham, W. (2018). 10 consumer trends to watch in 2018. *Director*, 9–10.

Hilken, T., Ruyter, K. D., Chylinski, M., Mahr, D., & Keeling, D. I. (2017). Augmenting the eye of the beholder: Exploring the strategic potential of augmented reality to enhance online service experiences. *Journal of the Academy of Marketing Science*, *45*(6), 884–905. doi:10.100711747-017-0541-x

Hill, S. (2005). *Mapping Multiliteracies: Children of the New Millennium Report of the Research Project 2002–2004*. University of South Australia and South Australian Department of Education and Children's Services.

Hirzy, E. C. (1996). *True Needs, True Partners: Museums and Schools Transforming Education*. Washington, DC: Institute of Museum Services.

Ho, C. M. L., Nelson, M. E., & Müeller-Wittig, W. (2011). Design and implementation of a student-generated virtual museum in a language curriculum to enhance collaborative multimodal meaning-making. *Computers & Education, 57*(1), 1083–1097. doi:10.1016/j.compedu.2010.12.003

Ho, C. M. L., Rappa, N. A., & Chee, Y. S. (2009). Designing and implementing virtual enactive role-play and structured argumentation: Promises and pitfalls. *Computer Assisted Language Learning, 22*(5), 381–408. doi:10.1080/09588220903184732

Holger, D. (2016, September 27). Report: VR adoption rates significantly jump in 2017. *VR Scout*. Retrieved on December 8, 2018 from https://vrscout.com/news/report-vr-adoption-rates-2017/

Hollins, P., & Robbins, S. (2018). The educational affordances of multi user virtual environments. In D. Heider (Ed.), *Living virtually: Researching new worlds*. New York: Peter Lang Publishing.

Horsfield, P. (2003). Continuities and discontinuities in ethical reflections on digital virtual reality. *Journal of Mass Media Ethics, 19*(3&4), 155–172. doi:10.1207/S15327728JMME1803&4_2

Hosman, R. (1999). *Are criteria for motion cueing and time delays possible?* Paper presented at the AIAA Modeling and Simulation Technologies Conference, Portland, OR. 10.2514/6.1999-4028

Hosman, R., & Advani, S. (2013). *Are criteria for motion cueing and time delays possible? Part 2*. Paper presented at the AIAA Modeling and Simulation Technologies Conference, Boston, MA. 10.2514/6.2013-4833

Hosman, R., Advani, S., & Haeck, N. (2002). *Integrated design of flight simulator motion cueing systems*. Paper presented at the Royal Aeronautical Society Conference on Flight Simulation, London, UK.

Hosman, R., & Advani, S. (2012). Status of the ICAO Objective Motion Cueing Test. *New Frontiers Conference Proceedings*.

Hosman, R., & Advani, S. (2016). Design and evaluation of the objective motion cueing test and criterion. *Aeronautical Journal, 120*(1227), 873–891. doi:10.1017/aer.2016.35

Hostetter, C., & Busch, M. (2013). Community matters: Social presence and learning outcomes. *The Journal of Scholarship of Teaching and Learning, 13*(1), 77–86.

Howell, D. R., Osternig, L. R., & Chou, L. S. (2015). Return to activity after concussion affects dual-task gait balance control recovery. *Medicine and Science in Sports and Exercise, 47*(4), 673–680. doi:10.1249/MSS.0000000000000462 PMID:25100340

Howell, D., Osternig, L., & Chou, L. (2015). Monitoring recovery of gait balance control following concussion using an accelerometer. *Journal of Biomechanics, 48*(12), 3364–3368. doi:10.1016/j.jbiomech.2015.06.014 PMID:26152463

Hsu, W.-Y. (2017). Brain-computer interface connected to telemedicine and telecommunication in virtual reality applications. *Telematics and Informatics, 34*(4), 224–238. doi:10.1016/j.tele.2016.01.003

Huang, H.-M., Rauch, U., & Liaw, S.-S. (2010). Investigating learners' attitudes toward virtual reality learning environments: Based on a constructivist approach. *Computers & Education, 55*(3), 1171–1182. doi:10.1016/j.compedu.2010.05.014

Huang, T.-L., & Liao, S. (2015). A model of acceptance of augmented-reality interactive technology: The moderating role of cognitive innovativeness. *Electronic Commerce Research*, *15*(2), 268–295. doi:10.100710660-014-9163-2

Huff, N., Hernandez, J. A., Fecteau, M., Zielinski, D., Brady, R., & LaBar, K. S. (2011). Revealing context-specific conditioned fear memories with full immersion virtual reality. *Frontiers in Behavioral Neuroscience*, *5*(75). doi:10.3389/fnbeh.2011.00075 PMID:22069384

Hwang, G. J., Wu, C. H., Tseng, J. C. R., & Huang, I. (2011). Development of a ubiquitous learning platform based on a real-time help-seeking mechanism. *British Journal of Educational Technology*, *42*(6), 992–1002. doi:10.1111/j.1467-8535.2010.01123.x

ICAO. (2009). Manual of criteria for the qualification of flight simulation training devices: Vol. 1. Aeroplanes (3rd ed.). International Civil Aviation Organization.

id Software. (2017, December 1). Doom VFR. Bethesda Softworks.

IDC. (2017, February 27). *Worldwide spending on augmented and virtual reality forecast to reach $13.9 billion in 2017, according to IDC*. Retrieved on November 19, 2017 from https://www.idc.com/getdoc.jsp?containerId=prUS42331217)

IKEA. (2017, September 12). *IKEA launches Ikea place, a new app that allows people to virtually place furniture in their home*. Retrieved on December 12, 2018 from https://www.ikea.com/us/en/about_ikea/newsitem/091217_IKEA_Launches_IKEA_Place

Impulse Gear. (2017, May 16). Farpoint. Sony Interactive Entertainment.

Infinadeck. (2017). *Infinadeck, the world's first true commercially viable omnidirectional treadmill*. Retrieved 01/10/2018, 2018, from http://www.infinadeck.com/

Inman, C. (2010). *Pre-service teachers in Second Life: Are digital natives prepared for a Web 2.0 experience?* (Doctoral Dissertation). Retrieved from ProQuest Dissertation Database.

International Data Corporation (IDC). (2018, September 20). *AR/VR headset shipments worldwide, commercial vs. Consumer, 2018 & 2022 (millions and CAGR)*. Retrieved on December 1, 2018 from http://totalaccess.emarketer.com/chart.aspx?r=222930

Iyer, B. (2015, December). Augmented-reality gallery enhances Singapore sights. *Campaign Asia-Pacific*, p. 31.

Jacobs, J. W., Prince, C., Hays, R. T., & Salas, E. (1990). *A meta-analysis of the flight simulator training research*. Orlando, FL: Naval Training Systems Center. doi:10.21236/ADA228733

Janeh, O., Langbehn, E., Steinicke, F., Bruder, G., Gulberti, A., & Poetter-Nerger, M. (2017). Walking in Virtual Reality: Effects of manipulated visual self-Motion on walking biomechanics. *ACM Transactions on Applied Perception*, *14*(2), 12. doi:10.1145/3022731

Jarmon, L., Traphagan, T., Mayrath, M., & Trivedi, A. (2009). Virtual world teaching, experiential learning, and assessment: An interdisciplinary communication course in Second Life. *Computers & Education*, *53*(1), 169–182. doi:10.1016/j.compedu.2009.01.010

Jarrier, E., & Bourgeon-Renault, D. (2012, Fall). Impact of mediation devices on the museum visit experience and on visitors' behavioural intentions. *International Journal of Arts Management*, *15*(1), 18–29.

Javornik, A. (2016). Augmented reality: Research agenda for studying the impact of its media characteristics on consumer behaviour. *Journal of Retailing and Consumer Services*, *30*, 252–261. doi:10.1016/j.jretconser.2016.02.004

Jerald, J. (2015). *The VR Book: Human-Centered Design for Virtual Reality* (T. Ozsu, Ed.). New York, NY: ACM Books. doi:10.1145/2792790

Jewitt, C., & Kress, G. (Eds.). (2003). *Multimodal Literacy*. New York: Peter Lang.

Johansson, A. (2018, June). 9 ethical problems with VR we still have to solve. *TNW.* Retrieved on December 10, 2018 from https://thenextweb.com/contributors/2018/2004/2018/2019-ethical-problems-vr-still-solve/

Johnson, B. (2018, May). The new reality. Augmented and virtual reality offer new ways to engage with customers. *SCT,* 80-82.

Johnson, L. (2017a, November 15). This horror movies campaign shows how VR can affect your body. *AdWeek.* Retrieved on November 15, 2017 from http://www.adweek.com/digital/this-horror-movies-campaign-shows-how-vr-can-affect-your-body/

Johnson, L. (2017b, July 26). Why brands like L'Oréal and Acura are betting big on augmented reality. *AdWeek.* Retrieved on November 15, 2017 from http://www.adweek.com/digital/why-brands-like-loreal-and-acura-are-betting-big-on-augmented-reality/

Johnson, L. (2017c, November 15). This horror movies campaign shows how VR can affect your body. *AdWeek.* Retrieved on November 15, 2017 from http://www.adweek.com/digital/this-horror-movies-campaign-shows-how-vr-can-affect-your-body/

Johnson, L. (2017d, June 23). Björk's real-time music video wins digital craft grand prix for breaking new ground with VR. *AdWeek.* Retrieved on November 15, 2017 from http://www.adweek.com/digital/bjorks-real-time-music-video-wins-digital-craft-grand-prix-for-breaking-new-ground-with-vr/

Johnson, J. (2011). *Second Life's future in education (Ph.D.).* Capella University.

Jones, B. (2017). *To raise teaching standards we must first improve the use of technology in the classroom.* Retrieved October, 2017, from The Telegraph Education section: http://www.telegraph.co.uk/education/2017/02/01/raise-teaching-standards-must-first- improve-use-technology-classroom/

Jones, G., & Christal, M. (2002). *The future of virtual museums: On-line, immersive, 3D environments.* Created Realities Group. Retrieved from: http://w.created-realities.com/pdf/Virtual_Museums.pdf

Jonsson, E., Seiger, Å., & Hirschfeld, H. (2004). One-leg stance in healthy young and elderly adults: A measure of postural steadiness? *Clinical Biomechanics (Bristol, Avon), 19*(7), 688–694. doi:10.1016/j.clinbiomech.2004.04.002 PMID:15288454

Kalantzis, M., & Cope, B. (2005). *Learning by Design.* Melbourne, VIC: Victorian Schools Innovation Commission and Common Ground.

Kalantzis, M., & Cope, B. (2012). *Literacies.* Cambridge, UK: Cambridge University Press. doi:10.1017/CBO9781139196581

Kalantzis, M., Cope, B., & Harvey, A. (2003). Assessing multiliteracies and the new basics. *Assessment in Education: Principles, Policy & Practice, 10*(1), 15–26. doi:10.1080/09695940301692

Kang, J. (2018, January). Virtual reality interfaces for interacting with three-dimensional graphs. *Wireless Personal Communications, 98*(2), 1931–1940. doi:10.100711277-017-4954-0

Kang, S., Norooz, L., Oguamanam, V., Plane, A. C., Clegg, T. L., & Froehlich, J. E. (2016). SharedPhys: Live physiological sensing, whole-body interaction, and large-screen visualizations to support shared inquiry experiences. In *Proceedings of the 15th International Conference on Interaction Design and Children* (pp. 275-287). ACM. 10.1145/2930674.2930710

Kapuire, G. K., Winschiers-Theophilus, H., Stanley, C., Maasz, D., Chamunorwa, M., Møller, R. H., & Gonzalez-Cabrero, D. (2017). Technologies to promote the inclusion of Indigenous knowledge holders in digital cultural heritage preservation. *International Conference on Culture & Computer Science*.

Karp, C. (2014). Digital Heritage in Digital Museums. *Museum*, *66*(1-4), 157–162. doi:10.1111/muse.12069

Kassaye, W. W. (2007). Virtual reality as source of advertising. *Journal of Website Promotion*, *2*(3/4), 103–124. doi:10.1080/15533610802174979

Kearsley, G., & Shneiderman, B. (1998). Engagement theory: A framework for technology-based teaching and learning. *Educational Technology*, *38*(5), 20–23.

Keeler, C. (2009). *Educational Virtual Museums Developed Using PowerPoint*. Retrieved July 14, 2016 from http://christykeeler.com/EducationalVirtualMuseums.html

Kellough, R. D., & Kellough, N. G. (2008). *Teaching Young Adolescents: Methods and Resources for Middle Grades Teaching* (5th ed.). Upper Saddle River, NJ: Pearson Merrill Prentice Hall.

Kendzierski, D., & DeCarlo, K. J. (1991). Physical activity enjoyment scale: Two validation studies. *Journal of Sport & Exercise Psychology*, *13*(1), 50–64. doi:10.1123/jsep.13.1.50

Kenny, L., Hattersley, C., Molins, B., Buckley, C., Povey, C., & Pellicano, E. (2015). Which terms should be used to describe autism? Perspectives from the UK autism community. *Autism*, *20*(4), 442–462. doi:10.1177/1362361315588200 PMID:26134030

Kerrebroeck, H. V., Brengman, M., & Willems, K. (2017). Escaping the crowd: An experimental study on the impact of a virtual reality experience in a shopping mall. *Computers in Human Behavior*, *77*, 437–450. doi:10.1016/j.chb.2017.07.019

Keshner, E. A., & Fung, J. (2017). The quest to apply VR technology to rehabilitation: Tribulations and treasures. *Journal of Vestibular Research: Equilibrium and Orientation*, *27*(1), 1–5. doi:10.3233/VES-170610 PMID:28387695

Ketelhut, D. J., & Nelson, B. C. (2016). Blending formal and informal learning environments: The case of SAVE science. In *Proceedings of the 10th European Conference on Games Based Learning, ECGBL 2016* (pp. 314-318). Dechema e.V.

Ketelhut, D. J., Nelson, B. C., Clarke, J., & Dede, C. (2010). A multi-user virtual environment for building and assessing higher order inquiry skills in science. *British Journal of Educational Technology*, *41*(1), 56–68. doi:10.1111/j.1467-8535.2009.01036.x

Kim, G., & Biocca, F. (2018, July 15-20). *Immersion in virtual reality can increase exercise motivation and physical performance*. Paper presented at the Virtual, Augmented and Mixed Reality: Applications in Health, Cultural Heritage, and Industry - 10th International Conference, VAMR 2018, Held as Part of HCI International 2018. 10.1007/978-3-319-91584-5_8

Kim, J., Lee, J., & Kim, S. (2017). The efficacy of cause-related marketing within a social network: The effects of congruency, corporate credibility, familiarity of cause brands, and perceived altruistic motive. *Journal of Marketing Communications*, *23*(5), 429-455. doi:10.1080/13527

Kim, K., Rosenthal, Z., Zielinski, D., & Brady, R. (2014). Effects of virtual environment platforms on emotional responses. *Computer Methods and Programs in Biomedicine*, *113*(3), 882–893. doi:10.1016/j.cmpb.2013.12.024 PMID:24440136

Kim, N., Phan, A. H., Erdenebat, M. U., Alam, A., Kwon, K. C., Piao, M. L., & Lee, J. H. (2013). 3D Display Technology. *Display and Imaging*, *1*, 73–95.

Kimpston, R. R., & Rogers, K. B. (1986). *A Framework for Curriculum Research*. Ontario Institute For Studies In Education/University of Toronto. Retrieved November 10, 2016, from Http://Www.Jstor.Org/Stable/1179432

Kirkwood, A. (2015, June). Teaching and learning with technology in higher education: blended and distance education needs "joined-up thinking" rather than technological determinism. *Open Learning: The Journal of Open, Distance and e-Learning*, 1–16.

Kiyokawa, K. (2007). An Introduction to Head Mounted Display for Augmented Reality. In M. Haller, M. Billinghurst, & B. Thomas (Eds.), *Emerging Technologies of Augmented Reality: Interfaces and Design* (pp. 43–63). Hershey, PA: Idea Group Publishing. doi:10.4018/978-1-59904-066-0.ch003

Klie, L. (2016, December 1). Virtual reality to become a true reality. *Destination CRM*. Retrieved on August 3, 2018 from https://www.destinationcrm.com/Articles/ReadArticle.aspx?ArticleID=115061

Klüver, M., Herrigel, C., Preuß, S., Schöner, H. P., & Hecht, H. (2015). Comparing the incidence of simulator sickness in five different driving simulators. *Proceedings of Driving Simulation Conference*.

Kolasinski, E. M. (1995). *Simulator sickness in virtual environments*. Technical Report 1027. U.S. Army Research Institute for Behavioral and Social Sciences.

Kolb, D. A. (1984). *Experiential Learning: Experience as the Source of Learning And Development*. Prentice-Hall.

Konetes, G. D. (2010). The function of intrinsic and extrinsic motivation in educational virtual games and simulations. *Journal of Emerging Technologies in Web Intelligence*, 2(1), 23–26. doi:10.4304/jetwi.2.1.23-26

Konstantinidis, A., Thrasyvoulos, T., Theodouli, T., & Pomportsis, A. (2010). Fostering collaborative learning in Second Life: Metaphors and affordances. *Computers & Education*, 55(2), 603–615. doi:10.1016/j.compedu.2010.02.021

Kress, G. R., & Van Leeuween, T. (1996). Reading images: The Grammar of Visual Design. New York: Routledge.

Kress, G. (1999). "English" at the crossroads: Rethinking curricula of communication in the context of the turn to the visual. In G. E. Hawisher & C. L. Selfe (Eds.), *Passions, Pedagogies, and 21ˢᵗ Century Technologies* (pp. 66–88). Logan, UT: Utah State University. doi:10.2307/j.ctt46nrfk.7

Kress, G. (2003). *Literacy in the New Media Age*. London: Routledge.

Kress, G. (2009). What is a mode? In C. Jewitt (Ed.), *The Routledge Handbook of Multimodal Analysis* (pp. 54–67). Abingdon, UK: Routledge.

Kress, G. (2010). *Multimodality: A Social Semiotic Approach to Contemporary Communication*. London: Routledge.

Kroes, M., Dunsmoor, J., Mackey, W., McClay, M., & Phelps, E. (2017). Context conditioning in humans using commercially available immersive Virtual Reality. *Scientific Reports*, 7(1), 8640. doi:10.103841598-017-08184-7 PMID:28819155

Küçük, S. (Ed.). (2012). *Serial and parallel robot manipulators - Kinematics, dynamics, control and optimization*. London, UK: InTech. doi:10.5772/2301

Kuhn, D., Black, J. B., Kesselman, A., & Kaplan, D. (2000). The development of cognitive skills to support inquiry learning. *Cognition and Instruction*, 18(4), 495–523. doi:10.1207/S1532690XCI1804_3

Kuo, A., & Rice, D. H. (2015). The impact of perceptual congruence on the effectiveness of cause-related marketing campaigns. *Journal of Consumer Psychology*, 25(1), 78–88. doi:10.1016/j.jcps.2014.06.002

Kuusela, H., & Paul, P. (2000). A comparison of concurrent and retrospective verbal protocol analysis. *The American Journal of Psychology*, 113(3), 387–404. doi:10.2307/1423365 PMID:10997234

Kyriacou, C. (2009). *Effective teaching in schools. Theory and practice*. Stanley Thornes Publishers Ltd.

Lafayette, J. (2017, October 16). Toyota revs up virtual reality efforts by sponsoring discovery's TRVLR. *Broadcasting & Cable*, p. 46.

Lajoie, Y., Teasdale, N., Bard, C., & Fleury, M. (1993). Attentional demands for static and dynamic equilibrium. *Experimental Brain Research*, *97*(1), 139–144. doi:10.1007/BF00228824 PMID:8131825

Lakento. (2018, October 18). House of Terror VR 360 Cardboard Horror Game. Google PlayStore.

Laker, S. R. (2015). Sports-Related Concussion. *Concussion and Head Injury*, *19*(41), 8–11. PMID:26122533

Lambert, J. L., & Fisher, J. L. (2013). Community of inquiry framework: Establishing community in an online course. *Journal of Interactive Online Learning*, *12*(1), 1–16.

Laposky, J. (2017, August 21). A virtual reality data crunch is coming. *Twice,* p. 8.

Lee, D., & Aronson, E. (1974). Visual propriceptive control of standing in human infants. *Perception & Psychophysics*, *15*(3), 529–532. doi:10.3758/BF03199297

Lee, D., & Lishman, L. (1977). Vision - the most efficient source of proprioceptive information for balance control. *Agressologie: Revue Internationale de Physio-Biologie et de Pharmacologie Appliquees Aux Effets de l'Agression, 18*, 83–94. PMID:22251

Lee, E. A.-L., & Wong, K. W. (2014). Learning with desktop virtual reality: Low spatial ability learners are more positively affected. *Computers & Education*, *79*, 49–58. doi:10.1016/j.compedu.2014.07.010

Lee, K. M., & Peng, W. (2006). What do we know about social and psychological effects of computer games? A comprehensive review of the current literature. In P. Vorderer & J. Bryant (Eds.), *Playing video games: Motives, responses, and consequences* (pp. 327–345). Hillsdale, NJ: Lawrence Erlbaum Associates.

Leonard, L., Withers, L. A., & Sherblom, J. C. (2011). Collaborating virtually: Using "Second Life" to teach collaboration. *Communication Teacher*, *25*(1), 42–47. doi:10.1080/17404622.2010.527297

Lesch, W. C., & Hazeltine, J. E. (2013). Secondary research, new product screening, and the marketing research course: An experiment in structured decision making. In J. Goodwin (Ed.), *Secondary data analysis* (pp. 1–16). Thousand Oaks, CA: Sage Publications, Inc.

Levoy, M., Pulli, K., Curless, B., Rusinkiewicz, S., Koller, D., Pereira, L., & Shade, J. (2000, July). The digital Michelangelo project: 3D scanning of large statues. In *Proceedings of the 27th annual conference on Computer graphics and interactive techniques* (pp. 131-144). ACM Press/Addison-Wesley Publishing Co. 10.1145/344779.344849

Levy, H. P. (2017, October 2). *Here's why CIOs will be the new executive leaders*. Gartner, Inc. Retrieved on December 7, 2018 from https://www.gartner.com/smarterwithgartner/heres-why-cios-will-be-the-new-executive-leaders/

Library of Congress-Federal Research Division. (2005, March). *Country profile: Taiwan*. Washington, DC: Library of Congress-Federal Research Division. Retrieved on December 15, 2018 from https://www.loc.gov/rr/frd/cs/profiles/Taiwan-new.pdf

Liddicoat, A. (2007). *Language Planning and Policy: Issues in Language Planning and Literacy*. Cromwell Press. doi:10.21832/9781853599781

Lim, F. V., O'Halloran, K. L., & Podlasov, A. (2012). Spatial pedagogy: Mapping meanings in the use of classroom space. *Cambridge Journal of Education*, *42*(2), 235–251. doi:10.1080/0305764X.2012.676629

Lincoln, Y. S., & Guba, E. G. (1985). *Naturalistic Inquiry*. Beverly Hills, CA: Sage Publications, Inc. doi:10.1016/0147-1767(85)90062-8

Lindberg, R., Seo, J., & Laine, T. H. (2016). Enhancing physical education with exergames and wearable technology. *IEEE Transactions on Learning Technologies*, *9*(4), 328–341. doi:10.1109/TLT.2016.2556671

Linder, W. (2009). *Digital photogrammetry*. Berlin: Springer. doi:10.1007/978-3-540-92725-9

Li, R. (2014). Why women see differently from the way men see? A review of sex differences in cognition and sports. *Journal of Sport and Health Science*, *3*(3), 155–162. doi:10.1016/j.jshs.2014.03.012 PMID:25520851

Liu, P. (2015, December 14). Cultural and creative businesses thriving in Taiwan. *Taiwanese Business Topics*. Retrieved on December 13, 2018 from https://topics.amcham.com.tw/2015/2012/cultural-and-creative-businesses-thriving-in-taiwan/

Lloyd, J. (2016, October). Contextualizing 3D Cultural Heritage. In *The Proceedings of Euro-Mediterranean Conference* (pp. 859-868). Springer International Publishing.

Loewus, L. (2017). How virtual reality is helping. *Education Week*, *37*(3), 1–2.

Longwell, T. (2018, September 4). Creative forces in VR at Venice Festival learn from the past. *Variety*. Retrieved on December 16, 2018 from https://variety.com/2018/film/festivals/creative-forces-in-vr-at-venice-festival-learn-from-the-past-1202926218/

Loop, E. (2017, November 5). *Catch marshmallows with Ben & Jerry's new Facebook AR filter!* Retrieved on November 19, 2017 from http://redtri.com/catch-marshmallows-with-ben-jerrys-new-facebook-ar-filter/)

Lorenzo, C. M., Sicilia, M. Á., & Sánchez, S. (2012). Studying the effectiveness of multi-user immersive environments for collaborative evaluation tasks. *Computers & Education*, *59*(4), 1361–1376. doi:10.1016/j.compedu.2012.06.002

Lou, C., & Alhabash, S. (2018). Understanding non-profit and for-profit social marketing on social media: The case of anti-texting while driving. *Journal of Promotion Management*, *24*(4), 484-510. doi:10.1080/10496491.10492017.11380109

Lowrie, T., & Jorgensen, R. (2011). Gender differences in students' mathematics game playing. *Computers & Education*, *57*(4), 2244–2248. doi:10.1016/j.compedu.2011.06.010

Lucke, S., & Heinze, J. (2015). The role of choice in cause-related marketing investigating the underlying mechanisms of cause and product involvement. *Procedia: Social and Behavioral Sciences*, *213*, 647–653. doi:10.1016/j.sbspro.2015.11.466

Lui, A., & Lamb, G. W. (2018). Artificial intelligence and augmented intelligence collaboration: Regaining trust and confidence in the financial sector. *Information & Communications Technology Law*, *27*(3), 267-283. doi:10.1080/13600834.13602018.11488659

Lui, D. P. Y., Szeto, G. P. Y., & Jones, A. Y. M. (2011). The pattern of electronic game use and related bodily discomfort in Hong Kong primary school children. *Computers & Education*, *57*(2), 1665–1674. doi:10.1016/j.compedu.2011.03.008

Luke, A., & Freebody, B. (1990). Literacies programs: Debates and demands in cultural context. *Prospect: Australian Journal of TESOL*, *5*(7), 7–16.

Luke, C. (2000). Cyber-schooling and technological change: Multiliteracies for new times. In B. Cope & M. Kalantzis (Eds.), *Multiliteracies: Literacy Learning and the Design of Social Futures* (pp. 69–91). London: Routledge.

Maass, A., Kollhorster, K., Riediger, A., MacDonald, V., & Lohaus, A. (2011). Effects of violent and nonviolent computer game content on memory performance in adolescents. *European Journal of Psychology of Education*, *26*(3), 339–353. doi:10.100710212-010-0047-0

Macklin, C., & Sharp, J. (2016). *Games, Design and Play: A detailed approach to iterative game design*. Boston, MA: Addison-Wesley Professional.

MacNeilage, P. R., Banks, M. S., Berger, D. R., & Bulthoff, H. H. (2007). A Bayesian model of the disambiguation of gravitoinertial force by visual cues. *Experimental Brain Research*, *179*(2), 263–290. doi:10.100700221-006-0792-0 PMID:17136526

Macromill. (2017, October 17). *Internet users in Japan who own a virtual reality headset*, by age, Sep 2017 (% of respondents in each group)*. Retrieved in December 1, 2018 from http://totalaccess.emarketer.com/chart.aspx?r=213870

Magazine, A. V. (2011, January). NHM turns to augmented reality. *AV Magazine (London)*, 5.

Maillet, É., Mathieu, L., & Sicotte, C. (2015). Modeling factors explaining the acceptance, actual use and satisfaction of nurses using an electronic patient record in acute care settings: An extension of the utaut. *International Journal of Medical Informatics*, *84*(1), 36–47. doi:10.1016/j.ijmedinf.2014.09.004 PMID:25288192

Makin, T. R., Holmes, N. P., & Ehrsson, H. H. (2008). On the other hand: Dummy hands and peripersonal space. *Behavioural Brain Research*, *191*(1), 1–10. doi:10.1016/j.bbr.2008.02.041 PMID:18423906

Malliarakis, C., Tomos, F., Shabalina, O., Mozelius, P., & Balan, O. C. (2015). How to build an ineffective serious game: Worst practices in serious game design. In *9th European Conference on Games Based Learning: ECGBL2015* (pp. 338-345). Steinkjer, Norway: Academic Conferences and Publishing Limited.

Mandinach, E. B., & Corno, L. (1985). Cognitive engagement variations among students of different ability level and sex in a computer problem solving game. *Sex Roles*, *13*(3), 241–251. doi:10.1007/BF00287914

Mariani, G. (2018). The cultural and creative industries. *Guillaume Mariani*. Retrieved on December 13, 2018 from https://www.guillaume-mariani.com/creative-industries/

Marketing Week. (2016, May 26). NHS launches first ever augmented reality billboard campaign to show power of blood donations. *Marketing Week*, p. 6.

Marketo. (n.d.). *Virtual reality: A fresh perspective for marketers*. Retrieved on November 24, 2018 from https://www.marketo.com/infographics/virtual-reality-a-fresh-perspective-for-marketers/

Martin, E. J. (2017, May/June). How virtual and augmented reality ads improve consumer engagement. *EContent (Wilton, Conn.)*, *5*, 8.

Mason, W. (2015, November 16). *Five Ways to Reduce Motion Sickness in VR*. Retrieved from https://uploadvr.com/five-ways-to-reduce-motion-sickness-in-vr/

Matter and Form. (2018). Retrieved from: https://matterandform.net/scanner

Mayer, R. E., & Moreno, R. (2003). Nine ways to reduce cognitive load in multimedia learning. *Educational Psychologist*, *38*(1), 43–52. doi:10.1207/S15326985EP3801_6

Mayrath, M. C., Traphagan, T., Jarmon, L., Trivedi, A., & Resta, P. (2010). Teaching with virtual worlds: Factors to consider for instructional use of Second Life. *Journal of Educational Computing Research*, *43*(4), 403–444. doi:10.2190/EC.43.4.a

McCarthy, B. (1987). *The 4MAT System: Teaching to Learning Styles with Right/left Mode Techniques*. Barrington, IL: Excel.

McCoog, I. (2008). *21st Century teaching and learning*. Retrieved November 2, 2018, from http://www.eric.ed.gov/ERICWebPortal/recordDetail?accno=ED502607

McEvoy, F. J. (2018, January 4). 10 ethical concerns that will shape the vr industry. *VB*. Retrieved on December 10, 2018 from https://venturebeat.com/2018/2001/2004/2010-ethical-concerns-that-will-shape-the-vr-industry/

McLean, A. (2018, June 26). Australia looks to capitalise on $150b AR and VR market opportunity. *ZDNet*. Retrieved on December 1, 2018 from https://www.zdnet.com/article/australia-looks-to-capitalise-on-2150b-ar-and-vr-market-opportunity/

McVey, M. H. (2008). Observations of expert communicators in immersive virtual worlds: Implications for synchronous discussion. *ALT-J. Research in Learning Technology*, *16*(3), 173–180. doi:10.3402/rlt.v16i3.10896

Mehrabi, M., Peek, E. M., Wuensche, B. C., & Lutteroth, C. (2013). Conferences in Research and Practice in Information Technology: Vol. 139. *Making 3D Work: A Classification of Visual Depth Cues, 3D Display Technologies and Their Applications*. Adelaide, Australia: CRPIT.

Melero, I., & Montaner, T. (2016). Cause-related marketing: An experimental study about how the product type and the perceived fit may influence the consumer response. *European Journal of Management and Business Economics*, *25*(3), 161–167. doi:10.1016/j.redeen.2016.07.001

Merchant, Z., Goetz, E. T., Cifuentes, L., Keeney-Kennicutt, W., & Davis, T. J. (2014). Effectiveness of virtual reality-based instruction on students' learning outcomes in K-12 and higher education: A meta-analysis. *Computers & Education*, *70*, 29–40. doi:10.1016/j.compedu.2013.07.033

Merleau-Ponty, M. (1968). The Visible and the Invisible (C. Lefort, J. Wild, J. M. Edie, Eds., & A. Lingis, Trans.). Evanston, IL: Northwestern University Press.

Merriam, S. B. (2009). *Qualitative research: A guide to design and implementation*. San Francisco, CA: Jossey-Bass.

Meshlab. (2018). Retrieved from: http://www.meshlab.net/

Metivier-Carreiro, K. A., & Lafollette, M. C. (1997, September). Commentary: Balancing cyberspace promise, privacy, and protection--tracking the debate. *Science Communication*, *19*(1), 3–20. doi:10.1177/1075547097019001001

Metz, R. (2015b, March 18). Virtual reality advertisements get in your face. *MIT Technology Review*. Retrieved on November 13, 2017 from https://www.technologyreview.com/s/535556/virtual-reality-advertisements-get-in-your-face/

Metz, R. (2015a, May/June). Augmented advertising. *MIT's Technology Review*, *118*(3), 21.

Meyers, E. M. (2009). Tip of the iceberg: Meaning, identity, and literacy in preteen virtual worlds. *Journal of Education for Library and Information Science*, *50*(4), 226–236.

Michaelsen, L. K., Knight, A. B., & Fink, L. D. (2004). *Team-Based Learning: A Transformative Use of Small Groups in College Teaching*. Sterling, VA: Stylus.

Michaelsen, L. K., & Sweet, M. (2008). The essential elements of team-based learning. *New Directions for Teaching and Learning*, *2008*(116), 7–27. doi:10.1002/tl.330

Microsoft. (2018, March 20). *What is mixed reality?* Retrieved on August 6, 2018 from https://docs.microsoft.com/en-us/windows/mixed-reality/mixed-reality

Milgram, P., Takemura, H., Utsumi, A., & Kishino, F. (1994). *Augmented reality: A class of displays on the reality-virtuality continuum*. Paper presented at the Telemanipulator and Telepresence Technologies. Boston, M.A

Milk, C. (2015). *How virtual reality can create the ultimate empathy machine. TED Talks: Chris Milk: How virtual reality can create the ultimate empathy machine*. TED Talks. Retrieved November 2016, from https://www.youtube.com/watch?v=iXHil1TPxvA

Mills, A. J., Durepos, G., & Wiebe, E. (2010). Explanatory case study. In Encyclopedia of case study research. Thousand Oaks, CA: Sage. doi:10.4135/9781412957397.n138

Mills, A. J., & Durepos, G. (2013). *Case study methods in business research* (Vols. 1–4). Thousand Oaks, CA: Sage Publications Ltd. doi:10.4135/9781446286166

Ministry of Culture (Taiwan). (2015, September 16). *Contents and scope of cultural creative industries.* Taipei, Taiwan: Ministry of Culture. Retrieved on December 13, 2018 from https://www.moc.gov.tw/information_311_20450.html

Ministry of Culture Taiwan. (2017). *2017 Taiwan cultural & creative industries annual report.* Taipei, Taiwan: Ministry of Culture. Retrieved on December 13, 2018 from http://cci.culture.tw/upload/cht/attachment/b131e555ec34a192be-359838c9a4eb07.pdf

Miyares, G. M. (2013). *Underachieving gifted science students and multi-user virtual environments (Ph.D.).* Fort Lauderdale, FL: Nova Southeastern University.

Mochizuki, L., Duarte, M., Amadio, A. C., Zatsiorsky, V. M., & Latash, M. L. (2006). Changes in postural sway and its fractions in conditions of postural instability. *Journal of Applied Biomechanics, 22*(1), 51–60. doi:10.1123/jab.22.1.51 PMID:16760567

Mohammadi, A., Asadi, H., Mohamed, S., Nelson, K., & Nahavandi, S. (2016). *MPC-based motion cueing algorithm with short prediction horizon using exponential weighting.* Paper presented at the Systems, Man, and Cybernetics (SMC), 2016 IEEE International Conference on. 10.1109/SMC.2016.7844292

Monllos, K. (October 1, 2017). Brands are doing more experiential marketing. Here's how they're measuring whether it's working. *AdWeek.* Retrieved on November 15, 2017 from http://www.adweek.com/brand-marketing/experiential-can-create-more-meaningful-relationships-with-consumers/

Montclair State University. (n.d.). Retrieved from https://www.montclair.edu/

Moreno, R. (2002). *Who Learns With Multiple Representation? Cognitive Theory of Ed-Media.* The World Conference On Educational Media And Hypermedia And Communications, Denver, CO.

Moreno, R., & Mayer, R. (2007). Interactive multimodal learning environments. *Educational Psychology Review, 19*(3), 309–325. doi:10.100710648-007-9047-2

Moreno, R., & Mayer, R. E. (2000). A coherence effect in multimedia learning: The case for minimizing irrelevant sounds in the design of multimedia instructional messages. *Journal of Education & Psychology, 92*(1), 117–125. doi:10.1037/0022-0663.92.1.117

Morgan, E. J. (2013). Virtual worlds: Integrating Second Life into the history classroom. *The History Teacher, 46*(4), 547–559.

Morley, M., Riesen, E., Burr, A., Clendinneng, D., Ogilvie, S., & Murray, M. A. (2015). Interprofessional education for pre-licensure learners in a multi-user virtual environment: Lessons learned from students, instructors, and administrators. In *ICERI2015: 8th International Conference of Education, Research and Innovation* (pp. 4796-4805). Seville, Spain: Academic Press.

Morrison McGill, R. (2013). *Professional development for teachers: how can we take it to the next level?* Retrieved from https://www.theguardian.com/teacher-network/teacher-blog/2013/jan/29/professional-development-teacher-training-needs

Mount, N. J., Chambers, C., Weaver, D., & Priestnall, G. (2009). Learner immersion engagement in the 3D virtual world: Principles emerging from the DELVE project. *Innovation in Teaching and Learning in Information and Computer Sciences, 8*(3), 40–55. doi:10.11120/ital.2009.08030040

Mueller, F., Agamanolis, S., Vetere, F., & Gibbs, M. R. (2009). A framework for exertion interactions over a distance. In *Proceedings of the 2009 ACM SIGGRAPH Symposium on Video Games, Sandbox '09* (pp. 143-150). New Orleans, LA: ACM. 10.1145/1581073.1581096

Mullin, B. (2016, January 6). *Virtual reality: A new frontier in journalism ethics*. Retrieved on December 10, 2018 from https://www.poynter.org/news/virtual-reality-new-frontier-journalism-ethics

Munumer, E., & Lerma, J. L. (2015, September). Fusion of 3D data from different image-based and range-based sources for efficient heritage recording. In Digital Heritage, 2015 (Vol. 1, pp. 83-86). IEEE.

Murphy, D., & Pitt, I. (2003). Spatial sound enhancing virtual story telling. In O. Balet, G. Subsol, & P. Torguet (Eds.), *Virtual Storytelling: Using Virtual Reality Technologies for Storytelling* (pp. 20–29). Avignon: Springer.

Museums Computer Group. (2011). *Homepage*. Retrieved August 13, 2018, from http://museumscomputergroup.org.uk/

Muybridge, E. (Director). (1878). *Sallie Gardner at a Gallop/The Horse in Motion* [Motion Picture]. Retrieved November 2016, from https://www.youtube.com/watch?v=IEqccPhsqgA

Nafarrete, J. (2016, November 1). HTC opens VIVELAND VR theme park in Taiwan. *Virtual Reality Pulse*. Retrieved on December 13, 2018 from http://www.virtualrealitypulse.com/taiwan/?open-article-id=5764515&article-title=htc-opens-viveland-vr-theme-park-in-taiwan&blog-domain=vrscout.com&blog-title=vrscout

Nahon, M. A., & Reid, L. D. (1990). Simulator motion-drive algorithms - A designer's perspective. *Journal of Guidance, Control, and Dynamics, 13*(2), 356–362. doi:10.2514/3.20557

Nahon, M. A., Reid, L. D., & Kirdeikis, J. (1992). Adaptive simulator motion software with supervisory control. *Journal of Guidance, Control, and Dynamics, 15*(2), 376–383. doi:10.2514/3.20846

Naimark, M., Lawrence, D., & McKee, J. (2016, June 22). *VR Cinematography Studies for Google*. Retrieved January 2017, from Medium: https://medium.com/@michaelnaimark/vr- cinematography-studies-for-google-8a2681317b3

National Education Radio. (2017, May 16). Mobile museum of Taiwan literature truck stops by national Taitung University with outdoor AR experiences. *Yahoo.News*. Retrieved on December 16, 2018 from https://tw.news.yahoo.com/%E2016%2096%2087%E2015%AD%B2018%E2018%A2011%2018C%E2015%2018B%2095%E2015%2018D%2019A%E2017%2089%A2019%E2019%A2014%A2018%E2015%2081%2019C%E2019%2019D%A2010%E2016%2019D%B2011%E2015%A2014%A2017-%E2019%A2016%2096%E2015%2089%B2015%E2018%BB%2018A%E2019%AB%2094%E2015%A2014%2096%E2017%2018E%A2019ar-113100831.html

National Taiwan Museum. (n.d.). *Images of the ocean: An exhibition of marine ecology photos with VR experiences*. Taipei, Taiwan: National Taiwan Museum. Retrieved on December 15, 2018 from https://event.culture.tw/NTM/portal/Registration/C0103MAction?useLanguage=tw&actId=70004

Nelson, B. C., & Erlandson, B. E. (2008). Managing cognitive load in educational multi-user virtual environments: Reflection on design practice. *Educational Technology Research and Development, 56*(5-6), 619–641. doi:10.100711423-007-9082-1

Nelson, B. C., & Ketelhut, D. J. (2007). Scientific inquiry in educational multi-user virtual environments. *Educational Psychology Review, 19*(3), 265–283. doi:10.100710648-007-9048-1

Neugnot-Cerioli, M., Gagner, C., & Beauchamp, M. H. (2015). The use of games in pediatric cognitive intervention: A systematic review. *International Journal of Physical Medicine & Rehabilitation, 3*(4), 1000286. doi:10.4172/2329-9096.1000286

New London Group. (1996). A pedagogy of multiliteracies: Designing social futures. *Harvard Educational Review, 66*(1), 60–92. doi:10.17763/haer.66.1.17370n67v22j160u

Newmann, F. M. (1996). *Authentic Achievement: Restructuring Schools for Intellectual Quality.* San Francisco, CA: Jossey-Bass.

Next Animation Studio. (2017, March 5). *Next Animation Studio partners with national museum of prehistory.* Retrieved on December 15, 2018 from https://eprnews.com/next-animation-studio-partners-with-national-museum-of-prehistory-87380/

Nextplayground guardian. (2015, November 3). Martell Singapore: Experience Martell air gallery. *Nextplayground Guardian.* Retrieved on December 16, 2018 from https://nextplayground.net/campaigns/martell-singapore-experience-martell-air-gallery/

Nickerson, J. V., Corter, J. E., Esche, S. K., & Chassapis, C. (2007). A model for evaluating the effectiveness of remote engineering laboratories and simulations in education. *Computers & Education, 49*(3), 708–725. doi:10.1016/j.compedu.2005.11.019

Nielsen, J. (2000). *Why you only need to test with 5 users.* Retrieved from: https://www.nngroup.com/articles/why-you-only-need-to-test-with-5-users/

Nielsen, J. (2012). *Usability 101: Introduction to usability.* Retrieved from: https://www.nngroup.com/articles/usability-101-introduction-to-usability/

Nielsen. (2016, September 22). *Reality check: A peek at the virtual audiences of tomorrow.* Retrieved on December 8, 2018 from https://www.nielsen.com/us/en/insights/news/2016/reality-check-a-peek-at-the-virtual-audiences-of-tomorrow.html

Nogueira, P. A., Torres, V., Rodrigues, R., Oliveira, E., & Nacke, L. E. (2016). Vanishing scares: Biofeedback modulation of affective player experiences in a procedural horror game. *Journal on Multimodal User Interfaces, 10*(1), 31–62. doi:10.100712193-015-0208-1

Norris, S. (2004). Multimodal Discourse Analysis: A conceptual framework. In P. Levine & R. Scollon (Eds.), *Discourse & Technology* (pp. 101–115). Washington, DC: Georgetown University Press.

Ntokos, K., & Eletheriou, O. (2017b). *Exploring Unreal Engine 4 VR Editor and Essentials of VR.* BirPacktPub.

Ntokos, K., & Eleutheriou, O. (2017a). *Creating a VR Shooter Game Using Optimized Techniques.* Birmingham, AL: PacktPub.

Nussli, N. (2014). *An investigation of special education teachers' perceptions of the effectiveness of a systematic 7-Step virtual worlds teacher training workshop for increasing social skills (Unpublished doctoral dissertation).* University of San Francisco. Retrieved from http://repository.usfca.edu/diss/113

Nussli, N., & Oh, K. (2017). Field research in Second Life: Strategies for discussion group facilitation and benefits of participation. In G. Panconesi & M. Guida (Eds.), *Handbook of Research on Collaborative Teaching Practice in Virtual Learning Environments* (pp. 348–373). Hershey, PA: IGI Global. doi:10.4018/978-1-5225-2426-7.ch018

Nussli, N., & Oh, K. (2018). Avatar-based group discussions in virtual worlds: Facilitation, communication modalities, & benefits of participation (Book Chapter Enhancement). *International Journal of Virtual and Personal Learning Environments, 8*(1), 1–14. doi:10.4018/IJVPLE.2018010101

O'Mahony, S. (2015). A proposed model for the approach to augmented reality deployment in marketing communications. *Procedia: Social and Behavioral Sciences, 175,* 227–235. doi:10.1016/j.sbspro.2015.01.1195

O'Toole, M. (1994/2010). *The Language of Displayed Art* (2nd ed.). London: Routledge.

Oculus, V. R. (2016). *Oculus Story Studio.* Retrieved September 2016, from Story Studio, https://storystudio.oculus.com/en-us/

Oculus. (2017). *Oculus / Developers.* Retrieved April 1, 2016, from https://developer3.oculus.com/documentation/audiosdk/0.10/concepts/audio-intro-mixing/

Olsson, T., & Salo, M. (2012). Narratives of satisfying and unsatisfying experiences of current mobile augmented reality applications. *Conference on Human Factors in Computing Systems Proceedings.* 10.1145/2207676.2208677

Open Simulator. (2018). *Grid list.* Retrieved November 16, 2018 from: http://opensimulator.org/wiki/Grid_List

Orr, K. K., Feret, B. M., Lemay, V. A., Cohen, L. B., Mac Donnell, C. P., Seeram, N., & Hume, A. L. (2015). Assessment of a hybrid team-based learning (TBL) format in a required self-care course. *Currents in Pharmacy Teaching and Learning, 7*(4), 470–475. doi:10.1016/j.cptl.2015.04.016

Ott, M., & Pozzi, F. (2011). Towards a new era for Cultural Heritage Education: Discussing the role of ICT. *Computers in Human Behavior, 27*(4), 1365–1371. doi:10.1016/j.chb.2010.07.031

Paas, F. (1992). Training strategies for attaining transfer of problem-solving skill in statistics: A cognitive load approach. *Journal of Educational Psychology, 84*(4), 429–434. doi:10.1037/0022-0663.84.4.429

Paas, F. G. W. C., Tuovinen, J. E., Tabbers, H., & Van Gerven, P. W. M. (2003). Cognitive load measurement as a means to advance cognitive load theory. *Educational Psychologist, 38*(1), 63–71. doi:10.1207/S15326985EP3801_8

Paas, F. G. W. C., & Van Merriënboer, J. J. G. (1993). The efficiency of instructional conditions: An approach to combine mental-effort and performance measures. *Human Factors, 35*(4), 737–743. doi:10.1177/001872089303500412

Paas, F. G. W. C., & Van Merriënboer, J. J. G. (1994). Variability of worked examples and transfer of geometrical problem solving skills: A cognitive-load approach. *Journal of Educational Psychology, 86*(1), 122–133. doi:10.1037/0022-0663.86.1.122

Page, L. R. (2000). *Brief history of flight simulation.* Paper presented at the SimTecT 2000 Proceedings, Sydney, NSW, Australia.

Pagés, R., Amplianitis, K., Monaghan, D., Ondřej, J., & Smolić, A. (2018). Affordable content creation for free-viewpoint video and VR/AR applications. *Journal of Visual Communication and Image Representation, 53*, 192–201. doi:10.1016/j.jvcir.2018.03.012

Pando, A. (2017, December 15). *Mixed reality will transform perceptions.* Retrieved on December 18, 2017 from https://www.forbes.com/sites/forbestechcouncil/2017/2012/2015/mixed-reality-will-transform-perceptions/#7539aff2478af

Pantano, E., Rese, A., & Baier, D. (2017). Enhancing the online decision-making process by using augmented reality: A two country comparison of youth markets. *Journal of Retailing and Consumer Services, 38*, 81–95. doi:10.1016/j.jretconser.2017.05.011

Pan, X., & Hamilton, A. F. C. (2018). Why and how to use virtual reality to study human social interaction: The challenges of exploring a new research landscape. *British Journal of Psychology, 109*(3), 395–417. doi:10.1111/bjop.12290 PMID:29504117

Pan, Z., Cheok, A. D., Yang, H., Zhu, J., & Shi, J. (2006). Virtual reality and mixed reality for virtual learning. *Computers & Graphics, 30*(1), 20–28. doi:10.1016/j.cag.2005.10.004

Park, K. S., & Kenyon, R. V. (1999). Effects of network characteristics on human performance in a collaborative virtual environment. In Proceedings of Virtual Reality (VR) (p. 104). Houston, TX: Academic Press. doi:10.1109/VR.1999.756940

Passig, D. (2015). Revisiting the Flynn effect through 3D immersive virtual reality (IVR). *Computers & Education, 88*, 327–342. doi:10.1016/j.compedu.2015.05.008

Patrizio, A. (2017, July 12). Virtual reality companies: Top 20 VR companies to watch. *Datamation*. Retrieved on December 9, 2018 from https://www.datamation.com/mobile-wireless/virtual-reality-companies-top-2020-vr-companies-to-watch-2011.html

Paura, A. (2009, March). Virtual reality creates ethical challenges for journalists. *Digital Journalism*. Retrieved on December 10, 2018 from https://ijnet.org/en/story/virtual-reality-creates-ethical-challenges-journalists

Pavlidis, G., Koutsoudis, A., Arnaoutoglou, F., Tsioukas, V., & Chamzas, C. (2007). Methods for 3D digitization of Cultural Heritage. *Journal of Cultural Heritage, 8*(1), 93–98. doi:10.1016/j.culher.2006.10.007

Pavlou, M., Quinn, C., Murray, K., Spyridakou, C., Faldon, M., & Bronstein, A. M. (2011). The effect of repeated visual motion stimuli on visual dependence and postural control in normal subjects. *Gait & Posture, 33*(1), 113–118. doi:10.1016/j.gaitpost.2010.10.085 PMID:21144753

Payne, A., Cole, K., Simon, K., Goodmaster, C., & Limp, F. (2009). *Designing the Next Generation Virtual Museum: Making 3D Artifacts Available for Viewing and Download. Center for Advanced Spatial Technologies, University of Arkansas*. GeoMarine, Inc.

Pedersen, I., Gale, N., Mirza-Babaei, P., & Reid, S. (2017). More than meets the eye: The benefits of augmented reality and holographic displays for digital cultural heritage. *Journal on Computing and Cultural Heritage, 10*(2), 11. doi:10.1145/3051480

Pena-Shaffa, J. B., & Nicholls, C. (2004). Analysing student interactions and meaning construction in computer bulletin board discussions. *Computers & Education, 42*(3), 243–265. doi:10.1016/j.compedu.2003.08.003

Peterka, R. J. (2002). Sensorimotor Integration in Human Postural Control. *Journal of Neurophysiology, 88*(3), 1097–1118. doi:10.1152/jn.2002.88.3.1097 PMID:12205132

Petrakou, A. (2010). Interacting through avatars: Virtual world as a context for online education. *Computers & Education, 54*(4), 1020–1027. doi:10.1016/j.compedu.2009.10.007

Petrock, V. (2018, April 25). *Virtual reality beyond gaming: Solving business problems in industries*. Retrieved on December 9, 2018 from https://www.emarketer.com/content/virtual-reality-beyond-gaming

Pettey, C. (2018, January 4). *Immersive technologies are moving closer to the edge of artificial intelligence*. Gartner, Inc. Retrieved on December 7, 2018 from https://www.gartner.com/smarterwithgartner/immersive-technologies-are-moving-closer-to-the-edge-of-artificial-intelligence/

Phan, K., & Daim, T. (2011). Exploring technology acceptance for mobile services. *Journal of Industrial Engineering and Management, 4*(2), 339–360. doi:10.3926/jiem.2011.v4n2.p339-360

Pieraccini, M., Guidi, G., & Atzeni, C. (2001). 3D digitizing of cultural heritage. *Journal of Cultural Heritage, 2*(1), 63–70. doi:10.1016/S1296-2074(01)01108-6

Pirker, J., Riffnaller-Schiefer, M., & Gütl, C. (2014). Motivational active learning: Engaging university students in computer science education. In *Proceedings of 19th Annual Conference on Innovation and Technology in Computer Science Education (ITiCSE '14)* (pp. 297–302). Uppsala, Sweden: ACM. 10.1145/2591708.2591750

Plass, J. L., Moreno, R., & Brünken, R. (Eds.). (2010). *Cognitive load theory*. Cambridge, UK: Cambridge University Press. doi:10.1017/CBO9780511844744

PLoS Biol. (2005). Mitochondrial DNA provides a link between Polynesians and indigenous Taiwanese. *PLoS Biol, 3*(8), e281. Retrieved on December 13, 2018 from https://www.ncbi.nlm.nih.gov/pmc/articles/PMC1166355/

Polgreen, E. (2014, November 19). Virtual reality is journalism's next frontier. *Columbia Journalism Review*. Retrieved on December 10, 2018 from https://www.cjr.org/innovations/virtual_reality_journalism.php

Pollard, A. (2002). *Reflective Teaching: Effective and Research-based Professional Practice*. London: Continuum.

Ponzo, S., Kirsch, L. P., Fotopoulou, A., & Jenkinson, P. M. (2018, March). Balancing body ownership: Visual capture of proprioception and affectivity during vestibular stimulation. *Neuropsychologia, 117*, 311–321. doi:10.1016/j.neuropsychologia.2018.06.020 PMID:29940194

Pool, D., Harder, G., & van Paassen, M. (2016). Effects of simulator motion feedback on training of skill-based control behavior. *Journal of Guidance, Control, and Dynamics, 39*(4), 889–902. doi:10.2514/1.G001603

Portales, C., Alonso-Monasterio, P., & Vinals, M. J. (2017). 3D virtual reconstruction and visualisation of the archaeological site Castellet de Bernabe (Lliria, Spain). Virtual Archaeology Review, 8(16), 75. doi:10.4995/var.2017.5890

Posey, G., Burgess, T., Eason, M., & Jones, Y. (2010, March). The Advantages and Disadvantages of the Virtual Classroom and the Role of the Teacher. In *Proceedings of Southwest Decision Sciences Institute Conference* (pp. 2-6). Decision Sciences Institute.

Potenziani, M., Callieri, M., Dellepiane, M., Corsini, M., Ponchio, F., & Scopigno, R. (2015). 3DHOP: 3D heritage online presenter. *Computers & Graphics, 52*, 129–141. doi:10.1016/j.cag.2015.07.001

Pouliot, N. A., Gosselin, C. M., & Nahon, M. A. (1998). Motion simulation capabilities of three-degree-of-freedom flight simulators. *Journal of Aircraft, 35*(1), 9–17. doi:10.2514/2.2283

Poushneh, A. (2018). Augmented reality in retail: A trade-off between user's control of access to personal information and augmentation quality. *Journal of Retailing and Consumer Services, 41*, 169–176. doi:10.1016/j.jretconser.2017.12.010

Powers, K. C., Kalmar, J. M., & Cinelli, M. E. (2014). Recovery of static stability following a concussion. *Gait & Posture, 39*(1), 611–614. doi:10.1016/j.gaitpost.2013.05.026 PMID:23810088

Prensky, M. (2001). Digital natives, digital immigrants part 1. *On the Horizon, 9*(5), 1–6. doi:10.1108/10748120110424816

Preziosa, A., Grassi, A., Gaggioli, A., & Riva, G. (2009). Therapeutic applications of the mobile phone. *British Journal of Guidance & Counselling, 37*(3), 313–325. doi:10.1080/03069880902957031

Pridmore, J., & Overocker, J. (2014, January). Privacy in virtual worlds: A US perspective. *Virtual World Research, 7*(1), Retrieved on December 12, 2018 from https://journals.tdl.org/jvwr/index.php/jvwr/article/view/7067

Prude, M. A. (2013). A classroom of bunnies, blimps, and werewolves. *ASIANetwork Exchange, 20*(2), 1–12.

Queiroz, A. C. M. N., Moreira, A., Alejandro, T. B., Tori, R., De Melo, V. V., De Souza Meirelles, F., & Da Silva Leme, M. I. (2018). *Virtual reality in marketing: Technological and psychological immersion*. Paper presented at the 24th Americas Conference on Information Systems 2018: Digital Disruption, AMCIS 2018, Louisiana State University (LSU), College of Business.

Rae, J., & Edwards, L. (2016, January). Virtual reality at the British Museum: What is the value of virtual reality environments for learning by children and young people, schools, and families? *Proceedings of MW2016: The Annual Conference Museums and the Web*.

Rausch, M., Simon, J. E., Starkey, C., & Grooms, D. R. (2018). Smartphone virtual reality to increase clinical balance assessment responsiveness. *Physical Therapy in Sport, 32*, 207–211. doi:10.1016/j.ptsp.2018.05.017 PMID:29803943

Rauschnabel, P. A. (2018). Virtually enhancing the real world with holograms: An exploration of expected gratifications of using augmented reality smart glasses. *Psychology and Marketing*, *35*(8), 557–572. doi:10.1002/mar.21106

RealityTechnology.com. (n.d.). *Reality technology market overview*. Retrieved on December 9, 2018 from https://www.realitytechnologies.com/market/

Red Storm Entertainment. (2017, May 30). Star Trek: Bridge Crew. Ubisoft.

Reid, L. D., & Nahon, M. A. (1985). *Flight simulation motion-base drive algorithms: Part 1 - Developing and testing the equations* (Vol. 296). University of Toronto: UTIAS.

Reid, L. D., & Nahon, M. A. (1986a). *Flight simulation motion-base drive algorithms: Part 2 - Selecting the system parameters* (Vol. 307). University of Toronto: UTIAS.

Reid, L. D., & Nahon, M. A. (1986b). *Flight simulation motion-base drive algorithms: Part 3 - Pilot evaluations*. University of Toronto: UTIAS.

Reid, L. D., & Nahon, M. A. (1988). Response of airline pilots to variations in flight simulator motion algorithms. *Journal of Aircraft*, *25*(7), 639–646. doi:10.2514/3.45635

Remondino, F., & El-Hakim, S. (2006). Image-based 3D modelling: A review. *The Photogrammetric Record*, *21*(115), 269–291. doi:10.1111/j.1477-9730.2006.00383.x

Rese, A., Baier, D., Geyer-Schulz, A., & Schreiber, S. (2017). How augmented reality apps are accepted by consumers: A comparative analysis using scales and opinions. *Technological Forecasting and Social Change*, *124*, 306–319. doi:10.1016/j.techfore.2016.10.010

Rese, A., Schreiber, S., & Baier, D. (2014). Technology acceptance modeling of augmented reality at the point of sale: Can surveys be replaced by an analysis of online reviews? *Journal of Retailing and Consumer Services*, *12*(5), 869–876. doi:10.1016/j.jretconser.2014.02.011

Research Methodology. (n.d.). *Case study*. Research Methodology. Retrieved on December 16, 2018 from https://research-methodology.net/research-methods/qualitative-research/case-studies/

ResearchAndMarkets.com. (2018, July 30). *Global augmented reality (AR) & virtual reality (VR) market outlook to 2023 by devices, component, application and geography*. Retrieved on August 2, 2018 from https://www.businesswire.com/news/home/20180730005663/en/

Reymond, G., & Kemeny, A. (2000). Motion cueing in the Renault driving simulator. *Vehicle System Dynamics: International Journal of Vehicle Mechanics and Mobility*, *34*(4), 249–259. doi:10.1076/vesd.34.4.249.2059

Reymond, G., Kemeny, A., Droulez, J., & Berthoz, A. (2001). Role of lateral acceleration in curve driving: Driver model and experiments on a real vehicle and a driving simulator. *Human Factors*, *43*(3), 483–495. doi:10.1518/001872001775898188 PMID:11866202

Richards, D., & Taylor, M. (2015). A comparison of learning gains when using a 2D simulation tool versus a 3D virtual world: An experiment to find the right representation involving the marginal value theorem. *Computers & Education*, *86*, 157–171. doi:10.1016/j.compedu.2015.03.009

Richey, R. C., Klein, J. D., & Nelson, W. A. (2004). *Developmental Research: Studies on Instructional Design and Development*. Retrieved September 21, 2018, from http://www.aect.org/edtech/41.pdf

Richey, R. C., & Klein, J. D. (2007). *Design and Development Research: Methods, Strategies, and Issues*. Lawrence Erlbraum Associates, Inc.

Rideout, V. J., Foehr, U. G., & Roberts, D. F. (2010). *Generation M²: Media in the Lives of 8- to 18-year-olds*. The Kaiser Family Foundation. Retrieved December 2, 2018, http://www.kff.org/other/event/generation-m2-media-in-the-lives-of/

Riedl, M. O., & Young, R. (2006). From linear story generation to branching story graphs. *IEEE Computer Graphics and Applications, 26*(3), 23–31. doi:10.1109/MCG.2006.56 PMID:16711214

Riedl, M., & Bulitko, V. (2012). Interactive narrative: An intelligent systems approach. *AI Magazine, 34*(1), 67. doi:10.1609/aimag.v34i1.2449

Ritz, L., & Buss, A. (2016). A framework for aligning instructional design strategies with affordances of CAVE immersive virtual reality systems. *TechTrends, 60*(6), 549–556. doi:10.100711528-016-0085-9

Riva, G., Wiederhold, B. K., Mantovani, F., & Gaggioli, A. (2011). Interreality: The experiential use of technology in the treatment of obesity. *Clinical Practice and Epidemiology in Mental Health, 4*(7), 51–61. doi:10.2174/1745017901107010051 PMID:21559236

Rizzotto, L. (2016, November 29). *The mixed reality revolution is here, and it'll change your world forever*. Retrieved on August 7, 2018 from https://medium.com/futurepi/the-mixed-reality-revolution-is-here-and-itll-change-your-world-forever-177b06dac792

Roberts, D., Wolff, R., Otto, O., & Steed, A. (2003). Constructing a Gazebo: Supporting teamwork in a tightly coupled, distributed task in virtual reality. *Presence (Cambridge, Mass.), 12*(6), 644–657. doi:10.1162/105474603322955932

Roberts, P., & Henderson, R. (2000, April). Information technology acceptance in a sample of government employees: A test of the technology acceptance model. *Interacting with Computers, 12*(5), 427–443. doi:10.1016/S0953-5438(98)00068-X

Rogers, E. (1967). *Diffusion of innovations*. New York, NY: Free Press.

Ross, S. M., & Morrison, G. R. (2004). Experimental research methods. Handbook of Research on Educational Communications and Technology, 2, 1021-43.

Rossetti, Y., Desmurget, M., & Prablanc, C. (1995). Vectorial coding of movement: Vision, proprioception, or both? *Journal of Neurophysiology, 74*(1), 457–463. doi:10.1152/jn.1995.74.1.457 PMID:7472347

Roussos, M., Johnson, A., Moher, T., Leigh, J., Vasilakis, C., & Barnes, C. (2006). Learning and building together in an immersive virtual world. *Presence (Cambridge, Mass.), 8*(3), 247–263. doi:10.1162/105474699566215

Rubin, J., & Chisnell, D. (2008). *Handbook of usability testing: how to plan, design, and conduct effective tests*. Indianapolis, IN: John Wiley & Sons.

Ryan, R. M., & Deci, E. L. (2000). Self-determination theory and the facilitation of intrinsic motivation, social development, and well-being. *American Psychologist, 55*(1), 68-78. doi:10.1037110003-066X.55.1.68

Ryan, M. D., & Hearn, G. (2010, August). Next-generation "filmmaking": New markets, new methods and new business models. *Media International Australia, 136*(1), 133–145. doi:10.1177/1329878X1013600115

Ryder, L. (2017, June 5). *Storm to perform: The 4 stages of team productivity*. Retrieved from Trello: https://blog.trello.com/form-storm-norm-perform-stages-of-team-productivity

Saavedra, A., & Opfer, V. (2012). *Teaching and Learning 21st Century Skills: Lessons from the Learning Sciences*. A Global Cities Education Network Report. New York: Asia Society. Retrieved August 13, 2018, from http://asiasociety.org/files/rand-0512report.pdf

Salisbury, I. G., & Limebeer, D. J. (2016). Optimal motion cueing for race cars. *IEEE Transactions on Control Systems Technology, 24*(1), 200–215. doi:10.1109/TCST.2015.2424161

Santos, P., Pena Serna, S., Stork, A., & Fellner, D. (2014). The potential of 3D internet in the cultural heritage domain. In M. Ioannides & E. Quak (Eds.), *A Roadmap in Digital Heritage Preservation on 3D Research Challenges in Cultural Heritage (Vol. 8355)*. New York, NY: Springer-Verlag. doi:10.1007/978-3-662-44630-0_1

Sauro, J. (2011). *A Practical guide to the system usability scale: Background, benchmarks & best practices*. Denver, CO: CreateSpace.

Savva, S. (2016a). *The potential of a museum-school partnership to support diversity and multiliteracies based pedagogy for the 21st century* (Unpublished PhD thesis). University of Leicester, UK.

Savva, S. (2016b). Re-imagining schooling: weaving the picture of school as an affinity space for 21st century through a multiliteracies lens. In Reimagining the Purpose of Schools and Educational Organisations (pp. 49-64). Springer Publishing.

Savva, S. (2013). Museum-based Multiliteracies and Learning for 21st Century Skills: A Preliminary Study. *The International Journal of the Inclusive Museum*, *6*(2), 117–130. doi:10.18848/1835-2014/CGP/v06i02/44444

Scheweibenz, W. (2004). Virtual Museums. *ICOM News*, *3*, 1.

Schmidt, B., & Stewart, S. (2010). Implementing the virtual world of Second Life into community nursing theory and clinical courses. *Nurse Educator*, *35*(2), 74–78. doi:10.1097/NNE.0b013e3181ced999 PMID:20173592

Schmierbach, M., Limperos, A. M., & Woolley, J. K. (2012). Feeling the need for (personalized) speed: How natural controls and customization contribute to enjoyment of a racing game through enhanced immersion. *Cyberpsychology, Behavior, and Social Networking*, *15*(7), 364–369. doi:10.1089/cyber.2012.0025 PMID:22687145

Scholz, J., & Smith, A. N. (2016). Augmented reality: Designing immersive experiences that maximize consumer engagement. *Business Horizons*, *59*(2), 149–161. doi:10.1016/j.bushor.2015.10.003

Schubert, M. (2016, March 10). Weightless. Itch.Io.

Schumann, P. L., Anderson, P. H., Scott, T. W., & Lawton, L. (2014, March). A framework for evaluating simulations as educational tools. In *Developments in Business Simulation and Experiential Learning: Proceedings of the Annual ABSEL conference (Vol. 28)*. Academic Press.

Schwarz, C. W. (2007). Two mitigation strategies for motion system limits in driving and flight simulators. *IEEE Transactions on Systems, Man, and Cybernetics. Part A, Systems and Humans*, *37*(4), 562–568. doi:10.1109/TSMCA.2007.897590

Science Circle in Second Life. (n.d.). Retrieved from http://maps.secondlife.com/secondlife/The%20Science%20Circle/188/64/56

Scott, C. L. (2015). *The Futures Of Learning 3: What Kind Of Pedagogies For The 21st Century? Education Research and Foresight*. Working Papers. United Nations Educational, Scientific and Cultural Organisation.

Scullion, J., Baxter, G., & Stansfield, M. (2015). UNITE: Enhancing students' self-efficacy through the use of a 3D virtual world. *Journal of Universal Computer Science*, *21*(12), 1635–1653. doi:10.3217/jucs-021-12-1635

Seitz, P. (2018, January 29). Augmented reality glasses still 23 years from consumer market. *Investors Business Daily*.

Seymour, N., Gallagher, A., Roman, S., O'Brien, M., Bansal, V., Andersen, D., & Satava, R. (2002). Virtual reality training improves operating room performance - Results of a randomized, double-blinded study. *Annals of Surgery*, *236*(4), 458–464. doi:10.1097/00000658-200210000-00008 PMID:12368674

Sheppard, B. (1993). *Building Museum and School Partnerships*. Washington, DC: The American Museum Association.

Sherman, W. R., & Craig, A. B. (2002). *Understanding virtual reality: Interface, application, and design.* San Francisco, CA: Morgan Kauffmann/Elsevier.

Shields, R. (2010, October 7). HarperCollins uses augmented reality to promote authors. *New Media Age*, 6.

Shin, D. (2018). Empathy and embodied experience in virtual environment: To what extent can virtual reality stimulate empathy and embodied experience? *Computers in Human Behavior*, *78*, 64–73. doi:10.1016/j.chb.2017.09.012

Shrindhar, S., & Herschman, N. (2017, October 23). How AR/VR can create a 'wow' experience at retail. *TWICE*, p. 14.

Sketchfab Controls. (2017). *Navigation and Controls.* Retrieved from: https://help.sketchfab.com/hc/en-us/articles/202509026-Navigation-and-Controls

Sketchfab. (2018). Retrieved from: https://sketchfab.com/

Slater, M. (2009). Place illusion and plausibility can lead to realistic behaviour in immersive virtual environments. *Philosophical Transactions of the Royal Society of London. Series B, Biological Sciences*, *364*(1535), 3549–3557. doi:10.1098/rstb.2009.0138 PMID:19884149

Slater, M. (2018). Immersion and the illusion of presence in virtual reality. *British Journal of Psychology*, *109*(3), 431–433. doi:10.1111/bjop.12305 PMID:29781508

Slater, M., Usoh, M., & Steed, A. (1994). Depth of presence in virtual environments. *Presence (Cambridge, Mass.)*, *3*(2), 130–144. doi:10.1162/pres.1994.3.2.130

Slater, M., & Wilbur, S. (1997). A Framework for Immersive Virtual Environments (FIVE): Speculation on the Role of Presence in Virtual Environments. *Presence (Cambridge, Mass.)*, *6*(6), 603–616. doi:10.1162/pres.1997.6.6.603

Smith, J., & Hu, R. (2013). Rethinking Teacher Education: Synchronizing Eastern and Western Views of Teaching and Learning to Promote 21st Century Skills and Global Perspectives. *Education Research and Perspectives*, *40*, 86–108.

So, H. J., & Brush, T. A. (2008). Student perceptions of collaborative learning, social presence and satisfaction in a blended learning environment: Relationships and critical factors. *Computers & Education*, *51*(1), 318–336. doi:10.1016/j.compedu.2007.05.009

Solent University. (2018). Retrieved from https://www.solent.ac.uk/about/our-history

Soltani, P. (2018). A SWOT analysis of virtual reality (VR) for seniors. In G. Guazzaroni (Ed.), *Virtual and augmented reality in mental health treatment.* Hershey, PA: IGI Global; doi:10.4018/978-1-5225-7168-1.ch006

Soltani, P., Figueiredo, P., Fernandes, R. J., & Vilas-Boas, J. P. (2016). Do player performance, real sport experience, and gender affect movement patterns during equivalent exergame? *Computers in Human Behavior*, *63*, 1–8. doi:10.1016/j.chb.2016.05.009

Soltani, P., Figueiredo, P., Fernandes, R. J., & Vilas-Boas, J. P. (2017a). Muscle activation behavior in a swimming exergame: Differences by experience and gaming velocity. *Physiology & Behavior*, *181*, 23–28. doi:10.1016/j.physbeh.2017.09.001 PMID:28882467

Soltani, P., Figueiredo, P., Ribeiro, J., Fernandes, R. J., & Vilas-Boas, J. P. (2017b). Physiological demands of a swimming-based video game: Influence of gender, swimming background, and exergame experience. *Scientific Reports*, *7*(1), 5247. doi:10.103841598-017-05583-8 PMID:28701720

Sony Interactive Entertainment. (2016, October 13). *PlayStation VR.* Retrieved from https://www.playstation.com/en-gb/explore/playstation-vr/

Sooai, A. G., Sumpeno, S., & Purnomo, M. H. (2016, April). User perception on 3D stereoscopic cultural heritage ancient collection. In *Proceedings of the 2nd International Conference in HCI and UX Indonesia 2016* (pp. 112-119). ACM. 10.1145/2898459.2898476

Spiegel, J. S. (2018, October). The ethics of virtual reality technology: Social hazards and public policy recommendations. *Science Engineering Ethics, 24*(5), 1537-1550. doi: 15 doi:10.100711948-11017-19979-y

Sploland in Second Life. (n.d.). Retrieved from http://maps.secondlife.com/secondlife/sploland/128/128/28

Spreng, R. N., McKinnon, M. C., Mar, R. A., & Levine, B. (2009). The Toronto empathy questionnaire: Scale development and initial validation of a factor-analytic solution to multiple empathy measures. *Journal of Personality Assessment, 91*(1), 62–71. doi:10.1080/00223890802484381 PMID:19085285

Stahl, K., Abdulsamad, G., Leimbach, K., & Vershinin, Y. A. (2014). *State of the art and simulation of motion cueing algorithms for a six degree of freedom driving simulator.* Paper presented at the 17th International Conference on Intelligent Transportation Systems (ITSC), Qingdao, China. 10.1109/ITSC.2014.6957745

Stein, C. (2016). Virtual reality design: How upcoming head-mounted displays change design paradigms of virtual reality worlds. *MediaTropes, 6*(1), 52–85.

Stein, E. W. (2014). *Designing Creative High Power Teams and Organizations: Beyond Leadership.* New York: Business Expert Press.

Stenger, M. (2017). *10 Ways Virtual Reality is Already Being used in Education.* InformEd. Retrieved from: https://www.opencolleges.edu.au/informed/edtech-integration/10-ways-virtual-reality-already-used-education/

Stevens, M., Flinn, A., & Shepherd, E. (2010). New frameworks for community engagement in the archive sector: From handing over to handing on. *Journal of Heritage Studies, 16*(1/2), 59–76. doi:10.1080/13527250903441770

Storey, V. A., & Wolf, A. A. (2010). Utilizing the platform of Second Life to teach future educators. *International Journal of Technology in Teaching and Learning, 6*(1), 58–70.

Strong, R. W., Silver, H. F., & Robinson, A. (1995). What do students want (and what really motivates them)? *Educational Leadership, 53*(1), 8–12.

Stroosma, O., Van Paassen, M. M., Mulder, M., Hosman, R., & Advani, S. (2013). *Applying the objective motion cueing test to a classical washout algorithm.* Paper presented at the AIAA Modeling and Simulation Technologies (MST) Conference, Boston, MA.

Su, M. J. (2017, November 7). Engaging audience through VR and AR technology in the national museum of natural science. *The Liberty Times.* Retrieved on December 16, 2018 from http://news.ltn.com.tw/news/life/breakingnews/2246155

Suciu, P. (2018, April). A new perception: Augmented reality is changing how newspapers (and readers) are seeing things. *Editor & Publisher (E&P),* 37-43.

Supermassive Games. (2016, October 13). Until Dawn: Rush of Blood. Sony Interactive Entertainment.

Susi, T., Johannesson, M., & Backlund, P. (2007). *Serious games: An overview* (Technical Report No. HS-IKI-TR-07-001). Skövde, Sweden: University of Skövde.

Sweller, J. (1988). Cognitive load during problem solving: Effects on learning. *Cognitive Science, 12*(2), 257–285. doi:10.120715516709cog1202_4

Sweller, J. (1999). *Instructional design in technical areas.* Camberwell, Australia: ACER Press.

Sweller, J. (2005). Implications of cognitive load theory for multimedia learning. In R. E. Mayer (Ed.), *The Cambridge handbook of multimedia learning* (pp. 19–30). New York, NY: Cambridge University Press. doi:10.1017/CBO9780511816819.003

Sylaiou, S., Kasapakis, V., & Dzardanova, E. (2018). Leveraging Mixed Reality Technologies to Enhance Museum Visitor Experiences. *International Conference on Intelligent Systems (IS)*, Madeira, Portugal.

Szymczyk, M. (2009, December 28). 2010: The year of augmented reality? *AdWeek*. Retrieved November 15, 2017 from http://www.adweek.com/brand-marketing/2010-year-augmented-reality-101138/

Taherdoost, H. (2017, October 5-6). A review of technology acceptance and adoption models and theories. *Procedia Manufacturing, 22*, 960-967.

Tait, E., MacLeod, M., Beel, D., Wallace, C., Mellish, C., & Taylor, S. (2013). Linking to the past: An analysis of community digital heritage initiatives. *Aslib Proceedings, 65*(6), 564–580. doi:10.1108/AP-05-2013-0039

Taiwan Cultural Creative Industries. (2018, August). *Cultural industries bimonthly: Information and trend analysis.* Taipei, Taiwan: Taiwan Cultural Creative Industries, Ministry of Culture. Retrieved on December 13, 2018 from http://cci.culture.tw/upload/cht/attachment/fed2d8ce1f2daae065f0155709146006.pdf

Taiwan Soft Power. (n.d.). Taiwan cultural & creative industry. *Taiwan Soft Power.* Retrieved on December 16, 2018 from http://www.humanrights.fi/TaiwanCulturalCreativeIndustries.htm

Tang, J. T., Lan, Y. J., & Chang, K. E. (2012). The influence of an online virtual situated environment on a Chinese learning community. *Knowledge Management & E-Learning: An International Journal, 4*(1), 51-62.

Tax'en, G., & Naeve, A. (2002). A system for exploring open issues in VR-based education. *Computers & Graphics, 26*(4), 593–598. doi:10.1016/S0097-8493(02)00112-7

TeachThoughtStaff. (2018, January 8). *10 Pros and Cons of a Flipped Classroom*. Retrieved from TeachThought: https://www.teachthought.com/learning/10-pros-cons-flipped-classroom/

Terras, M. (2015). So you want to reuse digital heritage content in a creative context? Good luck with that. *Art Libraries Journal, 40*(4), 33–37. doi:10.1017/S0307472200020502

The Coca-Cola Company (UK). (2013, January 17). *Coca-Cola Great Britain and WWF announce new arctic home campaign.* Retrieved on August 7, 2018 from https://www.coca-cola.co.uk/newsroom/press-releases/coca-cola-and-wwf-announce-new-arctic-home-campaign

The Coca-Cola Company. (2011, November 18). *Arctic home campaign fact sheet.* Retrieved on August 7, 2018 from https://www.coca-colacompany.com/stories/arctic-home-campaign-fact-sheet

The Shorty Social Good Awards. (2016). *Expedia dream adventures (winner in hospitality and travel).* Retrieved on August 3, 2018 from http://shortyawards.com/1st-socialgood/expedia-dream-adventures

The Webby Awards. (2017). Bullying in virtual reality. *The Webby Awards.* Retrieved on August 3, 2018 from https://www.webbyawards.com/winners/2017/advertising-media-pr/campaigns/best-cause-related-campaign/bullying-in-virtual-reality/

ThinkMobiles. (2018, April). *Augmented reality development companies in 2018.* Retrieved on December 9, 2018 from https://thinkmobiles.com/blog/augmented-reality-companies/

Tourville, S., & Forbes Agency Council. (2018, December 7). The power and promise of immersive technology in brand storytelling. *Forbes*. Retrieved on December 7, 2018 from https://www.forbes.com/sites/forbesagencycouncil/2018/2012/2007/the-power-and-promise-of-immersive-technology-in-brand-storytelling/?ss=leadership#49137b49 132e49167b49135

Trejaut, J. A., Kivisild, T., Loo, J. H., Lee, C. L., He, C. L., Hsu, C. J., & ... . (2005, August). Traces of archaic mitochondrial lineages persist in Austronesian-speaking Formosan populations. *PLoS Biol, 38*, e247. doi:10.1371/journal.pbio.0030247

Tsakiris, M. (2010). My body in the brain: A neurocognitive model of body-ownership. *Neuropsychologia, 48*(3), 703–712. doi:10.1016/j.neuropsychologia.2009.09.034 PMID:19819247

Tsang, C.-H. (2012). *The development of digitalizationat the national museum of prehistory, Taitung, Taiwan*. Taitung, Taiwan, Republic of China: National Museum of Prehistory. Retrieved on December 15, 2018 http://pnclink.org/annual/annual2003/programe/presenpdf/110727.pdf

Tsirliganis, N., Pavlidis, G., Koutsoudis, A., Papadopoulou, D., Tsompanopoulos, A., Stavroglou, K., & Chamzas, C. (2004). Archiving cultural objects in the 21st century. *Journal of Cultural Heritage, 5*(4), 379–384. doi:10.1016/j.culher.2004.04.001

Turner, T. L., & Hellbaum, R. F. (1986). LC shutter glasses provide 3-D display for simulated flight. *Information Display, 2*(9), 22–24.

Tweed, D., & Leung, A. (2018, September 17). Five Asia flashpoints to watch as U.S.-China trade war heats up. *Bloomberg*. Retrieved on December 1, 2018 from https://www.bloomberg.com/news/articles/2018-2009-2018/five-asia-flashpoints-to-watch-as-u-s-china-trade-war-heats-up

UK Creative Industry Council (CIC). (2018, November). UK creative industries -value. *UK Creative Industry Council (CIC)*. Retrieved on December 13, 2018 from http://www.thecreativeindustries.co.uk/resources/infographics

Usability Test. (2017). *Running a usability test*. U.S. Department of Health & Human Services. Retrieved from: https://www.usability.gov/how-to-and-tools/methods/running-usability-tests.html

Van der Akker, J. (2013). Curricular Development Research as a Specimen of Educational Design Research. In T. Plomp & N. Nieveen (Eds.), *Educational design research – part A: An introduction* (pp. 52–71). Enschede, The Netherlands: SLO.

Van Haren, R. (2010). Engaging Learner Diversity through Learning by Design. *E-Learning and Digital Media, 7*(3), 258–271. doi:10.2304/elea.2010.7.3.258

van Krevelen, R., & Poelman, R. (2010). A survey of augmented reality technologies, applications and limitations. *International Journal of Virtual Reality, 9*(1), 1–20.

Van Leeuwen, T. (2000). It was just like magic – a multimodal analysis of children's writing. *Linguistics and Education, 10*(3), 273–305. doi:10.1016/S0898-5898(99)00010-8

van Wyk, E., & de Villiers, R. (2009). Virtual reality training applications for the mining industry. *6th International Conference on Computer Graphics, Virtual Reality, Visualisation and Interaction in Africa*, (pp. 53-63). Academic Press. 10.1145/1503454.1503465

Vavoula, G., Sharples, M., Rudman, P., Meek, J., & Lonsdale, P. (2009). Myartspace: Design and evaluation of support for learning with multimedia phones between classrooms and museums. *Computers & Education, 53*(2), 286–299. doi:10.1016/j.compedu.2009.02.007

Venkatesh, V., & Davis, F. D. (2000). A theoretical extension of the technology acceptance model: Four longitudinal field studies. *Management Science, 46*(2), 186–204. doi:10.1287/mnsc.46.2.186.11926

Virtual Reality Society. (2018). *Semi-immersive virtual reality environments.* Retrieved Nov. 15, 2018 from: https://www.vrs.org.uk/virtual-reality-environments/semi-immersive.html

Virtuix. (2018). *Virtuix Omni Platform.* Retrieved 01/10/2018, 2018, from http://www.virtuix.com/product/omni-platform/

Virvou, M., & Katsionis, G. (2008). On the usability and likeability of virtual reality games for education: The case of VR-ENGAGE. *Computers & Education, 50*(1), 154–178. doi:10.1016/j.compedu.2006.04.004

Vrellis, I., Avouris, N., & Mikropoulos, T. A. (2016). Learning outcome, presence and satisfaction from a science activity in Second Life. *Australasian Journal of Educational Technology, 32*(1), 59–77. doi:10.14742/ajet.2164

Wagner, D. (2018). Retrieved from https://medium.com/@DAQRI/depth-cameras-for-mobile-ar-from-iphones-to-wearables-and-beyond-ea29758ec280

Walker, J. (2017, July 14). Virtual reality to create an 'internet of experience' by 2030. *Digital Journal.* Retrieved on August 3, 2018 from http://www.digitaljournal.com/tech-and-science/technology/virtual-reality-to-create-an-internet-of-experience-by-2030/article/497608

Walker, R., Voce, J., Nicholls, J., Swift, E., Ahmed, J., Horrigan, S., & Vincent, P. (2014). *2014 Survey of Technology Enhanced Learning for Higher Education in the UK.* Oxford, UK: UCISA.

Walsh, M. (2009). Pedagogic potentials of multimodal literacy. In W. H. L. Tan & R. Subramanian (Eds.), *Handbook of Research on New Media Literacy at the K-12 Level: Issues and Challenges.* Hershey, PA: IGI Global. doi:10.4018/978-1-60566-120-9.ch003

Wang, C. X., Anstadt, S., Goldman, J., & Lefaiver, M. L. M. (2014). Facilitating group discussions in Second Life. *MERLOT Journal of Online Learning and Teaching, 10*(1), 139–152.

Wang, F., & Hannafin, M. J. (2005). Design-based research and technology-enhanced learning environments. *Educational Technology Research and Development, 53*(4), 5–23. doi:10.1007/BF02504682

Watson, G. (2000). A synthesis of simulator sickness studies conducted in a high-fidelity driving simulator. In *Proceedings of Driving Simulation Conference* (pp. 69-78). Paris, France: Driving Simulation Association.

Wazlawick, R. S., Rosatelli, M. C., Ramos, E. M. F., Cybis, W., Storb, B. H., Schuhmacher, V. R. N., … Fagundes, L. C. (2001). Providing More Interactivity to Virtual Museums: A Proposal for a VR Authoring Tool. *Presence: Teleoperators and Virtual Environments, 10*(6), 647-656

We Are Social. (2018, January). *Digital in 2018.* Retrieved on December 1, 2018 from https://wearesocial.com/blog/2018/01/global-digital-report-2018

Webster, R. (2016). Declarative knowledge acquisition in immersive virtual learning environments. *Interactive Learning Environments, 24*(6), 1319–1333. doi:10.1080/10494820.2014.994533

Wei, C.-W., Chen, N.-S., & Kinshuk, S. (2012). A model for social presence in online classrooms. *Educational Technology Research and Development, 60*(3), 529–545. doi:10.100711423-012-9234-9

Weiser, M. (1991). The Computer for the 21st Century. *Scientific American, 265*(3), 66–75. doi:10.1038cientificameri can0991-94 PMID:1754874

Wentink, M., Valente Pais, R., Mayrhofer, M., Feenstra, P., & Bles, W. (2008). First curve driving experiments in the Desdemona simulator. *DSC Europe 08.*

What is the 'Flipped Classroom'? (2018). Retrieved from The University of Queensland: http://www.uq.edu.au/teach/flipped-classroom/what-is-fc.html

Whitehead, S., & Biddle, S. (2008). Adolescent girls' perceptions of physical activity: A focus group study. *European Physical Education Review, 14*(2), 243–262. doi:10.1177/1356336X08090708

Whiting, C., & Rugg, S. (2006). *Dynatomy: Dynamic human anatomy.* Champaign, IL: Human Kinetics.

Whittle, M. (2014). *Gait Analysis: An Introduction* (4th ed.). Burlington, VT: Elsevier Science.

Wigert, B., de Vreede, G., Boughzala, I., & Bououd, I. (2012). The role of the facilitator in virtual world collaboration. *Journal of Virtual Worlds Research, 5*(2), 1–18. doi:10.4101/jvwr.v5i2.6225

Williams, M. (2009, July 10). Advertisers test alimented reality's durability. *Campaign,* p. 9.

Williams, P., & Hobson, J. (1995). Virtual reality and tourism: Fact or fantasy? *Tourism Management, 16*(6), 423–427. doi:10.1016/0261-5177(95)00050-X

Wimpenny, K., Savin-Baden, M., Mawer, M., Steils, N., & Tombs, G. (2012). Unpacking frames of reference to inform the design of virtual world learning in higher education. *Australasian Journal of Educational Technology, 28*(3), 522–545. doi:10.14742/ajet.848

Winch, G., Ross-Johnston, R., Holliday, M., Ljungdahl, L., & March, P. (2006). *Literacy* (3rd ed.). New York: Oxford University Press.

Winter, D. (2005). *Biomechanics and motor control of human movement* (3rd ed.). Hoboken, NJ: John Wiley & Sons, Inc.

WIRED Brand Lab. (2018). Digital reality: The focus shifts from technology to opportunity. *Wired.* Retrieved on December 12, 2018 from https://www.wired.com/brandlab/2018/2002/digital-reality-focus-shifts-technology-opportunity/

Witkin, A., & Baraff, D. (1997). Physically based modeling: principles and practice. *SIGGRAPH '97 Course notes.* Retrieved 01/10/2018, 2018, from https://www.cs.cmu.edu/~baraff/sigcourse/

Won, A., Bailey, J., Bailenson, J., Tataru, C., Yoon, I., & Golianu, B. (2017). Immersive Virtual Reality for Pediatric Pain. *Children, 4*(7), 52. doi:10.3390/children4070052 PMID:28644422

Wortley, D. (2011). Immersive technologies and personalised learning: The influence of games-related technologies on 21st century learning. *Proceedings of the 4th Annual International Conference on Computer Games, Multimedia and Allied Technology, CGAT 2011 and 2nd Annual International Conference on Cloud Computing and Virtualization, CCV,* 74-78.

Wortley, D. (2011, April 25-26). *Immersive technologies and personalised learning: The influence of games-related technologies on 21st century learning.* Paper presented at the 4th Annual International Conference on Computer Games, Multimedia and Allied Technology, CGAT 2011 and 2nd Annual International Conference on Cloud Computing and Virtualization, CCV.

Yang, K. C. C. (Ed.). (2018). Multi-platform advertising strategies in the global marketplace. Hershey, PA: IGI-Global Publisher. doi:10.4018/978-1-5225-3114-2

Yang, M. J. (2018, November 17). Experiencing MacKay's daily life in Taiwan through VR and AR. *The Liberty Times.* Retrieved on December 15, 2018 from http://m.ltn.com.tw/news/life/breakingnews/2615715?utm_medium=M&utm_campaign=SHARE&utm_s

Yang, K. C. C., & Kang, Y. W. (2018). Integrating virtual reality and augmented reality into advertising campaigns: History, technology, and future trends. In N. Lee, X.-M. Wu, & A. El Rhalibi (Eds.), *Encyclopedia of computer graphics and games*. New York, NY: Springer. doi:10.1007/978-3-319-08234-9_132-1

Yee, N. (2006). Motivations for play in online games. *Cyberpsychology & Behavior, 9*(6), 772–775. doi:10.1089/cpb.2006.9.772 PMID:17201605

Yim, M. Y.-C., Chu, S.-C., & Sauer, P. L. (2017). Is augmented reality technology an effective tool for e-commerce? An interactivity and vividness perspective. *Journal of Interactive Marketing, 39*, 89–103. doi:10.1016/j.intmar.2017.04.001

Yin, R. K. (2003). *Case Study Research: Design and Methods*. Thousand Oaks, CA: Sage Publications.

Yoshimoto, M. (2003, December). The status of creative industries in Japan and policy recommendations for their promotion. *NLI Research*, 1-9.

Youngblut, C. (1998). *Educational Uses of Virtual Reality Technology*. Technical Report D2128. Institute for Defense Analysis, Alexandria, VA.

Young, M. F., Slota, S., Cutter, A. B., Jalette, G., Mullin, G., Lai, B., ... Yukhymenko, M. (2012). Our princess is in another castle: A review of trends in serious gaming for education. *Review of Educational Research, 82*(1), 61–89. doi:10.3102/0034654312436980

Youn, S., & Kim, H. (2018). Temporal duration and attribution process of cause-related marketing: Moderating roles of self-construal and product involvement. *International Journal of Advertising, 37*(2), 217-235. doi:10.1080/0265048 7.02652016.01225332

Zaharias, P.A. (2004). Usability and e-learning: the road towards integration. *eLearn Magazine, 2004*(6), 4.

Zaharias, P. A. (2006). Usability evaluation method for e-learning: Focus on motivation and learning. In *Proceedings of CHI 2006* (pp. 1571-1576), Montreal, Canada: ACM. 10.1145/1125451.1125738

Zastrow, J. (2016, December). Gamification meets meaningful play: An inside look. *Computers in Libraries*, 12–15.

Zhang, B. (2017). Design of mobile augmented reality game based on image recognition. *Journal on Image and Video Processing*, 90-110.

Zhong, Y. (2016). Explaining national identity shift in Taiwan. *Journal of Contemporary China, 25*(99), 336-352. doi:10.1080/10670564.10672015.11104866

Zwyno, M. S. (2003). Hypermedia instruction and learning outcomes at different levels of Bloom's taxonomy of cognitive domain. *Global Journal of Engineering Education, 7*(1), 59–70.

About the Contributors

Kenneth C. C. Yang, Ph.D. is Professor in the Department of Communication at the University of Texas at El Paso, USA. His research focuses on new media advertising, consumer behavior, and international advertising. Some of his many works have been published in International Cyberpsychology, Journal of Strategic Communication, International Journal of Consumer Marketing, Journal of Intercultural Communication Studies, Journal of Marketing Communication, and Telematics and Informatics.

* * *

Norita Ahmad is an Associate Professor of MIS at American University of Sharjah. She received her PhD in Decision Science Engineering Systems from Rensselaer Polytechnic Institute. Her research interest includes decision analysis, and technology adoption. She published in a variety of scholarly journals such as IT and People, IS Frontiers, Telematics and Informatics, Journal of Business Ethics and Journal of Knowledge Management.

Vince Briffa, artist, curator and academic, studied at the University of Leeds and the University of Central Lancashire in the UK. Produces gallery and site-specific artwork, objects and installations integrating traditional artistic practices with digital and electronic media. He has represented his country internationally and had his work exhibited in major museums and art galleries worldwide, including the 48th and the 58th editions of the Venice Biennale (1999 and 2019); the Pierides Museum of Contemporary Art in Nicosia, Cyprus; the Palais des Nations, United Nations Building, Geneva, Switzerland; the Museum of Modern Art, Vaduz, Liechtenstein; the Casoria Contemporary Art Museum, Naples, and Villa Manin Centre of Contemporary Art, Udine, Italy; MAC - Museo de Arte Contemporáneo de Santa Fe, Argentina; Palais Liechtenstein, Feldkirch, Austria; The Museum of Fine Arts, Cluj, Romania and the Museum of Modern Art, Tel Aviv, Israel amongst many others. He has also had commissioned projects at the Cork 2005, Pafos 2017, Valletta 2018 and Leeuwarden-Friesland 2018, European Capitals of Culture. His work forms part of numerous prestigious private and public collections. He is a Fellow of the Civitella Ranieri Foundation, New York and has also curated numerous exhibitions internationally including the NRW-Forum in Düsseldorf, and the Münchner Künstlerhaus, Munich, Germany; Les Rencontres, Arles, France; De Harmonie, Leeuwarden, the Netherlands; the Museum of Fine Arts, Valletta and Spazju Kreattiv, St. James Cavalier, Valletta, Malta amongst others. Briffa has published numerous papers and 3 books related to his art practice. As an academic, he is a Professor and the Head of Department of Digital Arts at the University of Malta.

Joseph Camilleri is an academic, currently lecturing narrative processes and concept art, filming and editing techniques at Saint Martin's Institute of Higher Education. He started his artistic career at the Malta National School of Arts, under the mentorship of prominent Maltese artists. His love for the arts took him on a journey, educating students in art and visual design at secondary and post-secondary levels. Joseph participated in several local exhibitions, but his love for technology led him to mould his artistic talents into more contemporary experimentation and hence he embarked towards a vision of filming in new media and experimentation in virtual reality, for educational and academic purposes. Reading for an MFA in Digital Arts enabled Joseph to understand further particular concepts which went a long way towards his self-discovery. He has recently started publishing his research on his fields of interest. He is currently working on projects which experiment with increasing empathy, through narrative techniques, in art and culture together with the Malta Philharmonic Orchestra, the Malta Arts Council, Heritage Malta and other entities from the private sector.

Vanessa Camilleri is an academic at the Department of Artificial Intelligence, Faculty of ICT, University of Malta. Her expertise is in the area of Human Computer Interactions, with a specialisation in Virtual Worlds and Serious Games. Her areas of interest include Virtual Reality applications for developing emotional intelligence values. Her previous experience in the area of education and pedagogy, as well as educational technologies and use of games for learning have contributed to her overall academic profile. Her main publications are in the areas of online learning and the use of innovative and emerging technologies for learning. She also has worked on a number of EU funded projects in the areas of game-based learning. More recently she has started working on developing virtual reality experiences for teaching and learning purposes related to various aspects of emotional intelligence.

Sergio Casas-Yrurzum has a master's degree in Computer Engineering and also a bachelor's degree in Telecommunications Engineering - Telematics Specialty. He received the Spanish National Award on University Studies in 2008. He received his PhD in Computational Mathematics at the University of Valencia in 2014. He works as a senior researcher in the Robotics Institute (IRTIC) of the University of Valencia, where he is also a part-time professor at the School of Engineering (ETSE). His expertise is in the simulation field with special focus on Virtual Reality, Augmented Reality and motion cueing.

Nicole Cuadro is an Adjunct Professor at the University of San Francisco, School of Education. She is currently completing her Doctoral work with an emphasis in Organization and Leadership. Nicole has over ten years of experience in the EdTech field, as a Technology Director, Technology Teacher, Professional Development presenter, and works as a Distance Learning Program Administrator.

Kevin Rose Dias is a Digital Analyst at MRM-McCann, Dubai. He obtained his bachelor of science in Mechanical Engineering and is pursuing a Masters of Business Administration at the American University of Sharjah. His research interests include data analytics and visualization.

Alexiei Dingli is an Associate Professor of Artificial Intelligence and Head of the Department of Artificial Intelligence within the Faculty of ICT at the University of Malta. He was also a founder member of the Google Developers Group Malta Section, the Web Science Research group, the International Game Developers Association (IGDA) Malta and of the Gaming group at the same University. He also heads the Gaming in Education group and used to represent the University of Malta on the BeSmartOnline initiative. He pursued his Ph.D. on the Semantic Web at the University of Sheffield in the UK under the supervision of Professor Yorick Wilks. His work was rated World Class by a panel of international experts whose chair was Professor James Handler (one of the creators of the Semantic Web) and was used as a core component of the application that won the Semantic Web challenge. His research in Mobile Technology and Smart Cities was also awarded a first prize by the European Space Agency and an e-Excellence Gold Seal at the prestigious CeBit Conference in Germany. His current project on Intelligent Transportation Systems has been shortlisted for another prize by the European Space Agency. He has published several posters, papers, book chapters and books in the area. He also pursued an MBA with the Grenoble Business School in France specialising on Technology Management. He is also the Mayor of Valletta, the Capital City of Malta. He was the Mayor who submitted the bid for Valletta to become the European Capital of Culture in 2018 and is a founding member of the Valletta 2018 foundation. He is also involved in other comities such as the Valletta Rehabilitation Committee, the Valletta Community Network, the Valletta Alive Foundation, etc in order to ensure the regeneration of the Capital City.

Miguel A. Garcia-Ruiz graduated in Computer Systems engineering and obtained his MSc in Computer Science from the University of Colima, Mexico. Miguel received his PhD in Computer Science and Artificial Intelligence from the Centre for Research in Cognitive Science (COGS), University of Sussex, UK. Dr. Miguel Garcia-Ruiz took a virtual reality workshop at Salford University, England, and a computer graphics techniques internship at the Madrid Polytechnic University, Spain. Dr. Miguel Garcia-Ruiz has published various books and many scientific papers in academic journals, and has directed a video documentary about an introduction to virtual reality. Dr. Miguel was an Assistant Professor with the College of Telematics, University of Colima, Mexico. Currently, Miguel is an Associate Professor with the Department of Mathematics and Computer Science from Algoma University, Canada. Dr. Garcia-Ruiz was a member of Mexico's National System of Researchers (SNI) of the National Council of Science and Technology (CONACYT), and was awarded the Innovation Educator of the Year, given by the Sault Ste. Marie Innovation Centre (SSMIC) in 2015.

Laura S. Gaytan-Lugo is a Research Professor at the University of Colima in Mexico, appointed at the School of Mechanical and Electrical Engineering. Her research focuses on human-computer interaction. Her research interests include serious games, user experience design, child-computer interaction and evaluation methods. She holds a PhD in Information Technologies from the University of Guadalajara, Mexico. She is a member of Mexico's National System of Researchers. She serves as a research vice-chair of the Latin American HCI Community and as an ACM SIGCHI Ambassador. She is part of the HCIxB community.

Foaad Haddod majors in Artificial Intelligence field and is currently at the final stage of an MSc programme at the Faculty of Information and Communications Technology at the University of Malta. He has a Bachelor's degree in Electrical and Electronic Engineering (Control) from Libya. Mr. Haddod also has about eight years of work experience working for different sectors including; Director of Information Technology and Documentation at UNISCO – Libya. Also, he worked as a Head of Evaluations and Follow—up department at the General Institute of Teachers' Training within the Ministry of Education in Libya. He is also a certified Microsoft IT trainer and has delivered a number of IT-related training courses to about 500 trainers working for different ministries in Tripoli – Libya. Mr. Haddod is very passionate about using virtual reality applications in different sectors and his current research interests and projects focus on its use within learning, education, and training.

Yowei Kang is currently an Assistant Professor in the Bachelor Degree Program in Oceanic Cultural Creative Design Industries at National Taiwan Ocean University, Taiwan. Dr. Kang's research interests focus on digital game technologies and rhetorical analysis. He has published and presented papers that examine digital discourses in MMORPGs, digital in-game literacy, persuasion in advertising, rhetoric of technology, and consumer behaviors.

Melisa Kaye, EdD, OTR/L, is an educator and occupational therapist. She teaches in the Educational Technology program at the University of San Francisco and in the Occupational Therapy department at Samuel Merritt University in Oakland, CA. Melisa has expertise in pediatric occupational therapy and is the founder and director of Firefly Center: Therapy Services for Children, a San Francisco Bay Area clinic. Dr. Kaye's teaching and research interests include multimedia learning, pedagogy and instruction in the digital age, sensory processing and integration, kindergarten readiness, work with individuals with Autism, trauma-informed care, and the development of cognitive and metacognitive skills.

Matthew Montebello is an associate professor at the Department of Intelligent Computer Systems at the Faculty of ICT, University of Malta. He heads the Agent Technology Research Group at departmental level, as well as coordinates a number of Interest Groups within the same faculty. Before joining the University in 1999 with a PhD in Computer Science he was already heavily involved in Education in secondary schools after graduating in 1990 at the University of Malta B.Ed.(Hons) degree. Having obtained an extensive teaching experience and having been involved with the introduction of computer labs through the Ministry of Education, he proceeded to follow the Computer Science domain when he pursued his post-graduate studies obtaining a Masters and a Doctorate at the Cardiff University in Wales in 1996 and 1998 respectively. Furthermore in 2009 and 2016 he also completed an M.A. and an Ed.D. (Higher Education) specialising in the application of artificial intelligence to e-learning.

Konstantinos Ntokos (BSc, Msc, PGCLTHE, FHEA) is a Lecturer in Computer Games Development, at Solent University of Southampton. He has over 8 years of experience in the games industry through his indie studio as a Gameplay/ AI Programmer and a deep love for vr games and horror games as both a gamer and a developer. Furthermore, he is a member of SIGN and BCS-AGSG Committees. His past work involved technical presentations for Microsoft, Instructional design and teaching for SAE Institute as a EU BSc Programme Lead and programming training at the Greek army as a Corporal. His research interests include horror games, emotions during gameplay, Virtual Reality, Artificial Intelligence, eLearning and Immersion.

Natalie Nussli, Ed.D., is a graduate from the University of San Francisco and the Monterey Institute of International Studies. She is now a faculty member at the University of Applied Sciences and Arts Northwestern Switzerland (FHNW) at the Institute of Primary Education where she currently trains pre- and in-service primary school teachers. Natalie emphasizes the importance of inquiry-based learning, reflective practice, and feedback processes in her teaching. Her research interests revolve around teacher training in three-dimensional virtual worlds, the use of avatar-based group discussions to promote online interaction and collaboration, the communication modalities in online learning, video-aided self-reflection, and the design of culturally responsive curricula in online learning environments.

Kevin Oh, Ph.D., is an associate professor and program coordinator at the University of San Francisco in the Learning and Instruction department. After completing his doctorate and a master's degree in special education at the University of Virginia, Kevin accepted a position at the University of San Francisco where he currently trains pre-service and in-service teachers in general education and special education programs. In his current position, Kevin emphasizes the importance of teacher training and the critical role of using data to provide important feedback for in-service teachers. In sum, he prepares teachers to utilize technology appropriately and effectively, and to investigate how technology can be integrated into the curriculum for high-need students with disabilities in urban school settings.

Cristina Portalés (PhD in Surveying and Geoinformation, with specialization in Augmented Reality, 2008; IEEE Computer Society member) has been recently (2012-2015) a Juan de la Cierva post-doc fellow at the Institute of Robotics and Information and Communication Technology (IRTIC) at Universitat de València (Spain), where she currently works as full PhD senior researcher. She was formerly graduated with a double degree: Engineer in Geodesy and Cartography from the Universidad Politécnica de Valencia (Spain) and MSc in Surveying and Geoinformation from the Technische Universität Wien (Austria), with the specialization in photogrammetry/computer vision. She obtained her first diploma degree (Bachelor) with honours, for having the best academic record, being awarded with the San Isidoro prize. She was an ERASMUS, PROMOE and Leonardo da Vinci research fellow at the Institute of Photogrammetry and Remote Sensing (Vienna, 1999-2002), a PhD research fellow at the Mixed Reality Laboratory of the University of Nottingham (UK, 2005) and at the Interaction and Entertainment Research Centre of the Nanyang University of Singapore (2006). She received an outstanding PhD. Award by the UPV. First woman receiving the EH Thompson Award (best paper), given by the Remote Sensing and Photogrammetry Society (2010). During 2008-2010 she worked at the Photogrammetry and Laser Scanning Research Group (GIFLE) of the UPV, and during 2011-2012 she at the Technological Institute of Optics, Colour and Imaging (AIDO), being primarily involved in computer-vision related projects and in the project FP7-SYDDARTA, coordinating the technical work of the WP dedicated to software implementation and carrying out managerial tasks. She has been designed (since 2014) as the proposal coordinator for her research group (ARTEC). She is author of more than 60 scientific publications including international conferences, high impact journals, books and book chapters. She has been invited speaker by Univ. Granada, Aula Natura, UNITEC (Honduras), RUVID & Univ. Gjøvik (Norway). She is S&T program committee of diverse international conferences (e.g. ACM SIGCHI ACE, GECCO), highlighting her involvement in the IEEE ISMAR (CORE A*) for taking decisions on the selected papers. She is also reviewer of scientific journals with impact factors (e.g. MDPI Sensors, Springer Journal of Digital Imaging, Elsevier Computers in Industry). Cristina has co-organized the successful ACM Advances in Computer Entertainment Technology Conference 2005. She is Deputy Editor of the scientific journal Multimodal Technologies and Interaction (MTI), and Editor in Chief of the International Journal of Virtual and Augmented Reality.

Pedro C. Santana-Mancilla is a Research professor from the School of Telematics at the University of Colima in Mexico. His research interest focus on HCI, ICT for elderly people and Software Engineering. Professor Santana currently serves as chair of the ACM SIGCHI Latin American HCI Community and in the board of the Mexican Association on Human Computer Interaction (AMexIHC). He has served as Officer of the Mexican ACM SIGCHI Chapter (CHI-Mexico) for several years and is a Senior Member of IEEE.

Markus Santoso holds a Ph.D. degree from Dongseo University, South Korea. His main research interests are Augmented and Virtual Reality, Wearable Technologies, NUI, UX/UI, and Serious-game Development. He graduated in 2013 and went to Erfurt, Germany to continue his research as a Postdoctoral Fellow at the Fraunhofer IDMT under a funding scheme from the European Research Consortium for Informatics and Mathematics (ERCIM). To enter this fellowship program, Dr. Santoso needed to compete with more than 300 PhDs worldwide; only 24 applications were approved. As an ERCIM fellow, Dr. Santoso had the opportunity to visit other well-known European research institutes as research intern such as INRIA MimeTIC at Rennes-France with a focus on VR and at VTT in Espoo-Finland doing research in AR. After that, Dr. Santoso conducted his 2nd postdoctoral with the LINDSAY Virtual Human Lab at the University of Calgary, Canada. He received an Eyes-high Postdoctoral fellowship and worked on the implementation of AR/MR for human anatomy illustration, medical education, and computational physiology. Dr. Santoso also had several industrial experiences with AR/VR-related startup companies in various capacities such as Head of Department of Licensing and Gamification Department at Octagon Studio. From Sept 2017 to July 2018, he worked as an Assistant Professor at Montclair State University and starting from July 2018 Dr. Santoso joins University of Florida. Dr. Santoso has various notable achievements such as 2nd and 3rd place at the SuperApp Korea 2012, a prestigious and competitive national mobile developer competition in South Korea. One of his Mobile AR Apps was selected as nominated for the Unity Developer Choice category at the Vuforia Vision Award 2015 by QUALCOMM. Markus also actively publishes his research at international conferences such as ACM SIGGRAPH Asia, VRIC Laval Virtual and others.

Stefania Savva is a Postdoctoral Research Fellow at Cyprus University of Technology, after securing €120,000 funding for two years awarded by the Research Promotion Foundation, under the RESTART Didaktor Program 2016-2020 (HORIZON 2020). Her post-doctoral research is entitled "Museum Affinity Spaces (MAS): Re-imagining Museum-School Partnerships for the 21st century through a Multiliteracies Lens". Stefania has completed a PhD in Museum Studies at the University of Leicester, UK in 2016, with a focus on developing innovative museum-school partnerships to support diversity and multiliteracies-based pedagogy for the 21st century. Following on from her undergraduate studies in Primary Education in Greece, she completed an MA in Art, Craft and Design Education in London in 2009, focusing on art education curriculum for social change and inclusion. Since 2012, Stefania has been working as a Research Associate of the Art and Design e-learning Lab at Cyprus University of Technology, supervised by Dr Nicos Souleles. Among her work there is the focus on projects and EU funded projects on Design for Social Change, Innovation and Entrepreneurship, whereas she has conducted research on the instructional use of iPads in Art & Design Education. Concurrently, she has been working with diverse children and adults since 2009, as part of her work as a primary teacher and museum educator. Stefania has a number of presentations in international conferences following Scholar

Grants received, while her work is featured in academic peer-reviewed journals and edited volumes. She has also three chapter manuscript publications on the way and two papers accepted, to be published in 2019. She is particularly fascinated by work in the field of inclusive museum learning, design thinking, technology-enhanced learning and social change.

Pooya Soltani is a postdoctoral researcher at Aix-Marseille University, France. With a holistic approach to physiology, biomechanics, and psychology, his research centers on virtual reality, exergames, and gamification to understand their efficacy in encouraging players to participate in physical activity and sports.

João Paulo Vilas-Boas is a full professor of biomechanics at the University of Porto, Portugal. He was a swimming coach for more than 20 years and elected 3 times as "Coach of the Year" of the Portuguese Swimming Coaches Association. He was a member of the board of the Portuguese Swimming Federation and is currently a board member of the Olympic Committee of Portugal.

Index

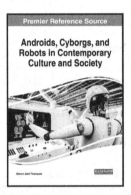

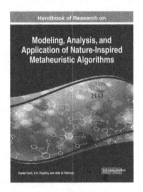

Ensure Quality Research is Introduced to the Academic Community

Become an IGI Global Reviewer for Authored Book Projects

Premier Reference Source

Emerging GIS Applications for Emergency and Disaster Management

Premier Reference Source

Managerial Strategies and Green Solutions for Project Sustainability

Premier Reference Source

Comparative Approaches to Using R and Python for Statistical Data Analysis

Premier Reference Source

Solutions for High-Touch Communications in a High-Tech World

The overall success of an authored book project is dependent on quality and timely reviews.

In this competitive age of scholarly publishing, constructive and timely feedback significantly expedites the turnaround time of manuscripts from submission to acceptance, allowing the publication and discovery of forward-thinking research at a much more expeditious rate. Several IGI Global authored book projects are currently seeking highly qualified experts in the field to fill vacancies on their respective editorial review boards:

Applications may be sent to:
development@igi-global.com

Applicants must have a doctorate (or an equivalent degree) as well as publishing and reviewing experience. Reviewers are asked to write reviews in a timely, collegial, and constructive manner. All reviewers will begin their role on an ad-hoc basis for a period of one year, and upon successful completion of this term can be considered for full editorial review board status, with the potential for a subsequent promotion to Associate Editor.

If you have a colleague that may be interested in this opportunity, we encourage you to share this information with them.

Printed in the United States
By Bookmasters